CHILD WELFARE

FOURTH EDITION

CHILD

WELFARE

POLICIES
A ——— N ——— D
PRACTICE

LELA B. COSTIN
School of Social Work, University of Illinois at Urbana-Champaign

CYNTHIA J. BELL
Superior Court of Los Angeles County

SUSAN W. DOWNS
School of Social Work, Wayne State University

Longman
New York & London

Child Welfare: Policies and Practice, Fourth Edition

Longman, 10 Bank Street, White Plains, N.Y. 10606

Associated companies:
Longman Group Ltd., London
Longman Cheshire Pty., Melbourne
Longman Paul Pty., Auckland
Copp Clark Pitman, Toronto

Permission for the following text citations is gratefully acknowledged. Pages 7–8: From *A Handbook of Child Welfare* by Joan Laird and Ann Hartman. Copyright © 1985 by The Free Press, a Division of Macmillan, Inc. Page 336: "Don't Want My Baby There," by J. C. Barden, February 5, 1990. Copyright © 1990 by The New York Times Company. Reprinted by permission. Page 410: "Foster Children in Life Course Perspective" by David Fanshel, Stephen J. Finch, and John F. Grundy. Child Welfare League of America, *Child Welfare,* Vol. 68, No. 5, September/October.

Senior editor: David J. Estrin
Production editor: Ann P. Kearns
Cover design: Renée Kilbride Edelman
Production supervisor: Anne P. Armeny

Library of Congress Cataloging-in-Publication Data

Costin, Lela B.
   Child welfare : policies and practice / Lela B. Costin, Cynthia J.
Bell, Susan Whitelaw Downs.—4th ed.
      p.   cm.
   Includes bibliographical references and indexes.
   ISBN 0-8013-0398-2
   1. Child welfare. 2. Child welfare—United States. I. Bell,
Cynthia Johnson. II. Downs, Susan. III. Title.
HV713.C67 1991
362.7′0973—dc20   90-45980
                                                CIP

5 6 7 8 9 10-MA-9594

Contents

Preface

This textbook presents concepts, policies, and practice in a broad field of child and family welfare. Material has been drawn from research findings, legislation, judicial decisions, other professional literature, and reports of social work practice. These subjects are examined in relation to the needs of children and their families, the major policies and programs of social services designed for them, and the policy issues that emerge for future planning. Our intent is to provide the student, undergraduate or graduate, with a substantive base of knowledge about child and family welfare policies and services.

The place of child welfare in the curricula of schools of social work is changing in response to broadened concepts of services for families and children within the human service community. In earlier years of social work education, child welfare was narrowly defined as a field of practice dealing mainly with children in foster care, in institutions, or in process of adoption, with some emphasis on protective services. Correspondingly, child welfare courses could be self-contained entities in a school's curriculum, combining policy and background knowledge with a large component of practice methods in this specialized field. Today, child welfare services have been redefined to include knowledge of the traditional child welfare services as well as a wide range of programs to support families and children and to prevent the need for out-of home care. Because this book addresses policies and programs directed at all families and children, the conceptual framework is appropriate not only for traditionally defined child welfare courses where the instructor may choose to use the content selectively; it is also especially suitable in the curricula of schools of social work who now

offer "concentrations" or "specializations" more broadly defined as "services to families, children, and youth" in which students are assigned to field placements in family service agencies, public and private child welfare agencies, the courts, and schools. Students in related specializations, for example, health and mental health services, for whom knowledge of public policy with respect to families is essential, often elect to enroll in child, family, and youth courses.

This text is useful as a reliable reference for new personnel entering into employment in child and family social agencies and as a tool for planned staff development programs. In some instances it can be helpful to citizens in our highly technological society who want to influence the environment in which social services are carried out.

More specifically, our major objectives are to help the reader (1) develop a vital concern for children, their potentialities, their family relationships, and their experiences within the neighborhood, school, and community; (2) identify problems necessitating child and family welfare services, and see how these problems are related to institutional gaps in the provision of appropriate services; (3) become familiar with the policies, practices, and goals of current child and family welfare programs and acquire a basis for evaluating them; (4) learn about how services to children and families interact with larger social and political structures and American cultural values, and the profound way these affect the goals and implementation of social policies; (5) identify some of the salient aspects of social work history that arose in response to rather narrowly conceived social and family/child problems and that still influence child and family welfare programs in this country; and (6) distinguish between child welfare practices based primarily on verified knowledge and those based mainly on custom and belief.

This book reflects our conviction that, to be effective in today's turbulent world, it is essential that we avoid an overly narrow, categorical view of the welfare of children and their families. Services for children and families must be broadly defined. It would be inaccurate to portray child welfare as a narrow band of traditional services quite apart from the larger societal context in which it finds its energy, focus, and niche. It would be irresponsible to ignore the impact of schools, the courts, and employment as major influences on the status of children and families. Therefore, full consideration is given to the basic core of child welfare services—family-based services for children in their own homes, including attention to the variety of family forms and special needs; services to protect children from neglect and abuse; foster care; adoption; child day care; and child advocacy. In addition, the text includes the legal framework that governs the affairs of children and young persons (an aspect of the child and family welfare system whose importance has burgeoned) as reflected in laws of guardianship and recent United States Supreme Court decisions, the organization and functioning of the juvenile court, and the sociolegal issues that emerge in matters of poverty, unwed parenting, child neglect and abuse, foster care, and adoption.

We also give attention to the state's authority in the regulation of children's out-of-home care (a neglected area of child welfare practice and an important one in view of the growing numbers of children who are receiving care outside their own homes), to the protection of children from exploitive labor situations, and to the provision of opportunity to youth through their public school experiences. These aspects of child welfare tend to be neglected in professional child welfare literature.

To make room in this book for new research findings and other significant aspects of child and family welfare programs that have arisen since the third edition, as well as to avoid a too cumbersome overall length, the chapter from the third edition entitled "Working in Child Welfare" has been omitted from this current edition.

All chapters in the fourth edition of *Child Welfare: Policies and Practice* have been carefully revised and updated to include current demographic data, findings from recent research, important new court decisions and legislation affecting the child and the family, and innovative demonstrations in recent child welfare practice, which reflects the renewed commitment to preserve a child's own home and enable parents to continue to maintain or resume care of their children.

The order of the chapters reflects our preference for providing the student with a beginning understanding of the legal framework of children's affairs before proceeding to a consideration of programs and issues. To emphasize the importance of basic services to intact families, many of whom are struggling to remain an intact unit, we move next to family-based services for children in their own homes. The following three chapters focus on essential matters that affect all families and often determine how well children and youth flourish—family income, children's daytime care, and the growing necessity among youth for effective schooling and opportunity for employment. In so ordering these early chapters, we have intended to provide a holistic perspective as a base for examining the demanding child welfare functions of protecting children and youth from abuse and neglect and of providing foster care and adoption. However, the chapters have been written to stand alone so that they can be ordered in a number of different ways to reflect the individual instructor's personal preferences in the construction of a child and family welfare course and teaching outline. In our teaching we have presented the chapters in different order for different groups of students. This book is highly adaptable in its organization.

At the end of each chapter are questions for individual study and for class discussion, as well as selected sources the instructor can use for lecture-discussion material, or the student for further independent study. For additional exploration of ideas, the references at the end of the text provide a substantial child welfare bibliography. The *Instructor's Manual* that accompanies the text has also been revised and updated.

In the course of preparing four editions of *Child Welfare: Policies and Practice,* we have incurred many debts to numerous colleagues, academicians in other disciplines, and professional social workers, who carry out the demanding work in child and family welfare. They have directed the way to new material and offered criticism and new insights that have been invaluable. We are also heavily indebted to our students, who are keen critics and who provide sometimes unexpected enlightenment and who represent for us the future of child welfare as an essential field of social work practice.

We express appreciation to Charles A. Rapp, University of Kansas, who as coauthor in the third edition of this book supplied new ideas and keen analysis of social problems and practice, much of which is still reflected in this edition. We are grateful as well to Jeannette Ingram, University of Illinois at Urbana-Champaign, who over the years, and always with competence, good humor, and friendship, has provided essential secretarial tasks, and to Anna Genus, Research Assistant, Wayne State University, for her dedication and skill in locating source materials.

CHILD WELFARE

CHAPTER 1

An Introduction to Child Welfare

In the green years of childhood the young begin their irreversible march into the future with the resolution and sweet calmness of innocence. The march of childhood goes on as long as the human race endures, an affirmation of new hope and the freshness of life that comes with every generation. The message proclaims another chance for mankind.

United Nation's Children's Fund

Chapter Outline

Child welfare as a specialized field of social work practice is vastly more complex than it was in the nineteenth century when our forebears confidently responded to problems of family functioning by "rescuing" children of poor par-ents and children of cruel parents and placing them in institutions of one kind or another. Over the years child welfare policies and practices developed in a pattern of gradual evolutionary growth. Historically, child welfare has

1

been a dominant and influential force in the development of the social work profession.

However, for more than three decades, rapid social change has placed heavy demands on child and family agencies for adaptations and innovations in services. These demands reflect public concern about the family, long regarded as society's best preventive institution and now showing the effects of rapid social, industrial, and economic dislocation. Some of these effects are manifested in alternative family forms and child-rearing patterns; in the greatly accelerated entry of women with very young children into the labor force; in the unprecedented growth of female-headed families and of teenage parenting; and in increased official reporting of child abuse and neglect. Other developments have heightened concern among the public and professionals in the child welfare system—the phenomenon of children with Acquired Immune Deficiency Syndrome (AIDS), children and families who are homeless, and the heavy damage to parents, children, and adolescents due to highly increased rates of drug use. All these developments, as well as new federal and state legislation and judicial decisions, have served to give a new face to much of child welfare practice, and to make more urgent the need for competent personnel in the system of child and family social services.

This book, then, is about children. It's about their needs and their problems. It's about our society and its influence on children, and therefore it is also a book about families, governments, agencies, and professionals. It's about what we do *for* children and what we do *to* children. It's also a book about how we can do better for the nation's children.

The welfare of children is dependent on the interaction between them and their environments. It is this focus that places the family at center stage because the family is the most dominant part of a child's environment. The family is the major instrument for providing for the welfare of children. The family is the primary social service agency in meeting social, educational, and health care needs. It is the family that negotiates with a larger environment to see that the child's needs are met. A larger society becomes involved when families are judged incapable of ensuring the child's welfare. This can occur because of the extraordinary needs of a special group of children, like handicapped children, which can easily overwhelm family resources. Or it can occur because families, owing to lack of resources or major dysfunctions, cannot meet even minimal standards of child care, as in the case of neglected or abused children.

A primary purpose of the field of social welfare is to strengthen family life. Within the wide range of social welfare programs, child welfare has a dual role in relation to children—''providing direct services primarily around special needs children; and advocating and forming policy to improve the lot of all children'' (Giovannoni, 1987, p. 253). Child welfare services represent one of society's organized expressions of conviction about the worth of the child and the family, as well as the child's rights as a developing human being and future citizen.

Social work has had a uniquely important role in the connection between children, families, and organized social welfare. The earliest activities of the profession were devoted to children and families. As Ann Hartman has described it:

> The profession has supported, replaced, taught, rehabilitated, treated, dismantled, abandoned, and embraced the family. To Mary Richmond [practitioner, teacher, and social work theoretician], the family was the central focus of social work's concern. The first professional practice journal was titled *The Family*. . . . The early child guidance workers focused their efforts on helping parents to be better parents, and the child-saving movement sought to rescue children by placing them with families. (1981, p. 7)

Child welfare continues to be the one field within social welfare in which social work is the dominant profession. More than most other social agencies, child welfare agencies are staffed and administered by professionals holding the title of social worker and are committed to the philosophy that the best way to help children is to support, strengthen, and supplement the efforts of families. Laird (1985) has offered this definition: "Ecologically oriented child welfare practice attends to, nurtures, and supports the biological family. Further, when it is necessary to substitute for the biological family, such practice dictates that every effort be made to preserve and protect important kinship ties. Intervention in families must be done with great care to avoid actions which could weaken the natural family, sap its vitality and strength, or force it to make difficult costly adjustments" (p. 177).

THE CHANGING AMERICAN FAMILY

Many observers have claimed that more changes have occurred in the American family over recent decades than ever before in our history. The changes have led some to pronounce that the American family is breaking down, losing its preeminent position in American society. The more prevalent belief is that the American family is merely adapting to a very different world than it experienced earlier. As one commentator has stated, "current family changes indicate American pluralism rather than family breakdown" ("Listening," 1980, p. 160). Regardless of the conclusions, few would argue that the last three decades have witnessed major changes in the family.

The U.S. Department of Commerce, Bureau of the Census (1989), has reported that in 1987 there were 70,895,000 children under the age of nineteen, which is a decrease of about 1,600,000 since 1980 and over 6 million since 1970. These figures reflect the decline in the fertility rate that began in the late 1960s. Census projections for the year 2000 suggest a continuing decline in these figures.

> *American families are adjusting to new economic realities and profoundly different family structures. All families have, to some extent, been affected by economic and social trends. . . . For the first time in more than forty years, families with children—especially young families—face an uncertain future with lowered expectations. (Rosewater, 1989, p. 4)*

Within the child population of 1987, some 3.4 percent were orphans, with neither a living father nor a living mother. These figures, however, reflect a decrease from 5.1 percent who were orphans in 1960 (U.S. Department of Commerce, 1989).

Divorce statistics suggest that America's families may be stabilizing to some extent. Divorce rates per 1,000 population fell to 4.8 percent in 1987, down from 5.0 percent in 1985 (U.S. Department of Commerce, 1989). However, given new normative societal standards that allow a generally high number of divorces, dramatic changes are unlikely.

Another change within American families is the unprecedented increase in the number of female-headed families. Since 1960, the number of families maintained by women has increased by 140 percent. By July 1988, one child out of every five did not live with both parents. Most of these children live with their mothers, 40 percent of whom had never married, and 30 percent who were divorced (*CDF Reports,* 1988a).

The increased participation of mothers in the labor force is another distinguishing feature of family life today. Impelled by the trend toward single parenthood, the women's rights movement, and the state of the economy, more women, especially women with children, entered or reentered the labor force in the 1970s than ever before in U.S. history. The trend has continued. Today 60 percent of all American six-year-olds have working mothers. Very troubling is the fact that only a minority of the children have safe, affordable, quality child care (*CDF Reports,* 1988a).

The last two decades have witnessed a large migration of people from northern urban areas to the south and west. There has also been a shift of people from large cities to medium- and small-sized areas. Even with these trends, however, most children and youth continue to live in or near a city. Further, the majority of urban nonwhite children live in central cities, while the majority of white children live in suburbs. Yet larger numbers of white than nonwhite children live in central cities. The latter statement illustrates the paradox of numbers versus proportions, which sometimes obscures other facts such as this: The majority of nonwhite children are poor, yet the majority of poor children are white.

PROBLEMS OF CHILDREN AND YOUNG PERSONS

Among the nation's children are millions who are living and growing up under economic, social, or psychological conditions that hinder their optimum development. Their problems are a reflection of interaction among their individual characteristics or those of their parents, factors associated with their particular family composition or situation, conditions within the neighborhood and community in which they live, and national issues and influences.

For many children there is destructive or poorly functioning family life due to poverty. This poverty may grow out of mental or physical illness or disability of parents, low educational levels and lack of marketable skills, or lack of access to employment because parents are not sufficiently mobile, which in turn is a condition that may be due to lack of housing near employment or lack of transportation to it. Other factors in a technological economy over

which an individual parent has no control contribute to high levels of unemployment.

Some families remain poor because they are headed by women with only low-level work skills who have young children at home to care for and whose only recourse is to an outworn, inadequate system of public assistance that maintains them and their families in poverty. Regardless of cause, poor families almost always experience two associated ills: inadequate housing and insufficient health services. In addition, children in crowded inner cities usually have only the street as a place for play, where they are often at the mercy of the hostilities and violence characterizing much of street life in the inner city. Safe areas to play may be similarly lacking in some isolated rural areas.

The 1980s brought to America in cities and in rural areas the phenomenon of "homelessness" for many thousands of children whose parents could no longer find nor sustain affordable housing. Many live in cars, shelters without privacy, rat-infested hotel rooms or abandoned buildings. The effects on children and family life have been devastating. These families lack basic health care; the children develop chronic illnesses as a result of nutritional deficits and poor sanitation. Many of the children are deprived of regular school attendance. Homelessness has become a precipitating factor in foster care placements and a barrier to family reunification.

Millions of youth confront a lack of opportunity to develop useful skills and find satisfying employment. The reason for this situation and the consequence has been stated thus: "As long as we continue to trap many young people in a low wage, unstable and generally unrewarding sector of the economy, increasing their stake in 'straight life' will be impossible" (Currie, 1982, p. 25).

Many of these problems in large part reflect the failure of the public school to educate its pupils in ways that are relevant to the complexity of life today and to generate a level of competence vital to successful social functioning and individual well-being. For many school children and youth the result is a diminishing desire to learn, inability to adapt to change, confusion about life goals, alienation from school and community, and antagonistic attitudes toward a society that has not solved its problems of war, poverty, unemployment, drugs, and racism. For many the open avenue is delinquency, which then is compounded by the inadequate treatment and rehabilitative resources available.

The 1960s brought attention to the problems of many "runaway" teenagers who left their own comfortable middle-class homes and migrated to cities to live among others like themselves. Many were seeking an escape from conflict with parents or the way of life of their parents. Some were seeking independence, individuality, or adventure away from what to them appeared as a no longer worthwhile environment. In the 1970s and 1980s larger proportions of the runaway children have come from low-income groups and have shown symptoms of long-term deprivation and disillusionment.

Parents, teachers, social workers, and other professionals have also had to face a lack of knowledge about how to help youth with the growing problem of alcohol and drug usage. "The United States has one of the highest prevalence rates of substance use by youth of any industrialized nation" (Girls Club, 1988, p. 8). Young people throughout the population experiment with all kinds of available drugs. The problems have appeared most noticeably among suburban upper-middle-class youth and among lower-class blacks and other minority groups. The growth in the numbers of young addicts and the increase in numbers of teenagers who die as a result illustrate the widespread danger of drug use.

A particularly poignant problem is evidenced in the rising number of infants born addicted to drugs. The babies' most common symptoms are associated with withdrawal from drugs—prematurity, underweight (no more than two to three pounds), muscle rigidity, inability to sleep, poor appetite, jerking convulsions, and peculiarly high-pitched and constant crying. In recent years, New York City made slow but steady progress in reducing its infant mortality rate, largely due to improved medical technology. But by the late 1980s, with the high incidence of cocaine abuse and AIDS, the rate had exceeded the national average of 10.8 per every 1,000 babies. Even more troubling, other large cities had higher rates (Gross, 1988).

Another tragic risk for children and families is illustrated in estimates that by 1991, some 10,000 to 20,000 children will be HIV-infected, statistics that lead to the prediction that children, youth, and families will make up the next wave of the AIDS epidemic ("AIDS reported," 1988). AIDS has already begun to produce a generation of orphans—thousands of children who are not infected but are losing their mothers and fathers to disability or death from AIDS (Lambert, 1989, July 17).

In the next decade, AIDS will touch every professional and advocate concerned about children and adolescents. . . . This problem will test our social and political systems. (Johnson, 1988, p. 27)

Although most children live with their own parents, who serve as their legal guardians, many children lack the protection of guardianship. These children are even more vulnerable to a disregard of their individual rights. They are without an adult protector, guide, or advocate. For thousands of children who must live in institutions or experience other forms of substitute care, their duly appointed guardian is an officer of the state or an administrator of a large child care agency. This practice fixes responsibility for the child but denies the opportunity for an ongoing personal relationship with his or her guardian.

Among many families who seek help in behalf of their children, the presenting problem is centered on faulty personality functioning within the family and conflict in the parent–child relationship or between husband and wife. Some parents are immature and overwhelmed with new or overdemanding responsibilities; others are poorly equipped with the knowledge needed today to give good care to children and maintain family balance. Despite greater availability of the means for birth control, many parents lack the help they want to plan the size of their families and use contraception effectively.

Some children's problems stem from their birth to teenage parents who are themselves immature, highly vulnerable to loss of continued schooling, and lacking in knowledge of how to care for their children as well as the financial means to do so.

Children are frequently brought to the attention of social agencies because there are complaints that they are neglected or abused by their parents or other caretakers. Such reports rose each year during the 1980s, and in the last three years of that decade, child fatalities due to child maltreatment increased (Child Welfare League, 1990). Federal funding and leadership has been inadequate to address the need of child protection. The solution to the problem of how to protect these children, yet maintain the family, continues to be elusive in too many cases. Some of these children must be enabled to live full time away from their own parents in foster homes or institutions.

The benefits to young children of early childhood education have been documented. Yet many children have no access to such programs. Quality programs for children's care and development generally are insufficient in number, posing a serious problem for families whose parents must be away from home during the day. America's delay in developing federal and state policy in response to the critical needs of working parents for safe, affordable, quality child care is in sharp contrast to the pattern in other industrialized countries.

Although adoption has been shown to be a successful solution for children who need new homes and loving, responsible parents, there are thousands who grow older as they wait for adoptive parents who do not materialize.

All of these problems directly affect the well-being of the nation's children and are appropriate for attention by child welfare agencies. Yet child welfare as a field of social work practice deals with only a small portion of the nation's children.

CLASSIFICATION OF SERVICES

Child welfare services, as they are traditionally organized, are designed to *support, supplement, or substitute for* the care given by parents. They have been classified as follows:

1. Services designed to support or reinforce the ability of parents to meet the child's needs, such as (1) *casework services in behalf of children in their own homes,* including direct casework with children and youth to help parents fulfill their parental roles and to help children in their social functioning; (2) *protective services,* provided on the initiative of community agencies which carry a delegated responsibility to protect children from conditions seriously detrimental to their welfare, when parents do not recognize their need for, nor seek, help; and (3) *services to unmarried parents,* to help them make decisions regarding the care or relinquishment of their child, to work out plans for caring for him or her, and to assist them in the solution of problems related to unmarried parenthood.

2. Services designed to supplement parental care or to compensate for certain inadequacies in such care, such as (1) *homemaker services* and (2) *day care services,* including both family and group day care.

3. Services designed to substitute for parental care, either partially or wholly, according to the child's individual needs and problems, such as (1) *foster family care service;* (2) *group care services,* as provided through emergency, shelter and detention care, children's institutions, residential treatment services for emo-

tionally disturbed children, training schools for delinquent children, institutions for physically handicapped children, including blind and deaf children, and institutions for mentally retarded children; and (3) *adoption services.*

The classification of child welfare services outlined above, formulated by the Child Welfare League of America (CWLA) and the U.S. Children's Bureau and published in 1959 after extended study, marked an official transition to a broader view of child welfare services, away from a narrow preoccupation with the provision of foster care and a neglect of services to children in their own homes that had dominated child welfare practice for so long. Since then, the CWLA, as a representative of child welfare agencies across the United States, has regularly revised the classification of services (most recently in 1984) but without fundamental changes in the categories of services or the scope of populations and problems to be addressed (Child Welfare League, 1984a).

However, the characteristics and needs of the family and child population and the nature of community and national life have continued to change. Certain urgent problems receive too little attention under such an organization of services. In the face of widespread unmet needs of children, the direction that is taken in planning services for children is crucial. Shall the available services continue in a pattern that is chiefly "residual" and therapeutic, that is, provided only when the natural channel for meeting an individual's needs (the family and the market economy) do not function adequately? This approach focuses on breakdown, economic depression, pathology, inadequacy, and need for treatment (Wilensky & Lebeaux, 1958).

The residual conception of social welfare emphasizes the provision of programs and services for people only after the primary group that usually functions has broken down. Services are provided in relation to an underlying assumption (although often denied or unacknowledged) that normal families, adequate and competent families, do not need help. Such an assumption influences legislative and administrative decisions. As a result the policy directions for a particular service often reflect restrictive and inconsistent attitudes, and negative views of people and their circumstances. Frequently services have been provided only after the family has endured hardship and trouble and the community has stood by while breakdown or family disintegration has been going on.

By contrast, an "institutional" conception of social welfare (or "developmental" view) holds that many "normal" and adequate families in today's complex technological society have common human needs and need help at various times; therefore services for children and families, in addition to being protective and therapeutic, should also be preventive and supplementary services, easily available without stigma—social supports necessary to help families meet the social realities of the present patterns of family and community living. Such a conception would include new social inventions to support, reinforce, and enhance family functioning, available to *all* people, not only those who are in some way a casualty of modern life and in need of protective or therapeutic services. Kahn has termed these kinds of social services "social utilities," to emphasize the notion of the user as citizen rather than client or patient (1965).

Given the potential for children and families in a broader classification of social services, why has the child welfare system continued in a mode of "residual" services? Meyer (1985) has supplied insight into this question:

Child Welfare is probably typical of all lasting social institutions in America. It has adapted to changes in society with sufficient energy to cope with external demands, yet its central purposes have remained essentially the same. Never a radical endeavor since its beginnings in America in the seventeenth century, the Child Welfare system has claimed a maintenance and residual function in the social service domain continually for over 300 years. It has changed its shape and its boundaries. It has redefined its goals and programs, but it has continued to perform in a narrow sector of society, escaping serious public judgments that were either excessively harsh or approving. . . . Child Welfare as a social institution, has, over the centuries, met a social need to provide supplementary or substitute parental care for children. This purpose is so necessary to society that . . . social criticism is always balanced by the need for the continuation of the service. . . . Child Welfare . . . has persisted because it has done the job society expected of it. (pp. 100–101)

Societal values play a significant role in determining the nature and goals of child welfare programs. Unlike the field of medicine where scientific evidence and the prestige of the medical profession have at times prevailed over public value preferences, "this is not the case in Child Welfare; even though society has allocated responsibility for the welfare of children to a social service community, it has not let go of its direct concern with the ideologies and outcomes of the services" (Meyer, 1985, p. 102).

Although the accepted classification of child welfare services has changed minimally, it is significant that within the classification, priorities have been reordered. "In theory, in-home services—designated primarily as supportive and supplementary—have always been given priority; the permanency planning movement has given such services priority in practice. Keeping the child in the home, providing the permanence and continuity of a caring relationship, is now more than ever before the sine qua non of child welfare services" (Kadushin, 1987, p. 269).

Left out in the current classification of services are the programs of public assistance labeled Aid to Families with Dependent Children (AFDC), the social insurance programs, delinquency programs, and regulatory programs applied to children's out-of-home care, all of which are mainly supplied by other state agencies. In the chapters that follow, attention will be given to these programs. Even though child welfare staff work within the boundaries of the residual classification of services, knowledge of these programs is essential for awareness of the larger context of child, family, and community life of which child welfare services are only a part.

RIGHTS AND RESPONSIBILITIES

All social services for children are based on certain assumptions about the relationships of a triad—*parent, child, society*. All the parts of the triad interact, with a constant shifting of balance, so that at certain times one part weighs more heavily than the others in terms of influencing the behavior and welfare of children.

Each of these—parent, child, society—at any given time, has certain rights and responsibilities. Child welfare services are predicated on the conclusion that at certain times the well-being of the child may be insufficiently attended to because of conflict in rights and roles, or inadequacies of, or pressing demands upon, any one of the parts of the triad.

Rights of Children

An essential question in any formulation of family social policy is the extent to which children have their own rights and interests independent of parents, with a claim to their recognition and enforcement. The *rights* of children stem from their status—dependent, immature individuals who require care, protection, and guidance to survive and flourish. The child, then, *needs* certain forms of care in order to move gradually toward assumption of adult roles in society. But there are differences between children's needs and rights. Even though a child's needs may be known and established, they are not necessarily assured by rights.

Children's needs are defined by current knowledge about the physical, psychological, and social development of the child. Rights,

"The most basic investments are those that protect our children against preventable diseases, hunger, homelessness, and unsafe child care." (CDF Reports, *1988a, p. 5, quoting Marian Wright Edelman)*

however, are based on a legal definition carrying a claim, or an "entitlement," and therefore enforceability. Statements of children's "needs" couched in language of "rights" are useful for defining goals in behalf of children, but they do not necessarily bring more enforceable rights.

The needs of children have been listed frequently and often with eloquence, and they have been attested to by impressive bodies of persons dedicated to the furtherance of the welfare of children. For example, the 1930 White House Conference on Child Health and Protection adopted a "Children's Charter," which enumerated nineteen separate "rights" for every child regardless of race, color, or situation. The Charter was printed attractively in blue and gold and hung on walls in many school buildings and churches. As can be seen from the following selected Charter aims, not all of these needs are yet fulfilled:

> For every child full preparation for his birth, his mother receiving prenatal, natal, and postnatal care; and the establishment of such protective measures as will make childbearing safer.
> For every child a dwelling place safe, sanitary, and wholesome, with reasonable provisions for privacy. . . .
> For every child who is in conflict with society the right to be dealt with intelligently as society's charge, not society's outcast. . . .
> For every child the right to grow up in a family with an adequate standard of living and the security of a stable income as the surest safeguard against social handicaps.

The General Assembly of the United Nations in 1951 proclaimed that humanity owes to

the child the best that it has to give and adopted an inspiring document, "Declaration of the Rights of the Child." A Children's Charter for the Seventies was presented at the White House Conference on Children in 1970. This statement again called attention to the rights and unmet needs of children in such areas as economic security, education, health, and social services. New aims also were expressed:

> For every child a community that ensures:
> "Freedom from pollution—clean air and water, safe foods, and the sights and sounds of a wholesome environment;
> Freedom from racism—social justice for all;
> Freedom from fear—the opportunity to move about safely."

In late 1989, the General Assembly of the United Nations, after ten years of negotiation, adopted an International Convention on the Rights of the Child. Issues that slowed negotiations included abortion, adoption, child labor, and the minimum age for military combat. The Convention included a child's right to a name, survival, education, and protection against exploitation and abuse, and safeguards against forcible separation of children from their parents ("U.N. Assembly," 1989, Nov. 21). These kinds of proclamations do not ensure enforceability, but they can be viewed as a constructive attempt to create international norms and inspire greater respect for children's rights.

In return for these commitments, children and young persons are expected to accept certain responsibilities to meet clear and consistent expectations of the adults responsible for them, to accept reasonable demands made on them, to develop a sense of personal accountability, to participate in voluntary work and various projects that exceed a narrow concept of service, and to take advantage of opportunities that help them develop their own sense of responsibility and capacity to alter society in constructive ways when they find it unacceptable.

Unfortunately, however, the child often is

regarded as an unproductive member of society with economic or social value only in the future. But as one study pointed out: "Children and young people are not a minority group to be given rights by the majority group as and when it wishes. They are part of society and should have the same rights as others. If they are different it is because they are not yet wholly integrated into society, but are preparing to be in it . . . , the adult of the future" (Berger, 1967, pp. 1–2).

In a consideration of the legal rights of children and youth, Brieland and Lemmon (1985) observed that "laws dealing with youths are characterized by paradoxes and inconsistencies." As one example: "Obligatory military service for eighteen-year-old males provided a strong impetus for establishment of eighteen as the minimum voting age as found in most states today. However, according other privileges to youths, such as the right to purchase liquor, has incurred strong opposition" (p. 15).

The law has created certain "privileges and disabilities" for persons who are still minors. The intent is to protect children from the consequences of their own lack of judgment, or to prevent them from acting where they lack sufficient maturity to act advisedly (Clark, 1968). Examples of the first purpose are found in the child's privilege to disaffirm contracts, or to have a guardian if he or she sues or is sued. An example of the second purpose is reflected in the child's inability to hold public office.

Advances in affirming the rights of the child have come about through recent court decisions such as *In re Gault* and *Kent v. United States,* which marked significant recognition of the rights of a minor who is alleged to be delinquent; *In re Winship* established the principle of proof beyond a reasonable doubt as a requirement for a finding of delinquency (see Chapter 3).

Levy v. Louisiana equalized the legal protections of the child born in and out of wedlock in relation to the mother in terms of wrongful death claims; *Gomez v. Perez* gave the nonmarital child the right of support from his or her father (see Chapter 5).

Goss v. Lopez and *Wood v. Strickland* extended due process rights to school pupils in danger of suspension. In addition, the opportunity of handicapped children for full and equal education programs was substantially advanced by federal legislation, the Education for All Handicapped Children Act of 1975. But a persisting ambivalence toward children on the part of the courts and other agencies of government is still evident, as in *Ingraham v. Wright,* which held that Eighth Amendment prohibitions against "cruel and unusual punishments" do not apply to children in school who may be subjected to severe and excessive corporal punishment (see Chapter 8).

In re Phillip B. and *Wisconsin v. Yoder* the court supported the parent's rights to decide on proper medical care and proper education, respectively. In *Carey v. Population Services International, et al.* the court limited parental authority in determining whether an adolescent can use contraception. *Bellotti v. Baird* ruled against a statute that required an unmarried minor to have parental or court consent before obtaining an abortion. In *Santosky v. Kramer* the court established higher standards for the state to meet when terminating parental rights. The rights of fathers of out-of-wedlock children in regard to adoption were supported by *Caban v. Mohammed* and *Stanley v. Illinois* but were not supported in *Quillon v. Walcott* (see Chapter 2).

These precedent-setting cases, and others as well, reflect competing interests: (1) greater autonomy for children at an earlier age versus increased parental control over children and accelerated state intervention into the lives of children to protect them from perceived risks or injury; (2) opposite goals of child autonomy versus child protection as found in rulings about medical decision making for children (Davis & Schwartz, 1987). The right of children to be dealt with as individuals continues to be given insufficient attention in the law, reflecting the complexity of equity within the triad of parent, child, society.

Rights and Responsibilities of Parents

Because heavy emphasis is placed upon the right of parents to plan and carry out their children's care, the likelihood that a child will receive protecting and growth-producing forms of care depends largely on the psychological capacities of his or her parents, the socioeconomic and sociolegal conditions which affect their ability to provide adequate care, and the kinds of support and aids which society provides to help parents meet their duties.

In our society the primary right and responsibility to care for children rests with their parents. As long as this care takes place in the child's own home and as long as it does not fall below a minimal standard demanded by a given community, then in most instances a wide range in quality and kind of care is tolerated, differences are accepted and valued as part of "our way of life," and the family is able to retain its privacy and independence.

These rights of parents and the ways in which they discharge the duties connected with these rights have crucial and far-reaching effects upon the child. Parents have the rights of guardianship by the fact that the child was born to them. Not all such rights accrue to natural parents, however—for instance, the right to guardianship of estate (see Chapter 2). Parents determine the "living pattern" and the standards of everyday conduct which influence the developing personality of the child. They can determine religion and may affect basic ethical values of the child. They influence the kind and extent of the child's education, the decision as to vocation, and the level of adult achievement. The quality of health care the child receives depends not only on the availability of health services in a particular community but also on the extent of knowledge the parents have and the choices made by them when medical care is needed. Even when guardianship is removed from parents, unless parental rights have been fully terminated by court action, certain rights (as well as the duty to support) remain, for example, the right of parents to notice of judicial proceedings involving the child and the right to give or withhold consent to the child's adoption.

Such far-reaching and well-entrenched rights of parents carry extensive responsibilities in relation to the child. Even though our society usually is willing to allow parents great latitude in the way they meet their responsibilities, parental duties are demanding ones. In those instances when the quality of parental care falls below the minimal level which a community will permit, usually the blame attached to parents is heavy. They will probably feel considerable censorship and rejection from the rest of their community.

The responsibilities of parenthood include (1) financial support—meeting the child's money needs in a society which looks with disfavor on economic dependency and inability of parents to keep the family economically self-supporting; (2) the provision of physical care—keeping the child safe from harm and injury and giving attention to his or her physical condition and health needs; (3) emotional care—for many parents a nebulous and poorly defined concept, carrying connotations of responsibility without knowledge of ways to meet it; and (4) a range of other parental duties, such as giving guidance and supervision to the young child as well as to the adolescent, promoting the growth of self-discipline, and setting forth clear parental and societal expectations which are adapted to the individual child's pace and ability. In addition, the right of parents to make certain major decisions for the child, for example, consent to medical care, to enlistment in the armed forces, and to marriage, is also a serious responsibility.

In their ordinary day-by-day activities, parents face myriad responsibilities and role expectations. Failure in this vital role usually is emotionally laden and defeating for adults, even for those who hide their feelings of inadequacy behind a facade of indifference, hostility, hurt, or bitterness.

There is increasing awareness of the heavy demands placed on adults in today's rapidly changing world with recognition of the frequent limitations of parental strength in an industrialized, urban society. Clearly the demands upon modern-day families call for more attention to the kinds of aids and new services which all parents need to enable them to succeed in their responsibilities.

Rights and Responsibilities of Society

To promote children's welfare, as well as to bring or maintain order in a modern way of life, society, through government, has the right and the responsibility to exercise authority to act in ways which benefit children.

One such power of the state is found in its use of *regulatory powers.* For the protection of children generally, the state can set up regulations that govern all parents, as in compulsory school attendance laws; it can impose regulations on third parties who employ children and young persons, or on doctors who may be required to apply silver nitrate to the eyes of newborn babies, or on merchants who may be prohibited from selling alcohol or tobacco to minors. Regulations may also be applied to foster parents and social welfare agencies who wish to give care to children, consisting of prescribed standards of care and treatment that all foster parents or child care agencies must adhere to. The intent in the state's use of its regulatory authority is to represent society's interest in all children through the application of broad powers to set standards applying to children generally, or all parents generally, or other adults acting in relation to children.

A second application of a state's right and responsibility to act in behalf of children is to intervene in the relationship of parent and child, and hence in the life of a particular family. When parental care falls below a level allowed for by law, or when a child or young person engages in delinquent acts prohibited by law, the state has a responsibility to intervene, that is, to exercise the ancient law of *parens patriae,* under which the court, acting as a protector of the dependent and immature child, uses its power to require a better level of care or treatment for a particular child. This may result in removal of the child from his or her own home to a foster home or institution.

A third kind of power of the state to act for children is its *authority to legislate for the development of various child welfare services.* For example, at the federal level, the government can tax for grant-in-aid programs so that, if certain conditions are met, states can receive federal money to aid in the development of their own plans of social services to children and their families. State governments have the power to adopt statutes providing for the development and financing of a range of social services on behalf of children, including the establishment of training schools and institutions for children needing foster care or treatment for special problems, or a public department of welfare specifically charged to develop and extend social work services to individual families. Although these public welfare departments cannot originate regulatory programs, they may be given the responsibility to administer them under the broad outlines of a regulatory statute, for example, the licensing of the means by which children are given out-of-home care; while social welfare agencies cannot modify the status relationship of parent and child (only the court can do so), they can serve as representatives of the community or of parents who are unable to carry their own responsibilities, in bringing attention to the needs of particular children who may require intervention of the state under the power of *parens patriae.*

The importance of the state's authority to legislate and spend for the development of social services to children and their families cannot be overemphasized. How successfully children are helped often depends on the extent to which the statutes of a state reflect modern knowledge about children and their changing world, respect for their rights, and readiness to tax and appropriate money for professional services and facilities to meet the needs of children.

PUBLIC SOCIAL POLICY

Differentiation from Social Goal, Social Action, and Social Issue

In the study of child welfare, we are primarily concerned with the impact of *public social policy* on the child and on family life developed by government through its judicial, legislative, and executive branches.

Although interrelated, social policy is a concept distinguishable from *social goal, social action,* and *social issue.* Social policy is a means to a social goal but not an end in itself. If it becomes so, it is usually illustrative of one of the pathologies to which bureaucracy is vulnerable.

Social action is often used to bring about a change in social policy as when a coalition of child advocates assemble and go together to the nation's capital to lobby vigorously for child care legislation. Sometimes, however, significant social policy is formulated without recognizable social action when knowledge is developed that suggests that public social policy is not meeting its responsibility for children. For example, the Head Start program was conceptualized against a backdrop of new scientific evidence about the nature of the child and how an individual child's intelligence develops. (The fact that attention to this new knowledge coincided with the political need of the Kennedy and Johnson administrations for a promising and appealing antipoverty program meant that the knowledge found tangible application in public social policy much sooner than it might have otherwise (Steiner, 1981).

A clear delineation of a social issue is an aid to social policy formulation, stating a social problem in terms of alternative solutions or lines of action and giving a focus for debate about what public policy should be. For example, a growing number of children are cared for outside their own homes while their mothers work. Many of these children are in substandard and unstimulating environments with poorly qualified caretakers. Although the public increasingly recognizes the need for regulation of these forms of child care, a central issue is whether standard setting and enforcement should be left to each of the states with maximum allowance for local or regional differences, or whether they should be assumed by the federal government as part of its effort to achieve fiscal accountability for use of child care funds and to raise the level of out-of-home care generally for young children. This issue, like others of public social policy for children, involves values, mores, economics, power relationships, and family functions and roles. Consequently, public social policy is arrived at through controversy, expressions of emotion, varying amounts of rationalizing of opinions and convictions, orderly and logical thinking, and ultimately compromise.

Differentiations within the Social Policy Field

As used here, social policy refers to official decisions about social issues or a broad principle of operation for carrying out a specific aspect of the social welfare system. Policies define such matters as the nature of the services or aid, who shall receive service, what the standards of practice shall be, and specific principles and procedures for carrying out a social welfare program. Antler (1985) states that "the concept of social policy evolved to describe the goals and actions of government in regulating or changing social relations." Social policies then, have the potential to "influence the direction of social change by providing incentives for certain functions and discouraging others" (p. 81).

The terms "social policy" and "social welfare policy" are sometimes used interchangeably. Antler (1985) distinguishes the two, however, defining social welfare policy as generally meaning government policy that addresses the social welfare system and its specified social services for individuals and families. Social policy "refers to a much larger range of public activities about which there is less specificity and consequently more room for different definitions" (p. 82).

Many social policies—ranging from those that stimulate the economy to those that support family planning, prenatal care, child health services, child care, preschool education, and improved schools—have a substantial role in strengthening families. (Schorr, 1988, p. 150)

Antler (1985) makes a further distinction between the related domains of social welfare policies: (1) child welfare policies guiding the programs in the child welfare system, and (2) other public policies that are directed toward families. The distinction between policy for children and policy for families is evident because the interests of children and those of their parents are in some instances incongruent, for example as played out in situations of runaway teenagers or child maltreatment. Antler characterizes child welfare policy as tending to be "residual, categorical," and aimed at a range of related but specific concerns such as child abuse, foster care, adoption. This is in contrast to family policy that is concerned with "a more expansive set of programs and social objectives" such as health, education, housing, and recreation (p. 85).

Families and Government

The family has been traditionally viewed in America as an inappropriate target for government planning and intervention except under the most compelling circumstances. Family policy issues raise fears, unresolved reluctance, and serious division within a population that has been wary of change in the relations of the family and the state. To some extent the reluctance of government to intervene into family life has given way to a perspective that encourages public involvement under certain conditions. When family dysfunction affects enough families, public or quasi-public efforts are initiated to fulfill the economic, physical, or emotional needs. "Family policy has to do with mechanisms for identifying family dysfunction, and with the organization of responsibility in public support systems: decisions about when public programs will take up the slack and the conditions under which they will do so" (Steiner, 1981, p. 9).

There are at least two reasons for this changing perspective. First, the changes, previously noted in this chapter, that have been taking place in American families have brought to many a growing fear that the family as an institution is breaking down. The declining role of the parent and the inevitably increasing role of the state have led to expectations in some quarters that the essential concerns of the family will be reflected in effective public social policy. Proponents for a more visible family policy believe that the importance of parental affection and a full parent-child relationship is not to be minimized, but neither is a positive role for government in the welfare of the child and his or her family. "Other factors determine the child's fate in the long term, and it is their interplay which is responsible for the prevailing ambivalence. But it is by the action of government that change will primarily be effected" ("Rights of the child," 1968, p. 10).

A second reason for the change in perspective has been the realization that virtually all governmental actions directly or indirectly affect families. Varying state and federal programs have an impact on family life even though family concerns were not a reason for their invention or directly considered in the formulation of their policies. For example, when government acts ineffectively to prevent the pollution of lake waters by the discharge of industrial waste, already scarce recreational areas that are important to family life are lost. Some urban renewal programs have cleared unsightly and overcrowded areas of a city and constructed modern buildings, but in doing so have ignored the established patterns of neighborhood life that had lifelong importance to some families. Public housing policy of the 1980s has created serious problems of homelessness for many parents and their children. Defense policy affects the family through the allocation of funds that cannot be used for domestic spending and the awarding of defense contracts affects unemployment in certain geographic areas. This more comprehensive view of the relationship between government actions and the family has led to a series of proposals for family impact analysis, that is, a requirement that new government laws and regulations be evaluated before passage for their effects on family well-being.

This is not to say that government can replace families or do what good families can do in nurturing and socializing children into useful adulthood. But by testing its policies of taxation, energy, transportation, housing, education, and income security for their effects on family life, government can add to the stability of the family—the unit of society this country still depends on for its basic child-rearing tasks.

Successful family social policy will require a balancing of the interests of children, their parents, and government. If this kind of collaboration were combined with a belief that generally children are helped most effectively through their parents, the result would be more service to the family and more power for the community's institutions and social agencies to work in behalf of children *with* parents, not *against* them.

Overview of Federal Policy

Family policy in the United States is chaotic and incoherent and defies brief analysis. The factors contributing to this confusion are multiple. First, the federal system of government divides responsibility between the federal government, fifty state governments, and a plethora of smaller units. Federal involvement with families has been a slow and incremental process whereby pieces of legislation were added one on top of the other without adequate attention to the relationships between policies or to any larger view of government-family relations.

A second reason for the incoherence is the scope of family policy. It involves health, education, housing, protection from abuse or crime, income security, recreation, and mental health. The complexity alone makes a comprehensive and integrated policy across domains virtually impossible.

Third, lack of agreement concerning family policy adds to the confusion. The debate over government involvement with families has shifted from whether it should occur to how and when it should occur. The debate becomes most intense when focused, not in the abstract, but on a specific problem or specific proposal. For example, abortion and contraception, public child care, and grounds for terminating parental rights have developed proponents and opponents who can be equally vociferous. The lack of unanimity has contributed to the fragmented and erratic nature of American policy toward families and reflects, in part, the impossibility of mandating a comprehensive family policy in our pluralistic society.

Federal legislation directed toward children and families can be evaluated on the basis of its adequacy. Adequacy refers to the ability of the legislation to accomplish what it sets out to do. For example, do assistance payments from Title IV of the Social Security Act, Aid to Families with Dependent Children (AFDC), provide a minimum but acceptable income for recipients? Does Title XX Social Services Block Grant provide enough funds to the states to protect children from abuse, neglect, and exploitation? Does the Women-Infant-Children's program (WIC) reach all the mothers and infants who need nutritional supplements?

Federal policy toward families is often inconsistent with regard to its end and means. For example, it has become clear that social welfare policy should support the social goal of keeping families together, ensuring that each child has a permanent home, and providing services in the least restrictive setting possible. This is one area where there seems to be a confluence of public opinion, judicial decisions, social work research, and public pronouncements by elected representatives. However, federal policy works against the achievement of this goal. As one example, Title IV-E of the Social Security Act provides large federal subsidies to foster care programs, while the Adoption Assistance Act of 1980, P. L. 96–272, was slow to be funded and is still only marginally funded. It is this latter legislation that is designed to facilitate arrangements for permanent homes for children.

It is the complexity of federal policy, its inadequacy in many areas, and its contradictions that have, in part, led to support for a comprehensive national family policy.

The Debate over Comprehensive National Family Policy

This country lacks a comprehensive and explicit national family social policy. This omission is apparent although we have moved toward a more extensive role for government as a positive force in directing social change. The great economic depression of the 1930s made it clear that governmental action was necessary to enable many individuals and families to cope with certain overwhelming problems and risks. Since then, legislative bodies at both the national and state levels have continued to enact provisions for new programs that have a significant effect on family life. For example, there has been far-reaching legislation on social insurance, public assistance, civil rights, housing, and employment. But this legislation has been directed primarily toward only one area of family life: its economic security. Moreover, this legislation largely reflects public policy in relation to the in-

dividual, with neglect of the family as a unit of attention and concern.

Antagonists of a comprehensive family policy contend that such a goal is both undesirable and not feasible. The negative aspects are seen in such a policy's "probable" discriminatory effects:

> Policies specifically directed at the family are an anathema in a free society. National policies are designed to regulate or guide social behavior, and governmental intervention into the area of family policy will inevitably encourage prescribed behavior for families. Families that comply with existing norms will be rewarded; nontraditional families and unmarried individuals are likely to be discriminated against in the allocation of governmental largess. (Barbaro, 1979, p. 457)

These projected effects are all the more troubling when one considers the great variation in what forms are labeled "family." Sussman (1971) identified at least twelve living arrangements that range from the traditional nuclear family to homosexual unions and communal groupings, which are generally viewed by the public as unacceptable. Developing a single family policy applying equally to each arrangement is probably impossible. Such difficulty was illustrated at the 1980 White House Conference on Families. Delegates were to produce a set of recommendations that would better support and strengthen families. The basis for doing so was a set of recommendations from the information gathered at seven national hearings and from 5,000 state recommendations, national organization recommendations, the results of a Gallup survey, and the delegates' own expertise and experience. The process was fraught with controversy and political jockeying that threatened to scuttle the conference. The center of the controversy was bitter division over how to define the family.

A different line of criticism concerning a national family policy focuses on the impossibility of formulating, passing, and implementing it. There is little consensus on the meaning of criteria such as "family well-being" or "strengthening families." For example, a program to provide child care can be viewed as supportive of the family because it allows a woman to combine family and work and allows the child a wide range of developmental experiences. However, the same proposal can be seen as antifamily because it invites second-class child rearing by taking the mother out of the home. The latter position was clearly stated by President Nixon when he vetoed a piece of child care legislation:

> Good public policy requires that we enhance rather than diminish parental authority and parental involvement with children. . . . For the Federal government to plunge headlong into supporting child development would commit the vast moral authority of the national government to the side of communal approaches to child rearing over against the family centered approach. (Nixon, 1971, Dec. 10)

Steiner (1981) has presented evidence of the "futility" of a national family policy and concludes that "family policy is unifying only as long as the details are avoided. When the details are confronted, family policy splits into innumerable components. It is many causes with many votaries" (p. 215).

THE ORGANIZATION OF SERVICES

Child welfare services usually are provided under the auspices of a social welfare agency—a formal organization existing to serve children and their families and organized under some sanction of society. Some of the agencies offer a variety of services to families and children; others are specialized in that they offer fewer services, or even only one.

Social welfare agencies providing service to children and their families are identified by various names, usually "child welfare agencies" or "family service agencies." Some carry both names, for example, Department of Children and Family Services. In an analysis of the institutional context of child welfare, Meyer (1985) has shed light on the conceptual separateness of child welfare services and family services despite their common professional knowledge and principles. Child welfare agencies and family agencies "have maintained rigid boundaries between each other. Their purposes, traditions, structure, funding sources, policies, and practices have always been different, and despite the current interest in family expressed in legislation and in agency policies, they remain apart." The result, Meyer asserts, is "a dysfunctional structure of services for both families and children." To understand how this separation came about, she cites the late nineteenth-century child-saving history of child welfare with its focus, not on maintaining intact families, but rather, on child placement as a way to protect children from their parents who were perceived by child-savers as inadequate or harmful. Another factor reinforced the separateness of child-centered versus family-centered services—the founding of two national organizations in the early twentieth century, the Child Welfare League of America and the Family Service Association of America, two bodies that have never found a way to join forces effectively. Meyer cites other factors as well that contribute to the failure to integrate child and family-based services: "unfortunate fragmentation in family and children's legislation and funding," which has influenced most public agencies to continue to keep their child welfare functions apart from their family services programs; and "the field of family services has not yet come to a clear determination of its particular function, making the more specifically articulated child welfare provisions more observable in the political and professional arenas" (Meyer, 1985, pp. 109, 110).

Mental health clinics also provide services to children and their families, as do public assistance agencies, neighborhood centers, and a variety of newer kinds of services, such as drop-in crisis counseling centers, "hotline" telephone counseling and referral services, and self-help groups such as Parents Anonymous, designed to support and aid child-abusing parents. Social work services for children are also provided in non-social-agency settings. For example, social workers frequently are employed in the public school to help pupils make maximum use of their educational opportunities. Probation officers attached to courts perform social work tasks in behalf of youthful law offenders. Social workers in hospitals and medical clinics work with physicians and nurses to try to ensure optimal benefits from medical services by giving attention to the social and emotional aspects of children's medical problems.

The organization offering the social service may be a "public" agency, or the services may be given under private auspices by a "voluntary" (philanthropic) agency or as a "proprietary" (commercial) venture. While both public and voluntary agencies are committed to broad, common goals in behalf of children, there are significant differences between the two forms of organization. Each has its separate legal base and means of financing its work; there are differences in the underlying philosophy and in the groups of children served. Proprietary services for children differ considerably from both public and voluntary child welfare services.

Child welfare agencies come in all shapes and sizes. Some agencies may employ only two to five people and provide a specialized service such as family treatment or adoption home placements. Some of the smaller agencies will have a few professionals and many volunteers or paraprofessionals like those in homemaker programs or in big brother and big sister programs. These small agencies are usually highly specialized or are located in sparsely populated rural areas where demand is small. They are usually privately operated.

Mental health centers, child guidance clinics, family service agencies, and youth service bureaus may all be mid-size agencies. These types of agencies are more likely to provide several child welfare services. For example, mental health centers may provide psychological assessment, family therapy, individual counseling, group work, and perhaps consultation to schools and the juvenile court. Family service agencies may provide homemakers, parenting education, and a variety of treatment options. These agencies would typically employ between eight and fifty people.

At the most complex end of the continuum are the large state child welfare agencies. They may employ thousands of people responsible for providing a wide range of services, geographically dispersed throughout the state. The budgets of such organizations can reach hundreds of millions of dollars a year. These state agencies have been delegated public responsibility for the protection and care of children and authority over life-determining decisions for children and families who come under their mandate.

Public Child Welfare Services

Legal Base and Financing. The public child welfare agency is established by the passage of law—a particular statute that defines the agency's responsibilities for providing a welfare service for children and their families. This statute, desirably, is sufficiently broad and flexible to permit and encourage continuing program development and adaptation to the changing times and needs of children. A public child welfare program has a spread of legal authorization in that its purpose and structure is defined not only by a specific statute but also by a body of related law, for example, a law which determines the status, rights, responsibilities, and relationships of children and their parents or establishes other relevant services and procedures, such as schools, juvenile courts, health agencies, veterans agencies, or social insurance programs.

The provision of basic child welfare services is an acknowledged responsibility of government in the United States.

> Government, because it is the instrumentality representative of all the people, has an underlying responsibility for making public social services *available* for all children by the same concept that governs provision for public education. ("Statement of principles," 1950, p. 11).

The passage of the Social Security Act of 1935 greatly extended the assumption of responsibility by government for social services and other programs of support to children and their families. The early principle of financial aid to help keep families intact, embodied in mothers' pension laws in various states, was extended into the Social Security Act by the Aid to Dependent Children program, Title IV of the act. This program provides grants to the states for a program of financial assistance to maintain children in their own homes or homes of relatives. The Social Security Act, Title IV-B, also contains provision for child welfare services through federal grants to the states for the purpose of establishing, extending, and strengthening services for the protection and care of homeless, dependent, and neglected children or children in danger of becoming delinquent. Amendments following the initial passage of the Social Security Act have broadened the kinds of services which are provided for children.

Public welfare services for children and families are financed by taxation—federal, state, or local, or some combination of these sources. Most government expenditures for children are made by or channeled through some unit of the Department of Health and Human Services (DHHS). Federal funds provide a significant proportion of the total expenditures for children's programs, particularly in such programs as public assistance, social insurance, Medicaid, Head Start, and maternal and child health services. In other areas of expenditures for children, for example, elementary and sec-

ondary education, states and localities contribute a larger proportion (Kahn, 1977).

By 1961, public agencies were carrying responsibility for most of the children requiring financial assistance and for two-thirds of those receiving other child welfare services (Turitz & Smith, 1965). This trend has continued. But in spite of broadened definitions of child welfare and increasing assumption of responsibility by government for child welfare services, comprehensive child welfare services—that is, the full range of social services for all children who need them—are still lacking in all communities.

The principle of local responsibility is well entrenched in the history of social welfare. Local and state influences have always been strong in child welfare programs because children and their families are closely linked to other concerns that traditionally have been regarded as the responsibility of the various states. For example, marriage, divorce, guardianship, custody, adoption, juvenile delinquency, and treatment of the mentally ill are all principally matters for legislation by the separate states. Sectarian influences, which have been strong in child welfare programs, to a considerable degree reflect local interests and influences. Undoubtedly there is still a strong strain of folk belief that planning and carrying out programs for the welfare of children require only a good heart, abundant energy, and common sense—qualities that local officials can find among their friends, relatives, and other citizens within their various communities. The persistence of such a belief has retarded recognition of the complexities of present-day program planning and financing, and of the competence and special knowledge needed to plan and administer effective child welfare services.

For various reasons, then, the idea that local government is the proper unit to organize child welfare services has never been wholly disavowed in this country. Nevertheless, "local" came to encompass wider geographical boundaries, and the Social Security Act increased pressures for greater federal control of standards in program planning, administration, and financing.

Background of Federal-State-Local Relationships.   In the early years of this nation, individuals who could not maintain themselves or their families were considered the responsibility of the local township. Some children were mentally retarded; some were physically handicapped. Some were orphaned by epidemics and other disasters of the frontier. Some showed incorrigible behavior. The methods of treatment within a community, however, were simple. The youngest children who required support by the town were "farmed out" to the lowest bidder—a family that agreed to give care to the child for a small, regular sum of money or goods. Able-bodied, older children were usually indentured, that is, placed under contract with a citizen of the town who agreed to maintain a child and teach him or her a trade or other gainful occupation in return for the profit from the child's labor. Others were often sent to live in the dreary, unsanitary almshouses with the adult misfits of the town—the mentally ill, the mentally deficient, lawbreakers, and the aged and infirm.

Gradually it was recognized that children need a different type of care from adults and more than the "security" provided by a master under a contract of indenture. At the same time the states had begun to assume responsibility for certain classes of the poor, those the local units of government were unwilling or unable to care for, such as persons without legal settlement or disabled veterans. Children, too, began to benefit from this assumption of responsibility by the state. Specialized state institutions were established: "reform" schools and training schools for children who were blind, deaf, or mentally deficient. This increased activity underscored the need for a central agency at the state level to coordinate the administration of these welfare programs that local units of government had been unable to finance or administer. Massa-

chusetts, in 1863, was the first state to establish such a central agency, a State Board of Charities, for the supervision of all state charities.

In the latter part of the nineteenth century national leadership in behalf of children was growing. The twentieth century brought the beginnings of a period of social reform in which the federal government showed its commitment to the welfare of the child and assumed certain responsibilities for child welfare programming. It was a tempestuous, challenging period in the development of social welfare. Today's child welfare workers owe much to the early national leaders—Jane Addams, Julia Lathrop, Lillian Wald, Florence Kelley, Grace and Edith Abbott, and others—who labored with such dedication for the protection and enhancement of child life. These were among the influential persons who brought about the establishment of the juvenile court, the passage of mothers' pension laws among the states, child labor legislation, and the inauguration of the White House conferences.

The first such conference, called thereafter at ten-year intervals by the President of the United States, was held in 1909 under the leadership of President Theodore Roosevelt, who invited leading workers in the field of child welfare from all over the United States to come to the White House to confer on "Care of Dependent Children." Recognition was given thereby to the need for national policy in regard to children in place of local efforts and piecemeal legislation in the various states. Among the recommendations of the first conference was one calling for the establishment of a federal children's agency. As a result the Children's Bureau was enacted into law on April 9, 1912, by congressional legislation charging the new federal agency to "investigate and report . . . upon all matters pertaining to the welfare of children and child life among all classes of our people. . . ." (Bradbury & Oettinger, 1962, p. 1). Fact-finding, investigation, and reporting were the original purposes of the bureau. In addition, the bureau staff assumed considerable responsibility for consultation with the states in an attempt to stimulate and guide their efforts to develop better programs of child welfare. (See Chapter 12 for a fuller account of the Children's Bureau as a child advocacy agency.) Under the Social Security Act in 1935, Title IV-B, the Children's Bureau was given responsibility for administering a grant-in-aid program for three types of services: maternal and child health programs modeled after the provisions of the earlier Sheppard-Towner Act, services for crippled children, and child welfare services.

The pattern of administration and financing was intended to strengthen state planning and services without imposing a program from the federal level. Through use of its power to tax and spend for social welfare purposes, the federal government offers money to the various states for the development of children's social services. A state must submit a written plan and agree to meet certain conditions, for example, to follow merit system principles in employing personnel and to use the funds for certain defined purposes. The Children's Bureau was given responsibility for providing consultation and attempting to stimulate better programs in the states and localities. States, in turn, retained their powers to plan and administer their own welfare services for children.

In the years since the passage of the Social Security Act, the federal government has assumed an increasing share of the financing as well as responsibility for technical and professional consultation in the development of state child welfare programs. Its role in standard setting is of great importance: the setting of conditions under which states can receive federal money to carry out their child welfare programs and the program goals that must be met within specified time limits.

Nevertheless, the primary responsibility for administering public child welfare services rests upon the states and their regional and local subdivisions. In 1975 Congress amended the Social Security Act by creating Title XX, under which social services (including a range of child and family welfare services) were to be provided for persons receiving cash payments under Aid to Families with Dependent Children (AFDC) or Supplemental Security Income (SSI) and for specially defined low-income families. The new title reversed the trend toward greater centralization at the federal level by transferring a large measure of administration and policy-making powers to states and localities, for example, in decisions as to what programs to fund, the extent of funding, the method of service delivery, eligibility standards, and methods of monitoring and evaluating programs (Mott, 1976).

Voluntary Child Welfare Services

A voluntary child and family welfare agency receives its authorization from a group of responsible citizens who undertake to assume responsibility for a defined and limited part of a community's social services for children. They may form a corporate body and obtain a legal charter by showing that a need for a particular service exists and a group of citizens is ready to support the activity. Some of these interested citizens are selected to serve as members of a board of directors with certain policy-making and advisory responsibilities in relation to a professional social work staff. In theory the interested and responsible citizen group can terminate the service when it chooses. Although voluntary agencies play a significant role for children in many communities, the best estimates indicate that only about 10 percent of child welfare expenditures are voluntary (Kahn, 1977).

A voluntary agency may serve only one community or a group of communities. It frequently has a cooperative relationship with a local, federated, fund-raising corporation (for example, the United Fund) and a community council of social agencies that strives to plan and coordinate social work activities in a community. The voluntary agency, even though locally financed and administered, may (as may a public agency) have an affiliation with a voluntary national agency, such as the Child Welfare League of America (CWLA), which provides some direction and consultation in program planning. The voluntary agency that provides out-of-home care for children is usually subject to the regulatory authority of the state and must establish its eligibility for a license certifying that it meets certain standards of child care.

Background of Voluntary Child Welfare Services. Voluntary agencies giving service to children have a long history in this country. To a large extent they had their beginnings in the desire of people to fulfill neighborly obligations. Many of the earliest institutions for children, established before 1850, grew out of some specific cause of distress, for example, epidemics of cholera or yellow fever, or wars between Indians and early settlers, which left children orphaned and destitute. Concerned citizens would then undertake to organize a group of people to care for the children in need. Examples include the Ursuline Convent in New Orleans, where ten Sisters in 1729 undertook the care of ten girls who had been orphaned by Indian massacres; an asylum for the care and education of destitute girls, established in Baltimore in 1799 by St. Paul's Church; institutions in various states called Protestant Orphan Asylums, which came into being to care for children orphaned in the cholera epidemic of the 1830s; the Female Humane Association in Virginia, which was the outgrowth of the interest of a group of citizens in 1788 who met to organize for the relief of the "strangers who were then coming in increasing numbers into a growing town on one of the main highways of the nation" (Lundberg, 1947, p. 58).

By 1800, eight such institutions had been founded; by 1824, eighteen more had come into being; and by 1850, an additional ninety had been established (Lundberg, 1947). Many of these later became child-placing agencies, extending their care of children into foster homes in the communities or taking on other community activities.

The latter half of the nineteenth century brought an era of "child-saving" activities. The intent was to save children from conditions of crime, vice, and poverty, often expressed in such terms as these: to "diminish the victims of the spoiler and save the perishing"; to "rescue from vice and degradation the morally exposed children"; or to shelter, educate, and protect the "waifs and strays of the gutter" (Lundberg, 1947, p. 71). These societies, found first in the cities of the eastern seaboard, took many children into care and placed them in free foster homes. An example is the Children's Aid Society of New York City, founded in 1853 by the Reverend Charles Loring Brace. Similar movements developed elsewhere, as in the child-saving work of the Reverend Martin Van Buren Van Arsdale, who lectured and took up collections for homeless children and took over the protection of neglected girls, who were first cared for in his own home. He helped found what is now called the Children's Home and Aid Society of Illinois.

In addition to the intent of the new voluntary agencies to protect harmless children orphaned by disaster and to save others from a life of crime and moral degradation, a third concern was protection of children from neglect and cruelty. Where laws existed for the protection of children from cruelty and abuse, they were poorly enforced. The New York Society for the Prevention of Cruelty to Children (NYSPCC)—the first of its sort—was formed in 1875 to rescue children from cruelty and inhuman treatment and to bring about enforcement of existing laws and passage of new laws. These functions were seen as beyond the purposes of the existing institutions and agencies described above (see Chapter 9 for an account of the NYSPCC as an early child advocacy agency).

The latter part of the nineteenth century brought still another kind of voluntary agency that pioneered in many kinds of service to families and children. Settlement houses such as Jane Addams's famous Hull House in Chicago and Lillian Wald's Henry Street Settlement in New

York were notable examples. Founded with broad aims and open to all the inhabitants of the neighborhood, focused on the needs of families and the preservation and enhancement of human dignity, skill, and values, attuned to the social forces which buffeted poor people, most of whom were immigrants of various nationalities and religions—these early settlements demonstrated new services for families and children and worked steadfastly for social reform and an assumption of public responsibility for social welfare programs.

Voluntary Agencies' Choice of Service.   Traditionally, the particular services given by a voluntary agency have related to the special interests of its sponsoring citizens and the kinds of programs they believe are desirable for a community. Particularly in the field of children's services, many of the voluntary agencies have been sponsored by sectarian interests and have chosen to serve, largely or completely, those children who belong to a particular religious group.

When voluntary agencies in a community define intake policies narrowly along religious or racial definitions, certain negative results are likely. One such result may be unequal services for those children whom the voluntary agencies are unable or unwilling to serve. This is a particular hazard in communities where voluntary agencies have been able to draw in financial and professional resources disproportionate to those available to the public agencies who do serve these children. But even with a well-staffed and well-financed public service the result may still be an unequal de facto segregated service if large numbers of nonwhite children are left to the care of public agencies.

The voluntary agency's authorization from the community to collect contributions and provide services obligates it to greater accountability to the public and less individualization and freedom of choice in program than was acceptable in the early part of the century. A state requirement that voluntary agencies must be licensed to provide out-of-home care for children does result in some voluntary agency accountability, as does the practice of a state department of public welfare that specifies conditions and standards that must be met by the voluntary agency if the public agency is to "purchase care" from it for a particular child for whom the public agency is responsible.

Society today has heavy strains on community resources, and the urgency and complexity of social needs among families are great; furthermore, the voluntary agency's base of financial support usually includes public tax monies, increasing its responsibility to account for its program not only in terms of its daily practice but also in its relationship to community planning for children.

The voluntary agency clearly has an obligation to go beyond a laudable purpose as it selects its function from an array of needs within a community. It should implement a set of policies serving the interests of the community's children, and the choice of function and policies should reflect responsible community planning and the priority needs of all the community's children.

Public–Voluntary Agency Cooperation

Shared Financing.   In theory, voluntary welfare agencies are financed completely by voluntary contributions from citizens. That private agencies should be voluntarily supported has been stated as a corollary principle to the stand that public funds should be expended under the control of public agencies, with full and complete accounting to the people (Branscombe, 1953).

However, the practice of channeling public tax monies to voluntary agencies has a long history, going back to the early 1800s and increasing in the latter quarter of the nineteenth century when a variety of voluntary agencies were established for purposes of "child-saving" and "child rescue." Many such agencies depended for a considerable part of their annual income on the receipt of public money. This support was sometimes in the form of a subsidy—a lump sum to be applied to the agency's operating budget. More recently the usual method has been a per capita payment by a public agency for the care of, or services to, a particular child, the amount determined in various ways.

Until the 1960s extensive funding by government to nonprofit child welfare agencies was an exception to the norm. Then the demand began to rise significantly for social services to a wider range of families and children with especially difficult problems. A survey in the early 1970s of child welfare services in twenty-five states found that purchase of service arrangements ranged widely depending on the traditional role of private agencies, the availability of private agency resources, and the adequacy of state funding. In many states, purchase policies and procedures were not well documented.

Nevertheless, the practice of purchase seemed to be growing with increasing involvement of public welfare with the private sector ("Child welfare in 25 States," 1976). An Urban Institute study found that purchase services had become the predominant mode of service delivery nationally (Benton et al., 1978). By the fiscal year 1982, more than 40 percent of funds of nonprofit child welfare agencies were from public sources (Kimmich, 1985). The author of a comprehensive study of thirty child and family agencies was led to assert that "the growing use of purchase-of-service contracts between government and nonprofit child welfare agencies" was perhaps "the most critical development within child welfare policy during the last 25 years affecting the response of child welfare service organizations to children in need." The danger cited was that the increase in public contracting with voluntary agencies for services "is restructuring the relationship between government and nonprofit child welfare agencies, leading to greater government intervention and influence in nonprofit agencies" (S. R. Smith, 1989, pp. 289, 290).

What explains this very substantial growth in the practice of public purchase of voluntary services for children and families? S. R. Smith (1989) identified some coinciding factors. In the 1960s and 1970s federal funds for purchase of social services from nonprofit agencies expanded. With funds now available, emphasis at both the federal and state levels of social services administration urged "quick program start-up" rather than rigorous examination and monitoring of voluntary agency programs (p. 292). In fact, the state social welfare departments at that point had limited resources for monitoring. In addition, many of the voluntary child welfare agencies had a traditional and firm claim on their service areas, leaving the public agencies in a disadvantaged position and likely to accept the preferences of the nonprofit agencies.

The changed political and economic currents of the 1980s substantially shifted the relationship between the public and voluntary sectors of social welfare. Federal funds for social services were cut seriously, even as the need for services increased, especially in the areas of child abuse and neglect, foster care, and child care for children of working parents. Voluntary agencies became more financially vulnerable and were forced to become more competitive in seeking purchase contracts from the public agencies. State agencies had improved their situation in terms of management and accountability, making it feasible to develop new initiatives toward the voluntary agencies that increased the influence of the public agency in decisions about accepting children for services and defining what these should be (S. R. Smith, 1989).

The pattern of shared financing presents a complicated issue. The public authority has the broad responsibility for services required to meet the needs of children and their families and is guided by "norms of equity," that is, fairness reflected in "equivalent services across geographic regions, services to the neediest clients, and nondiscrimination in the provision of services." Voluntary agencies, in contrast, are responsive to "clients who are deemed to be consistent with the basic mission of their organizations (S. R. Smith, 1989, p. 291). If that level of appropriateness for services is established, then a child may receive a variety of intensive and beneficial services. Public agencies sometimes claim that such a pattern of selecting children to help who fit the organizational mission results in unnecessarily long treatment that deprives other waiting children of services. The voluntary agency in turn sees this treatment as representing their commitment to make utmost efforts in behalf of the child and the family accepted for access to their services (S. R. Smith, 1989).

The purchase of care and service appeals to public agencies on the grounds that it provides increased service flexibility, program innovation, and in many instances lower service cost (S. R. Smith, 1989). However, although a system of purchase may be the most feasible way for a public agency to meet its service obligations and ensure that all children are served, any system of shared financing establishes a mutual dependence between the public and private agencies involved and presents each with potential problems. One of the gravest is the danger that the public agency may depend on discharging its responsibility through payments to voluntary agencies, thus retarding the proper growth of public services. In addition, the public agency may be hard-pressed to demonstrate its accountability for the expenditure of such public funds when the service actually is provided by another agency. The public agency must determine that the service purchased is indeed what a particular child or family needs; the service must be provided on an economically and professionally sound basis—no public agency should purchase substandard service. In addition, there is the problem of how cost should be computed; for example, what part of the private agency's capital investment in its physical plan should be considered?

The voluntary agency also is faced with potential problems. It may come to depend on the receipt of tax funds for significant proportions of its operating budget, thus threatening its tra-

ditional freedom to select whom it will serve and the type of program it will offer. Pressured by the public agency to develop service priorities according to equity principles—services first to families and children who are most disadvantaged or at greatest risk—their extensive use of purchase-of-care contracts clearly restricts the discretion of nonprofit agencies as to whom they serve. Further, the voluntary agency may fear gradual intervention in policy making as the public agency seeks to achieve accountability for the use of its funds and to ensure a level of care that meets its standard (S. R. Smith, 1989).

In any case, if purchase of care is employed as one means of financing a community's social services for children, it should be carried out within a framework of community planning if it is to further the welfare of children and their families.

Proprietary Child Welfare Services

Purchase of child welfare services is sometimes contracted between a public agency and a *proprietary for-profit* agency. For-profit contracting occurs mainly in the provision of child care for working parents; a high majority of such contracting is with nonprofit agencies (S. R. Smith, 1989, p. 297). Very large numbers of other children have care arranged and carried out for them independently of any social welfare agency. Some parents answer ads in the newspaper or learn through other more casual means of someone who will give care to their children during the day. Most of the available child care centers and family day care homes are operated as commercial ventures. Some families have found their own homemaker to bring into the home during periods of crisis and the mothers' absence. Some parents find a foster home and make arrangements for others to care for their children. Many children are placed in adoptive homes without the planning or supervision of a social welfare agency; this is very often arranged by an attorney for a fee or by other intermediaries.

Not enough is known about the quality of care and the experiences of children through these various independent arrangements. For many such children, there are poor quality of care, instability, and even abuse. However, some parents, particularly those with initiative, sound judgment, and financial resources, have been able to make satisfactory, independent arrangements for some aspects of their children's care.

Further systematic study of existing forms of independent care of children is needed, with attention not only to their hazards but also to the factors contributing to a successful experience for children and families. Such study could provide a basis for new experimentation in the development of independent care as well as a basis for giving direction to parents who want to use independent forms of care. Such study could also provide important information to state licensing authorities in the reformulation of mandatory licensing standards for child care facilities.

TRENDS AND ISSUES

Comprehensive Services for Children, Youth, and Families

"The generation of children growing up in the United States today faces a different world from the one in which its parents were reared. Sweeping economic and demographic changes since the 1960s have fundamentally altered traditional assumptions about the family and have changed significantly the way American families work, the way they live, and the world in which their children grow and learn" (Rosewater, 1989).

The impact of these changes is mirrored in the recognition that traditional child welfare services are not comprehensive enough to meet the social welfare needs of large numbers of today's children, youth, and families. In

Kadushin's assessment, the need for and the legitimacy of the existing child welfare programs are unquestioned; they perform functions that the public sees as essential and is willing to support (1987). At the same time, the boundaries of the child welfare system are being challenged and there is growing pressure to expand practice into a broader range of family-based services.

From a two-year study of both public and private agencies in states and counties across the country, Kamerman and Kahn (1989) reported findings from agency efforts to deliver alternative social services to children, youth and families. Their findings were sobering. Child protective services, the researchers asserted, "today constitute the core public child and family services," in effect " 'driving' the public agency and often taking over child welfare entirely." Further, most of the protective services that were offered were organized around "investigation and risk assessment rather than treatment" (p. 11). Consequently, in the very numerous instances where the allegations of abuse were not substantiated, no help to the family was available, even though urgent problems of family maintenance and child-rearing practices were common. In many instances "the only other social service provided is foster care, which in turn serves mostly abuse and neglect cases" (p. 10).

A repeated theme that emerged in Kamerman and Kahn's interviews was that "the social service system has become so constricted that children can gain access to help only if they have been abused or severely neglected, are found delinquent, or run away. Doorways for 'less serious' or differently defined problems are closed" (p. 9).

"The mounting crisis of our children and our families is a rebuke to everything America professes to be." (CDF Reports, 1990, quoting Marian Wright Edelman, p. 8)

Some of the factors that have contributed to this situation can be identified. One was the unprecedented attack on social programs by the Reagan administration and the heavy retrenchment in federal support for social programs, which had dire effects on children, youth, and families. For example, federal aid for handicapped education in fiscal year 1980 was over $1 billion, whereas Reagan proposed a ceiling for fiscal year 1984 of $845 million. The Women-Infant-Children's program was maintained over the proposal of the executive branch of the government to abolish it. Similarly, the Early and Periodic Screening, Diagnosis, and Treatment program, an effort to provide health testing and immunization for children, was proposed for abolishment, but the proposal was defeated in Congress. Food stamps and the school lunch program were reduced and more restrictive eligibility standards established. Another proposal was made to relax child labor laws for fourteen- and fifteen-year-olds so that they could work more hours. Support for research focused on children and families was significantly reduced. No major initiative in support of children was forthcoming and responsibility for social programs was increasingly transferred to the states.

Another major factor that has made it difficult to know what has been happening to children is the lack of overall statistics about the number of children and families receiving child welfare services in each part of the system, and the nature of those services. Nor has there been in the last decade any synthesis of various minimal sets of data that do exist. As a result, a comprehensive analysis of the issues of children, youth, and families is absent (Kadushin, 1987; Rosewater, 1989). Given the inadequacy of data and the confusing inconsistency of language in what does exist, we are left with "extraordinary categorical fragmentation, *not* a holistic overview" (Kamerman & Kahn, 1989, p. 36).

Another factor in influencing the present lack of clarity with respect to services for children, youth, and families has been unanticipated effects of two separate pieces of federal legislation: (1) P. L. 100–294, the Child Abuse Prevention and Treatment Act of 1974, which provides assistance to states to enable them to identify and treat instances of child abuse and neglect, and (2) P. L. 96–272, the Adoption Assistance and Child Welfare Act of 1980, which endorsed and supports (in limited amounts) efforts to find adoptive families for children who, for a variety of reasons, are unable to live with their own parents. The new philosophy of the Adoption Act was applauded, as had been the federal effort to help the child welfare system to identify and prevent child abuse and neglect. The proponents of both strategies were in agreement about the need for a more broadly defined child and family services system. Nevertheless, from their recent findings with respect to current child and family welfare practice, Kamerman and Kahn (1989) identified "dual pressures" in the efforts to implement the two branches of federal legislation: On the one hand, a mandate to identify and investigate each of the rapidly escalating reports of abuse and neglect; and on the other hand, a new philosophy and service framework to facilitate moving children out of foster homes and into permanent adoptive homes. In Kamerman and Kahn's view, one result has been a denigration of foster care of all types and a decline in the numbers of foster families. This decline occurred despite clear evidence that some children need placement away from their own families, perhaps for some time before being returned to their own homes, and despite current research that confirms earlier findings that long-term foster care can be beneficial to some children. Compounding the problem is the scarcity of supportive and supplementary services for parents who have been reported to be abusive or neglectful.

An encouraging finding from the Kamerman and Kahn study (1989) was the discovery of a number of states and counties that have expanded their child welfare services by developing a broader range of services focused on the whole family rather than individual members. These new practices are sometimes termed "family-preservation" services. In some instances they are used, not only when placement is imminent, but are also offered to highly vulnerable families where children are at risk but not yet necessarily in crisis.

It is encouraging that these new directions toward a comprehensive system of social services for children, youth, and families appear to be spreading. Nevertheless, without reliable financial resources and clear public policy commitment, the child welfare system will continue to be unable to meet the pressing needs of groups of children with problems different from those provided in the traditional pattern of services. These groups include seriously troubled older youth, young adolescents, some very young children, and youth who in earlier years would be in institutions but are now in the community (Kamerman & Kahn, 1989, p. 19).

The loss of federal commitment to social services in the 1980s was severely detrimental to the welfare of children and families. One positive development in increased federal interest for planning for children and families is found in the work of the House of Representatives' Select Committee on Children, Youth and Families, established by Congress in 1982. Through its hearings, the Committee has sought expert testimony with respect to the problems and issues affecting U.S. children and their families, and has disseminated the findings. The founding in 1974 of the Children's Defense Fund (see Chapter 12), which pursues an active program of child advocacy, has also added significantly to an understanding of the difficult issues and possible solutions.

The Role of the Social Work Profession in Child Welfare

"During the 1950s and 1960s child welfare as a specialization was clearly identified administratively and conceptually in large public welfare agencies. It enjoyed a special recognition and status as a highly professional sector of social work. Recently, however, child welfare has lost some of its elite status. As units were divided, reallocated, and merged almost into nonexistence, child welfare was no longer able to maintain its unique identity and clearly defined, specialized visibility in public agencies" (Kadushin, 1987, p. 272).

Kamerman and Kahn (1989) also cite some of the conditions within the child welfare system that have weakened its status and the effectiveness of its services: (1) growth in the numbers of very difficult cases along with a decline in the numbers of professional staff; (2) a perception of deprofessionalization on the part of staff emanating from a decline in autonomy and flexibility, which in turn stems from demanding accountability tasks imposed by child abuse requirements; (3) a downgrading of positions by reclassification of professional to nonprofessional, accompanied by further declining salaries, making the positions less attractive to the professional staff; and (4) a loss in the availability of social work professionals for child welfare positions in some communities (pp. 24–25).

Meyer (1984) has observed that "the entire field of child welfare, broadly defined, is the one in which social work has been the predominant discipline." Its research has been "prodigious and exemplary." More than all other fields of social work practice, child welfare is "most familiar . . . to the public, to Congress, and to social work recruits." Child welfare is the only field of practice in which social workers have long been in control of their own programs. Meyer challenged the social work profession to reassume its vital responsibility for the entire field of child welfare (p. 499).

In Kadushin's view, whether this recovery can be accomplished "will depend on the ability of the profession to establish convincingly that professional knowledge, skill, and expertise, acquired by social workers as a consequence of professional training, are clearly superior to service provided by nonprofessionals. As yet, the profession has failed to provide clear evidence that such is the case" (1987, p. 274).

FOR STUDY AND DISCUSSION

1. What is meant by public social policy? Give examples in addition to those mentioned in the text that directly or indirectly affect children and family life. Draw from your knowledge of your own community.

2. Debate the merits of a comprehensive national family policy. Include both desirability and feasibility in the arguments.

3. In broad but specific terms, delineate services that should be included in a system of comprehensive services for children, youth, and families. Give reasons that support your choices.

4. Keeping in mind the differences between *rights* and *needs* of children, what do you believe should be the rights of children in our society? The rights of parents? The duty that corresponds to each right?

5. Enumerate, with examples, the powers of government society employs to further the well-being of children and their families.

6. Discuss differences between public, voluntary, and proprietary child welfare agencies in terms of philosophy, financing, and authorization from society.

7. What problematic aspects are associated with public purchase of care and services from nonprofit and for-profit agencies?

FOR ADDITIONAL STUDY

Child Welfare League of America. (1988a). *Report of the CWLA task force on children and HIV infection. Initial guidelines.* Washington, DC: Author.

Davis, M., & Schwartz, M. D. (1987). *Children's rights and the law.* Lexington, MA: Lexington Books.

Freeman, E. M., & Pennekamp, M. (1988). *Social work practice: Toward a child, family, school, community perspective.* Springfield, IL: C. C. Thomas.

Girls Clubs of America (1988). *Facts and reflections on girls and substance abuse.* New York: Author.

Hutchings, J. J. (1988). Pediatric AIDS: An overview. *Children Today, 17*(3), 4–7.

Johnson, K. (1988). *Teens and AIDS: Opportunities for prevention.* Washington, DC: Children's Defense Fund.

Schorr, L. B. (1988). *Within our reach. Breaking the cycle of disadvantage.* New York: Anchor Press.

CHAPTER 2

Children's Guardianship

Guardianship establishes a relation which may well affect the whole life of a child.

Irving Weissman

Chapter Outline

The integrity of the parent-child relationship has been long shielded by a tradition of family privacy and the presumption that parents will act in their children's best interests. Nevertheless, state laws allow intervention into family life when there is evidence that parents are unable or unwilling to provide their children with proper guardianship. In such instances guardianship can be involuntarily transferred from parents and vested in public or private child welfare agencies or individuals.

Legal ramifications of the parent-child relationship are demanding more and more attention from social workers traditionally concerned about the protection of children. Various public constituencies, often with different values and philosophies, want to safeguard the family by developing public social policy. Some advocates for the family favor policy that reaffirms the traditional presumption that parents will act in their child's best interests, and that safeguards the rights of parents by stringent tests to justify the termination of parental rights. Some other child and family advocates place greater reliance on policy that advocates the legal rights of children as distinct from those of their parents. Society's response currently is an ambivalent one—sometimes leaning in the direction of parent rights and in other instances in the direction of child rights. Most child and family advocates prefer an approach to treating family problems that represents the "least intrusive intervention" appropriate to the family's and child's needs.

Social workers play a variety of roles in relation to the court process. They may file petitions, conduct social and family assessments, investigate facts, provide information to the court at intake, prepare child witnesses for court, testify as expert witnesses, and serve as guardian *ad litem*. Pending court disposition, social workers offer services to families in the home and community, with the intent of keeping the family together and functional. In-home or out-of-home services may be given to children to enhance their safety and welfare. Short-term transfer of guardianship can contribute to the well-being of children while their parents receive treatment or learn parenting skills. In situations where children cannot live with parents and adoption is not appropriate, long-term transfer of guardianship is a preferred permanency outcome.

Guardianship issues arise as well in divorce actions. Social workers often serve as mediators in resolving custody conflicts between parents seeking divorce. When mediation does not result in a custody agreement, social workers may serve as custody evaluators and make recommendations to the judge.

Guardianship often has been insufficiently understood as a resource for children, and its potential for contributing to the well-being of many children has been neglected. Guardianship is a *concept,* a *practice* in child welfare, and a *policy issue.* In any sense guardianship is of central importance to the life events of children, particularly those who have come into the care of the state or are at risk of doing so.

THE NATURE OF GUARDIANSHIP AND CUSTODY

Distinguished from *in loco parentis*

Awards of guardianship and custody constitute a method of providing legal protections for children and young persons. ("Transfer" or "assignment" of guardianship and custody are newer terms used by some courts instead of "awards," which connotes a win/lose orientation.) Guardianship and custody are distinguished from the concept of *in loco parentis,* by which someone acts informally as a parent or gives care to a child. *In loco parentis* is not an official relationship in that it carries no continuing obligation toward the child. Sometimes parents hand over their child to a succession of caretakers and finally abandon him or her to the care of a willing person, who, in turn, assumes parental rights and duties. But under the informal authority of *in loco parentis* the child lacks the legal security that an award of guardianship or custody supplies. A caretaker *in loco parentis* is not bound to responsibility for the child. The child is vulnerable to abandonment again or to being turned over carelessly to someone else.

Guardianship and Custody Differentiated

The terms "guardianship" and "custody" are somewhat overlapping in definition and therefore frequently confused. While there are differences in the rights and responsibilities of each, an award of either custody or guardianship involves substantially the same questions; in either action, the decision must be based on a concern as to what the welfare of the child requires. That an award of custody or guardianship must be made so as to promote the child's best interests is a principle that can be applied to a range of conflicts.

When children do not have necessary protections assured through their parents, guardianship may become a legal substitute for the relationship of parent to child. Guardianship laws are based on the recognition that children are too immature and inexperienced to care for themselves or to manage their own affairs, so this responsibility must be entrusted to others. Parents, as natural guardians, have the first right and responsibility to provide for their children's care and management. For most children, their own parents adequately fulfill the responsibilities of guardian and custodian. But when a child loses the protection of parents through death or incapacity, or when the guardianship afforded by a parent falls short of what society requires as a minimal standard of care, the state may supplement or substitute for the parental effort through the court's appointment of a guardian.

Guardians, then, are those individuals whom the law charges with the overall care and management of the person or the property, or both, of a child during his or her minority. Guardians have broad powers for decision making and authoritative action in matters that have long-term effects on a child's development and future. Persons selected to serve as guardians are supplied by the court with written authorization (*letters of guardianship*), which enables them legally to act with or represent their *wards* (the minors involved) and by so doing to protect those wards through sound decisions, advice, guidance, or direct authoritative action in their behalf. Guardians have a continuing obligation toward their wards for the duration of appointment or until the children reach majority age.

Custody implies having the physical possession of the child, including responsibility to provide immediate care, supervision, guidance, and discipline in day-to-day living. Guardianship carries greater rights and responsibilities than does custody for the major or more significant decisions about the child's care. Guardians frequently have custody of their wards, but not necessarily so; custody may be entrusted to a natural parent, a relative, or a foster parent at the same time that guardianship is vested in another person.

Most controversy over custody comes about as a part of a divorce action involving the necessity of deciding with which parent a child shall live. Divorce statutes in all states make provision for awards of custody of children of the marriage. Some jurisdictions no longer use the adversarial term "custody," and favor instead "allocating parental responsibilities" or "parenting plans following divorce." Changing sex roles are reflected in the court's greater readiness to avoid the old presumption that mothers should be preferred in awarding custody of children. Fathers now often seek and gain custody of their children.

Joint custody is another option—a court-approved agreement between parents that provides for joint decision making concerning a child's education, medical treatment, religious training, and care. In some joint arrangements, physical custody is also shared. In addition, if a child's best interests require it, custody may be granted to someone other than one of the parents. Generally in such situations relatives or friends are given preference over social agencies.

The most frequent social work roles in custody actions arising from divorce are mediation with parents to arrive at the best plan for the child, or failing that, carrying out a family evaluation and recommending a particular custody or time share arrangement to the judge. Many children experience very undesirable instability arising from a continual transfer between parents, particularly when parents try to relitigate custody disputes and use the child as a weapon against one another.

Some authorities in child welfare matters have taken a controversial point of view about the custody of children of divorced parents.

Their recommendations are made out of concern for many children's difficulties in maintaining satisfactory contact with two parents who do not have a positive relationship with each other, the frequent discontinuity in visits from or to the "other" parent, the incidence of children being shifted back and forth between competing parents merely to comply with what may prove to be tentative decisions, and the likelihood conflicts of loyalty that threaten the child's relationship with both parents. A custody decision, these authors state, should be final, not subject to modification. They place primary emphasis on the security of an ongoing relationship between the child and the parent awarded custody. Therefore, the custodial parent would decide under what conditions he or she wishes to raise the child. The noncustodial parent would have no legal and enforceable right to visit; the parent having custody would decide whether and under what circumstances such visits might be desirable for the child. To avoid having children become, in a sense, an "award for damages" at the conclusion of a divorce action, all disputes between parents about custody of their children should be resolved in proceedings held prior to a determination of the merits of the divorce or separation action itself. Because children in divorce actions cannot be adequately represented by the advocates of either of the parents, some suggest that children should have legal representation as persons in their own right (Goldstein et al., 1973, pp. 37–38, 46–47, 67, 79; Edwards, 1985, p. 4).

Given the increasing incidence of a variety of shared custody arrangements by divorced parents, these recommendations tend to provoke opposition. Persons who wish to see more attention focused on the best interests of children of divorced parents may respond more positively to guidelines developed and put into practice by Judge Robert Hansen of the Family Court in Milwaukee County. In order to encourage reconciliation of parents, to arrive at custody arrangements that are in a child's best interests, and to call attention to the child's need for a guardian *ad litem* in divorce actions, Judge Hansen developed a "Bill of Rights of Children in Divorce Actions." These guidelines include the right of the child to have a positive and constructive relationship with both parents, to know the noncustodial parent, to receive love and guidance from that parent through adequate visitations, and to have periodic review of custodial arrangements as changed circumstances of the parents or the needs of the child may require (Brieland & Lemmon, 1985).

Background of Guardianship Law

Legislation concerning guardianship in this country was written for the most part within the pattern of English law; it was frequently among the first enacted by the new states. In general the American states developed a simpler form of guardianship than the English system. English law had provided for at least ten kinds of guardianship, but many of these were never included in American law (*Mauro v. Ritchie,* 1827; Weissman, 1949, pp. 15–16). Some trend was discernible in this country toward intervention in the parent-child relationship in order to protect the child in matters other than the management of property, but for the most part this tendency reflected the early citizens' view of a parent's duty as something that should be enforced. The intervention, then, was more to enforce parental duty than to bring about other care or protection for the child.

*Whatever may be their precise impact, neither the Fourteenth Amendment nor the Bill of Rights is for adults alone. (*In re Gault, *1967)*

Nevertheless, in the history of guardianship in America, increasing emphasis can be found on the welfare of the child as a first consideration. No longer is the child viewed as the "property" of parents, but as an individual with the right to grow and to develop his or her own unique capacities. Parents are regarded by the community as being entrusted with the rearing of children to become responsible and useful members of society. Consequently, parental power may be limited by state supervision (Rheinstein, 1958, p. 16). The Children's Bureau stated this position: All children are entitled to an individual guardian "by birth or adoption or a judicially appointed guardian." This guardian is responsible for safeguarding the child's interests, making important decisions in her or his life, and maintaining a personal relationship with the child (Children's Bureau, 1961, p. 3). It is, then, a source of concern that large numbers of children are living in homes of nonrelatives or in institutions without adequate provision of legal guardianship. In some states children are brought into custody by one of society's social agencies or institutions but without guardianship of person being judicially appointed. Thus the nonrelative caretakers of these children stand *in loco parentis,* and the children risk discontinuity in their lives (Williams, 1980). In addition, such children can be subjected to neglect or exploitation if they have no personal guardian who speaks and questions for them or asks for evidence from time to time that the care and treatment being provided is appropriate and in their own particular best interests.

In summary, the best use of guardianship and custody is based on these principles: (1) Children are individuals with the right to the development of their fullest capacities; (2) parents, as natural guardians, have the first right and responsibility to give care and protection to their children; (3) when children lose their parents or when parental efforts fall short of society's minimum standards, the state has the authority and responsibility to provide substitute care and protection through appointment of a legal guardian or custodian; (4) the responsibility for transfer of guardianship is properly a judicial responsibility and as such is an inherent part of our dem-

ocratic system; and lastly (5) all children who need it are entitled to a judicially appointed guardian who will safeguard their interests and make important decisions in their lives, and with whom they can can have a personal relationship.

KINDS OF GUARDIANS—DUTIES, RIGHTS, RESTRICTIONS

The power to appoint a guardian derives from laws within each of the separate states. In spite of the variation that separate state laws imply, the natural guardianship of parents uniformly has been given great weight and has been preferred generally to judicial (or court-appointed) guardianship.

Natural Guardianship

Guardianship "by nature" refers to the private, legal relationship of parent and child. Natural guardianship provides the pattern for other forms of guardianship and carries all the parental rights and responsibilities that were discussed in Chapter 1.

However, the control vested in the parent as guardian usually extends only to the person of the child; to assume control over the property of the child, the parent usually must be appointed to this authority by court action. Natural guardianship does not devolve on other relatives. Parents cannot on their own transfer their guardianship to someone else, nor is guardianship an absolute right of parents. Always the welfare of the child is the primary consideration, and natural guardianship may be interrupted by court intervention when just cause is shown.

There are important differences between the rights and responsibilities of parents and those of a court-appointed guardian. Guardianship through court appointment is subject to the continuing supervision of the court; natural guardianship is not. Guardianship, unlike parenthood, does not involve the duty to support and educate the ward except from his or her own estate, nor does it carry the right to the ward's earnings and services. Children under court-appointed guardianship continue in their right to inherit from their parents; they do not have the right to inherit from their guardians. Parents have the right to choose where their child shall live as long as the care given does not fall below the minimal standards demanded by the community. In contrast, a guardian of person may exercise choice as to a foster home or institutional placement for a child without specific court approval; but because the guardian and ward are subject to the continuing supervision of the court, the guardian may not change the ward's home without court approval if such a change would remove the ward from the jurisdiction of the court.

Although parents cannot transfer their rights of guardianship to someone else, generally they can extend their rights of natural guardianship through the provision of a *testamentary guardian*. This term refers to the naming of a guardian for their child by parents in a last will and testament. This is a voluntary, independent act of parents who may exercise free choice as to the person they want named as guardian of person or estate or both in the event of their own deaths. This form of guardianship generally requires court approval before the guardians assume their responsibilities, and they then become subject to the supervision of the court, as is true for other court-appointed guardians. Only a parent, that is, the mother or father of a child born within a marriage, or the mother of a nonmarital child, can name a testamentary guardian; other relatives such as grandparent, aunt, or uncle cannot exercise this right in behalf of the child. Neither can the testamentary guardian delegate his or her guardianship to someone else.

When parents' guardianship of their child is interrupted by court intervention and awarded to someone else, it constitutes a very substantial limitation on parental rights. But even with the naming of a guardian, unless the parent-child relationship has been fully terminated by judicial decree, there are still certain rights and responsibilities that the parent retains. These include, but are not necessarily limited to (1) the right of reasonable visitation, that is, the right to visit his or her child regularly at a convenient place for a long enough period of time for the visit to be mutually satisfying for both the parent and the child; (2) the right to consent or refuse to consent to adoption; (3) the right to determine the child's religious affiliation; (4) the responsibility for financial support of the child; and (5) the right to ask for judicial review of the case and reinstatement of guardianship.

When there is reason to sever parental rights completely and irrevocably, a final judicial determination is indicated—*termination proceedings* dissolving the last legal ties between parent and child. "Generally, termination is appropriate only if there is a need to decisively and permanently end all parent-child contacts" (Hardin, 1983, p. 133).

A judicial, or court-appointed guardian may be a guardian of person, guardian of estate, or guardian *ad litem*.

Guardian of Person

This kind of judicial guardianship most approximates that of a child's own parents. Like the parent, the guardian of person becomes responsible for the care and control of the child. A guardian of person has the right and responsibility of legal custody unless custody has been vested in another individual or in an authorized social agency or institution.

The guardian of person is entrusted with important decisions of the kind which have a permanent effect on the child's life. These decisions may concern choice of a foster home or institution, or kind of medical care, including permission for major medical, psychiatric, and surgical treatment; or decisions about education, employment, permission for marriage, and permission for entry into the armed forces; and the right to represent the child in legal actions. In certain instances, the guardian of person may have been invested by court action with the power to consent to the adoption of the minor when the parent-child relationship has been *fully terminated* by judicial decree.

Like parents, guardians of person do not have the right to receive and manage property which their wards may acquire unless specifically authorized to do so, usually by appointment to guardian of estate. Because the same person is often appointed to both duties—control of person and estate—the different functions of the two offices are frequently confused.

Guardian of Estate

This form of guardianship creates a means by which a minor can deal in the business world. Guardians of estate are in a sense trustees or administrators. Specifically, they have power to govern the estate and act for their wards in matters involving property. The office makes possible the mortgage or sale of property and frees resources for the rearing of the child that would otherwise be tied up during the ward's minority.

However, the responsibility of a guardian of property should not extend to the expenditure of a ward's small maintenance income, for example, Social Security or veteran's benefits, since these kinds of funds will usually be needed for the child's daily living. For this kind of decision making and supervision, private personal guardians are needed (A. D. Smith, 1955, p. 150).

Guardians of estate are persons of presumed integrity and are subject to the continuing supervision of the court through periodic accounting. Unless the guardian of estate is also named guardian of person, the guardian does not have the right to interfere in personal affairs of the minor, but must confine his or her activities to the management of the estate.

A major study of guardianship (Weissman, 1949) found that some guardians appeared to have distinctly individual conceptions of their jobs, sometimes because the court had not explained the office. An inability to distinguish clearly between guardianship of person and guardianship of estate appeared to be a common source of misunderstanding and difficulty.

Betrayals of the element of trust by guardians have been many, but none more unconscionable than the plundering of American-Indian children's inheritance that occurred in 1901–1905 when the federal government mandated a division of the land within The Indian Territory (now Oklahoma) owned by five autonomous Indian tribes (Debo, 1940). According to ancient Indian custom, the tribes held their land under a communal and self-sustaining economic order. The new compulsory division of the land was based on an individualistic conception of property ownership that was foreign to their previous experience. The result was unexpected problems of human adjustment as well as new opportunities for exploitation by white men, termed "grafters," who dealt in Indian land by illegal conveyances.

The division of tribal property among all its citizens brought many minor children into possession of estates varying in value from an average farm to great speculative wealth of land with the potential of producing oil. Many of the children's parents were too inexperienced to qualify before a federal court as guardians of their own children's estates. As a result white men individually secured appointment as guardians of a large number of children and controlled their assets with minimal court supervision. By means of collusion with real estate dealers and a series of legal fictions, these guardians illegally appropriated children's property at enormous profit. The children continued to be supported from their parents' own shrinking assets, or were living in orphanages maintained by large expenditures from federal and tribal funds. Of this violation of child rights, the historian Angie Debo observed that "no other children had ever been so rich and so defenseless" (Debo, 1940, p. 109).

Guardian *ad litem*

This form of guardianship has a temporary and specific nature making it different from the substitute parental relationship in other forms of guardianship. Courts have a responsibility to see that children and young persons have the services of a guardian when issues affecting them directly are being adjudicated. Commonly, parents may be represented by counsel and the social agency will have a legal representative present. When the needs and interests of a child are also at stake, it cannot be assumed that either parent or agency will necessarily be able to focus squarely on the best interests of the child. To that end, a guardian *ad litem* can be appointed by a court to serve in a particular litigation to which a minor is a party for the purpose of representing and protecting that child's interests.

Traditionally it was believed that a guardian *ad litem* was needed only to protect the property of a minor or an incompetent adult. However, in recent years widespread support has developed for expanding the role. The concepts of guardian *ad litem* and of the power to appoint such a guardian are firmly established in the judicial system and are ready resources when concerns of children are brought to the attention of the court (Gittis, 1988; Schwartz, 1987; Hardin, 1986–87; Edwards, 1985; Eitzen, 1985; Bross & Munson, 1980; Genden, 1976).

When Is a Guardian **ad litem** *Useful?*   Proponents of child rights see various types of litigation in which appointment of a guardian *ad litem* would be beneficial. Primary among these are the following situations (Genden, 1976, pp. 570–580):

1. *Situations in which the child's liberty is at stake,* as in juvenile delinquency or status offense disposition hearings (that is, at the point the court decides what treatment plan will be as-

signed to the minor), and in instances in which parents voluntarily commit their children to a mental institution. The interests of a young person charged with delinquent behavior or with "incorrigibility" (in need of supervision) may not coincide with those of parents. A child alleged by parents to be beyond control may sometimes have a single basis for defense—one based on an inadequate home environment or rejection by parents. Parents, probation officers, and social workers sometimes yield to an easy remedy for a difficult young person by resorting to institutional placement, which means a loss of liberty. The agents of society, ostensibly acting in behalf of children, sometimes display quite unfriendly, even antagonistic attitudes toward minors in delinquency hearings.

A similar risk occurs when parents agree to seek voluntary commitment of a child to a mental hospital. Once committed, the child cannot act on her or his own to leave the confined setting. Questions are being raised more often about the adequacy of treatment in closed institutions of different kinds where children and youth are placed without adequate attention to their special needs and access to an effective advocate.

2. *Divorce litigation involving decisions about child custody and financial support.* Traditionally children's interests have not been individualized effectively in divorce.

> The importance of assessing the individual child's strengths, vulnerabilities, concerns, and wishes must be emphasized, particularly when parents are in dispute over the children. Parents at the time of divorce often have competing perceptions of the children's needs, problems and adjustment to the divorce and their particular living arrangements. A parent's perceptions of the child's adjustment may be distorted by the parent's own satisfaction or dissatisfaction. Frequently, the parent who sought the divorce views the child as coping better than the person who opposed it. Similarly, a parent who sought a particular custody arrangement and who is satisfied with it may see the child as adjusting

well, while the other parent sees the child as troubled. (Steinman, 1984, p. 126)

The question of child support following divorce is a crucial one for children. Either parent may seek to have financial payments designated as alimony rather than child support, a mother because alimony is not restricted in its use as are child support payments, a father because alimony can be deducted from income for tax purposes. Subsequent marriages often affect support payments. A guardian *ad litem* is often the only way to assure that the child's critical financial interests are given attention (Paquin, 1987–1988, p. 286; Genden, 1976, p. 573).

Despite the slowing of the divorce rate, more public attention is being given to the special needs of children of divorce. The Uniform Marriage and Divorce Act includes a provision for the appointment of a guardian *ad litem* for children whose parents divorce. Thirty-three states or jurisdictions have some provision for advocacy for children in private custody disputes (Blakesley, 1988, p. 16). Under some state laws, social work mediators can recommend that the court appoint a guardian *ad litem* for a child whose best interests cannot be protected in child custody mediation because the parents cannot focus on the child's needs.

3. *Nondivorce custody proceedings.* Such proceedings serve the interests of children most appropriately if there is a guardian *ad litem* appointed for their protection. Examples include decisions about foster family placement, termination of parental rights, and adoption. A major step has been taken in assuring independent advocacy for the abused and neglected child when the investigation of suspected abuse and neglect results in judicial proceedings. Among the conditions that states must meet to receive federal funds under the Child Abuse Prevention and Treatment Act of 1974 is the stipulation that a guardian *ad litem* must be appointed to represent each child who is the subject of an abuse and neglect court hearing. The act served as a significant impetus for state legislation. All states and the District of Columbia have enacted provisions for guardian *ad litem* representation for the child alleged to be neglected or abused.

4. *Paternity suits.* In such suits children have significant interests at stake that merit special advocacy: entitlement to welfare benefits, paternal support, inheritance, wrongful death claims, and in addition, risk of the stigma of "illegitimacy." Appointment of a guardian or guardian *ad litem* to represent the child in paternity proceedings is required by the Uniform Parentage Act. The Act has been adopted in 20 states (Bross & Munson, 1980, p. 574).

5. *Actions to compel nonessential medical treatment or access to education.* This is an area where a guardian *ad litem* may be needed but where courts have been reluctant to inquire as to the views of the child. With increased public recognition of the needs of handicapped children, the state more frequently is bringing action to insist on medical treatment rejected by parents. For example, a probation department in California alleged that a twelve-year-old boy suffering from Down's syndrome was not provided with the necessities of life and requested that he be declared a dependent child in order to receive cardiac surgery for a congenital defect. Medical evidence was submitted to establish that if the heart defect was not corrected, damage to the lungs would increase with a progressive loss of energy and vitality, followed by a bed-to-chair existence and, subsequently, death. Although the court acknowledged that the state is justified in intervening when parents fail to provide adequate medical care, it said as well that substantial justification must be offered before abridging parental autonomy. The court denied the probation department's request to proceed with medical treatment, holding that testimony had shown that surgery for this boy was more serious than the average because of his particular pulmonary problems and the possibility of more postoperative problems common to children with Down's syndrome. Further, the court held that it had no duty to inform the boy

of his right to counsel and independent advocacy because he was adequately represented by a deputy district attorney present at the hearing (*In re Phillip B.*, 1957).

An interesting example from education is found in *Wisconsin v. Yoder,* in which Amish parents objected to compulsory education laws that would force their children to attend public high schools. Their objections reflected their belief that the "worldly" environment of the high school would undermine their religious faith and distinct cultural way of life. The United States Supreme Court acted on the presumption that the children as individuals did not have views adverse to those of their parents and found in favor of the Amish parents. Justice William Douglas dissented in a significant statement of the right of mature children to be heard as separate individuals and to express desires that might conflict with their parents' notion of religious duty. He cited the basic premise of child advocacy: that children may have interests separate and distinct from those of either their parents or the state (*Wisconsin v. Yoder,* 1972).

Duties and Skills.   Commonly, the state statutes that require or permit the appointment of a guardian *ad litem* offer little guidance as to duties, often containing only the vague phrase that responsibilities include "protection of the child's interests." A guardian *ad litem* may in fact be required to function in at least four separate roles, as (1) an investigator of background information for the judge, (2) an advocate of the child's rights and interests, (3) a counsel who helps the child in the expression of his or her wishes in court, and (4) a court watchdog who submits a written report at disposition, assures that the child's best interests are protected in dispute resolutions, and oversees that court orders are followed (Davidson & Gerlach, 1984).

Which of these roles are filled, and how effectively, depends heavily on how promptly the guardian *ad litem* is appointed and how much time is given to perform the duties. Beyond this, success depends on the extent to which the guardian possesses special professional and personal skills. A working knowledge of the structure and rules of the juvenile court is needed, as distinct from substantive expertise in juvenile law. At the same time the guardian *ad litem* must acknowledge the complexity of the situation, recognize the limits of his or her own knowledge, and seek consultation as needed to incorporate the expertise of others. Most often children need from a guardian *ad litem* not so much expertise in litigation as familiarity with nonlegal resources and competence in bringing them to bear upon their problems. Perhaps most crucial of all is the ability of the guardian *ad litem* to present innovative solutions to the child's unsatisfactory situation.

In addition to these essential skills, a guardian *ad litem* to be effective must understand children—how they think and express themselves, when they are holding back matters of major concern to them—and know how to interview them in a caring and sensitive way. "Advocates should let their child clients know that the advocate's role is to voice the child's needs and to represent his or her interests before the court. However, it should be made clear to the child that the judge or referee makes the final decisions about placement and the need for court intervention to protect the child. Clarifying the respective roles and responsibilities of the child advocate and the judge, as well as explaining the degree to which a child can influence the court's decision, will help children to deal with loyalty conflicts, guilt feelings, or fears about potential punishment for exposing family 'secrets.' Client counseling can only be successful when advocates . . . (1) adequately explain to the child what to expect of the court process; (2) assess the child's understanding of the court and agency involvement; and (3) clarify the child's expressed wishes regarding the outcome of their case" (Duquette, 1988a, pp. 257–258).

Guardians *ad litem* have a duty to promote the child's best interests, and in carrying out that duty could conceivably go against the child's wishes. Some states assign a child counsel rather than a guardian *ad litem*. Counsel in contrast to guardian *ad litem* is bound by the child's own determination of best interests if the child is capable of considered judgment. A dilemma may confront the child's representative when courts combine the roles of child's counsel and guardian *ad litem*.

Who Should Be Appointed?   Although the requirement that a guardian *ad litem* be an attorney is not always mandated by statute, juvenile court judges have tended to appoint only from among attorneys, frequently relying on overburdened public defenders. As the juvenile court has become more attentive to legal procedures and due process safeguards, the layperson serving as guardian *ad litem* needs commensurate training and supervision to recognize the many procedures available to protect the legal rights of the child.

However, others point out that the role of temporary guardian and advocate, which requires a departure from the traditional legal role, is difficult for lawyers trained in the adversarial process (Solender, 1976, p. 465). Although an attorney may have legal expertise, other needed qualities are not within the competence of large segments of the legal profession. These qualities include knowledge of human development, the kinds of personal and other professional skills discussed above, and the ability to locate and assess available treatment alternatives. Thus some maintain: "Every guardian *ad litem* must have access to legal expertise, but it does not follow that every guardian *ad litem* should be an attorney" (Fraser & Martin, 1976, p. 465).

A North Carolina statewide study examined characteristics associated with effectiveness of guardians *ad litem*. During a period when only attorneys could serve in that capacity, 210 randomly selected juvenile court records involving 375 children were studied. On the basis that

removal from home should be an outcome of last resort, to be used only if lesser intervention was not possible, the standard of effectiveness was stated to be preventing a child's removal from home or return of a child to home. It was found that individual characteristics of guardians *ad litem* (preparation time, race, experience in the role, and age) rather than the presence of a guardian *ad litem* per se, were associated with more effective representation of children. More work hours spent on preparation of the case tended to expedite a child's return from placement. When guardians *ad litem* were racially matched, the risk of custody removal from parents was reduced. Guardians *ad litem* who had less experience with neglect cases kept more children in their homes. Younger guardians newly out of law school were more aggressive in substantially reducing the likelihood of a child's being removed from home (Kelley & Ramsey, 1982–1983, p. 406).

Use of Social Workers as Guardians ad litem.   Social workers are appointed guardians *ad litem* under laws that implicitly acknowledge that such skills are pertinent insofar as guardian *ad litem* duties are not primarily legal in nature. Appointments of social workers are made possible because the federal law mandating such appointments for abuse and/or neglect hearings does not require that the guardian *ad litem* be an attorney.

In criminal child abuse cases, the social work guardian *ad litem* is charged with responsibility to protect the child from the defendant, help the child prepare effective testimony, and shield the child victim from any emotional harm in the criminal court system. For example, the social worker may object to the child being harassed during cross-examination or may persuade the court to accept a child's out-of-court statement rather than testimony. The *ad litem* can move for the removal of the defendant from the child's home. The nonattorney guardian *ad litem* should identify basic litigation goals, such as avoiding traumatic questioning or protecting the child from intimidation by a defendant who is a family member. The attorney and guardian *ad litem* may need to collaborate in exploring the legal alternatives and their likely impact'' (Hardin, 1986–1987, p. 704).

Use of Volunteers as Guardians ad litem. Since 1977, in Seattle, Washington, King County has had in place a guardian *ad litem* program as part of the administrative structure of the juvenile court (Neraas, 1983, p. 862). The program has served as a substitute for court-appointed lawyers and was intended to overcome two disadvantages in the old system of providing independent representation: (1) the cost of paying lawyer's fees, which were becoming prohibitive, and (2) the fact that few lawyers were equipped to offer the thorough investigation of the child's total life situation, necessary to arrive at a plan for the child in a permanent care arrangement.

Volunteers were recruited on a continuing basis from the community at large, beginning with a major effort at a university-sponsored child neglect and abuse conference that brought together persons from varied disciplines, all with an interest in child welfare. Training seminars were used (1) to give an overview of the volunteer role within the juvenile court system; (2) to develop specific legal skills such as writing recommendations to the court, testifying, and responding to cross-examination; (3) to practice communication skills for obtaining all necessary information; and (4) to learn the art of maintaining an independent stance. Before receiving a case assignment, a volunteer received a three-hour orientation. Training took place in an actual courtroom to familiarize the volunteer with the legal environment and to give immediacy to the training materials. Follow-up monthly seminars on relevant topics were held.

In carrying out the social investigation, the volunteer guardian interviewed parents, social workers, teachers, counselors, and others who had knowledge of the child. Children who were old enough were interviewed extensively, and very young children were observed. The volunteer guardian was free to consult with the program director and practicing attorneys interested in the program. The latter also could be called upon to represent the volunteer guardian in instances in which the guardian's recommendations were likely to be seriously contested.

Major factors accounting for the program's success were (1) its cost-effectiveness, (2) its credibility with judges because of the volunteer guardian's independent and open-minded position, (3) the planned and continuing training, (4) a sensitive matching of volunteer capabilities to child needs, (5) ongoing legal and social consultation made available to volunteer guardians, (6) the matching of racial and ethnic background of the child to that of the guardian, (7) the level of qualification of the volunteers at the point they entered the program, and (8) the cooperation of professional staff of social agencies with whom the program staff and volunteers had worked to maintain effective relationships (Ray-Bettineski, 1978). Since the onset of the King County program, sixty jurisdictions in twenty-seven states have created similar programs (Neraas, 1983, p. 862).

Detriments and Risks in Guardian ad litem. The high cost of proper independent representation for children whose interests are at stake in court is a critical detriment to authentic protection for them. This barrier is likely to remain a potent one in the present economy so long as courts retain their preference for appointing members of the law profession where fees are competitively high.

Perhaps even more hazardous to the welfare of children is the ease with which the guardian *ad litem* concept can be corrupted into a pro forma gesture that makes a farce of the court's traditional concern for the child's best interests. The League of Women Voters conducted a year-long "court-watching" project in Illinois in which more than 24,000 juvenile court proceedings before 102 judges were observed and reported. Objective data were computerized and narrative data analyzed. A major concern was the quality of representation for juveniles. While public defenders acting as guardian *ad litem* in some counties were credited with appearing with a well-prepared case, too frequently the public defender had never talked to the child or youth or even seen the case file before the court hearing. Stacks of papers on the social history and juvenile court reports were gone over in five to ten minutes when the case was called. Sometimes the public defender's only contact with the family or the youth was a hurried conference in the hallway just before court convened. The presence of the juvenile in court too often seemed to be overlooked in an impersonal environment of adults discussing the case as though the young person were not present. Many times the minor was not addressed, nor was her or his name even mentioned. Even when judges gave sound explanations to juveniles and asked if they had any questions, without earlier preparation by the guardian *ad litem* no questions came (League of Women Voters, 1981).

Another concern about the provision of independent advocacy for children in court is the fear that it may serve to increase trauma for children, propelling them more centrally into a conflict-laden situation in which they feel pressed to take an open stand against the wishes of parents (Genden, 1976, p. 594).

In view of the costs and other risks, some concerned professionals take the position that the appointment of a child advocate in court should not be mandatory, but should be done on an individual basis. Then when appointed, a guardian *ad litem* would be expected to carry out the full spirit and intent of independent advocacy. An alternative would be an initial naming of a guardian *ad litem* who would withdraw

if it became evident that the interests of the child were being effectively represented (Genden, 1976, p. 594-595).

WHO SHOULD BE APPOINTED GUARDIAN OF PERSON?

Preferences Stated in Statutes

In the early days of this country, children needing court-appointed guardians generally were orphans, or children abandoned by their parents, or children whose property required protection. Such instances came under the jurisdiction of the probate courts in the various states. The guardianship needs of orphans or abandoned children did not present the probate court with complex conflicts of interest between allegedly neglecting parents and society's concerns for the welfare of children. However, in the latter part of the nineteenth and the early twentieth century, the child-saving and child rescue movements focused attention on children with problems and needs different from those of property interests—children neglected and abused by their parents or guardians, children held by their parents to be incorrigible and beyond their control, children committing offenses against the law, and children needing specialized care and education in institutions.

With the founding of the juvenile court in Illinois in 1899 and its rapid spread into other states, problems of guardianship rights and responsibilities were referred to the new specialized court. With its emphasis on social services and rehabilitation, the juvenile court appeared more suited than the probate court to deal with conflicting claims of parents and the state as well as the residual rights of parents after natural guardianship was modified.

An examination today of the states' probate court statutes relating to guardianship still reveals a section dealing with the question of who should be appointed to the office of guardian. An example can be cited from the California Probate Code:

> Sec. 1407. Order of Preference of Right to Guardianship. Of persons equally entitled in other respects to the guardianship of a minor, preference is to be given as follows:
>
> 1. To a parent;
> 2. To one who was indicated by the wishes of a deceased parent;
> 3. To one who already stands in the position of a trustee of a fund to be applied to the child's support;
> 4. To a relative;
> 5. If the child has already been declared to be a ward or dependent child of the juvenile court, to the probation officer of said court. (*Statutes of California*, 1931)

The intent of the court to safeguard the rights of natural parents is discernible above in the stated preference of assignment to parents, persons nominated by parents, or to relatives. The historical shift toward naming guardians from among the agents of the state is also noted in the reference to the probation officer of the juvenile court.

Preferences of Standard-setting Agencies

National agencies have cited preferred categories of persons to serve as children's court-appointed guardians of person. The U.S. Children's Bureau statement of 1966 still stands unchallenged in principle, although not in practice, with its emphasis on the importance of personal ties between children and their guardians.

> In the selection of a *guardian of the person* of a child, the court should give preference to a brother or sister, a relative, godparent, or close family friend. . . . The appointment of such a person would more likely assure a closer personal relationship to the child. In the event that the court is unable to appoint one of the persons in the preferred category above, the court may select a clergyman, physician, or attorney who lives in the child's community and who has demonstrated his interest in and concern for the welfare of children. (Sheridan, 1966, pp. 94–95)

Thus, the choice of person to serve as guardian should favor the maintenance of family and community ties. Further, these standards assume, when appointment of a guardian of person is found necessary, a person in the preferred category can be found—an assumption that challenges social workers and the community to recruit more suitable candidates for children's guardians.

The Court as Guardian

The phrase "a ward of the court" is misleading since properly the court itself does not act as guardian. The judicial function is not to *act* as guardian but to appoint guardians and thereby bring about guardian-ward relationships.

With insufficient numbers of private citizens easily available to serve as guardians, a court may routinely name its juvenile probation officer as guardian. This practice may seem expeditious since the probation officer is easily available and accountable to the court. But there are more important considerations. Is the probation officer necessarily the best person to be given the responsibility for the particular child? Are the needs and interests of the child appropriate to the probation officer's regularly assigned duties?

Social Agency as Guardian

The guardianship of substantial numbers of children is vested in administrative officers, or other staff members of state departments of public welfare, or other charitable agencies or institutions in a community. In such instances, the guardian usually delegates his or her responsibilities to others in the agency, frequently to the child's social worker, since administrative officers cannot possibly have personal relationships with these numerous children.

Guardianship such as this has been defended on the basis that it provides the agency with the authority it needs to carry out a plan of care and treatment for children, many of whom have various physical and emotional illnesses with special treatment needs, and further, that it is necessary for social agencies to act as guardians in view of the difficulty in getting responsible citizens in their private capacities to act as guardians of person.

But some observers find the practice of administrative guardianship of children to be a flawed concept. They cite the rapid growth of administrative agencies, the multiple and heavy tasks assigned to them by social legislation, the lack of inside questioning about their assumptions and practices. "There is grave danger that children will belong to the state rather than their families and to themselves" (Liggett, 1958, p. 46). More recent authorities affirm that social agencies "do not and cannot provide the actual day-to-day care for the child." Responsibility for daily and continuing care falls to foster parents and other child care workers who may have little regard for parent-child ties. "Dependent children should be in the care of individuals who do not deny the existence of biological parents nor the ties that children may have with them" (Leashore, 1984–1985, p. 200).

The essence of these statements is that guardianship is not a professional function; guardianship requires a personal relationship. While guardians should receive relevant information particular to their ward's condition, they do not need to be experts on the condition, nor do they need to be the ones to provide treatment. A guardian is a child's advocate, not always impartial, not always wholly knowledgeable about the child's problem, but constant, fulfilling a relationship with stated rights and responsibilities. Guardians must be aware of their legal responsibilities to their wards. Theirs is an authoritative relationship, one in which, as guardians, they are responsible for the management and supervision of large aspects of a particular child's private life and matters of personal concern to the child.

If social workers do act as children's guardians, and they may find it necessary to do so for some time to come, their function as guardian with its judicial responsibilities and controls must be separated from their function as professional helper with its administrative responsibilities and controls. A social worker deals with defined and limited areas of a child's life, those relevant to the child's condition as they may be perceived and diagnosed as problems, or at least as areas of needed help. Social workers have professional, not personal, goals; their skills include techniques of treatment, and use of themselves in a professional capacity. They are accountable, not judicially to a court, but administratively to the social agency that employs them.

The recommended policy of the Children's Bureau states succinctly:

> No person employed by or associated with an agency holding *legal custody* of the child, such as a caseworker or a board member, should be appointed as guardian of the person, since this would clearly involve a conflict of duties and interests. (Sheridan, 1966, p. 95)

Other practical objections have been voiced, particularly in relation to guardianship of increasing numbers of children by superintendents of public institutions such as state mental hospitals or institutions for the retarded. In practice such a system of public guardianship tends to become a routine and stereotyped one rather than one that provides a socially significant use of guardianship. In addition, society may be lulled into the belief that all the interests of the children concerned are being protected, whereas, in reality, in many cases only a modicum of protection is afforded (Begab & Goldberg, 1962, pp. 21–25).

If the office of guardian is to be used properly in a democratic society to ensure the rights of children, public welfare staff may need to use aggressive and innovative ways to recruit private individuals to carry out the tasks of guardian, and remove the obstacles to the ability of such citizens to serve children as personal, private guardians.

Investigating the Proposed Guardian's Suitability

Of special importance is the court's responsibility to obtain a social investigation of the proposed guardian's suitability to assume the role and responsibilities of guardian to the particular child involved. In some states the statutes provide that a social investigation is mandatory before a guardian is appointed, but in many other states the decision to secure a social investigation is left to the discretion of the judge.

Judicial appointment of a guardian should take place only after careful investigation, even in those cases where an adult already has possession of a child and seeks to defend a claim to the child by reason of *in loco parentis*. Our society does not regard a transfer of a piece of land or other valued property as a casual transaction and requires an individual to obtain a legal title for the control of such property. Human relationships between adult and child are far more complex, and the resulting influences on the child are long-term.

Continuing Supervision

Courts, generally, attempt to establish instrumentalities and relationships that will become self-operative, that is, will require little or no continuing supervision. Citizen groups frequently recommend that courts require periodic reports of the guardian on each child's situation. Many courts maintain no contact with guardians, who often appear to be under no requirement to account for their actions in relation to their wards. To a large extent this lack of supervision is attributable to insufficient court staff and is most apparent in the lack of supervision of guardians of the person. Guardians of the estate, like other trustees of money, are usually required to file inventories and make periodic accountings. But in any case, the court

maintains continuing legal jurisdiction during the period of guardianship and *may* require the guardian of person to report periodically.

All parties to the guardianship are free to return to the court for clarification of authority, status, or individual responsibility. Persons most likely to request a review are the child's parents, who may be seeking the return of the child to their own home and guardianship; the guardian, who may be requesting termination of guardianship; or a social worker who seeks termination of parental rights in order to place a child in an adoptive home. Within the past decade, as part of the new effort to find permanent homes for all children now in foster care, the practice of "court review" has increased.

Guardianship as a Social Instrument

In this country we are making no generally effective use of the legal institution of guardianship. Perhaps a potentiality has been overlooked because guardianship has been regarded as a matter of legal formality with little to offer that is relevant to the day-to-day social well-being of a child. Children are seldom in personal interaction with responsible adults in the particular relationship of guardian and ward unless there is an estate to be managed.

But is guardianship a child care resource that could be used more productively? Can the relationship of guardian and ward be used to contribute to the well-being of many of the nation's children who are now deprived of their own parents and who need substitute parents?

These become significant questions in the face of evidence of large numbers of children who cannot be cared for by their own parents, who have no experience with or constructive relationship with these parents, who live for long periods in institutions or temporary shelters, and who lose the expected benefits of foster care because they are moved frequently from one place to another. These are children who need stable relationships with adults and continuity in their living situation. In addition, many are children for whom adoption is not an alternative. For example, they may belong to sibling groups for whom a single adoptive home is not feasible. Or they may be children whose natural parents cannot care for them but who are unwilling to relinquish them for adoption; children who for various reasons were difficult to place for adoption in infancy, are now older, and have little chance for adoption; or children old enough to remember their parents and to cherish their own identity.

Two approaches to strengthening guardianship protections will be considered: (1) an award of guardianship to a private individual as an alternative form of child care for selected children and (2) the use of a child care agency staff member as a reliable and active guardian (the use of the concept of "parental force").

Guardianship by Private Individuals

Taylor (1966, pp. 417–423) and more recently Leashore (1984–1985, p. 400) maintain that the formal and personal relationship of guardian and ward is an appropriate status for selected children, one that could help to sustain ties to biological families and communities. In some instances the practice could strengthen ties through parental selection of the guardian and facilitated parental visitation. Using guardianship as a child care resource would require that it be regarded as an alternative form of permanency planning along with foster care and adoption. As a form of care for particular children, it would be distinguishable by certain attributes. For example, a guardian would be recruited, investigated, and recommended to the court by social agencies to assure that children are placed in the care of responsible, competent caretakers.

Guardians, in the course of the social agency study of their suitability, would be helped to become familiar with the availability of social services if they become troubled or in need of consultation in relation to their child care undertaking; the service of social agencies would be used in the same way as other citizens and parents use the community's professional services.

Socially provided money payments would be necessary for the support of children who require a guardian and have no estate of their own or other souces of support. In writing about the great potential in the use of guradianship for children, Smith (1955) recognized that private guardians could not be provided free. All forms of child care, he said, have values not translated into dollars and cents. "The belief . . . that personal guardians should not be paid stems largely from the inadequacies of the present system and the failure to encourage effective methods of insuring an awakened sense of guardianship responsibility" (p. 151). Relatives who lack monetary resources may have an interest in giving care as private guardians with the potential of reducing identity loss in children. In such instances, as Leashore recognized, a subsidized guardianship program "would enable those most interested to fill the gap in the child's family structure. For those who argue that subsidized guardianship is costly, it must be noted that it is also costly to maintain children in foster care" (1984–1985, p. 390).

Additional merits in the relationship of guardian and ward for selected children might be these: The child would be living with a person in a situation where authority is less likely to be divided, as it is in a foster home with foster parents accountable to an agency social worker; this factor might encourage some adults to offer child care who have not wished to become agency foster parents. And children could more easily understand their relationship to legally appointed guardians, identify it, and explain the variance in surname between themselves and their guardians.

There is need for study and demonstrations by child welfare agencies as to whether such a use of guardianship, as an alternative child care resource, might open additional homes for children. Such study would require "conviction on the part of child welfare agencies and social workers that guardianship is worthy of exploration along with the possibilities of adoption and other forms of substitute care" (Taylor, 1966, p. 419).

Serious obstacles commonly cited to such innovation include (1) the costs of financial payments to guardians and the unlikelihood of such allocations in the current political, social, and economic climate, and (2) doubts as to the feasibility of recruiting significant numbers of capable, trustworthy adults who would be willing to take on such a serious commitment to individual children.

"Parental Force" as an Agency Practice

The second proposal for using guardianship as a means of furthering the well-being of selected children is based on the concept of "parental force," a term selected to connote a responsible, conscientious, and emotionally involved legal guardian (Robinson, 1950; Barnes, 1967).

Children and adolescents who are referred to child-caring agencies are often seriously emotionally disturbed. Their behavior has become intolerable in their own communities, and in addition to foster care, they require psychotherapeutic treatment, in either an outpatient clinic or a residential center. These children's needs for adequate guardianship often have been lost sight of and given little or no consideration because of their difficult behavior and the attendant problems for the social agency of maintaining them in foster care and securing some of a community's scarce psychotherapeutic services for them.

Attempts to find ways to help such children more effectively led to the recognition by the Iowa Children's Home Society that negligence in the implementation of guardianship contributes to the child's and adolescent's inability to utilize otherwise well-conceived treatment programs, and that it was necessary to attend to a child's need for adequate and consistent parenting *before* seeking any kind of treatment for him or her. A plan was sought that would be applicable to children whether they live in foster homes,

group homes, state training schools, or residential treatment centers, and workable as well in the face of staff turnover, which precludes any guarantee that the same social worker will always be available to the child.

The resulting proposal of a "parental force" program was based on several principles (Barnes, 1967; Zober & Taber, 1965): (1) A conscientious guardian is needed by any child, particularly by one who has experienced the loss of a parent or guardian, and never more so than when a child is required to undergo and participate in psychotherapy; (2) in the case of a child without a family, proper guardianship comes ahead of treatment, not only because parents are more important to a child than professional helpers, but also because treatment cannot be effective unless proper guardianship is established first; (3) establishment of conscientious and reliable guardianship of a child, that is, the use of parental force, gives meaning to the psychotherapy and facilitates it in many ways; and (4) the presence of an enduring parental force permits flexibility in treatment plans and a long-term approach to the child's problems.

The proposal evolved from these principles calls for a duly appointed child-caring agency to act as a child's guardian, not perfunctorily, but actively as his or her advocate through the vicissitudes of foster care and treatment, with the change in living arrangements and in agency social workers that appears almost inevitable in the lives of seriously disturbed foster children and adolescents. Assigned social workers, as representatives of the agency and its parental force, act in the guardianship role and assume a direct and active part in children's lives. They visit the children, seek better understanding and communication with them, plan with them for their future, encourage them, but in all, do not seek to be neutral. They react frankly to children in everyday practical problems of school, dress, and conduct, and as a parent would, guard them against any abuse or poor practices, even to the point of removing them from treatment situations that are not working well. In turn, the children's therapists are freed from carrying any of the parental role and are enabled to provide treatment more effectively. The appointed agency remains the responsible, continuing, and accountable parental force, or guardian, in the children's individual lives for as long as they need it—until they can return to a natural parent, go into adoption, or become self-maintaining.

Children need models rather than critics. (Joubert, 1842)

Emancipation of Minors

Partial or complete "emancipation" is a means by which in some instances a young person can be legally released from parental custody and control and thereafter be considered an adult for most purposes. Although state statutes vary, criteria used frequently to justify an action of emancipation are these: the youth is living separately from parents, is self-supporting, has joined the military, is married. Emancipation may empower a minor to transact business such as buying or selling property, sue or be sued, enlist in the military, and consent to medical, psychological, or social work services (Horowitz & Davidson, 1984, p. 152).

The doctrine of emancipation is not new; it existed in common law times. Traditionally, however, the courts declared a minor emancipated only in particular cases involving individual circumstances distinct from those that might be more generally found among youth. To the extent that emancipation cases commonly involved minors in the eighteen to twenty-one age group, the overall significance of the emancipation doctrine was diminished by the adoption of eighteen years, rather than twenty-one, as the age of majority. In more recent years, legislation in some states has allowed persons under eighteen years of age to petition the court for a determination of emancipation. A typical example appears in the California Civil Code that permits "a child fourteen or older to petition the court for emancipation on a showing that the child lives separately and apart from the parents with the parents' consent and is self-supporting. . . . The petition is granted if the court finds the information contained in it to be true and that emancipation would not be adverse to the child's best interest" (Davis & Schwartz, 1987, p. 40).

Emancipation may be an appropriate plan for a youth with an impaired parent-child relationship but no need for an ongoing guardian. Nineteen states have emancipation statutes allowing youth or their parents to file for an emancipated status. In the first year of the state of Connecticut's emancipation law, more parents requested emancipation than did young persons, and more girls than boys (Henry, 1981, p. 24).

GUARDIANSHIP POLICY: SUPREME COURT DECISIONS

Laws of guardianship for children went relatively unchanged for hundreds of years, with modifications confined mainly to moving from the father as sole guardian to a sharing of guardianship with the mother, and allowing married women to be named guardian (Taylor, 1935, p. 25). With increased attention in the nineteenth century to the nature of motherhood and the mother's role during a child's young years, the presumption developed that in "the tender years" of a child's life, the mother was the preferred custodian. Beyond these developments, parent-child relations and responsibilities were regarded as generally unsuitable subjects for public policy making. However, in the decade of the 1960s and continuing to the present, government has enunciated principles in judicial decisions that have become the basis for new public policy in relation to guardianship rights of parents, as well as the rights of minors independent of parental interests.

Parental rights were so absolute in American tradition and law that child welfare played a timid role in the protection of children from neglect and abuse within their homes. Throughout recorded history the unquestioned power of parents imposed many forms of destructive permanence on their children. (Polier, 1989, p. 65)

Child advocates have studied the pattern reflected in the new surge of Supreme Court decisions directly focused on the affairs of children and parents and tend to see an inconsistent line of legal reasoning. They claim two persistent problems of legal theory related to child rights: (1) an ambivalence about placing limits on parental control, and (2) a failure on the part of the state to take into account the interests of children and to give competent children a chance to speak for themselves (Rodham, 1973).

The reasoning of the Supreme Court is complex. The justices have said clearly that the child, merely on account of his or her minority status, is not beyond the protection of the Constitution. In some cases the Court has concluded that the child's right to due process is the same as that of an adult, particularly in matters of threat to liberty or property interests. But also it has rejected "the uncritical assumption that the constitutional rights of children are indistinguishable from those of adults," or that under the law children can never be treated differently from adults (*Bellotti v. Baird,* 1979, pp. 3038, 3044). The problem becomes one of achieving a just and workable balance in parent-child-society conflicts.

U.S. Supreme court cases not only reveal rights of parents and their offspring, but also the Court's *view of children*—their needs, protections, and capabilities. The court's justices have offered three principles that guide their reasoning and justify the conclusion that the

constitutional rights of children cannot be unequivocally equated with those of adults: "the peculiar vulnerability of children; their inability to make critical decisions in an informed, mature manner; and the importance of the parental role in child-rearing" (*Bellotti v. Baird,* 1979, p. 3043). In the words of former Justice Felix Frankfurter: "Children have a very special place in life which law should reflect. Legal theories and their phrasing in other cases readily leads to fallacious reasoning if uncritically transferred to determination of a State's duty toward children" (*Bellotti v. Baird,* 1979, p. 3035). It follows that although children are generally protected by the same constitutional guarantees as adults, the state is allowed to adjust its legal system to accord with children's vulnerability and the unique role of the family; constitutional principles must be applied flexibly and sensitively to the special needs of children and parents. Given this framework for legal reasoning in relation to child rights, the ambivalence perceived by child advocates (that is, a dichotomy of rights bestowed and rights denied) becomes more understandable, if not fully acceptable, to proponents of the children's cause.

Discussed below are recent Supreme Court rulings that affect public policy in the often conflicting needs and goals of parents, children, and society. Some of these cases are weighted in the direction of reinforcing the guardianship rights of parents in the upbringing of their children. Some clearly extend the legal rights of minors; others limit their freedom. In all of them the influences and interests of society are apparent.

Parental Rights Reinforced

The Supreme Court repeatedly has emphasized the guiding role of parents in the upbringing of their children and the responsibility of parents to "inculcate and pass down many of our most cherished values, moral and cultural" (*Bellotti v. Baird,* 1979). This "unique role" of the family, the Court has said, entitles biological parents to substantive due process protections and, although not without dissent among the justices, justifies limitations on the freedom of minors.

A long-awaited Supreme Court decision was made in *Parham v. J. R.* (1979), a case from Georgia testing the rights of parents to institutionalize their children and of the state to institutionalize its wards without due process procedures in behalf of the child. More than thirty states had statutes that allowed children to be "voluntarily" committed to institutions as mental patients, making children the only class of people who could be deprived of their liberty in this manner without a hearing (Franek, 1980, p. 376).

J. R. represented children in the custody of the state. J. L., another child whose situation was considered at the same time, represented a class of children in the custody of parents at the time of commitment. The differences in their guardianship status at the time of commitment was held not to require different procedures. J. R. had been in seven different foster homes, and during this time he had shown disruptive behavior. At the same time of his commitment, he was said to be showing "unsocialized, aggressive reaction of childhood." J. L. was said to be suffering a condition termed "hyperkinetic reaction of childhood."

The Supreme Court concluded that the traditional presumption that natural bonds of affection lead parents to act in the best interests of their children should apply. Parents should retain a substantial if not the dominant role in the decision to voluntarily commit their children to an institution. Furthermore, Georgia law provided for informal medical review 30 days after admission to state hospitals, and the Court underscored as protection to the child the authority of doctors to make medical judgments. Thus the decision reinforced not only the authority of parents and agents of the state over children, but also the authority of the medical profession in confining children for medical treatment.

Justice Brennan, speaking for the minority justices, noted that even under ideal circumstances, psychiatric diagnosis and decisions about therapy are uncertain; that when a child is institutionalized by his or her parents, there has already been a break in family autonomy; and that parental authority should not stand in the way of a child's constitutional rights. Further, children held in mental hospitals are "not only deprived of physical liberty; they are also deprived of friends, family, and community, and at risk of stigma as well. They live in unnatural surroundings under the continuous and detailed control of strangers." Brennan questioned the traditional presumption that parents will act in their child's best interests when making commitment decisions, and said "a child who has been ousted from his family has even greater need for an independent advocate" (*Parham v. J. R.,* 1979).

A decision in *Santosky v. Kramer* (1982) is of critical concern to professionals who are aware of the thousands of children who languish in foster homes and institutions, whose parents are unable or unwilling to resume their care, and who are denied a permanent home through adoption because of legal difficulties in fully terminating parental rights. The Santoskys had lost custody of their three older children on a petition of the local department of social services after episodes of physical abuse. The children, one of them only a few days old, were placed in foster care where they remained for more than seven years.

A New York law that came under challenge stipulated that the state could terminate the rights of parents over their objection if the child or children involved were found to be "permanently neglected." To make that finding under the New York law the state would have to show that for more than a year after the children came into state custody the agency had "made diligent efforts to encourage and strengthen the parental relationship," and that during that period the parents failed "substantially and continuously or repeatedly to maintain contact with or plan for the future of the child although physically and financially able to do so" (*Santosky v. Kramer,* 1982, p. 4334).

While the Santosky children were in foster care, the department of social services offered the parents training by a mother's aide, a nutritional aide, and a public health nurse and counseling at a family planning clinic. In addition, psychiatric treatment and vocational training were offered to the father and counseling at a family service center to the mother. Eventually the department filed a termination petition after finding the parents' response to their efforts "marginal at best": they wholly disregarded some of the available services and used others only sporadically. Infrequent visits between parents and children had been "at best superficial and devoid of any real emotional content" (*Santosky v. Kramer,* 1982, p. 4342–4343). When the family court terminated parental rights, freeing the three children for adoption, the parents appealed, thus bringing the situation finally before the United States Supreme Court.

The majority justices declined to express any view on the merits of the Santoskys' claim or that of the department of social services. Instead they saw the appropriate question before them to be the standard of proof that should be used to fully terminate parental rights.

The most stringent standard is "evidence beyond a reasonable doubt," used in findings of juvenile delinquency and in terminations of parental rights under the Indian Child Welfare Act of 1978. A less strict standard is "clear and convincing evidence," which at the time the New York case reached the Supreme Court was being applied in thirty-three states. Least stringent is "a fair preponderance of the evidence," usually interpreted to mean that the evidence presented is "more probable than not." It was this latter level of proof that was being used in New York.

The justices, in a five-to-four decision, ruled that the due process clause of the Fourteenth Amendment demands more than "a fair preponderance of the evidence" before terminating irrevocably the parent-child relationship.

Allegations must be supported by at least "clear and convincing evidence."

Four justices dissented from the majority decision on two grounds. First, the "myopic scrutiny of the standard of proof" by the majority justices had blinded them to the extensive procedural protections included in New York law that must be accorded parents before children can be brought into foster care. In addition, the order to place children out of their own parents' home is reviewed every eighteen months by the family court. Further, the state's diligent but unsuccessful efforts over four years to reunite the family had been disregarded in the majority opinion—all procedures and services which, the minority justices said, made the New York approach "fundamentally fair." The second part of the dissent held that by separating out one narrow provision of the New York process and holding it unconstitutional, the majority had invited "further court intrusion into every facet of state and family law . . . an area traditionally entrusted to state care" (*Santosky v. Kramer,* 1982, p. 4345).

Child advocates and social welfare professionals who are particularly concerned about getting neglected and abused children out of the limbo of unstable foster care and into permanent adoptive homes fear greatly heightened difficulty under the stringent standard of "clear and convincing evidence," now applicable to all the states.

Guardianship Rights of the Unwed Father

Within the past two decades the unwed father has gained legal recognition of some aspects of guardianship of his nonmarital child. In adoption hearings in which parental rights are terminated, the right of certain fathers to veto the adoption of their nonmarital children is protected constitutionally. A chain of U.S. Supreme Court cases has established that the father must have developed a significant and personal relationship with his nonmarital child to warrant constitutional protection in adoption proceedings. To date, the fact of biological relationship alone between father and nonmarital child does not merit protection. Unwed fathers must "grasp the opportunity" of their biological connection to their child to form an actual parenting relationship. What is protected, then, is a "liberty interest" in a "developed parent–child relationship resulting from the father's shouldering significant responsibility with respect to daily supervision, education, protection and care of his child that has been recognized as an interest with due process safeguards" (Gitlin, 1987, p. 2). Three Supreme Court decisions have addressed the interests of the unwed father.

Stanley v. Illinois (1972) dealt with the rights of an unwed father who had lived with the mother of his nonmarital children, provided some financial support, and served in the parental role. After the death of the mother, the children were declared dependent and made wards of the state. The father was excluded from a voice in the state's effort to place his children in adoptive homes. The Supreme Court decided the case in relation to procedural due process and ruled that the parental rights of the unwed father could not be disregarded unless he was found to be an "unfit parent." In this case, Stanley's parent–child relationship over the lifetime of his children developed a guardianship interest of constitutionally protected stature.

The imprecise language of the decision led to legal uncertainties and resulted in considerable ambiguity for adoption agencies. Experts in family law concluded that conflicting interpretations of *Stanley v. Illinois* made the adoptive process more cumbersome and raised more questions than it answered with reference to the substantive nature of the unmarried father's parental rights and the mandated procedures that adoption agencies are required to follow (Krause, 1981, p. 414; Weinhaus, 1980–1981).

In early 1978 the Supreme Court in *Quillon v. Walcott* upheld a Georgia law that denied fathers of nonmarital children the right to challenge their children's adoptions. In doing so the court distinguished the Stanley case from the Georgia situation by noting that in the latter the father had never exercised custody over his child nor assumed any significant responsibility for the child's daily care, protection, supervision, or education. For eleven years he had not availed himself of the opportunity under Georgia law to legitimate his nonmarital child and thus gain full parental rights. He had come forward only when the mother's husband sought to adopt the child. Krause concluded that Quillon, with its irrelevance to the vast majority of adoptive situations, "did little to clarify the murky situation in which the adoption industry had found itself after *Stanley*" (Krause, 1981, p. 146). In any case the court appeared to have reasoned that a father who had never established either a legal or a familial bond with his child did not have a fundamental constitutionally protected right.

The concept of familial bond was reinforced in an additional case, *Caban v. Mohammed,* (1979) which involved a father who had lived with the mother of their two children, whose name appeared on the birth certificate of each, who had contributed to their support, and even after the mother left with the children to marry another man, continued to see them frequently. The mother's new husband subsequently sought to adopt the children with the mother's consent but without the consent of the biological father. Emphasizing the substantial de facto relationship the biological father had maintained with his children, the Supreme Court disallowed the mother's right to consent to adoption of her children without attention to the biological father's wishes.

The court's decision, however, clouded what at first impression appeared to be an acknowledgment of an unqualified right for the concerned unwed father who had been actively involved with his children. Instead of focusing only on legal distinctions and consequent injustices between unmarried and married fathers in relation to their children, the majority justices made a gender-based distinction between mothers and fathers, introducing sex discrimination as a factor in their judgment. Krause termed this development a highly unfortunate example of faulty logic that may have unhappy consequences for the rights of the nonmarital child. "The child is not and should not be concerned with whether its father, for rational legislative purposes, is the equal of its mother. The child is concerned with whether its legal position rationally differs from that of its legitimate half-sibling!" Similarly, the unmarried father should be compared with the married father, not with the unmarried mother (Krause, 1981, pp. 149–150).

Substantial uncertainty still persists as to the rights of the unwed father to his nonmarital children. In summary, however, it can be said that unmarried fathers do not have the same constitutional protections as married fathers. Nor do unmarried fathers have the same procedural advantages as do unmarried mothers. For the unwed father to be able to veto the adoption or contend for custody or visitation, he must have had a "significant relationship" with his child.

The Rights of Minors versus Parental Prerogatives

No issue of child-parent-society rights and responsibilities has attracted and sustained more controversy than the question of the minor's right to control her own reproductive capacities by access to contraception or abortion. In *Carey v. Population Service* (1977), the U.S. Supreme Court struck down a New York statute that prohibited the sale and distribution of contraceptives (except by a physician) to minors under the age of sixteen. In the majority decision the Court stated that "the right to privacy in connection with decisions affecting procreation extended to minors as well as to adults" and that inhibiting minors' privacy rights was valid only to serve "a significant state interest," one that would not be present in the case of an adult. There was substantial doubt, the Court said, that limiting access to contraception would in fact act as a meaningful deterrent to sexual activity among the young, as had been contended.

The decision did not abate the controversy. Congress subsequently amended Title X of the Public Health Service Act that governed the federal funding of family planning services. The statutory amendment required that such federally funded programs encourage "family participation" in the provision of contraceptive services "to the extent practical." The Reagan administration, through the secretary of Health and Human Services, stated its intent to implement the amendment by requiring programs to notify the parents of "unemancipated minors" who sought contraceptive services. Criticism and support for the proposed regulations came from many sides. Planned Parenthood Federation announced that in the event the new regulation was put into effect, it stood ready to ask the court for an immediate injunction and a hearing to prevent its implementation (Planned Parenthood, 1982).

In *Roe v. Wade* (1973) the Supreme Court had given constitutional protection to the right of women to choose abortion early in pregnancy. Three years later, in *Planned Parenthood of Central Missouri v. Danforth* (1976), the court held that the state does not have constitutional authority to give a third party, such as a spouse or parent or person *in loco parentis,* an absolute and possibly arbitrary veto over the decision of a pregnant patient and her physician. Some other states continued to legislate in an attempt to restrict the *minor's right* to abortion when she lacked the consent of parents.

The U.S. Supreme Court heard from Massachusetts' highest court an appeal of *Bellotti v. Baird* (1979) concerning a statute that required a pregnant unmarried minor to have the consent of her parents or the permission of a judge of a state court of general jurisdiction before obtaining an abortion. The action was brought on behalf of a class of "mature and fully competent" unmarried minors "who have adequate capacity to give a valid and informed consent to abortion" and who do not wish to involve their parents. The Court affirmed the desirability of fostering parental involvement in a minor's large decisions and noted that deference to parents may be appropriate with respect to a range of choices facing a minor. However, the Court said, the abortion decision differs from other decisions that may be made during minority, ones that often can safely be postponed in deference to the preferences of parents. In the event of pregnancy, the adolescent has only a matter of weeks in which to make a decision. Given her probable education, employment skills, financial resources, and emotional maturity, unwed motherhood may be "exceptionally burdensome." The Court found the Massachusetts statute unconstitutional because no matter how informed and competent a minor might be, her decision could in every instance be subject to consent of both parents or a superior court judge, and with reference to Danforth, thus subject to an absolute and possibly an arbitrary veto.

Although the Court had now twice struck down state laws requiring parental consent to a minor's abortion, some states sought to circumvent the ruling by enacting legislation that mandated *notice* to parents, rather than consent. Utah's statute required a physician to notify parents, "if possible," before performing an abortion on a minor or face criminal penalties. A challenge to the law came in *H. L. v. Matheson et al.* (1981). A fifteen-year-old pregnant girl, living with her parents, had been advised by her physician that an abortion would be in her best medical interests. Because of the criminal liability involved, he refused to perform the abortion without notifying her parents.

The Court upheld the constitutionality of the Utah law as it applied to "unemancipated minors," those not married or self-supporting, still dependent on their parents and living at home, with no claim or showing of being "mature" enough to make informed decisions on a matter with such "medical, emotional and psychological consequences." The majority decision stated that for girls such as H. L., "the stat-

ute plainly serves the important considerations of family integrity and protecting adolescents." Further, the Court said, although it had formerly held that a state may not constitutionally legislate a blanket and unreviewable power of parents to veto their daughter's abortion, a "mere requirement of parental notice" does not violate the rights of an immature, dependent minor.

Matheson avoided deciding if parental notice laws imposed on mature minors would be constitutionally permitted. A different practice with the mature minor was implied, however, leaving open the need for a procedure for the pregnant minor to demonstrate sufficient maturity to make the abortion decision herself, or to establish that an abortion was in her best interests despite her immaturity.

In early July, 1989, the U.S. Supreme Court in a 5–4 ruling upheld a restrictive Missouri law on abortion (*Webster v. Reproductive Health Service*). In doing so, the Court stopped short of overturning the *Roe v. Wade* decision of 1972 that had established a woman's constitutional right to obtain an abortion, but gave the States the right to impose new restrictions on abortion. A question left unanswered by the decision was the status of a minor's right to give evidence of her maturity and to receive an abortion. The result was to turn political fallout from the decision to the state legislatures and in the view of many, to open the way to further restrictions on abortion (Dionne, 1989; Greenhouse, 1989b).

Until the 1989 Missouri case was heard by the Supreme Court, overall, minors had gained more in reproductive rights, in terms of autonomy distinct from parental and state intervention, than in other areas of medical attention and health. However, the Court agreed to hear in its next term two cases (from Minnesota and Ohio) that concerned the minor's right to seek abortion without parental notification. By the time these cases were acted upon by the Supreme Court on June 25, 1990, thirty-two states had passed legislation requiring some form of parental involvement in teenagers' abortion decisions. Some states were considering such legislation (Greenhouse, 1990b, p. 1).

In *Ohio v. Akron Center for Reproductive Health* (1990), the Court upheld the Ohio law that requires pregnant unmarried teenagers under age eighteen years to notify at least one parent or get a judge's permission before terminating a pregnancy. To obtain judicial consent, the minor must present "clear and convincing proof that she has sufficient maturity and information to make the abortion decision herself, that one of her parents has engaged in a pattern of physical, emotional, or sexual abuse against her, or that notice is not in her best interests."

In the case of *Hodgson v. Minnesota* (1990), the Court upheld Minnesota's requirement that all unmarried teenagers under eighteen years must notify both parents and wait forty-eight hours before terminating a pregnancy. This law, the most restrictive in the country, required the pregnant teenager to notify both parents even though a parent may never have lived with the teenager or have had legal custody of her. The legislation was saved from unconstitutionality, the court said, because the state provided an alternative—a judicial hearing for pregnant girls who do not want to inform their parents of their decision. The alternative court procedure requires the minor either to demonstrate her maturity, or to show that an abortion without notification of parents would be in her best interests.

The Minnesota law, passed in 1981, had been barred from enforcement by a lower court order in 1986. Unrebutted evidence leading to this order showed that only half of minors in Minnesota live with both biological parents; other extensive testimony had claimed particularly harmful effects of the two-parent notice requirement on both the minor and the custodial parent. The notifying process had not reestablished useful relations between the minor and the absent parent. In addition the forced notification often left the custodial parent resentful of the perceived intrusion of the absent parent, and sometimes fearful of loss of custody rights or, in some cases, renewed intrafamily violence. During the period of enforcement of the law, all but 15 of 3,573 judicial bypass petitions were granted. The judges who adjudicated over 90 percent of these petitions had given evidence to the lower court that none of the hearings demonstrated positive effects of the law. Common reactions of the minor to the judicial hearing were anxiety, shame, fear, and sometimes major trauma to the girl or a parent as well ("Excerpts from the court's ruling," 1990, p. 13).

Proponents of the two-parent notification have claimed that it reinforces family values by promoting the role of parents in the care and upbringing of their children and that the intent has always been to foster the welfare of the child. Opponents have seen the legislation as an overly demanding standard, one directed at the plight and special vulnerability of young pregnant girls. Commentary following the Supreme Court decisions indicated that it appeared evident that "there is no longer a majority on the Court that views abortion as a fundamental constitutional right, but the Justices have still not settled on a standard for analyzing obstacles to abortion" (Greenhouse, 1990b, p. 1).

TRENDS AND ISSUES

Least Intrusive and Appropriate Intervention

The lack of clear public policy in relation to guardianship of children is apparent in the recent major Supreme Court decisions discussed above. The current Court has been criticized for its difficulty in articulating a consistent method of legal analysis with respect to the parent-child relationship and the rights of parents versus the role of the state. Despite some gains, large areas of disagreement and inconsistency emerge that cloud the Court's line of reasoning. Parents, child advocates, and other professionals are left to deplore what appears as nonproductive ambivalence about placing limits on parental control or granting rights to minors. The tangled strands in public policy with respect to the family and the child tend to influence social agencies to move slowly and to adopt at times a more legalistic approach to resolution of parent and child problems than may be necessary.

Divisions in thought are found not only in court rulings and other forms of public policy, but in public thought as well. Child and family policy has become a volatile field for proponents of the far right and the far left. In between the two extremes are many parents, professionals, and other citizens who are working to maintain a constructive and growth-producing balance in the triad of parent-child-society roles and responsibilities. For them the issue is how to advance the rights of children, strengthen family life, and apply the *least intrusive appropriate intervention* to parent-child-societal problems.

Freeing Children for Permanent Homes

One of the important gains in child welfare policy and practice in the past decade has been in the area of "permanency planning" for children caught in the limbo of an unstable foster care system. Effective efforts in many states have helped former neglecting and abusing families to rehabilitate their homes for the return of their children, or, where these efforts are unsuccessful, have established children in permanent homes through adoption, guardianship, or other forms of permanent care.

For many such children, even the best professional efforts will not make their biological parents able or willing to care for them. Gathering evidence to establish a legal basis for terminating parental rights has seldom been easy, given the complexities in parent-child relationships and the contradictory strengths and weaknesses of many individuals, particularly those who have at least once given a level of care to their children that has justified society's assumption of guardianship. With the newly established public policy of "clear and convincing

evidence" as a standard of proof to terminate parental rights, the difficulties will be compounded, especially in states that previously relied on a lesser standard of proof.

To continue to serve children who need a permanent home, it is important that social agencies and professionals further refine their skills in working with parents who have lost their children into foster care. It is equally important that they maintain a focus on the common goals of society's child welfare agencies and its courts, refusing to see one or the other as the adversary and making a sound effort to establish constructive working relationships between child welfare agency staff and court staff.

Guardianship Administration

The need for improved guardianship administration can scarcely be overstated. The more frequent use of guardian *ad litem* provides an example of the need. So does the long-term practice of administrative guardianship of children by state agencies and other large organizations.

The high cost of proper independent advocacy for children before the court and the disastrous tendency for the use of guardian *ad litem* to become simply a pro forma process are two unresolved problems in improving legal protection for children before the court. Alternative practices in the use of guardian *ad litem* need to be tried out and evaluated. Cost factors would surely argue for further use of trained volunteers as well as of professional social workers who could readily gain competence in the role and, under prevailing salary levels, provide the service at less cost than is required in the use of attorneys.

Much more attention needs to be given by professionals to developing sensitive and caring ways of preparing children for court experiences, helping them to speak for themselves, and offering them guidance in avoiding the cruel pitfall of finding themselves feeling compelled to take an open stand against their parents, as happens often, for example, with children in divorce custody contests or in incest situations.

The social distance between state guardians of person and the children whose lives guardianship affects continues to be an unresolved issue. The need to reduce that social distance and find ways to give children a continuing personal relationship to their court-appointed guardians is perhaps greater today than ever before, given the instability of the foster care system, the instabilities in their own parents' lives, and the prevailing state agency practice of emancipating wards from guardianship at age eighteen. Even when states have changed organizational structures to decentralize the administration of state guardianship to some extent, the guardian role tends to remain a reactive one—responding to various requests of the child's social workers, such as giving permission for AIDS testing before placement, use of psychotropic medication, or to withhold "heroic measures" in the hospital. Decisions are made too often only after review of reports and records and with minimum or no direct communication with the child. Such a role falls short of the proactive advocacy stance inherent in the concept of guardian.

If the need to find ways to give children a continuing personal relationship with their court-appointed guardians is very real, so are the difficulties in doing so given (1) the untested question as to whether private persons would come forward to act as guardians of children with difficulties, (2) the probable resistance of large agencies to sharing with private citizens the authority underlying agency services, and (3) the costs that would occur in implementing a new method of "paying people to parent."

The use made of guardianship is, indeed, a test of the extent of a country's freedom in that it reflects how a nation regards and acts toward those individuals who are least able to act for themselves and maintain the prerogatives of their private lives. A child, by the fact of immaturity and inexperience, is one of these vulnerable individuals. Guardianship, properly administered, is not an infringement of rights or an invasion of the individual's privacy, but a safeguard to personal rights and privacy, and a protection when the likely alternative is complete assumption of responsibility for the individual by organizations, officials, or professional persons.

Besides an improvement in guardianship administration, there must be an extension of basic preventive social services to families and children—services that will strengthen the child's own home and make guardianship away from parents unnecessary. These services must be interrelated and easily available to families as soon as they are needed. Such an extension of the preventive social services will reduce the frequency with which court-appointed guardianship is needed for children and will enhance the use of guardianship when it is required.

FOR STUDY AND DISCUSSION

1. What do you see as the specific protections which well-administered guardianship affords a child?
2. Develop an explanation that makes clear why matters involving a transfer of a child's guardianship are appropriate for adjudication by a court.
3. Differentiate the duties, rights, and restrictions of the various kinds of duties discussed.
4. How do the interests protected by the child's guardian *ad litem* differ from the interests protected by the child's *legal counsel?* Does a child need both a legal counsel and a guardian *ad litem?* Why or why not, and in what situations?
5. Explain what is meant by (a) establishing jurisdiction, (b) establishing guardianship within the statutes, and (c) the social investigation in the process of appointing a guardian.
6. Go to the library to read in its entirety one of the United States Supreme Court decisions dis-

cussed in the text. Then, with other students, an-
alyze the line of reasoning used by the majority
and the minority justices. How does such reasoning square with your own conception of a
just balance in parent-child-society rights and
responsibilities?

FOR ADDITIONAL STUDY

Abbott, G. (1938). *The child and the state,* Vol. 1, Pt.
1. Chicago: University of Chicago Press, pp. 3–76.

American Bar Association. (1981). *Protecting children through the legal system.* Washington, DC:
Author.

Breckinridge, S. P. (1934). *The family and the state.*
Chicago: University of Chicago Press.

Condelli, L. (1988). *National evaluation of the impact of guardians* ad litem *in child abuse or neglect
judicial proceedings.* Washington, DC: Administration for Children, Youth and Families.

Deardurff, D. D. (1986). Representing the interests
of the abused and neglected child: The guardian *ad
litem* and access to confidential information. *University of Dayton Law Review, 11*(3).

Goldstein, J., Freud, A., & Solnit, A. J. (1979). *Before the best interests of the child.* New York: Free
Press.

Goldstein, J., Freud, A., & Solnit, A. J. (1986). *In
the best interests of the child.* New York: Free
Press.

Hardin, M. (1985). Families, children, and the law. In
J. Laird, and A. Hartman (Eds.), *A handbook of
child welfare. Context, knowledge, and practice*
(pp. 213–236). New York: Free Press.

Krause, H. (1983). *Family law. Cases and materials.*
St. Paul, MN: West Publishing.

Woerner, J. G. (1897). *A treatise on the American
law of guardianship of minors and persons of un-
sound mind.* Boston: Little, Brown.

CHAPTER 3

The Child and the Court

Let us speak less of the duties of children and more of their rights.

Jean-Jacques Rousseau

Chapter Outline

Juvenile courts were created by a legal and social work cooperative venture. In a spirit of mission, late nineteenth- and early twentieth-century social reformers enjoined the "child welfare" purpose to that of "youth correction." Historical factors in large measure account for the highly complex commingling of the child welfare system and the juvenile justice system that exists today: "The most significant fact about the history of juvenile justice is that it evolved simultaneously with the child welfare system. Most of its defects and its virtues derive from that fact" (Flicker, 1977, p. 27).

Perhaps no social institution was founded with higher hopes for its contribution to justice for children than the juvenile court. In the last three decades, however, it has been a center of controversy. Its philosophy, procedures, and achievements have undergone scrutiny, challenge, and demands for radical change. At the heart of the controversy are differences over the proper purpose and focus of the juvenile court. Should it be primarily concerned with *rehabilitation and treatment* of young persons coming before it or with guarantees of *constitutional due process procedures?* The question attracts proponents to both sides, and the intensity of the differences is at the center of many of the most perplexing decisions that child welfare professionals are called on to make.

Out of the controversy have come some constructive attempts to find ways to serve the needs and rights of children who are brought before the court. In the past three decades, more than three-fourths of the states have enacted changes in their juvenile codes. A movement has grown to exclude status offenses (acts that if committed by an adult would not be a crime) from the jurisdiction of the juvenile court. A major piece of federal legislation, the Juvenile Justice and Delinquency Prevention Act of 1974 (P. L. 93–415, amended 1977), is designed to improve policies and practices that affect youth in the justice system. This legislation marked a significant change in the role of the federal government, which heretofore had left the juvenile court to operate as a state and local institution except for being subject to decisions of the United States Supreme Court. A national assessment of juvenile courts in light of the federal legislation led to this conclusion: "The changes legislated . . . may well be of the same magnitude as those at the beginning of the century" (Sarri & Hasenfeld, 1976, p. 5).

BACKGROUND OF THE JUVENILE COURT

Philosophy and Purpose

From its inception, the juvenile court has had high aims, combined with heavy responsibilities. Its purpose was conceived of as protection and rehabilitation of the child in place of indictment and punishment. It was based on a philosophy of "individualized justice," which directs the application of law to social ends by individualization, that is, by "dealing with each case as in great measure unique and yet . . . on a basis of principle derived from experience . . . developed by reason" (Pound, 1950, p. 36). The intent was a humanitarian one, based on the conviction that the individual child and his or her needs rather than an offense and its legal penalty should be the focus of consideration.

The concern of the juvenile court founders was directed toward the youthful lawbreaker and children whose circumstances were likely to lead them into delinquency, rather than those who were grossly neglected or in need of other protections. As one of the early founders stated:

> It is particularly in dealing with those children who have broken the law or who are leading the kind of life which will inevitably result in such breach, that the new and distinctive features of the juvenile court legislation appear. (Mack, 1909–1910, p. 106)

Judge Julian Mack, one of the early leaders in the juvenile court movement, described procedures prior to the passage of juvenile court legislation:

> Our common criminal law did not differentiate between the adult and the minor who had reached the age of criminal responsibility, seven at common law and in some of our states, ten in others, with a chance of escape up to twelve, if lacking in mental and moral maturity. The majesty and dignity of the state demanded vindication for infractions from both alike. . . . The

child was arrested, put into prison, indicted by the grand jury, tried by a petit jury, under all the forms and technicalities of our criminal law, with the aim of ascertaining whether it had done the specific act—nothing else—and if it had, then of visiting the punishment of the state upon it. (Mack, 1909–1910, p. 106)

An early description of the aims and the humanitarian concerns of the new court will serve to draw the contrast between the old and the new philosophy:

[E]mphasis is laid, not on the act done by the child, but on the social fact and circumstances that are really the inducing causes of the child's appearance in court. The particular offense which was the immediate and proximate cause of the proceedings is considered only as one of the many other factors surrounding the child. The purpose of the proceeding here is not punishment but correction of conditions, care and protection of the child and prevention of a recurrence through the constructive work of the court. Conservation of the child, as a valuable asset of the community, is the dominant note. (Flexner & Baldwin, 1914, pp. 6–7)

To implement such a philosophy, the juvenile court was of necessity a court of equity, one intended to temper the strict application of the law to the individual needs of the child. Its justice represented a departure from the concept of justice personified by the traditional symbol: a statue of a woman holding a balanced scale. In one scale, the crime is measured, and in the other, the punishment. When the two sides of the scale balance evenly, then, it was held, justice prevails. This symbol of justice wears a blindfold so that she cannot be influenced by the wealth or poverty of the accused, or other individual characteristics or station in life. She is blind to individual differences, all objective and evenhanded. There were historical reasons for this symbol. It marked a revolt against the tyranny and the inequities of earlier centuries when law was made and interpreted differently for

nobles and peasants, rich and poor. It marked a claim of the ordinary person for equal treatment before the law.

But in the philosophy of the juvenile court, the blindfold was, in effect, stripped from the symbol of justice. The characteristics of the child became crucial to the judge, who was under obligation to examine the child and a particular situation with all its differences and to turn away from a scrutiny of the offense and its legal penalty. Julia Lathrop, one of the juvenile court's early founders, said that the outstanding contribution of the juvenile court was that "it made the child visible" (Lundberg, 1947, p. 119).

Founding

The first juvenile court in the United States was created in Illinois on April 2, 1899. The attainment of this significant and far-reaching piece of legislation came through cooperation among a group of discerning and energetic social workers in Chicago, lawyers for the Chicago Bar Association, and civic leaders from various organizations, particularly the Chicago Woman's Club.

Logic, and history, and custom, and standards of right conduct, are the forces which singly shape the progress of the law. Which of these forces shall dominate in any case, must depend largely upon the comparative importance or value of the social interests that will be thereby promoted or impaired. (Cardozo, 1921, p. 112)

The leading female reformer among those who assumed responsibility for securing the juvenile court was a social worker, Julia C. Lathrop. An early resident of Hull House, she had been challenged by the spirit and potentiality of youth and distressed at the careless and neglectful treatment of many of them.

As a member of the State Board of Charities, Julia Lathrop visited the various institutions of the state, including orphanages and poorhouses where children were living in distressing conditions, often because they had been in difficulty with the law. At this same time the Chicago Woman's Club, under the leadership of a civic clubwoman, Lucy L. Flower, was making consistent efforts in behalf of delinquent children in Chicago. Club committees had worked to bring about improvements in the conditions of police stations and jails where children were held; they had worked for a truant's special school and supported compulsory education. In 1895, the club had sponsored the drafting of a bill to legislate a separate court for children with a probation department, but had set it aside when they were advised such a law would be found unconstitutional. However, they did not abandon the idea and continued to agitate for reform.

In 1898, at the annual meeting of the Illinois State Conference of Charities, Julia Lathrop gave leadership in planning an entire conference program on the topic "The Children of the State." Different organizations were found to be considering legislative proposals for benefits to children. The various groups merged their efforts and appointed a committee to secure the cooperation of the Chicago Bar Association to bring about a draft of a juvenile court act. While there were many revisions, the bill that emerged was approved as a Bar Association bill and introduced into the state legislature (Lathrop, 1925, pp. 290–297).

The task of proposing and testifying in behalf of the juvenile court bill was assigned to the lawyers, while the woman's club took major responsibility for securing support for the bill (Rosenheim, 1962, pp. 18–19).

This initial piece of legislation, which served as a model for legislation in other states, was broadly entitled "An Act to Regulate the Treatment and Control of Dependent, Neglected, and Delinquent Children." Thereafter, children who violated laws or ordinances were classified as delinquents instead of criminals. As a means of ensuring protection and special con-

sideration of children coming before the court, and as a reaction against the rigid formalities of the civil and criminal courts, certain special procedures were installed.

> Sections of the act called for private informal hearings; protection of court records from publicity; detention of children apart from adults; and the appointment of a probation staff. A catalogue of threatening conditions revealed the meaning of "dependency and neglect." The delinquency definition, a model of simplicity in the original act, covered only those who violated state statutes or municipal ordinances. (Rosenheim, 1962, p. 8)

A Chicago citizen's committee, known as the Juvenile Court Committee, was formed, and voluntary funds were raised to pay probation officers until the law was amended six years later to provide payment of salaries by the county. The committee also maintained a detention home, where children could be held pending disposition by the court. The first juvenile court was housed in the county building until a new structure was erected diagonally across from Hull House, permitting Hull House residents opportunities to watch and advise on the progress of this new social experiment (Addams, 1935, p. 136).

The new act was considered a magnificent accomplishment, attained against the weight and opposition of tradition. Jane Addams believed that the new court brought such change that

> there was almost a change in *mores* when the Juvenile Court was established. The child was brought before the judge with no one to prosecute him and no one to defend him—the judge and all concerned were merely trying to find out what could be done on his behalf. (Addams, 1935, p. 137)

Roscoe Pound said that the juvenile court represented "the greatest advance in judicial history since the Magna Carta" (National Probation and Parole Association, 1957, p. 127). The movement had strong appeal to individual citizens and to groups working in behalf of children. This exciting concept of justice for children and the new legal machinery for helping them was achieved during a period of support for social reforms generally and special interest in the needs of children, a factor that helped to speed the creation of juvenile courts in other states.

By 1910, juvenile court laws had been passed by thirty-four states, the District of Columbia, and Hawaii; by 1917, only three states lacked such legislation (Lundberg, 1947, pp. 116–117). By 1945, all states plus the District of Columbia, Hawaii, Alaska, and Puerto Rico had enacted juvenile court legislation, and Congress had authorized similar procedures for use in the federal courts (Nutt, 1949, p. 270).

Just as the juvenile court movement spread among the various states of the United States, it also came to be enacted in much of the world. England provided for a juvenile court in 1908, followed by the countries of Europe. Most of the Latin American nations have enacted such legislation, as well as Canada, Australia, India, the Soviet Union, Japan, Israel, and some of the African countries (A. K. Smith, 1951).

Antecedents of the New Court

The roots of the juvenile court have been traced to a number of early developments and influences. Among these were legal precedents found in criminal law and in the law of equity.

The distinction between children and adults had already been sharply drawn in criminal cases prior to the passage of the juvenile court laws. Because children under the age of seven were considered too young to understand the nature and consequences of their act, they were below the "age of responsibility" and hence could not be held accountable and punishable. Pound claimed, therefore, that the new court

arose on the criminal side of the courts because of the revolts of those judges' consciences from legal rules that required trial of children over seven as criminals and sentence of children over fourteen to penalties provided for adult offenders. (Pound, 1923, pp. 134–135)

By the time of the juvenile court movement the age of responsibility had been raised above seven in some states—for example, to ten in Illinois, and reformers were agitating for even older children to be removed from criminal court jurisdiction. One point of view, then, about the direct ancestry of the juvenile court is that juvenile court legislation extended the age of responsibility to sixteen or eighteen years, and by so doing "has merely widened the application of the common law rule. But in doing so it has, in effect, built a new structure upon the old foundations" (Flexner & Oppenheimer, 1922, p. 8).

Another view, however, is that the juvenile court grew directly out of the court of chancery with an application of its power of *parens patriae* traceable to English common law, developing from the feudal system of land tenure (Mack, 1909–1910, pp. 104–109). In early times the king, as *parens patriae* (father of his country), had the responsibility to maintain and defend his people in return for their services and obedience, and, in addition, he had the right to assume protection of all children in his realm. However, this parental interest was directed mainly toward those who had property, and while in theory the king was protector of all the children, whether born serf or lord, in actuality he exercised the right only in matters of the supervision of a minor child's estate. His intent was to control the income from the land and conserve it for the ruling class.

But when the feudal system disappeared, the king assumed somewhat broader duties toward minor children. To meet his duty, the king delegated responsibility to his chancellor, as keeper of his conscience. The chancery courts were courts of equity; that is, their purpose was to produce equitable solutions to disputes between persons in the kingdom by tempering the strict application of the law which was found to be too narrow or rigid to be applied automatically.

Although the chancellor tended to use his authority over minors only when a property right was involved, exceptions began to reinforce a wider application of the doctrine of *parens patriae* to include protection of children who were thought to be receiving poor parental care. For example, the poet Shelley was deprived of his children because he declared himself to be an atheist (*Shelley v. Westbrooke,* 1817). Lord Wellesley's children were taken away from him in 1827 because of his dissolute conduct, which included "general ill treatment of his wife, an adulterous connection, the encouragement of the children in habits of swearing, and keeping low company" (*Wellesley v. Wellesley,* 1827). But in spite of such examples, the doctrine of *parens patriae* continued to be used mostly as a profitable right of a guardian when property was involved or to enforce parental duty; it was not applied to children whose distress was the result of their own delinquent acts.

To name the courts of chancery as the direct forebear of the juvenile court, particularly in its delinquency jurisdiction, is to apply a legal rationale after the fact. Rosenheim (1962, p. 6) has noted that the doctrine of *parens patriae* offered to the proponents of a juvenile court act

> just the theoretical justification for nonpunitive, individualized handling of offenders that they were seeking . . . and thus extended its application far beyond the propertied wards in whose behalf it had previously been invoked.

Perhaps, as one authority has concluded:

> The most that may be claimed in giving equity the credit for the juvenile court idea seems to be that much the same general motive that gave rise to equity itself in the history of English law is involved in the origin of the juvenile court. (Glueck & Glueck, 1934, p. 15)

In addition to the legal precedents in criminal law and in the courts of chancery, some of the roots of the juvenile court were found in court procedures in use in a few states before the passage of the juvenile court laws, for example, provisions for private hearings, separate court records, and a place of detention apart from the adult prisons, where the child could await trial.

The development of probation service in Massachusetts also preceded the establishment of the juvenile court. In 1869, a law was enacted which charged an agent of the State Board of Charities to attend the hearing of any child on trial in a criminal court, to arrange care with a private family instead of commitment to a reformatory if this was in the child's interest, and to visit the child at intervals (Board of State Charities, 1869, p. 174). The passage of juvenile court laws, of course, provided considerable impetus for further extensions of probation services among all the states. These services were seen as among the most important of all the benefits to children provided by the new court. Over time, the concept of probation, with its direct relationship to social casework theory, had a critical influence on the direction in which the juvenile courts developed in this country, and on the issues raised about the administrative rather than judicial coloration of most of the juvenile courts.

The Early Question of Constitutionality

Some opposition to the initial passage of the acts came from members of the bar who believed that the court procedures, although intended to protect children, actually took away their constitutional rights. Nevertheless, by insisting that juvenile proceedings were not adversary, the constitutionality of the juvenile court statutes was firmly established by a series of court decisions in which the courts substantially reinforced and extended the doctrine of *parens patriae* to include juvenile delinquents. In all the leading test cases, the *parens patriae* tenet was called up and used to justify the state's authority in the new acts even though this old doctrine had not been a direct antecedent of the juvenile court (Flexner & Oppenheimer, 1922, pp. 9–12; Lou, 1927, pp. 9–12).

The first major test of the constitutionality of juvenile court procedures was that of the Pennsylvania Act of 1903. An excerpt from the decision is illustrative of the philosophy that prevailed.

> To save a child from becoming a criminal, or from continuing in a career of crime, to end in maturer years in public punishment and disgrace, the legislature surely may provide for the salvation of such a child, if its parents or guardian be unable or unwilling to do so, by bringing it into one of the courts of the state without any process at all, for the purpose of subjecting it to the state's guardianship and protection. . . . There is no probability, in the proper administration of the law, of the child's liberty being unduly invaded. Every statute which is designed to give protection, care, and training to children, as a needed substitute for parental authority and performance of parental duty, is but a recognition of the duty of the state, as the legitimate guardian and protector of children where other guardianship fails. No constitutional right is violated. (*Commonwealth v. Fisher,* 1905)

Most of the early attacks on the juvenile court that resulted in tests of constitutionality came about because with the informal proceedings of the new court, young people could lose their freedom for acts defined in criminal law as misdemeanors even though 'there was no provision for trial by jury, or open hearings, or legal counsel for the child, or other protections that state constitutions guaranteed adults charged with crimes. But when the new juvenile court statutes were challenged on constitutional grounds, the state supreme courts successively upheld them on the basis that the juvenile court was not a criminal court and no child was brought before the juvenile court under arrest and on trial for a crime; hence, constitutional guarantees accorded defendants in criminal cases did not apply to juvenile procedures. The weight of decision was an overwhelming endorsement of the new laws.

Practically, this meant that the child or youth was brought under the power of the juvenile court without the legal safeguards an adult accused of law violations claimed as a constitutional right. These safeguards are embodied in such procedures as open hearings, right to counsel, proof beyond a reasonable doubt, limitations on the use of hearsay evidence, protection against self-incrimination, and right to bail. This practice of failing to provide the minor with these constitutionally guaranteed protections eventually led to extensive criticism of the juvenile court, on the basis that the rights of the child should be no less highly regarded and no less strictly observed than those of an adult in any court.

The criticism was present early in the juvenile court movement although outweighed by the greater enthusiasm. For example, Edward Lindsey, writing in 1914, voiced his concern that fundamental legal questions were being overlooked. He pointed out that juvenile court cases involved questions of status, that is, questions of rights and obligations of individuals to each other and to social and political groups, such as the family, the state, and society in general. He believed that many of the provisions of the juvenile court acts were clearly in conflict with constitutional provisions.

Lindsey predicted that a period of criticism of the juvenile court would succeed the period of high praise and that when this happened, the features of the acts that were out of harmony with the existing legal system would be eliminated (Lindsey, 1914, pp. 140–148).

Why did the early decisions on constitutionality of the new laws go so wholeheartedly in favor of the movement? One reason might lie in the desire of judges to uphold the new laws simply because of the social purposes they were intended to further. For example, consider the judge's introductory comment in his decision sustaining the Missouri Juvenile Court Act of

1903 when the act was challenged after an eight-year-old boy had been sentenced to the state reform school:

> We confess, at the outset, that the wise and beneficent purposes sought to be accomplished by this act—the prevention of crime, and the upbuilding of a good and useful citizenship—tend, at least to the creation of a desire to uphold it. (*Ex parte Loving,* 1903)

Lindsey (1914, pp. 144–145) believed that public opinion favoring juvenile court legislation had "infected the court" and had led it to try to find a legal ground for sustaining the acts. He also observed that, in the majority of cases, the persons involved were handicapped by poverty or ignorance in challenging the action against them. He noted that the acts are "not applied to the dominant social class" and believed that if they ever were so applied, changes would be made.

When the period of criticism came in the 1960s (discussed at greater length later in this chapter), it brought revisions to the popularly held conception of the benign nature of the late-nineteenth-century child-saving movement of which the juvenile court was one outgrowth. For example, Platt (1969) concluded that an accurate understanding of the juvenile court has been limited by a sentimental interpretation of history. The juvenile court, in his view, was not so much a break with the past as it was simply the creation of a new specialized institution that could carry out traditional legal policies more effectively and flexibly. Further, Platt observed, child saving was a middle-class movement, and although it was organized in behalf of those less fortunately placed in the social order, it reflected dominant class interests and was an affirmation of faith in traditional institutions and values—parental authority, home, education, rural life—all of which in the late nineteenth century appeared threatened by the growth of immigration, urbanism, and industrialization. The founders were unwilling to acknowledge

economic inequalities in the referral of youth and their parents to the new court even though the child behaviors selected for court action were ones primarily attributed to the children of lower class or immigrant families, for example, drinking, begging, roaming the streets, frequenting dance halls, sexuality, fighting, and incorrigibility. The reformers held paternalistic attitudes toward delinquent youth, but their decisions and actions in relation to these youth were aimed at social control and backed up by force. Further, Platt noted, child savers assumed that there was a harmony of interest between delinquent youth and the agencies of social control. This assumption contributed to a blurring of the distinction between dependency and delinquency, a restriction of youthful autonomy and premature independence, and an invention of new categories of child misbehavior that were in actuality aimed at defining, regulating, and maintaining the dependent status of youth.

JUVENILE COURT JURISDICTION

Statutory Definitions of Jurisdiction

In juvenile court practice, the jurisdiction of a court (that is, the legal authority to hear and decide a particular case) is determined by the statutes of the particular state in which it is located, and the judge must confine his or her authority to those situations authorized by law.

The *age* of the young person under question is a primary factor that enters into a decision as to whether a juvenile court has jurisdiction. In most states (thirty-three) the maximum age for original jurisdiction is seventeen years. In twelve other states it is sixteen years, and in the remaining states the court can assume jurisdiction only for children fifteen years of age or under. Although the age at which courts can assume original jurisdiction may be seventeen, sixteen, or fifteen years, most states (forty-one) give the juvenile court continuing jurisdiction over juvenile offenders until they reach the age of twenty-one. Status offense jurisdiction generally continues until age seventeen or eighteen (Bird et al., 1984). Setting a lower maximum age for males than for females has been common in state statutes, but this practice has now been declared unconstitutional in state courts (Levin & Sarri, 1974, pp. 14–17).

In this country the juvenile court is given jurisdiction in the following types of situations.

1. *Instances in which children or young persons are alleged to be delinquent,* that is, to have violated any federal or state law, or municipal ordinance. While most states continue to categorize juvenile lawbreakers as "delinquents," statutes in some states have been revised to use what are regarded as less stigmatizing labels—"offenders," or "wards of the court." It is interesting that the term "delinquent" was chosen by the juvenile court founders because it was considered to be free of the taint that attaches to criminal behavior. Given today's high degree of public concern and outcry about youth who commit very serious crimes, it is also of interest that the Institute of Judicial Administration and the American Bar Association (hereafter referred to as the IJA-ABA Joint Commission) considered a motion to call juvenile offenders "juvenile criminals." The motion was defeated for three reasons: "Developmental differences of children must be recognized in dealing with juvenile crime; abandonment of the term 'delinquency' would be too abrupt and politically unpalatable . . . , and a 'juvenile criminal' label could produce a more rigid, punitive community response to youthful crime" (Flicker, 1977, p. 51).

The definition of delinquency is fairly clear-cut. States may vary somewhat by excluding certain minor offenses such as vagrancy or loitering, or by treating traffic offenses differently depending on whether they are heard in traffic court or juvenile court. Some differentiate between misdemeanors and felonies for offenders under and over sixteen. However, the primary criterion in defining delinquency is whether the act would be a crime if committed by an adult.

Nearly all states have some provision to permit a juvenile court to waive jurisdiction in the case of major offenses and to transfer a young person to the criminal court for adjudication. A significant decision by the U.S. Supreme Court (*Kent v. United States,* 1966) had to do with a youth's constitutional rights during a transfer, or waiver, from the juvenile court to the criminal court. The decision emphasized the necessity for the basic requirements of due process and fairness to obtain in juvenile hearings and specified that the juvenile court must hold a hearing on the matter of waiver, provide the young person with counsel at this hearing, and make the juvenile court records available to his or her counsel.

Theoretically, to grant such a waiver the judge is expected to consider the youth's age at the time of the offense and the seriousness of the alleged offense (such as whether it was against the person or property). After these initial determinations, courts should satisfy further criteria set forth in juvenile codes. These may include "the existence of a *prima facie* case of guilt; the prior record of the child; the juvenile's response to prior treatment efforts; the mental state of the youth; the amenability of the child to treatment and rehabilitation; and the availability of the means for treatment and rehabilitation" (Shepherd, 1988). Further, before waiving its jurisdiction and thus permitting a child to be tried as an adult, the juvenile court should see that a social study is made, a hearing is held, and it is determined that the existing juvenile facilities in the state are inappropriate and cannot be developed, or that acceptable treatment is not available in the private sector, or that the safety of the community requires the youth to be restrained for a period beyond maturity (Sheridan, 1966, pp. 34–35; Heck et al. 1985, p. 31).

2. *Instances in which children or young persons are in need of supervision,* that is, are alleged to be beyond the control of their parents, guardians, or other lawful custodians, and

display patterns of conduct deemed incorrigible, uncontrollable, or likely to develop into more serious and dangerous behavior. These situations are sometimes referred to as "status offenses" because the conduct that brings the child before the court is held to be illegal only because of the child's age and would not be regarded as illegal if he or she were not a minor. Examples of status offenses include truancy, running away, curfew violations, sexual promiscuity, undesirable companions, and disobedience to parents.

Only six states still deal with the numerous noncriminal misbehaviors called status offenses under the classification of delinquency. Others have created a separate classification. The first to do so was New York, which in 1962 differentiated status offenses from the more serious offenses of delinquency by creating a category called "persons in need of supervision." Other states followed and began referring to such children as persons (or minors, or children) in need of supervision and using the acronyms PINS, MINS, or CHINS. "By 1980, some thirty-five states either had a separate status offense category or prescribed different dispositional alternatives for status offenders than for delinquents" (Dodson, 1984, p. 157). Four states now include status offenses in their abuse, neglect, and dependency category, rendering the child welfare system responsible for services.

The new classifications were intended to remove the stigma associated with the term "juvenile delinquent" and to call attention to the need to develop appropriate new treatments. Neither intent has succeeded well. The MINS label denotes a youth's contact with the court and is troublesome to her or him. And the courts, rehabilitation experts, and community agencies have far to go in showing an ability to deal effectively with traditional adolescent behavior problems in coercive treatment programs that are linked to the court.

Maintaining status offenses within the jurisdiction of the juvenile court remains highly controversial. Some authorities challenge the wisdom and justice of authorizing the juvenile court to assume jurisdiction over youth who behave in ways encompassed under such general terms as "incorrigibility" or "in need of supervision." There is a danger that such imprecise terms will invite vague allegations and actions, with results that are inappropriate to the best interests of children. Given the scope, vagueness, and equivocal language of the statutes in many states, almost any child could be brought within the jurisdiction of the juvenile court. Evidence of the high proportion of MINS who are kept in detention centers for indefinite periods of time or committed to correctional institutions and mixed with delinquents, contrary to federal law, has led to a search for alternatives to the juvenile court process, with an emphasis on "diversion" of minors alleged to be in need of supervision—diversion away from the juvenile justice system to community agencies and programs. Unless there is neglect or delinquency that is clearly manifest, or at least some plain demonstration that a child's behavior is so far beyond the control of parents as to endanger the child or others, the community's responsibility should be to provide control or supervision by a private person or treatment by one of the community's service agencies in lieu of a status offense adjudication (Dodson, 1984, p. 165; Sarri & Hasenfeld, 1976; Levin & Sarri, 1974; Klapmuts, 1972, pp. 21–26).

A Juvenile Justice Standards Project, sponsored by the IJA-ABA Joint Commission, recommended that status offenders be eliminated from court jurisdiction. Yet it took note of certain intransigent situations of noncriminal juvenile misconduct where strictly noncoercive community remedies might not be effective. Consequently, the commission recommended limited court intervention for a juvenile status offender found in circumstances that constitute a substantial and immediate danger to her or his physical safety. Some adolescents are deeply involved in family conflict, or are runaways from home and adamantly refuse to return. Some with very serious behavior disorders may not seek help voluntarily even after being referred, or families may not cooperate. In such instances the commission recommended the use of "limited custody" in a temporary nonsecure residential facility (Flicker, 1977, pp. 67–68). Thus the commission illustrated an ambivalence about turning over some implacable youths to strictly noncoercive and voluntary community remedies, an ambivalence common to many juvenile judges and citizens of the community.

3. *Instances in which the quality of the care and protection a child receives is at question,* that is, when the child is classified as "dependent," "neglected," "abused." Dependent children generally lack proper guardianship because their parents are dead or unable to provide acceptable care because of some established mental or physical incapacity. The statutes may also provide for a parent to assent to a finding of dependency for a child so that he or she can be placed in an adoptive home.

As in the case of dependent children, those classified as neglected are subject to the jurisdiction of the court as it carries out its function of protecting the child on behalf of society. Whereas a child's dependency status reflects inability on the part of a parent to act as a proper guardian, *neglect* implies acts of omission that cause harm or injury to a child (Caulfield & Horowitz, 1987, p. 1). There has usually been some parental behavior that has a recognizably harmful effect on the child, such as failing to provide necessary physical care, leaving young children unsupervised and alone at home, maintaining the home in conditions of filth, clothing children inadequately in extreme weather, or neglecting their basic medical needs. Neglected children may also include those whose parents, guardians, or custodians allegedly have neglected to provide them with support or education, as required by law; or those who have been abandoned by their parents or guardians or custodians (an extreme form of neglect); or those whose environment is in some other way injurious to their welfare. No child, however, should be subject to the jurisdiction of the court

for economic reasons alone. Unless there is clear evidence of an element of neglect in the child's care, parents should be eligible to receive financial assistance to care for their children without the intervention of the court.

Abuse of children is intentional, nonaccidental use of physical force by parents or other caretakers. (See Chapter 9 for fuller discussion of the difficulties in finding an adequate definition of child neglect and abuse.) As can be seen, the categories are sometimes overlapping.

> Parental neglect can precipitate delinquent conduct and the delinquent child may have been subjected to hostility and child abuse in the home. The neglected child may also be a delinquent who has not yet been caught. (Brieland & Lemmon, 1985, p. 139)

4. *Additional situations* formerly found elsewhere in law are also recommended for inclusion in the jurisdiction of the juvenile court for easier access to the benefits of a social study and report to the court. (Social study was recognized from the beginning of the juvenile court as one of its important and distinguishing characteristics.) These situations include certain actions concerning children's legal status and rights or those of their parents, all of which require social study for their determination: (1) adoption of a minor, (2) termination of the legal child-parent relationship, (3) appointment of a guardian of the person of a minor, and (4) determination of the legal custody of any child or the transfer to institutions of legal custody of mentally retarded children or children with severe physical disabilities or emotional problems.

The role of the court in such matters is predicated upon the principle that the care and control of one person by another should be assured only on a legally responsible basis. The court's interest and authority is not to take over the making of decisions among human beings in their relationships to each other, but to assure that the individual has the means of decision and that choices are safeguarded.

Other Determinants of Jurisdiction

In addition to state statutory definitions that determine the kinds of children's situations brought under juvenile court jurisdiction, other elements in a community help to determine what kinds of problems will reach the court. Ones discussed here include actions and attitudes of *police, lawyers, judges, and citizens of the community*.

The screening power of police is the most significant factor in the handling of juvenile offenses. Almost all delinquency cases reaching the juvenile court are referred by the police. Parents initiate most of the status offense cases by referrals to police. From this welter of cases, the police screen out many before they get to court through a largely ad hoc discretionary process. In encounters with juveniles, police act without the statutory constraints required in the handling of adult offenses. Thus they wield considerable power. It is that element of informal, unstructured discretionary power that makes exchanges between minors and police so critical. To bring some uniformity to the process, the IJA-ABA standards would require that "police authority to take juveniles into custody be specifically authorized by statute" (*Standards relating to police,* 1980, p. 44).

Before referral to the court, good practice suggests that police use the least restrictive and appropriate alternative, and voluntary referrals to community services over mandatory ones. However, even though the formulation of standards and guidelines is an important step in improved handling of juvenile cases, how often these guidelines are used varies considerably.

Several studies of police behavior show a tendency to detain and refer status offenders to court more often than delinquents, and to detain girls more frequently than boys (Chesney-Lind, 1988, p. 154). These findings may suggest that police tend at times to see themselves in a parental or guardian role rather than that of officer. Subjective judgments by police may adversely affect young persons in one of two ways.

If referral to court is made on the basis of an unsubstantiated evaluation, minors may be mislabeled as delinquents or status offenders and then respond by behaving as expected. If the police choose to release the minor, he or she may be denied corrective services intended to terminate delinquent behaviors.

Studies suggest, however, that some agreement exists among police about *basic* criteria to use in deciding what action to take: (1) severity of the delinquent act, (2) frequency of the juvenile's involvement in delinquency, (3) community attitudes toward delinquency, and (4) the demeanor of minors in their encounters with police. In addition, police are often influenced by their personal view of the effectiveness of correctional agencies. Practical matters also play a part; for example, referral to court for detention is "strongly related to simple geographical accessibility to a secure detention facility" (Pappenfort & Young, 1980, p. 10). Knowledge of community services is pivotal since juvenile officers are uniquely positioned to refer youth for longer term help to family counseling services, mental health and youth service agencies. A close liaison of social workers and juvenile officers, including social workers in police departments, accrues to the benefit of youth through information sharing on agency programs and services.

In contrast to the handling of delinquency cases, there is little formal information on the administration of dependency and neglect cases at the police level. Although there is not as discernible a regulatory system, it is known that not all such cases that come to the attention of the police are referred to court. Reliable information is needed as to how police engage in extensive regulation of the handling of neglect and abuse of children (Handler & Rosenheim, 1966, p. 9).

How can the acknowledged benefits of informal, pre-judicial handling of youthful offenders be ensured and the evils so often accompanying informal "screening" be minimized? As a step toward this goal, selected police officers should be designated to deal with cases involving children. These police officers should receive special training, and criteria should be agreed upon by police and juvenile court staff for deciding whether a given case should go to court, be referred to other community agencies, or be dealt with in other ways (Myren & Swanson, 1962, p. 28).

A *lawyer* who represents one of the parties may influence the definitions of neglect or delinquency that will prevail by raising questions about the alleged situation and clarifying legal issues.

Judges are a powerful contributor to a community's definition of neglect or delinquency. While they must carry out their responsibilities within the statutory definition of their jurisdiction, statutes are necessarily couched in such general language as to encompass a wide range of situations. Therefore, they must interpret the meaning and intent of the law, and in so doing, may exercise considerable individual discretion by reflecting particular points of view about human behavior and social influences.

An individual community also contributes to the definition of delinquency or neglect by its explicit or implicit identification of child and adult behaviors it disapproves of or considers harmful. In addition, the kinds of parents or youthful offenders who come before the court may also be influenced by a community's proportion of poor families, already disadvantaged and less able to assert their rights or handle their problems by the use of private resources.

Particularly in matters of neglect, usually more difficult to prove or disprove than single acts of delinquency or abuse, an improved definition is needed. In a discussion of children under the law, Rodham (1973, p. 514) noted that "a common complaint about the exercise of discretion in neglect cases is that alien values, usually middle-class, are used to judge a family's child-rearing practices." She suggests that one way to counter that complaint when neglect is alleged is to entrust the required discretion to "persons representing the milieu in which a family lives. Boards composed of citizens representing identifiable constituencies— racial, religious, ethnic, geographical—could make the initial decision regarding intervention or review judicial decisions." Too often communities lack defensible criteria for intervention in family life, and as a result, people in similar situations are not treated equitably.

CONDITIONS THAT AFFECT THE COURT'S ATTAINMENT FOR CHILDREN

Multilevel Administrative Relationships

Certain characteristics of the juvenile court as a social institution tend to limit or complicate its effectiveness. The juvenile court is a specialized unit in state judicial systems, although it is typically city- or county-based. Its basic mandates are defined by the state legislature, and its proceedings can be reviewed by higher courts. But at the same time it is an institution highly dependent on local persons and organizations. This dependency complicates its relationships to state-level bodies and, with the passage of the Juvenile Justice and Delinquency Prevention Act of 1974, to the federal level of government as well. For example, its finances are largely provided by local government so that local approval is needed to sustain its operation budget. Judges usually occupy their positions as long as they can win the endorsement of the local electorate. The clientele of the court is supplied mainly by referrals from local police or social agencies. The success of the court's disposition plans depends in large measure on the policies and resources of local organizations. Not enough appropriate social services and treatment resources exist to aid in the rehabilitation of children and families, yet the juvenile court often experiences critical pressures from local agencies who may have conflicting expectations of the court, or who may impose demands for prompt solutions to their referrals of some of the community's most difficult situations. The judge and the judge's staff must somehow harmonize these multilevel relationships required by mandates from the United States Supreme Court, the state legislature, and the pressures for action by the locality (Vinter, 1967, pp. 84–90). To this end, juvenile court judges need to act as advocates and catalysts in developing community programs for children in liaison with schools, businesses, and industry, and also ensure that the most efficient use is made of existing resources and financial support for the court (National Council of Juvenile and Family Court Judges, 1984). Inadequate financing in the majority of juvenile courts directly affects the quality and quantity of staff that can be recruited.

A Family Court

Although the juvenile court handles most of the jurisdiction of cases involving children, the concept of the family court—one with jurisdiction over a broad range of family problems—has received widespread approval although very incomplete implementation.

Most juvenile courts have been given a jurisdiction narrower than the scope of family problems. For example, juvenile courts, typically, have not been given jurisdiction over the custody of children involved in divorce actions. In some states adoption can be granted without the attention of the juvenile court. In some, the probate court may retain its power to appoint guardians of the person and to award custody to the guardian. Situations of family conflict, manifesting a labyrinth of social and emotional symptoms, often find their way into a number of courts at the same time. The results are wasted court resources, inconsistent decisions, and continued unsolved problems and stress for families.

The aim of a family court is to group and unify services to families and children requiring the attention of a court, so that the totality of family-related controversies can be dealt with systematically and consistently. These family matters include jurisdiction over (1) children alleged to be dependent, delinquent, neglected, or in need of supervision; (2) adults alleged to have contributed to the delinquency of a minor; (3) couples seeking a divorce, especially when there are children whose custody must be decided; (4) matters of financial support and visitation; (5) establishment of paternity; and (6) the adoption of a minor.

Advocates of the family court point out that all these kinds of situations have common elements and require access to social study and decision making based on the best interests of the children involved. For example, the problems of dependent, neglected, or delinquent children frequently are not very different from those children who are the victims of a bitter contest for custody by divorcing parents. A mother of dependent children may need attention to a cluster of legal and social problems, for example, establishing paternity, securing support, and securing a divorce so that future children can be legitimated through remarriage. Scarce court resources are wasted, and the individuals involved receive less effective attention when their problems are dealt with fragmentally.

Why have family courts not flourished? Generally, the concept has been endorsed by nationally organized groups, such as the American Bar Association and the National Council on Crime and Delinquency, as well as by numerous individual legal experts. But relatively few family courts have been established, and there is great variation among those that do exist. Some of them can be said to have only some of the elements of a family court; others are regarded only as a step in the direction of a family court; still others are termed family courts only by the addition of a marriage counseling service.

The slow growth of family courts is attributable to resistance to change from staff of present courts, opposition from some juvenile court judges who fear the loss of the juvenile court concept, mistaken conflicts between legal and social points of view, and a prevailing lack of reliance upon behavioral science among court personnel and community persons who are in a position to influence the establishment of a family court. Another deterrent arises from a consideration of the sheer volume of litigation involved, with a diminution of interest in the face of already insufficient numbers of trained personnel and rehabilitative resources.

In any case, the concept of a family court will not be self-fulfilling. To be successful, solutions must be found to the same problems that now beset the juvenile court, for example, inadequate financing, lack of sufficient numbers of competent staff, lack of treatment resources, and problems in providing due process protections in highly complex family situations.

Casefinding

Courts do not act as casefinders. Generally a court concerns itself with children only when it is petitioned to do so because some conflict of interest exists. For example, sometimes the reported observations of neighbors or teachers strongly suggest that parents are failing to provide food for their children, or are not supervising them properly, or are inflicting cruel punishment on them; then a conflict of interest exists between parents, who have certain rights and responsibilities to their children, and society, which has other rights and responsibilities. Or if a parent arranges for a person to care for his or her child and then neglects a continuing responsibility for support or visitation, and if that caretaker forms an attachment to the child and a concern for its welfare and decides to petition the court for guardianship of the child, then a conflict of interest exists between the petitioner and the child's parent.

But such illustrations imply that someone in the community has been responsive to the conflict of interest to the extent that the court is requested to give its attention to the matter. Since a court does not initiate its cases, but acts only on what is brought before it, the responsibility clearly rests on citizens of a community, and particularly on staff members of its authorized social agencies, to discover and refer to the court those children who need its attention.

Judges and Probation Officers— Qualifications and Roles

Relatively little factual information about the persons who carry out the functions of the court, particularly the judges, was available until data were gathered for a "national profile" of the approximately 3,000 judges who were handling juvenile court duties in this country (McCune & Skoler, 1965). The survey was later replicated (K. C. Smith, 1974.) What emerged, as it had a decade earlier, was a picture of the juvenile court judge group as having family and marital stability, experience in the parent role, a commitment to societal and middle-class norms, and a taking on of their judicial position after having held other public offices and community responsibilities—conditions that many persons would say are appropriate to the functions and the attainment of judicial status. An important change during the intervening decade was found in the amount and kind of educational preparation for judgeship. In 1973, 82 percent of the judges had had three or more years of law school compared with 69 percent a decade earlier. In a later survey (Sarri & Hasenfeld, 1976), 96 percent of the judges in charge of juveniles were reported to have a law degree—a high percentage explained by the fact that counties below 50,000 in population were not studied, thus somewhat biasing the findings toward areas where higher levels of legal education are required.

Juvenile matters were still a relatively minor part of their work loads as judges. Most spent one-fourth or less of their time on juvenile cases (K. C. Smith, 1974)—a fact suggesting, as it had a decade earlier, that the juvenile court had been "integrated into the existing judicial structure without recognition of the complexity of the job assignment'' (McCune & Skoler, 1965).

The most striking finding from Smith's survey was that today's juvenile court judges are faced with the same unsolved pressing problems as were their predecessors a decade ago. Judges (both rural and metropolitan, young and old) continued to rank their top four problems as (1) inadequate facilities for detention or shelter care pending disposition, (2) insufficient foster home placement facilities, (3) inadequate or insufficient training in correctional institutions, and (4) insufficient probation or social service staff. This agreement seemed especially important in view of the fact that about three-fourths of the judges were not in their judge position a decade earlier and so had not participated in the McCune and Skoler study. Smith concluded:

> What is strikingly evident is that the nation's juvenile court judges . . . are looking for, but not finding alternatives to incarcerating juveniles. Further it is evident that the nation's juvenile court judges want more and better dispositional alternatives for young offenders. (K. C. Smith, 1974, p. 38)

When McDonough (1976) examined the characteristics of court staff in counties with populations over 50,000, she found that about 85 percent of the probation officers were required to have a bachelor's degree and, at the time of the survey, 92 percent possessed that degree. Only in 2 percent of the courts was a master's degree required for the position of probation officer. Disturbingly, in 13 percent of the courts a high school education or less was reported to be acceptable. Even though the overall proportion of probation officers with a bachelor's degree was high, less than half had had professional training in criminal justice, corrections, or social work. When characteristics of all court staff were examined (judges, administrators, probation supervisors, line probation officers, and detention supervisors), as a group they were middle-aged, white, male, and married—a profile disproportionate to the ratios by sex and race of the young persons who were referred to and processed by the court.

A recent study in a large industrial state suggests that at least in characteristics of age and sex, there has been change: Juvenile probation officers were found to be younger (mean age of thirty-five years) and of equal numbers of male and females (Colley et al., 1987).

Probation officers in Sarri's national sample (1976, p. 158) reported a median caseload of 55 juveniles; 25 percent reported a more manageable number, 35 or fewer per worker, but there were also caseloads reported in excess of 100 per worker, obviously making it difficult to offer intensive counseling or referral.

Colley and coworkers (1987) found caseloads that were somewhat more favorable. About one-half of juvenile probation officers carried fifty or fewer cases. Still, the most frequently reported client caseload was thirty juveniles. The designation of caseload numbers is somewhat arbitrary. Numbers are more meaningful if they are associated with the disparate tasks that juvenile probation officers perform and are adjusted by the time demands of certain functions. For example, the time required for intake and predisposition investigation may justify a smaller caseload than probation supervisory services (*Standards relating to the juvenile*, 1980, p. 18).

In any case, inappropriately high caseloads increase the likelihood that probation officers will limit their social investigations to readily obtainable facts, checklist reports from school or other agencies, and an interview with the child and one parent. Yet this social investigation in most instances is the only or principal material on which the judge bases the disposition.

Probation officers deal with such problems as school attendance and other school-related situations, troublesome juvenile behavior in the community, youth employment, and alcohol and drug abuse. Yet well-developed channels for appropriate goal-directed collaboration with community agencies are generally lacking. When probation officers were asked what the community expected the court or probation officer to do in relation to juvenile offenders, their replies indicated their view that the community expected probation officers to remove offenders from the community, protect the community at any cost, and make examples of those who commit serious offenses. These probation officers seemed to expect little support for considering the needs of the individual young person or trying to keep the young offender in the community (Sarri, 1976, pp. 160–166).

Nevertheless, new trends are changing the face of probation and its traditional underpinnings. Recent developments in probation services include the development of recidivism prediction instruments, intensive probation, new approaches to caseload management, and other interventions to stimulate modified behavior among delinquents. Dobbert (1987, pp. 29–33) has proposed that probation be made a therapeutic intervention rather than a law enforcement function. His model, Positive Contingency Probation Management, relies on identification and diagnosis of conditions that precipitated the individual youth's delinquent behavior. The youth enters a contract, agrees to undertake activities specially designed to counteract his or her delinquent behavior, with desired behavior rewarded through shortened probation. Using indeterminate probation sentences, the length of probation can be contingent on the actions of the youth. As a consequence, "probation becomes the responsibility of the probationer, and not the probation officer" (p. 32). This model has the potential to free probation officer time for other therapeutic and community organization efforts.

In summary, courts for children are not properly or adequately staffed. Despite gains, at least 18 percent of the judges lack basic professional credentials to preside over any court; all of them have insufficient time to devote to excessive work loads. Yet current state of the art standards for selected judges reflect the demands of an increasingly complex juvenile court. There are new expectations in judge qualifications: special interest in the social and legal problems of children, youth, and families; sensitivity toward minority groups who may come before the court; an appreciation of divergent lifestyles; and capability to evaluate the testimony of children and of expert witnesses concerning children (Standards relating to the juvenile, 1980, p. 19).

There are insufficient numbers of probation staff with current and appropriate training, frequent confusion about the nature of probation service, and a lack of collaboration with related community agencies. At best the probation officer often is faced with conflicting role demands—to investigate a delinquent act or a charge of neglect and present evidence against the child or parent, and concurrently or later secure the child's or parent's trust through a supporting, accepting treatment relationship.

Judges and probation staff make up only a part of the personnel in the juvenile justice system. An array of other participants are involved as well—police, attorneys, physicians, correctional authorities, school officials, child welfare and mental health professionals, and other service providers. The list is open-ended, depending on the particular community. A basic problem is that "too many people and organizations are involved and no one is coordinating their activities . . . an important facet of the overall inability of the participants to achieve a clear understanding of their respective roles" (Flicker, 1977, p. 39). The absence of a coordinating authority over the parts of the system contributes to inefficiency and waste of resources.

Parents and juveniles are also participants in the juvenile justice system. The young person supposedly is the central figure. Yet minors are presumed to be incapable of making decisions for themselves. Thus parents are expected to act on their behalf. The IJA-ABA Joint Commission cites two dilemmas or contradictions that these conditions create: (1) If the young person is in court at least partly because of parental inadequacies or behaviors (even to the point of being the petitioner, as is frequently the case with status offenders), why is the parent considered to be a qualified advocate for the child's interests? (2) If minors are to be brought into court and held responsible for their acts, why are they usually held to be incapable of speaking for themselves? How effective can a judicial proceeding be from the minor's point of view if she or he has been a passive observer, denied a true participant's role? (Flicker, 1977).

More optimistically, many juvenile and family courts are discovering social science research from which to fashion criteria for determining when juveniles can be presumed competent to testify in court about their observations and their desires in decisions affecting their lives (Bell, 1988).

Facilities Available in the Court and Community

Court facilities for care and protection of children are commonly called "shelter" and "detention" homes. Shelters are "nonsecurity" facilities, usually provided in temporary foster homes or open institutions. Children in shelters often are there because they have been found abandoned or seriously neglected by their parents and are taken to the shelter by police or social agency representatives pending the attention of the court. Shelters are also appropriate for emotionally disturbed children who must be removed from their own homes pending court disposition because of a critical crisis growing out of strained relationships between child and parents. In addition, shelter care is suitable for children alleged to have committed delinquent acts when they cannot remain in their own homes and when a "security" type of care is not required for the protection of the community.

Detention care implies "secure custody" and is used for children awaiting court action, usually those alleged to have committed a delinquent act or a status offense. Detention in the juvenile justice system is vastly overused, espe-

cially for status offenders. Reasons given for holding young persons in detention are to ensure their appearance in court, to prevent them from committing further offenses harmful to themselves or the community, and to move them out of dangerous situations quickly pending a court hearing.

The use of secure detention decreased between 1975 and 1983. This decline, however, has not been uniform across all juvenile offenses. By 1983 a higher proportion of delinquency cases were securely detained than in 1975, but the use of secure facilities for status offenders plummeted in the same time period from 40 percent to 11 percent (Snyder, 1987, p. 46).

A serious shortage of good detention and shelter facilities exists, with frequent overcrowding in those that are available. Large numbers of communities, particularly in rural areas, have no detention or shelter facilities at all. As a result, children awaiting juvenile court hearings frequently are held in jails. Juveniles are jailed not only in rural areas, where more appropriate detention facilities are limited, but in urban areas as well, where a greater range of alternative facilities exists. Jails hold juveniles in nearly all states, signaling a national rather than a regional occurrence (Levin & Sarri, 1974, pp. 25–36). The last annual count of the number of children and young persons held in jails was in 1984. According to the Annual Survey of Jails, 95,580 juveniles entered jails; nearly 17 percent were girls (Chesney-Lind, 1988, p. 150). It appears that juvenile jailing has increased rather sharply in the past five years or more after a long period of gradual decline from the nineteenth into the twentieth century.

Using jails for children, even for those who must be kept in secure custody, cannot be defended. Jails are a part of the system of criminal justice and do not reflect the rehabilitative philosophy of the juvenile court. Children confined in jails are undesirably either placed in isolation or else exposed to adult lawbreakers or various kinds of persons abandoned by society. Jails used for children often do not provide even adequate physical care. Overcrowding, poor diet, no facilities for exercise, inadequate sanitation, and even cruelty and sexual abuse—all these conditions are not uncommon.

The tragedy of children held in jail is compounded by the fact that many of them pose no actual threat to society; they are in dire need of society's help.

A typical detainee is a male living in a metropolitan area. Relatively few detainees are represented by an attorney at a detention hearing even though they have a right to counsel. Although the large majority of young persons held in jail or detention facilities are males, females have a higher probability of being detained. The highest rate of detention occurs among females charged with *status offenses,* particularly those accused of running away, sexual promiscuity, or incorrigibility. Although males are more often charged with crimes against property or persons, females charged with status offenses are at significantly greater risk of loss of liberty through detention or jailing. Race appears to be a factor in this differential treatment, but as a factor it interacts with sex and social class in ways that obscure a clear-cut pattern (Sarri, 1974, p. 5; 1983; Milton et al., 1977).

Very often detention facilities are used as dumping grounds for unwanted children, who may be detained without understanding why. Consider the following statement of a thirteen-year-old girl:

I was sitting on the front steps of my grandmother's house. My father said, "Put your shoes on. I'm going to take you downtown with me." We got into the car and we went to the police station and I kept asking him, "What are we doing here?" Then one of the policemen took me and told me to wait in this little room. I was waiting for my father to finish his business, and then I looked out the window and I saw him walking toward the car. I screamed at him, "Where was he going? Why was he leaving me?" He never turned around. He just kept walking to the car and then he got in the car and drove off. He never told me I was an "incorrigi-

ble child" . . . I didn't know I had any problems or what they were. I just knew he left me there. From there I was sent to the Youth Studies Center and from there to Slaten Farms . . . and then on to all the rest of the joints. . . . (Burkhart, 1975, p. 5)

Holding status offenders in jails is sometimes defended on the basis that no detention or other facilities are available—a reason clearly suggesting that too little attention has been given to providing more appropriate alternatives. Misuse of detention centers that do exist is common, compounding the shortage of adequate facilities and damaging children who should not be so confined. Children who need basic care and protection, such as are provided appropriately in a shelter facility, should not be held in detention. Children who can be allowed to remain in their own homes pending court action should not be kept in either shelters or detention centers for any reason, and especially not for punishment, for example, "to teach a child a lesson," or for the convenience of court personnel in making a social study, or law enforcement officers in investigating offenses by others.

The passage of the Juvenile Justice and Delinquency Prevention Act of 1974 has effected change in practice. Further impact of this legislation is expected to continue to reduce institutionalization of status offenders as well as jailing of delinquent youth. For states to be eligible for federal funds, the act requires that they may use only shelter facilities for status offenders and not detention or correctional facilities. Further, the act provides that juveniles alleged to be or found to be delinquent shall not be confined in any institution in which they have regular contact with adults who are charged with or have been convicted of a crime.

The crucial lack of enough adequate treatment facilities for neglected and delinquent children when they are ready to leave shelter or detention care means that for many, their stay in such facilities stretches into months as the court staff or social agency staff "shop" for a therapeutic placement. While the lack of appropriate treatment facilities is widespread and affects almost all groups, it impinges most harshly on nonwhite children or children of mixed parentage. Polier has evaluated the difficulties in carrying out sound treatment recommendations thus:

> The lack of appropriate services and facilities for delinquent children and to a much greater extent for neglected children has contributed more than any other single factor to negating the purpose of the court. (Polier, 1964, p. 30)

Racist and Sexist Influences in Decision Making

Racism and sexism are long-standing influences in the delivery of services to dependent, neglected, and delinquent children. Fewer community supports and treatment alternatives have been made available for females and minorities, thus leaving those who are brought before the court at greater risk of being removed from their own homes for reasons of dependency and neglect. Such malevolent tendencies are mirrored in the correctional system, where female and nonwhite children are at much higher risk of being apprehended by police, screened into the juvenile justice system, and placed in an institution, particularly a correctional institution. Furthermore, they are more likely to be confined in such institutions for longer periods of time.

Corrective legislation for one minority group—American Indian children—was passed in 1978 (The Indian Child Welfare Act, P. L. 95–608). Its intent was to curb an excessive rate of placement of Indian children in non-Indian foster and adoptive homes. The legislation came about after years of agitation by Indian groups and other advocates of civil liberties who maintained that out-of-home placements contributed to disruption of tribal culture and identity confusion on the part of Indian children. The scope of the problem was set forth as follows:

In the States of North and South Dakota, approximately seventeen times as many Indian children as white children, on a per capita basis, are living in foster homes.

In Montana, Indian children are placed in foster homes at ten times the national foster home placement rate.

In Minnesota, the rate of foster home placement of Indian children is four and one-half times greater than that of non-Indian children. . . .

While one out of two hundred children nationally are not in their natural homes, one out of every nine Indian children in North Dakota, South Dakota and Nebraska are not in their natural homes; they are either in foster homes, institutions, boarding facilities or adoptive homes. Thus Indian children in those states are removed from their homes at a rate more than twenty times the national average. ("Scope of the problem," 1974, p. 3)

Indian family advocates charged institutional bias on the part of social agencies and courts who dealt with Indian families in crisis. They spoke effectively for the extended family, which is a basic part of the Indian way of life, and for the rights of Native American grandparents to serve as guardians of children.

The federal legislation was a significant social policy development, unique in acknowledging and protecting cultural values and self-determination of a minority group within the larger American society. In passing the legislation, Congress stated that the policy of the nation was to promote the stability and security of Indian tribes and families by establishing minimum federal standards for the removal of Indian children from their families. The placement of such children in foster homes hereafter would reflect Indian preferences for placement in priority order: extended family; homes licensed by a nontribal entity; or institutions approved by an Indian tribe. Tribal courts were given jurisdiction over child custody proceedings involving most Indian children. Custody proceedings would include all foster care or adoptive placements of Indian children resulting from abuse or neglect, termination of parental rights, or status offenses of running away, truancy and curfew proceedings from the state courts to the tribal courts. Government would provide for assistance to tribes in developing and operating child and family service programs.

Before foster placement could take place two conditions would have to be met. First, child welfare workers would have to show that active provision of remedial and rehabilitative services to keep the Indian family intact was unsuccessful. Second, expert testimony by child welfare workers or other appropriate professionals would have to show convincingly the likelihood of serious emotional or physical damage to the child in the present living arrangement.

By no means have all problems been resolved in the implementation of the legislation. There is often a lack of effective coordination between tribal and state court personnel at all levels. Because of the law's vague definition of "Indian child," and because cases can remain in state court for "good cause," it is likely that significant numbers of Indian children enter foster and adoptive homes. Furthermore, Indian parents who live some distance from the reservation often do not return for the tribal court hearing. One explanation lies in the entrenched belief of many Indian parents that foster placement inevitably means the end of their relationship with their children. Many such parents grew up in foster care themselves and, with such beliefs, simply drift out of their children's lives. Interrupting such a cycle is difficult (Dietrich, 1982).

A current and first national study of the effects of the Indian Child Welfare Act found that in many states, public agencies and state courts are "making significant efforts" to comply with the Act's requirements even though some are not implementing the Act uniformly. An overall conclusion of the study was on a positive note: "Indian children's rights to their tribal and cultural heritage are being protected better than in the past, and the role of Indian parents and

tribes in protecting those rights has been strengthened" (Plantz et al., 1989, p. 28).

The ways in which decision makers in the juvenile justice system treat girls differently from boys has been recognized for some time (Sarri, 1974; 1976; 1983; Sarri & Hasenfeld, 1976; Milton et al., 1977). Girls are more likely than are boys to be referred to court by parents and by police. They are referred for less serious offenses. Girls are routinely referred to court for sexual misbehavior, while boys are seldom so referred. Girls are at greater risk of detention, and in the disposition phase of the court process are less likely to be entered into community programs and more at risk of institutionalization in a severely restricted environment. Fewer alternative programs have been developed for girls than for boys, so that the chance is increased that they will be removed from their own homes. Once institutionalized, girls are afforded fewer services and learning opportunities than are boys.

Attaching a criminal label to girls for behavior that is tolerated among boys constitutes not only unfair treatment but a clear attempt at conditioning girls to their "proper" place. (Figueira-McDonough, 1985b, p. 285)

Such practices have led to allegations of sexism in law enforcement, particularly evident in the handling of female status offenses, such as running away, sexual activity, uncontrollability, and other behavior that represent to many a deviation from female-appropriate behavior. That this differential treatment is a result of discrimination has been rejected by some who argue that girls and boys involve themselves in different kinds of delinquent behavior and that official statistics simply reflect this fact.

To obtain valid information about delinquent behavior of both girls and boys, Figueira-McDonough (1985) studied self-reports of 2,000 tenth-graders. No evidence of gender specialization in delinquent behavior was found. "Virtually the same proportion of girls and boys were involved in status offenses and other acts identified as part of adolescent subculture . . . behaviors that aim to challenge adult authority and are often imitations of adult roles that have been defined illegitimate for adolescents" (p. 277). The incidence of such offenses was almost the same for males and females, except for sexual activities, a behavior more often reported by boys and more often leading to arrest of girls despite lower incidence. Evidence reflected a greater involvement of males than females in property and violent offenses. No evidence emerged of greater involvement of females in status offenses.

A conclusion that emerged was that "the criteria used by the juvenile justice system in handling girls cannot be justified in terms of effective or fair control of delinquency. They appear, instead, to serve the purpose of punishing 'female-inappropriate activities.' "

The potential for change is contained in the Juvenile Justice and Delinquency Prevention Act. Federal funds are available for developing alternative programs for juvenile offenders. The act states specifically that assistance must be made available to "all disadvantaged youth, including . . . females" (P. L. 93–415, 1974).

COURT PROCEDURES

An orderly process involving four steps should be followed when a child comes to the attention of the court: *intake, adjudication, study* or *social investigation,* and *disposition.*

Intake procedures usually begin when a minor is arrested by police or other authorized personnel, or when a complaint about a child's behavior or welfare is made by a member of the community. This person may be a parent or other relative of the child; a person acted against, such as a property owner; a school official; or some other concerned citizen. The complaint may be made to and initially explored by such representatives of the community as a so-

cial worker in a protective agency, a school social worker, or the police or probation officer.

Particularly in cases of parental neglect and abuse, social agencies and the juvenile court should establish clear-cut policies to effect a constructive referral of those situations in which legal action seems necessary. This practice will simplify and make more objective the probation officer's screening of referrals to determine if the protection of the child or the community requires the authority of the court. Without adequate screening a juvenile court may be burdened with cases that should never have reached the court.

The complaint may lead to the filing of a petition—a sworn statement to the court alleging certain acts or conditions, for example, that a child is abused by his or her parents, or has committed a delinquent act, or is left unsupervised by parents. As soon as possible after a petition has been filed, a date should be set for a hearing. The child's parents or guardians should be notified of the petition and the time of the hearing, with instructions to appear with the child.

Before the court can adjudicate the conflict, the judge must first establish jurisdiction, that is, make clear the basis for the court's authority to hear and decide the case. The right and authority of the court to act under its legislated power to judge certain issues must be made evident. The court does so by ascertaining certain facts, such as the age of the child, where he or she lives, and, if neglect or delinquency is alleged, where and when the alleged acts took place. If these established facts accord with a kind of situation over which the court has been given authority by statute, then it may proceed with the case.

The *adjudication* takes place in a court hearing and clearly requires the application of legal skills. Here the court weighs the facts, properly presented under the rules of evidence, and decides whether the child is, under the law, delinquent, neglected, or dependent, or in need of supervision or an award of custody or guardianship. The decision must be made within the framework of the existing law, not within the framework of the judge's personal discretion or preferred action. Only then is the state justified in making a change in the child's legal status and assuming responsibility for certain aspects of his or her upbringing.

Until the alleged act is judged and the child's legal status determined, the court has no authority to make any disposition, that is, to prescribe or carry out a treatment plan. Further, the alleged act should be adjudicated on the evidence submitted separately and prior to the consideration of the social investigation report, which should bear only on the treatment plan.

The *study* or *social investigation* is to help the court make intelligent and constructive plans in relation to the child and his or her family. It may be carried out by the probation staff or by a social agency as a service to the court. In any case it is important that the court have all the facts necessary to act properly in the best interest of the child.

The primary purpose of a social study is to provide an important basis for judgment in the last step of the court process, that is, the disposition. If the social investigation also has produced facts relevant to the adjudication, as may happen particularly in cases of neglect, these facts should be presented separately as legal evidence and should be clearly directed toward helping the judge determine the truth of the acts or conditions alleged in the petition. For example, did the youth indeed commit a delinquent act under the law? Does neglect or abuse of the child truly exist? But the social study properly is directed toward the disposition, presenting facts and evaluations that help the judge determine what treatment plan should be decided upon.

The *disposition* is, in essence, the decision as to how the child shall be treated, that is, what is to be ordered or arranged for him or her following the adjudication. Four dispositions are most common.

1. No further action is needed and therefore the case is closed, as in instances of a single minor delinquent act or status offense when it is believed that the family is able to prevent further misconduct on the part of the child.

2. The child is found to be delinquent or guilty of a status offense and is placed on probation and permitted to remain in the community under the official supervision of the court.

3. The child is found to be neglected or abused and is allowed to remain at home under the protective supervision of a probation officer or a social agency.

4. The child, either delinquent, guilty of a status offense, neglected or abused, may be placed out of the home for protection, care, and treatment. (In these instances there is usually a transfer of official custody or guardianship.)

Placements may be in foster homes, institutions for dependent children, residential treatment institutions, or state training schools. The most careful consideration should be given to the decision to place a child out of his or her own home. Removing a child or youth from family and community is a critical act and should be ordered only if it is shown that protective supervision by a social agency or probation cannot be used successfully.

FORCES THAT PRECIPITATED CRITICISM

Procedural Deficiencies

We return now to the central question posed at the beginning of this chapter—should the juvenile court be primarily concerned with the rehabilitation and treatment of young persons coming before it, or with guarantees of constitutional due process procedures for juveniles? In this section we will review the kinds of criticism leveled at the juvenile justice system when the period of enthusiasm about the new court ended, as Lindsey (1914) had predicted it would. Then we will examine the actions of the United States Supreme Court that followed those years of heavy criticism—actions taken in an effort to correct features of juvenile procedures that were out of harmony with the existing legal system.

At the time of the founding of the juvenile court, relatively few persons questioned that the benevolent intent of the state was sufficient to protect children without extending them the full constitutional guarantees of due process of law. But just as attention came to be focused on the juvenile court's lack of success due to inadequate staff and scarcity of rehabilitative facilities in the community, so was increasing concern voiced over the court's differences from the usual adversary system of justice and the resulting variations in procedures. It became evident that procedural inadequacies had increased the vulnerability of children and the extent of the state's failure to meet its obligations to them. All through the 1950s and 1960s, finally culminating in the Kent and Gault decisions of the United States Supreme Court, heavy criticisms were directed toward the court's handling of the child at each of the four procedural steps.

In the intake phase, youth and their parents frequently had not been informed of their right to counsel. Young children had been questioned without their parents present, sometimes even before parents had been informed that their child was in difficulty with the law. Children had been fingerprinted, often unnecessarily, in an apparent effort to protect the community, but without attention to protecting children against indiscriminate use of their prints in later life.

The absence of suitable facilities had led to the use of jails for children in the intake stage of the juvenile court process. Even suitable detention facilities often had been used inappropriately when children could have remained at home pending adjudication and disposition—a practice that reflects a serious encroachment on the child's liberty and the parental right to custody.

The social investigation, designed as a basis for helping the judge make informed decisions at the dispositional hearing, often was sparse or superficial, thus negating its purpose. Or it was misused, such as when it unnecessarily invaded the privacy of the child or family, or was introduced inappropriately into the adjudication hearing.

Many of the criticisms of juvenile court procedures centered on the way the hearing was conducted. Often its dual purpose of adjudication and disposition had been lost sight of, particularly if two separate hearings were not held. By merging a consideration of whether the facts alleged in the petition were true (through information presented under the rules of evidence) with a consideration of social data relevant to disposition (which may include opinions, hearsay evidence, and evaluation of the child's potentiality for treatment), the juvenile court, it was charged, too often had assumed control over children improperly. That this might have been prompted by a desire to help children did not change the disservice done them through lack of regard for their constitutional rights.

The charge that the juvenile court had not protected the constitutional rights of the children and their families appeared especially serious in the light of additional findings (Beemsterboer, 1960; Ellrod & Melaney, 1950; Elson, 1962; Handler, 1965; Rubin, 1952). Clear proof of charges had been often lacking even though the result was undesirable "labeling" of the child, or loss of liberty through commitment to training schools. Frequently there had been no transcripts of court proceedings, or incomplete ones, which made an appeal to a higher court difficult. Too often there had been failure on the part of the state to provide true rehabilitative facilities following the removal of a child from parental custody, what Ketcham (1962) termed substitution of "governmental for parental neglect." In fact, such lacks had led some lawyers to term the juvenile court a "star chamber," the term used to describe those courts in the history of law in which proceedings were conducted in secret with no checks and balances for the judges' autonomy.

These concerns led to increasing attention to the necessary and constructive role lawyers can play in the children's courts. Lawyers had not always been interested in such cases, but in the past they had been actively discouraged from appearing in juvenile court. It was believed their presence complicated the proceedings and contributed little or nothing to the interests of justice (Lou, 1927). Increasingly, however, the child's right to counsel at all points of the court process was acknowledged. Certainly at the adjudication and disposition stages, an attorney should be available to the child and his or her parents to represent their interests.

Without a lawyer to represent the child, the judge is left to act as prosecutor, defense lawyer, and impartial arbiter, all necessary functions but difficult ones to join. In addition, lawyers can present arguments for points of view that poorly educated parents might assert, were they gifted with communication skills. A lawyer speaking up and making points clearly can help to explain to parents the aims of the court, renew respect for the law, and give support to children and parents, which helps to decrease their feelings of alienation (Paulsen, 1966).

There were other charges during the 1960s that the juvenile court had failed to protect the child in the course of the hearing. Despite promises that juvenile court records were confidential and would not be used in ways that place future social or legal obstacles before the youth, juvenile court records often had been made available almost routinely on request to a wide variety of governmental and nongovernmental agencies (Ketcham, 1962; Kahn, 1953).

Children had sometimes been unprotected in the matter of publicity in juvenile court proceedings. The right of the news media to report on court hearings grows out of the constitutional guarantee of freedom of the press and a right to a fair trial. While a free press most assuredly has the responsibility to print the news, balance is required, especially when children are involved. On the one hand, juvenile courts should not be shielded from legitimate criticism, which sometimes grows out of the presence of reporters at hearings; complete exclusion of the press leads to a loss of benefits that go with openness and public scrutiny. On the other hand, children and families had been harmed and further alienated from society where there was no protection from undesirable publicity and needless labeling arising from unrestricted publication of names, addresses, or photographs (Geis, 1958).

There were numerous complaints about the lack of regard for the child's and parent's rights during the disposition phase of the juvenile court procedures. Some grew out of the wide discretionary power given to judges and the resulting inequities in the outcomes for children. This wide latitude in dispositions is based on the court's philosophy that the judge should act in relation to the interests of the child rather than the seriousness of the act. Therefore, judges act at the disposition phase with few or no rules to guide them. Wide disparity in the treatment ordered for accused youth is not surprising, for example, one youth being put on probation for a serious offense and another committed to an institution for a minor act. Polier's study of the New York City Juvenile Court produced evidence of the way variations in the attitudes and decisions of judges affected the lives of children. The judges who sat in juvenile term at rotated intervals varied greatly in the extent to which they determined cases:

> Twelve judges rotated; each served four or five weeks. The rate of dismissal of children charged with delinquency varied from 2.2 per cent by one judge to 24.9 per cent by another judge; the average was 13.8 per cent. Where neglect was alleged, the rate of dismissal varied from 0.5 per cent to 23.1 per cent; the average was 3.3 per cent. (Polier, 1964, p. 2)

Harsh, coercive punishment applied to youthful offenders disproportionate to the seriousness of their misconduct was common. A World Health Organization study of juvenile delinquency produced this statement: ''Few fields exist in which more serious coercive measures are applied, on such flimsy objective evidence, than in that of juvenile delinquency" (Bovet, 1951, p. 79).

Paulsen (1966) cited evidence of the way the flexible powers of the juvenile courts had been misused in connection with civil rights demonstrators. Juveniles had been arrested and threatened with imprisonment if they participated further in demonstrations, placed on probation with the condition that they not associate with certain civil rights leaders, and committed to state training schools or confined in county jails for extended periods without bail or hearing.

It was also charged that the child's and family's rights were unprotected in the matter of "unofficial" or "informal" handling of cases. These terms refer to the practice of making a treatment disposition without the filing of a petition or official establishment of the right of the court to intercede. The practice protects the child from "a record" or "a label" as delinquent, and enables the court to offer a needed social service to the family. A judge's desire for approval from the community may lead him or her to favor unofficial handling because it keeps the reported delinquency rates lower. However, the practice can lead to a jeopardous confusion of judicial and administrative duties, and increases the danger of an unjustified application of the authority of the state to intervene in the parent-child relationship (Sheridan, 1966; Fradkin, 1962).

Another criticism was noted: some children, committed to a training school, had later been transferred to a penal institution. This raised questions of constitutionality "since it permits a 'delinquent' act to enlarge into a 'crime' and results in the punishment of a child for a 'crime' even though he has not been tried under the safeguards prescribed for criminal trial" (Sheridan, 1966).

In summary, criticisms of the court's procedures in relation to juvenile cases were extensive during the 1950s and 1960s. All these documented criticisms added to a growing weight of opinion that children's constitutional rights were being violated and they were receiving neither justice nor rehabilitation.

Forces for Change

Two major concerns helped to bring renewed attention to correcting the faults of the juvenile courts. One was the upsurge of interest in the legal rights of poor persons. Decisions of the United States Supreme Court in relation to the legal treatment of adults (*Gideon v. Wainright,* 1963; *Miranda v. Arizona,* 1966; *Escobedo v. Illinois,* 1964), programs such as Mobilization for Youth, and local endeavors to provide legal services for the poor, developed under the Economic Opportunity Act, all helped to focus citizen attention on the essential legal protections under the Constitution, which too frequently had been denied to poor families. It was apparent that the juvenile court had always dealt more with children of parents who were poor, with the result that poor children had always been in greater danger of court-ordered separation from their parents than had children belonging to higher socioeconomic groups. Judge Julian Mack wrote in 1910:

> Most of the children who come before the court are, naturally, the children of the poor. In many cases these parents are foreigners, frequently unable to speak English, and without an understanding of American methods and views.

Judge Mack followed this statement with a prescription for the paternalistic approach of the time, an approach embodying such qualities as "kindly assistance," "tact," "forbearance," and "sympathy" (pp. 116–117).

A disproportionate number of poor families were still coming before the juvenile court. More persons began to recognize that to avoid perpetuating a distinct class treatment of poor children, continuing attention must be given to ways to move into court practice those procedures that protect the constitutional rights of all children and their parents, and treat children equitably before the law.

Juvenile Courts are in a position to demonstrate that the most pervasive and damaging form of discrimination against youth in this country arises from their poverty. (Polier, 1989, p. 163)

A second major concern that focused attention on the functioning of the juvenile court was community awareness of the pernicious problems of certain youth and their families. It was increasingly evident from the kinds of situations being referred to the court that there were groups of youth all over the country who were seriously destructive and harmful to the lives and property of others. In addition, large numbers of socially disorganized families were identified, particularly in urban areas. Their chronic abuse or neglect of their children and their pervasive inability to sustain an adequate level of parental functioning marshaled public alarm over the likelihood of such life patterns being perpetuated in the children of these families.

Not only were existing programs of rehabilitation in short supply, but also those that were available frequently proved unsuited to and ineffective in regard to the needs and problems of these disturbed young people and malfunctioning families. Massive action using new social inventions would be necessary to treat and rehabilitate these individuals, both before and after they came to the attention of the court. It was apparent to many that, in addition to major changes in the rehabilitative programs the juvenile court could rely on, social and economic change must also attack the root causes of delinquency and family disorganization—change that would improve housing, employment opportunities, schools, and family counseling centers.

Supreme Court Decisions: New Procedural Directions

In the significant Kent case, referred to earlier in this chapter, Supreme Court Justice Abe Fortas cogently pinpointed two of the major problems before the juvenile court—the lack of constitutional guarantees as well as rehabilitative treatment resources:

There is much evidence that some juvenile courts . . . lack the personnel, facilities and techniques to perform adequately as representatives of the state in a *parens patriae* capacity, at least with respect to children charged with law violation. There is evidence, in fact, that there may be grounds for concern that the child receives the worst of both worlds: that he gets neither the protections accorded to adults nor the solicitous care and regenerative treatment postulated for children. (*Kent v. United States,* 1966)

The second major United States Supreme Court decision in relation to procedural protections for juveniles was *In re Gault* (1967), a case appealed from the Supreme Court of Arizona by the parents of a fifteen-year-old boy. The circumstances were as follows.

About ten o'clock one morning, Gerald Gault and another boy were taken into custody by a sheriff. Gerald was then still subject to a six-months' probation order that was a result of his having been in the company of another boy who had stolen a wallet from a woman's purse. On this morning Gerald was taken into custody and placed in the Children's Detention Home as a result of a verbal complaint by a neighbor, Mrs. Cook, who charged that Gerald and his friend had made an obscene telephone call to her, with lewd or indecent statements—remarks that were characterized in the United States Supreme Court opinion as "of the irritatingly offensive, adolescent, sex variety."

Gerald's father and mother were both at work at the time he was picked up. No notice that Gerald was being taken into custody was left at the home, nor were other steps taken to advise them that their son had been arrested.

When the mother arrived home after work (the father was working out of town), the older brother, who had also returned, was sent to look for Gerald at a friend's house, where he apparently learned that Gerald had been picked up by the sheriff. Gerald's mother and brother went to the detention home and talked with the deputy probation officer, who was also superintendent of the detention home, who told them "why Jerry was there" and that there would be a hearing the next afternoon.

The next day, the day of the hearing, the probation officer filed a petition. It was not served on the Gaults, and they never saw it until over two months later. The petition contained no factual basis for initiating the action, only specifying that "said minor is under the age of 18 years and in need of the protection of this Honorable Court" and that "said minor is a delinquent minor."

Gerald's mother and brother went to the court hearing. The complainant, Mrs. Cook, was not there. No one was sworn in to give testimony, and there was no transcript of recording or memorandum made of what was said at the hearing. Gerald was questioned by the judge about the alleged telephone call to Mrs. Cook. Later, when the hearing was reviewed, there were differences in what the participants remembered had been said and particularly in what Gerald had admitted to—only dialing the number and then handing the phone to his friend, making at least one lewd statement, or making all the remarks in the telephone call. In any case, at the conclusion of the hearing, the judge said he would "think about it." Gerald was taken back to the detention home.

After three or four days, Gerald was released from the detention home and allowed to return home with no explanation given as to why he had been kept there or why he was being released.

On the day of Gerald's release, Mrs. Gault received a note from the probation officer, written on plain paper, setting a time for "future hearings on Gerald's delinquency." Gerald's mother, father, and older brother went to the hearing. Again the complainant, Mrs. Cook, was not there, and when Gerald's mother asked for her to be summoned so she could identify

which boy had actually talked to her by telephone, the judge said it was not necessary. The judge had never spoken to Mrs. Cook, and the probation officer had had only one telephone conversation with her.

At the close of the second hearing, Gerald was committed as a juvenile delinquent to the state industrial school "for the period of his minority," that is, until he would be twenty-one years of age.

In the majority opinion of the United States Supreme Court, Justice Fortas stated, "Juvenile court history has again demonstrated that unbridled discretion, however benevolently motivated, is frequently a poor substitute for principle and procedure." The essential difference in the handling of Gerald's case and a criminal case was that the "safeguards available to adults were discarded in Gerald's case. The summary procedures as well as the long commitment were possible because Gerald was fifteen years of age instead of over eighteen." In other words, if Gerald had been over eighteen, he would not have been subject to juvenile court proceedings. His maximum punishment for the particular offense involved would have been a fine of $5 to $50 or imprisonment in jail for not more than two months. But instead he was committed to a state training school for a maximum of six years.

The decision noted:

It is of no constitutional consequence—and of limited practical meaning—that the institution to which he is committed is called an Industrial School. The fact of the matter is that, however euphemistic the title, a "receiving home" or an "industrial school" for juveniles is an institution of confinement in which the child is incarcerated for a greater or lesser time.

The possibility of such loss of liberty whether for children or adults, the Supreme Court said further, requires basic protections through "due process of law." While the Court made it clear that juvenile court proceedings on an adjudication of delinquency need not conform to all the requirements of a criminal trial, or even of the usual administrative hearing, such action must measure up to the essentials of due process and fair treatment guaranteed by the Fourteenth Amendment to the Constitution. Specifically (1) the child and his or her parents must be given written *notice* of a scheduled hearing sufficiently in advance to provide opportunity to prepare for the hearing, and this notice must set forth the alleged misconduct "with particularity"; (2) the child and his or her parents must be notified of the child's right to be *represented by counsel* retained by them, or if they are unable to afford this, counsel will be appointed to represent the child; (3) the constitutional *privilege against self-incrimination* (the right to remain silent instead of admitting or confessing) is applicable in the case of juveniles as well as adults; and (4) the child or young person has a *right to confront and cross-examine* witnesses who appear against him or her.

The Gault decision left certain questions unsettled. For example, the desirability of a transcript or record of facts and transactions during the hearing was acknowledged but not explicitly required. In addition, the decision on Gault dealt only with the application of due process protections during the adjudication stage of juvenile court procedures, not with the disposition stage or with the required protections during the intake, or prejudicial stage, when the child is extremely vulnerable to a misuse of authority.

Three other U.S. Supreme Court decisions are important in shaping the adjudication phase of a delinquency procedure. *In re Winship* (1970) established the principle of proof beyond a reasonable doubt as a requirement for a finding of delinquency (although not necessarily for finding a child "in need of supervision"). While *Winship* affirmed a required level of proof for minors, two other decisions, *McKeiver v. Pennsylvania* (1971) and *Schall v. Martin* (1984), were in the direction of limiting the legal rights of a minor. *McKeiver* held that the due process

clause of the Fourteenth Amendment does not require jury trials for youth charged with delinquent acts that could result in incarceration, leading to the criticism that *McKeiver* "continues the tradition of conceptual oscillation when juvenile court procedure is at issue . . ." resulting in "the extension of some rights and the denial of others" (Schultz & Cohen, 1976, p. 28). The *Schall* court decided that pretrial detention to protect an accused juvenile and society from the "serious risk" of pretrial crime is compatible with the "fundamental fairness" demanded by the Due Process Clause. The interest of the state in promoting juvenile welfare is a *parens patriae* interest, and is what "makes a juvenile proceeding fundamentally different from an adult criminal trial" (*Schall*, 1984, pp. 253, 263). Liberty can therefore be circumscribed by the power of *parens patriae*.

The doctrine of *parens patriae* found further expression in the first Supreme Court decision establishing a standard in the *dispositional* stage of juvenile proceedings. *Thompson v. Oklahoma* (1988) overturned the death penalty for a boy who was fifteen at the time he participated in the brutal murder of his former brother-in-law. The Court's majority held that to execute a person who was under sixteen at the time of committing a crime was cruel and unusual punishment and therefore unconstitutional. The court distinguished juveniles from adults in terms of a basic assumption of society about children as a class: "We assume that they do not yet act as adults do, and thus we act in their interest. . . . It would be ironic if these assumptions that we so readily make about children as a class—about their inherent difference from adults in their capacity as agents, as choosers, as shapers of their own lives—were suddenly unavailable in determining whether it is cruel and unusual to treat children the same as adults for purposes of inflicting capital punishment" (*Thompson,* 1988, p. 2693, n. 23).

The precedent-setting cases that have been discussed here affirm that in instances of alleged delinquency, juveniles are granted legal rights differentiated from those of adults, and at the same time are afforded due process protections. But the right to constitutional safeguards has not always assured their observance. Nor are constitutional safeguards, important as these are, sufficient to solve the varied and complex problems of all the very troubled children who come before the court. Many will still need to have care, daily protection, and psychotherapeutic treatment arranged. Vital though it is to develop and perfect a concept of due process suitable for juvenile proceedings, to achieve the goals of procedural reform there must also be attention to other deficiencies in the juvenile court and in the social agencies of the community. Significantly, to the extent that the U.S. Supreme Court decisions are fully implemented, a large body of minor cases are directed away from the court for handling, providing considerable challenge to traditional child welfare agencies to assume a clear and effective responsibility for status offenders and other youth at risk of involvement with the law.

ALTERNATIVES TO THE JUVENILE JUSTICE SYSTEM

The Status Offender Issue

A heated controversy among policy makers has to do with whether status offenders should be removed from the juvenile court jurisdiction and their problems dealt with by schools and social welfare agencies. Arguments cited in support of doing so usually focus on the misapplication of judicial power and the injustice that often results when the punishment is out of proportion to the offense, for example, supposedly benevolent incarceration for offenses as distinctly noncriminal as truancy or being on the streets after curfew. The proponents of policy change also cite the harm done to youths by the stigma of having participated in the judicial process. They maintain as well that the juvenile jus-

tice system clearly lacks the capability to resolve individual behavior problems typical of minors in need of supervision. On the other hand, juvenile court judges in many states strongly oppose the proposal to remove status offenders from their authority and have lobbied effectively against it.

The status offender concept can be traced back to colonial America, where the family was held strictly responsible for serving as the primary socializing agent of children. Parents were held accountable for training the child into patterns of life acceptable to the community, and children, in turn, were expected to obey their parents. These prescriptions were written into laws that became the archetypes of modern status offense laws. The homogeneous colonial culture underwent social change in the face of immigration and urbanization. Skepticism began to be expressed about the family as the traditional agency of socialization and social control. The juvenile court was only one movement by the state, although a powerful one, to assume the role of surrogate parent.

Nine decades after the forming of the juvenile court, youth policy planners are questioning whether any quasi-legal means of regulating childhood can take the place of the family as the *primary* source of nurture and support for the child. The juvenile justice system, many contend, has been vested with overwhelming and sometimes quite unrealistic expectations. Its institutional limitations must be acknowledged and efforts made to reeducate the public about the responsibilities the family and the community must accept, particularly in relation to children in need of supervision (C. P. Smith et al., 1980, p. 160).

The status offender problem is persistent despite the efforts of the National Institute of Juvenile Justice and Delinquency Prevention (NIJJDP) and the various states to improve the handling of minors in need of supervision. An assessment by NIJJDP of the current state of knowledge concerning status offenders found that they continue to be involved in a significant portion of juvenile arrests, intake and court procedures, and detention homes and other institutional placements. Wide variation in state status offense legislation exists, negating any assumption that decisions are being made on uniform principles and procedures. Dealing with non-criminal adolescent behavior is a significant issue in most states. Four major obstacles to more effective policy development and implementation were identified (C. P. Smith et al., 1980).

The first major obstacle is *lack of consensus* as to the approach to take. The juvenile justice system is given contradictory mandates—to protect the rights of the individual juvenile and to protect the community from the misconduct of youth acting out their problems. Thus the court is faced with the dichotomous roles of socializing agent and protector of child rights versus coercive control agent. This constraint is felt particularly in relation to status offenders.

A second major obstacle to progressive status offender policy is found in the *tensions between the divergent agencies that make up the juvenile justice system.* Conflict between agencies often arises when one agency pursues ends perceived as threatening to the interests of the other. An example: Attempts on a large scale in some states to remove status offenders from institutions have often been adamantly opposed by the court and other law enforcement agencies who see the move as one that will dilute their jurisdictional authority and eliminate staff positions. On the other hand, top-level personnel in child welfare and other human service agencies may approve a proposal to deinstitutionalize status offenders and see it not only as a recognition and reinforcement of their treatment philosophy, but also as a source of increased client population, budget, and staff. In the absence in most states of a well-organized and funded constituency for children's interests, one that reflects the views of families, youth, and child development experts, legislators may be prone to rely on the perceptions and preferences of segments of the juvenile justice complex, without

recognizing that they are responding to only one part of a much larger system.

Bureaucratic manipulation by juvenile justice system agencies after legislation is passed has also been identified as an obstacle to improved handling of status offenders. For example, the NIJJDP found evidence of interference with policy ranging from "situations where status offenders were being held in maximum security isolation, to instances where police were intentionally ignoring citizen complaints regarding status offense behavior problems" (C. P. Smith et al., 1980, pp. 168–169). This conduct represented an attempt to bring pressure on legislators to reinstitute police authority to arrest and hold such youths in secure detention facilities. Without adequate monitoring and enforcement procedures, innovative policy advances may never be reflected authentically in practice. "Worse yet, what often happens is that the programs are deemed failures for reasons unrelated to their conceptual or practical value."

Perhaps the most serious obstacle to better handling of the status offender is reflected in a *lack of uniform data and in overall inadequacies of the juvenile justice information systems.* Substantive information is either lacking or unreliable about the characteristics and numbers of status offenders, their differences and similarities compared with delinquent youth, and the various ways they are handled by the juvenile justice system. All these deficiencies in information lead to policy for status offenders that is made on unverified assumptions or by default (C. P. Smith et al., 1980, pp. 169–170).

A question for which there is still insufficient empirical evidence is whether status offenders in actuality are so different from delinquents as to justify separate handling and different treatment programs. Some of the proponents for removing status offenders from juvenile court jurisdiction have based their position on the claim that minors in need of supervision are indeed different and do not tend to engage in acts that are classified as delinquent. Further, they say that any later, more serious behavior is linked to the stigmatizing consequences of court processing. Some researchers have challenged these assertions.

Thomas (1976, pp. 449, 454) examined the offense history of more than 2,000 juvenile offenders over a five-year period. He found an overall low rate of recidivism—72 percent had four official contacts. He concluded that "any suggestion that formal court appearances are so stigmatizing that they encourage recidivism is difficult to substantiate." Thomas's analysis also showed substantial shifts in the classifications assigned to behavior when the youths did return to court. For example, over 59 percent of reappearing status offenders subsequently were involved with misdemeanors or felonies, leading him to reject any contention that youth initially charged as status offenders will remain status offenders in later court encounters. He concluded that "knowledge of the type of behavior which brought about an initial court appearance is an exceedingly poor predictor of whether a juvenile would reappear and, if so, the type of misconduct that would prompt the reappearance."

Fjeld and coworkers (1981) studied in detail ninety-two consecutive psychological referrals from a juvenile court and, with findings not very different from Thomas's study, concluded that status offenders and delinquents cannot be clearly distinguished, that the two groups are unpredictable in their behavior, and that they are not substantially different enough that separate handling is necessary or desirable.

Diversion

The widening disenchantment with the juvenile court has led to a search for ways to divert youth from the traditional juvenile justice system by providing much needed dispositional alternatives. The concept and practice of "diversion"—channeling referrals away from the court toward community-based, noncourt institutions—has received much attention. Diversion is not new, however. Large numbers of young

persons coming to the attention of police and other law enforcement officers have always been released informally without arrest or referral elsewhere. What is new in the idea of diversion is the thrust for "planned" diversion to enable children to remain outside the juvenile justice system; in practice, diversion goes further. Linking diversion to the development of alternative programs means that children may be directed away from the juvenile court but into other forms of coercive intervention on the part of society.

The strong interest in developing programs has produced some confusion as to the meaning of "diversion" with applications of the term to situations varying from a police warning to postadjudication probation. To clarify the term, the Office of Juvenile Justice and Delinquency Prevention established these criteria: Diversion means "a process by which youth who would otherwise be adjudicated are referred out of the juvenile justice system sometime after apprehension and prior to adjudication" (DeAngelo, 1988, p. 24).

Most often, diversion follows one of two alternatives: (1) the youth is released to the custody of her or his parents or guardian; (2) the youth agrees to participate in a program designed to help youthful offenders with their problems and keep them from becoming further involved in the system (DeAngelo, 1988, p. 21). Common referrals are to special schools, mental health centers, other social welfare programs, or law enforcement agencies that appear able to offer constructive help to the individual child or family. In some communities, special programs such as youth service bureaus have been developed to provide counseling, education, recreation, job training, and placement. Mediation programs are a recently developed alternative to traditional procedures involving status offenders. Various models of court-connected juvenile mediation have proved to be effective. Most have been developed on the assumption that dysfunctional relationships within the family are common in minor delinquency cases and that the youth's behavior is not likely to change unless family relationships are addressed and modified (D'Amico, 1986; Phear, 1985; Galaway, 1988).

Diversion is a concept that has attracted various followers as a means of giving an overburdened court the flexibility it must have to cope with its very heavy demands for service. Persons who hold little confidence in the outcomes of juvenile court intervention have tended to see diversion as something of a panacea. In contrast, Nejelski (1976) considers the practice of diversion with considerable caution, pointing out that diversion is not necessarily prevention. A preventive program would be directed to a broad range of children so that they might not at some future time come to the attention of the court at all. He sees the distinction between prevention and diversion as important because of the danger that a false sense of having engaged in the prevention of delinquency through use of a diversionary program may retard the quest for true reform. Discretionary screening of cases in the juvenile court process has always most detrimentally affected poor children and minority groups. If not properly studied, diversion may have the unfortunate result of postponing more basic reform that would make state intervention into the lives of children unnecessary.

An objective of diversion programs has been not only to keep youth from further progressing into the juvenile justice system. Another aim has been to reduce detrimental stigma that has attached to juvenile offenders. Anderson and Schoen (1985) have identified three forms of negative stigmatization to which juvenile offenders are at risk: One is *personal* stigma where labeled youth identify with the label, which then becomes a catalyst to further delinquency. Negative *social* effects appear when stereotyped youth distinguish themselves from the larger society and begin to identify with deviate subcultures associated with criminal value systems. *Organizational* processes, such as negative discretionary practices associated with serious

offenders, often reflect on status offenders as well. From a review of the literature designed to document diversion's positive and negative effects on juveniles, and particularly status offenders, Anderson and Schoen (1985, p. 20) found that "diversion's effect on stigmatization of status offenders has been researched only from an organizational perspective"—restricted to effects on the youth of the juvenile justice *system*. Yet the literature affirms that all three sources of stigma adversely affect status offenders. The outcomes of diversion on the various forms of stigma to which juvenile and status offenders are subject has not been adequately researched, leaving diversion's stigma-reduction capability inconclusive.

Reliable and valid data about alternative programs for status offenders are often unavailable because of a lack of clearly stated program goals or underlying theoretical positions, poorly articulated methods, and the absence of a systematic needs assessment of the target population. An exception is a study of first-time juvenile offenders who, in contrast to a control group, received special treatment including counseling, informal (unofficial) probation, and appropriate referrals to other community agencies. Findings showed a significant decrease in court appearances of the status offenders who received treatment, and a reduced likelihood of their return as criminal offenders (Stewart et al., 1986).

Nevertheless, results of many diversion efforts have not been encouraging. One benefit, however, is strongly suggested from limited data. Noninstitutional community-based services have shown the potential to deliver needed services at less cost than the cost of juvenile justice processing (Reamer & Shireman, 1981).

Alternatives to the Use of Secure Detention

Criteria established by the National Council on Crime and Delinquency for admission of children and youth into secure detention emphasize that detention should not be used "unless failure to do so would be likely to place the child or the community in danger" (Pappenfort & Young, 1980, p. 99). In all jurisdictions courts are faced at times with children who, after arrest or some other form of intake, cannot be returned home. In such instances secure detention is often misused. The reasons given in justification are numerous: (1) a child's psychiatric and neurological problems require attention, and no alternative to detention is available; (2) neglected and dependent children are sometimes classified as children in need of supervision and detained, pointing up in another way the common characteristics of status offenders and other children before the court; (3) some youth must be detained to prevent the chance of their committing a delinquent act or engaging in incorrigible behavior while awaiting adjudication; (4) some children go into secure detention only because there is no other place for them to stay; and (5) some children who present little or no danger to themselves or the community go into detention so that they can be readily referred into services that otherwise would not be available to them (Pappenfort & Young, 1980; Reamer & Shireman, 1981).

A national study of juvenile detention observes that "inconsistent criteria [for use of detention] can create a chaotic pattern of referral. . . . Failure of detention intake to control and rationalize those referrals is probably the most serious obstacle to providing a respectable detention service" (Pappenfort & Young, 1980, p. 8).

Many jurisdictions are attempting to avoid inappropriate use of detention by developing strict criteria for its use, by reviewing early the detention decisions by a juvenile court judge, and by developing nonresidential and residential alternatives. Home detention is one such alternative. Youths are released to their parents to await court hearings with supervision by a youth worker attached to the court's probation department. The youth worker is responsible for helping the juvenile avoid committing new offenses and making sure that he or she appears in court.

From their national assessment of alternatives to the use of secure detention, Pappenfort and Young concluded that home detention programs appear to work well for many youths who would ordinarily be detained securely. In relative terms they are inexpensive. But there is no inherent magic in a home detention program. Regardless of the prevailing judicial philosophy, in large measure success "is enhanced by consensus regarding the program's purpose among the presiding judge, the director of court services (or court probation officer), the superintendent of the severe detention center, and the director or supervisor of the alternative program. When a consensus is present a program prospers and . . . program failures remain low" (Pappenfort & Young, 1980, pp. 69–70).

Residential group homes also are used as alternatives to detention and are frequently directed toward runaway children, a type of status offender generally considered to be troublesome to deal with effectively. Some group homes have relied on the "attention home" concept, described thus:

> The term attention as distinct from detention, signifies an environment which accentuates the positive aspects of community interaction with young offenders. The homes are structured enough for necessary control of juveniles, but far less restrictive and less punishing than jail. In fact, the atmosphere is made as homelike as possible—to give youngsters exactly what the term describes—attention. (Kaersvang, 1972, p. 3)

Pappenfort and Young found it difficult to be sure what factors were responsible for the success of the attention homes studied, but suggested these reasons: "The programs are residential and so remove status offenders from tension-ridden homes. Simulated homelike environments that provide both structure and personal caring by staff may lower anxiety and its impulsive expression. The noticeably high levels of community support may give the staffs and the youths confidence that the programs can help" (1980, p. 80). The adaptability of the attention home to needs in less densely populated areas is an advantage. The concept and structure can be adapted to serve different categories of juveniles needing residential care—care and mixed usage can be a benefit to smaller jurisdictions.

Another alternative to detention is found in some jurisdictions in which foster parents are paid an annual salary to make their homes available for youths on a short-term basis. The foster parent role is to provide care and supervision as well as companionship to troubled youth awaiting court hearings.

Each of these types of alternative programs was included in Pappenfort and Young's study. They found wide differences between the programs in terms of the type of offender served and how the service was offered. They arrived at two tentative conclusions: (1) "Programs used as alternatives to secure detention can be used for many youths who would otherwise be placed in secure detention with a relatively small risk of failure." (2) "The *type* of program used does not appear as critical as *how* it is used by the jurisdiction" (1980, p. 80).

Deinstitutionalization

The decade or more of concern about due process protections for children, as well as a sobering awareness of the need to redefine and limit expectations of the juvenile justice system, has led to greater efforts to keep children in their own homes and own communities whenever possible. The new interest in "deinstitutionalization" is part of a move to diminish the range of intervention into family life. This interest is reflected not only in the juvenile justice system but throughout the child welfare system as well—in efforts to develop more effective and easily available supportive services to children in their own homes; in efforts to help abusing and neglecting parents to improve their level of child care; in child guidance centers, where out-of-home care for emotionally disturbed children is less often or more cautiously recommended;

and in foster care programs, where more attention is being paid to monitoring a child's experiences in foster care and working with the parents to help bring about a home sufficiently rehabilitated that they can resume the care of their children. Throughout the helping professions preferences are being stated for new alternatives to judicial methods of dealing with children who are in trouble with the law or with their own parents.

A first large-scale demonstration of deinstitutionalization of children and youth in a state's correctional system occurred in Massachusetts after major investigations of youth corrections by executive and legislative commissions, followed by reform legislation in 1969 (Coates et al., 1978). The intent was to implement quickly a policy of closing down the traditional training schools and to shift care and treatment of the youth of such schools to a network of community-based services—group homes, halfway houses, individually assigned advocates, the purchase of services from voluntary agencies, work programs in forestry camps, and to a limited extent the use of small security units in detention centers.

The rationale for the new policy was built around a belief, based on research evidence, that the basic ideology of the traditional training school for youth offenders was destructive and that these institutions represented a negative last resort of the courts for reinforcing adult authority, one that relied on confinement and punitive deprivation to teach obedience and conformity to adult expectations. As a result the correctional institutions served to confirm and consolidate socially destructive definitions of young people in trouble, close off opportunities to them, and make it more difficult for them to reenter community life and avoid future and more serious offenses against the law. Further, it was observed, the traditional correctional institution served to alienate youth from the larger society and produced antiauthority peer group subcultures that became self-defeating to the rehabilitation of youth.

Serious difficulties were encountered in implementing the new policy of deinstitutionalization. Any system that depends primarily on entrenched institutions has to deal with attitudes resistant to change: (1) concern on the part of institutional staff about job security; (2) interest on the part of outside professional groups who differ about the form rehabilitation programs should take; (3) inertia, ignorance, and divided opinion on the part of the public about how delinquent youth should be treated; (4) wide acceptance by many groups of the idea that law offenders must to some degree be coerced to participate in treatment programs and that some type of punitive, maximum-security facility is necessary and must be visible as a symbol to act as a deterrent; and (5) inflexibility on the part of administrators and public officials with regard to the transfer of funds from an established program to a new one.

Despite these obstacles and heated controversy, by 1973 the six training schools for committed juvenile offenders in Massachusetts were closed. Follow-up data suggest that

> as a whole, the provision of alternatives to institutionalization produced recidivism rates only slightly different than those following institutional care. However, in areas of the state in which programs had been developed which emphasized the retention and strengthening of youths' positive ties to persons and institutions in the community, indications were that greater success was achieved. (Reamer & Shireman, 1981, p. 33)

Alternatives are not necessarily community-based simply because they are located outside of an institution. They may be "merely islands within a community." In contrast, Reamer and Shireman (1981, pp. 28–29) define a community-based program as "of the community as well as in it," a program that "attempts to increase and enhance the quality of contact youths have with families, schools, peers, recreational and cultural programs and the world of work."

A considerable decrease in the number of juveniles held in public correctional training schools occurred in the years 1965 to 1978, a decrease that was significant considering that those same years saw a growth in the total juvenile population and very high increases in numbers of youths arrested (Reamer & Shireman, 1981). Despite the success of alternatives to secure detention, a decade later an increased reliance on incarceration of youths was reported. Of all juveniles in public facilities in 1987, 80 percent were held in secure or locked settings (Allen-Hagen, 1988, p. 4). The greater likelihood of incarceration for juveniles has other ramifications. Risk of confinement in locked settings may be increased by the fact that a majority of juveniles prosecuted as delinquents are not represented by legal counsel (Feld, 1987, p. 531). Public sentiment has been to "get tough" with juvenile delinquents rather than preserve their legal counsel. Yet the public fear of juvenile offenses is incongruent with actual trends. Serious juvenile offenders comprise only 4 percent of all delinquents. The number of juveniles held for serious, violent offenses has dropped 11 percent since 1983 (Allen-Hagen, 1988, p. 1).

SOCIAL WORK ROLES AND THE JUVENILE COURT

Increasingly, social workers in child welfare settings are expected to refine their competence with respect to the legal framework of children's affairs. To be effective a social worker must possess an ability to think logically, recognize legal evidence as distinct from social evidence, demonstrate a working knowledge of relevant statutes and court decisions that shape public policy in the children's realm, and help clients who are called to testify in court (Brieland & Lemmon, 1985). More often than formerly, social workers are required to gather and organize evidence and present direct testimony as a proponent of the client's best interests.

Social workers who are well-trained and experienced and who possess an expertise in child and family problem-solving can be qualified as neutral expert witnesses to assist the judge or jury. "Clinical social workers, particularly those with experience working with child welfare agencies, are generally more expert than psychologists and psychiatrists on the conditions in the home and environment that contribute to family stresses and to family strengths. Social workers are generally more able to marshall community resources that may help the family with its problems" (Duquette, 1983, p. 494). Situations in which social workers have qualified as experts include child custody in neglect and abuse cases; child custody in divorce; termination of parental rights; juvenile delinquency; and, most recently, assessment of a defendant's mental state and competency to stand trial (Gothard, 1989, pp. 66–67).

In child welfare settings, judicial processes and social work processes often appear entangled, yet they are distinct. The confusion is partly historical. Mothers' pensions, a reform of the early twentieth century (see Chapter 6) was in many states given to the juvenile court to administer, even though it clearly was a service program that required social work skills. Legislators wanted their new social program to avoid the stigma of public relief, so they were inclined to give its administration to the juvenile court, still a new and popular institution. Compounding this mixture of administrative and judicial functions was the tendency for many juvenile courts, because of a lack of foster care services, to develop their own foster care programs as part of their probation service, or rely on a set pattern of committing children to favored institutions. Thus there came to be an administrative dominance over the children's court, a system supposed to be judicial in nature.

Judges and social workers both have contributed to this confusion. Social workers inclined to think they knew best about children's needs often tried to influence judges in their adjudicative decisions. Judges who thought that

When the juvenile court and Child Welfare agency assume control and responsibility concerning a child, the result is both an erosion of parental responsibilities and a fragmentation of control and responsibility concerning the child. (Hardin, 1985, p. 232)

they knew best often dictated treatment plans for children without regard for the social worker investigations and knowledge of appropriate dispositional alternatives. A commonly overlooked factor that contributed to the eventual reassessment of juvenile court functions was the growth of social work as a profession. As social workers began developing their own principles and strategies, distinctions between legal activities and social work activities become more apparent.

Conflict between the child welfare system and the juvenile justice system was invited by the basic differences in the kinds of information that each system accepts as valid and acts upon. The courts in their judicial function are charged to determine the facts that can be proved with certainty, and then to apply the appropriate legal rules to these facts. Rules of legal evidence were shaped with the jury in mind and the need to assist it by separating out confusing or conflicting information and focusing only on that which has high probative value.

Social workers in their administrative functions are required to marshal not only legal evidence, but social evidence as well that will influence the treatment plan. Social workers may have to rely on an accumulation of evidence, some of which has slight probative value. Some situations of children and families do not yield clear legal evidence, and yet they must be served by a social agency. Because the questions at issue in such cases are often not simple, social workers, in attempting to apply the least intrusive intervention, may rely on a variety of information, some of which is hearsay evidence or other information acquired informally. In such cases they look for repeated patterns of parent and child behavior and environmental influences. The fact that the treatment plan may not rest on a basis of clear proof of its appropriateness means that social workers are charged especially to give very careful scrutiny and evaluation to the reliability of any item of social evidence that is used in a way that affects the rights of children and families and their ability to direct their own lives.

The professions of law and social work have collaborated in the development of a position statement that lays out the respective roles of social workers and lawyers (Brieland & Lemmon, 1985, pp. 163–165). Courses in social work and law are being reintroduced into the curriculum of professional social work education. Family and child welfare agencies are finding it necessary to include consulting attorneys on their staffs and to provide in-service training programs to enable social workers to improve their relationships with the juvenile court.

When social workers understand the nature of evidence, and the court process, and become skillful in finding and organizing facts, and integrate this knowledge and skill into their social work values and approaches to helping, they vastly increase the probability that their efforts will be effective in securing justice for the child.

TRENDS AND ISSUES

Due Process versus Rehabilitation

Should the juvenile court reflect a model of justice based mainly on protection and rehabilitation of persons coming before it, or one based on constitutional guarantees of due process and a strict reliance on legal evidence? Most of today's controversy about the combination of legal and social functions in the juvenile court is contained in that question, cited at the beginning of this chapter.

Today's controversy actually began in the first decade after the new court was founded in 1899. Very early critics, including some disillusioned reformers, alleged that the juvenile court was not living up to their expectations. The criticism was slow to build, but by the late 1950s it was producing a stream of articles, other literature, and press commentary (Pettibone et al., 1981, pp. 12–13). Significant attempts to establish national standards and heightened dissatisfaction with the juvenile court among various sectors of society have brought the controversy to a point where it has been said that "the very existence of a separate juvenile justice system is seriously being debated today" (Horowitz & Davidson, 1984, p. 468).

Nevertheless, a continuing separate existence for the juvenile court has been affirmed by recent Supreme Court cases. Its pronouncements imply that no choice need be made between due process procedures and rehabilitation for juveniles. Adult legal protections for youth are largely defined for the *adjudicatory* phase only. The dispositional hearing allows for a thorough "review of the child's social history and for his individualized treatment" (*In re Winship,* 1970, at 366). Further, the Court has said, the flexibility and informality of the juvenile court make it uniquely suitable for young persons (*Schall,* 1984, at 2630). By not imposing all formalities of the criminal adjudication of adults upon the juvenile court (jury trial, bail), the Supreme Court in effect has validated the need for a juvenile court.. In the most recent cases before the Supreme Court involving minors, protection of youth is a recurring theme under the doctrine of *parens patriae.*

A consideration of this controversy and the Court's position makes it evident that constructive attempts are essential on the part of the legal and child welfare systems to find ways to better serve the needs and rights of children who are brought before the juvenile court.

Status Offenders—Whose Responsibility?

One of the most debated issues before the public is whether the juvenile court should strip away its rehabilitative and treatment dimension with respect to status offenders and turn responsibility for these youth over to noncoercive community-based services. Concern is expressed that the traditional responsibility of the family for control of children's misbehavior is being seriously weakened by a too ready transfer of responsibility to bureaucratic discretion. Within an increasingly adversarial context, it is said, the juvenile justice system is being forced to deal with delinquents and status offenders alike.

The issue of jurisdiction over status offenders is complicated by research findings on the question of whether status offenders are more similar than different from delinquent youth. So far the weight of evidence strongly suggests that youth tend to be concurrently involved in both delinquent and status offense behavior. Such findings imply that it is not possible at this time to differentiate involvement in status offenses from involvement in delinquency, at least in less serious delinquency. "There seem to be two major categories of illegal involvement . . . one is petty illegal behavior, which includes status offenses and less serious delinquency, and the other is serious delinquency." In other words, "one can infer that there are not behaviorally distinct groups of status offenders and of delinquents, [and that] . . . the most significant difference in *behavior* is between youngsters who engage in status offenses and less serious delinquency and those who engage in serious delinquency" (Weis et al., 1980, p. 99).

Such findings suggest that the juvenile justice system should treat the two categories of petty and serious offenders differentially. Some recommend that jurisdiction over status offenders should be restricted, or perhaps abandoned, and so should it be over less serious delinquents. Appropriate dispositional decisions by the court and treatment alternatives in the community for status offenders and for less seriously delinquent youth may well be the same (Weis et al., 1980).

Serious Offenders and Drug Use

A major departure from the view that the juvenile justice system's purpose is to protect and re-

habilitate juvenile offenders is reflected in changing policy recommendations with respect to serious juvenile crime (Heck et al., 1985).

Recent studies have shown that "frequent use and abuse of drugs is more common among youths who engage in chronic delinquent behavior than among other adolescents. Data collected in 1980 in . . . a self-report study of a national probability sample of adolescents showed that nearly 50 percent of serious juvenile offenders (who admitted having committed three or more index offenses in the past year) were also multiple, illicit drug users. Eighty-two percent of these chronic serious offenders reported use, beyond experimentation, of at least one illicit drug" (Hawkins et al., 1988, pp. 258–259).

While it appears that some degree of delinquency and occasional use of alcohol and marijuana are relatively widespread among American adolescents, "the factors that lead to these behaviors are likely to be quite different from factors that lead to serious and persistent delinquency or to frequent use of illicit drugs." The majority of the juveniles who enter the juvenile justice system are not serious, habitual offenders. But the relatively small group of drug-using chronic offenders "is responsible for a disproportionate number of violent crimes and property crimes and for large social and economic costs to society" (Hawkins et al., 1988, p. 259).

To many persons concerned about the juvenile justice system, these conditions illustrate an inherent contradiction in the responsibility of the juvenile court—to protect and rehabilitate the youth who come to the attention of the court versus the obligation of the court to preserve the social order. Given these divergent interests, the National Council of Juvenile and Family Court Judges endorsed a number of recommendations relating to the problem of serious juvenile crime, the first of which was this: "*Serious Juvenile Offenders Should Be Held Accountable by the Courts.* The primary focus of the juvenile court for the disposition of serious, chronic or violent juvenile offenders should be accountability. Dispositions of such offenders should be proportionate to the injury done and the culpability of the juvenile and to the prior record of adjudication, if any." The Council added that "the principal purpose of the juvenile justice court system is to protect the public," and qualified this position only by the statement, "Although rehabilitation is a primary goal of the court, it is not the sole objective and not always appropriate" (Heck et al., 1985, p. 29).

On the national scene as well as in many states, a battle cry was raised against "violent juveniles." The achievements of the late 1960s and early 1970s in securing more humane treatment of incarcerated youth were undermined by the new focus on drug users and runaways, and the decreased Federal funding for community services. Hostility toward violent youths was reflected in indifference to what happened to them once "put away." (Polier, 1989, p. 41)

In recognition of the sometimes inappropriate efforts of the juvenile court to rehabilitate the juvenile offender, the Council further recommended that "*Offenders Unamenable to Juvenile Treatment Should be Transferred.*" In other words, "if a juvenile commits a crime which is, for one reason or another, beyond the limits of juvenile court, that juvenile should be waived to criminal court" (Heck et al., 1985, p. 31).

The Council recommended as well that "*Substance Abuse Programs Should be Provided for Juveniles* and . . . made part of the dispositional plan for those offenders whose criminal conduct is determined to be related to substance abuse." A difficulty in developing such programs was cited as the limited data available in the juvenile justice system on this type of juvenile who is drug/alcohol involved (Heck et al., 1985, p. 34).

Hawkins and coworkers (1988, pp. 269–270) have identified a variety of risk factors for delinquency and drug abuse that have relevancy for prevention programs. They cite the ethical problem in labeling and treating individuals as predelinquents or future drug users and suggest

an alternative strategy. "Rather than targeting individuals . . . prevention programs can target neighborhoods, schools, or communities where risk factors for delinquent behavior and drug abuse are prevalent."

Community Readiness to Support Alternative Programs

Community-based alternatives to judicial handling of youthful offenders are dependent on the willingness of community residents to support them. The term "community-based" implies an intention to enable troubled youth to retain their ties to persons in the community, to move about and communicate freely within the community, and to experience some degree of acceptance from others in the community. Yet community residents often object to plans for alternative programs. Such proposals, especially for residential programs, often bring prompt and vigorous opposition on the assumption that the kind of youth served would be a danger to the surrounding neighborhood. Somewhat paradoxically, professional interests and federal guidelines that favor community-based alternatives came at a time when many citizens were expressing intense fear about delinquency and crime, and state legislatures were enacting more restrictive laws affecting the handling of law offenders generally.

Reamer and Shireman have concluded that

proponents of alternative programs cannot afford to regard these two sentiments as independent phenomena that require separate responses. The fear of crime and delinquency itself represents one of the most serious threats to the future of alternative programs. . . . Legislators and administrators cannot afford to ignore the concern of citizens that public safety should be guaranteed first and foremost. The tension between the shift toward diversion and deinstitutionalization and community tolerance is a precarious one that demands thoughtful attention. (1981, pp. 38–39)

There is a delicate balance between the protection of legitimate community concerns (state interest) and the freedom of young persons from coercive intervention (individual liberty). Thus policy makers are presented with a renewed responsibility to address an enduring issue (Flicker, 1977, p. 109).

FOR STUDY AND DISCUSSION

1. Explain and evaluate the aims and guiding philosophy of the early founders of the juvenile court.
2. Give arguments to support either the traditional rehabilitative model of the juvenile court, or a model based on constitutional guarantees of due process and legal justice.
3. Obtain a copy of the juvenile court act in your state or some other. Evaluate it in these terms:
   a. What is the expressed intent of the act? How well does this intent reflect a modern juvenile court philosophy?
   b. Compare its definitions of classes of children who come under the jurisdiction discussed in this chapter.
   c. What indications are there in the statute that the child's constitutional rights shall be respected?
   d. How adequate are the act's provisions in regard to personnel and services of the court?
4. What are some of the principal sociolegal differences between children and youth who are (a) dependent, (b) neglected, (c) abused, (d) delinquent, (e) guilty of a status offense, or (f) whose custody is at stake because of divorce? What are some of their similar characteristics?
5. What is the difference in jurisdiction between a juvenile and a family court, and what are some of the likely benefits of a well-staffed family court?
6. What were the principal findings of the six U.S. Supreme Court decisions discussed in this chapter? What have been the major implications of these decisions for the court and for the community?
7. What are the possible role conflicts of social workers serving as probation officer, juvenile police officer, corrections worker, or other juvenile institution employee?
8. Should youthful offenders have the adult criminal protections of determinate (time-limited) sentences, jury trials, and bail? Make the case pro and con. Justify your conclusions.
9. How would you design an "ideal" diversion program? What would be its features? Why? How could stigma be averted?

FOR ADDITIONAL STUDY

Breckinridge, S., & Abbott, E. (1912). *The delinquent child and the home.* New York: Russell Sage Foundation.

Croxton, T. A., Churchill, S. R., & Fellin, P. (1988). Counseling minors without parental consent. *Child Welfare, 67*(1), 3–14.

Curtis, P. A., & Lutkus, A. M. (1985). Client confidentiality in policy social work settings. *Social Work, 30*(4), 355–360.

Dranoff, S. F., & Cohen, M. Y. (1987). Psychiatrists, psychologists, and social workers: Getting the most out of experts. *Family Advocate, 10*(1), 20–23.

Gibelman, M., & Demone, H. W., Jr. (1989). The social worker as mediator in the legal system. *Social Casework, 70*(1), 28–36.

Moss, D. C. (1987, June 1). *In re Gault* now 20, but . . . juveniles still underrepresented by lawyers in proceedings. *ABA Journal, 73,* 29.

Polier, J. W. (1989). *Juvenile justice in double jeopardy. The distanced community and vengeful retribution.* Hillsdale, NJ: Lawrence Erlbaum Associates. New York: National Council on Crime and Delinquency.

Soler, M. (1988, Dec. 1). An introduction to children's rights. *ABA Journal, 74,* 52–56.

Stein, T. J. (1991). *Child welfare and the law.* New York: Longman.

CHAPTER 4

The Regulation of Children's Out-of-Home Care

No agency can do its duty by the children for whom it is responsible without adequate inspection and study. . . . No state can do its duty by the people of the commonwealth that fails adequately to supervise the organizations and institutions . . . which . . . are caring for . . . its children.

W. H. Slingerland

Chapter Outline

REGULATION IN CHILD WELFARE PRACTICE

Public concern about the places and conditions of children's out-of-own-home care has been present since this country's early beginnings. Although varying in form, today all of the states have statutory provisions for the regulation of out-of-home care of children. The intent of governmental regulation is to safeguard children from harm and prevent ills that might befall them from poor care and supervision. Regulation is an action of government to bring an activity in the private sector (in this case the places where and the means by which children are cared for outside their own homes) under the control of constituted authority and to require compliance with agreed-upon expectations.

The regulatory function, with its preventive, community-oriented function, is differentiated from protective services, which come into play after a report of neglect or abuse is received by a designated child protection agency (see Chapter 9). The two functions intersect only when neglect or abuse is reported to be occurring in a regulated facility.

THE NATURE AND PURPOSE OF LICENSING

Licensing as a child welfare responsibility rests on state statutory provisions. This use of regulatory authority by the state to safeguard children is an attempt to ensure that children receive acceptable care with the basic essentials for healthy growth and development. The principal means employed in regulation include (1) an identification of substandard situations in the care of children, (2) the use of positive and negative sanctions to assure effective implementation of the licensing statute, and (3) the provision of assistance to the caretakers by means of consultation and other educational measures aimed toward remedying unacceptable conditions of care or enabling caretakers to exceed the prescribed conditions.

The intent is not to *prohibit* parents from arranging care for their children elsewhere, or to prohibit well-meaning individuals from giving or sponsoring care to unrelated children. The intent is to *regulate* the conditions under which such children are cared for and to establish a standard—a floor of protection—for care outside their own homes. This emphasis on regulation is recognized in Ernst Freund's statement:

> The primary legislative thought in licensing is not prohibition but regulation, to be made effective by the formal general denial of a right which is then made individually available by an administrative act of approval, certification, consent or permit. (1935, p. 447).

The legislature applies this regulatory authority to the field of child welfare by identifying a form of care of children which, if unregulated, appears to be contrary to the public interest, for example, day care of children outside their own homes. This form of child care is then prohibited generally; on individual application and approval of that application, it may be permitted specifically and a license issued to sanction the operation of a particular child care facility. The issuance of a license is certification that a person, an agency, or an institution meets certain specified standards.

Licensing is one of the activities affecting the standard of care that children receive. . . . Its mission is to require services in which the safety and well-being of children are givens. (Terpstra, 1989, p. 442)

The legal mandatory standards for issuance of a license are a baseline for an agency's care of children. These standards reflect what the public recognizes, requires, and supports as overall safeguards necessary for children. Licensing also can serve to set in motion a process to raise those standards through education, consultation, and community planning. The long-term success of a licensing program depends in large measure on the extent to which persons giving care to children or planning community child care services can be helped to "internalize" the standards and to identify with the philosophy and goals of progressive child welfare practice. When this occurs, the groundwork has been laid for an upward revision of official, publicly endorsed licensing standards. But even in those cases in which persons who care for children are incapable of achieving any real identification with child welfare goals, a holding to agreed-upon requirements for licensing guarantees that safeguards are placed around children through the caretaker's overall reasonable compliance with standards.

Why Licensing Is Necessary

Licensing of certain services is common to many occupations and activities today. For the most part it is taken for granted. We expect doctors, nurses, lawyers, and teachers to be licensed or certified. We expect, too, that the places or facilities in which persons give services to the public will be regulated and inspected for conformity to certain standards. These facilities may be hospitals, schools, restaurants, or barber and beauty shops. Communities are expected to provide safe water supplies and neighborhoods free of fire and health risks. One of the means used to insure such protection to the public is authorized study and inspection.

Whether we are considering the licensing of a physician to give medical services, or a restaurant owner to prepare and serve food to the public, or a child care operator or social agency to give care to unrelated children outside their own homes, the regulation of such facilities is expected because there are risks involved in the use of services or goods. The private citizen, though possibly competent to, lacks the means to evaluate those services and to enforce adequate standards of operation. The increasing incidence of

children's care away from their own parents as a result of the realities of present-day living patterns further justifies the state's responsibility in such matters.

Source of Legal Authority

Government's responsibility to protect the rights and welfare of citizens rests on a benevolent exercise of the police powers of the state. When the facility or service to be regulated is a child-caring one, regulation is sometimes also termed an exercise of the doctrine of *parens patriae*. To cite *parens patriae* as theoretical justification for licensing is probably to apply an appealing legal rationale after the fact, just as seems to have been done in naming *parens patriae* as a direct forebear of the juvenile court. Social workers are accustomed to responding positively to the familiar explanation of *parens patriae* when the state acts as protector or ultimate guardian in matters affecting the welfare of children. In contrast, acknowledging a relationship between their social work activities and an exercise of a state's police power, however benevolent, often strikes them as dissonant to their methods. The distinction between *parens patriae* and police power is confounded further by the fact that state statutes and judicial decisions cite the *parens patriae* doctrine in relation to safeguards and protections for dependent and neglected children.

What can be said with some certainty is that licensing is utilized to achieve the *purposes* of *parens patriae,* and in that sense licensing is a manifestation of that doctrine. The state is empowered to use licensing, however, through an application of police power.

The Status of the Applicant for Licensing

Services subject to licensing are recognized by most citizens as having value to them, and the persons who are permitted to supply these services acquire a particular status; that is, they are designated as having permission to give a recognized service to the community. This kind of status also devolves upon licensees who are certified to give child care services. Such persons, then, are not clients, as social workers use that term; they have not come to the licensing agency to seek help with personal problems, and whatever may be their particular set of personal needs, it is inappropriate to view the application for license as a basis for the provision of casework services. Instead, the application signifies their desire to give a public service and a readiness to be evaluated.

The supervision that is given following issuance of a license, for example, supervision of a licensed foster mother, is different from that supplied by a social worker who carries direct responsibility for a particular child in a foster home. If the licensee is a voluntary agency or institution, the supervision supplied as a part of licensing is not administrative supervision such as is found in the relationship of a state agency to a related local agency. (The various parts of the licensing process will be discussed at a later point in this chapter.)

Where Children Are Cared For

When children are cared for in places other than their own homes and by persons unrelated to them, this care is recognized as a private act that has a public purpose. The forms of care for children away from their parents can be viewed in Table 4.1.

All four forms of care may be under public or private auspices. (Private agencies may be either voluntary or proprietary.) Larger numbers of children are cared for under proprietary (or commercial) auspices than in agency facilities, both public and voluntary. Examples are child care centers and nursery schools operating as a business venture, or family day care homes advertised in a newspaper, or foster mothers who find children to care for by some other informal means.

There has been a shift in the kinds of applications licensing agencies are receiving. In contrast to a time when most applicants were representatives of religious, philanthropic, nonprofit groups, the majority of applicants now are entrepreneurs offering child care as a business service for profit in response to the rise in numbers of working mothers. This shift has meant that licensing workers must give attention to different purposes and orientations of applicants and acquire a wider knowledge in relation to administration, the structure of the community, and public relations.

Because licensing in all its various forms deals with the regulation of private enterprise that serves a public purpose, child care licensing is directly applicable to the private forms of care, that is, voluntary agencies and proprietary facilities, and not to public agencies. Without question, the care given to children in public facilities should also be subject to scrutiny and should be of at least equal quality to that provided under private auspices. However, the method of administrative supervision is generally regarded as a more appropriate and flexible means of public control than would be the licensing of an agency that had been created by

TABLE 4.1. Forms of Care for Children

	Small Group	Large Group
Part of day (supplemental to parental care)	Family day care	Group day care (centers, nursery schools, day camps)
All day (substitute for parental care)	Foster family home (24-hour) Group home (24-hour)	Group institutional care (residential centers, camp, and large-group children's institutions)

legislative action. Administrative self-monitoring by public institutions and agencies has not always been effective, however, leading to proposals for administratively separate monitoring offices charged with evaluating public child care programs, providing consultation aimed at improved methods of care, and reporting to department heads and to the public.

Whom Does Licensing Serve?

The regulation of the places and means used to care for children away from home is especially important since children separated from their families constitute a vulnerable group. The protection that licensing of child care facilities offers is extended to both children and their parents. The child cannot control the circumstances that bring about his or her placement nor the conditions under which care is offered. If the care given is neglectful or unsuitable, a child can be seriously harmed. For many children the only external protection against gross physical abuse or severe emotional neglect is a requirement that agencies or individuals must be licensed to give care to them outside their own homes, and to be licensed, certain standards of care must be met. Furthermore, in the normal, everyday life of increasing numbers of children, some care away from their parents is needed. The requirement of licensing is a protection that supports and enhances the possibility that this care will provide a happy, successful experience for them.

Parents, as well, are vulnerable when they need to arrange care away from themselves for their children. It takes time and knowledge to make sound evaluations about the adequacy of a facility or its program, or the competence and reliability of its personnel. Parents may lack the information or experience to enable them to make a sound judgment about where and how their child will be cared for. They may be under emotional or environmental stresses that complicate their ability to make safe decisions when outside care must be arranged. A well-administered licensing program assures parents and concerned citizens that children are being offered care in facilities meeting specified basic standards of care—standards that the general public endorses and requires, through statutes or formal regulations, as at least minimal protections to children.

Licensing also provides safeguards and service to the individuals or agencies providing care. Foster parents, child care center operators, or institution boards and staff who have met requirements for a license are protected by the assurance that they are not unintentionally creating specified hazards for children or for themselves. In addition, the fact of having met requirements for issuance of a license is public recognition that they are operating within the law and providing an acceptable standard of care. Perhaps the most telling benefit to providers is that the requirements of licensing serve as a deterrent to ruthless competition from programs that are poorly conceived and poorly carried out.

The Administrative Setting for Child Care Licensing

Licensing responsibility is an appropriate administrative function belonging to the executive branch of government. The department of public welfare (or its equivalent) is the most common state agency to be made responsible for administering the child care licensing program although in seven states, departments of public health have the legal regulatory responsibility for day care centers. Some city health departments are responsible for formulating, implementing, and enforcing day care center standards within their municipal boundaries (Class & Norris, 1981).

Assigning child care licensing to the public welfare department is related to its broad base of child welfare activity, including direct services and community planning in behalf of children. But other departments of state government are drawn in as cooperating departments because of their specialized knowledge, which can be utilized to help protect children—health, sanitation, nutrition, education, and safety (fire zoning and building codes).

Certain problems are common among the states' administrative departments. Chief among these problems is some continuing confusion about the nature and purpose of licensing in relation to children's out-of-home care, regardless of whether that care takes place in foster homes, group homes, institutions, or other child care facilities. Class has presented the thesis that social workers have failed to see child care licensing as a preventive program, although it is basically one of the few truly preventive programs in the American welfare system. He has cited several factors that have confused the perception of licensing as preventive (Class, 1968):

1. Historically, licensing was wrongly used as a "false front" to deal with serious protective care situations; it still is seen by many as a protective service in behalf of individual children rather than as a community service to maintain and enhance an adequate norm or standard of care for all the community's children outside their own homes.

2. The administrative location of child care licensing, and the concomitant stereotypes about public welfare clients and services, have colored the public's image of the licensing function so that it does not have the prestige and operational effectiveness necessary for the sound development of a preventive program.

3. The licensing function has been combined or confused administratively with agency home-finding and child placement operations. In such instances licensing staff workers often have had no knowledge or appreciation of the potentiality in child care licensing; lacking an orientation to regulatory programs, they have relied on their social work skills in child placement supervision.

To move toward a recognition of child care licensing for what it is—a preventive welfare service—Class has proposed four imperative actions: (1) Mandatory licensing standards must be scientifically validated; that is, the licensing authority must be able to establish by research or technical findings the needs for each requirement and its relationship to specific preventive goals. (2) Licensing standards must become widely known and accepted as patterns of expected behavior through broad community education programs. (3) The overt use of authority inherent in the licensing program must be accepted administratively, and serious consideration given to necessary enforcement operations. (4) New attention must be given to understanding and effectively implementing the tasks in supervision of and consultation with the licensee (Class, 1968).

HISTORICAL BACKGROUND

Public concern about children's out-of-home care can be traced back to colonial America. Although not regulatory in nature, colonial poor laws vested overseers of the poor with responsibilities in relation to the indenture of dependent, delinquent, and neglected children, a form of out-of-home care for children. The appearance in the latter half of the nineteenth century of free foster homes, "boarding" homes, and voluntary institutions for children (termed "orphanages") was followed by concern about distressing conditions of care in many of these child care arrangements. As early as 1863 Massachusetts gave responsibility to its State Board of Charities for inspection and reporting (although not licensing) of certain types of child care facilities. Other state boards of charities also became interested in the safeguards needed when children were placed in foster homes or institutions. Pressure mounted for a state-supervised system of foster care, and various states that had experienced difficulties in relation to children placed in foster homes or institutions within their jurisdiction began to press for some form of control of interstate placements.

In 1885 Pennsylvania passed a foster care licensing law, making it a misdemeanor for any person to engage in the business of offering care to more than two children under the age of three without a license from the mayor of the town, the justice of the peace, or the magistrate of the locality. Massachusetts passed a similar law in 1892. In 1887 the New York Board of Charities authorized town overseers of the poor to remove children from institutions receiving public subsidies if the care given was unsatisfactory (Class, 1968).

The continuing demand for state inspection and control was expressed by both local and state groups and by members of the National Conference of Charities and Correction. It was apparent that there was need not only for state inspection and supervision, but also for provision to prevent the establishment of inferior facilities or to bring about the discontinuance of organizations falling below standard (Fraser, 1937).

The recommendations of three national child welfare conferences are noteworthy as an indication of a growing recognition of the need for state control of the places and means used to care for children. The first, the White House Conference of 1909, concluded that it was

> sound public policy that the State, through its duly authorized representative, should inspect the work of all agencies which care for dependent children, whether by institutional or by home finding methods, and whether supported by public or private funds. Such inspection should be made by trained agents, should be thorough, and the results thereof should be reported to the responsible authorities of the institution or agency concerned. (Children's Bureau, 1926, p. 62)

This resolution stopped short of recommending a program of licensing by the state, and considered a report, following an inspection, to the institution concerned to be sufficient.

The second national conference that made significant recommendations for a state authority in child care was the Washington and Regional Conference on Child Welfare, which, in 1919, resolved that the

> state board of charities or a similar supervisory body should be responsible for the regular inspection and licensing of every institution, agency, or association, incorporated or otherwise, which receives or cares for mothers with children or children . . . and should have authority to revoke such license for cause and to prescribe forms of registration and report. (Children's Bureau, 1919, p. 10)

The White House Conference of 1930 again recommended that the

> state, through a welfare or other appropriate department, should maintain effective supervision over all institutions and agencies having the care of variously handicapped children; and should set up and enforce, through licensing or other forms of direction or control, at least minimum standards of work so as to insure to children under institutional care or in foster homes—either free or at board—proper care, education and protection. (*White House Conference 1930,* 1931, p. 280)

Interest in licensing developed further, as shown by the reports of the children's code commissions appointed in many states to study and recommend laws to bring about better care of children. Additional states began to enact licensing legislation until, by 1937, licensing laws providing for state supervision and control had been passed by the legislatures of thirty-seven states (Fraser, 1937, p. 5). Much of the early support for licensing laws came from voluntary agencies that were giving a relatively high level of care to children and therefore sought protection from the threatening growth of poorer agencies and institutions.

> Early licensing programs were weak, characterized by administrative unreality. Licensing agencies were not clear as to their responsibilities and did not seem to know how to use legal counsel or the courts to clarify and define their powers.

Personnel were insufficient or lacking altogether, and there was little recognition of the need for particularization of skills. Even so, many abuses, including the notorious "baby farms," were corrected. (Hughes et al., 1962, p. 10)

Today all the states have some kind of statutory provision for licensing in the field of child care. The laws differ from state to state, reflecting local conditions and the kind of public opinion prevailing at the time of enactment. From her national study of the state of child care regulation, Morgan observes that "the most striking characteristic of child care regulation in the United States is its diversity" (1987, p. 1).

THE ELEMENTS OF A SOUND LICENSING LAW

A welfare licensing statute, to be effective, must be carefully written; it provides the basic framework for the administrative department. Therefore, the effectiveness of the intended protection for children is dependent in large measure on the strengths of the licensing act passed by the state legislature.

Since the statute has been passed by the elected representatives of the people of the state, it is taken to express the concern of the general public about children in certain circumstances, and the public's desire that protection be given to children who are dependent on the care of others.

> Like other forms of social legislation, a welfare licensing law generally comes into being at the point where a social problem has assumed proportions too large to be controlled by informal, voluntary methods. Since its basic feature is a prohibition, it must have public approval and support in order to be enforceable, and there must be a sufficient number of persons willing to meet requirements to make possible the closing of substandard facilities. (Binder & Class, 1958, p. 267)

The strength of a licensing law can be evaluated by the following six criteria.

Statement of Purpose

The purpose of the act should be stated clearly and should include some indication of the interests served by the law. If the statement of the law's purpose reflects the general philosophy behind the act, conveyed in simple and nontechnical language, it serves as an aid in interpreting the law's intent.

> Regardless of the quality of administration the agency is prepared to give, a statute should make clear the legislative intent. If it does not, it will deflect political and social pressures that should properly be dealt with by the law-making body, turning them into licensing instrumentality. When successfully administered, welfare licensing represents a continuous balancing of the individual rights of persons who wish to engage in a particular activity against the welfare of the group to be protected. The law should, therefore, give some indication of the point at which individual rights must yield before the general welfare. (Binder & Class, 1958, p. 267)

What Activity Is Prohibited

A second criterion used to evaluate the soundness of a licensing law is the extent to which it makes clear the activities that are prohibited so that interested citizens can ascertain whether they are affected and subject to license. Such a determination will depend on the *definitions* contained in the act. For example, terms such as "child" or "related," while generally understood, need to be specifically defined for the purposes of the act. Even more, there is a need for definitions of terms when a general public understanding may not be present as in terms such as "facility for child care."

Usually the legislature provides for some exceptions to the prohibitions. For example, some states permit foster mothers to care for only one unrelated child, or for several children from one family, without being required to qualify for a license. From his long experience with regulatory administration, Norris Class has taken the position that if exemptions are made, licensing should in any case be required in all instances where the caretaker accepts for care two or more children from two or more families. Courts are reluctant to enforce anything more stringent, seeing anything less as informal neighborliness. Two or more children from two or more families is, on the face of it, a more complex situation (Class, 1982).

Constitutionality

Sometimes the strength of a licensing law is determined by a test of constitutionality. If the persons affected by the act believe that its provisions run counter to their fundamental rights, they may contest the validity of the act in court. If the statute is upheld by the judicial review, the base for the licensing activity is clarified and strengthened. If a suit is won by those who challenge the act, the entire statute, or particular sections of it, may be declared invalid.

The Means for Implementation

A further test of the strength of a licensing law depends on the extent to which the department charged with administering the act is given the tools to do an effective job. The administering agency cannot go beyond the dictates of the law, but it is obligated to carry out to the fullest extent the intent and provisions of the law. If insufficient funds are appropriated by the legislature, the program will be a disappointment for all who are interested in effective regulation of child care facilities.

If the administering department is to be effective over time, the law must give it clear power to deny or to revoke a license in those situations where an inadequate facility for children is being planned or unsatisfactory care is being given.

Rights and Responsibilities of the Licensee

To what extent are the responsibilities and rights of the licensee clearly stated? For example, does the law make clear that the licensee has responsibility for certain kinds of record keeping, and for permitting the licensing staff to enter and inspect the facility? Is the licensee protected by a clear statement of the grounds that the licensing department can use to deny or revoke a license? Is the penalty for operating without a license set forth in the law? Is the licensee entitled to an administrative hearing when a license is denied or revoked?

Provision for Citizen and Parental Participation

Is there provision for citizens of the community, especially parents of children in out-of-home care, to assume responsibility in child care regulation? Does the law provide for a representative advisory board to assist the licensing department in the development of mandatory rules and regulations? Perhaps the best test of citizen participation is the extent to which parents, as consumers of child care, are given an authentic voice in the adoption of mandatory rules and regulations that are applied to their children's care. Are public hearings held before final adoption of a set of regulations so that persons directly affected by the law can come forward and register their agreement or disagreement? And is there provision for citizens to take action to require or force a dilatory licensing authority to discharge its responsibility?

Another way to assure participation of parents and other citizens in the regulatory function is to give names of licensed operators to new applicants for a license, and to urge licensed operators to invite new applicants to visit their facilities, so that new applicants may see what constitutes approved child care service. Another technique used profitably is the use of a second review by licensed providers when new applicants for a license are at risk of being denied permission to operate. The aim in all these techniques is to broaden the concept of citizen participation and to use the strength of licensed child care providers to extend the base of qualified child care in the community.

Licensing is a state consumer protection system. Some states enlist parents actively in monitoring whether requirements are met. (Morgan, 1987, p. 7–1)

Removing barriers to visiting licensed child care facilities opens up opportunities for citizen awareness of the quality of child care in the community. For children in full-time care outside their own homes, visits by parents have special meaning and potential for enabling their children to leave the foster care system. Monitoring of agency requirements for parental visiting is essential.

THE NATURE OF LICENSING RULES

Official Mandatory Requirements

Licensing standards are mandatory requirements for operating a child care home or institution or other child care facility. These requirements represent a floor under the quality of child care services below which no facility should be authorized to care for children. The role of the licensing worker in relation to these rules is to see that they are complied with before a license is issued. To this extent, but not exclusively, the licensing worker is a specialized type of law enforcement officer.

Licensing requirements, as *mandatory* standards, necessarily imply some limitation on individual choice. In turn, this limitation may imply a conflict between the right of an applicant or holder of a license and the interests of those the licensing law is designed to safeguard:

children and their parents. The task of successful licensing, then, becomes the reconciliation of the welfare *needs* of those served and the *interests* of the groups or individuals who are subject to licensing. At the same time there must be agreement by the licensing staff as to what is acceptable throughout the administering department as conformity. Otherwise there can be no consistent application of standards.

To effect this reconciliation of needs and interests, the administering agency must operate from a set of policies that are consistently interpreted to licensees by the licensing staff, and at the same time flexibly applied to the individual situation at issue. Staff development programs are essential to give licensing workers an understanding of the agency's consistent expectations in the application of standards and at the same time, a grasp of the limits within which they may use individual discretion in determining when an applicant has met standards acceptably. This is necessary because an evaluation of conditions in the care of children cannot be arrived at through automatic, precise judgments. Questions arise such as: "What is sufficient shade in a play area?" "When does the presence of older children interfere with or distract from a program for younger children?" "If the day care mother is obligated to observe the child carefully when he or she arrives in the morning for any sign of illness, what observations should be made?" In all these examples, the decision may relate to characteristics within an individual situation or require a balancing of the effects of a number of variables.

Some controversy exists as to the extent to which mandatory rules should be made very specific, thus limiting individual discretion on the part of the licensing worker, or broad and general, allowing assessment of compliance according to a particular set of circumstances. Stumbras (1971, p. 18) favors greater specificity in the language of mandatory standards. To be effective, he says, licensing standards must be (1) understandable to any citizen, (2) specific enough that it is clear what must or must not be done, (3) enforceable in the sense that a particular standard can be measured or judged, and (4) complete enough to offer the protection needed by children.

In any case discretionary judgments on the part of the licensing worker as to whether requirements are met cannot be made arbitrarily. They must be related to the rules from a frame of reference supplied by the agency, and interpreted to licensees with consistency.

Almost all licensing requirements have pros and cons. The various interests of the provider of a service, its users, and society must be considered. Since opinions of specialists as to what constitutes good child care are subject to change, conflict is likely between the rights of the applicant for a license and the interests of children and their parents, those the licensing law is designed primarily to safeguard.

Recommended Standards

Some licensing laws provide for recommended standards to be used as objectives or desirable goals for licensees. These desirable goals are based on practice approved by child care experts and are used in consultation with child care personnel to try to raise the level of care given to children. They are distinct, however, from the mandatory rules used as a measure in a decision to issue or withhold a license.

Regulatory experts tend to object when a licensing agency promulgates recommended or "desirable goal" standards. Doing so, they say, can confuse the basic function of licensing—the consistent application and enforcement of mandatory requirements applicable to all child care facilities. Developing and distributing recommended higher-level standards is an appropriate function for standard-setting agencies, such as the Child Welfare League of America (CWLA) and the National Association for the Education of Young Children (NAEYC). Such standards may become unofficial goals for many persons involved in different ways in organizing or offering child care services. However, they are not the same as mandatory licensing requirements.

Additional Classification of Standards

Whether mandatory or recommended, standards can be classified further. Some are tangible standards related to *physical aspects of growth and development,* mainly in the field of health and safety. Numerous examples can be found in mandatory requirements, such as: "Electrical outlets that are within reach of children shall have protective coverings. There shall be no exposed or uninsulated wiring" (*Licensing standards for day care homes,* 1985, Sec. 406.8).

Then some other standards are concerned with a *desirable psychological maturation.* These are usually seen as intangible standards; they can be found in mandatory or recommended requirements. For example: "Each child shall be given the opportunity to develop social relationships through participation in schools, and other community and group activities. Each child shall have the opportunity to invite friends to the foster home and to visit in the home of friends" (*Licensing standards for foster family homes,* 1987, Sec. 402.16).

Finally, standards contributing to achievement or *self-realization* of the child are usually found in desirable or recommended standards rather than as requirements. For example: "Children's verbalization of emotions and ideas is both a goal for and an indicator of a good quality program. While preverbal children will naturally communicate physically, staff members redirect their actions constructively and encourage verbal expression" (Bredekamp, 1987, p. 10).

How Standards Are Formulated

The formulation of standards should be accomplished with cooperation between the licensing authority and the groups affected. Since licensing standards are mandatory, they become, in effect, "little laws." That is, they prescribe behavior, demand conformity, and carry sanctions. Such an application of authority, to be successful, must be accepted as reasonable by the persons to whom it is applied. In deciding what constitutes adequate child care, some issues are debatable, and since the licensing department which administers the law is not a representative body, it must seek a variety of viewpoints and sources of knowledge. Then the differences in opinions or evaluation of facts must be reconciled in writing the standards.

For an effective application of the licensing authority, the administering agency must be concerned not only with the content of the standards but also with the process by which these standards are developed. Jambor has identified three constructs or methods for the development of state licensing standards: (1) procedural due process, (2) partnership, and (3) interest representation. He finds interest representation the most suitable to child care licensing (Jambor, 1964).

When interest representation is the method, a usual beginning is for the state agency to create, by invitation, an advisory committee to meet and study together in order to assist in developing the standards. Different persons and groups have important roles in such a committee. Some are chosen because they are especially knowledgeable about child care, or because they speak with authority for some large part of the child care field—agency or institution executives, board members, or professionals from related fields. Some persons may be chosen as "reactors and interpreters." Often these are responsible and vocal citizens. Some committee members represent the regulated group, such as child care center operators or agency foster parents. In addition, the advisory committee usually includes personnel from related public services, such as health, fire, or sanitation departments, whose knowledge of services may be needed not only in formulation of standards but also in enforcement. It is important that licensing standards be consistent with requirements of other related departments in the state.

Through the deliberations of the licensing department and its advisory committee, a tentative set of standards is constructed, predicated upon knowledge of what is necessary for the well-being of a child. After the various points of view and interest have been considered and reconciled, the department formulates the draft of a statement of standards.

At this point there should be hearings. Notice must be given to representatives of affected interests that the state intends to adopt rules, and an opportunity for them to be heard is scheduled. Agencies and persons who are affected can then respond to the notice and exercise their right to be heard. Individuals may speak for their own interests. Sometimes private agencies organize into an association and have a representative speak for them.

The state department has an obligation to give careful and serious consideration to all suggestions or objections that are offered. Then comes the final decision on standards and official adoption of them by the state agency that has been given responsibility for administering the licensing law, followed by their publication and promulgation.

To be successful, a licensing program must be concerned with review and revision of requirements. There is a danger of bureaucratic formalism in which standards are formulated or continued in licensing practice only because they have historical precedence (Meyer, 1968). In addition, there is the tendency to concentrate on "lower-level" objectives, for example, trained personnel, proper organization of boards, or the physical facilities, all important but not always clearly directed toward children's needs (Wolins, 1968). Can enforceable standards somehow be formulated that are tied to the child's identity as a family member, with a focus on family concerns? Fanshel (1975a) has found evidence that parental visitation is a key indicator of the likelihood of children's discharge from foster care. He advocates that records of parental visits be kept in a readily available computerized information system, and that agency practice in regard to parental visitation be carefully monitored as part of the licensing function.

As soon as the licensing program is put into operation, experience begins to show where the rules are unworkable, insufficient, or outdated. Front-line licensing staff—those persons who carry out licensing studies and offer supervision to licensed facilities—have a principal role to play in the revision of standards. They have important information to channel to policy makers about the changing picture in licensing and current needs. Essentially the same process is followed in revising requirements as in the initial formulation—study, tentative proposals, representation by interest groups, notice to the public, and official adoption.

When rules are revised, it is generally expected that requirements will be kept applicable and reasonable but also that they will be revised to require increased safeguards in care for children. Scientific breakthroughs in knowledge, for example in health practices, are usually effective as an impetus to higher-level safeguards. So is the expenditure of money—to fund special projects, to subsidize higher-level services, or to provide aid to states in meeting the increased costs of complying with higher standards.

Even so, upgrading requirements can be difficult to achieve even after there is agreement that the public is ready to support higher standards. For example, in one state the administering department and its advisory committee were in agreement that the licensing requirements for children's institutions should be rewritten to require higher levels of education for houseparents because they have many hours of supervision and direct interaction with children and are often the staff workers with the lowest levels of education and training. Before this higher level of training could be required, however, it had to be determined whether it was fair to expect institutions currently meeting the mandatory requirements to meet new ones. This meant the following questions had to be considered: In view of the kinds of available personnel in the service fields, could institutions obtain personnel for this necessary position if higher levels of education were required? Could the institutions meet the increased costs of obtaining personnel with higher qualifications? Could the houseparents who had served for a number of years and to whom the institutions felt obligated be released from duty to attend academic courses, workshops, or other training sessions? Under what auspices could these courses be made available, especially in the less populated parts of the state, where a number of children's institutions are located?

Other barriers to revising standards upward arise out of vested interests on the part of child care providers who have met an initial set of standards, have organized and budgeted their service in relation to that set of standards, and as a result tend to be resistant to change.

Any regulatory policy by government at any level is based on trade-offs between cost and quality. The general public must support the goal of the regulation, and be willing to pay a price. (Morgan, 1987, p. 14–1)

The expectation that mandatory requirements for licensing will be regularly adjusted upward poses other problems. Licensing is focused on the idea of adherence to a baseline through a set of requirements applied consistently to all child care situations subject to licensing, rather than on an evaluation of the actual alternatives for children's care in particular instances. When such alternatives are considered, a child in a neglectful home may appear better off even in a very marginal day care facility. The community tends to view enforceable requirements in relation to whether a child's situation is improved by the available alternative child care arrangement. If it appears to be, this alternative tends to become the public's baseline even if the base is less than that required by licensing standards or less than that endorsed generally as good child care.

Morgan has taken the point of view that to say that the licensing process in and of itself can result in a raising of mandatory standards is "more than a little misleading." The claim arose, she stated, because licensing workers who have social work training are uncomfortable with the regulatory function and wish to see the service conform to goals that they have been taught. In addition, the claim is based on the early days of licensing, when there were enough voluntary social service providers in the community willing to meet higher standards.

> At that point, and only at that point, was it feasible for licensing agencies to raise their requirements. This experience suggests that licensing is not the force which raises the quality of care in the community. Other means of raising quality, such as public education, staff training, increased commitment of funds, and voluntary accreditation, must precede the raising of quality through licensing requirements. Licensing must be the basic and essential tool in *maintaining* a specific level of quality. (1971, p. 47)

Such are some of the varying and complex considerations that frequently enter into a revision of licensing standards toward a higher level of child care. As a result, improved standards, even though they are revised upward, still represent compromise and only a gradual move toward child welfare goals.

THE LICENSING PROCESS

What is the work of the licensing staff member? What is the process by which agencies, institutions, foster homes, or child care centers are determined to be suitable or unsuitable for issuance of a license?

"Process" may be defined as a series of operations consciously effected, in a successive or simultaneous manner, in order to achieve a given goal or set of goals. While all the operations or phases are interrelated and must be properly integrated, each phase has its own unique purpose or function.

The licensing process includes five steps: (1) *application,* (2) *assessment* based on investigation and inspection, (3) *approval or rejection* for issuance of a license based on a determination of facts, (4) *supervision of and consultation with* the licensee, and (5) *termination* of a license. The steps cannot be carried out successfully by a mechanical application of rules and regulations. A dynamic use of the licensing provisions calls for staff workers who are perceptive, understanding, and supportive of those who want to give child care. It requires skill in observation and interviewing, the use of individual judgment free of caprice or rigidity, and an ability to arrive at a decision as to whether a license should be issued, this decision being based on careful study and presentation of evidence.

Application

The goal of the application phase of the licensing process is to bring the persons who want to give child care under the jurisdiction of the licensing statute and to enable them to present a readiness to cooperate with the study procedures. To achieve this goal, the licensing worker must help would-be licensees to explore what they want to do and are able to do. This requires the worker to give information as a basis for a realistic understanding of what is involved in qualifying for a license, to explain and interpret the provisions of the licensing law and its underlying philosophy, to give information about the nature of the requirements, to communicate and convey a specific understanding of what is expected, and to provide forms and clarify the procedures to be followed.

Assessment

The goal of the assessment phase is the determination and evaluation of facts as a basis for deciding whether a license is to be issued. To achieve this goal, the licensing worker must assess the applicant's situation in relation to the official requirements. This implies the necessity of inquiring fully into many aspects of the proposed care which is subject to regulation. In addition, the applicant must be told where requirements are and are not met and should be given some guidance as to how they might be met. While the primary responsibility of the worker is to determine whether the foster mother, day care operator, or institution board can be given a license to operate, that does not preclude helping the applicant find ways to meet requirements. In doing so, the licensing worker's role is somewhat analogous to that of the probation officer, who is a "friend of the child in court."

Recommendation regarding Issuance

The goal of the third step in the licensing process—recommendation for approval or rejection of a license—is to come to a decision as to whether or not to grant "official permission" (through issuance of a license) to the applicant to care for children outside their own homes. This requires a summary judgment related to the requirements. The obviously qualified and the obviously unsuited applicant offer few problems; the borderline applicant presents many problems in decision making. It is in relation to the marginal applicant that the community need for child care spaces may bring pressure for concessions in the direction of issuance of license, thus creating stress for the licensing worker in the decision-making process.

When the summary judgment is complete, a decision to grant or not to grant a license, and evidence to support this judgment, must be entered into a written record. Because of the statutory basis of the licensing function, the evidence relating to the applicant's qualification for a license must be documented. "Feeling" that an applicant is suitable or unsuitable is insufficient; evidence must be obtained and recorded to show that specific standards are or are not met.

Then either the approval or the decision to deny a license must be conveyed to the appli-

cant. In the case of approval, the worker's future role in supervision and consultation should be discussed. If the decision is to deny a license, then valid reasons must be given. If a license is issued with certain conditions, these should be made clear, for example, the number or the ages of children that the facility may accommodate.

Individual applicants are entitled to a fair and impartial hearing if they wish to challenge the denial of a license, and in turn, the licensing authority must refer to the proper law enforcement agency if the denial is upheld and the child care operation begins or continues anyway. The willingness of the licensing workers and the administering department to use authority is essential to enforcement of the legislation.

Supervision and Consultation

The fourth step in the licensing process—supervision of and consultation with the licensee—can be the key to dynamic accomplishments in child care licensing, but too often it is forgotten or ignored. The primary goal of supervision is to assure through visits, interviews, and inspection that the licensee continues to meet requirements. It is especially necessary in borderline situations after a license has been issued, when outside circumstances, or unexpected demands, or laxness on the part of the licensee may allow the care given to children to fall below mandatory standards. Licensing supervision implies constituted authority as well as the authority deriving from the worker's knowledge and competence. Supervision is initiated by the licensing department; the worker perceives and states the problem.

In a plea for more precise language, Terpstra (1985, p. 3) maintains that the term, "supervision" of licensees is "misleading" in that it implies a relationship that in fact does not exist. Licensing staff, he points out, do not have a supervisory or administrative authority over licensees. Instead, they "monitor" programs to determine whether they continue to be in compliance with regulatory requirements. When compliance is found to be lacking, the licensing staff may take negative licensing action. Monitoring is essential. It can occur during the initial licensing study, intermittent visits (announced or unannounced) and during compliance investigations.

Difficulties are often widespread in maintaining compliance. In communities where there are not enough child care facilities, licensing staff are at risk of becoming too responsive to the supply-and-demand component in out-of-home care. When this attitude is coupled with an administrative reluctance to use authority in the supervision of marginal licensees or in the termination of licenses, the result is a perfunctory and ineffective service for children. Often these problems reflect a lack of full or enthusiastic acceptance of licensing as a social work service by social workers and the field of child welfare. Frequently, a lack of sufficient staff and a discontinuity in administrative assignment of responsibility for licensing result in a jagged and incomplete implementation of the licensing statute. Such a staffing pattern often arises from a lack of administrative backing for full acceptance of the licensing function. When this occurs, licensing staffs suffer from feelings of lesser status, and feel less commitment to, and reward for, their work in comparison to other staff assignments more focused on treatment, pathology, or crisis situations.

If there is a productive relationship between the worker and the licensee, consultation develops out of supervision. The goals of consultation are to help the licensee meet standards and to move beyond minimum standards through the use of advice or help in finding improved ways of caring for children. Frequently this involves motivating or supporting the caretaking persons to exceed mandatory standards, or supplying information from a knowledge of resources that a licensee may use to work through a problem or situation in connection with child care. The worker's consultative role

also carries the obligation to bring unmet needs of children and gaps in services to the attention of planning groups and other professional persons in the community.

In consultation the authority derives only from the worker's knowledge and competence. The licensee usually initiates the problem for discussion; he or she sees the situation to some extent as a problem even in the beginning. While some consultation comes about naturally as a result of interaction between the licensing worker and the caregiver, more is dependent on the competence of the worker in using consciously applied skills.

For personnel who perform the supervisory tasks of measuring conformity to standards and monitoring continued compliance—tasks that are often taxing and not personally rewarding—the consultative role can provide "a form of job enrichment." There are, however, potential problems in assigning supervision and consultation to the same licensing worker. One suggested problem has been that the opportunity to provide consultation may act to impose advice on child care providers who have not asked for it, and may reinforce a disinclination on the part of the licensing worker to apply mandatory standards firmly, especially in facilities where compliance with standards is marginal (Lounsbury & Hall, 1976).

In a study of supervision and consultation in child care institutions serving dependent, delinquent, and emotionally disturbed children, Polenz (1970) found that the licensing worker's constituted authority for enforcing standards did not interfere with providing consultation to the licensee. Support for this finding also came from a later study of child care that addressed two questions: (1) whether the supervision function interferes with the consultation function in the licensor's role, and (2) whether a licensor's orientation toward providing consultation is linked with a disinclination to enforce standards (Lounsbury & Hall, 1976).

In answer to the first question, it appeared

that the licensing staff had not attempted to use their regulatory authority to influence child care providers to use the advice they gave through consultative activities. The primary reservation about consultation voiced by child care providers was that the licensing workers often seemed to have inadequate training in matters of child development, which diluted the worth of their recommendations.

In answer to the second research question, Lounsbury and Hall's data partially confirmed that an orientation toward consultation is associated with a lower level of supervisory activity. Licensing workers' high level of interest in providing consultation correlated negatively with frequency of licensing denial and nonrenewal and with the number of facilities perceived as warranting a suspension or revocation of a license. This conflict between supervisory and consultative tasks was most evident in the prelicense phase. Problems may include (1) complaints by licensing administrators that licensing staff spend too much time with applicants who should be given a firm decision about issuance of a license, (2) complaints by day care operators about unnecessary delay in the initial stage of seeking a license, and (3) perhaps most serious, the possibility that marginal applicants may continue to care for a number of children while their study in unnecessarily prolonged.

In the late 1970s and early 1980s, the use of consultation by licensing staff expanded, and then began to diminish, partly due to cutbacks in financing licensing staff. Consultation as a function of licensing was still seen as appropriate, but there was some uncertainty as to the degree or level at which it could be maintained.

Another major development contributed to less consultation being offered by licensing staff—a significant expansion of child care Information and Referral (I&R) services. These new consulting services were a response to "the difficulties parents have in finding affordable, decent child care in a fragmented delivery system." In a sense, I&Rs "organized child care access" (Kahn & Kamerman, 1987, pp. 37, 55).

However, the I&Rs not only offer consultation to parents. They may supply information to potential child care providers about the requirements of licensing or registration, pinpoint areas of child care need for providers who wish to expand their operations, or recruit and advise persons who are interested in beginning a child care service—centers or family day care homes.

These new sources to which providers of child care can turn have lessened significantly the pressure on licensing staff to be consultants. However, helping a new applicant for a license find constructive ways to meet the legal requirements clearly remains a basic licensing task (Freebury, 1988, p. 1).

Termination

The last step in the licensing process is referred to as the termination phase. Some licensees voluntarily discontinue child-caring operations and do not ask to have their licenses renewed. This is often true of foster parents as well as family day care providers. There has been little systematic study of the reasons for the termination of child care. In view of the crucial need for child-caring resources, two questions should be answered when a resource is discontinued: (1) Was the quality of care such that the termination represents a loss to children who need care and to the community that needs more licensed facilities? (2) If more service had been available from the state licensing agency or from community social services, might the child care provider have continued his or her work with children?

In some instances the licensing agency is confronted with the necessity of seeking revocation of the license, thus bringing about the involuntary termination of the child-caring operation. This action may grow out of evidence obtained through ongoing supervision of the facility, following issuance of a license, or evidence growing out of investigation of complaints. As in the case of denial of a license, when complaints are received that, upon investigation, lead to the necessity for revocation of a license, there must be a readiness to act promptly and responsibly in the application of the authority of the licensing agency.

The licensing of child care facilities, when performed with conviction and skill, has within it a "dynamic for change" and is increasingly accepted as an effective method of safeguarding children needing care outside their own homes. However, to be truly preventive of harm to children and effective in encouraging improved community planning for children, licensing departments must find ways to define obligations broadly. They must do more than just carry out the application and assessment phases of the licensing process with periodic, perfunctory renewals of licenses. The total regulatory process must be used to ensure the licensing function a place in the network of child welfare services.

RELATED FORMS OF REGULATION

Accreditation

Licensing of child care facilities differs from accreditation, although both are forms of regulation. Although the regulatory agency that administers the licensing law and the voluntary accrediting agency (such as the Child Welfare League of America or the National Association for the Education of Young Children) seek to improve the level of care for children outside their own homes, they move toward this goal by different means.

The authority of the regulatory agency to investigate and license a child care facility is applicable to all persons or institutions or agencies that fall under the particular definition of child care facility provided by the licensing statute. As a result, all of these child care facilities must meet the prescribed requirements in order to operate. If the child care facility does not meet the mandatory requirements for licensing, the regulatory agency must enforce its rules and the unlicensed facility cannot legally continue to operate. Since the licensing agency administers a statute passed by the people of the state, it is accountable to all the persons in that state and their elected representatives.

An accrediting agency sets those standards required for accreditation, as well as desired or recommended standards that give guidelines for better professional practice. These standards apply to child care agencies choosing to seek the status of accreditation and to participate in such a system of self-regulation. (Achieving accreditation does not exempt individuals and agencies from the jurisdiction of the licensing statute and its requirements.) If the agency that seeks accreditation does not meet the prescribed standards, it is excluded from accreditation or membership in the standard-setting organization, but is not prohibited from continuing to operate. In turn, the accrediting organization can ignore the substandard facility and concentrate on the development of institutions and agencies that demonstrate a better service. The accrediting agency is accountable, not to an electorate, but to its membership, or to the profession it represents.

Registration

In recent years a number of states have begun to consider and evaluate different ways of regulating family day care. Concern has grown about the high costs of licensing day care homes in view of the limited safeguards achieved for children. Only a small proportion of day care homes actually caring for children are brought to the attention of the licensing agency—perhaps about 10 to 15 percent. Family day care is a first choice of many working mothers, and some studies show that much of it is stable and useful to both children and parents (Collins & Watson, 1976). Nevertheless, most family day care, whether beneficial or harmful, is socially invisible to the general public and to the licensing agency. In fact, if licensing authorities actively undertook to study and evaluate all the homes now giving care to unrelated children, the endeavor would be beyond the capacities of administrative departments as now constituted. This is in contrast to day care centers, child-placing agencies, and child care institutions that by their nature are more easily identified in a community and brought under the jurisdiction of a licensing statute.

Regulating family day care is an administrative challenge, since at least 10 homes must be regulated to protect the same number of children as would be covered in one inspection visit to a typical center. (Morgan, 1987, p. 2–1)

Other aspects of family day care tend to increase resistance to licensing. When parent consumers are satisfied with day care arrangements they have made informally for their child and the care takes place in the privacy of someone else's home, they as well as the caretakers tend to see the licensing investigation and the presence of the licensing worker as an intrusion. In addition, because many day care homes go unlicensed, some citizens take the point of view that licensing of family day care is discriminatory.

The alternative form of regulation that receives the most consideration and demonstration is "registration." Sixteen states have now adopted registration as the means to regulate family day care (Morgan, 1987, p. 2–1). The idea of registration is based on the assumption that most family day care providers want to comply with the law and that most of them are in substantial if not complete compliance with the family day care mandatory requirements. This approach to regulation operates somewhat as follows: Persons giving family day care to one or a small number of children are required to make this fact known to the state's regulatory agency, that is, to register the day care operation and report the names of children being cared for. The regulatory agency is then responsible for supplying the child care provider with a statement of the mandatory forms to be completed for registration, and other literature

deemed to be helpful to anyone caring for young children. Day care providers are instructed to review the requirements carefully, assess their own degree of compliance, and report the degree of conformity to the regulatory agency. Day care providers may also be required to provide statements from references about their suitability to provide family day care. In addition, they must supply the parents of the children they care for with a copy of the mandatory requirements and the means by which complaints can be made to the regulatory agency. Intentional false self-certification carries a penalty. After registration day care providers are given access to consultative resources for improving their child care endeavors. The regulatory agency also makes inspection visits to randomly selected registered day care homes to determine if substantial conformity to standards does in fact exist and, when necessary, to help day care providers overcome obstacles to meeting standards. All complaints that are received about standards violations are followed up promptly with on-site inspection and evaluation.

To be successful the regulatory agency must promulgate family day care standards widely. It must also carry out a continuing program of interpretation to the public of required standards of care, the role of the regulatory agency, and ways in which parents can select appropriate day care, monitor it, and report complaints.

Advantages of registration to family day care over licensing that have been cited include these: (1) Regulatory staff members are freed to concentrate on problem homes rather than on routine inspections; (2) parents are looked to for a greater role in evaluating day care homes; (3) to the extent that heretofore-unlicensed family day care providers respond to the publicity about registration, more caretakers are treated equally under the law; (4) family day care becomes more socially visible, so that it is more feasible to measure its extent and to evaluate and strengthen its characteristics.

Disadvantages that are cited include the

following: (1) For success, registration relies heavily on parent and community awareness and involvement; (2) family day care providers may be unable to assess their compliance with standards correctly or may do so falsely, hoping not to receive a randomly scheduled spot-check inspection; (3) registration is too simplistic, an after-the-fact form of regulation that negates the opportunity to involve the caretaker in the meaning of standards and the availability of consultation; (4) random sampling and spot checking of registered homes is a form of selective enforcement. It is valuable mainly as a research device for constructive child care planning, but it is limited as a regulatory enforcement strategy.

The Michigan Department of Social Services completed a two-year project designed to determine whether registration of family day care homes is a more appropriate type of regulatory system than licensing from the operational viewpoint of effectiveness, efficiency, and economy (State of Michigan, 1977). In matching sets of counties, three approaches to family day care regulation were compared: (1) registration, including staff training, mass media information, and child care information provided to day care providers; (2) licensing, using a form of enrichment of traditional practice through staff training, mass media information, and the provision of information identical or equal to that provided in registration; and (3) licensing as generally practiced.

The findings were as follows:

1. The greatest increase in the number of homes regulated was reported in registered counties; this fact suggests that the registration process increases the number of homes regulated in comparison with the licensing process. This finding tended to be more characteristic of larger counties than of smaller ones.

2. A higher percentage of homes in violation of regulations were found in registration counties than in licensing counties. Smaller licensing counties had a higher percentage of violations than larger counties.

3. Only a few regulations tended to be violated in registration counties, whereas in licensing counties a wide variety of standards were found to be violated.

4. When costs of the various regulatory approaches were compared in areas of personnel, transportation, training, and information programs, and when costs were controlled for the size of the county, the least expensive form of regulation per home was registration—50 percent less expensive in large counties and 25 percent less in small counties.

5. Few differences emerged in attitudes of providers to the form of regulation applied to them; there was no clear preference in favor of registration. Each group appeared relatively pleased with the regulatory process they encountered.

The project investigators concluded that the demonstration had shown registration to be easier, less expensive, and capable of regulating more homes. However, it did not provide as much compliance as licensing. The consequent choice seemed to be between a registration process covering more homes at less cost but less effectively (registration) or a process covering fewer homes at higher cost but more effectively (licensing).

On the basis of the project findings, the Department of Social Services recommended to the state legislature that registration be utilized statewide as the method of regulating family day care homes; that the change be reflected in an amended regulatory statute; and, in order to reduce the rate of violation in registered homes, that applicants be requested to submit proof of freedom from communicable tuberculosis before registering, that more stress be placed on the importance of compliance at the time of registration, and that stronger emphasis be given to regulatory supervision through an increased number of random, on-site, spot-check visits.

The distinction between licensing family day care homes and relying on a system of registration is less clear than was envisioned when registration began to be used. A commonly used criterion for distinguishing registration from licensing has been the frequency of monitoring visits after registration or licensing. Most states that adopted registration planned that "random rotating visits would be made to a percentage of the homes to assure compliance with the requirements." Systematic monitoring has also been regarded as an important part of the licensing function. Nevertheless, Morgan's national study has shown that some states that register, visit all homes; some states that license, do not visit at all after the licensing study is completed. "The frequency of visits may vary from none to several times a year regardless of whether a state licenses or registers" (Morgan, 1987, p. 2–2).

Data are absent as yet as to the extent that registration has met two significant expectations of its proponents. These were that (1) registration would appeal to family day care providers to the extent that a very substantial proportion of the underground family day care industry would become visible, and that (2) research would follow experience with registration and produce significant data for use in child care planning.

A positive indication of the meaning of registration of family day care providers is reflected in Texas, where there are forty-six Registered Family Day Care Associations. These organizations were formed in different localities by the caregivers themselves. The initial reasons for forming such associations have varied. Among them were (1) a need for some kind of formal public recognition of their service, (2) the opportunity to share experiences and give mutual support, (3) the belief that a formal organization would strengthen their exchanges with city officials, and (4) an interest to bring in guest speakers as a means of continuing training for their work (Winsted, 1989).

The need for training of family day care providers has been largely ignored. Twenty-eight states do not require experience or any form of education for family day care providers. An encouraging development is that twelve states now require preservice training and nine

states have an ongoing training requirement (Morgan, 1987, p. 6).

Purchase of Care

Some children have care arranged for them through a "purchase contract" using governmental funds and negotiated between the licensing agency and the selected child care provider. The purchase of out-of-home care and services for children from voluntary agencies by public welfare agencies offers a potential means to regulate child care and move it to higher levels than can be enforced under the mandatory standards of licensing. Public agencies that wish to match the needs of individual children for whom they are responsible with the most appropriate services to meet those needs can evaluate and classify available services into levels of merit beyond the requirements for licensing. This formal or informal classification scheme can then be used in making decisions as to when care and services should be purchased from other agencies or be supplied by the public agency.

The alternative of purchase of care under these conditions becomes a means to increase the benefits of care and service for individual children as well as an incentive to voluntary agencies to improve their existing services or to develop new and innovative ones within a community network of services. However, purchase of care will not yield these benefits if the public agency has not developed its own set of basic services and is dependent on purchase of care for meeting the needs of children for whom it is responsible.

FEDERAL INTEREST IN CHILD CARE REGULATION

Even before the 1960s the Children's Bureau of the Department of Health, Education, and Welfare (DHEW) had become concerned about the numbers of children being cared for in unregulated and often substandard day care. It had become apparent, too, that a surprising array of federal agencies had some involvement with the provision of day care through such legislation as the Elementary and Secondary Education Act of 1965, the Vocational Education Act of 1963, the Education Professions Development Act, the Manpower Training and Development Act, and the Economic Opportunity Act. In addition, the Women's Bureau of the DHEW, under the direction of Mary Dublin Keyserling, was urgently concerned about standards for children's out-of-home daytime care; the Department of Housing and Urban Development had included day care in its Model Cities program; the Department of Agriculture was involved through its surplus food program; and even the Department of Defense had a concern with day care centers on military bases (although these facilities continue to be privately funded and subject to neither federal nor state standards) (Cooper, 1976; Federal Interagency, 1968).

The need for coordination could not be ignored. The result was the appointment of a Federal Panel on Early Childhood with representatives from a variety of departments and agencies, and the development in 1968 of a set of standards—the Federal Interagency Day Care Requirements (FIDCR)—applicable to all day care programs receiving federal funds. Five aspects of quality day care were given specific attention: child-staff ratios, parent participation, mental health services, physical health services, and delivery mechanisms and costs.

Following this major step in expression of federal concern for the quantity and quality of day care in the United States, attention turned to problems connected with state licensing codes. Under the 1962 amendments to the Social Security Act, only day care facilities that met state licensing requirements could receive federal aid. Although all states had some kind of child care licensing,

> some states had codes so strict and elaborate that they raised provider costs prohibitively; others had codes so lax that child care specialists

considered them wholly inadequate to guarantee even a bare minimum of protection for children. Also, many of the codes constituted jungles of confusing, even contradictory requirements and red tape that had a tendency to discourage would-be care providers and thus reduce the amount of care available nationwide. Finally, if the government was going to increase its support of day care, some measure of the cost implication of state licensing codes was needed. (Cooper, 1976, p. 31)

Officials in DHEW's Children's Bureau and the Office of Child Development (OCD) were concerned about the effect of expanding day care with federal funds while state licensing standards were so varying and poorly enforced. They started work on analyzing existing state laws and preparing model licensing codes that states could be encouraged to adopt (U.S. Department of Health, Education, and Welfare, 1971a; 1971b; 1972). The project, carried out from 1970 to 1972, encompassed the points of view and expertise of state and local leaders, federal officials, attorneys, legislators, fire safety marshals, zoning experts and city planners, public health and child development experts, licensing program administrators, day care operators, and parents of children in day care. Representatives from all these groups were brought together to debate, to consult, and finally to agree on drafts of model directions for more effective state licensing practices in behalf of all children in day care. The intent was to "design an effective safety net and at the same time to remove all unnecessary barriers at the state level to swift expansion of day care services" (Cooper, 1976, p. 34).

The model licensing code project encountered serious obstacles before its completion, and the results have been disappointing. It did, however, act as a catalyst in focusing attention on the urgency of improving child care regulation at the state level, and in the view of some has been an important force in making inroads against the antiquated licensing statutes and practices in some states (Cohen & Zigler, n.d.).

Concern with the provision and quality of day care began to focus on the need for revisions in the FIDCR, and in early 1970 the Federal Panel on Early Childhood was again convened for that purpose. A variety of issues entered into the revision process. Imprecisions in language, intended to ensure flexibility in application, had made the standards difficult to enforce. The standards were primarily concerned with center care of the preschool child, to the neglect of attention to children in family day care, schoolage children needing out-of-school-hours day care, and infants. Drafters of the 1968 FIDCR had held that infants should not be in group day care, but working mothers continued to make such arrangements. There were differences of opinion about child-staff ratios and staff qualifications. Persons primarily concerned with quality day care wanted higher staff requirements. But if requirements for staff were too strict, costs would become excessive and limit the availability of day care. The debate over quality versus effective use of limited funds was persistent. Another issue that entered into attempts to revise the 1968 FIDCR was defining an appropriate role for parents. Minority and advocacy groups wanted a stronger role in day care policy making, but by 1972 resistance to this had grown among persons who believed that many in these groups were less interested in child care programs than in using day care policy to gain political influence within their communities.

Progress proved to be difficult to achieve. Changes in personnel at the federal level, overlapping and duplicating assignments, and major disagreements on the issue of quality versus effective use of limited funds and on the best means of enforcement eventually polarized the participants in the revision of FIDCR. In the absence of broad-based support needed for action by Congress on a revised set of requirements in 1972, revisions of FIDCR were stalemated and sent into limbo within the Office of Management and Budget (Cooper, 1976; Cohen & Zigler, n.d.).

The passage of Title XX in 1974 reopened the matter of federal participation in child care standards and enforcement by giving the secretary of DHEW power to revise the FIDCR after first submitting to Congress a study of their "appropriateness." By 1980, the decade of research and debate had brought about acceptance of minimum standards to be implemented on October 1, 1981 and applied to all federally supported child care programs.

Before that date, however, the Reagan administration changed the total picture. Federal administration representatives went on record as opposing any form of regulation of federally funded child care. The Omnibus Budget Reconciliation Act of 1981 (OBRA) amended Title XX of the Social Security Act and in doing so created the Social Service Block Grant (SSBG). By this action, federal standards were effectively eliminated along with all other Title XX requirements that had been imposed on federally funded child care. Child care facilities now were required only to adhere to state licensing standards in order to receive federal money (Kahn & Kamerman, 1987).

The development of federal standards yielded some benefits. During the long debate, to some extent the FIDCR had emerged as a desirable norm; more states by 1981 were in compliance or close to it. And although most child care services would not have been subject to the FIDCR in any case, the federal standards had provided some guidelines for the country as to what minimum standards should be. At the same time, "eliminating federal regulations undoubtedly led some large commercial chains to expand into states with standards that are low enough to insure the operator a profit" (Kahn & Kamerman, 1987, p. 103).

TRENDS AND ISSUES

The Limits of Licensing

The experience with FIDCR disappointed many people and left them troubled about the need of the federal government to achieve fiscal responsibility in its funding of child care and to require compliance with agreed-upon standards. The question was left, however, as to just what direction federal leadership should take and by what means. Contradictory viewpoints have been summed up thus: "Some advocates, impatient with the complexity of the regulatory system and the range of standards, believe there should be national standards. Others believe that another layer of standards would add a further barrier, increased costs, and reduced citizen involvement in standards" (Morgan, 1987, p. 1).

Some advocates hope to see the original FIDCR implemented eventually with only minimal and appropriate revisions. Some others, although favoring federal standard setting, believe that in the last analysis, the comprehensive federal standards were a mistake. They doubt that the federal government will attempt again to impose comprehensive standards on resistant states. They cite the size of the country and the wide diversity of opinion among and within states as to an acceptable role of government in family life. These child care advocates would seek a smaller number of standards tied to federal funding—basic standards whose benefits have been shown from systematic research. Such a core of essential standards would focus on these areas: staff–child ratios; group size; staff qualifications and inservice training; parent involvement through advisory groups and parental drop-in access to their children's care; and prohibition of corporal punishment. Health and safety standards, some believe, could be left to local and state government where such standards have been in place for some time; a second layer of such requirements would be cumbersome.

The controversy raises the issue as to what the limits of licensing are. Some would say that too much has been expected of licensing as a means of assuring "quality" child care. The police power (from which child care regulation derives its authority) justifies rules at a level that the citizens of the state have agreed is essential to safeguard children from harm. To go beyond

that level and attempt to use licensing as a means of assuring "quality care" is to invite definitional problems about which child care experts, as well as the general public, are likely to disagree.

Much of the thrust to make licensing go beyond its sociolegal conceptual base is attributable to two influences. The first is found in vestiges of the historical confusion within the field of social work about the distinctive functions of child care regulation and child protective services. In the first half of the century, in a climate that placed high value on social treatment programs, as child protective services were conceptualized to be, professional social workers resisted the use of constituted authority inherent in regulatory administration. They saw it as posing a threat to positive treatment relationships they sought to develop in protective services. The result was ineffective enforcement of licensing requirements, which was followed first by dissatisfaction with standards in children's out-of-home care and then by an expressed need to raise requirements for licensing, even though existing ones had not been enforced.

A second influence in the quality-care issue comes from the search by child development experts for an established authority to use in bringing standards of day care closer to their knowledge-based child care goals. The effort to improve levels of child care is worthy, but the vehicle of licensing as a means to do so has limitations.

The standards for licensing are not professional statements of good practice. . . . [They] are requirements, not goals to be pursued. (Morgan, 1987, p. 3)

Licensing serves the purpose of establishing minimal standards that, if enforced, will assure basic safeguards for children. Within the constraints of public distrust of governmental intervention into matters directly affecting the prerogatives of families, perhaps child care regulation cannot go beyond enforcing a "life safety'' level of care. A dynamic, yet systematic, enforcement of a life safety level implies the need to seek agreement on a core set of minimal standards within a hierarchy of standards that, if enforced, will provide safety for children from risks of fire and other physical and sanitation safety hazards; safe levels of nutrition; and some assurance of activities and experiences for healthy growth and development through requirements of basic credentials on the part of caretakers.

Roles and Distinctions between Licensing and Child Protection

With increased publicity about sexual abuse and other forms of abuse that occur in child care centers, day care homes, foster homes, and child care institutions, a major issue has emerged: What are proper investigative roles for licensing staff and for child protection personnel? The clouded distinction is a problem among most or all states. Abuse literature has focused mainly on in-home abuse rather than out-of-home child care facilities, leaving investigation procedures and standards largely unspecified or confused.

Freebury (1989) has identified wide variation in existing practice among the states. In Michigan, licensing staff are assigned sole responsibility for all out-of-home abuse reports. Texas has a separate unit within the licensing unit, wholly separate from other licensing functions. In California a more cooperative plan is in place—a special unit from the licensing staff in conjunction with staff from child protection. Maine, in turn, has a separate unit assigned to the licensing unit but staffed by child protection workers.

In a national study of sexual abuse in child care facilities (family, center-based, or preschool, but excluding residential facilities), Finkelhor et al. (1988) drew from a roster of all cases of sexual abuse in day care reported nationally during the period January 1, 1983, through December 1985. To be included in the study, reports of abuse had to have been substantiated by at least one of the agencies as-

signed to investigate the incident. Data were collected on all such cases. In addition, an in-depth analysis was carried out of a random sample of 43 of the cases.

Among the factors studied was the process of investigation that followed the allegation of abuse. The researchers found that a variety of different agencies "crossed paths, sometimes cooperatively, sometimes uncooperatively" as they carried out an investigation. Three principal types of investigations were identified: "(1) In *child welfare solo,* the whole investigation was carried out by child protection agencies; (2) in *parallel investigation,* two or more agencies (most commonly child protection and police) conducted simultaneous, often overlapping investigations with frequently conflicting goals and methods; (3) in *multi-disciplinary teams,* agencies worked together and established goals and methods collaboratively." Perhaps not surprisingly, clear evidence showed that multi-disciplinary teams were most successful. This was true in terms of objective outcomes, satisfaction on the part of the investigators, and most significantly, the impact on the children (Finkelhor et al., 1988, p. 8).

Common problems confronted all the investigators. These include (1) ambiguity in the children's statements; (2) professional and public prejudice about children's credibility; (3) relationships of the investigators and the parents of victimized children, who despite shared desire to protect the child, often found themselves in adversarial relationships; (4) frequent lack of cooperation by the facility under investigation; (5) complicating media attention; (6) and organizational problems such as lack of resources and proper training or experience with respect to sexual abuse (Finkelhor et al., 1988, p. 9).

Actions taken by the licensing agency after the investigation was completed are of interest. In one-third of the cases, the license was revoked. In another third the license became provisional pending specific changes in the facility, with the license to be revoked if the required changes did not occur. Somewhat surprisingly, 54 percent of all facilities with substantiated abuse remained open. Many of these were instances of single perpetrators who were not employees or had been dismissed from employment after the disclosure of involvement in the abuse. In those instances, licensing agencies reasoned that the facility had not been clearly at fault and could continue to operate if appropriate means were taken to prevent reoccurrences. The researchers recommended that intense and specialized training be offered and required for all staff who were assigned to sexual abuse investigative teams (Finkelhor et al., 1988, pp. 9, 14).

New Interest in Health Requirements

Concern has grown about the extent to which child care facilities contribute to the spread of infectious diseases. Especially for centers with infants in care, the question is urgent. As a result many states have revised their health licensing requirements to address key health-related issues.

Licensing policies have shifted with respect to the question as to whether mildly ill children should be excluded from child care until they are fully recovered. Heretofore, general practice has been to notify parents and isolate the child until a parent can arrive to take the child home. However, public health experts now tend to support standards that do not require exclusion of most mildly ill children. Twenty-two states now permit children with mild respiratory or other minor illnesses to attend child care centers. Thirty states allow mildly ill children to be in small licensed day care homes. Ten states specify particular illnesses for which exclusion is required (Morgan, 1987, pp. 10–1 through 10–3).

Frequent handwashing is known to be a most effective procedure for reducing the spread of disease and is particularly important for centers with large numbers of children. Although many states are clarifying their regulations in this area, the rules in sixteen states do not refer to handwashing. Space for changing diapers should be located where there is a source of running water if procedures for washing can realistically assure cleanliness. Yet only twenty-eight states require centers to have fresh running water in the infant changing room (Morgan, 1987, p. 10–3).

It is possible for states to reduce the spread of disease by requiring immunization. "If it is nationally desirable to reach all children in day care with immunization, this goal is close to being achieved." Only three states do not have an immunization requirement for infant/toddler preschool children. Nine states do not have an immunization licensing requirement of family day care (Morgan, 1987, p. 9–1).

Another critical health question with respect to licensing rules and state child placement policies addresses the care of children with AIDS who are placed in full-time care in foster homes and institutions. Complex questions include the matter of testing children for AIDS—testing at admission? testing regularly when in care or at discharge? testing all children or only those known to be at risk of AIDS? The role of confidentiality and its implications for physicians, providers, and parents, and liability risks assumed by the state or foster care provider are also critical issues that urgently need consideration (Freebury, 1988, pp. 10–11).

The American Public Health Association, in collaboration with the American Academy of Pediatrics is engaged in an effort to develop national performance standards in health, nutrition, safety, and sanitation for out-of-home child care programs, based on sound epidemiological principles and practices. The standards are expected to delineate criteria between minimal requirements and the ideal that can serve as a national reference code to guide regulatory agencies as they seek to upgrade state and local child care licensing requirements (Hawks, 1988).

Requests for Exemption from Licensing

Reference was made earlier to legislative practice in some states of allowing certain exemptions from licensing of out-of-home child care. These exemptions mostly have reflected accepted notions of informal neighborliness in caring for children. In recent years, however, an increasing number of religious organizations, especially fundamentalist Christian churches, have sought exemptions from child care licensure. By arguing that church-affiliated centers are instructional programs and a part of the religious ministry, they hold that only the church should decide the qualifications of "those who minister to children." Further, they maintain that their child care programs are "an arm of the church" and an expression of free exercise of religion. They claim exemption from licensing by reason of the separation of church and state guaranteed in the U.S. Constitution (Sanger, 1985).

Some states have responded by amending their statutes to exempt child care centers operated by religious organizations from complying with some or all of the standards that other centers are legally required to meet, including compliance with fire and safety codes. Critical issues are contained in this development, and center owners and staff, parents, educational organizations, church leaders, lawyers, state officials, and legislators have lined up on both sides of the issue (Sanger, 1985, p. 5).

Not only do secular child care centers oppose these exemptions, but also a number of long-established religious organizations, such as the National Council of Churches of Christ, the National Conference of Catholic Charities, the National Lutheran Council, and the Salvation Army. Churches affiliated with these organizations have responded to the crisis of child care for working mothers by sponsoring a significant proportion of out-of-home child care. In these endeavors they have usually not sought exemption from regulation and have stated that the requirements from which other church-run centers seek exemption "have nothing to do with religious freedom, but rather address the welfare of children" (Sanger, 1985, p. 3).

Embedded in the controversy is resistance by certain religious groups to prohibition of corporal punishment, which some claim is "mandated by scripture" (Sanger, 1985, p. 15). Licensing standards in 32 states now prohibit corporal punishment in family day care, and do the same for center care in 39 states (Morgan, 1987, p. 8-1). Requirements that prohibit corporal punishment are based on research showing it to be an ineffective method of enabling children to learn to assume responsibility for their own behavior, a disciplinary practice that only demonstrates the use of aggression and violence as a problem-solving method.

In a study of child care licensing standards among the states relative to discipline of children generally and corporal punishment specifically, using questionnaires and field interviews, Norris Class (1981) tentatively concluded that "objections to no corporal standards (and even to other types of discipline constraints) . . . seem frequently to come from facilities sponsored (or directly administered) by so-called 'conservative' church groups." From his inquiry Class forecast that "resistance to no corporal punishment standards by certain religious groups will likely increase in the immediate future" (p. 4).

Since Class made that prediction, certain religious groups have regularly launched efforts to obtain or expand religious exemptions. Lawmakers who must vote on such exemptions experience strong political pressure, making compromise a way out in an effort to accommodate both sides (Sanger, 1985, p. 34).

Legislative compromise has taken three forms. One is based on the principle of "substantial compliance." Exemptions are granted for *some* of the regulations that religious organizations say infringe on their religious practices. In response, proponents of licensing point out that *all* regulatory standards are basic but minimal standards, and that each of them has to do with some aspect of children's well-being. Exemptions undermine the comprehensive yet minimal protections for children in out-of-home care (Sanger, 1985, p. 34).

A second type of compromise is to provide for "notice" to parents that their children are receiving care in an exempt facility. In effect this permits parents to agree to lower standards than those for children in other out-of-home care facilities. The content of the "notice" often lacks sufficient information to enable a parent to make an informed choice (Sanger, 1985, pp. 35–37).

A third compromise is to offer exemptions to a wider category of child care centers in an effort to reduce political opposition from nonexempt centers who are economically disadvantaged by having to conform to a range of requirements. Exemptions from serving meals, supplying cribs and space for each child's belongings, specific numbers of staff persons, prescribed space and other requirements add up to a substantial economic benefit for one sector of a competitive industry (Sanger, 1985, pp. 34–37).

Those who seek exemptions and those who oppose them each argue that the other is in violation of the First Amendment of the Constitution: "Congress shall make no law respecting an establishment of religion, or prohibiting the free exercise thereof. . . ." Religious day care centers, seeking exemption, focus on the promise of "free exercise of religion." Secular centers and their proponents focus on the prohibition of "establishment of religion," and hold that by granting exemptions, the state is clearly favoring religion in violation of the constitutionally protected separation of church and state. Thus each group views the same act of government as a violation of the Constitution, but for different reasons.

The issue becomes public in one of several ways. (1) In states with religious exemptions, nonexempt centers may sue the state for violating the "Establishment" clause of the First Amendment. (2) In states that require all centers to meet licensing requirements, fundamentalist centers may refuse to apply for a license or renew an existing one. The state regulatory body then takes the center to court for operating without a license. The center then claims a violation of free exercise of religion. (3) In states without exemptions, fundamentalist groups engage in intense lobbying efforts to obtain them, asserting the religious freedom of child care center operators (Sanger, 1985, p. 4).

Opponents of exemptions counter these tactics by arguing that the state has a "compelling interest" in protecting the safety and health of children in out-of-home care, and that licensing is a significant means to further that protection. They assert that total separation of church and state is not feasible and that there are essential forms of state supervision. Further, they say that supporting uniform licensing regulations is not an antichurch position in that licensing statutes neither prohibit nor discourage religious activities that occur in many licensed church-run centers through lessons, songs, prayer, and decor (Sanger, 1985).

Setting acceptable boundaries of governmental involvement in a range of religious practices has presented complex problems to lawmakers and courts for many years. The search for a neutral course between the two clauses of the First Amendment is nowhere more important than in the context of protection of children in out-of-home care.

FOR STUDY AND DISCUSSION

1. Some applicants for a child care license, as well as other citizens, view the licensing requirements as an "invasion of privacy." State and discuss the arguments that could be used on both sides of this question. Following this discussion, formulate an answer you would give to an acquaintance who asks you why the licensing statute is necessary and what purpose it serves.

2. Obtain a copy of the child care licensing statute of your state. What are its apparent strengths and weaknesses in relation to the criteria for evaluating a licensing law?

3. Obtain a copy of a set of licensing standards used in your state for one of the child care facilities, for example, foster home, child care center, child-placing agency, or institution. Evaluate these standards as to the rationale for their being mandatory. To what extent do they address current regulatory issues discussed in this chapter?

4. Debate with other students the various alternatives for the federal government with respect to a role in child care regulation.

5. Consider the magnitude of unregulated family day care, the purpose served, and the needs and capabilities of parents who use this form of out-of-home care. Cite positive and negative aspects of registration as a means of preventing harm to children in family day care.

6. Consider the matter of granting exemptions from child care regulation. With other students, debate the issue as it was presented in the chapter.

FOR ADDITIONAL STUDY

Nelson, J. R. (1982). The politics of federal day care regulation. In Zigler, E. F., & Gordon, E. W., Eds. *Day care: Scientific and social policy issues,* pp. 267–306. Dover, MA: Auburn House.

Morgan, G. (1987). *The national state of child care regulation 1986.* Watertown, MA: Work/Family Directions, Inc.

National Association for the Education of Young Children (1987). *The growing crisis in child care: Quality, compensation, and affordability in early childhood programs.* Washington, DC: Author.

Kahn, A. J., & Kamerman, S. B. (1987). *Child care:* *Facing the hard choices.* Dover, MA: Auburn House.

Association for Regulatory Administration in Human Services (1988). *A licensing curriculum.* Richmond, VA.: Author.

Terpstra, J. (1989). Day care standards and licensing. *Child Welfare, 68*(4), 437–442.

Phillips, D., Lande, J., & Goldberg, M. (1990). The state of child care regulation: A comparative analysis. *Early Childhood Research Quarterly, 5*(2), 151–179.

CHAPTER 5

Services for Children and Families in Their Own Homes

The little world of childhood with its familiar surroundings is a model of the greater world. The more intensively the family has stamped its character upon the child, the more it will tend to feel and see its earlier miniature world again in the bigger world of adult life.

Carl Gustav Jung

Chapter Outline

NEW INTEREST IN SERVICES IN CHILDREN'S OWN HOMES

For most of the twentieth century, professionals in the human services have recognized the importance of a child's own home. Yet efforts to conceptualize and develop social services to preserve, strengthen, and enhance family life and the quality of the child's environment have lagged. Society's reliance on the family for essential nurturance and guidance of the nation's children has not been accompanied by necessary changes in social and economic policies and preventive social provisions. As a result, social agencies tend to be overwhelmed with demands from families and children in crisis.

If you care about children, then care about families. (Emlen, 1978, p. 1)

In recent decades much of the general public has voiced alarm about what it perceives as increasing breakdown of the family system. Professionals have responded with keener awareness of the important meaning to the child of his or her own home and the need to develop more and better family-based social services. Their efforts are visible in the movement within the foster care system to get children out of foster care and into permanent homes (see Chapter 10) as well as in the numerous demonstrations and social service projects that are aimed at providing timely supportive services to families before breakdown occurs (Stehno, 1986).

The gradual trend toward more services for children and parents within their own homes reflects such factors as these.

1. Serious social problems arising from an urban culture that make it clear that many families, even normal, self-supporting ones, cannot cope unaided with many of the demands and strains of daily life.

2. Modified patterns of family life seen in changing life-styles and norms governing (1) male-female relationships, (2) teenage parenting, (3) rising divorce rates, and (4) increased expectations that children will be accorded rights that were formerly denied them.

3. New awareness of violence in marriage, particularly among couples with inadequate means, heavy stresses, and dependent children.

4. Problems encountered in providing a sufficient number of stable foster care facilities for children who clearly need better care than they receive from their own parents.

5. Difficulties experienced in attempting to return children successfully from foster care to their own families, or in finding other homes for them, and an awareness that some children in foster care could have remained at home if their parents had had access to supportive services.

6. Increasing reluctance on the part of social workers to assume responsibility for removing children from their homes, even when their situations are recognized as hazardous to their well-being.

7. Changes in other fields of practice that have influenced the nature of family situations and child welfare concerns. For example, community mental health care makes long absences of mentally ill parents from home less likely than in the past. However, their behavior and the treatment process may still generate considerable stress for family members, which social services could help to alleviate.

8. Legislated amendments to the Social Security Act that have emphasized social services to low-income families and legally defined "family services," and other family-based legislation such as the Indian Child Welfare Act and the Adoption Assistance and Child Welfare Act.

PROBLEMS TOWARD WHICH SERVICES ARE DIRECTED

Many parents cannot provide an environment conducive to the positive functioning of their children. The kinds of problems they face are numerous and may vary widely in their characteristics, duration, and degree of gravity. Their causes and symptoms are interrelated and frequently overlapping.

Naturally Occurring Stress in Family Life

Many "normal" events in the course of family life can become problems that create tensions and demand an extraordinary output of physical or emotional energy on the part of one or more family members. Whether these events produce growth or generate more serious problems depends not only on the capacities of family members but also on the extent of available outside resources and opportunities.

Hazardous life events that may produce such stress include the following:

1. A parent moving to a new job and, in so doing, requiring family members to give up a familiar home, find an identity in a new community, make new friends, and change schools may create adjustment pressures.

2. Early childbirth, especially combined with insufficient education, frequently results in a lowered standard of living and overwhelming pressures to postpone personal gratification.

3. A long season of contagious and confining illnesses among young children in a family without outside help may burden a mother excessively and create or intensify marital tensions.

4. The death of a child, learning of an unwanted pregnancy, the birth of a handicapped child, or the death of a parent's own mother or father usually requires a particular and demanding adjustment.

5. The youngest child entering school, the oldest child leaving home, a mother entering the labor market, or the addition of a grandparent or other relative into the household may thrust the family into a changed pattern of living.

Continuing Constraints on Parental Capabilities

Many children are denied constructive experiences and opportunities because of inadequate parental care.

1. For many parents the overriding problem is *poverty* and all its accompaniments (see Chapter 6)—poor health; low educational levels; unemployment or underemployment; substandard housing; discrimination; lack of playgrounds, libraries, and other public facilities; loneliness; alienation from the mainstream of society; and individual depression and lack of hope.

2. Families with *only one parent* may be handicapped in providing a suitable child-rearing environment and normal family relationships. The parent may be overwhelmed with the total responsibility for home management and rearing of children. There may be lack of adequate adult models of both sexes, insufficient financial and emotional support, difficulties in visiting arrangements by the absent parent, or trauma to other members if the parent's absence is due to death.

3. *Mental deficiency or mental or physical illness of parents* may sharply limit their capacity to care for their children.

4. In some families the problems are exemplified by *interpersonal conflicts between family members*. Marital conflict may be threatening family unity or endangering a child's emotional balance. In other instances, there is conflict or a lack of satisfying relationships between a parent and a particular child, or among siblings.

If there is anything that we wish to change in a child, we should first examine it and see if it is not something that could better be changed in ourselves. (C. G. Jung, 1939, p. 285)

---

5. *Parents with serious behavior problems* may cause deleterious conditions within a family and impair a child's chance to develop normally. At all socioeconomic levels a parent may steal or lie, have destructive attitudes that affect success in employment, be addicted to drugs or alcohol, or be sexually exploitive or aggressively hostile. In recent years a long-standing problem has been documented—violence in marriage—a pattern that has proved difficult to interrupt and modify.

6. Many persons have been poorly prepared for parental responsibilities and show *family management problems:* for example, inability to handle income efficiently, obtain and keep appropriate housing, organize and execute housekeeping tasks, get children to school regularly and on time, or protect them from health hazards. Parents frequently have not learned successful methods of child rearing, and their ignorance is reflected in damaging methods of discipline or supervision. They may be unprepared for the responsibility of planning and controlling family size, and may have difficulty in seeking or using contraceptive methods. Inadequate preparation for parenthood, resulting in dissatisfactions in the parental role, may stem from psychological problems of adjustment to the requirements, rewards, and penalties of parenthood.

Behaviors Centered in Children

Physical and mental conditions and behavior in children often constitute a problem toward which services are directed.

1. Some children have *special needs* as a result of mental handicaps, physically disabling conditions, severe emotional disturbances, or chronic illness. They often experience parental rejection, feelings of inferiority, isolation from other children, lack of normal play, or separation from parents in order to receive treatment or education. A lack of appropriate treatment resources and social services compounds their problems and generates new ones for them, their parents, and the community.

2. Some children who are without easily observable or serious physical or mental impairment nevertheless show symptoms of *disturbed functioning or development*. These symptoms may reflect trouble in parent-child relationships or in other aspects of home or community life.

In turn, the disturbed behavior and other troublesome symptoms may produce new inabilities to function successfully on the part of both the children and their parents. These symptoms and exacerbated behaviors may take the form of temper tantrums, moodiness, jealousy, or simply a general aura of unhappiness. Some children have no friends or interest in school; they often do not acquire the basic competencies needed in today's world. Young people who have come to feel alienated from their families, schools, or communities may resist supervision, get into trouble with authority in their communities, engage in irresponsible or deviant sexual behavior, or use harmful drugs. A considerable number of them "run away" from their parents' homes.

Community Characteristics

Conditions within a community, a state, or the nation often are unfavorable to family life and infringe upon the needs and rights of children and youth. In such instances, services in behalf of children should be directed toward these community characteristics. Inadequate social provisions to support or supplement family life may be related to a number of factors within the community: (1) leadership that fails to provide sound and imaginative social planning; (2) inadequate financing and ineffective information and referral services for established programs; (3) negative community attitudes toward certain groups of people or problems, exemplified by discriminatory practices toward minority groups, absence of fair employment opportunities, a stigma attached to persons unable to support themselves financially, an indifference to conditions of child neglect, or repressive disapproval of young persons who actively protest what they see as critical malconditions of society; (4) lack of appropriate channels for the expression of opinion about the community by all groups in its population; (5) failure on the part of interlocking community institutions, which may be reflected in authoritarian methods by

police officers, a preponderance of unqualified court personnel, or public school policies and practices that create problems for large numbers of pupils and contribute to their failure.

THE MANY FACES OF FAMILY LIFE

The "traditional" family form, two married parents caring for one or more children born within their marriage, with the father as the essential wage earner and the mother the chief child caretaker at home, is no longer the norm. The rapid rise in divorce and in out-of-wedlock births and the large-scale entrance of mothers into the labor force have changed the composition of most families. Only 73 percent of families with children in America were made up of two-parent couples in 1988, compared to 87 percent in 1970 (see Figure 5.1). The number of unmarried couples living together rose from 532,000 in 1970 to 2,588,000 in 1988; however, these couples only comprised about 3 percent of all households (Saluter, 1989).

All family forms have parenting and child care needs in common, whether that family unit is the "traditional" one cited above, an intact family with two working parents, a single-parent family, a stepparent family, a teenage-parent family, or a homosexual-parent family. However, the "new" forms of family life usually carry additional demands or have needs and problems that become intensified, making even more evident the importance of access to supportive social services.

SINGLE-PARENT FAMILIES

Demographic Factors

In 1988, about one-fourth of the nation's children lived with only one parent (15.3 million children under the age of eighteen). The Census Bureau estimates that 60 percent of all American children, at some time before they reach

Two-parent groups

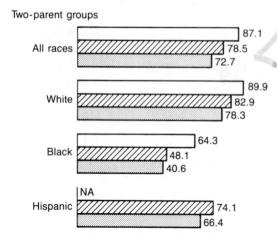

One-parent groups (mother/child)

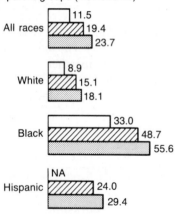

One-parent groups (father/child)

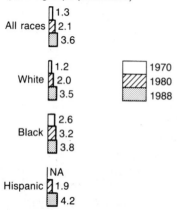

adulthood, will live in single-parent households. This is a large increase from 1970, when only 12 percent, or 8.2 million children, lived with a single parent (Saluter, 1989). Of all children living with one parent in 1988, 88 percent lived with their mothers as the single parent; the rest were about equally divided between those living with their fathers and those living with other relatives (Rawlings, 1989).

These findings illustrate the effect of large increases in out-of-wedlock births, but even more the higher rates of *marital instability, the predominant source of fatherless households.* Thirty-eight percent of the children living with a single parent had divorced parents, and another 25 percent had parents who were separated. Thirty-one percent were children of parents who never married, and 6 percent had a widowed parent (Rawlings, 1989).

Children of color are more likely than white children to live with a single parent. In 1988, 54 percent of all black children and 30 percent of Hispanic children lived with one parent, while 19 percent of white children were in single-parent households (Saluter, 1989). Black single-parent families differ from their white counterparts in several ways. For black families, the largest contributor to single parenthood is not marital dissolution but births of children to unmarried parents. Also, in comparison to white women, black women are less likely to marry after the birth of a child or remarry after divorce, and so they stay single parents longer (Nichols-Casebolt, 1988). Five of every six black children are likely to experience single-parent family life before reaching age eighteen (Bumpass, 1984).

Figure 5.1. Change in Composition of Family Groups with Children, by Race and Hispanic Origin; 1988, 1980, and 1970 (in percent). (*Source:* S. W. Rawlings. [1989]. "Single Parents and Their Children." In U.S. Department of Commerce, Bureau of the Census, *Studies in Marriage and the Family, Current Population Reports* [Special studies series P-23, No. 162]. Washington, DC: U.S. Government Printing Office, p. 15.)

Families headed by women do not constitute a new phenomenon, having been present throughout history. Nevertheless, the recent acceleration in the number of such families and awareness of the special problems that many of them face have attracted national concern.

The needs of single-parent families are not markedly different from those of all other families. At the same time, because of the responsibility of single parents to carry out the duties of child care and family decision making without a marital partner, and because of the higher probability that family income will be limited, normal needs and problems may become harder to deal with.

Economic Problems of Single-Parent Families

Single parenthood has pervasive and negative effects on the income and employment of the family head—usually a woman. Limited economic resources—not enough money—and the continuing pressure to balance one financial need against another are an especially troublesome aspect of daily life for most single parents.

Approximately half of all mother-only families in the United States are poor, if we use the U.S. Census Bureau definition of poverty. Mother-only families have higher poverty rates than any other type of family (disabled, aged, two-parent). Also, in comparison to other types of families, the poverty experienced by female-headed families is more severe and lasts a longer time (Garfinkel & McLanahan, 1986, pp. 11–26). The combined trends of an increase in the number of mother-only families and the decline in their living standards relative to other kinds of families are captured in the phrase, the "feminization of poverty."

Divorce creates economic stress for single-mother families whether or not they fall below the poverty line, as defined by the U.S. Census Bureau. The income of mothers and their children a year after divorce falls to about two-thirds or lower of their predivorce income (Gar-finkel & McLanahan, 1986). Although one might expect that the separating of one household into two would cause a decline in income for both divorcing parties, in fact divorced fathers experience much less of a drop than do their ex-wives. Some evidence suggests that fathers may be better off financially after the divorce than they were before (Weitzman, 1985).

One reason for post-divorce loss of income in single-mother households is that the mother's earnings become the major source of family income, accounting for 60 to 70 percent of total income (Garfinkel & McLanahan, 1986, pp. 18–22). Her ability to earn a good living wage in the labor market becomes critical to her family's economic well-being, but, unfortunately, women have a lower earning capacity than men. Among full-time year-round workers, women earn about 60 percent as much as men, a ratio that has held constant for the last thirty years. Partly, this difference is explained by different work patterns between men and women. Women are less likely to work continuously because they take time off to have and rear children. Their lower earnings capacity cannot be explained entirely by fewer years of work experience, however. Over half the gender wage gap is due probably to discrimination against women in the labor market (Garfinkel & Mc-Lanahan, 1986, p. 23).

Brandwein and her colleagues (1974), in their analysis of the literature on the social situation of divorced women and their children, concluded that the economic loss divorced women and their children experience is attributable largely to economic discrimination against women in the labor market, a practice maintained by a persistent assumption in society that women do not or should not support families and can expect at every class and income level to depend on their husbands for the major support of themselves and their children. This long-held attitude is used to justify a segregated labor market in which women are concentrated in low-paying and insecure jobs with minimal opportunity for new job training and career advancement. Even in two-parent homes, working wives usually find it necessary to look to their husbands for the larger share of the family income. Women who become single heads of families lose the economic strength that they had before divorce when both husband and wife were working, with the husband earning the larger amount.

Given the widespread practice of keeping women in poorly paying occupations, divorce usually means the departure of the principal earner for the family. Even though fathers retain legal responsibility for child support following divorce, in most instances child support payments from them are not sufficient to keep divorced women and their children at their previous standard of living. Only about 40 percent of absent white fathers and 19 percent of absent black fathers paid child support in 1982. The lower level of support from black fathers was due mainly to their lower incomes (Garfinkel & McLanahan, 1986). In 1988, efforts of the states to collect child support payments yielded only 24 percent of the child support obligations (Children's Defense Fund, 1990, p. 99).

Attitudinal and system barriers have hindered the development of an effective child support system in the United States. Until recently, responsibility for maintaining the child support system rested with the courts. The legal system was ineffective in compelling absent parents to pay regularly and repeatedly the relatively small sums of money for the support of their children. Because the court enforcement system did not work well, and in some instances because they held sexist attitudes, many judges were apathetic about taking action against men for nonsupport, or, if they did so, ordered only minimal portions of the father's income to be paid for child support. In turn, single parents with day-to-day child care, domestic burdens, and employment problems usually had insufficient time and money to try to sustain alimony or child support payments through a reluctant court system (Cassetty, 1982; Stuart, 1986).

The Title IV-D Child Support Enforcement amendments to the Social Security Act in 1974 and subsequent amendments in 1984 and 1988 have strengthened the public system for collecting child support (see Chapter 6).

The families of black single mothers are at even greater economic risk than single mother families in general. Black single mothers have 30 percent less income than their white counterparts, and must stretch their income among more children. Sixty-one percent of black single-mother families have incomes below the poverty line. These mothers have greater difficulty than white women in working because of their relatively younger age, lower level of education, greater number of children, and younger age of children. Although more black single mothers worked in 1984 than in 1970, the percentage below the poverty line remained unchanged during that time, testifying to the low earning capacity of many black mothers (Nichols-Casebolt, 1988).

The rise of African-American families headed by women is "due in part to the increasing economic anomie of Black men." (Joe and Yu, 1986, p. 235)

Not only do black single mothers earn less as a group than their white counterparts, they are less apt to receive support from their children's fathers. Black male joblessness, caused largely by a loss of manufacturing and other labor-intensive jobs in the U.S. economy, has contributed to the increase in the number of black single-mother families and to their continued impoverishment.

Greater job opportunities for black men would increase black women's marriage possibilities, decrease the numbers of black single-parent families, and reduce the poverty and welfare dependency of these families. In addition, enhancing black men's economic opportunities could have a significant effect on the poverty status of women who remain or become single parents, because the economic insecurity of black fathers is a major reason for the low child support payments currently received by black mothers. (Nichols-Casebolt, 1988, p. 311)

The growing but still relatively small fraction of fathers who become single parents of families often also face economic problems. Although they usually have higher earnings than their divorced wives, have been employed longer, and have more opportunity for upward career mobility, they too must cope with combining child care and work. A 1982 survey of a national, nonrandom sample of 1,136 fathers who had custody of their minor children found that combining work with child rearing was difficult for nearly four out of five fathers. "Job mobility, earning power, freedom to work late, job performance, and job advancement are all negatively affected. Some fathers had to quit or were fired" (Greif, 1985, p. 181).

The effects of sustained loss of income for single-parent families are much the same as those that any family experiences in such economic circumstances. Less money coming in over time means a lowered standard of living, often a move to less desirable housing and a poorer neighborhood, perhaps lowered educational opportunities for children in less well supported schools, and modified aspirations. The expense of day care, the scarcity of jobs, even low-paying jobs, and the difficult circumstances of women's employment and men's commitments are compounding factors.

It would appear, in short, that single-parent families need more income than they are capable of earning or collecting, at least during the difficult periods when children are young or when the father's remarriage precedes the mother's. . . . These economic problems ought to be the main concern of policymakers who worry about the children of marital disruption. (Bane, 1979)

Social and Psychological Aspects of Single-Parent Family Life

Not enough is known about single parenthood as an operating social system, that is, how single women and men cope with their situations, and what the variables are that determine their abilities to respond to the demands on them and overcome the constraints they experience. As has been discussed, we do know that the marked decline in income that occurs when a single-parent family is created and the lowered standard of living that follows complicate the process of transition from a two-parent to a single-parent family. There are other problems, also, in the process of transition.

The parent who becomes the single head of a family must find a way to assume the authority role responsibly if the family is not to experience various levels of disintegration. She or he must represent the family interests to society at large, interpret society to the children, and be a figure of authority and discipline for them.

Some women do this readily and may even perceive the role as giving them a degree of power and independence that they were denied in marriage or in their own parents' home. But some other women lack training and experience for this new role and are not comfortable with it. In such instances sometimes an older child or an adult sibling is expected to fill in for the mother (Brown, 1988). Mothers who find it difficult to assume the authority role as head of the family and who are also faced with harassing economic problems may feel pushed into remarriage as a solution, even if conditions in the new union may be less than positive (Brandwein et al., 1974).

The combined responsibility for employment and child care creates considerable stress for most single-parent families. Family needs are mostly ignored in industrial decision making about the conditions of work. Most work situations are still organized on an implicit assumption of fathers at work and mothers at home, despite the labor market's reliance on women to fill many jobs. The rigidity of full-time employment, the requirement of a continuous eight-hour day, and the paucity of flexible working arrangements provide evidence of this persistent and outworn assumption.

Child care for working parents is often a complex set of arrangements. Efforts to maintain these arrangements are even more stressful for the single parent. In addition, the mother usually finds herself alone with housekeeping and home-maintenance tasks, ones that before her divorce she shared to some extent and in various ways with her spouse. The loss of that shared responsibility for home maintenance means that work may remain undone or have to be paid for out of scarce resources. Husbands often looked after the children when mothers did errands, went shopping, or got out of the house to see friends. The loss of help with a variety of domestic tasks leaves single mothers even more dependent than other parents on informal organizations such as baby-sitting pools, play groups, relatives, or even a doubling up of households with other single mothers. Single fathers have some advantage in that their average larger income makes it more feasible for them to hire housework and baby-sitting services. In addition, relatives tend to provide such help to men more readily than to women (Kurdek, 1988; Lindblad-Goldberg, 1987).

Perhaps most hazardous for the single parent is loneliness and a feeling of isolation in the absence of emotional support from a partner who shares responsibility for the family and its well-being (Wallerstein, 1986). The problem has been stated this way:

> The importance of positive emotional support from other people cannot be overemphasized when children are a 24-hour responsibility. . . . Children cannot provide emotional support—their love is demanding of the parent, rather than supportive. A great, and often overlooked, strength of the two-parent family is the presence of two *adult* members, each providing the other

with aid in decision making, psychological support, replacement during illness or absence—someone to take over part of the burden. The solo parent not only has to fulfill all family functions, but has no relief from her or his burden. (Brandwein et al., 1974, p. 507)

The psychosocial environment in the single-parent home is an important factor in the post-divorce adjustment of children. Socially competent children of divorce tend to be living with a parent who acts authoritatively. If the mother and the children's father continue to maintain a cooperative parenting relationship, this can enhance the mother's ability to maintain an authoritative parenting role and yield benefits to the children, reassured of their father's continuing concern for them (Heath & Mackinnon, 1988). Many divorced fathers do remain involved with their children and play significant parental roles during their children's growing-up years.

However, the reality for a growing number of families is a "disappearing father," one who absents himself from his children, emotionally and financially. Using both cross-sectional and longitudinal data from three successive waves of the National Survey of Children, researchers have studied over time the dynamics of paternal involvement following separation or divorce. The findings given here were reached from an eleven-year-long study, through the years 1976 to 1987. The studies were of more than 1,000 children in disrupted families nationwide. The sample was a representative one for such factors as race, geography, income, and education. The children were first interviewed in middle childhood (Furstenberg & Harris, 1990).

Findings from the national surveys identified a high level of paternal disengagement from their children, with sharp declines in contact at all three cross-sections. The loss was especially evident among children whose fathers moved out when they were quite young; many of these children lose contact with their fathers for most or all of their childhood. Close to half of the children living apart from their fathers had not seen them in the previous year. Most of the children who had had some contact with their fathers saw or heard from them only sporadically. Letters and telephone calls were infrequent. Only a sixth of the children had seen their fathers once a week or more in the past year. More than half had never been in their father's home, and in a typical month, only a fifth said that they had stayed overnight at their father's house (Furstenberg & Harris, 1990, p. 4).

Black children experienced greater instability in their contact with fathers than whites, but fathers of all races began to lose contact with their children at increasing rates the longer they were out of the home. Children of mothers who had more than high school education experienced greater continuity in contact with fathers than did those of less-educated mothers (Furstenberg & Harris, 1990, p. 9).

Many of the fathers appeared to regard childrearing "as part of a bundle of marital responsibilities attached to the household where they reside." Once the marriage was broken and the fathers living away, they appeared unable to differentiate their continuing responsibility and relations with their children from their changed relationship with the mother. The paternal bond began to wither. Sometimes this was a result of geographic distances, personal misunderstandings or distrust on the part of one or both of the divorcing parents. Frequently fathers chose an alternative: moving their allegiance to a new household, either by starting a new family or acquiring an existing one. Shifting loyalties and competing obligations tend to leave biological children with only a symbolic relation to their father. In turn, some children find father figures in stepparents who offer emotional and material support that the biological father does not provide (Furstenberg & Harris, 1990, p. 16).

Some of the proponents of the Family Support Act of 1988 hoped that compelling fathers to meet their financial obligations to their families would also "strengthen the social and emotional bonds between men and their offspring."

Furstenberg and Harris believe such gains are likely to be modest. They cite the real limitations on nonresidential fatherhood. The act may well increase the level of child support payment, but it is not likely to bring absent fathers back into the family (Furstenberg & Harris, 1990, p. 19).

Some Special Risks of Single-Parent Children

Some children can be helped by their parents to understand the circumstances that brought about their single-parent family, so that they are spared unnecessary disruption in their lives. Shared custody arrangements between divorced or separated parents are becoming common. Some work well, enabling parents to continue to share responsibility for their children's growing-up years and enabling children to maintain close relationships with both parents. But in some other instances of shared custody, children experience a serious sense of discontinuity and lack of belonging to either parent. Some children become pawns in bitter quarrels between divorcing parents and are caught in their parents' unresolved problems.

Child Snatching.   The kidnapping of a child or children by noncustodial parents in divorce has increased sharply, influenced by the higher rate of divorce and the larger number of contested custody actions. The practice is pervasive—found among all social classes and racial groups. The incidence of child snatching is hard to estimate. From the results of a 1982 Harris telephone survey of 3,745 respondents, Gelles (1984) estimated that between 313,000 and 626,000 child snatching episodes occur each year.

The problem, so detrimental to the affected children, has been a difficult one to bring under control because of inadequacies in the law. Because lawmakers eschewed the use of criminal procedures to solve what were perceived as domestic disputes, the Federal Kidnapping Act passed in 1971 excludes parents who abduct their own children, leaving the FBI an un-empowered source of help to aggrieved parents. Several states have attacked the problem by making snatching a felony. More states have en-acted the Uniform Child Custody Jurisdiction Act (UCCJA), which mandates that one state honor a court custody decision made in another state and assigns court costs, attorney fees, and travel expenses against the kidnapping parent. Nevertheless, most states offer only the possibil-ity of a contempt of court citation against the child snatcher, a power that is valid only within the boundaries of the state. As a result most snatched children are taken to another state (or another country) that is known as a "safe state," one in which child snatching is not a fel-ony and where the UCCJA is not in force. For this reason some custodial parents are seeking an amendment to the Federal Kidnapping Act to end parental immunity from charges of criminal behavior (Hoff, 1980).

A report on children seen clinically follow-ing their return to the custodial parent indicated that reactions to the abduction varied consider-ably among children. Length of time that the victims were sequestered seemed related to sub-sequent adjustment, with those whose abduc-tion lasted longer than six months at risk for se-vere psychological trauma (Agopian, 1984). A child abducted without his or her consent at best has had personal liberty interfered with and is apt to feel like a piece of property to be quar-reled over. Some children seen by clinicians are reported to have become deeply confused and distrustful of parent figures, with an intensifica-tion of the trauma they endured during conflict between their parents in a contested custody ac-tion. Some children, as they may do in other sit-uations, take on feelings of guilt for their parents' troubled and objectionable behavior. The risks are even greater when the snatching in-volves violence toward the person attempting to protect the child, and sometimes toward the children themselves (Lewis, 1978).

An organization formed to work for the re-moval of sex bias in the judicial system, called M.E.N. (Men's Equality Now) of the U.S.A., Inc., has attempted to bring about passage of the UCCJA in more states. In addition it has had some success in retrieving children snatched by noncustodial parents. Its success is possible in states that follow legitimate custody proce-dures embodied in the UCCJA (Lewis, 1978).

The need is very great for more profes-sional services to parents considering divorce to help them understand the economic conse-quences and reach a custody decision that each can accept, one that is the best alternative for the child. In recent years social workers in some family and child social agencies and in court ser-vices have been providing such help.

Unequal Rights for Children Born outside of Marriage.   For hundreds of years children of unwed parents (termed "bastards" and later "illegitimate" children) suffered hardships growing out of unequal legal protection. The United States Supreme Court traditionally al-lowed the states broad discretion in the treat-ment of out-of-wedlock children. However, be-ginning in 1968 and continuing into the present, the Court has rendered a substantial number of decisions that recognize or expand the rights of these children. Some of these judicial decisions will be discussed here.

The legal equality of the child born out of marriage as a matter of constitutional law was first significantly advanced by a landmark deci-sion of the United States Supreme Court in 1968 (*Levy v. Louisiana,* 1968). Louise Levy, a black mother, had died in the Charity Hospital of New Orleans. Her children's guardian tried to sue the hospital, the physician, and the insur-ance companies, alleging negligence and wrong-ful death. The Louisiana courts rejected the suit on the grounds that out-of-wedlock children had no cause of action for the wrongful death of a parent. The Supreme Court overturned this decision and used the equal protection clause of the Fourteenth Amendment to equalize the legal protection of children born inside of marriage and those born outside of marriage, in terms of wrongful-death claims.

While this decision eliminated the few remaining legal distinctions, in relation to their mothers, between children born inside of marriage and those born outside of marriage, the significant question of whether equal protection would be extended to the *father*–child relationship remained. There has been progress, although certain categories of legislation are still unfavorable to the child or remain ambiguous.

1. *Support:* Even though most states obligate the unwed father to provide financial support for his child, the child of married parents generally has broader rights as to both the level of support and the duration of the father's obligation. A Texas case was brought to the court to test whether it was a violation of the equal protection clause for Texas to deny an out-of-wedlock child the right to support from the biological father while granting that right to children born within marriage. The decision was that if a state has imposed the obligation of a child's support upon the father, then it cannot grant the benefit to some children while denying it to others (*Gomez v. Perez,* 1973).

A later attempt in Texas to restrict the rights of children of unwed fathers was found unconstitutional as well. In this instance it was a statute that barred all paternity suits filed after a child's first birthday. The "unrealistically short time limitation" deprived children of an adequate opportunity to obtain support (*Mills v. Habluetzel,* 1982).

2. *Inheritance:* Most states have treated children born inside and outside of marriage differently when disposing of a deceased person's property. In 1977 the Supreme Court decided that it was unconstitutional for states to deny a share of an inheritance to children for whom paternity had been formally established (*Trimble v. Gordon,* 1977).

3. *Welfare laws:* Federal welfare laws have been revised in an attempt to eliminate discrimination against the child of unwed parents, as in the 1965 amendments to the Social Security

Act. However, until recently state welfare provisions could still leave the child ineligible for benefits from a father's insured status, for example, workers' compensation laws. In 1972 the Court declared that to deny such benefits to dependent, even though unacknowledged, children violated the equal protection clause of the Fourteenth Amendment. Unacknowledged children, the Court said, also suffer from the loss of a parent, just as do children born in wedlock or out of wedlock but later acknowledged (*Weber v. Aetna Casualty & Surety Co.,* 1972). The next year the Supreme Court found unconstitutional a New Jersey public assistance program that limited benefits to two-parent married families and their children and said that family support under the program must also be supplied for unwed parents (*New Jersey Welfare Rights Organization v. Cahill,* 1973).

In still another case a challenge was brought to an application for disability benefits for three children of Ramon Jiminez, disabled from work. Disability benefits had been allowed only for the oldest child, who was already born at the time the father became disabled and eligible for benefits. Benefits were disallowed for the children born later. The United States Supreme Court held that the presumption of nondependency for disability benefits was unconstitutional when it excluded children from benefits who were in fact dependent and who could prove paternity and when the statute's purpose was to provide *needed* support, not *lost* support (*Jimenez v. Weinberger,* 1974).

4. *Custody, visitation, and adoption:* The child born outside of marriage has no clear right to the father's name, or to his company, or to a familiar relationship with him. As for giving consent to adoption, recent court decisions have left the father's rights unclear (see Chapter 11).

In reaching these decisions, the United States Supreme Court has sought to reduce or eliminate penalties against children whose parents are unmarried. However, the line of reasoning it has employed is complex and has not provided a consistent method of analysis of the rights of children born out of marriage or of the obligations and rights of their fathers.

The states can eliminate the legal distinction between children born inside of marriage and those born outside of marriage by enacting a simple statutory provision, contained in the Uniform Parentage Act, which considers every child to be the legitimate offspring of his or her biological parents. Although not all states have adopted this statutory provision, Court decisions and the child support legislation enacted since 1974 by the U.S. Congress indicate that a consensus has emerged that nonmarital children, like children born in wedlock, should receive support from their fathers ("New uniform act," 1989).

The implication of these court decisions for social service providers and for the courts is that important benefits accrue to children for whom paternity has been established. These benefits may include: Social Security payments, dependent allowance and educational benefits from the armed services, health insurance, benefits from worker's compensation, and child support. Children who know the identity of their fathers can get valuable genetic information and medical history. Knowing one's biological heritage may also have psychosocial benefits (Wattenberg, 1987).

In spite of potential benefits, agencies and courts are lagging in assisting families to establish paternity for their children. In 1987, paternity was established for about 25 percent of all births to unmarried women, an increase of only 15 percent since 1981 (Children's Defense Fund, 1990, p. 89). A recent study of paternity adjudication found several reasons why many children still do not have legally established paternity. Agency staff and the children's mothers and fathers often do not know the procedures for handling paternity matters nor the benefits to the child of formally establishing paternity. Court procedures may be confusing, expensive, and not clearly formulated. If the father is young and in school, and cannot provide financial support for several years, agencies may not see the value of establishing paternity. Public information and media campaigns are needed to educate the community that paternity adjudication has important, long-lasting benefits for nonmarital children. Agencies should routinely provide sensitive, facilitative counseling to unmarried mothers and fathers, to explain the importance of paternity adjudication to the child, the legal process, procedures concerning blood tests, and the rights of all parties (Wattenberg, 1987).

FAMILIES CREATED BY BIRTHS OUTSIDE OF MARRIAGE

The birth of children outside of marriage has been regarded as a serious problem for hundreds of years. Despite present-day "enlightened" attitudes toward sex, out-of-wedlock births in this country engender a high degree of concern that has become intensified because of the vastly increased percentages of babies that are currently being born to unwed mothers.

Incidence of Births outside of Marriage

In the past five decades the total number of out-of-wedlock births has increased sharply. To some extent this increase is a manifestation of a long-term trend in overall birth rates, reflecting changes in the number of women of childbearing age, in their age distribution, in marriage rates, and in average family size. Higher rates for inner cities also reflect, to a very considerable extent, population redistribution rather than true increases in rate. As middle-income groups have moved out to suburbia, leaving the inner city to low socioeconomic groups, figures for out-of-wedlock births appear unreasonably high for those selected inner-city areas, but tell less of the overall increase in out-of-wedlock births for a total metropolitan area.

Nevertheless, it is clear that nonmarital births are making up an ever-larger proportion of all babies born during the year. In 1970, nonmarital infants comprised 11 percent of all births; this percentage increased to 17 percent in 1979 and to 25 percent in 1987 ("Births to the unwed," 1981; Children's Defense Fund, 1990, p. 88). States vary in the percentage of births that are to the unwed and also in the rate at which this percentage is increasing, as Table 5.1 shows.

Among births to black women in 1986, 61 percent were out-of-wedlock. The comparable figure for white births was 16 percent (Hughes et al., 1989, p. 26). National figures on unwed motherhood do not directly relate the incidence to socioeconomic level. However, it appears that the majority of reported out-of-wedlock births occur among women in low-income groups. If this is true, then because large portions of the black population have low incomes, differences between black and white groups in rates of out-of-wedlock births may reflect differences between socioeconomic levels as much as or more than between racial groups.

The increased practice of unwed mothers' keeping their babies to rear themselves instead of releasing them for adoption has significantly heightened public concern about the future of these families. The practice has long been common among blacks and is now more common among whites. The fact that high proportions of these new families are headed by teenagers has become a central social issue. Teenage parenting will be examined at some length in a later section of this chapter.

In view of the high degree of concern engendered by the incidence of out-of-wedlock births and in view of the many unanswered questions about causation and appropriate societal responses to the phenomenon, it is enlightening to examine some of the earlier views about unmarried parents and professional responses to the problem.

Historical Aspects

Emphasis on Protection of the Child.   In their historical works on unmarried parenthood, Ripple (1953) and Shapiro (1966) pointed out that during the first two or three decades of this century, research studies of out-of-wedlock pregnancy were limited in design and the data collected were analyzed inadequately in most instances. The result was that early investigators tended to reach conclusions and advocate actions that simply reiterated prevailing beliefs.

Early explanations for births outside of marriage laid stress on environmental histories as found in case records. These explanations were generally a list of conditions or circumstances in the life situations of the unwed mothers with whom social workers dealt. One commonly accepted description of causes, in 1918, listed these factors: bad home conditions, bad environment, bad companions, feeblemindedness, and sexual suggestibility (Kammerer, 1918). A decade later another study of out-of-wedlock births still stated that the most important causes of out-of-wedlock births were "low standards of behavior" and "bad home conditions" characterized by broken homes, incompetent mothers, drunken fathers, and sexual irregularities, leading to various delinquencies in the children (Barrett, 1929, pp. 25–31). Environmental conditions such as poverty and overcrowding were acknowledged as influential but probably not seen as real causes of pregnancy out of wedlock. Rather, they were thought to intensify bad conditions already existing in the home. The primary causation was considered to be the unwed woman's failure to develop "personal control" over "physiological drives," which in turn led to behavior resulting in pregnancy.

Treatment of the unwed mother early in this century reflected reliance on such a philosophy of causation. Services were based on these principles laid down by the founder of the National Florence Crittenton Mission: (1) Isolation of the unwed girl from the immoral influences of the outside world is an important element in her rehabilitation; (2) the experience of motherhood itself "is often the means of regeneration; hence the mother must be kept with the child *for the influence it will have upon her*" [italics

TABLE 5.1. Births to Unmarried Women

Definition of Adequate Progress: Has the state experienced a smaller increase in the percent of births that were to unmarried women than has the nation as a whole?

	Percentage of Births That Were to Unmarried Mothers				1980–1987 Change		Is State's Progress Adequate?
	1980	Rank	1987	Rank	Percentage	Rank	
United States Total	18.4	—	24.5	—	33.2	—	Yes 22/No 29
Alabama	22.2	41	26.8	38	20.7	7	Yes
Alaska	15.6	24	22.0	26	41.0	30	No
Arizona	18.7	34	27.2	39	45.5	38	No
Arkansas	20.5	38	24.6	33	20.0	6	Yes
California	21.4	40	27.2	39	27.1	17	Yes
Colorado	13.0	11	18.9	12	45.4	37	No
Connecticut	17.9	33	23.5	30	31.3	19	Yes
Delaware	24.2	48	27.7	42	14.5	3	Yes
District of Columbia	56.5	51	59.7	51	5.7	1	Yes
Florida	23.0	43	27.5	41	19.6	5	Yes
Georgia	23.2	45	28.0	43	20.7	7	Yes
Hawaii	17.6	29	21.3	24	21.0	9	Yes
Idaho	7.9	2	13.0	2	64.6	48	No
Illinois	22.5	42	28.1	44	24.9	12	Yes
Indiana	15.5	23	22.0	26	41.9	31	No
Iowa	10.3	5	16.2	6	57.3	46	No
Kansas	12.3	9	17.2	10	39.8	28	No
Kentucky	15.1	22	20.7	18	37.1	26	No
Louisiana	23.4	46	31.9	49	36.3	25	No
Maine	13.9	18	19.8	16	42.4	32	No
Maryland	25.2	49	31.5	48	25.0	13	Yes
Massachusetts	15.7	25	20.9	22	33.1	22	Yes
Michigan	16.2	28	20.4	17	25.9	15	Yes
Minnesota	11.4	7	17.1	9	50.0	41	No
Mississippi	28.0	50	35.1	50	25.4	14	Yes
Missouri	17.6	29	23.7	32	34.7	24	No
Montana	12.5	10	19.4	14	55.2	45	No
Nebraska	11.6	8	16.8	8	44.8	35	No
Nevada	13.5	15	16.4	7	21.5	10	Yes
New Hampshire	11.0	6	14.7	4	33.6	23	No
New Jersey	21.1	39	23.5	30	11.4	2	Yes
New Mexico	16.1	27	29.6	46	83.9	50	No
New York	23.8	47	29.7	47	24.8	11	Yes
North Carolina	19.0	35	24.9	34	31.1	18	Yes
North Dakota	9.2	4	13.9	3	51.1	42	No
Ohio	17.8	32	24.9	34	39.9	29	No
Oklahoma	14.0	20	20.7	18	47.9	39	No
Oregon	14.8	21	22.4	28	51.4	43	No
Pennsylvania	17.7	31	25.3	36	42.9	33	No
Rhode Island	15.7	25	21.8	25	38.9	27	No
South Carolina	23.0	43	29.0	45	26.1	16	Yes
South Dakota	13.4	14	19.4	14	44.8	35	No
Tennessee	19.9	37	26.3	37	32.2	21	Yes
Texas	13.3	13	19.0	13	42.9	33	No
Utah	6.2	1	11.1	1	79.0	49	No
Vermont	13.7	17	18.0	11	31.4	20	Yes
Virginia	19.2	36	22.8	29	18.8	4	Yes
Washington	13.6	16	20.8	21	52.9	44	No
West Virginia	13.1	12	21.1	23	61.1	47	No
Wisconsin	13.9	18	20.7	18	48.9	40	No
Wyoming	8.2	3	15.8	5	92.7	51	No

(*Source:* Children's Defense Fund. [1990]. *Children 1990: A Report Card, Briefing Book, and Action Primer.* Washington, DC: Children's Defense Fund, p. 88.)

added]; and (3) the child born outside of marriage should remain with its mother because it needs the maternal care that "only a mother can give" (Barrett, 1929, pp. 49–50, 182).

By the 1920s the prevailing belief clearly was that unwed mothers should keep and rear their children. A focus on child protection had emerged. The aim of social workers was for the child to receive support and care as nearly as possible like that received by the legitimate child under normal family conditions. Social work treatment programs, therefore, were directed toward removing or compensating for the differences between the two groups of children that were legally or socially imposed.

This focus on the protection of the child was reflected in the resolutions of the 1920 Conferences on Illegitimacy, where the view was expressed that "the rightful status of every child" required a mother's care and a father's support, and that the mother should be aided in such a way as "to restore her standing and enable her to care for her child with decent dignity" (Children's Bureau, 1921, p. 7).

Various influences contributed to this protective concern for the child of unwed parents and the principle that the mother should keep and rear her child:

1. The twentieth century had introduced a period of new attention to children and awareness of their special needs, expressed in legislation, in numerous conferences, and in research studies. It was not surprising that out-of-wedlock children began to receive more attention in their own right, apart from the behaviors and needs of their mothers.

2. In addition to the earlier notion that motherhood was a beneficial and restorative experience for the mother, more had now been learned about the importance of maternal care for the child and the part which the mother-child relationship played in the child's development. It seemed important in new ways for the child to be reared by his or her mother, even though the family was incomplete.

3. Concern had developed over infant mortality rates in this country. One contributing cause of infant deaths was believed to be artificial methods of feeding from unsanitary milk supplies in contrast to the preferred method of breast feeding. If unwed mothers were not separated from their babies, it was assumed, infants would be breast-fed and the death rate for children reduced as a consequence.

4. Adoption practices, which were not well developed in the 1920s, did not provide an alternative solution to the child's need for maternal care. Generally, there was some suspicion of adoption, perhaps relating to the fact that it was not as common then as today and was not regarded particularly as a solution to infertility—the social purpose it later came to serve. In any case, infants who were adopted usually were not out-of-wedlock children, but more often were marital children of large, impoverished families.

All these factors contributed to a conviction that out-of-wedlock children must be protected, that they should be cared for by the mother, and that society was obligated to ensure conditions suitable for child care.

One major approach of the second and third decades of this century was an attempt to give the out-of-wedlock child the needed protection through legislation. Examples of some of the legislation and actions growing out of this period are as follows: (1) Maryland, in 1915, prohibited the separation of infants from their mothers while they were under six months of age unless it was necessitated by the illness of the mother or the child; (2) Milwaukee health departments, under their authority to license child-caring agencies and foster homes, delegated to a voluntary children's agency the responsibility to investigate and approve all requests for placement of infants under six months of age; (3) Minnesota's State Board of Control in 1928 set as a condition for licensing maternity homes and hospitals that the staff require unmarried mothers to remain in the institution and to nurse their infants for at least three months; (4) Newark health department nurses were expected to visit mothers and urge them to breast-feed their babies (Rosenberg & Donohue, 1925; Drury, n.d., pp. 99–104, 190–191).

In addition to these legislative efforts, voluntary agencies who served the individual unwed mother developed certain policies and practices in an attempt to ensure that the children stayed with their mothers. Policies provided generally for an agency system of authoritative supervision of the mother and child. It was reasoned that the child had a stronger chance for a normal family life if agency supervision was provided for "an extended period."

One part of agency supervision was an attempt to secure financial support for the mother. Since the child's right to support from the father was part of the child's "rightful status," and since agency funds to help the mother and child were limited, agencies usually participated actively in efforts to secure paternal support.

Another significant part of agency supervision grew out of the importance attached to breast-feeding the child for its first six months. In order to breast-feed a baby, the mother had to be assured of financial support and a living arrangement that would give her free time to care for her child. One common solution was for the mother to stay in a maternity home with the child for the first three months. But then she had to be helped to secure a protected living situation for herself and her child during the last three months of the nursing period. Lacking a more adequate alternative, unmarried mothers usually were placed with their babies in "good" private family homes, preferably in the country, to give domestic service. This practical solution had been in use since the latter part of the nineteenth century, since it was the only generally available employment that could be counted on to assure the mother an opportunity to nurse her baby.

After the nursing period, agencies usually expected that the mother might seek other suitable employment and a new living arrangement. The most approved arrangement was for the mother to live with her baby in her family's home, or with relatives or friends, or even in a boarding home, so long as the baby was with her. As an alternative, the child might live with the mother's family or board with a foster family until the mother could arrange to give care herself. Adoption was least favored; the best ultimate solution was considered to be the mother's marriage to a man who would accept her child.

In summary, then, until the 1930s, social work literature predominantly focused on the protection of the child based on these premises: Unwed mothers should care for their children in early infancy and should breast-feed them. They should retain permanent responsibility for their rearing. Paternity should be established and the father held to a responsibility for financial support. Agencies should implement protective legislation and carry out a program of authoritative supervision of the mother and child.

The Unwed Parent as Client. Another treatment formulation to be applied to unmarried parent situations was emerging to challenge the near unanimity of opinion that had prevailed in a primary focus on the child. The new, competing approach reflected the changing nature of social casework practice, which increasingly utilized psychoanalytic theories of behavior. It implied a fresh interest in the mother herself as an agency client, a divergence of opinion as to whether she should keep her child, and a decline in the primary intent to protect the child by preserving the mother-child relationship and the mother's continuing care of the child.

As a result, two markedly differing formulations were found in an approach to unwed parenthood and each was endorsed by a distinct group of social workers. The leaders of the previous decades continued to advocate the more authoritative approach of legislation, court service, and individual case "supervision," while agency workers providing casework services began to use an approach based on a philosophy of psychodynamically oriented individualization.

Some social agency staffs were convinced that "the usual lot of the illegitimate child whose mother had kept him is that of a succession of changes from one cheap boarding home to another during the early formative years of his life" and that

> the policy of encouraging the mother to keep the custody of her child during the first months of his life is without social value unless adequate and satisfactory facilities, either public or private, are provided for the mother so that she can actually remain with her child during the nursing period. (Reed, 1934, p. 89)

As a result some social workers began to emphasize that the decision to keep or surrender her child was the mother's, and that they, as representatives of social agencies, must be prepared to accept either outcome. This policy meant that the agency had to have alternative plans of care for the mother to consider for her child. Perhaps it is not surprising that agencies began to respond to an increasing interest in adoption and a demand for infants to meet the requests of would-be adoptive parents.

Various factors probably contributed to the increased demand for adoptable infants during this period, for example, the lower birth rates during the 1930s, the decline in the extended family, and the effects of assistance programs enabling widowed or divorced mothers of dependent children to keep the family together and, consequently, limited the supply of adoptable children. The result was increasing acceptability and desirability of adoption for the out-of-wedlock child.

As adoption became a more acceptable alternative form of care for an out-of-wedlock baby, maternity homes became somewhat less restrictive, perhaps because unmarried mothers were in a better position to resist the requirements and rigid expectations of such a setting, for example, compulsory periods of residence made even longer for those who came destitute and, consequently, were required to stay on to "work out" the expenses of their care.

In addition to the growing belief that the mother should make her own decision about the child, with adoption as an increasingly acceptable solution, another change was reflected in individualized casework practice—an increasing emphasis on secrecy about the pregnancy. While earlier maternity homes had favored isolation of the unmarried mother as a means of furthering her rehabilitation through separation from her former life, this practice had not ensured secrecy about her pregnancy. Indeed, it could not, since the goal was to have her resume life in the community with her child. The newer emphasis on secrecy was to provide anonymity so that the unwed mother would be protected from social censure. Reed was critical of this practice and noted certain disadvantageous effects. It led to an unwillingness on the part of agencies to initiate or even allow the unmarried mother to initiate paternity actions because of the likelihood of publicity. It led some agencies to a policy of regarding the alleged father as of no importance to the situation, or at least to a policy of nonrecognition of the father as a means of "helping the girl to forget a disagreeable experience." It led in some instances to an agency's usurpation of parental duties, as when a young unwed mother was deliberately separated from her own parents to shield her from severe parental blame or from some other manifestation of disturbance in her relationship with her own parents (Reed, 1934, pp. 48–51, 157).

One obstacle to the new philosophy of individualization lay in public opinion and in the opinion of the medical and legal professions, which on the whole endorsed adoption as a general solution to out-of-wedlock births even when it was not in accordance with the unmarried mother's wishes or capabilities. The social work profession, on the other hand, was affected by a legacy of reluctance to separate the mother and child and a fear of the finality of adoption (Ripple, 1953, pp. 104–105). More serious obstacles were contained in the laws and regulations in various states requiring that paternity be established and that the mother keep the child in her care for the early months of its life.

Services to unmarried mothers in the 1930s, then, went on in such a climate of conflicting purposes and philosophy. In 1938, however, the Children's Bureau released a statement that approved a more flexible approach: While breast feeding was advantageous to a child's health, it sometimes had complicating social and emotional effects on the unmarried parenthood situation; and since methods of artificial feeding were now improved, specific case plans should depend on individual evaluation of an unmarried mother's total situation (Children's Bureau, 1938). Within the next few years all states revoked the legislation or regulations that had led to enforced care of the child by the mother.

Clearly, by the end of the 1930s, the mother had emerged as the central client, and some interest was being shown in the father as an individual and as someone in need of service.

The Psychological Nature of Unwed Parenthood.

Social work literature of the 1940s began to reflect a heavy emphasis on the psychological nature of unmarried parenthood. Social factors were seen as unimportant or at least secondary, not only in causation but in treatment formulations as well. Psychiatrists reinforced a growing conviction that unmarried mothers were almost always neurotic and incapable of providing good care for their children. Their problems and motivations were deeply embedded in the powerful emotions of their own early childhood. The best treatment, then, was psychotherapy for the unwed woman and adoption for her child.

This dual theme of unmarried parenthood as a psychological disorder and the desirability of adoption appeared even more strongly during the 1950s. The literature is replete with references to the serious emotional maladjustment of the unmarried mother; the pregnancy as a result of psychic pressures with which she cannot deal, comparable to neurotic symptoms and delinquent behavior; and giving up the baby as a positive solution, with the unmarried mother who has the poorest potential for becoming a happy individual being the one most apt to keep the infant. With such agreement on the psychological pathology of the unmarried mother and the desirability of adoption, agencies acquired a conviction that not only should the baby be placed for adoption, but also the earlier the decision was made, the better for all concerned. It was believed that the unwed client, after the birth of the baby, wished to dissociate herself from the agency that had been concerned with her pregnancy. And in any case most agencies lacked the resources to continue service very long after delivery.

Doubts about a Unidimensional Causation.

For some time social workers involved in work with unmarried mothers relied largely on a psychological explanation of out-of-wedlock pregnancy. The social work profession was heavily committed already to an application of psychoanalytic principles in its casework method and thus looked less at social forces that might be contributing to out-of-wedlock pregnancy. However, as Perlman pointed out, an element of circular thinking was operating. Those individuals who came to social agencies because of out-of-wedlock pregnancy represented a particular group, those who had no close sources of concrete help and emotional support. It was not surprising, then, that some of them had psychological problems, perhaps exacerbated by anger, faultfinding, and disappointment in the parent-daughter relationship that the very crisis of unwanted pregnancy had called forth. It was these individuals who were most often selected for referral to a psychiatrist for consultation. This selective emphasis in turn reinforced psychiatric interest in the problem and influenced social work literature (Perlman, 1964, p. 291).

Bernstein called attention to the limited applicability of the theory and the fact that the emphasis on a single point of view was restricting the kinds of treatment offered. She claimed that social workers had not considered the influence of cultural factors sufficiently and urged that the profession be ready to accept multiple theories of causation and to give up the stereotyped image of the unmarried mother to which social workers had uncritically committed themselves. "We need to think in terms of hypotheses to be truly tested rather than closed systems of explanation for which we are impelled to find substantiating evidence" (Bernstein, 1960).

Others suggested that the conviction about the value of adoption was carried too far, often injecting bias into the approach to an individual unwed mother (Leyendecker, 1958). Some concern was expressed about possible harm to new mothers who surrendered their infants without any sense of fulfillment in the maternal role (Bye, 1959). Particularly indefensible and contradictory, some stated, was agency readiness to help unmarried mothers surrender normal infants while reserving the right to hold them responsible for the care of their children should they prove unadoptable because of some physical or mental defect (Leyendecker, 1958). Others called attention to an inconsistency in observance of a child's and mother's rights when paternity proceedings were instituted if the child was being kept by the mother, but not if adoption was being planned.

Doubts became stronger. Bernstein observed the limited social work involvement with most unwed mothers, particularly among the voluntary agencies, which were serving largely only one sample of the unwed mother population (Bernstein, 1963). The absence of service to large numbers of unwed mothers was related to the racial and socioeconomic characteristics of the unserved groups. Many voluntary child-placing agencies had tended to define their function in terms of adoption, and maternity homes increasingly had given priority to service for unwed clients who planned to relinquish their babies for adoption. Since the decision to keep a child is related to low socioeconomic (and thereby racial) factors, black and other nonwhite unwed mothers received less than their share of community services.

Shapiro, in her study of social distance factors as they affect service to unwed parents, traced over time a pattern of ambivalence when social workers attempted to come to terms with the racial component of the problem of out-of-wedlock pregnancy (Shapiro, 1966, pp. 28–35). For example, Reed found that black families were more likely to keep a child with its mother and that social workers believed the black unmarried mother was less likely to wish to surrender her child because of her "natural affection," fewer social pressures, and the presence of relatives who were likely to be willing to help her. At the same time social workers acknowledged that

> facilities existing for the care of the dependent Negro child are far less adequate than the same facilities for the dependent white child, and that, even if the Negro unmarried mother should wish to surrender her child, she would have more difficulty in doing so. (Reed, 1934)

Most social workers continued to assume that black children of unwed parents were accepted in a matter-of-fact way, that they were not faced with social ostracism, and that the black community's readiness to care for its children should be seen as a positive innate characteristic rather than as a response to a lack of social services. Some social workers questioned these broad generalizations, however. Davis, at the United States Children's Bureau, warned that the common assumption that blacks accept unwed pregnancies leads to the premise that no action needs to be taken in behalf of black children (Davis, 1948).

Limited research on this question does not appear to substantiate the existence of a subculture in this country that approves of out-of-wedlock birth or finds it an easily acceptable pattern of family life. For example, in a study of child-rearing practices among low-income families, Lewis found little support for the assertion that there was a distinct population of unmarried mothers or a cult of unwed motherhood in a particular population, or that unwed mothers preferred to be unwed, or that low-income groups, newcomers, and certain ethnic minorities were not troubled by out-of-wedlock births. "In general," Lewis concluded, "value is attached to legitimate birth, although in a given situation, this value may be superseded by another important value, or its realization may be thwarted by practical considerations" (Lewis, 1961, p. 86).

Other studies bore out the findings that most unmarried mothers in low-income groups did not condone having children outside of marriage. Such a pattern of family life was not accepted as normal by the female heads of the families—they recognized their handicaps in rearing children and wanted a more stable pattern of family life (Osili & Parker, 1957; Greenleigh, 1960; Herzog, 1964; McCabe et al., 1965; Sauber & Rubinstein, 1965; Crumidy & Jacobziner, 1966; Bernard, 1966; Shapiro, 1967).

However, in the early decades of this century the social work profession had only superficial contact with these groups of unwed families. Such a situation reinforced a discriminatory pattern of agency services.

TEENAGE PARENTING

In the 1970s and continuing into the 1980s the old concern about unwed mothers was expanded into an explosive controversy about teenage sexuality and teenage parenting. The focus of services and research was shifted to adolescent childbearing. As parenting by teenagers became more publicly visible, its growth in numbers, its causal patterns, the conditions associated with it, and its consequences became a matter of keen concern in America.

Incidence

It has come to be generally acknowledged that sexual activity and pregnancy among adolescents are not confined to any one racial, ethnic, or social group. Instead, teenage parents are found in all parts of the country, rural and urban, and among families of all races, religious denominations, and socioeconomic groups. Because of the young age of these new parents and their general unreadiness for the responsibility of parenthood, public concern has greatly heightened.

Birth rates to teenage women have fluctuated over the past forty years, and the causes of the fluctuations are not completely understood. Births to teenagers increased steadily from 1950 to 1970; in the peak year 1970, some 656,000 children of teenage mothers were born. Numbers then declined through the mid-1980s; in 1985, only 477,700 infants were born to teenagers (Children's Defense Fund, 1988). A recent study by the National Center for Health Statistics indicates that births to teenage mothers began to increase again in the late 1980s. The birth rate among fifteen-, sixteen-, and seventeen-year-olds showed the sharpest rise, with an increase of 10 percent from 1986 to 1988. About one in thirty women between fifteen and seventeen had a baby in 1988, giving birth to a total of 168,000 infants. This was the highest number in a decade but still below the 230,000 recorded in 1972, the year before the U.S. Supreme Court overturned state laws against abortion (Barringer, 1990).

Factors affecting these trends are complex and contradictory. Premarital sexual activity has increased among teenagers, rising sharply during the 1970s and tapering off in the 1980s, when about 42 percent of teenage women were sexually active. This increase in sexual activity occurred concurrently with a decline in teenage births; these seemingly contradictory trends are explained by teenagers' increased use of contraceptives and abortion. Estimates are that, if teenagers had maintained the relatively low rates of contraceptive use and abortion that they had in the early 1970s, there would have been 200,000 more births in 1984 than actually occurred (Children's Defense Fund, 1988c). The upturn in teenage birth rates in the late 1980s may be caused by teenagers' perception that abortions were becoming harder to obtain, though the link between changes in state abortion laws and birth rates is not clear (Barringer, 1990).

From the early 1970s to the mid-1980s, when the number of teenage births declined, the percentage of those births that occurred to unmarried mothers increased (see Figure 5.2). In 1970, only 31 percent of teenage mothers were unmarried; by 1985 that figure had increased to 59 percent; and, by 1988, about two-thirds of teenagers giving birth in that year were unmarried (Barringer, 1990).

Clearly, marriage rates among pregnant teenagers have been declining faster than teenage birth rates. In 1970, about 12 percent of teenage girls and 4 percent of teenage boys were married. By 1984, the comparable figures were 7 percent for adolescent girls and 2 percent for teenage boys. Today's teenagers are less likely than those in earlier years to abstain from sexual intercourse until marriage. Once pregnant, they are less likely than earlier cohorts to marry. The day of the forced marriage to maintain a conventional status appears to be almost over (Children's Defense Fund, 1988c).

From a review of social and psychological research about adolescent childbearing, Chilman (1980) noted that most of the enormous increase in systematic study on the subject during the 1970s and 1980s was an outgrowth of a highly publicized belief that the nation was confronted with a dangerous "epidemic" of teenage pregnancies. The notion of an epidemic overlooked the declining (though still high) birth rate for adolescent teenagers. Chilman found positive and negative outcomes flowing from concern about a teenage pregnancy epidemic. Positively, it had increased public awareness and acceptance of the need for contraceptive services and education about sexuality and had stimulated federal funds for such services and for research. Negatively, however, the "cri-

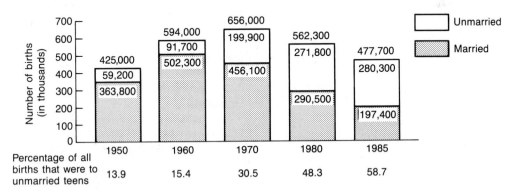

- After peaking in 1970, the number of births to teens has declined steadily. But the proportion of teen births that were to unmarried teens has been growing.
- In 1960, 15.4 percent of all teen births were to unmarried teens. By 1970, the proportion had doubled. By 1985, it had almost doubled again—58.7 percent of teen births were to unmarried teens. The proportion crossed the 50 percent mark in 1982.

Figure 5.2. Births to Teens Younger Than Twenty by Marital Status, United States, 1950–1985. (*Source:* National Center for Health Statistics. [1988c, Jan./March]. *Teenage Pregnancy: An Advocate's Guide to the Numbers.* Washington, DC: Children's Defense Fund, p. 11. [Calculations by the Children's Defense Fund.])

sis'' approach was sexist in its focus on the prob-
lem-laden, sexually active female; it clouded the
realities of birthrate statistics; and it ''directed
attention away from the more fundamental social and economic problems that warped the
lives of so many teenagers during the 1970s, especially if they came from minority group, low-
income backgrounds'' (Chilman, 1980).

---

*Why did the dominant society fail to recognize
the seriousness of the problem of unmarried
teenage parenthood until its ''own'' were affected by the situation? (Gould, 1991)*

Associated Conditions and Causes

One of the methodological limitations of much
of the research on teenage parenting is that con-
founding variables are often confused with
causes of adolescent childbearing. Low achievement at school, race, social class, intrafamilial
relationships, and other conditions that were
part of the characteristics or environment of
these young people prior to becoming pregnant
may be moderately or highly correlated with
teenage pregnancy, but are not necessarily
''causes'' of it (Abrahamse et al., 1988). Attempts to identify the characteristics of individuals who are most likely to become pregnant
during their teenage years have demonstrated
the futility of searching for a unique psychological profile common to most or all pregnant adolescents, or a single explanation such as peer
group pressure or ignorance about the use of
contraception (Chilman, 1980). Nevertheless,
from her review of relevant research, Phipps-
Yonas concluded that ''if we consider all of the
points at which a choice is made along the path
that leads to teenage motherhood, it is possible
to build the case that it is the least appropriate
candidate for that role who moves forward at
each conjunction'' (Phipps-Yonas, 1980).

In an intensive five-year longitudinal study
of unplanned parenthood among teenagers,
Furstenberg traced the life events of pregnant
adolescents who came to an out-patient clinic of
Sinai Hospital in Baltimore for prenatal care
(Furstenberg, 1976). The sample was low-income, largely black, under eighteen years of
age, and pregnant for the first time. During the
five years of the study, Furstenberg held interviews with 421 girls during their pregnancies and
again at one, three, and five years after delivery.
He also interviewed 350 of the prospective
grandmothers who were visited in their own
homes. A contrast sample of 361 former classmates who had similar backgrounds to those of
the pregnant teenagers but who had not become
pregnant was also studied. In addition, an effort
was made to interview as many of the adolescent
fathers as could be located (35 percent of them).
Furstenberg's findings about what had led these
unmarried teenagers to become pregnant contrasted with the old assumption that such pregnancies occur because the girl is motivated consciously or unconsciously to have a baby.
Instead the evidence led him to conclude that
most of the teenagers studied did not set out to
have a child out of marriage. They did not engage in sexual intercourse for that purpose.
They were not brought into motherhood by
some prior commitment to it. Most had drifted
into it. How or why had this drift occurred?

These girls had experienced considerable
pressure to engage in sexual relations once they
began dating. Even though some had misgiv-
ings, peer influence tended to neutralize restrictive norms. In addition, parents had tacitly
encouraged them to conceal their sexual activity; parents had ignored indications that their
daughters were sexually active, perhaps because
they did not know how to act effectively against
it. In any case, a subtle directive for concealment had left the girls without the controls that
might otherwise have been exercised by the family. One result was that contraception was usually left up to the male and consistent use of
birth control was rare. The pregnancy was generally unwelcome, but the stage had been set for

most of the adolescents and the parents to accommodate themselves to the impending birth. In this light, Furstenberg noted, one can understand why teenagers often claim that pregnancy is something that "just happens" even though they insist they did not want to have a child (Furstenberg, 1976, pp. 37–59).

In further efforts to understand the causes of teenage pregnancy and childbirth, researchers have examined behaviors and conditions that appear to be associated with participation in nonmarital sexual intercourse, use of contraception, and abortion. Participation in nonmarital intercourse among adolescent girls has been found to be correlated with such *social situational factors* as low level of religiousness, norms favoring equality between the sexes, permissive sexual norms in the larger society, racism and poverty, migration from rural to urban areas, lower social class, and single-parent low-income families. *Psychological variables* have included desire for affection, low educational goals and achievement, deviant attitudes, strained parent-child relationships, and little parent-child communication. For male adolescents, many of the same relationships appeared, except that peer group pressure was more salient, as were the use of drugs and alcohol, aggression, and high levels of activity (Chilman, 1980).

Associated with failure of teenagers to use contraception or to use it effectively were such *demographic variables* as lower social class, minority group membership, nonattendance at college, and fundamentalist Protestant affiliation. *Situational variables* included not being in a consistent, committed relationship, not having experienced a pregnancy, having intercourse sporadically and without prior plan, not having contraception available when needed, and not having access to contraception services that could be obtained without parental consent. *Psychological variables* included desire for pregnancy, stemming from high fertility values; ignorance of pregnancy risks; fatalistic attitudes; powerlessness; passive dependency; traditional female-role attitudes; low ego strength; and risk-taking, pleasure-oriented attitudes (Chilman, 1980).

In summarizing these variables, Chilman indicated that socioeconomic status, race, and ethnicity have a greater importance than such a summary can show. "Research reveals that poverty status often breeds attitudes of fatalism, powerlessness, alienation, a sense of personal incompetence and hopelessness in respect to striving for high educational and occupational goals. This is especially apt to be true when racism combines with poverty to reduce one's life chances" (Chilman, 1980, p. 797).

A limited number of studies on characteristics of adolescents and use of abortion found that those who chose abortion tended to come from intact, non-Catholic, and nonwelfare families. They were doing well in school before the pregnancy, had relatively high educational goals, were self-confident, and came from white-collar or skilled-working-class families. Later data, however, also showed increased use of abortion by those poor enough to be eligible for Medicaid (Chilman, 1980).

This array of variables associated with participation in sexual relations, use of contraception, and abortion again points to the fact that no single explanation of teenage parenting is sufficient. More needs to be known about how and why different variables combine into patterns of behavior and conditions that "cause" a particular adolescent to become pregnant and to give birth.

A frequently heard explanation for adolescent childbearing is that some girls become pregnant in order to receive Aid to Families with Dependent Children. Several competent studies, one using New York data and others based on national data, have concluded that women do not give birth in order to be eligible for welfare. Once pregnant, however, the availability of financial assistance tends to increase the alternatives for decision making, because it lessens the pressure to marry, have an abortion, or use adoption (Chilman, 1980; Allen & Pittman, 1986).

Race and Ethnicity.   White teenagers account for the majority (68%) of births to adolescents. However, black and Hispanic teenagers are more likely than white teenagers to become parents. In 1985, black teens accounted for 15 percent of the population of adolescents in the United States, but 29 percent of births to teens; Hispanic teens accounted for 9 percent of the population, but 13 percent of teen births. The disproportionate number of minority teen births is not primarily caused by racial differences in rates of premarital sexual activity, but is related to differences in poverty rates, education, employment and earnings potential, and differences in contraceptive use (Children's Defense Fund, 1988c). Distinctive family structures and sociocultural factors also may be associated with black teenage pregnancy (Franklin, 1988).

Black teen births are of special concern to the black community and other advocates of black children because a large number occur to mothers who are not married (90%) and because nearly half (45%) occur to adolescents in the younger end of the age spectrum, age seventeen or younger. These factors exacerbate the health, economic, social, and educational consequences of teenage pregnancy (Randolph & Gesche, 1986). In 1985, over one birth in every five to a black woman was to an adolescent (Children's Defense Fund, 1988).

The high rate of births to black teens is a problem partly because of other changes also taking place in black families. Ladner (1985) points out that the black grandmother traditionally assumed some of the responsibility for the care of nonmarital grandchildren. However, the declining age of black unmarried mothers has resulted in a generation of very young black grandmothers, who may understandably prefer to take advantage of the opportunities for education and employment now available to them rather than staying home with the grandchil-

dren. The consequence of the changing role of grandparents is that teenage mothers "are growing up more isolated than any generation before them. . . . Without the support of their parents, without the continued nurturance teenage mothers received from their own mothers in the past, as they nurtured their babies, these girls today are physically isolated and emotionally deprived of the continued socialization they so desperately need" (Ladner, 1985, p. 19).

Among Hispanics, the profile of teenage parenthood varies according to subgroup. About 30 percent of all births among Puerto Ricans are to women under age twenty. A very high proportion, 74 percent, of Puerto Rican teenage mothers in the United States are unmarried (Children's Defense Fund, 1988). Reliable information on abortion rates and contraceptive use among this group is lacking. Studies suggest that the attitude of the adolescent's own mother is critical, as her acceptance or rejection of the forthcoming child may strongly influence her daughter's decision to abort or carry to term (Ortiz & Vazquez-Nuttall, 1987).

In Puerto Rico, the cultural norm is for teen pregnancies to lead quickly to marriage, and this norm survives among many who have emigrated to the mainland. For these families, the pregnancy of an unwed daughter is apt to create a crisis. It is not accurate to assume that the high rate of unwed parenthood among Puerto Ricans in the United States reflects acceptance of this life style (Gutierrez, 1987).

As with Puerto Ricans, among Mexican-Americans about 30 percent of all births occur to women under twenty. However, over half of these teenage mothers are married. Cuban and South and Central American groups have smaller proportions of births to unmarried teenage mothers than other Hispanic groups or whites (Children's Defense Fund, 1988).

Consequences

In considering the consequences of teenage parenting, it must be kept in mind that underlying factors that were present in the lives of these new parents prior to pregnancy and childbirth may also be present afterwards. Thus behavior and conditions, such as the variables discussed above as correlates of becoming pregnant and giving birth, may later be observed and assumed to be outcomes of teenage parenting, instead of simply being later manifestations of patterns present or in formation much earlier. Nevertheless, the teenager who becomes a parent is vulnerable to a range of new high-risk factors, risks to herself and to her infant as well.

Health. Negative effects on the health of the teenager who bears children have received considerable research attention. Early studies reported a high rate of obstetrical complications of all types for girls eighteen years of age or younger. More recent work has raised doubts as to the extent to which rates of childbirth complications among adolescents can be attributed to age and gynecological immaturity per se. Girls younger than fifteen do tend to have more obstetrical difficulties that are not explained by factors other than physiological and anatomical immaturity. But for most adolescent childbearers, negative health consequences more clearly reflect poor nutrition, lack of health care prior to pregnancy, and inadequate prenatal care—factors more associated with socioeconomic status than age per se. The negative health consequences found in earlier studies tend to disappear when quality medical care and nutrition are made available, a finding that argues strongly for free or low-cost health services for adolescents (Chilman, 1980; Phipps-Yonas, 1980).

Many pregnant teenagers do not have access to prenatal care early and regularly enough for optimal protection of their own health and that of their unborn infant. Even when care is available, teenagers often are reluctant to seek it out and use it consistently. Many of the tasks of pregnancy are burdensome to adolescents, leading them to ignore critical elements of care. The need to maintain a consistent nutritious diet affords a significant example. Lack of timely

prenatal care is a primary factor in maternal complications of birth, such as prematurity, toxemia, hypertension, and syphilis. The significant correlation between lack of adequate prenatal care and prematurity is extended as well to infant death rates. Many of today's pregnant teenagers have experienced lifelong deprivation in their environment, which has meant poor nutrition, poor childhood and adolescent health care, and lack of education about health care and pregnancy. These deficits in the environment are potent influences in determining the degree of health risk and the outcomes of teenage pregnancy.

Education. Pregnant teenagers face another tangible risk: the increased likelihood that their education will be interrupted or terminated. The loss of the student role, essential educational experience, and the ability to retain and realize aspirations is one of the critical ways in which pregnant teenagers are at greater risk than are their classmates who do not become pregnant.

Often the pregnant schoolgirl who drops out was already a marginal student (Furstenberg, 1976). Nevertheless, motivated and average-achieving students have been enabled to continue in school during and after their pregnancies if they have the support of school personnel and educational program adaptations. To focus exclusively on earlier marginality places disproportionate responsibility on the student and overlooks the responsibility of the school system to find ways to help these at-risk adolescents to avoid dropping out. Despite court rulings that pregnant school-age girls are entitled to continue their education, they still constitute a group that schools exclude from, or unofficially discourage from continuing in, educational programs by means of subtle messages from teachers and administrators. Most often termination of education comes about without counseling or referral for help with problems or a plan for the resumption of education (Children's Defense Fund, 1974). This situation contrasts with that of young fathers of unborn children, who are rarely excluded from educational programs as a result of their actions. Such practices ignore the vital importance of education for these young women and the stake society has in seeing that they continue to learn and move toward more adequate adult functioning.

A teenage mother, excluded from school, is apt to be denied access to all adult roles. Particularly because she is young and immature, she may be urged to choose abortion or give up the baby for adoption without attention to a plan for her own future. If she keeps the baby, her own mother may take on the maternal responsibilities for its care, with the result that the teenage mother is cast into a role more like that of a sibling to her child. Denied a maternal role and a student role as well, she finds herself too young or unskilled for stable employment. Fortunately, there are an increasing number of notable exceptions among school systems, where programs have been installed to help the pregnant student continue her education (Pittman et al., 1989).

Marriage and Economic Disadvantage. Early marriage has been shown to be closely associated with leaving school. The pregnant schoolgirl who does not marry and continues to live with her parents, who provide help with child care and other support, has a far better chance of continuing her schooling and avoiding dependence on public assistance (Chilman, 1980; Phipps-Yonas, 1980; Furstenberg, 1976). The husbands of teenage mothers are also likely to have less education and occupational preparation than is true for their classmates who avoided childbirth. Thus the new family unit begins with both parents lacking sufficient formal education to achieve a stable position in the labor market. In such situations the new family is at risk of economic disadvantage or dependence from the time the child is born (Alan Guttmacher Institute, 1981).

Childbearing Pattern and Child Maltreatment. Research findings tell us that between 17 percent

and 47 percent of teens who become pregnant experience an additional pregnancy during the teen years. Teenage mothers who have more children over a short period of time are likely to be younger and to be doing less well in school than those who do not have additional children (Balassone, 1988).

Given the risks that accompany the birth of a first child to a teenager, it seems reasonable to expect that negative outcomes would be intensified when successive pregnancies come swiftly. In a comparison of 118 AFDC mothers who had abused or neglected their children with 281 mothers on AFDC with no history of child maltreatment, Zuravin (1988) found that, among these poor, single mothers, large family size was related to maltreatment. The researcher postulates that for many of the families, it was the increased stress brought about by trying to manage a large family on a very limited income that precipitated the abuse or neglect. The study points out the importance of helping young, low-income teenage mothers avoid closely spaced, subsequent pregnancies.

Marital Disruption. Teenage marriages are at least twice as likely to end in divorce or permanent separation than are marriages postponed until the partners are in their twenties. This is true for early marriages with or without adolescent pregnancy. However, even though early marriage itself appears to be the key variable in future marital disruption, research has suggested that early childbearing also may be associated with later marital trouble (Alan Guttmacher Institute, 1981; Chilman, 1980). Certainly, early marriage occasioned by pregnancy provides an unstable beginning and suggests that without a union based on a firm commitment before the pregnancy, the chance for a lasting marriage is at best uncertain.

As a result of the pattern of divorce and separation, the Guttmacher Institute estimated that "by age eight, 70 percent of children firstborn to women at age 17 or younger have spent part of their childhood in a single-parent household. This compared to 41 percent of the children first-born to women at age 18–19, and about 25 percent of children first-born to women in their 20s.'' Moreover, young mothers are far less likely to receive financial help from absent fathers (Alan Guttmacher Institute, 1981; Danziger & Nichols-Casebolt, 1987–1988).

Developmental Risks to the Children of Teenagers. Concern is expressed frequently about the developmental dangers to children of very young mothers. In a follow-up investigation Oppel and Royston studied eighty-six mothers who had given birth before the age of eighteen and the same number of mothers who had given birth at eighteen years of age or older. Each young mother was matched with an older mother by socioeconomic status, race, birth weight of the child, and number of previous live births. Comparisons were made on nurturing behavior, family composition, and physical, social, and psychological characteristics of their children from birth to ten years of age.

The findings supported the view that the youth of adolescent mothers contributed to less adequate nurture of children and to deficits in their physical, social, and psychological development. Although all the children in the study had been released to the mother from the hospital following delivery, the younger mothers were less likely to remain with their child, and their children were at greater risk of being reared by persons other than their own parents. The younger mothers tended to be less anxious than the older ones and to believe that their young children should be allowed to act independently. They were less emotionally and behaviorally involved with their young children. In turn, the children of the younger mothers were more likely to be outgoing than were the children of the older mothers, as well as being more distractable and more prone to acting out difficulties. They were also more likely to be underweight and shorter than the children of the older mothers, to be at a lower level in reading, and to have a lower IQ. Because of the matched-pair method used in the research, it was unlikely that these differences were found because of differences such as race or socioeconomic status (Oppel & Royston, 1971).

Chilman (1980) summarized six studies carried out between 1970 and 1980 that showed correlations between adolescent childbearing and developmental outcomes of the resulting children. Significantly lower scores in *cognitive development,* compared with other children, were found among children of teenage mothers. However, the differences were lessened in studies that controlled for adverse effects of poverty, racism, and family headship. Sons appeared to be more adversely affected than daughters. Another adult in the home appeared to reduce adverse cognitive development.

A statistically significant proportion of the children of teenagers were rated as having behavioral problems. Again this was more likely among sons. A larger proportion of children of adolescent mothers, compared with other children, were found to be slow in *overall development,* with boys again being particularly affected.

Differences were found in *educational achievement.* By age seven, children of teenage mothers were more likely to have repeated a grade in school. Boys had lower reading scores and were rated in larger proportions as having learning disabilities. School adjustment problems of the children of teenage mothers were more likely to increase, with more serious behavior and school problems being apparent by adolescence.

With respect to family structure, a slight tendency was found for the children, when they became teenagers, to repeat the parental pattern of early childbearing, a finding that held even when the effects of racism, poverty, and family headship were statistically controlled (Chilman, 1980).

In his Baltimore study, Furstenberg found that half of the mothers of the pregnant teenagers had given birth before age eighteen, and one-fourth of them had borne a child outside of marriage. In reflecting upon this finding, Bolton observed:

> This modeling effect, when combined with the restrictions in occupational and educational aspirations which often accompany the adolescent pregnancy, may convince the lower socioeconomic status adolescents that an inescapable life pattern has been established for them by pregnancy. This acceptance of what life has dealt them has been cited as a major reason behind the repetition of the adolescent pregnancy cycle across generations of lower socioeconomic status families. This is a cycle that is more easily entered by the poor adolescent and one which is much more difficult for that adolescent to escape. (Furstenberg, 1976; Bolton, 1980)

The Teenage Mother and Her Family. Only limited research has focused on teenage parenting within the context of the adolescent mother's family of origin. Yet it is important to learn how the family serves the adolescent when pregnancy is acknowledged and how her parents, siblings, and other close relatives are affected. Furstenberg recognized the importance of such research, given the family's important role as sexual socializer, its part in decision making about actions to be taken relative to the pregnancy, and the significant role the family often plays in child care. Using a secondary analysis based on his longitudinal Baltimore study, a study of welfare mothers and working mothers in Camden, New Jersey, and a limited number of case studies from the Child Guidance Clinic of Philadelphia, he examined the "burdens and benefits" of the impact of early childbearing on the family (Furstenberg, 1980).

Findings showed clearly that help from family members had brought benefits both to the adolescent mother and to her child, at least in the short run. For the young mothers in the investigations, the family had been "the most significant refuge for the adolescent childbearers" at the time immediately following birth, as well as, for some, a later refuge from failed marriages (Fustenberg, 1980). Remaining with relatives, particularly in a couple-headed household as against a female-headed household, offered the young mother a better chance to remain in school and more economic resources, which in turn either enabled the grandmother to stay at home and provide child care or enabled the family to purchase day care. Female-headed households, in contrast, had smaller quarters and were more likely to be on welfare, or at least in very strained economic resources, which acted as incentives for the adolescent mother to move out.

Staying with the family facilitated a division of labor in child care through collaborative arrangements that provided care for the infant and at the same time protected the young mother from the full impact of premature parental responsibilities. Thus, as Furstenberg stated it, such families served as a system of apprenticeship to early childbearers (Furstenberg, 1980).

Major changes in a family system require a realignment among its members. A major task for members of the household was to decide just how to integrate the child into the family as a family member, and whether to incorporate the father of the child into the family system. Fathers who wanted access to their children were not always accorded that right, and sometimes the adolescent mother was burdened with the necessity of dealing with the competing interests of the father and the grandparents. The adolescent mother often found herself in the position of requiring continued mothering at the same time as she tried to function as a mother herself. Sometimes the adolescent found herself accorded new respect for her status as a mother and encountered expectations that she behave maturely.

Other research has also found that the role changes and realignments of subsystems within the family, occasioned by the birth of a child, can be experienced by the teenage mother and other family members as both stressful and very helpful at the same time (de Anda & Becerra, 1984; Nathanson et al., 1986; Thompson, 1986).

Support from the child's father, in the form of visits, financial contributions, and help with the child's daily care, can significantly contribute to the psychological well-being of the mother (Martin & Baenan, 1987). For a young mother particularly, the positive involvement of a male partner "fulfills the need for connectedness which affirms one's identity, provides a sense of security, and communicates attachment" (Thompson, 1986).

Adolescent Fathers

In the consideration of teenage parenting, the father, for the most part, has been ignored or merely singled out for blame and generally has been treated with insufficient regard for his rights and duties in relation to the mother and their child. When he has been included in planning for the mother's care or in decisions about the future care of the child, it has been chiefly for purposes of securing financial support or establishing paternity legally in order to force responsibility upon him. It is frequently assumed that he will escape his obligations if he can and that the mother is a victim of his aggressive and irresponsible sexual exploitation. Until recently, there has been little acknowledgement of the possibility that he may want to fulfill his responsibilities when his sexual activity results in the conception of a life, or that he may face problems in connection with the pregnancy with which he needs help. Nor has there been much recognition of the significant fact that an out-of-wedlock child has rights and needs in relation to both of its parents.

Even with indication in the literature of increasing interest in the father as a partner in teenage parenting, the father's own needs, potentials, and problems in relation to the child and the adolescent mother remain largely unknown and of less concern generally than those of the mother. Parke and coworkers (1980) attribute the general neglect of the father on the part of social scientists and professionals to a variety of factors. They cite theories of infant development that emphasize the primacy of the mother-infant relationship, false notions about the "biological preparedness" of mothers, and a concomitant assumption that the father's role is of little importance in infancy and early childhood. These attitudes toward the male parenting role generally are particularly detrimental in relation to adolescent parenting. They are intensified by the persistent sexist notion that problems of childbearing and child rearing belong to women, and that the male partner in teenage pregnancy is at best exploitive with nothing to contribute to the mother and child.

Compared to the information available on teenage mothers, very little is known about young fathers. Fewer adolescent boys than girls become parents, since teenage females tend to be about two years younger than their male partners. Among fathers of children born to teenage mothers, perhaps as few as 30 percent are under twenty years of age (Adams & Pittman, 1988; Robinson, 1988).

---

*Our nation cannot reduce teen pregnancy unless we can find ways to get young males to do their part in preventing this problem. ". . . Most guys [said a teenage boy] the way they show they're a man is by getting over—having sex. You want to be like the rest of the guys. . . . My basic thing was getting over, not worrying about birth control—pills, condoms, nothing like that." (*CDF Reports, 1988, p. 1)*

Recent research highlights some of the sexual attitudes and behaviors of adolescent males that may contribute to the high rate of nonmarital births to teenage parents. Studies suggest that, in comparison to girls, teenage boys initiate sexual intercourse at a younger age, rank sex as a higher priority, are less likely to require commitment from a partner before engaging in sexual activity, and are more likely to feel proud of themselves for having lost their virginity (Pittman & Adams, 1988).

Unfortunately, this higher rate of sexual interest and activity is not matched with competency in contraceptive use. Boys tend to use contraceptives less than girls, partly because boys tend to start intercourse at a younger age and are more likely to have sex without a committed relationship, factors that are associated with lower use of contraceptives. Boys tend to know less about pregnancy risk and contraceptives than girls and, in particular, often are misinformed about condoms or do not know how to use them. Girls, on the other hand, often have more information about contraceptives and more interest in preventing pregnancy, but embarrassment at appearing knowledgeable about sex prohibits them from acting on their information. Girls still conform to the double standard that condemns females for appearing sexually experienced (Pittman & Adams, 1988).

Young, unmarried fathers often have characteristics that make it difficult for them to fulfill their paternal role responsibly. In comparison to all young men, those who are unmarried fathers tend to have less education, and are more likely to have dropped out of high school. They more frequently have been involved in illegal activity, been suspended from school, and have exhibited other problem behaviors. They are more likely to be unemployed and, if working, to be in low-paying jobs. Many live with extended family members, perhaps because of their reduced financial circumstances (Adams & Pittman, 1988).

Fathers indicate a willingness to accept responsibility for their children in a number of ways. Marriage, the traditional way in which a long-term commitment is expressed, has declined among teenage parents during the past fifteen years. About 66 percent of teenage mothers do marry within a year of their child's birth, however, which suggests that a substantial number of young people are willing to express parental responsibility in this way. Fathers may also express an intention to fulfill the parental role by acknowledging paternity and paying child support. Information is lacking on the numbers of young mothers who establish paternity or receive legally mandated support, but it is likely that most do not. An unknown number of young fathers acknowledge paternity informally, by letting their relationship to the mother and child be known in the community and perhaps by paying support. This may be a common pattern in minority and rural communities (Adams & Pittman, 1988).

Substantial numbers of teenage mothers continue to see the fathers of their children on a regular basis. Some fathers who see the mother also visit the child. Some who have been isolated from the child eventually establish a common living arrangement and a satisfactory father-child relationship. These paternal assumptions of responsibility, signifying some degree of support and stable relationship with the mother and child, are not found in the majority of teenage parenting situations that have been studied. However, the small but significant element of paternal involvement has tended to be either ignored or discounted in the literature on teenage parenting (Furstenberg, 1976; Lorenzi et al., 1977; Nettleton & Cline, 1975).

The Decision to Parent or to Choose Adoption

Adolescent single mothers today are deciding to keep their babies far more often than was true before the great increase in teenage sexual activity and childbirth. In 1982, only 5 percent of teenage mothers released their children for adoption, a percentage that had not changed substantially since the mid-1970s (Bachrach, 1986). This development has sharply reduced the number of infants available to adults who wish to adopt and has heightened the concern within the community about teenage parenting. Social agencies are pressed to find explanations of the causes of this significant shift away from adoption.

In the mid-1970s, Grow (1979) studied the characteristics of mothers who kept their babies and those who chose adoption. The study focused on factors that in earlier studies had distinguished the two groups. The subjects were white unwed women having their first birth and were between fourteen and twenty-four years of age at the time of delivery. Of the 210 mothers in the study, 182 kept their children; the other 28 chose adoption. The latter were interviewed in their homes about a month after the child's birth. Follow-up interviews were held three years later. The study found some consistencies and some differences when contrasted with earlier findings.

> Consistent with earlier findings, more of the keeping than surrendering mothers were from parental homes broken by divorce or separation, were more often nonstudents, had less education, had sought help earlier, had known the putative father longer and were more likely to have maintained contact with him. Unlike earlier reported findings, the keeping mothers were younger than their counterparts and were more likely to have lived with parents or relatives during pregnancy. (Grow, 1979, p. 369)

Mothers who kept their babies received significantly more help from their family, the baby's father, and from their best friend than was true of mothers who chose adoption.

The shift seen in the late 1960s to a lack of association between the adolescent mother's religion and her decision about whether to keep the child or surrender it for adoption was sustained in Grow's study. And in contrast to earlier studies, there was no difference in socioeconomic status between keeping and surrendering mothers. Significantly, no differences were found in the emotional health of the two groups. "Women who kept their children were no more or no less disturbed than those who decided to surrender" (Grow, 1979, p. 367).

Women who chose adoption appeared to be more committed to traditional values about motherhood and marriage, for example, believing that it is better to be married when rearing children. Grow concluded that the desire to keep a child or use adoption, rather than being

attributed to psychological explanations or deviancy, is instead related to the extent to which the mother has been exposed to and has accepted the traditional social milieu. The very much larger number of mothers who keep their children may reflect significant changes in social values.

A national survey of American families in 1982 found that white teenagers were much more likely to release their children for adoption than were black adolescent mothers. White mothers were more likely to relinquish their children if their own fathers had some college education, than if their fathers had not completed high school. Since teenagers who have well-educated fathers often expect to continue their education and move into satisfying occupations, it may be that those who get pregnant believe that motherhood would conflict with their future plans, and so are more likely to release their children for adoption (Bachrach, 1986).

Barth (1987) surveyed a nonrandom sample of 106 young, mainly white, teenagers who were in one of twelve school-age parent programs in five states. The purpose of the survey was to find out what teenagers knew about adoption, the experiences they had had, and their attitudes and beliefs about releasing children for adoption. Very few of the mothers had seriously considered adoption and only two had children living away from them. The mothers strongly believed that if they had chosen adoption, they would always wonder about their child in the future; the prospect of never knowing how their child was faring was a powerful influence on their decision not to pursue adoption. The concept of open adoption, in which the relinquishing mother retains some connection to the developing child, appealed to some of the mothers as a way of reducing uncertainty about their child's future (see Chapter 11).

The participants reported that, on average, adoption had been discussed about twice during the time that they had attended a school-age parent program. About a quarter said that adoption had never been discussed in their program. Yet as the author points out, "fully understanding the available opportunities and procedures for adoption requires a lot of thought and discussion" (Barth, 1987, p. 330).

The extent to which adolescents are informed about adoption and would be more receptive to adoption if they were given a more accurate understanding of it was of interest in another study (Mech, 1984; 1988a). In a part of this study, data were collected from fifty-seven health facilities claiming to offer pregnancy counseling services. About 14,400 pregnant teenagers came to these facilities during a one-year period for pregnancy testing and prenatal care. Because most health facilities do not emphasize adoption as an alternative, these facilities offered a unique opportunity to devise a model for communicating balanced information to pregnant adolescents about choices: keeping the baby, placing for adoption, or seeking abortion. Predemonstration study had shown that many of the health facility counselors had little conviction that adolescent parenting was a desirable decision, although, paradoxically, they asserted firm support to teenagers who decided to parent. They tended to believe that few pregnant teenagers wanted information about adoption. Many of the counselors were uninformed about adoption procedures and unable to make a clear distinction between agency adoptions and those arranged privately (Mech, 1984: 1988a).

An inventory-based counseling model for communicating about adoption with pregnant adolescents was developed to identify those adolescents who appeared interested and were willing to consider an adoption plan. They were provided with information about adoption, access to an adoption agency, and, as well, were given support for their interest in adoption. These pregnant teenagers were encouraged to discuss adoption with birthparents who had chosen to place their child, with adoptive parents, and an agency social worker. Group sessions were provided with a focus on decision-making during pregnancy. Findings showed that the adoption screening procedures, in conjunction with the counseling supports, were associated with low but important increases in adoption placement rates. The program was most effective with white adolescents who recorded a placement rate of 15.7 percent. For nonwhite adolescents (52 percent of the sample) the overall relinquishment rate was only 2.1 percent. The combination of limited availability of adoptive homes for black infants coupled with a shortage of black staff to provide adoption counseling posed barriers for minority adolescents who might want to place children for adoption in nonrelative homes (Mech, 1988a, p. 5).

More research is badly needed to further clarify factors associated with a teenager's decision on how to resolve a pregnancy, and ways in which pregnancy counseling services can support the mother's efforts to explore options available to her.

FAMILIES WITH LESBIAN MOTHERS

Among the nontraditional family forms is one under scrutiny as to its suitability for child rearing—the family headed by a lesbian mother. Little is known about this kind of family. The lack of knowledge may partially explain common fears about such a family and the stigma that attaches to it. Social workers in child welfare are being called on more frequently than in the past for advice and guidance in relation to families headed by lesbian mothers, particularly in matters of child custody. Thus, social workers are challenged to learn about lesbianism and motherhood and its implications for the lives of children.

Incidence

In an examination of issues in lesbianism and motherhood, Ellen Lewin (1981) notes that arriving at population figures for homosexuals is highly problematic, given the stigma they face as a group. She cites the work of Kinsey and co-workers (1948; 1953) to show the complexity of determining how many persons are heterosexual or homosexual. The Kinsey Heterosexual-Homosexual Rating Scale has been useful for avoiding an unduly rigid bipolar method of classification and allowing sexual orientation to be more usefully conceptualized as a continuum between two extremes. With this scale, the proportion of lesbians in the young adult population may be estimated as somewhere between 1 and 20 percent, depending on what portion of the Kinsey scale is taken to denote "homosexual." In a conservative use of those data, Hoeffer in 1978 suggested that the lesbian mother population was about 3 percent of the 6.6 million families headed by females in that year, or about 200,000 individuals (Hoeffer, 1978).

Community Attitudes

In a more socially tolerant climate brought about by changes in sex mores and in the rights of women, homosexuals' need for secrecy about themselves has been reduced, particularly in urban areas. Lesbian mothers, as well as lesbians without children, now find more support for their sexual identification. However, this support often is elusive. Women who seek to provide foster care or adoption as a route to parenthood have a sharply reduced chance of doing so if the decision maker in an agency knows that the applicant is lesbian. In a discussion of cultural and clinical issues in lesbian families, Hall points out that "resolutions affirming the right of gay people to be considered as prospective foster and adoptive parents have been supported by a substantial portion of the memberships of both the National Association of Social Workers and the American Psychological Association; however, these professional endorsements have yet to be translated into general practice" (Hall, 1978). Lesbian mothers in the process of divorce are at high risk of losing their children in custody contests. Even when homosexuality is not specified as legal grounds for denial of custody, judges typically rule against them under their own interpretation of "the best interests of the child."

Judges appear to be more inclined to grant custody to the lesbian mother if she has not publicly acknowledged her homosexuality, if she is not engaged in political activism, if she leads a conventional life in other respects, and if her children are of preschool age and are female. The reservation about lesbian mothers' rearing male children apparently extends as well to community networks that usually support lesbian mothers. Even when custody is awarded to the mother, judges often attach conditions, for example, that she end her association with her lover or limit it by not seeing her in the presence of her children (Hall, 1978). The assumption is that lesbianism, in and of itself, is to be strictly scrutinized in matters of child custody. For instance, the California Court of Appeals ruled in 1959 that the trial judge had acted incorrectly when he excluded evidence of the mother's lesbianism and stated that the court was obliged to inquire into the "moral character, acts, conduct and disposition" of the mother (*Immerman v. Immerman,* 1959). The censure of homosexuality as an unhealthy influence on the developing child is seen also in actions by other institutions of the community when they deny employment to teachers or health practitioners who are gay or lesbian.

Underlying these attitudes is a series of largely untested stereotyped beliefs: (1) The child reared in a lesbian home will lack traditional role models and will be more likely than others to become homosexual; (2) the child will be harmed by the stigma that attaches to the mother and inevitably extends to the child; (3) the child is at risk of sexual abuse by the mother or her friends; and (4) lesbianism will compete with and undermine the provision of maternal care, thus impairing the child's overall growth and development (Lewin, 1981).

Behind these fears is a view of lesbianism as indicative of an inherent pathology that would dominate all other aspects of family interaction. As yet little research has addressed lesbianism and the questions raised by the court and others in the community. Some studies, however, raise doubts about the validity of the stereotypes and assumptions.

Studies of Lesbian Mothers

In a review of recent research on lesbianism, Lewin cited separate studies that showed that when factors such as socioeconomic status, age of children, birth order, family constellation, and length of absence of the father or the adult male were rigorously controlled, the children of lesbian mothers were not different from children of heterosexual single or divorced mothers in any of these dimensions: gender-identity confusion, inappropriate gender-role behavior, psychopathology, and heterosexual-homosexual orientation (Lewin, 1981). Less research has been done on the day-to-day experiences of lesbian mothers as they act as family heads, provide child care, and handle problems that arise as part of those activities.

To help fill that gap, Lewin carried out in-depth semistructured interviews with eighty mothers in their own homes. Forty-three of the mothers were lesbian and thirty-seven were heterosexual. All had been formerly married and had children ranging in age from one to eighteen. Informants were obtained through personal referrals and through responses to publicity about the study. The focus of the interview was primarily on the adaptive strategies these mothers relied on, the influence of their sexual identification on the kinds of resources made available to them, and the choices they made in utilizing these resources. The interview covered a range of issues—economic problems, interpersonal support systems, institutional support systems, and the mothers' own beliefs and values about their maternal situation. Among the findings were these:

1. *The lesbian mothers, as did the heterosexual mothers, defined their identity by a variety of affiliations.* Their sexual identification was of primary interest to outsiders, but the mothers frequently reported that other factors of their identity were more telling than their sexual orientation. To cite an example: One lesbian mother

> was more intensely involved in the world of a therapeutic self-help group . . . and with a variety of religious activities . . : than with anything that might be viewed as the gay life. Her friends represented those she had met through her spiritual involvements and included other members of the self-help organization (both gay and straight), both of her ex-husbands, a heterosexual room-mate (also a single mother), and several relatives (all heterosexual). Although her identification as a lesbian was unambiguous, she experienced it as only one among several sources of personal definition. (Lewin, 1981, p. 8)

2. *Lesbian and heterosexual mothers were most strikingly similar in the means by which they established and maintained similar kinds of support systems.* Whenever possible, both groups of mothers depended heavily on family relationships with parents, brothers, and sisters as primary sources of reliable child care and economic and emotional support.

3. *Despite tensions in their relationships with former husbands, both groups of mothers, heterosexual and lesbian, tended to try to strengthen the ties in order to reinforce continuity in child support payments.* For both groups of mothers the payments were very important as a necessary supplement to their own earnings. Nevertheless, about half of the mothers in each group reported significant difficulties in obtaining agreed-upon financial help. The need to keep payments coming influenced many of them to try to maintain a civil relationship with their ex-husbands. The expense of legal action and a fear that it might invite some kind of retaliation or a child custody suit led many of them to reject the option of legal action to try to improve their financial situations. Fear of precipitating a

custody suit was especially acute among the lesbian mothers.

4. *Each group of mothers sought to strengthen their children's relationship with their father.* About three-fourths of the mothers in each group looked to their ex-husbands as a central source of male role modeling. Both groups also relied on other male family members as sources of masculine influence.

In summary, Lewin's study showed that the only source of systematic difference between the families headed by a single lesbian mother and those headed by a single heterosexual mother was "the stress which fear of loss of custody produces for the lesbian mothers—and the often conflict-laden adaptations they make to this special source of vulnerability" (Lewin, 1981, pp. 11–12).

The generally positive findings of Lewin's study should be accepted cautiously. The study had certain limitations. The sample of mothers interviewed was small and not necessarily representative. In addition, the researcher did not report the means by which she analyzed the extensive data from lengthy semistructured interviews. Not knowing the means of data analysis complicates an evaluation of the procedures and the findings.

A recent legal development is the emergence in the courts of custody disputes between lesbian partners with children. In situations where a child was planned for and conceived within the context of a lesbian relationship, both partners may feel that they have a parental relationship with the child, though only one is the biological parent. These separating families face a special challenge, the lack of established legal doctrines to guide courts in settling these disputes while protecting children and their parents. In the past, generally courts have not heard custody cases involving lesbian parents, since the birth mother is presumed to be the suitable custodial parent. However, in 1989, custody and visitation disputes between birth mothers and their separated partners were heard in courts in Los Angeles, New York, and Maryland. Court decisions from these cases may have implications for separating gay male couples and for stepparents as well as lesbian couples (Margolick, 1990, p. 1).

Additional research is needed to understand more fully the range of adaptive behaviors that all single parents use to cope with the demands and stress in their situations. More studies are also needed of the children of lesbian mothers, for example, to learn what understanding and degree of acceptance they have with peers, teachers, and others that may reflect either an accepting or rejecting response to lesbianism, and to learn about the nature of their relationships with their biological fathers.

Social Work Roles

Most of the roles for social workers in relation to lesbian mothers and their children are the same as those that are important for all families, particularly for single-parent families. The matter of threats to custody in viable lesbian homes is an area in which social workers are likely to be called on increasingly to provide counseling, guidance, and assistance in legal contests. In addition, social workers have a role to play in clarifying and negating the persistent stereotypes about homosexuality and in lending support to the legitimacy of the lesbian mother's choice of life-style. As is true of all single parents, and especially lesbian single parents, their problems of everyday life are compounded by an unsupportive society.

STEPPARENT FAMILIES

The current high rate of divorce followed by new marriage has resulted in a major and no longer unusual social phenomenon, the family made up of children and one or two stepparents. These families are variously termed "remarried," "reconstituted," or "blended" families. Their composition varies and can include a stepmother with no children married to a man with children, a stepfather with no children married to a woman with children, or a man with children married to a woman with children.

Accurate demographic data about stepparent families in the United States are not available. However, it is known that the number of such families has sharply increased in recent decades. Based on Census Bureau estimates, about one quarter of children today will live with a stepparent before they are grown. Stepchildren make up about 15 percent of all children who live in married-couple families (Miller & Moorman, 1989).

Distinctive Aspects

While many of the characteristics and problems of family life in the stepparent family are the same as those found in other family forms, certain factors within it are distinctive (Sager et al., 1980).

1.   The family is created without the usual pattern of evolutionary growth.

2.   Commonly there is an ex-spouse, and often ex-grandparents, who, although "outsiders," seek to influence the new family system.

3.   Children often have mixed loyalties to old and new parents; parents in turn often feel guilt and ambivalence toward the children or ex-spouse—feelings that complicate family life.

4.   Children are at risk of residual problems from marital conflict or desertion by a parent.

5.   Children, who usually are not given a choice, may not want to be a part of the newly formed family.

6.   Children who move back and forth between households carry many kinds of messages, some of which accentuate differences in value systems between the different households with which the child is connected.

7.   Role confusion for all family members is characteristic of the newly formed stepfamily.

The recency with which the stepparent family has come to be regarded as a major family form conditions the state of research on impor-

tant questions. Much of the literature on stepparents is found in popular books and articles, often written by a stepparent who offers her or his own prescriptions for solving family problems. The research is still limited in quality and quantity, even though the stepparent family has become a common kinship form. For example, longitudinal studies with large random samples are lacking. Despite these limitations, some findings of significant interest have emerged (Sager et al., 1980).

"Stick out the hard times and don't underestimate your personal strength. Talk a lot—try to listen, but keep on talking." (A stepparent, quoted in Dahl et al., 1987, p. 3)

Common Developmental Tasks in Forming Stepparent Families

Persons in families undergoing reorganization are faced with problems of adaptation in an attempt to handle a new and complicated network of relationships and to fit the disparate family parts into a new structure. Despite the strengths in many stepparent families, certain stresses tend to emerge quickly when formation of the family begins. "There are feelings of confusion and ambivalence as roles are experienced quite differently from similar roles in first marriages. There is the hesitation of the new spouses to make firm commitments, to deal openly with difficulties, and their dismay at how quickly parenting issues emerge between them. Concern over stepchildren and ex-spouses underscores the complexity, ambiguity, and overload of new roles" (Kleinman et al., 1979, p. 78).

From their clinical work of evaluating and treating stepparent families, Kleinman et al. (1979) have identified some common developmental tasks with which such families often struggle. One task seems to be primary: *mourning the loss of the previous family*. If this process is not undertaken and handled successfully, it can present a major interference to establishing a strong family unit.

> The process involves the gradual giving up of the wish for parental reunion and the hope of intimacy with the other biological parent which was possible when all were living together. This relinquishing of a previous set of relationships usually has to occur in the face of continuing . . . variable and frequently unpredictable contact with the parent or spouse. For the parent this involves the difficult task of giving up the marital relationship while maintaining a "fellow parent" interaction with the ex-spouse. For the child it involves the equally hard task of giving up the intimate, daily parental-child relationship while adapting to a less close, less frequent but still ongoing relationship. (Kleinman et al., 1979, p. 80)

Often children wish to deny that the changes are final, leading them to split off the negative emotions about the parent now denied to them and to direct their feelings toward the stepparent or the biological parent with whom they live. Kleinman and coworkers suggest a helpful means of hastening the mourning process—an open sharing of memories by the members of each original family unit. Learning about each other's past and making it a part of the new unit can have a beneficial consolidating effect (Kleinman et al., 1979).

The Marital Relationship

The new marital relationship is critical in its strong influence on the degree to which the new family achieves cohesiveness. Frequently the new marriage is affected by the intrusion of unresolved feelings and conflicts left over from the first marriage. Hostility toward a former spouse can stir up anger that is then injected into the new relationship. Sometimes one or both partners have entered into the new marriage impulsively, and when it quickly becomes apparent that it will not solve all the emotional, economic, and child care problems, as may have

been envisioned, disenchantment takes over. Such pressures reduce the extent to which the two spouses can openly discuss their differences, desires, and needs. In such instances the couple may feel an inordinate need to succeed in the new union and to present an image of a family free of problems.

The immediate need for the stepparent to assume a parenting role in relation to the spouse's children and share his or her love with stepchildren can intrude into the marital relationship. The parents' time alone with each other is often very limited. Success in new parenting depends largely, of course, on the abilities and willingness of the stepparent to fulfill the role. Much also depends, however, on the actual willingness of the spouse to accept the other's role and authority in relation to his or her biological children.

Child and Parent Relationships

In the early stages of family formation children are often more demanding and dependent. They may feel confused and unhappy about the changes and fearful of the future. Long-standing interactional patterns come into play, illustrating that how children fared in the first family and during its dissolution will affect the new marital couple's ability to have success in forming a new family (Sager et al., 1980).

A common reaction of children is resentment toward the stepparent, who already may have her or his own doubts about the legitimacy of the stepparent role. For authentic and supportive attachments to develop, problems such as these must be resolved. Researchers have emphasized the importance of the child's relationship to the custodial biological parent on whom much responsibility rests for providing appropriate supportive relationships during the period of stress and dissolution of the first family and for facilitating the child's transition into new family relationships (Kelly & Wallerstein, 1977; Tessman, 1978).

The roles of stepmother and stepfather are

ambiguous, and few guidelines have been offered to women for overcoming the stepmother stereotype. Draughon (1975) proposed three choices of role for a stepmother: primary mother, other mother, and friend. The choice to be made depends in large measure on the child's dependency needs and relationship with the biological mother. When a child continues to feel a primary attachment to her, then the stepmother may be better advised to play the role of friend. However, in that role, the stepmother will still have to set rules and establish her authority when the child visits or lives in the stepmother's home.

Stepfathers also have undefined roles. In the early part of the century, stepfathers usually married widows and their role as "father" was clearly recognized. But with stepparent families today most often being the result of divorce, stepfathers too have problems. One that often causes trouble is the matter of discipline. A new stepfather's style of discipline may be different from what the children know. The mother may be ambivalent about how much and what kind of help she wants with discipline, thus leaving the stepfather to feel that he is being given double messages that invite him to retreat into passivity. Parents who care for their children from birth work out a relationship and a mode of discipline over a span of years. Stepparents are faced with situations to which they must respond without the background of time together (Visher & Visher, 1978).

Stepfathers often report strong feelings of guilt about leaving the children of a previous marriage to become the stepfather of other children. Sometimes the guilt is so urgent that it interferes with their ability to form supportive and affectionate relationships with stepchildren (Visher & Visher, 1978).

Sexual conflicts have been noted in professional work with stepparent families. In the less cohesive stepfamily, as compared with the nuclear family, sexuality within the unit can be a greater source of tension, with the incest taboo being weakened by the nonbiological relationships:

> Young children in a stepfamily may develop strong affectional feelings for one another, which may be obscured by fighting and discord to combat the unacceptable attraction. Teenagers who have not grown up together may suddenly find themselves in a variety of intimate living situations, at a time when they are very curious and fascinated by sexual concerns. They may develop strong sexual fantasies and attractions for each other. Previously repressed impulses may be awakened by virtue of the non-blood relationship. . . . The affections between the newly married couple may stimulate thoughts of sexuality in some cases. (Visher & Visher, 1978, pp. 260–261)

Current Myths about Stepparent Families

A recurring theme in the literature on stepparent families is the existence of ancient as well as contemporary myths that make it harder for stepparent families to successfully handle their family developmental tasks and that reduce a therapist's effectiveness in working with stepfamilies. The myth of the "wicked stepmother" is ancient and universal. There are also contemporary myths. Visher and Visher (1978) have discussed four:

1. *Stepfamilies are nuclear families.* In fact, death and divorce bring about dissolution of the nuclear family. The stepparent family should be seen as a structural variation with its own organization and potentially solvable problems.

2. *Death of the ex-spouse and parent makes stepparenting easier.* Whether adjustment is easier or harder because a family member was lost to death rather than divorce, in both situations the family experiences pain. Better methods need to be developed to help stepfamilies cope with whatever residual problems there may be.

3. *Stepchildren are easier to handle when*

not living in the home. In situations where a child's behavior is very upsetting and often overwhelming to a stepparent, it is tempting to believe that it would be easier if the child only visited, rather than lived with, the stepparent. "When the stepchildren live in the home, the stepparents and their spouses may have a relatively constant level of unpleasant tension. Where the stepchildren live elsewhere and visit only occasionally, anxiety, which is a common reaction to anticipated stress, builds up ahead of each painful encounter." Each situation brings great stress (Visher & Visher, 1978, p. 256).

4. *Love happens instantly.* The myth of "instant love," that is, an expectation that stepparents will love their stepchildren almost at once, falls most heavily on the stepmother as the person traditionally responsible for nurturance and affection. In response, many stepmothers feel a very heavy demand to show early success with their stepchildren. Some have done well with their own children only to find the stepparent experience very different and unrewarding. Even warm and loving women can find themselves in situations where they appear to be the "wicked stepmother" (McGoldrick & Carter, 1988).

The Need for Stepparent Family Services

Despite the problems of the stepparent family that have been discussed, it should be kept in mind that it is an established and viable family form that serves many children well in their growing years. Like the single-parent family, society has been slow to recognize its importance and the need to develop supportive services in its behalf.

Stepparents are required to cope with complicated and emotionally demanding situations. Without others with whom to share these problems, tensions persist. Sometimes the primary service need is for marital counseling with individual couples. In numerous instances, however, the primary need of stepparents and their

children is an opportunity to share feelings and experiences with other stepparents and stepchildren (Dahl et al., 1987).

MINORITY FAMILIES

The effectiveness of family-based services offered to minority families depends in large measure on the extent to which the services have been planned and offered within the context of a family's own cultural, racial, and ethnic identity. Child welfare services focus on family functioning and child-rearing practices. Any group's cultural or ethnic identity is most clearly reflected within the family. Whether the services offered are based on an understanding of ethnically determined behaviors and cultural differences will be a potent influence on the use made of them. Ethnicity is significant in determining how different groups define normality and social competence. The way in which a family structures and manages a particular situation reveals practical strategies it has developed over time to manage many aspects of daily life. However, the usefulness of these strategies may not be readily understood by a social worker who is charged to assess family functioning but is unfamiliar with the culture.

Including minority persons as professional, paraprofessional, and volunteer participants in family-based programs serving minority populations is essential to an accurate interpretation of how ethnicity affects a family's life-style, child-rearing practices, and the community norms. Having at least one member of the service team who shares the family's culture facilitates empathetic communication and understanding and gives credibility to the services being offered. Also, it becomes more feasible to handle some of the ethical considerations that arise whenever social workers go into the homes of children and work intensively with family members in their natural context. "Issues such as intrusiveness, subtle coercion, or violations of a family's values may jeopardize program goals if not recognized by workers who are sensitive to the family's life style and values." In addition, a service team that has at least one member who shares a family's culture makes it possible "to distinguish between child care practices which are genuinely detrimental and those which may simply represent variations from practices in the larger society. When working with the families of all children at risk of out-of-home placement, cultural sensitivity is a potentially powerful service factor" (National Resource Center, 1982).

The African-American Family

Among the 11 percent of American families that are African-American, great diversity exists. Country of origin, level of acculturation, religion, and socioeconomic status combine to create families that differ in life-style and values. However, all black families in America share the experience of color discrimination. Racism and oppression have prevented African-Americans from moving into the mainstream of American life. The strengths of black families are credited with helping those of African-American descent to advance in education, income, and employment, despite the almost overwhelming obstacle of discrimination (Hines & Boyd-Franklin, 1982; Nobles, 1988).

If we are going to serve Black children and families, we have to understand how Blacks are simultaneously like every family in this country, like some other families, and like no other family at all. The professional helping person has to be able to assess at what point they are dealing with universalities and at what point they are dealing with unique issues. (Solomon, 1985, p. 10)

Three aspects of black family and community life that have helped African-Americans survive in America are role flexibility of family members, the extended family support system, and the church. Black parents are able to take on a range of roles within the family, regardless of gender; fathers and mothers both expect to work outside the home and to care for children and the home, though women do seem to assume more responsibility for child-rearing (Hall & King, 1982). This flexibility has enabled black families to survive the undermining of the male role as family provider, caused by discriminatory employment practices (Pinderhughes, 1982).

The concept of role sharing extends to children as well as grandparents and other extended family members, who may take instrumental and affective roles in the family. Freeman cites the advantages and potential difficulties for children of role sharing in the family. "Such patterns tend to broaden each child's role network and teach him or her responsibility for others in the 'group'—those within the same cultural context. In assessment, however, distinctions must be made between these normative cultural expectations within black families, and dysfunctional circumstances involving child neglect . . ." (Freeman, 1990, p. 58).

Social workers and other professionals especially need an understanding of the extended family ties found in black communities. Stack (1974) used an anthropological approach to study kinship among black families and the collective adaptations to poverty that they have developed within their own sociocultural network. She focused on ways in which blacks in a poor urban neighborhood ordered and dealt with the world in which they lived and the nature of their collective responses to poverty. She identified and described the nature of the informal exchange systems of reciprocal sharing and mutual help. These exchange systems operated among alliances of individuals who regularly shared essential help and resources of various kinds, such as material goods, transportation, and child care. She concluded that black family life could not be understood without a grasp of its strong kinship bonds and the practical and often ingenious ways in which kinship members worked together in a circle of mutual help.

In efforts to understand and reinforce the benefits of reciprocal exchange systems among black families, social workers need to keep in mind that kinship networks are beset often with strains, setbacks, and contradictions that over time bring limits to progress. "To survive urban culture is far different . . . from participating in it" (Martin & Martin, 1978). Social work efforts to help families only by trying to change them overlook the persistent forces over which black families have no control, for example, the extensive joblessness among their youth. Mediating, advocating, and facilitating, rather than clinical approaches, are more appropriate in such instances.

The black church has been the predominant cultural institution of Americans of African descent. With the continuing decay of inner city neighborhoods, black churches have renewed their commitment to residents in these areas by expanding the range of social services they provide (Lewin, 1988a). After-school programs, food pantries, clothing exchanges, and tutorial services for school children are common. Innovative programs are being developed in many churches to help adolescents make the transition to manhood, through sports, recreation, opportunities for exchanges with adult role models, and group sessions devoted to health, spirituality, family life, and the special problems of black men. A Chicago church established the "One Church, One Child" program to encourage black families to adopt black children. Churches in thirty-one states have replicated the program and been responsible for 8,000 adoptions (Lewin, 1988). The philosophy of this program is that the shortage of African-American adoptive families was a problem "that could not be solved by the state. The people in the Black community themselves had to do it and the churches are the life blood of the Black community" ("One Church, One Child," 1984, p. 23). Social workers may find that churches and religious leaders are important allies in their work

with black families (Davis & Proctor, 1989, p. 78).

The Native-American Family

After centuries of decline, the population of Native Americans in the United States is again increasing. In 1980, the Census reported over one million Indians, half of whom were under age eighteen (Kessel & Robbins, 1984). The introduction of modern medical services in rural areas has helped lower infant mortality rates, and improved adaptations to modern living have increased somewhat the longevity of adults (Attneave, 1982). With these population changes, it is likely that the stresses and problems of young families will become of increasing interest to agencies involved with Native Americans.

Traditional Indian culture was diverse, with an estimated 200 different nations at the time of first European contact in the 1600s (Spicer, 1980). In spite of much variation, it is broadly true that each nation provided natural systems to safeguard children and promote their healthy development. Children were raised in an extended family environment that included three or more generations; separate households of cousins, aunts, and uncles; and nonrelatives who became incorporated into the family (Red Horse, 1980). Aunts, uncles and grandparents had specific roles and responsibilities in regard to the family's children, and were also ready to help if the parents became overburdened, incapacitated, or died. Children could form bonds to several parental figures who offered affection, education in proper behavior, and various role models (Attneave, 1982). Spiritual beliefs reinforced the value of children as a special gift from the Creator (Cross, 1986).

The conquest of America by Western culture drastically altered tribal life. The loss of land separated families so that the extended family system could no longer provide a nurturing environment for children. Adults lost their traditional occupations and their ability to be role models as competent providers. Women's domestic skills made it easier for them than for Indian men to find work in the economy of the dominant culture, both on and off the reservation. The massive unemployment of Indian men has resulted in an increase of single-mother families (Attneave, 1982). Alcohol, introduced by early explorers to Native American cultures with no social context to control its use, has plagued Indian families. Sixty deaths due to alcoholism per 100,000 individuals is reported for Indians; the comparable number for the general population in the United States is nine (Lamarine, 1988). For Indian and non-Indian families alike, alcoholism is associated with higher rates of family problems, child maltreatment, and developmental disabilities.

Native-American families historically have been at great risk of family breakup through government programs and policies. Indian boarding schools, established in the late nineteenth century by the Bureau of Indian Affairs, were designed to "separate a child from his reservation and family, strip him of his tribal lore and mores, force the complete abandonment of his native language, and prepare him in such a way that he would never return to his people" (Indian Education, 1969). Consequently, Indian children were often forcibly removed from their homes, given English names, required to speak English, and in many instances not allowed to return home. A devastating effect of this program was that young people grew up with no experience of family life and no parental role models to guide their own efforts to establish families after they were grown and had left the schools (Johnson, 1981).

Through the years Indian children continued to be at highest risk of out-of-home placement of children in any racial or cultural group, with placement rates reported to be twenty times higher than that of white children (Johnson, 1981). Little regard was given to the unique character of the Indian family and sociocultural aspects of life on the reservation, and children were removed from their families often because of poverty, poor housing, and problems that could have been resolved had adequate family services been available. The foster and adoptive homes were mainly non-Indian, at least partly because Indian families often could not meet the housing and income requirements to qualify as substitute homes. Many non-Indian foster and adoptive families provided loving and caring homes, but the children were inevitably deprived of the opportunities needed to incorporate their cultural heritage into their personal identity. By the 1970s, it is estimated that a quarter of all Indian children were not living with their families, but were in boarding schools, or foster or adoptive homes (Johnson, 1981). This great loss of Indian children to their cultural heritage gave impetus to the passage of the Indian Child Welfare Act of 1978, federal legislation intended to restore and preserve Indian families (see Chapter 3).

In spite of adversity, Indian culture and Indian families endure. Present day Indians are survivors who have learned to adapt to an alien culture. A 1974 study of urban Indian families found that many were coping and managing successfully. These families tended to be open to learning and using the technology and social norms of white culture. Significantly, maintaining interest in tribal folkways, language, and values was also associated with successful adaptation to urban life (Attneave, 1982). A study of Indian women in rural North Dakota who were affiliated with Head Start found that their family and personal relationships were characterized by mutual respect and helpfulness. The women were optimistic and courageous, and were "certain they could make plans work" (Light & Martin, 1986).

In recent years, the interest of government and industry has focused on certain tribes that own land rich in energy and other natural resources. Resource development on Indian lands is changing social and economic conditions of life on reservations, and may result in greater

economic and political power for Native American groups in relation to the dominant society (Snipp, 1986).

The Mexican-American Family

Like other minority groups, the Mexican-American family is frequently perceived through a veil of myths and stereotypes. One such view is of a *macho*-dominated authoritarian family. Another is a more sympathetic, even romanticized view of a warm, nurturing, cohesive environment. Both views hold that the Mexican-American family is characterized by "(1) male dominance; (2) rigid sex-age grading so that the older order the younger, and the men order the women; (3) clearly established patterns of help and mutual aid among family members; and (4) a strong familistic orientation whereby individual needs are subordinated to collective needs" (Maraude, 1980, p. 485). Given this general agreement about basic characteristics, the differences emerge in the kinds of interpretations and evaluations given them.

Familism is a characteristic strongly emphasized in discussions of Mexican-American family life—the family as a central source of emotional support through close bonds not only with immediate family members, but with grandparents, aunts, uncles, cousins, and family friends (Rothman et al., 1985). A study of young children aged seven to thirteen in a Houston *barrio* concluded that "in the child's eye-view the central feature is home, and the people at home" (Maraude, 1980, p. 487). Grandparents are influential in the lives of children, less as authority figures than as sources of love and warmth and nurturance. Familism also means a lessening of sharp distinctions between relatives and friends. Relatives can be friends, and friends are symbolically accepted as part of the family.

The mother in Mexican-American family life is critically important in intrafamily relationships despite the common characterization of the father as the unquestioned authority in the family. Maraude holds that this mostly unquestioned characterization is derived from the formal aspects of Mexican-American culture without regard for its more subtle and informal nuances. "The male may officially be the ultimate authority but he is frequently aloof or uninvolved in family matters. The father tends to be warm and affectionate when children are little, but as they enter puberty, relations between him and his family become more tenuous" (Maraude, 1980, p. 487). To his children, the Mexican-American father may be perceived as a somewhat distant authority figure, reflecting a remoteness that may result from his long hours away from home. The mother, however, plays a critical role in the daily life of her children, performing many tasks for and with them in a relationship characterized most often by warmth and affection. The informal but significant authority she projects during these interchanges and the role she plays in perpetuating the language and cultural values of the family should not be overlooked by social workers offering services to the family (Maraude, 1980).

As applies to all kinds of family groups, there is no one Mexican-American family type, but a number of types that vary by geographic region, how recently the family came to the United States, rural-urban differences, socioeconomic status, education, frequency of contact with newly arrived relatives or friends, and other factors. In addition, Mexican-American families, like other families, are subject to the powerful influences of a highly technological and urban population that in time modify traditional roles in family life. To be effective in working with all families, social workers must free themselves of preconceived notions of minority family life.

The Asian-American Family

World War II marked the beginning of a significant increase in the numbers of Asian-American families in the United States (Kim et al., 1981). Since then nearly a quarter of a million women from Japan, Korea, the Philippines, Thailand, and Vietnam have met and married American men in military service in their countries and eventually emigrated with them to the United States. As long as the couple stayed in the country of the woman's birth, necessary cultural adjustments were minimal. She was still close to her own family and able to rely on her own language and to follow familiar customs. The husband's work at a military base went on as usual, and military benefits for dependents gave financial stability in a country with a lower cost of living than in the United States. In this interlude both husband and wife could avoid facing their unrealistic expectations of the marriage.

> Many of these men discovered that in their relationships to Oriental women their feelings, comfort and welfare were given precedence. Thus for the first time they felt accepted by solicitous, unquestioning women who respected them. . . . Handicapped by a language barrier, by an ignorance of American culture, and by limited social experiences, these women failed to view the men in realistic terms; they considered them masculine and potential security-giving mates. . . . Marriage to American soldiers symbolized eternal security and happiness, an insurance against suffering and want. (Kim et al., 1981, p. 15)

Behind these expectations lay vast differences in philosophies, religion, and cultural mores between Eastern and Western ways of living.

When the time came to go together to the United States to establish a home, and in many instances a new form of work for the husband, the couple faced unexpected and heavy demands in its transition to life in this country. Cultural differences and cultural adjustment tasks fell most heavily on the wife, a stranger in an entirely new culture.

Learning English for daily interaction can be extremely difficult for many Asians because of quite different language roots and structures.

When the Asian wife arrives in the United States, she loses her major means of communication with others. As one Asian wife expressed it to her social worker:

> All of a sudden, I became deaf and mute at the moment the plane landed in the United States. For one thing, everyone treats me like a child because my English is poor. Some treat me like an idiot, but I cannot tell them how I feel. The worst is the feeling I get when I don't understand what is being said to me. I get upset and suspicious of everyone, including my husband. Often I feel like I am about to explode! Sometimes I think I am going crazy. (Kim et al., 1981, p. 41)

The poor use of English complicates all her other pressing tasks—learning the mechanics of everyday life such as shopping for the family's necessities, enrolling her children in school, interacting with neighbors, and using public and private services in her community. At the same time she must find a way to handle sometimes profound homesickness, value conflicts, and cultural clashes with her husband. A frequent source of tension arises in conflicts in child-rearing practices, an area where the Asian mother expects to feel competent and to have her motherhood valued. If her husband objects to what seems to him a too-lenient and indulgent approach to child rearing, her sense of adequacy is further threatened.

The husband is the key to his Asian wife's adjustment. Much depends on the extent to which he can give her emotional support as well as guide and teach her appropriate ways to respond to each new situation. Some do this sucessfully, with the marriage becoming more enriching and the family unit stronger as it learns to take advantage of a greater range of cultural choices in everyday living. However, not every husband of an Asian woman can meet the responsibilities of facilitating her adjustment. Some lack empathy with her difficulties and fail to see the tremendous demands made on her. If the husband has married his wife with the expectation that she will be docile and look after all his needs without his having to reciprocate, he may fear her Americanization and discourage her in open or subtle ways from activities that would make her more self-sufficient. Thus the dependence the wife experiences on coming to a new country is reinforced, and she as well as her children pays a high price for her social and psychological isolation.

From work with Asian wives of American servicemen through the National Committee Concerned with Asian Wives of U.S. Servicemen, Kim and coworkers reported that wife battering afflicts a sizable number of such marriages. They cited the Inspector General's Report on Domestic Violence, which identified military service as occupationally conducive to domestic violence. Contributing factors were the authoritarian setting of the military, its use of physical force in training, and stress within families who are required to move frequently (Inspector General, 1979).

The National Committee cited above serves as a spearhead for social services to Asian-American families through advocacy, public education, and consultation. It has recommended appropriate and culturally sensitive procedures for work with Asian families, particularly the wives and mothers who come to women's shelters, hospital emergency rooms, the police, the clergy, and other sources of possible help.

SERVICES FOR CHILDREN AND FAMILIES

Evidence has accumulated that many foster placements could have been prevented if prompt and supportive services had been directed to the problems in the child's own family, community, and culture. This awareness has led to an intensified interest in developing more and better services to children in their own homes. These include a range of social services to support family life—homemaker services, day care, counsel-

ling, support groups, crisis centers and shelters, respite care, and other services.

Despite the recognition of the need for programs that will enable families to function more adequately and to remain intact, proposals have lagged as to how supportive services should be defined, operated, and fit into a comprehensive pattern. For example, the Child Welfare League of America over the years has developed and promulgated standards for such services as foster family care, group homes, institutional care for children, homemaker services, and day care. Only recently, however, have standards been developed for social work services for children in their own homes (Child Welfare League, 1984b).

Several factors help explain this gap. First, child welfare agencies have had relatively limited experience in offering services to intact families. Second, serious social problems in the late 1960s and 1970s thrust social work theory and practice into a transitional phase, with social workers having differing conceptions of social welfare, placing varying degrees of emphasis on clinical and social factors in the causation and treatment of problems, and holding a wide variety of views about appropriate roles for agencies offering social services to families. Third, a specific kind of service may have either preventive, protective, or therapeutic purposes, or perhaps all of these. For example, a social agency may appropriately supply homemaker service to one family in order to prevent problems from arising and to enhance normal family functioning. For another family this same service may supply daily care that will protect children from threatened neglect or abuse. In a third family, homemaker service may be part of a therapeutic plan for parents or other family members.

The National Resource Center on Family-Based Services has conceptualized a set of services that have the potential to be family-focused and to strengthen and maintain troubled families (see Figure 5.3). Choices among the various services should be extended through the

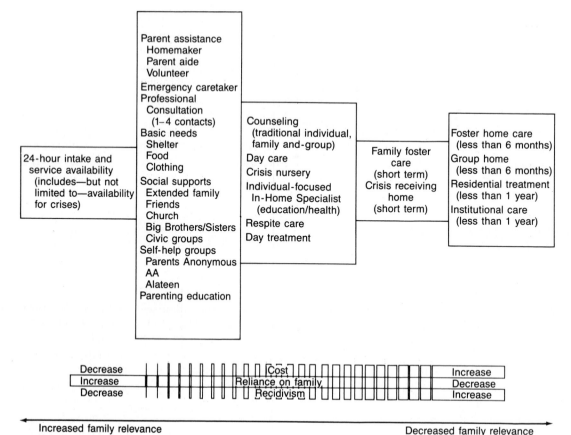

Figure 5.3. Potentially Family-focused Services. (*Source:* National Resource Center on Family-Based Services. [1982, Spring]. *Prevention Report,* p. 2.)

coordination of a home-based worker. It will be apparent that the services shown in the figure can be used in ways that are preventive, protective, or therapeutic, depending on the problems addressed and the timing of the intervention.

Kinds of Services Offered

Preventive Services. These services are designed to ensure conditions in families and communities that reduce overall risks of social distress and offer opportunity for normal maturation of children and effective social functioning of all family members. The primary aim is to prevent situations from becoming unfavorable

or hazardous to the well-being of children and to avert the emergence of individual problems. Some of the attributes of preventive social services follow (Class, 1968b).

1. Preventive social services are oriented to the future. Their purpose is to prevent pathology, rather than to combat or cope with harmful elements that already have attacked or adversely affected the child or family, as is true of protective services and of therapeutic services. Because they are services offered in advance of an identified harmful event, they contain an essential component of teaching and learning in relation to recognized and accepted norms of family life. They utilize educational techniques not only in

delivering services to families but also in teaching the community about the possible injurious influences in family life that can be prevented.

2. Preventive services are planned and carried out, not in relation to an individual child or an individual family in distress, but in relation to a larger population—a target group within which individual families and children share common risks. The intent is to maintain community standards that reduce risks in family life and which further the normal development and well-being of children. Directed toward the naturally occurring needs of children and their families in a given population, these services are especially important when disturbances in the community or in families are likely to generate problems for children. Therefore, programs must be readily available, not on the basis of an individual social worker's discretion as to whether a particular child or family can respond to and profit from the service, but as a matter of right to all individuals or families in a certain situation. Although a social worker may point out to a family the preventive resources of the community that are available, it should also be possible for any family to recognize its own eligibility on the basis of known, easily measurable, and objective criteria—for example, it lives within a flexibly prescribed neighborhood; it has children of certain age categories; the mother is working (without regard to her motivation for doing so); or it includes a physically or mentally handicapped child.

3. A preventive program utilizes a scientific approach. To be effective over time, a service designed to prevent problems of social functioning must be founded on evidence gained through systematic inquiry about empirical relationships—by knowledge of what action truly prevents specified conditions. For example, programs for young children's daytime care and development are needed that will foster optimal intellectual development and help overcome deficits brought about by early deprivation. To plan and successfully carry out such programs, one must first determine through sci-

entific investigation the cu methods which, under spe likely to reach these deve. tive goals for children.

4. Preventive social services interventive, in the sense that to be successtu. forestalling harmful events or influences in people's lives, the social workers who administer these services must sometimes involve themselves in private situations and exercise considerable initiative in reaching people, particularly those who most need the services. Interventive techniques are needed, especially in relation to persons who do not see the need for services or who have come to believe that their situation cannot be changed or that no one is interested in helping them.

This assumption of responsibility for reaching out to people and encouraging them to use services is based on certain convictions. Most parents want to care for their children adequately, although they may need help in doing so. In a highly industrialized society, increasing numbers of parents have a need for social services if acceptable norms or standards of child care are to prevail generally. Most people, even those in very stressful situations, have substantial strengths that can be called forth and used so that they can direct their own lives along lines of normal family life and balanced well-being. A timely provision of "social utilities" does not increase dependency, but in fact tends to increase people's self-reliance, competence, and feelings of compatibility with society.

The vision of greater justice for neglected and delinquent children and youth can endure and grow only if America provides far more preventive and supportive services for all young people. (Polier, 1989, p. 163)

Social workers frequently speak of their services as "preventive" in the sense that by their actions they aim to prevent problems from erging that are more serious than the ones eir clients currently face. Such a use of the term may simply reflect their desire to extend services of significant value to clients and their future. However, the kinds of preventive social services for children and families that have been described here are in a very early stage of development in this country. They are insufficient in number, usually have an uncertain or time-limited financial base, and have served for the most part as experiments or demonstrations.

Protective Services. Many of the existing services for children in their own homes are protective services. As discussed in Chapter 9, these are involuntary—they are not sought out by parents. Instead, they stem from intervention by a sanctioned agency when children are reported or found to be neglected, abused, or at high risk in their caretaking situation. In these circumstances parents must effect improvement in their caretaking or endanger their right to keep their children.

Therapeutic Services. These stem from the identification of a serious problem, the development of an assessment, and the engagement of an individual or group in a course of social treatment whose goal is to stimulate change from maladaptive functioning to more adaptive behavior. People may seek these therapeutic services on their own initiative or be strongly encouraged to seek help; in any case, in varying ways and degrees they acknowledge a problem and choose to engage themselves in the treatment process. Typical examples are the casework treatment of a seriously emotionally disturbed boy or girl, the group work treatment of a number of children with similar handicapping behavior problems, the treatment of a mentally ill parent in an outpatient facility or hospital setting, and therapy based on the interaction of family members as a vital part of both the cause and the treatment of the family problems. Therapeutic services are essential for the deeply troubled family or the seriously upset young person.

These services are specialized and relatively well developed among the agencies offering family and child welfare services; however, too frequently such services are not available in communities where children and families most need them.

Auspices and Settings

Services for children and families in their own homes may be given by public or private agencies, whether profit or nonprofit, and in a variety of settings. Their purpose may be to help children with their own problems or to strengthen their family life. They may be given by child welfare or family service units of public welfare departments, by voluntary family service agencies, by neighborhood service centers, by settlement houses, by child guidance clinics or other mental health agencies, and by courts, hospitals, and schools.

The fact that services in behalf of children can be offered by such a variety of agencies may make it possible to meet the particular needs of a child. On the other hand, the variety of agencies complicates the planning of services and the achieving of accountability. This is particularly true if the first agency to which the family goes does not coordinate its work with that of other agencies in the community, or does not continue its service to the child or family as long as it may be helpful or until the service of a more appropriate agency can be arranged. Counseling and therapy in various forms are a major means of helping children in their own homes. These services may be carried on with an individual parent or child, a family unit, or a group of parents or children.

Casework with Individual Parents

This has been a principal method in child welfare and family services. The social worker usually arrives at an assessment early in the course of regularly scheduled interviews. Through attempts to help the parent identify the problem causing stress in the family, understand some of its roots, and recognize the feelings and behaviors the problem produces, the social worker hopes to make the parent (and indirectly other family members) able to act more effectively. Social workers may lend strong emotional support to parents. They may attempt to clarify the situation by identifying troublesome components of the unhappy family situation and the alternative actions the parents may take. They may offer interpretations of the parents' feelings and behaviors and help them to gain insight into the behaviors that react on family members.

From their knowledge of the community and its resources, social workers may also offer information and suggestions about opportunities that can benefit parents or other family members. They may refer the parents to another social agency for a specialized service, prepare written summaries of the family situation and the basis for referral, and sometimes continue as a liaison between the family and the new agency until service gets underway. They may act directly on behalf of the parents by accompanying them in stressful situations, such as when they must ask for supplementary financial assistance or confront a negligent landlord about repairs. They may teach effective ways of getting attention to legitimate requests for service in the community or act on the parents' behalf by speaking for them and actively pressing for attention to their rights and needs.

Social workers may perform other tasks or employ other innovative techniques, but at all stages of the service, they seek to involve parents in an assumption of responsibility for the solution to family problems.

Crisis Intervention.   This approach looks for the source of the client's difficulty in the social situation rather than in personal pathology (Lufton, 1982). Proponents believe that effective professional intervention at crisis points can help clients resolve the immediate problem and prevent more serious problems from arising later on. Because family members are usually more motivated to use help at a point of crisis, when their usual coping patterns have proved inadequate, a social worker has an opportunity to help family members improve their performance of social roles and strengthen their ability to solve problems.

In one program, for example, crisis workers are teamed with police to respond to calls of spouse abuse. The workers may be able to help the parties resolve the immediate domestic problem, or they may help the victim find safe emergency housing. Over the longer run, they support and encourage victims through legal processes if the assailant is being criminally prosecuted. The workers also can help abused wives make permanent changes in their living situation when they feel ready to do so (Fein & Knaut, 1986). This program illustrates that preventive intervention at a point of crisis not only capitalizes on people's readiness to use help; it can also mobilize and coordinate community and agency resources on behalf of families with multiple needs.

Treatment for the Individual Child

Children are often interviewed or observed by social workers outside the presence of their parents for the purpose of making a social study and evaluation as a basis for recommending certain actions in their behalf. But many children can best be helped by participating directly in the modification of their troubling behavior, in which case a social worker may give therapy to the individual child. Therapy is offered on the assumption that the child is a person in his or her own right, that the child's behavior is not just a reflection of the parents' problems, and that the child is an important actor in the situation, one capable of significant self-expression in words or deeds.

Kelly and Wallerstein (1976) observed and reported the impact of divorce on children as seen in a divorce counseling program of a mental health center. They studied behavior exhibited shortly after the initial parental separation, and again one year later. One aim of their work was to develop clinical interventions specific to divorce for children of different ages. Although the experience of each child was individual, common types of responses were identified among children between the ages of seven and ten. These initial responses included sadness and grieving, fear, feelings of deprivation, and fantasies of responsibility and reconciliation. Following is an example of a child who expressed his sorrow within the supportive structure of the counseling interviews:

> Roger, age seven, started the first hour by asking if the therapist had heard the "bad news" of the divorce. He felt "very, very sad about the split" but maintained he couldn't cry. "I have to hold it in, 'cause I'd be crying all the time." Roger observed it would be very embarrassing to cry at school. He mournfully related how he gets his own breakfast and lunch because his mother didn't get up in the morning like she used to. "She must be sick." Roger knew there was trouble from the beginning: "They only knew each other two days and they *should* have known each other at least nine days before getting married." He sadly recounted to the therapist his unsuccessful efforts to break up his parents' fights.

Some children openly acknowledge their feeling of primary responsibility for the divorce:

> Eight-year-old Debbie, psychologically intact yet saddened and bewildered by her mother's decision to divorce, anxiously admitted that her failure to relay an important message from one parent to the other had precipitated an intensely heated argument leading to the divorce. The therapist's efforts to explore the parent's divorce action with Debbie and provide some reassurance of her innocence were met with considerable skepticism.
>
> Another child blamed his father for the divorce, but then suddenly asked, "You don't think I caused that old divorce, do you?" In a later session, he told the therapist that his father left "because I'm dumb."

A year later most of the children's responses had modified. Intense pain had lessened and been replaced by a sad, resigned acceptance of the divorce as final. Children as young as five or six tended to cling to fantasies of the father's return (Kelly & Wallerstein, 1976).

Social-Cognitive Treatment. The term "social-cognitive" refers to a set of techniques for promoting sociobehavioral and cognitive changes in children. The therapist, or child helper, supports the child's efforts to increase her social and cognitive skills. Social skills include accepting the influence of adults and others in authority, engaging in reciprocally enjoyable social exchanges with friends, and resolving conflict appropriately. The child helper may teach the child cognitive strategies such as anger-management training, social problem solving, and self-instruction. The latter includes the ability to set goals, make commitments to reach those goals, evaluate one's own progress, and manage one's wishes and desires. This approach recognizes the significance on behavior of the social environment and of the attitudes and coping skills that children have learned (Barth, 1986a, pp. 4, 5, 20, 21).

The helping process is structured as a sequence of tasks, from initial contact, through identifying the problems, developing a treatment plan, completing a plan, evaluation, and termination (Barth, 1986a, pp. 32–33). The intervention will have both social and cognitive aspects. If, for example, a teenager has a habit of skipping school, the child helper might involve the family, the school, and the community in establishing a coordinated strategy, with consistent reinforcers for the desired behavior. Parents, attendance officers, and proprietors of popular teenage hangouts can all help the child to decide to go to school rather than spend the day elsewhere.

In designing cognitive interventions, the child helper understands that "students may believe that school success will not accrue to them regardless of their effort or skill. Older youth especially often judge themselves to be victims of teachers' arbitrariness or prejudice. These beliefs are stubborn. Antidotes to such belief systems are not always successful, but some cognitive strategies have promise. . . . The child helper can encourage students to identify students similar to themselves—that is, those of the same race, with similarly cut hair, or with a history of trouble—who are achieving success. This may help make success seem more possible and advance a discussion of the coping strategies that others use to manage in a sometimes hostile environment. Cognitive rehearsal of successful interactions in such environments may also forward reentry into the classroom'' (Barth, 1986a, p. 246).

Other Work with Children. Social workers blend theories and techniques in various ways to help children reach certain developmental goals, learn about themselves and the world about them, utilize opportunities, meet an unexpected crisis, or resolve a conflict that impairs their social functioning.

They may apply principles of ego psychology to provide a supportive casework service to a child to help him or her during a stressful ordeal, such as a period of extended and frightening medical care. In such an instance the goal may be to modify the child's disabling feelings and behavior and strengthen the ego's capacity to endure and adapt to frustration.

Social workers act as casefinders in the early detection of children's problems. They seek to discover or develop opportunities for children in the community. They refer them for a variety of community services, for recreational programs, music and art activities, or health services. Sometimes they seek a relatively simple service, such as the assignment of a volunteer who offers a child companionable friendship and new experiences. Sometimes the need is complex, and social workers must bring together a combination of resources and professional personnel to collaborate in behalf of a child. In a variety of ways they seek to discover children's strengths and reinforce these in their daily lives.

Family Therapy

Sometimes distress revolving around a particular child in a family or some problem that a family encounters lends itself most effectively to a form of family therapy, or family unit treatment.

The varying forms of family therapy are based on the view that family life is a system of relationships between people. The goals are directly related to the well-being of children and the enhancement of their learning and growth opportunities. For example, the goals may be to open communication between family members, educate them as to how to get along within the family and the community, help parents to take on sound child-rearing practices, and clarify and stabilize family roles.

Family therapy may provide several advantages: attention to each individual member as well as the family as a whole; an opportunity for the reenactment of crucial themes within a family and a broader and more balanced diagnostic view of the strengths and weaknesses in the family; a reduction of the pressure on a single family member, particularly a child who may have been singled out by other family members as their special problem; and an increase in the probability that improvement in a child's behavior and direction of growth will be sustained by changes and adaptations within the total family pattern of interaction (Leader, 1969).

Adaptations in family therapy have been made in order to bring services to some families with urgent problems who generally do not use existing services. For example, the Mental Hygiene Clinic of the Henry Street Settlement in New York City undertook an experimental approach to bringing mental health services to low-income families in ways they could use. Because persons from this social class appeared to need mental health services keenly but had often not followed through with service offered in traditional ways, for example, appointments in the office and formal interviews, treatment was shifted from the clinic to the home in a series of regularly scheduled but nonthreatening friendly visits.

The social worker's role was either to act as a catalyst to dramatize the particular conflict or to break into the destructive pattern as it occurred. Then the social worker demonstrated ways and means of settling differences, with family members testing out and talking about the new methods. This excerpt from a case record is illustrative:

The Cs are a Chinese family living in a crowded, four-room slum tenement. Mr. C. is fifteen years older than his wife and there are four school-age children, the oldest 12 and the youngest 6. . . . Tom, the 9-year-old, . . . had violent, uncontrollable temper outbursts, during which he would run out of the school building. His 10-year-old brother Danny was released a few months ago from a state hospital and, except for his readmission to school, there was little follow-up by the after-care clinic in assessing his problems or needs in readjustment to the family and community. . . .

Typical forms of discipline used by the parents were to isolate the children when they got into fights, beat them in explosive fits of anger, or tell them that Danny was crazy and should be left alone. . . .

The worker's visits were planned at a time when all family members were present, which was before the evening meal. The children were always around the kitchen table ready to begin a game or to work with clay. In the first few sessions Mr. C. would sit nearby but not participate except to criticize or correct the children, and Mrs. C. would continue preparing the evening meal, with one eye on the table to see what was going on. During this period, too, considerable attention was diverted toward Danny, who, in keeping with the parental discipline of isolating him, hung back and would not come into the

room. He finally came in after some tentative moves.

In the games or other activities Danny did quite well in learning to share materials and adult attention while the worker was present. Yet, as the time approached to terminate the session, he would invariably provoke one of the other children. During one session he claimed he won a game of cards, although Tom was the real winner. Mrs. C. immediately pushed the winning cards to Danny in order to avert the tantrum she anticipated. Tom, furious, ran off in tears. Enlisting the parents' help, the worker brought Tom back, gently but firmly, and the issue was discussed before everybody. As this was clarified, other grievances between the brothers were brought out. Danny had broken a table that Tom had made in the settlement woodshop and proudly taken home. The parents claimed it was beyond repair. The worker had the table brought in, looked over, and repaired then and there, with Danny's help.

In succeeding weeks, incidents such as these and others typical in the lives of children who are in rivalry and angry with each other were either observed or reported during the activity sessions. Each time the worker would encourage each to tell his version and bring out his feelings, and each time the grievance or dispute would either be settled to everybody's satisfaction or it would be evident that angry feelings were in better control. (Levine, 1964, pp. 24–25)

This approach of "treatment in the home" had parallels with more traditional family casework and family therapy in that it included the provision of concrete services, focused on the whole family, and attempted to build on whatever family strengths could be detected. However, these clients could not be viewed as "motivated" in the usual sense; modification of behavior patterns through some level of insight therapy was not attempted.

The Henry Street experiment "did effect concrete changes in the way parents responded to and dealt with their children, and . . . these changes are reflected in the improved behavior of the children" (Levine, 1964, p. 28).

Group Work Approaches

Some parents and children have needs that lend themselves to social group work. Social workers may bring together a number of parents or children who can be expected to profit from an association together under social work or other trained guidance. Group work may be the only service offered, or it may be used as a supplement to casework with individuals or to community work.

In selecting persons for groups, the intent is to make possible a climate of acceptance and support as an aid to learning, and the emergence of a process of meaningful interaction within the group. For some persons the group provides security in which they are confronted. Groups may be formed of parents who share common problems or demands, for example, parents of mentally retarded children, mothers of one-parent families, and parents who are facing difficulties with adolescent behavior. Groups may also be chosen by sex, for example, mothers' clubs for AFDC recipients; or by age level, for example, groups of teenage parents.

Some group work carries a strong component of counseling or therapy and is directed primarily toward problems in a participant's personality and interpersonal relationships. Some other work with groups may be termed family life education, which focuses more directly on the imparting of knowledge to parents that can be expected to have a positive effect on family life. Some groups are fused with elements of both education and counseling (Berry, 1988).

Services for Families with a Handicapped Member

Families whose members have disabilities face the same stresses as other families—single parenthood, geographic mobility, and attenuated extended family ties. In addition, families with a disabled member face other stresses; they must find special services needed by the disabled person and deal with a range of service professionals; and they often must direct special attention to the tasks of balancing their lives and supporting the needs of *all* family members. Too often service professionals assume that families with a disabled member are dysfunctional and inadequate. Particularly if the disability is severe emotional illness, professionals may assume that the family is the source of the problem. This assumption adds to the family's already considerable burdens (Will, 1988).

For many years, children with serious mental or physical disorders were institutionalized. Their disabilities were thought to require expert treatment in a highly specialized environment. Treatment plans often excluded parents either purposely or by default. Since the 1960s, public policy changes have caused a shift away from institutional care and toward community-based supports for families. This change recognizes that families with a disabled member can sustain satisfying family life with the right kind of external supports (Friesen et al., 1988).

The National Institute of Mental Health is sponsoring projects to help states design and try out family-centered services for families with a severely emotionally disturbed child. These projects value individualized service plans, in which the needs of the child and family dictate the mix of services provided. They also value the personal dignity of the children and families served, respecting their wishes and goals, and involving them as vital partners in all aspects of the service plan (Stroul & Friedman, 1988). Services may include child care, crisis intervention, legal assistance, housing, recreation, homemaker services, parent education, counseling, transportation, therapeutic camping, respite care, educational programs, and vocational counseling. With the help of these projects, families organize themselves and meet together for social support, information sharing, and advocacy efforts directed toward local and state governing bodies. Through informal parent-to-parent interaction and more formalized self-help organizations, parents benefit from knowing they are not alone and can make positive changes in their lives.

Services for Teenage Mothers

Working with adolescent mothers is characterized by the special aspects of their teenage status that seem incongruous with motherhood. Most adolescents are in a stage of personality development that, with its rapid contrasts in maturity and immaturity and varying degrees of rebellion against adult authority, confronts the social worker with special problems in understanding which of the young mother's reactions are normal responses for an adolescent and which are unduly distorted by the early pregnancy. The stress the teenage mother feels is apt to be intensified by the fact that she has to adapt herself to disharmonious roles, that of young adolescent and that of mother (Bucholz & Gol, 1986).

Across the country numerous programs have been established in an effort to respond to the special needs of pregnant teenagers, particularly during the prenatal period. In many instances positive outcomes have been shown. Yet it has become clear that these benefits are very likely to be short-lived if no effort is made to maintain contact with the teenage mother after delivery (Young et al., 1975; Furstenberg, 1976; Klerman & Jekel, 1977; Olds et al., 1986, 1988; Vecchiolla & Maza, 1989).

The Need for Services beyond Delivery. Some programs are now providing a range of assertive postpartum services in order to preserve gains made during the prenatal period, particularly with regard to using contraception, staying in school, and retaining early goals. Crittenton Hastings House in Boston is one agency that became aware through its own experience of the need for long-term services. Hastings House has offered a prenatal program to pregnant teenagers since 1973 (Cartoof, 1978). The program is designed especially for teenagers who usually drop out of school on becoming pregnant, who do not seek prenatal care until late in pregnancy, and who seldom receive social services. The program offers the adolescent a comprehensive service under one roof: daily transportation to and from the center; academic instruction by the Boston School Department; education about prenatal care, parenting, and sexuality; medical care provided in the center by Boston City and Boston Lying-in hospitals; individual and group counseling; two meals each day; and evening discussion groups for the teenager's parents.

In a 1978 study of the Hastings House program it was found that, of the population served, one in four had had a previous pregnancy; 84 percent reported that they had knowledge of birth control methods, but only 30 percent had used contraception, with only 2 percent of these using any method consistently. Almost all indicated that the pregnancy was unintended. Records of the program over time indicated that after childbearing about 80 percent of the young mothers returned to school, 67 percent had plans to continue into college or some career preparation, and over two-thirds reported use of contraception. However, a follow-up two years later showed almost half of the mothers had dropped out of school and half had had at least one more unplanned pregnancy. These statistics impelled the agency to extend service well into the postpartum period and to be assertive in offering a range of services, whether or not the new mother had asked for such help.

> The basic plan of the follow-up service is simple. A home visit is made to each mother on the average of once every three months, for assessment purposes. In an in-depth interview, the worker inquires about school attendance, birth control usage and employment intentions. If the mother reveals a problem, a service plan is devised. The worker not only refers the girl to an appropriate resource, but explains the referral process, makes the necessary contacts, and accompanies the client to the resource. (Cartoof, 1978, p. 663)

The follow-up procedures are supplemented by other services—job and day care referrals, registration for an academic or training program, and abortion referrals when indicated. In addition, advocacy interventions are also employed. For example:

> When day care centers have no openings, the worker may negotiate a baby-sitting arrangement with families in the neighborhood. Contacting minority recruitment members of the personnel departments of local banks and businesses may open jobs for young women. Visiting a high school guidance counselor to advocate for a special academic plan for a particular student may pave the way for her to get needed services. (Cartoof, 1978, pp. 663–664)

Detailed statistics and narrative records on the first seventy-seven participants in the extended program gave evidence of gains in maintaining school attendance, avoiding repeated pregnancies, and in finding employment. The 22 percent of the mothers who conceived again illustrated a problem common to many teenagers: difficulty in using birth control pills effectively.

Family Life and Sex Education Programs. The high rates of teenage premarital births indicate clearly that sex education programs are reaching many adolescents either too late or ineffectively. Evidence is at hand that 50 percent of premature adolescent pregnancies occur within six months after the girl has become sexually active, and that 20 percent of these pregnancies occur within the first month of sexual activity (Zabin et al., 1979). Too often teenagers become sexually active without planning for consistent use of contraception. More positively, among those who did use contraception during their first experience with sexual intercourse, 70 percent of them continued to use birth control methods whenever they engaged in sex (Zelnik & Kanter, 1978) thus illustrating the importance of more effective programs of sex education and contraceptive counseling.

Public polls through the 1970s showed increasing numbers of adults favoring sex education within the schools. Yet there is also evidence that most sex education courses have little impact on preventing premature births (Chilman, 1978). In a study of sexual and contraceptive experiences of young women in the United States, an attempt was made to determine how effective sex education was in informing young women about the menstrual cycle. Those who had had a course in which the menstrual cycle was discussed were more knowledgeable and more able to correctly perceive the time of greatest pregnancy risk than were those who had not had such a course. However, the differences were not great (Zelnik & Kanter, 1977). A curriculum that presents information only is clearly not enough in an area where so much depends on personal and social attitudes and behaviors.

Although public opinion generally has supported giving adolescents access to contraception, doing so is far more controversial than simply providing information. Schools usually confine their programs to the latter. However, in 1973 a program was established in a public high school in St. Paul, Minnesota, where an in-school health clinic offered gynecological services. Participation was slow in the beginning. To increase use of the services, a decision was made to include athletic, job, and college physical examinations and a weight-control program as well. These programs were enthusiastically accepted by students of both sexes and brought increased requests for contraceptive counseling among individuals who had not wanted their motives for using the clinic to be obvious.

Follow-up studies of this program indicate that it has helped to alleviate problems associated with teenage sexuality. The program is credited with reducing the rate of teenage pregnancy, increasing the school retention rate of pregnant and parenting teens, and helping students sustain competent use of contraceptives. The program attributes its success to its "'open door' policy that allows for daily contact with the service team, a convenient location, accessible staff, flexibility, and a wide range of available services" (Pittman & Govan, 1986, p. 9).

Today many school-based clinics exist, most of which offer a comprehensive array of health and mental health services in the school building during the school day (Harold, 1988). Those opposed to the clinics are concerned that, by virtue of their location at the school, they implicitly condone sexual behavior among adolescents. They believe that the clinics may encourage youth to become sexually active who otherwise would not. Opponents of school-based clinics suggest alternative programs emphasizing abstinence and teaching parents how to communicate with their children about sex (DeBlasio, 1988).

Chilman argues for reconceptualizing sex education programs as guidance for living as a male or female in a rapidly changing society. She observes that sexual behaviors are linked to many personal characteristics, for example, level of self-esteem, sense of competence, ego strength, personal values, family relationships, and peer group associations. Sex education programs should be offered within an atmosphere of respect and sensitivity to both sexes with open sharing of ideas and feelings. Prescriptions of how males and females ought to behave because of their gender should be avoided (Chilman, 1978).

Homemaker Service

Homemaker service in behalf of children is provided by a governmental or nonprofit health or welfare agency to enable children to receive care in their own homes when their mother for any number of reasons cannot fully meet her maternal and homemaking responsibilities. In such instances, the agency provides a "homemaker" (sometimes called a "home-health aide"), a woman trained in child care and in home management who comes into the home for a few hours or more a day, or perhaps 24 hours a day, to perform a variety of tasks to help the family maintain itself. In addition to the help provided by the homemaker, the sponsoring agency tries to facilitate use of other social or health services by family members as may be needed. Homemaker service was originally conceived of as a short-term emergency service to hold families together during a crisis. While it still serves this purpose, the present-day conception of this service permits its application to a broader range of situations and to all socioeconomic groups. Its purposes may be preventive (and educational), protective, or therapeutic (Child Welfare League, 1959).

Philosophy. Homemaker service is predicated on the conviction that, given certain safeguards, children are best cared for and happiest living in their own homes. Homemaker service, therefore, is an organized expression of society's wish to strengthen and safeguard the homes and family lives of children and their parents.

A community's definition of homemaker service should be broad and applicable to different problem situations and family life-styles. For many the crisis is a temporary and naturally occurring event in the family life cycle, for example, hospitalization of the mother at childbirth. During such a brief disruption of normal family life, the availability of a homemaker is a preventive measure and should exist in a community as a social utility, easily available for families to use as a normal support. Some family situations are more serious, and the provision of a homemaker to assist parents is part of a social agency plan to protect children from neglect or abuse, or it is part of some other form of family therapy. In these situations a greater measure of social work evaluation and casework service is required.

Homemaker service is an economical service in relation to most out-of-home care for children, as well as in relation to its preservation of the social values of family life.

When Homemaker Service Is Appropriate. Homemaker service can be helpful in a variety of situations. In some the mother is absent from the home. In others she is present but unable to meet her responsibilities fully. In either case, the homemaker's function is to help the family maintain itself and improve its level of functioning.

The mother may be absent because of physical or mental illness that makes hospitalization necessary. Or she may find it imperative to be away from home because of the illness of a close relative, perhaps her own parent, where she is needed to give solace or nursing care. Sometimes a mother temporarily deserts her family because of marital discord or discouragement with continuing and overwhelming burdens. A capable and accepting homemaker may serve to hold the family together and minimize the stress felt by the children until the mother has returned or the father has made other arrangements for their care. Sometimes both parents temporarily abandon children, and a homemaker can be used to spare them the added trauma of leaving familiar surroundings and entering into shelter care during the immediate period when authorities are trying to locate their parents or make other arrangements for their long-term care. Homemakers have also been used most beneficially when a mother dies, to enable a father to hold his family together within its own home, particularly during the difficult period of adjustment to a way of life without the mother.

Homemaker service is also a useful resource in homes when a mother needs to learn better household practices or child care. She may lack the knowledge or motivation needed to meet her responsibilities; an accepting and competent homemaker can demonstrate ways of fulfilling her role more effectively and, in so doing, provide support and encouragement that nourish her motivation. Sometimes a mother's excessively poor housekeeping threatens the family with eviction; a homemaker can stave off this action while she teaches the mother to perform more adequately.

Homemaker service can provide a better-organized and happier home environment for some families with young children who are retarded or have other marked handicaps. Often there is psychological turmoil within the family during the early reaction to the child's handicap, or the demands of the handicapped child may consume the parents' energies. The introduction of a homemaker into the family can provide warmth and support that may enable parents to mobilize themselves more constructively. A homemaker also may be effective in supplying reliable observations of the child's level of development that can aid the parents and the social agency to develop a sound plan for his or her care and treatment.

If a child in the family has a long-term illness, perhaps a terminal one, a homemaker may supply additional help and support that enables the parents to maintain a balance with the other children in the family.

A homemaker can be of great help to an isolated mother who is the head of a family of young children, permitting her some time off for necessary errands, friendships, or attendance at training courses.

Homemakers have demonstrated creative ways of working with the mothers and children of agricultural migrant workers to help them improve their living conditions in regard to sanitation, nutrition, and child care.

Assessment. Homemaker service has been in use since the turn of the century, and has demonstrated its value. States have been given authority to purchase such service or to develop their own. Nevertheless, homemaker service is still insufficiently provided. Even though homemaker service has been shown to be feasible in rural areas, it continues to be primarily an urban service.

The preventive, protective, and therapeutic usefulness of homemaker service has been demonstrated in a variety of socioeconomic groups and problem situations. It has kept together families during a period of crisis and avoided unhappy alternatives—haphazard care of children by neighbors, or children scattered among relatives or left alone and unsupervised. Homemaker service can be provided at less cost in terms of both money and human stress than can foster care, particularly when there are several children in the family. It is unfortunate, therefore, that the service is so insufficiently supplied to all segments of the population.

Family-based Services

As will be seen in Chapter 10, child welfare agencies have poured great effort and many resources in the last two decades into getting children out of foster care and into permanent homes—reunited with their own families or established in adoptive homes or other permanent arrangements. In doing so, they have realized that most of the process entailed in family reunification would be appropriate as a means to ensure that children never have to leave their own homes. This realization has led to a reaffirmation of a long-standing social work principle, that society should have "a willingness to invest at least as much in a child's own family as society is willing to pay for out-of-home care for that child. This philosophy addresses the immense service vacuum which often exists between minimal services in the home and 24-hour care" (National Resource Center on Family-Based Services, 1982).

The term "family-based services" refers to a range of programs intended to preserve and strengthen family life. In spite of great diversity among the numerous (200 to 300) family-based service programs in the United States, all tend to share the following features. The whole family is regarded as the client, with attention to the interdependence of family members and to the transactions between the family and its social context. Services tend to be short-term and intensive, and are usually offered in the family's home. Often, a team of professionals and paraprofessionals works with the family, rather than an individual caseworker. The team offers a comprehensive array of services, based on the needs of the family, with extensive use of community resources (Annotated Directory, 1986; Hutchinson, 1986; Nelson et al., 1988).

Family-based services have their origins in traditionally practiced social work with families, which has always emphasized visits to the family's home, mobilization of natural helping networks and coordination of community services, and the provision of concrete and supportive services to help maintain the child in the home. This traditional mode of helping families has been greatly strengthened by the theory and practice base of the interdisciplinary family therapy movement, particularly the contribution of general systems theory to structural and family systems models of family treatment. Using these practice models, social workers are able to intervene more effectively in highly dysfunctional family systems (Strean, 1978).

The principle that children should be raised in their own families if possible, and that foster care should be used only if the child's well-being is seriously threatened at home, is reflected in P.L. 96-272, the Adoption Assistance and Child Welfare Act. The U.S. Congress passed this historic legislation in 1980, although implementation was somewhat delayed until the administrative regulations were promulgated in 1983. An essential feature of this complicated and far-reaching law is the fiscal incentives it offers states to provide family support services both to prevent the need to place children in foster care and to hasten family reunification for children who must be placed. The law also requires judges to determine that the social agency made "reasonable efforts" to preserve the family before the child is placed in foster care, or the federal government will not financially support the foster care placement (Sudia, 1986). This Act has given federal endorsement to locally developed family-based services.

The SCAN program (Supportive Child Adult Network) exemplifies one way that the common philosophy and program features of family-based services can be shaped. Evolving in 1977 from a multidisciplinary child protection team, by 1986 the program had become one of the largest voluntary agencies in Philadelphia to offer a family-centered approach to prevent child abuse and neglect. The target population for the approximately 500 families served each year are the mainly black, single parents living in substandard inner city housing. Families chosen are generally those for whom the public child protection agency has confirmed a report of abuse or neglect and therefore is requiring that the family participate in the program, or where the family was cleared of maltreatment charges but has been referred to receive services voluntarily. The families have an average of three or four children, of whom one is likely to be an infant. The children are likely to have unmet health needs, behavior problems, and difficulties at school. Many of their mothers suffer significant depression or abuse alcohol or drugs, and about a quarter function at a low intellectual level. They are often unaware of their children's needs, and all are at risk for child abuse and neglect. The program's intent is to strengthen the family's functioning so that the children can remain at home and not require foster care placement (Tatara et al., 1986).

The staff consist of master's and bachelor's level social workers, nurses, and paraprofessionals, with consultation from physicians and psychologists. Social workers provide protective casework, family counseling, and teach everyday living skills, using task-focused treatment plans developed jointly with the family. Spending time with the family and participating in the daily routine are considered essential to building a trusting relationship and provide occasions for modeling life skills in such areas as child management, shopping, and home maintenance. A special feature of this program is the nursing unit, which provides health information to parents and links families with health providers. Workers connect families with community services by accompanying them to other agencies and acting as advocates. The families are seen two to four hours a week, for a period ranging usually from nine to fifteen months. After termination, all families continue to receive health care at a weekly clinic (Tatara et al., 1986).

Research on effectiveness of family-based programs has been hampered by the difficulty in identifying appropriate control groups, loosely defined program goals, lack of instruments to measure the complex and elusive changes in family functioning, and wide variation across programs regarding client and service characteristics (Frankel, 1988). However, a recent evaluation of eleven family-based services in six states has provided information on worker, client, and service characteristics of the programs, and factors associated with program success (Nelson et al., 1988). The study found that 75 percent to 96 percent of the families in the different programs did not experience separation during the service period. Other indicators of success were that the majority of families achieved at least half of their treatment goals, and comparison of pre- and posttest scores of family functioning revealed that over 80 percent of the families showed moderate or high improvement during the time they received services.

The evaluation also identified family and service characteristics associated with whether or not a child was placed out of the home after the intervention began. As expected, families with more problems, older children, lower functioning children and caretakers, and previous placement history were more at risk for placement. The study found a surprising degree of association between service and family characteristics and case outcome. Programs offering more focused, shorter term involvement to lower risk families tended also to prevent placement in a high proportion of cases. Programs offering more comprehensive, long-term services to higher risk families were likely to experience higher placement rates. The study concludes that length and intensity of treatment and mode of service delivery must be matched to the client population served, and that no simple formulations can ensure a high success rate (Nelson et al., 1988).

Neighborhood-based Services

Neighborhood-based centers offer a range of services to families in a specific geographical area. In this respect, they differ from many agencies, which offer a specialized service, such as job counseling, or serve a particular problem population, such as teenage mothers, but do not limit their services to one neighborhood. The centers are reminiscent of the early settlement houses. They strive to create a friendly, non-stigmatizing atmosphere, inviting drop-ins and informal exchanges among staff and local visitors. They may develop programs in response to local need, and, like the settlements, they see their mission as improving community life and neighborhood conditions, as well as helping individuals and families.

Traditionally, settlement houses and community centers have offered an array of preventive and family support services, including opportunities for all age groups, from preschoolers to seniors, to socialize and engage in recreational activities together. Nursery schools, parent education programs, after-school care and tutorial services, job counseling, chemical addiction treatment and prevention groups, and youth sports and recreational programs are common. Centers also frequently administer clothing and food banks, and offer emergency housing and fuel assistance to community residents. Staff may act as advocates and mediators for residents with schools, the welfare department, the employment office, and other complex service organizations.

An innovative center in Brooklyn, New York, is the Center for Family Life, sponsored by St. Christopher-Ottilie, a voluntary child welfare agency. A special feature of this Center is that it combines a spectrum of traditional preventive services, including those listed above, with specialized, intensive, child welfare services. The Center offers child protective services, intensive family counseling, foster care, and family preservation and reunification services to the subgroup of neighborhood residents with serious problems of family functioning (McGowan, 1989).

Combining the services traditionally offered by a community center with those of a child welfare agency has important advantages for families who need child welfare services. These families are offered a continuum of services, from occasional socializing events to intensive counseling and substitute care, in one easily accessible setting. This allows Center staff to adjust the intensity and mix of services provided to meet the changing needs of the family over time. For the children who must go into temporary foster care, the center provides foster families in the child's own neighborhood, which lessens the disruption of placement, permits the child to remain with her school and friends, and eases arrangements for visiting with parents. Intensive services to parents are initiated immediately, with the goal of rapid reunification, in order to normalize and abbreviate the disruption of foster care (McGowan, 1989).

The Center for Family Life has been operating since 1978 but is still too new for any formal evaluation to have been completed. It seems replicable to other communities. The evaluator of this program points out that not only the program features, but also the quality of the Center's skillful and dedicated leadership, may be important components of the program's apparent success (McGowan, 1989).

TRENDS AND ISSUES

In considering issues embedded in the need for this country to address itself constructively to problems of family life, several conditions repeatedly emerge: the disadvantaged economic position of women in our society; a persistent view of female-headed families as a deviant family form, an attitude that burdens any attempt at social planning for single-parent families; and the penalties to many thousands of children who grow up without a father in their home.

This country has been reluctant to formulate any kind of integrated public policy on the family. The reluctance is strongest in relation to alternative family forms. One belief that underlies this stance is that making services and support readily available represents a dangerous sanction of divorce and births outside of marriage. The evidence is in the other direction: restrictive welfare policies and the withholding of help and support to families does not decrease marital dissolution or teenage parenting; it only compounds the noxious pressures that trap many families in a disadvantaged status for which they can find no exit.

Economic Loss to Single-Parent Families

Economic loss is inherent in the status of single-parent households. As Ross and Sawhill have pointed out:

> Whatever their prior income status (and many were middle class), women and children who form their own families run a high risk of poverty. Almost half of them are poor and a similar proportion spend some time on welfare. Indeed, the poverty population is coming increasingly to be dominated by female-headed families. . . . No one who is concerned about poverty or about distributional equity in our society can ignore the disadvantaged position of the group. (Ross & Sawhill, 1975, p. 3)

Central to any resolution of this disadvantage is the pressing need for flexible and easily available child care facilities and for training and equal opportunities for women. Such provisions support the concept of the family as the most effective preventive institution in our society.

Parental Responsibility for Support

Inherent in this issue is the question of basic economic rights of children. As a class, children are in special need of a minimal standard of living so that they can grow and develop physically, emotionally, and intellectually. The extent of parental responsibility for an acceptable level of economic support and the proper role of the public in relation to child laws and enforcement mechanisms are unresolved questions.

In the past, governmental efforts to enforce child support payments have been applied mostly to welfare families headed by women, although the problem of adequate child support from absent fathers is pervasive. Many women are not awarded child support payments at all, and others do not receive the amount to which they are legally entitled (Garfinkel & Sorenson, 1982). Moreover, divorced men are more likely to remarry than are their former wives, and in so doing, they incur new obligations that further reduce the economic support they provide their former households. The Family Support Act of 1988 increases the federal role in establishing paternity, setting child support awards, and enforcing payment from absent parents, and is intended to apply to all single-parent families, whether or not they receive welfare. However, the law leaves the states considerable discretion in implementation, and many important details remain unresolved (see Chapter 6).

The matter of economic security of children is further complicated by a prevailing perception of the single-parent family as a temporary stage of the family that will be changed by remarriage, or marriage, of the single parent. However, many single parents choose to remain single, or for numerous other reasons do not marry and gain greater economic security.

The issue remains: What should be a unified approach to income security for children in single-parent families? The need is urgent for a fair and general system.

Early Childbearing and the Family

As has been discussed earlier, the family system has been overlooked in many of the service approaches to teenage parenting. Programs have mainly focused on the adolescent mother or her child without attention to the potential benefits to be gained by working with other members of her family. Yet a theme that emerges in the literature of teenage parenting is the crucial role played by the teenager's mother, particularly as an agent of sexual socialization, as a counselor in decision making about the pregnancy, and as a primary figure in the early care of the child (Furstenburg, 1980; Young et al., 1980; de Anda & Becerra, 1984; Thompson, 1986). Little effort has been made, however, to channel resources to the families of teenagers at risk of pregnancy. Nor have service providers taken into account the impact on parents of their teenage daughter's pregnancy. In particular, the mothers of pregnant adolescents need concrete community support in efforts to help their daughters. Greater effort should be made to involve them in the programs developed and directed toward the young mothers.

The Need for Preventive Programs

Social workers concerned with children and families endure frustration in their work from an unresolved and compelling question: With the ongoing demand for treatment programs to deal with crises and very serious problems in family functioning, which currently absorbs most of the resources of social agencies, how can they be enabled to turn effective attention to preventive programs?

Solving problems is usually highly dependent on their early detection. Yet the inability on the part of social workers to reach families before problems become serious is common. We know that large numbers of children may be placed in jeopardy primarily because of their status. Generally, preschool children are more vulnerable to a range of health and developmental problems than other children. Adolescence brings special hazards. Children living with unmarried mothers encounter legal and social disabilities. Teenage parents are most often woefully unprepared for the responsibilities of parenthood. Babies born prematurely are at higher risk than others. Families that are fatherless lose the benefits and constructive influences that a father can bring to a family. Social services for groups of children such as these should not be delayed. Their availability should be a matter of right.

Social workers bear a responsibility to serve as advocates for groups of children and families with unmet needs and to work for change in the existing pattern of social services.

FOR STUDY AND DISCUSSION

1. Give arguments for and against a family policy that integrates the needs of single-parent families of all types with those of the more traditional family form.

2. Think of examples of preventive services that exist or could be developed for each of these groups: families that for whatever reason have only one parent; teenage-parent families; children experiencing divorce; adolescents in conflict with their parents; newly created stepfamilies; minority families (specify which minority). Show how each example is consistent with the attributes of preventive services discussed in this chapter.

3. For an ethnic or racial minority with which you are familiar, consider: the group's definition of family; child rearing and family interaction pat-

terns; and attitudes and values concerning families, family roles, and children. How have adaptations to dominant American society affected family functioning of members of this culture? How would you design ethnically sensitive preventive services for families of this group?

4. Visit a planned parenthood clinic. Ask the personnel to explain the services and procedures. How well are the alternatives presented: becoming sexually active; using contraception; having an abortion; choosing adoption?

5. Discuss how service to teenage parents might be improved through greater attention to their families. What problems, issues, alternatives, and possible consequences would you want to give attention to in counseling sessions with teenage pregnant girls and expectant fathers?

6. Find out if there is a family-based service in your community. If there is, learn the auspices under which it operates, the number of families it serves, the range of services it offers, eligibility requirements, and its goals for families. Make a tentative evaluation of the extent to which its services are likely to prevent foster care and make lasting improvements in family functioning. If there is no family-based service, try to identify reasons for its absence from the community's social services.

FOR ADDITIONAL STUDY

Children's Defense Fund. (1988). *Teenage pregnancy: An advocate's guide to the numbers.* Washington, DC: Children's Defense Fund, Adolescent Pregnancy Prevention Clearinghouse.

Furstenberg, F. F., Jr. (1976). *Unplanned parenthood: The social consequences of teenage childbearing.* New York: Free Press, 1976.

Garfinkel, I., & McLanahan, S. S. (1986). *Single mothers and their children.* Washington, DC: Urban Institute Press.

McGoldrick, M., Pearce, J. K., & Giordano, J. (1982). *Ethnicity and family therapy.* New York: Guilford Press.

Nelson, K., et al. (1988). *Family based services: Factors contributing to success and failure in family based child welfare services, final report.* Iowa City: National Resource Center on Family Based Services, University of Iowa, School of Social Work.

Thernstrom, S., Orlov, A., & Handlin, O. (Eds). (1980). *Harvard encyclopedia of American ethnic groups.* Cambridge, MA: Harvard University Press.

Wattenberg, E. (1987). Establishing paternity for nonmarital children. *Public Welfare, 45*(3), 8–13.

Wattenberg, E. (1990). Unmarried fathers: Perplexing questions. *Children Today, 19*(2), 25–30.

CHAPTER 6

Family Income
and the Child's Welfare

In the midst of affluence, child poverty casts a lengthening shadow.

Children's Defense Fund

Chapter Outline

The fundamental relationship of family income security to child welfare was recognized in 1909 when the participants of the first White House Conference on the Care of Dependent Children stated the principle that the child's own home should not be broken up for reasons of poverty and urged that money aid be given to maintain suitable homes for the rearing of children. Yet poverty rates among children in the United States are higher than in any of five other industrial countries—Australia, Canada, Sweden, United Kingdom, and West Germany (Smeeding & Torrey, 1988)—and higher today than at any time since the early 1960s, clear evidence of failure to ensure basic security to millions of America's children. Theoretically, America has a "safety net" that is assumed to ease the plight of poverty. In fact we have an increasingly inadequate patchwork of different programs that have never been able to keep many families from destitution.

Unfortunately, outmoded attitudes and opinions toward the poor continue to retard progress in ending poverty. These restrictive views generally hold that it is the nature of the poor to be poor, that they have particular characteristics inevitably predisposing them to poverty and precluding effective societal remedies. Such a frame of reference ignores the poverty-inducing impact of a set of environmental circumstances or forces over which an individual has little or no control.

After two decades of periodic attempts to reform the public welfare system, Congress passed and President Reagan signed into law the Family Support Act of 1988—P.L. 100–485. In this chapter we will review the provisions of this attempt at "welfare reform" and evaluate its strengths and weaknesses for reducing poverty among children and their families. First, however, we will consider the nature of poverty among children, its extent, causes and effects, and the principles and policies of governmental income maintenance programs (principally social insurance and public assistance). Because an understanding of the provisions of the new legislation is best arrived at from an awareness of a larger context, attention will be given to historical perspectives of the development of income maintenance programs in the United States.

NATURE OF POVERTY AMONG CHILDREN

Extent

The magnitude of poverty among the families of children and youth is evident from regularly issued reports of the United States Census Bureau. The federal government's poverty-level index represents an attempt to classify families as being above or below an income level required to support an average family of a given composition at the lowest level consistent with the standards of living prevailing in this country. The index currently in use was adopted in 1969 and is updated each year to reflect changes in the Consumer Price Index.

In the middle 1960s, census counts of the number of persons living in poverty showed a decline from the number so designated in 1959. But the census figures released in 1976 documented a halt in significant progress in reducing poverty in the United States. Poverty had not declined but had increased substantially (U.S. Department of Commerce, 1976).

Continuing losses in the battle against poverty are startlingly clear in census figures for 1987. From these data the Children's Defense Fund derived these findings:

> Among all children (up to 18 years old) in America, one out of five is poor.
> Among infants and toddlers younger than three, one in four is poor.
> Among children in families headed by young adults (younger than 30) one in three is poor.
> Among black children, nearly one out of two is poor. (Children's Defense Fund, 1989, pp. 16–17)

In 1987, almost 12,500,000 children were in families with income below the poverty level.

The burden falls disproportionately on families headed by women, on children and young adults, and on minority groups. Among the poor children, 15 percent were white, 39 percent were Hispanic, and 45 percent were black (U.S. Department of Commerce, 1989, pp. 454–455).

An especially troubling pattern within the poverty statistics for all American families is the increasing rise in poverty among parents younger than twenty-five years. During the early 1980s poverty rose among young families at a rate far higher than any other age group, reaching 30 percent by 1985 (Johnson & Sum, 1987, pp. 14–15).

Factors Contributing to the Growth in Poverty

The 1980s demonstrated America's changed role in international economic leadership. The national level of production slowed seriously, leaving in its wake widespread employment dis-

location that fell most heavily on families already economically disadvantaged. A significant number of persons entering the poverty ranks were blue-collar families who had previously had comfortable incomes, but had lost their employment because of the decline of jobs in heavy manufacturing industries. A slack economy was cited as the chief reason for the upswing in numbers of poor persons. Cutbacks by the Reagan administration in appropriations for various forms of social assistance programs were also cited as having forced some marginal-income families back into poverty (Herbers, 1982, July 20).

Many Americans work but remain poor, often because they cannot find full-time work. A compounding factor is the eroded value of the minimum wage, held constant between 1981 and 1989 despite the continuing rise in the cost of living (see Figure 6.1). Then, in a congressional compromise, the wage-floor was raised from $3.35 to $3.80 to begin on April 1, 1990, and to

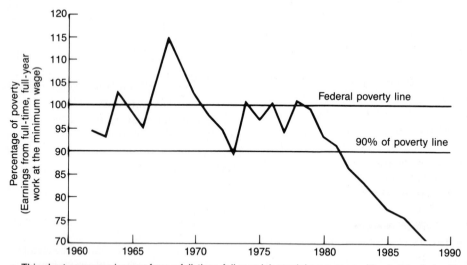

• This chart compares income from a full-time, full-year job at minimum wage with what the federal government says a family of three needs for poverty-level subsistence. The minimum wage has been losing ground to inflation since 1978 and now provides only 71 percent of the family's poverty-level needs. The 1988 poverty line is estimated.

Figure 6.1. Losing Ground: Minimum Wage and Poverty. (*Source:* Children's Defense Fund. [1989]. *A Vision for America's Future: An Agenda for the 1990s: A Children's Defense Budget.* Washington, DC: Children's Defense Fund, p. 19.)

$4.25 to begin a year later. A controversial provision was a 90-day wage for first-time employees at the old rate, rising then for that group of employees to $3.61 in 1991.

Certain characteristics make some people especially vulnerable to the threat of poverty. Furthermore, these characteristics tend frequently to be found together, and when this is so, the risk of poverty is heavier. As seen earlier in this chapter, *nonwhite status* increases the risk of poverty. Another factor is *large families.* The child growing up in a family with more than a few brothers and sisters is at greater risk of poverty, particularly if the family is vulnerable on some other count as well. *Single-parent families headed by a woman* bear an increased likelihood of poverty. Nonwhite families more often have a woman at the head, linking two situations accompanied by a high risk of poverty. *Change in family composition,* particularly through divorce, is a significant factor underlying low economic status, given the history of difficulty in enforcement of child support by the noncustodial parent.

In families of the "working poor," the problem is *low earning power of the parents.* Sometimes they are unable to find or keep a job or have only irregular employment. Frequently a poor family is headed by a parent who has worked steadily through the years, but still his or her family lives in poverty. Often the parent's work is unskilled, requiring long hours at low pay. And always if the head of the family is under twenty-five years of age and especially if she or he is black, the likelihood of unemployment or underemployment is greater than for the middle-age group.

Of special concern are the children of *migrant farm workers,* who occupy the lowest level of any major group in the American economy. An estimated 175,000 to 255,000 children under eighteen years of age move about with their parents during the crop seasons. A similar number have parents in the migrant stream but do not travel with them. Year after year these parents are unable to achieve even the barest minimum

income necessary for wholesome family life. Like them, their children are trapped in a vicious circle of unending poverty and rootlessness (American Friends, 1976).

The relationship of *low levels of education* to unemployment and poverty is well known. The direct bearing of education on job potential becomes greater each year with automated industry heightening the risk of a lifetime of poverty for youth who have insufficient education. Many young people living in poor families do not finish high school and begin at age sixteen to swell the ranks of the unemployed. School dropouts tend to marry early, thus stepping up the risk of enduring poverty.

The timing and circumstances of *marriage and childbearing* are of critical importance to future family income. The relationship of early marriage to low income is not just a circumstance of the first few years following marriage. As the size of the family grows and older children's needs expand, it becomes harder to match earnings with family needs. Early childbearing frequently forces the parents to make occupational decisions without sufficient education or real choice and is likely to supply a continual experience of poverty for the new family unit (Schorr, 1966).

The risk to family income arising from low levels of education and early marriage is not related only to the education of a male head of family. Teenage mothers and other women with little education have few skills to fall back on if they are deprived of the support of their children's father.

Effects of Poverty on Children and Parents

"There can be no doubt that social conditions such as wealth or poverty have profound effects on children's development" (Stone & Church, 1984). The unfavorable influences of poverty begin early for children and continue for a long time—too often through all their lives.

All children should be able to expect certain

basic needs to be met—those for food, clothing, health care, and adequate housing. The fact is that many children do not have these basic needs satisfied. The *provision of food* is one of the first duties that parents attend to, even though it means going without or postponing the fulfillment of other wants and desires in the family. Even so, we know that many children go hungry to school each day. The food they do receive only partially supplies them with the basic nutrients for proper growth.

"Children are dying every day in this country. They die in accidents that occur when no adult is watching over them; they die at birth, because of insufficient or nonexistent prenatal health care; they die of malnutrition, or drugs, or preventable diseases—but the root cause is poverty." (Tomkins, 1989, p. 74, quoting Marian Wright Edelman)

The extent to which poor children are *inadequately clothed* is less apparent. Perhaps in the midst of our abundant material goods, many poor parents can somehow obtain clothing for their children that is at least minimally adequate. Even so, in any big city school system and in poor rural schools, some children come to school poorly clothed or miss days of school for lack of a pair of shoes or a winter coat.

More factual knowledge is available about poor children and health care. Progress in maternal and child health, which had moved steadily forward in the 1960s and 1970s, fell behind in the following decade. A strong indicator is the infant mortality rate, which in 1986 was 10.4 deaths for 1,000 live births, leaving the United States ranking thirteenth, with a higher rate than such countries as Spain, Ireland, Japan, West Germany, and France (Children's Defense Fund, 1989, p. 5). Furthermore, despite medical advances, infant mortality rates in impoverished areas of our major cities are almost double the national average (Wilkenson, 1987). Almost one

in four American babies is born with its mother having had no prenatal care in the early stages of pregnancy (*CDF Reports,* 1987a, p. 11).

Children in poor families lack proper medical care. Increasing numbers of women and children have no form of health insurance and no way to pay health bills. Low-wage jobs frequently carry no health benefits (Children's Defense Fund, 1989, pp. 7–9). Among poor preschoolers, between 34 and 45 percent are not adequately immunized against serious but preventable diseases, for example, measles or diphtheria (*CDF Reports,* 1987a, p. 11). Poverty, ignorance, and lack of access to proper care contribute to this state of affairs.

Another significant and far-reaching effect of poverty is seen in the impact of early social environment on the *development of intelligence.* Crucial and limiting effects of poverty restrict poor children's ability to profit from their right to academic learning and to grasp their determining opportunity for educational attainment. In view of contemporary understanding of the way in which children develop intellectually, it is not surprising to find that many children of the poor enter school unready to make use of the opportunity for learning (see Chapter 8).

Poor children frequently live in seriously *inadequate housing.* Sources of stress to which the individual cannot adapt occur frequently in the housing of poor families—crowding, dilapidation, and high noise level. Inadequate housing relates directly to the incidence of certain illnesses. Acute respiratory infections and diseases of the skin are related to crowding, inadequate facilities for washing, multiple use of toilet facilities, and inadequate heating or ventilation. Other health hazards are evident in the minor digestive diseases related to poor facilities for cold storage of food and inadequate toilet and water facilities. Some children experience lead poisoning from eating peeling paint in their neglected tenements (Schorr, 1966). Most serious of all with respect to inadequacy of housing is the effects of *homelessness* on children and their parents.

Homeless Children and Their Parents

Extent. The growing phenomenon of a large homeless population in America has shocked much of the public, reflected in terms such as "a national disgrace" and "a moral outrage." From a study by the Institute of Medicine requested by Congress, at least 100,000 children are estimated to be homeless on any given night. This estimate does not include children who have run away or been pushed out by parents, some of them pregnant or already a parent, all of whom are in need of shelter. An estimated 250,000 people are believed to be homeless; 1.3 million to 2 million are homeless for one night or more sometime in the year. Most disturbing: Children under the age of eighteen, usually in families headed by a woman, are "the fastest growing group among the many sub-populations of the homeless" (Boffey, 1988, p. 12).

In this enormously wealthy country, homelessness is a national disgrace. It is a metaphor and a symptom—a metaphor for an irresponsible and careless society, a symptom that something is very wrong in the land of the free and the home of the brave. (Hartman, 1989)

Causes. The fundamental cause of homelessness in America is the sharp decline in construction of low-income housing during the 1980s. This development contrasted significantly with the previous three decades. Following the end of World War II, Congress passed bipartisan legislation, the National Housing Act of 1949, with the stated goal of "a decent home for every American family." Under the act, the federal government supported housing programs that maintained a reasonable balance between supply and demand for low-cost housing. By 1980 some $32 billion was budgeted annually for the building of housing for low- or moderate-income families. In the 1980s of the Reagan administration, low-income housing allocations fell sharply. By 1989 public concern about homelessness was at a new height and federal allocations rose to $7.5 billion, a level that was still 77 percent less than the 1980 level. The loss of housing for the poor was exacerbated by the "gentrification" that appeared in the late 1970s. Public funds were supplied to convert low-cost housing into homes for those with significantly higher incomes. Goals of gentrification had merit—slum clearance, an enlarged tax base, and revitalization of urban villages. Nevertheless, housing that poor families and many working people could afford was depleted and not replaced (Hayes, 1989, pp. 60–61).

Characteristics of Homeless Children and Parents. Many homeless families are sheltered in old hotels. One of these is the Martinique in New York City, where 400 families are housed. A City Council report described them thus:

> The average family consists of a mother and three children. Thirty-four percent of the families became homeless after eviction by a landlord, forty-seven percent after being doubled up with other families or otherwise living in overcrowded conditions, nineteen percent after living in substandard housing. Fifty percent of the heads of households reported that they had once held full-time jobs. Seventy percent had, since coming to the Martinique, visited at least five places to rent that they could not afford or from which they had been turned away by landlords who did not want children or welfare recipients. (Kozol, 1988a, p. 66)

From his repeated visits and interviews with the homeless in the Martinique, Kozol reported that it "is not the worst of the hotels for homeless families. . . . Because its tenants have refrigerators— . . . a precious item for the mother of a newborn—some residents consider it to be one of the better shelters in the city" (p. 66). Nevertheless, typically the room in which a family lives is crowded with no place to sit except on beds or the floor, dreary, devoid of fresh air, dimly lit or lit by the stark light of fluorescent tubes in the ceiling, lead paint peeling everywhere. Toilets often overflow leaving sewage on the floor; cockroaches are abundant; elevators frequently don't work. Children have no place to play; when they look out the window from the room that is their home, they look down on a narrow alley strewn with broken glass or at the towering wall of another hotel (Kozol, 1988a).

As part of a larger study of homeless families in fourteen Massachusetts shelters (two-thirds of the shelters statewide), Bassuk and Rubin (1987) collected clinical information about 156 children by means of interviews with members of 82 families. Data collected covered demographics, medical and psychiatric status, nature of family and peer relationships, participation in day care, Head Start, or a school program, and school adjustment. Their descriptive findings indicated that a majority of the children were "suffering developmental delays, severe anxiety, and learning difficulties." About half of the children were in need of psychiatric referral and evaluation. The preschoolers showed multiple impairments. The school-age children had serious problems that needed immediate attention. The lack of a home was a source of shame for the children. "The new and often chaotic environment of the shelter; the lack of privacy, structure, and routine; and the acute stress experienced by their mothers contribute to the children's distress." Parents appeared to be aware of their children's trouble but lacked a way of dealing with it. "When one is preoccupied with concerns about survival, there is little energy for attention to anything else" (pp. 284, 285).

The children's problems had begun before the current homelessness. Many had experienced a cycle of residential instability stemming from severe poverty and/or homelessness. The researchers concluded that "the data support that homelessness is becoming intergenerational. As each year goes by without stable housing and appropriate services for these families, the fate of the children, especially the pre-schoolers, becomes increasingly uncertain. One can only imagine what the legacy and experience of homelessness will mean for these children as adults" (Bassuk & Rubin, 1987, p. 265).

GOVERNMENTAL INCOME MAINTENANCE PROGRAMS

Various factors influence the extent to which individuals are free to compete and earn. Family income varies with such factors as the extent to which the head of the family possesses marketable skills, social class, the way in which he or she may be affected by a color caste system, and the satisfaction or lack of it received from work. Low income and poverty are not the lot of a family by rational choice. These conditions can arise from inequities of the market and other institutional inadequacies outside the control of the individual.

Human behavior is complex, and the development of an individual's innate capacities depends in large part on the degree to which a hierarchy of needs has been progressively satisfied. At least a minimum level of guaranteed security is necessary if children are to attain the goals society holds for them. If the source of income within a family is undependable and critically inadequate, then the individual and the family must always be bound down to meeting the physiological needs of bare subsistence.

There should be no implication of inadequacy in the need for outside help; an attachment of stigma is unwarranted. The family can no longer be held fully responsible for what happens to it. Children cannot realize the fruits of a democratic commitment to the ideals of liberty, equality, and fair opportunity unless some system exists that protects them and their families against the hazards of poverty with its resulting social insecurity.

The principal programs by which people in this country have used the instrument of government to assure some measure of income security to themselves and their families reflect two different approaches to meeting income needs: a guaranteed minimum security provided by a program of social insurance based on earned right; and a system of public assistance, or relief, based on an investigation of the individual's economic means and proven need.

Social Insurance

The term "social insurance" refers to programs established by law for the purpose of assuring financial benefits, related to earlier compulsory contributions, when an individual or family experiences loss of income due to specified risks. Social insurance is based on the idea of self-help and prevention of poverty and its resultant serious problems.

When people vote to utilize government as a means of assuring minimum income security for themselves, they must further decide what groups of people will be eligible to participate in the plan, what conditions they must meet to receive benefits, what risks to income are to be insured against, and how the plan shall be financed and administered. In this country our largest social insurance programs are provided for by the Social Security Act and its amendments. Let us consider first the old age, survivors, disability, and health insurance provisions (OASDHI) of this act as these affect families and children.

OASDHI. Everyone in the country can and must participate in the OASDHI system if he or she works in "covered" occupations. (Nine-tenths of all employed people are in "covered" work.) If men and women work for specified periods of time during which they and their employers each contribute equally through the payment of taxes (a certain percentage of the employee's earnings), then they are insured against certain risks—specifically the loss of income when they retire, or become disabled, or die, or need hospital and medical care after they are aged. They and their family members are eligible to receive benefits when such loss of income occurs.

The program is financed by payroll deductions from earnings, matched in like amounts by the employer, or by a payment by self-employed persons. The rate of taxation has been increased regularly to cover costs as new groups of employees have been brought under the definition of covered employment, or benefits increased, or new risks identified and written into the law. Not all of an employed person's income is necessarily taxed since it is not the intent of the program to insure for complete replacement of earnings. However, the maximum annual earnings subject to Social Security taxes has been increased from time to time, thereby improving the program's financial base and making it possible for workers to receive benefits more reasonably related to their actual earnings. The program is federally administered by the Social Security Administration of the Department of Health and Human Services (DHHS) and its regional offices. The employee's tax payments are paid to the federal government and deposited into a trust fund. The benefits that are paid out and the cost of administering the program are financed entirely by the taxes paid by employees, employers, and self-employed persons, thus reinforcing the concept of self-help and earned right on which the program is based.

Four decades after the initial legislation, however, the financing of the Social Security system needed evaluation. Trust fund reserves, though still substantial, showed signs in 1975 of shrinkage as the system began to pay out more than it was taking in through Social Security taxes. High rates of unemployment meant that fewer employees and employers were paying into the system than expected. Older workers, on becoming unemployed, tended to retire, thus accelerating a demand upon benefits. The unanticipated high rate of inflation brought corresponding benefit increases in line with the annual rise in the Consumer Price Index. In addition, the number of people claiming disability benefits rose unexpectedly, perhaps because more people learned about the relatively new disability provisions in the Social Security system.

In late 1977 federal legislation was enacted to "save the Social Security system" by substantially increasing payroll deductions and the taxable earning base. Those measures proved inadequate as high inflation and unemployment continued to climb. By 1982 the Social Security Administration faced a serious cash-flow problem because benefit rates are tied to rising prices while payroll taxes are tied to earnings of the work force, and taxable earnings were not keeping up with inflationary prices. The Social Security system does not set aside money to cover future payments. Instead it relies on current revenues from wages to pay current retirees.

In late 1982 Congress set up a bipartisan Society Security Reform Commission to propose financing mechanisms. A year later Congress enacted P.L. 98–21, the Social Security Act Amendments of 1983, a complex and sweeping reform package expected to shore up and bring about an actuarial balance in social security for the next seventy-five years. Three basic approaches were taken to assure this goal: Increasing revenue coming into the Social Security Trust Funds, decreasing benefits paid out, and slowing the rate of retirements (Ozawa, 1984).

Revenue was increased by a variety of means, including bringing under compulsory coverage employee groups who previously had not participated in the system, or who had done so only by choice. These included a wide range of federal employees, state and local government employees, and employees of nonprofit organizations. In addition, the tax rate for self-employed persons was raised to a level equal to the combined employer–employee rate. Interfund borrowing was authorized among the trust funds of Old Age and Survivors Insurance (OASI), Disability Insurance (DI), and Health Insurance (HI), a step taken to give greater flexibility to meet any short-term financial difficulties (Ozawa, 1984).

In addition, a number of steps were taken to slow the growth in benefit payments by means of some technical modifications and one very new approach—taxing part of an individual's income from Social Security benefits when that taxpayer's income exceeded certain base amounts, specifically $32,000 for married taxpayers who file jointly and $25,000 for a single taxpayer. The new measure was expected to save $27 billion in Social Security costs between 1983 and 1989 (Ozawa, 1984).

A third strategy to strengthen the Social Security system was applied—efforts to decrease the rate of people retiring. For example, the age at which workers can receive full benefits was raised to 67 years, to be accomplished in two steps by the year 2022. Other inducements were enacted as well to encourage potential retirees to stay in the labor force, paying into the Social Security system rather than retiring and claiming their benefits (Ozawa, 1984).

Substantial numbers of children receive benefits under the OASDHI program. In 1987, 3,244,000 children received monthly benefits averaging slightly over $352 for children whose fathers were dead, $216 for children of retired fathers, and $146 for children of disabled workers (U.S. Department of Commerce, 1989, p. 354).

Unemployment Insurance.   A second program of social insurance provided for in the Social Security Act is unemployment compensation, later termed unemployment insurance (UI). It is intended to provide partial protection against loss of income due to unemployment of workers who are usually regularly working or looking for work. UI is based on the idea that, generally, workers are dependent on their employers for a job and thus are faced with the risk of unemployment. To be eligible, workers must have accrued a certain number of "wage credits" to demonstrate that they have been recently and regularly a part of the labor force. They must be able and willing to work in suitable employment and must register at a local public employment office. Payments are made for a specified and limited number of weeks, usually for at least 26 weeks. The program is administered by the states, and the result is considerable variation in eligibility conditions, the amounts and duration of benefits, and the relationship of benefits to reemployment training. The unemployment insurance program is financed almost entirely by the employer, who pays a payroll tax. This fact reflects a philosophy in this country that the employer has very substantial responsibility for, and ability to regulate, worker security.

The fact that the unemployment payment is only partial replacement of income is reflected in the amounts of the benefits. For example, in 1987 the average weekly paid benefits among all the states was $140, with a range of $174 in Massachusetts and $98 in Tennessee (U.S. Department of Commerce, 1989, p. 300).

"Working more to take home less is not a measure of social or economic progress in American society." (William T. Grant Foundation, 1988, p. 15, quoting A. Sum)

Despite low benefits and their limited duration, until the 1980s many families, with the help of benefit payments, were enabled to get through a period of crisis, even though it left them with debts or lessened net assets. However, changes in the labor market and new eligibility restrictions have left the program far less well-equipped to minimize the effects of unemployment. Although most workers are employed in jobs covered by the UI system, fewer qualify for benefits when they become unemployed. For example, in 1975 more than two-thirds of all unemployed workers received benefits. In 1980 proportions had slipped to under half. By 1986 only 35 percent of all unemployed workers received UI benefits. Many of the jobless workers had not worked long enough or steadily enough to be eligible for benefits, or they remained unemployed for a longer time than the benefits last. In addition, in the early 1980s extensions of payments to persons out of work for longer periods were curtailed sharply. Those most vulnerable to unemployment—young families, women, and minorities—were particularly affected (Children's Defense Fund, 1987, p. 81).

Workers' Compensation. A third form of social insurance in the United States contributing to family income security is workers' compensation, or industrial accident insurance, directed toward alleviating loss of income arising from a worker's injuries on the job or death from fatal work-related injuries. Each state has its own law administered by an independent agency, the state's department of labor, or a court. This form of social insurance, which is the oldest in the United States, has to a large extent been dominated by private insurance characteristics. It is financed almost entirely by employers. Not all workers in the various states are covered, and there is very great variation from state to state in the kinds and amounts of benefits.

Veterans' Benefits. A fourth system of benefits and services that has general similarities to social insurance (but many differences as well) encompasses a variety of programs for veterans of military service. These persons were one of the earliest groups for which the colonies and later the states assumed responsibility. The different programs today give a strong underpinning to income security for many families of veterans. For example, the government offers persons in military service low-cost life insurance for the protection of their families. In addition, the federal government pays benefits to the dependents of veterans who die in military service. Disability benefits are provided to the veteran who loses earning power as a result of injury or disease resulting from military service; hospitalization and medical care are provided. Certain educational benefits are also available to veterans when their education or training was interrupted or delayed by military service. Sons and daughters of a veteran who dies in service are also eligible for benefits so that they can be assured of opportunity to attain an education that their parent might otherwise have provided. In addition, the federal government helps veterans obtain credit on favorable terms in order to provide adequate housing for their families or loans to undertake a business or farming venture, thus reinforcing future family income security. All of these benefits are provided as a matter of earned right, based not so much on financial contribution as on a felt obligation the American people have expressed in legislation.

Principles and Policies of Social Insurance

The social insurance programs in this country are intended to provide a base, a floor of protection, on which individual citizens can build additional security and the kind of life to which they aspire. Six principles on which these insurance programs are based will be discussed: benefits provided as a matter of right, a system financed by special taxation, nearly universal coverage, compulsory participation, wage-related benefits, and a family emphasis.

Income Security as a Right. The economic benefits received by an individual are not regarded as benevolent charity but as justifiable and essential protection to which each citizen is entitled. The target is the distress and loss of personal dignity and well-being caused by insufficient earnings arising from various identified causes. The benefits are awarded and accepted without stigma attached. The fact that the conditions of eligibility to benefits are derived from an objective assessment of an individual's work record, rather than from an investigation of present condition of need, gives the right to benefits a social and political support that public assistance has never had.

Financing by Special Taxation. The citizen's right to benefits is augmented further by a second principle: The system is financed by special taxes paid by employees and their employers, or in certain programs by the employers alone. Therefore, in addition to the moral right, the citizen is given a legal right based on participation through tax payments to the insurance system and safeguarded by an established appeals machinery. The benefits paid are regarded as fulfillment of a contract between citizens and their government.

The decision to finance the program in this way was intended not only to make the program financially sound, but also to give citizens a clear responsibility for their own system of protection and a vested interest that claims their attention and leads them to scrutinize future program directions. The right to social insurance benefits is, in the last analysis, as much a political fact as a strict legal right. The right derives from statutes that can be changed; and although the tax is compulsory, for it to be imposed there must be strong public support among persons so taxed, generally because they associate the taxation with specified future benefits. The result is a strong moral commitment for government to use the special tax funds for no other purpose.

Schlesinger has recorded that, at the time of the initial formulation of the Social Security legislation, some of President Franklin Roosevelt's advisers argued against employee contributions, pointing out that the employer would shift the payroll tax to the consumer in any case, so that employees would already pay their share, and that the employee's payment meant that the system would be financed by those who could least afford it. President Roosevelt, however, wanted the social insurance programs to be a self-supporting system, financed by special taxes, rather than out of the general tax revenue. Years later, Schlesinger records, Roosevelt explained:

> [T]hose taxes were never a problem of economics. They are politics all the way through. We put those payroll contributions there so as to give the contributors a legal, moral, and political right to collect their pensions and their unemployment benefits. (1959, pp. 308–309)

Universal Coverage. As a third principle, the system moves toward citizenwide or nearly universal coverage. In a democratic country characterized by high social mobility, all citizens should be eligible to participate in the system and receive benefits without regard to social class or levels of income. This conviction has influenced the American people to amend the original legislation from time to time in order to extend the number of groups who are eligible to participate.

Compulsory Participation. Not only do citizens have the right to participate in the system; they are also obligated to do so to assure its success. A fourth principle, then, is that of compulsory participation. At first it may seem that a system of protection that compels citizens to participate is undemocratic and intrudes into the right to manage one's own affairs. However, if government is to foster conditions that make it possible for all individuals to exercise their personal rights, some degree of individual free choice must be given up. A system of social insurance that provides protection against broad and costly risks to which large numbers of persons are vulnerable must have a broad base for its financing. If only those persons who are most apt to need the benefits chose to participate and contribute, then the assured group would be heavily weighted with "high-risk" persons, making the system unduly expensive. Furthermore, the loss of income that results in poverty among large numbers of citizens becomes a threat to the security of all citizens of a nation. Citizens cannot be left to choose whether to remain uninsured at the risk of becoming dependent on the rest of society; in addition, wide-scale poverty is a social ill arising from broad multiple and interrelated causes. Therefore the responsibility must be shared.

Wage-related Benefits. A fifth principle of the American system of social insurance specifies that the benefits are wage-related; that is, the amount of income an individual receives back

depends, within limits, on the amount of money he or she has paid into the system over the years. The principle is borrowed from private insurance with its concept of "equity," signifying a rightful claim based on the money value of an interest in a property. It is applied to the social insurance system in recognition of the belief that a worker's individual efforts should be rewarded (thereby reinforcing motivation from within) and that the amount of security provided should take into account those differences that have prevailed among people in their occupation, work pattern, and resultant earnings. But at the same time, the system was founded to increase the security of all citizens, particularly those least able to protect themselves and their families against the hazards of complete loss of income or low wages over their lifetimes. Therefore, even though the benefits are wage-related in the spirit of "equity," they are also geared toward "adequacy," a level that is lawfully and reasonably sufficient to meet the program's social objective of minimal income security for all. To achieve this social objective, therefore, new groups of people have sometimes been given coverage in the program without their having paid into the system proportionately to others, for example, people already old when the legislation is passed. Another example is legislation to raise all benefits to meet increased costs of living even though no additional contributions were made by those who are receiving payments. In addition, dependents or survivors of wage earners are provided benefits even though the wage earner who provided for them through contributions was not required to make additional payments simply because he or she had dependents.

Eveline Burns points out that our social insurance programs were designed to deal with a social problem, and so attention to "adequacy" must persist.

Those who are concerned about equity may, however, take some comfort from the fact that, even so, the method of determining the benefit amount still yields relatively larger benefits to the individual with long and continuous coverage. (1956, p. 33)

The problem is one of achieving a reasonable balance between equity and adequacy, with recognition that a reasonable level of adequacy must be considered essential and weighted as necessary to achieve the program's social objectives.

The Earned Income Tax Credit (EITC). As a measure in the direction of "adequacy," an earned income tax credit was legislated in 1975 to offset the social security taxes paid by low-income families. The credit "is available only to *working* poor people with dependent children. In 1987, some four million families with less than $6,000 in earned income were entitled to a 14 percent credit, or a maximum of $851. . . . The subsidy gradually decreases as income increases, disappearing entirely at $15,432." Merits of the system include these: It is easily administered, using the same computer system that withholds payroll and income taxes to add the amount of the tax credit to weekly paychecks; because it doesn't raise employers' costs or risk workers' jobs, there is little motive for evasion by either party; the credit can be directly targeted to the working poor ("A smarter way," 1988, p. 20).

As enacted, the EITC was not tied to family size. There is currently considerable support for increasing the maximum credit and linking it to the number of children in a household in order to further enhance this very generally approved measure and to reinforce the adequacy of the benefit.

The Family Emphasized. An additional principle contained in the social insurance programs of some countries is only partially observed in the American program: the family as the focal unit for insured protection against a wide range of hazards. Although the system provides for benefits to the minor children of retired workers or to dependent children of insured workers who die prematurely or become disabled, these provisions were not contained in the original legislation. The amendments of 1939 provided for benefits to the survivors or dependents of the insured wage earner, thus giving a family and child welfare facet to what had been regarded as "old age" insurance.

But our unemployment insurance benefits in most states are not computed in relation to differential family responsibilities; nor do we yet provide socially insured medical care for all members of a family, or meet other unavoidable and heavy demands on family income.

Relatively little attention in this country has been focused on children's allowances, sometimes called family allowances, a form of social insurance long found in all other industrialized countries. Such programs provide cash payments to a parent, most often the mother, without a requirement to prove need or low income. Specific provisions and policies vary from one country to another, but "the one feature that is common to all schemes is that they do something about childhood poverty that is due to sheer size of family" (Burns, 1968, p. 10).

Assessment. The incomplete recognition of the family as the focal unit for economic protection is part of a general lag in America in developing social insurance as a means of providing for income security. Our first workers' compensation laws passed in 1911 were reform measures aimed as much toward fixing responsibility and stimulating the employer to improve safety conditions in industry as toward serving as a base of income security. While countries in Europe were evolving systems of social insurance in the latter part of the nineteenth and early twentieth century, not until the Depression of the 1930s did we see a system of social insurance as an essential means for protecting citizens against distress caused by lack of earnings.

For example, a program of old age and survivors' insurance was legislated in Germany in 1889 (in contrast to 1935 and 1939 in America), and it was followed within less than twenty-five years by similar programs in five other major European countries. A similar pattern holds for social insurance against occupational hazards, sickness, and unemployment.

There are several reasons for our later use of social insurance. Our philosophy of rugged individualism and personal responsibility retarded our readiness to consider the use of government to insure for a floor of protection to all citizens. And indeed, until almost the beginning of the twentieth century, there was a frontier where many kinds of people were needed and could succeed through their own efforts and through mutual aid with other newcomers. Also, until the 1930s our country had not faced the kind of devastating and tenacious economic crisis that finally forced us to acknowledge that the old idea of personal responsibility, without at least minimal guaranteed security, was no longer tenable.

We began our system of social insurance slowly, seeing problems of unemployment and lack of resources in retirement as the most pressing problems. The choice was made to enact the most urgently needed provisions first, and as experience was gained, to build a stronger system through succeeding amendments to the legislation. Our early provisions and policies reflected the environment in which they were formulated. It follows that policies and programs today cannot remain static; they must continually be re-evaluated and reformulated in light of the changing environment within which the nation's people live and work.

Without doubt our social insurance programs as a method of income protection have generally been approved of by most Americans. The payments have had a favorable effect on the national economy by helping to sustain purchasing power and to even out fluctuations in national income levels; benefits have enabled many families to face the crisis brought about by loss of income with minimal disruption to their lives; the margin of security against future risks has provided a base on which many parents have been able to build additional protection for themselves and their families through supplementary private pension and insurance plans; through amendments to the original legislation the programs have been broadened to cover more risks and extend benefits to more people.

Firmer evidence about the role of Social Security in reducing income inequality is found in a comprehensive and rigorous study of 1986 data by the Census Bureau. The study found that Social Security is the most effective weapon the federal government has for reducing the inequality of Americans' income. In the preceding eight years, Social Security reduced the poverty level from 21.2 percent to 14.9 percent. (A family of four was classified "poor" if it had an annual cash income of less than $11,210.) Further, the Census Bureau found that programs that pay benefits regardless of financial needs lowered income inequalities and poverty four times more than programs based on a needs test (Pear, 1988).

Nevertheless, our social insurance programs are not sufficient to protect those persons most vulnerable to poverty. Children whose parents are the lowest earners are the least protected. Yet, as Wilbur J. Cohen pointed out, because the objectives of our Social Security system are much broader than merely preventing poverty, its actual and potential contribution to reducing poverty is often overlooked, particularly if it were used more effectively in combination with other approaches toward this goal.

Any attempt to deal with a problem as broad as poverty requires the combined and coordinated efforts of many programs. Economic growth, improved education and training, more effective manpower policies, and more adequate income maintenance programs must all be pursued if poverty is to be reduced and eventually abolished. In view of the gigantic contribution Social Security has already made in preventing and reducing poverty and in view of the vast number of people these programs can effectively reach, they must be considered as one of the systems through which the reduction of poverty can be pursued (Cohen, 1977).

Persons concerned about the degree of family protection in our Social Security system should take note of the way in which Social Security benefits still reflect the obsolete concept of a woman as a dependent of her husband, rather than as an economic partner, as she is in over half of the marriages today. Although the great upsurge in the number of working mothers is a product of the latter half of the twentieth century, women (and daughters) have always performed work required by the nation's economy—on farms and plantations, and in our earliest factories and mills. Women and children in the two great waves of nineteenth- and twentieth-century immigration expected to work, and industry expected that they would do so.

Male retired workers consistently average monthly Social Security benefits well above those of female retired workers. This situation reflects the traditionally low wages paid to women and the greater chance of irregular employment because of their childrearing and childbearing responsibilities. Mothers who remain at home for whatever reason perform a range of necessary services—housekeeping, cooking, laundry, and child care. Yet these forms of work are not considered work for Social Security coverage that in the event of her death or disability may become vitally important to her family. A divorced homemaker loses her right to a wife's or widow's benefits unless she has been married at least ten years at the time of divorce (changed from twenty years as recently as January 1979)—a requirement that leaves many women with minor children still in their care.

Clearly the idea of the family as a unit for protection has been slow to enter fully into the philosophy of social insurance in this country.

Public Assistance—Aid to Families with Dependent Children

For families who are either uninsured or insufficiently insured, our country provides a system of public assistance. The term "public assistance" refers to tax-supported programs of financial aid to individuals and families based on established need. These include the categorical aid programs in which federal monies are used—Aid to Families with Dependent Children (AFDC), and the Supplementary Security Income programs (SSI) of Old Age Assistance (OAA), Aid to the Blind, and Aid to the Permanently and Totally Disabled. The term also includes state-financed or locally financed programs of general assistance designed to meet the needs of poor persons not eligible for one of the categorical programs.

Medicaid, a federal-state provision of medical care for AFDC recipients and other specified medically needy persons is another program of public assistance. In 1985, 19,204,000 individuals were provided medical care under the Medicaid program (U.S. Department of Commerce, 1989, p. 362). At its enactment in 1965, Medicaid (Title XIX of the Social Security Act) was viewed as a gateway to vastly improved health care for needy children. However, experience with the program has shown that the legislation has not been the wide-open gate to improved health care for children that some thought it to be at the time of its passage. Explanations include the considerable discretion in setting eligibility limits and medical coverage that states are allowed and the limitations of state resources and priorities. Although Medicaid has been the means of bringing medical services to many AFDC families, health care for low-income families remains inadequate.

The food stamp program is another component of public assistance. Its purposes are to (1) improve the nutritional adequacy of low-income persons, (2) stimulate a market for farm products, and (3) supplement income. The program is found in all states and in 1987 served an average of 19.1 million persons each month (U.S. Department of Commerce, 1989, p. 364). Growing costs of the food stamp program prompted Congress to direct the U.S. Department of Agriculture to investigate the causes. Findings showed that between May 1989, and May 1990, the number of applicants for food stamps had risen by 1.2 million, with increases in 44 states and the District of Columbia. The growth in food stamp recipients "strongly correlated" with a concurrent increase in the AFDC program (Pear, 1990, Aug. 20).

For some poor women, the Women-Infant-Children program (WIC) provides prenatal care and diet supplements. A report from the Federal Center for Disease Control concludes that the rate of anemia among poor children in WIC programs decreased almost two-thirds from 1975 to 1985. Another study, a five-year evaluation by the Department of Agriculture, showed that WIC programs of appropriate quality reduce fetal and early infant deaths and help to ensure normal birth weight. Infants of below normal birth weight require intensive care, and frequently have to be rehospitalized during the first year of life. Some are born with handicaps that require costly continuing medical care. It is tragic that limited financing restricts the WIC program to barely half of those eligible (Wisdom, 1987, Oct. 14). Policy makers should consider the value of sound investment principles and the cost-effectiveness of prevention.

The discussion in this section will focus on the AFDC program, provided for under Title IV of the Social Security Act, since this is the basic public assistance program that reaches needy families with young children.

Purpose. AFDC is a cooperative program between federal and state governments for the purpose of maintaining income to families in which children have been deprived of parental support for certain reasons, specifically a parent's death, continued absence from home,

mental or physical incapacity, and unemployment of the father. The intent has been to provide financial assistance when a family has no income or insufficient income and to do so in ways that will enable children to remain in their own homes, where they can be reared by at least one of their parents or by relatives.

To achieve these purposes, three main forms of assistance are provided: (1) cash payments, which in 1986 averaged $355 per month per family, ranging from $114 in Alabama to $565 in Alaska and $532 in California (U.S. Department of Commerce, 1989, p. 367), amounts that are intended to cover food, clothing, shelter, and other basic expenses; (2) medical and other remedial care through payments directly to hospitals, physicians, dentists, and others; and (3) social services, such as counseling in relation to personal problems, help in finding better housing, homemaker services, day care for children, and referral to community resources.

Financing. The program is financed by a sharing of costs between the federal and state governments. More specifically the federal government offers to each of the various states, on a matching-formula basis, a grant-in-aid to supplement or balance state funds that are appropriated for the program. Revisions of the reimbursement formula have occurred a number of times since the passage of the Social Security Act, increasing the share of total cost paid by the federal government depending on the nature of the specific expenditures.

Extent of the Program. In 1987, 3,734,000 families, containing 10,882,000 recipients, including 7,296,000 children, received AFDC payments. AFDC involved the largest number of people of any of the categorical assistance programs and had the highest expenditures in money payments to recipients (U.S. Department of Commerce, 1989, p. 366).

Even in the face of the large numbers aided by AFDC, not all poor children are in families receiving AFDC help. Furthermore, most families who are aided by the AFDC payments are provided with income still well below the poverty-level index. The great bulk of the AFDC caseload is made up of families headed by a woman, always among the most vulnerable to poverty.

The AFDC program has been viewed increasingly with suspicion, disappointment, and distaste, and from time to time has come under bitter attack, a state of affairs that influenced Congress to legislate the Family Support Act of 1988 as an attempt to bring about "welfare reform." Although the AFDC program is large and costly, the help provided to many families is seriously inadequate and leaves many of their problems untreated. The general public has noted the increasing numbers of AFDC families who are fatherless because of desertion or births outside of marriage and concludes that the program rewards irresponsibility and therefore encourages parents to fail in their duties. The large portion of black families in AFDC caseloads provides some critics with a chance to express racial prejudice. Claims of "fraud" and excessive payments to ineligible parents are common even though ineligibility rates have declined from 16.5 percent in 1973 to 7.3 percent in the period October 1981 to March 1982 (Carrera, 1987, p. 130), a rate not unexpected in such an administratively complex program.

As a step toward achieving a valid basis for evaluation of the AFDC program as a method of assuring family income security to needy families, a review of the background of the program and its original philosophy will be useful.

Background of the AFDC Programs

Mothers' Pensions.   Activity on the part of social reformers of the early 1900s and resolutions of the first White House Conference on the Care of Dependent Children in 1909 highlighted concern about poor children who lost their own homes because of their parents' inability to support them. At this time there was a new aware-

ness of the importance of a child's own home and her or his need for family life experiences that found expression in the following resolution of the conference:

> Home life is the highest and finest product of civilization. It is the great molding force of mind and of character. Children should not be deprived of it except for urgent and compelling reasons. . . . Except in unusual circumstances, the home should not be broken up for reasons of poverty. (*Proceedings,* 1909, pp. 9–10)

Reaction against old methods of public outdoor relief (assistance to persons living in their own homes rather than in institutions) contributed to support for a new and special form of financial aid for mothers. Public relief, when it was given, reluctantly, consisted mostly of coal or grocery orders or emergency medical care. In some communities, notably Philadelphia, Washington, Baltimore, San Francisco, and Brooklyn, public relief offices had been abolished either because of public disapproval of maladministration or because of the opposition of private agencies. Although private agencies sometimes had the funds for emergency help to widows, they provided them with no permanent security.

Some of the impetus to preserve the child's own home through the payment of public funds to mothers of dependent children was a reaction to the institutionalization of young children. The early juvenile courts, given jurisdiction over children alleged to be dependent, usually had no way to assist a "poor but competent" mother with public funds except to place the children in an institution, thus freeing the mother to go to work outside her home. Not only was there concern over children's loss of their home; public officials also realized that paying for children to live in an institution was costlier than furnishing a small amount of aid to them in their own home.

The increasing legislation among states to prohibit or regulate child labor and the passage of compulsory school attendance laws were additional factors leading to the passage of mothers' pension laws. A child of nine or ten years of age was no longer free to quit school and go to work in factories and mines to help his or her widowed mother feed and care for younger brothers and sisters (see Chapter 8).

All these reasons then—(1) concern about preservation of the values of the child's own home, (2) reaction against old methods of public out-of-home relief, (3) reaction against institutionalization as an only resource when children were found to be dependent by the juvenile court, and (4) the development of child labor and compulsory school attendance laws in some states—gave weight to the growing argument early in the twentieth century for a special form of assistance for mothers whose children were deprived of parental support.

Mothers' pension laws were not passed without controversy, however. There was much debate over the merits of public versus private relief programs. Early social workers who were closely identified with private welfare efforts questioned that any form of public relief could be well-administered with adequate salaries and freedom from political interference. There was fear that a new form of public assistance would dry up the sources of charity and pauperize the families involved.

Much of the controversy was rooted in the fear that a family program of public assistance could not be restricted to "worthy" parents; others of "poor character" might also claim its help. Inherent in the controversy was reluctance to enact any legislation that would appear to relieve fathers of responsibility for their children's support. It was feared that the substance of family life would be seriously weakened, and irresponsibility and immorality would be encouraged. For example, in 1912, Mary Richmond objected to the new movement:

> So far from being a forward step, 'funds to parents' is a backward one—public funds not to widows only, mark you, but . . . funds to the families of those who have deserted and are going to desert. (G. Abbott, 1938, Vol. 2, p. 232)

Homer Folks, secretary of the New York State Charities Aid Association, cautiously endorsed a system of public relief for widows, but echoed concern that

> to pension desertion or illegitimacy would, undoubtedly, have the effect of a premium upon these crimes against society. . . . It is a great deal more difficult to determine the worthiness of such mothers than of the widow, and a great deal more dangerous for the State to attempt relief on any large scale. (*Report of the Commission,* 1914, p. 21)

Nevertheless, there was support for the concept of public responsibility for aid to needy children, popular distaste for the practice of removing children from their own homes for reasons of poverty, and belief that honest, efficient, and service-oriented public welfare (a term not yet in general use) could be created. Illinois passed the first statewide mothers' pension law in 1911, the Funds to Parents Act. Two years later twenty states had passed such legislation; ten years after the Illinois act, forty states had enacted such laws.

In many states, following the pattern of Illinois, administration of the laws was given to the new and still popular juvenile courts rather than to the local public relief officials. It was believed that such a move would remove the new program from the stigma of public relief, thus enhancing its benefits to mothers and children and increasing public support for the program. Another reason was the element of social control inherent in the planning. There was, for example, concern about working mothers and an assumed link to juvenile delinquency. It was intended that some surveillance of parental care would accompany receipt of the new benefits.

Two main problems emerged to plague the effectiveness of the mothers' pension movement: (1) the enactment of laws by the various states did not necessarily ensure that a program would be put into effect; and (2) there were conflicts concerning what kinds of mothers were entitled to public assistance under the new program.

The first of these problems was often born of the fact that the state legislation was "permissive" or "enabling" legislation; that is, local units of government *could* establish programs and expend public funds for such a purpose. Whether a local unit of government chose to do so depended on local leadership, prevailing attitudes on the question of families who lacked paternal support, and the financial ability of a county or township to support such a program.

Concerning the second problem: Even though the original proposals for mothers' pensions in 1911 by the Chicago reformers had no "suitability" or morality provisions, it had become generally agreed that it was necessary to separate out the deserving and worthy mothers for receipt of funds. This was attempted by one of two means. States could define by law the particular status required to be an eligible mother, that is, widows only, or other categories as well, such as deserted, divorced, or separated mothers, mothers whose husbands were imprisoned or mentally or physically disabled, or, most questionable of all, unmarried mothers. The second means was to carry out an investigation of the character of each mother who applied to make sure that she was "physically, mentally, and morally fit" to rear her children. Local welfare workers were inclined to protect the public acceptability of the program by a more restrictive screening of applications than the legislation required. A Children's Bureau study of the administration of mothers' pensions in the various states showed that in 1931, 82 percent of those given aid were children of widows (U.S. Children's Bureau, 1933, p. 25).

In addition, mothers considered to be worthy and fit usually turned out to be white. The Children's Bureau study referred to above showed that 96 percent of the mothers were white, 3 percent were black, and 1 percent were of other racial background. About half of these black mothers were in only two states, Ohio and Pennsylvania; in other states black mothers received aid in proportions vastly less than their makeup in the general population of the state (U.S. Children's Bureau, 1933, pp. 1, 3, 26, 27).

In her study of "suitable home" policies as they are reflected in today's program of AFDC, Winifred Bell summed up the mothers' pension movement thus:

> The "suitable home" concept implied a partnership between the states and dependent mothers: the state committed itself to provide sufficient financial support to enable mothers to maintain "suitable homes"; the mothers, in turn, agreed to be "fit" and "proper" custodians of their children.
>
> This was the ideal that social planners envisaged as they drafted state statutes and helped to evolve programs and policies. They feared the consequences of opening the door to public support too widely, of taking over parental responsibility, or of supporting any but the most upright and promising families. So they selected families with great care and held them, so far as possible, to rigorous standards of adult behavior and child supervision. . . .
>
> Undoubtedly, the "suitable home" policies protected the program itself from criticism and thereby helped to attract some public support that might otherwise have been alienated. . . . The host society was embarking cautiously on an experiment, and while the premature death of a good father had been an acknowledged tragedy for generations, there was little or no collective concern for childhood deprivation resulting from parental indolence or misbehavior. . . .
>
> The very vagueness of the "suitable home" eligibility conditions guaranteed their adaptability to local and regional mores. . . . Local workers were relied upon to infuse the terms with meaning, and, in doing so, they tended to restrict the programs to nice Anglo-Saxon widows and . . . to protect their young programs from Negro and unmarried mothers who might well attract criticism.
>
> In appraising the function of the policies in

these early years, it is important to note that the idea that absolute poverty could be eliminated was not yet current in the nation. . . . Under the circumstances existing in the early twentieth century, in fact, anything other than an "elite" program, intimately based in parochial and regional values . . . might have not survived. (Bell, 1965, pp. 17–19)

Thus it was that leaders working in behalf of children when the Social Security Act was being written began with a legacy of purposeful, humanitarian effort in behalf of dependent children and belief in the concept of public responsibility. But this was interlaced with unresolved administrative problems of shared state and local responsibility and complicating, amibivalent attitudes about suitable homes.

Children's Concerns in the Enactment of the Social Security Act.

Edwin E. Witte (1963), in his account of the history of the Committee on Economic Security appointed by President Franklin Roosevelt (which lasted from 1934 to 1935), and of the drafting of the Social Security Act, details some of the background of the decisions on administration and financing of the new aid to dependent children program. Children's concerns were not part of the charge to the Committee on Economic Security. Problems of adults that had been brought about by catastrophic unemployment and loss of earnings to support families and aged persons made up the more urgent demands. After the committee began its work, representatives of the Children's Bureau (notably Katharine Lenroot and Martha Eliot) were charged with undertaking necessary background studies for an aid to dependent children (ADC) program. It was expected that this would be administered by the Children's Bureau. But in the final stage of the preparation of the report of the Committee on Economic Security, representatives of the Federal Emergency Relief Administration (most prominently Aubrey J. Williams and Josephine Brown) took the position that ADC was chiefly public assistance,

as opposed to a child welfare service. This significant distinction reflected a focus on the large numbers of families that had been disrupted by the nation's economic crisis; the purpose of the new program of aid was not so much to offer a new kind of child-centered service as to make needed income available to mothers so that they could be restored to carrying out their own normal adult responsibilities to their children. As a result the administration of the federal grants for ADC was vested in the Social Security Board along with the other categorical assistance programs.

Grants to the states for ADC programs were initially limited to one-third of the states' expenditures, in contrast to more generous matching for OAA. Witte reports that this disparity

was acknowledged to be a justified criticism, but there was so little interest on the part of any of the members in the aid to dependent children that no one thereafter made a motion to strike out the restriction. (1963, p. 164)

An additional disparity between categories in level of assistance grants grew out of the fact that the amounts of ADC grants were modeled after the amounts of pensions payable to children of servicemen who had lost their lives in World War I. In doing so, Congress completely overlooked that under the Veterans' Pension Act a grant was made for the widow. In the original ADC legislation, the mother, or other adult caretaker, who was awarded a grant to take care of her children had nothing included in the grant for her own maintenance. Not until 1950 was this omission corrected by amendment to the Social Security Act. Steiner, in discussing the separate levels of support between ADC and OAA, states:

The cynical explanation that adults vote, and that children do not, is too pat. . . . The ADC program began at a comparative disadvantage because of the pressing nature of the old age problem in 1935. Equity between the child and adult categories was not considered and rejected but rather was never considered in those terms. Although the Social Security Act has come to be considered a comprehensive package approach to the problems of economic security, the legislative and political histories of its origin suggest that the approach was more a collection of separate specifics for problems separately considered than a big comprehensive approach to interrelated problems. . . . The ADC and OAA categories tended to be separately compartmentalized from the outset. Levels of support were separately developed. (Steiner, 1966, pp. 24–25)

Minimum concern about the ADC program continued during the early years after the passage of the Social Security Act, largely because the program fit the acceptable model carried over from the mothers' pension movement—public support for the involuntary dependency of "worthy" mothers, that is, widows, and their dependent children. A conflict in the underlying philosophy of the program did not yet have to be faced, but its outlines could be found in the combination of old and new values on which the ADC program was being built.

There was the old allegiance to moralistic evaluation of good and bad homes, with strong undertones of stigma attached to poverty. The stigma, with its aura of immorality, was especially marked when mothers and children were poor as a result of family breakdown characterized by desertion, divorce, and especially illegitimacy. In addition, the belief was still strong that meeting dependency needs adequately would aggravate and perpetuate dependency.

In contrast, however, new emphasis was being given to the value of a child's own family, the importance of a mother's being enabled to maintain a home in which she could continue to rear her children in her own way, and recognition that children and youth are indeed a chief resource of the nation. There was strong conviction on the part of social workers who helped to develop and carry out the new depression-born programs that relief should be given in ways that

preserve the dignity and sense of self-worth of the nation's people. Newer understanding of the dynamics of behavior was making it clear that a certain degree of security and fulfilled needs is essential to achieving or maintaining independence. The family's right to economic security was emphasized. Public assistance was recognized to be a rightful public responsibility, with open acknowledgment that voluntary agencies, faced with national crisis, could not meet the economic needs of all.

Principles and Policies of AFDC

Federal and State Roles in Program Definition. As a condition for receiving the grant-in-aid, the state must first present to the Department of Health and Human Services (DHHS) a plan for an AFDC program that meets certain requirements, that is, assures that certain principles and policies will be applied in carrying out the program in that state. The DHHS has the power to recommend that federal funds be withheld from any state failing to comply with the Social Security Act generally or with its own approved state plan.

Nevertheless, "welfare" traditionally has been regarded as a responsibility of state and local governments, and from the beginning of the Social Security Act, states have retained considerable leeway in shaping their programs. The administration of the programs depends on extensive interaction and agreement between responsible agencies and officials at different governmental levels, in contrast to OASDHI and veterans' benefits, which are federally administered. As a result the individual preferences of the various states have had a very significant impact on the AFDC programs. Generally, federal policies have been aimed toward the states if federal money grants are to be given; in turn, states have been left to set other eligibility requirements so long as they are not in contradiction to the federal requirements, and in doing so, to establish policies permitting a restrictive pursuit of the program's aim if social and economic conditions within a state dictate this.

As examples of the kinds of definitions left to the states, consider the following: "Incapacity" of a parent includes what kind and duration of disability? How shall it be determined? "Continued absence from home," if it is to be used as a qualifying condition, must be further defined; that is, how long must a father have been absent? For what reasons? Is he in prison? Has he deserted his family? Are his whereabouts unknown? Must he have been absent from the home for some length of time for his family to qualify for assistance, regardless of whether he is in prison or has deserted? Or does the reason for his absence affect how quickly his family may establish their eligibility for assistance?

But perhaps the most crucial definitions left largely to the individual states have been the determinations of what constitutes "need" in a particular family, how it shall be proved, and what level or standard of living shall be provided by an assistance grant once the individual family establishes its eligibility. These kinds of determinations in each state are influenced by the prevailing concept of need with its attendant social attitudes and values, the economic resources of the particular state that can be used in developing a strong welfare program, and the political history of the AFDC program in that state.

It is not surprising, then, that there has been from the beginning of the AFDC program very wide variation among the states as to their policies and standards of assistance.

In discussing the results of the federal agency's lack of power to insist on payment standards providing at least a minimum standard of living, Steiner pointed out that more recent federal grant-in-aid programs in other fields are far lass permissive, and exacting federal standards have become commonplace.

Thus, federal money for highways or for urban removal can be withheld until there is state or local compliance with minimum standards. Yet, funds that may not be provided to support the cost of a highway that is too narrow or a building that is inadequately wired may be provided to support relief benefits below minimum standards of health and decency. (Steiner, 1966, p. 247)

Policy Changes to Make the Program More Adequate. Generally, the preceding were the policies the federal government expected states to follow until 1950. Since then some significant changes have been made to extend benefits to more persons in need and to make the help given more adequate, changes that were essential to the child welfare purposes of the program but added to both cost and size. For example, in 1950, a *caretaker grant* was belatedly approved in Congress to permit inclusion in the family budget of the mother's essential needs. In 1962, provision was made to allow a *grant for a second parent* in the home, such as an incapacitated father. In 1961, to help combat the effects of periodic recessions, states were given the option of extending the AFDC program to families whose children were deprived of parental support because of a *parent's unemployment.* In an attempt to give protective care to children receiving AFDC when their home was found to be unsuitable by a court, Congress in 1961 enacted legislation to permit the extension of AFDC payments to children placed in *foster homes.*

Changing Composition of AFDC Population. After 1950 concern about the AFDC program began to mount. Steiner identifies the "withering-away fallacy" as a major reason for delayed concern about the assistance programs (1966, pp. 18–47). At the time of the inclusion of survivors' benefits in the social insurance system, it was expected that as more children became eligible for benefits in the event of their father's death, fewer children would need to be cared for under ADC. It was widely believed that public assistance was only supplementary to the social insurance system and that as coverage for social insurance was extended to more wage earners, the need for supplementary public assistance programs would end—wither away.

The OASDHI program affected AFDC, but not by taking away the need for a children's public assistance program. Rather, the effect was to change the nature of the AFDC caseload. The shift has been dramatic. For example:

> In 1936, death of a parent was the largest single reason for dependency of all ADC children. By June 1948, death was still the reason for 24 percent of all ADC cases and in November 1953, for 17 percent of all cases. But by the end of 1960 it was the critical reason in less than 11 percent of all ADC families. (Burgess & Price, 1963, p. 190)

The social insurance program, along with a continuing decline in mortality rates for younger adults, undoubtedly contributed to a shift in principal reasons for AFDC eligibility away from the death or disability of a parent. At the same time social and economic conditions created new reasons for dependency, causing the AFDC program to grow, costs to increase, and major qualifying conditions for eligibility to become desertion, separation, divorce, and unmarried parenthood.

> Even those who were not sanguine about a diminishing public assistance load—and there were a few—could not have anticipated all the real reasons why public assistance would not wither away. Who could anticipate in the late 1930s that inflation would make social insurance inadequate for those depending on it; that death of the father would be replaced by illegitimacy and desertion as the real hard-core ADC problems—risks for which there is no public insurance program; that unemployment compensation designed to protect against temporary unemployment would not be able to protect a worker rendered permanently obsolete by a machine; that southern Negroes would move in waves to the northern industrial states and find the combination of technology and discrimination to be overpowering; and that the failure of social insurance to give protection against the

catastrophes of prolonged and expensive illness or permanent disability would add to the costs of public assistance? (Steiner, 1966, pp. 22, 23)

As criticism about AFDC mounted, new policies, more restrictive ones, were enacted.

Disclosure of Information

In the 1940s attention turned to the growing costs of public assistance with frequent charges in the news that people were receiving AFDC unnecessarily, either because of maladministration of the program or the refusal of relatives to contribute. In 1950 the Jenner amendment was enacted, which provided for the disclosure of AFDC records under certain conditions. The Social Security Act had been amended in 1939 to ensure the confidentiality of information about applicants and recipients. The intent had been to protect against public embarrassment or exploitation by unscrupulous advertisers or politicians. Those who supported the Jenner amendment claimed that access to names of public assistance recipients and the amounts of aid being given them would effectively persuade persons to get off the relief rolls and find jobs or else persuade relatives to help their needy family members. The Jenner amendment permitted the states to define their own conditions for allowing the public to examine disbursement records (names and amounts of assistance, not the agency casework records) so long as the information about recipients was not used for commercial or political purposes.

The legislation was supported for a number of reasons. Steiner suggests that confidentiality became a target because it could be attacked and eliminated without really endangering the basic principle of providing a minimum measure of the necessities of life for unemployables lacking these necessities. In addition, "vigorous attack came from the press which has a vested interest in 'the public's right to know' that is comparable to the vested interest of welfare professionals in confidentiality." And further, newspaper and magazine opponents to confidentiality had important "assistance from the states' rights adherents" (Steiner, 1966, pp. 93, 94).

The effects of the Jenner amendment appeared to be minimal. A year after its passage it was of little interest. Steiner notes, however, that the confidentiality dispute was of great political importance, symbolic of what was to come. Why? For one reason, the action served as a kind of turning point in the activities and authority of the federal agency in relation to state policy makers, suggesting that politicians could be as influential as welfare professionals in the making of relief policy, and diminishing the threat of federal withholding of funds. Further, it brought added strength to those groups who oppose more liberalized eligibility policy for public assistance, and it demonstrated the separate channels in which welfare professionals and politicians usually move (Steiner, 1966, pp. 97–98).

Enforcement of Parental Support

Orders for child support payments traditionally have been left to state laws and local enforcement agencies. These child support efforts "grew up as the prosecutorial, punitive side of state welfare systems, acting primarily as a debt collection program for recovering welfare costs" (Savage, 1987, p. 5). Concern about non-support of children by parents emerged as a federal issue in 1950 when Congress enacted an additional condition the states had to meet in order to receive matching funds—the so-called NOLEO (notice to law enforcement officials) amendment, which required the state AFDC agency to notify the appropriate law enforcement authority of all cases where AFDC was provided for children who had been deserted by a parent. Its purpose was to facilitate efforts to locate the father and enforce his obligation for support payments. Desertion was a growing problem, and attention was being focused on it as a less socially acceptable reason for needing public aid than death or disability, or even imprisonment of the father. The requirement was based on the assumption that the wife, as well as her husband, had some responsibility for his desertion. Therefore, it was permissible to make eligibility for assistance dependent on her cooperation with law enforcement officers by furnishing information that might help to locate her husband.

The NOLEO amendment represented the result of a conflict between two public policies and reflected ambivalence on the part of the general public and lawmakers toward these two points of view. On the one hand, it is considered socially desirable, indicative of a public good, to support and protect the nation's dependent children. On the other hand, fathers should not be relieved of their parental responsibilities.

The action required by the NOLEO amendment seemed to many social workers to be in direct conflict with the basic purpose of AFDC legislation, which was to protect the interests of future citizens by providing support for needy children. If a mother refused to comply with the requirement, then she would be denied help for her children. Reasons why she might choose not to cooperate were varied. She might hope for a reconciliation with her husband and fear that some action would antagonize him further. If her husband had been punitive, she might fear retaliation. She might worry about the effect of such action on her children's attitudes toward her or their father. She might hold attitudes toward authority that make her reluctant to cooperate with law enforcement officials.

In a study of the nature and effects of the NOLEO amendment McKeany pointed out that the legislation had added a new function to the traditional ones of the public welfare agency, which are to meet need and provide service. The legislation had made the welfare agency "a vehicle of social compulsion" (McKeany, 1960, p. 67).

The NOLEO amendment was a compromise in that only "notice" to law enforcement officers that aid was being given the child was required of the welfare agency and any action taken after the notice was received depended on local law enforcement policies and practices. Once notice was given, the welfare agency could give aid, provided that other eligibility requirements were met. The public wanted to force fathers to resume a socially acceptable pattern of responsibility and at the same time to avoid depriving children of public aid when it was needed. Nevertheless, the amendment was significant in this way: the "condition prescribed by NOLEO was a mild one, but it made clear that special behavior not applicable to non-welfare recipients—in this case mandatory reporting of desertion—would be expected for recipients" (Steiner, 1966, p. 117). Many found objectionable the selection of public assistance recipients for special sanctions or enforcement of responsibilities that supposedly apply to all.

One nationwide study on the effects of the NOLEO amendment showed only modest achievement in obtaining money payments from fathers. Many of the same difficulties welfare agencies had experienced prior to NOLEO persisted in attempts to secure voluntary support (Kaplan, 1958). From similar findings, McKeany (1960, p. 121) concluded that "once the family breaks up, the chances of securing adequate and regular support from the father and of conserving his feeling of responsibility for his children are greatly diminished. . . . the most effective approach to the problem of nonsupport can be made through measures which foster a sense of parental responsibility and prevent, or at least reduce, family breakdown."

Nevertheless, public sentiment for enforcement of parental duties continued to build. By 1973 almost half of the children on the AFDC program had parents who were separated or divorced. This was a primary factor in bringing about the passage in 1975 of the Child Support Enforcement Act, Title IV-D of the Social Security Act, which offered financial incentives to states to establish a standard means for establishing paternity, locating parents, and obtaining child support.

An additional step in implementing a fed-

eral parent-locator service was taken when the DHEW agreed to supply individual Social Security numbers to the states. Although records of the Internal Revenue Service, the Pentagon, and the Veterans Administration had already been made available to states to track down absent fathers, the Social Security Administration had resisted giving out Social Security numbers, contending that doing so was in violation of federal privacy laws. Under heavy pressure, however, the Social Security commissioner reversed his position in early 1976 and agreed to supply Social Security numbers to the states for the purpose of implementing child support enforcement programs (*New York Times,* 1976, April 7).

Concern about parental failure to support dependent children continued to be voiced. In February 1982, the Department of Health and Human Services issued regulations to provide for deducting delinquent support payments from federal income tax refunds owed to absent parents of children receiving AFDC payments. The new policy is jointly administered by the Internal Revenue Service (IRS) and the Office of Child Support Enforcement. An example of how it is implemented follows: From his income tax report, a parent expects to receive a refund of $400. However, he has been more than three months delinquent in support payments totaling $300. Consequently he will receive a refund of only $100. By late 1982, forty-seven states and the District of Columbia had submitted 550,000 cases for forwarding to the IRS (*Social Security Bulletin,* 1982, April).

Congress took another step toward securing parental support in 1984. A degree of consensus had emerged that the entire child support system condoned parental irresponsibility. In this new attempt, the objective went beyond reducing welfare costs and caseloads by applying the new legislation not only to parents on welfare but to all noncustodial parents who were delinquent in child support payments. The legislation required states to develop guidelines to determine child support awards and have them in place by October 1. The legislation was weak, however, by its failure to make the standards binding on local courts, leaving the negotiations for support vulnerable to manipulation by lawyers, judges, or other interested parties (Garfinkel & McLanahan, 1986, pp. 135–136).

Despite the new concern about delinquent child support payments and the new efforts, in 1985 "only 61 percent of the 8.8 million women raising at least one child whose father was absent from the home had been awarded child support. And of those with court orders, only 38 percent received the full amount due. One third received nothing" (Savage, 1987, p. 9).

This history of four decades of national ineffectiveness in enforcing parental support of children was a key factor in bringing about new federal legislation in 1988—The Child Support Standards Act, P.L. 100–485. The enacted changes were intended to require (1) noncustodial parents of every income level to meet their legal obligations for child support; and (2) the states to assume fuller responsibility for implementing an effective system of child support enforcement. Major changes reflected in the legislation were these (Lewin, 1988b, p. 8):

1. Employers are required to withhold wages for child support owed by their employees. Wage withholding was to be implemented for Title IV-D cases beginning November 1, 1990, and on or after January 1, 1990 for all new or modified support orders issues.

2. States are required to develop procedures for establishing paternity for all children in AFDC homes and, with enhanced federal financial incentives, to use genetic testing in cases where paternity is contested.

3. States are required to establish and abide by specific formulas that determine child support amounts. Exceptions can be made when there is a clear finding that the amount of the support payment places an unfair burden on the noncusto-

dial parent. One example is a disabled father who needs a larger share of his income for special needs related to his disability.

4. States are expected to pursue effectively absent parents who fall behind in their support payments, and by October 1, 1995 to have statewide tracking systems in place.

5. The states are required to review child support awards whenever review is requested or every three years when families are receiving public assistance.

6. The Department of Health and Human Services was instructed to establish time lines for states to assure prompt attention to key tasks, such as (a) distributing to families the support payments collected in their behalf, (b) responding to requests to locate absent parents, (c) establishing paternity, and (d) setting and enforcing standardized formulas for the amount of a parent's payment rather than relying on individual decisions of judges.

The new legislation allowed the states considerable discretion in establishing their formulas for levels of support. Some are expected to prefer a formula that sets percentages of the noncustodial parent's income. Some other states prefer more flexible formulas, arguing that flat percentages are not sensitive to the needs of a particular family. To avoid this inflexibility, the state might use a formula that takes into account individual family factors such as cost of child care, medical expenses, the ages of the children, and then arrive at an amount it takes per year to support that family. Support payments would then be established by taking into account the proportionate income of each parent (Lewin, 1988b, p. 8).

An early warning with respect to institutionalized goals came from the Children's Defense Fund: "Child support enforcement, practiced at its best, will not eliminate child poverty or the need for other assistance programs (Savage, 1987, p. 3). A well-administered program, however, can be expected to improve the economic level of many families.

"Suitable Home" Policy.   The Social Security Act, as originally enacted, did not cite the condition of a child's home as a factor affecting his or her acceptability for aid. It was expected that children in unsuitable homes, those where they were abused, exploited, or neglected, would be dealt with under the child-protective statutes in the various states. But very early, in an effort to extend aid in ways that were consistent with local customs and beliefs, some states specified in their AFDC plans that assistance would be granted only if the children were living in a "suitable home." The stated goal was to protect children from care in a poor environment, a goal consistent with the highest aims of the original AFDC legislation. Whatever the intent, the effect was to control the size of the caseload, its costs, and its composition in such terms as race and marital status. "The traditional sanction against immorality or race was preserved, while severely neglectful parents were sometimes treated with surprising clemency" (Bell, 1965, p. 182).

In defining eligibility, if public accountability for state purposes is to be assured, the criteria for eligibility must be defined clearly and precisely. But "suitable homes" requirements are vague and imprecise, subject to a wide range of interpretation, and dependent on personal discretion exercised under circumstances where individual belief can play a strong part. Even years of experience in administering such policies left them undefinable. Particular guidelines for judgment were never well laid out for staff workers. "With no uniform guides, welfare workers tended to fall back on the tried and tested status attributes of birth and color" (Bell, 1965, p. 42).

The full impact of the growth in application of suitable home policies did not occur, however, until 1960, when the governor of Louisiana signed a law, based on earlier Mississippi practice that had gone unchallenged, which required welfare workers to enforce immediately a new eligibility requirement: to deny or suspend assistance to homes in which the adult caretaker was living with, but not legally married to, a member of the opposite sex or in which the mother had had an illegitimate child since receiving ADC, or was illegitimately pregnant, or had had a total of two or more illegitimate children at any time. Within three months, assistance had been terminated in a total of 6,235 cases involving 23,300 children. Usually no written notice was given to the recipients, nor were they notified of their right to a hearing. The children continued to live in "unsuitable" homes, made more so by even crueler poverty.

The Louisiana action attracted attention from aroused citizens from all over the country (and other countries as well). Voluntary agencies formally protested, for example, the Child Welfare League of America, the Urban League, and the American Civil Liberties Union. It was claimed that the Louisiana law was in violation of the intent and spirit of the Social Security Act (which was to provide aid for needy persons, not to police morality) and that it denied equal protection of the law by setting up unreasonable classifications and denying a fair hearing.

The DHEW scheduled a hearing on the Louisiana action, with the eventual result that the secretary issued a ruling (the Fleming rule), effective September 1, 1962, that state plans for AFDC may not impose an eligibility condition that would deny assistance to a needy child on the basis that the home in which the child lives is unsuitable if the child continues to reside in the home, exposed to the same environment. Efforts must be made, in other words, either to improve the home conditions or to make arrangements for the child elsewhere through the usual authoritative channels for intervening in parental rights. Congress then formalized this action further by including the same stipulations as part of the 1962 amendments to the Social Security Act. As a result, "suitable home" policies are not unlawful and do not prevent a state from receiving federal funds, provided that attention is given to improving the home conditions of children or finding appropriate foster placements for them.

Substitute Parents. An additional policy emerged in various state plans in the 1950s, the substitute parent provision, a policy -distinct from the suitable home policy but with the same or similar consequences. These policies were found most often in states that had not extended AFDC to unemployed fathers in the home. The "substitute parent" policy rests on an arbitrary redefinition of the word "parent." Under its aegis, families were deprived of AFDC payments on the claim that the mother was maintaining a relationship in her home with a male, a "substitute father"—a person unrelated to the children by blood or marriage and regarded as a substitute parent without determination as to whether he was actively providing for the children or was legally liable for support. The effect, where such a policy was systematically enforced, was to require an AFDC mother whose husband was dead or divorced, or had deserted, to prove that she was not engaged in a "continuing relationship" with a man with whom she might wish to develop a friendship, and that sexual intercourse was not a part of their relationship, even though there were "frequent visits."

The "substitute parent" policies, sometimes referred to as "man-in-the-house" rules, led to a practice known as the "midnight raid" or "welfare search." Even though the avowed purpose was to check the recipient's eligibility for public assistance, these visits were regarded by many as violating the privacy of the home and being humiliating and degrading to recipients (Source materials, 1963).

In 1968 the United States Supreme Court unanimously held in relation to a substitute father policy in Alabama that the regulation was invalid as inconsistent with Title IV of the Social Security Act. The "worthy" poor concept had been discarded, the Chief Justice said, by the DHEW's Fleming rule and subsequent amendments to the Social Security Act that provided for rehabilitative measures as a way of dealing with unsuitable homes instead of measures that punish children by disqualifying them from public aid (*King v. Smith,* 1968).

Residence Requirements. Another controversial policy of long standing came to an end by Supreme Court action in 1969. The Social Security Act, in recognition of the long history of "settlement" or residence laws, had permitted states to require a period of residence within the state as a condition of eligibility as long as it did not exceed one year. The purpose was to inhibit migration by needy persons into a state with higher welfare benefits. Most states did so require, until these residence stipulations for persons seeking public assistance under the various titles of the Social Security Act were declared unconstitutional by the U. S. Supreme Court (*Shapiro v. Thompson,* 1969).

In the decision the Court affirmed that

> the nature of our Federal Union and our constitutional concepts of personal liberty unite to require that all citizens be free to travel throughout the length and breadth of our land uninhibited by statutes, rules, or regulations which unreasonably burden or restrict this movement.

After the Supreme Court decision, state welfare agencies were queried about trends in assistance payments to recipients who previously would have been classed as nonresident (Lourie & Brody, 1970). Answers indicated that there had been no radical changes in assistance caseloads. States with relatively high levels of public assistance did not attract a disproportionate number of nonresidents. This fact appeared to affirm what social workers had long held—that poor people move for reasons much like those of the general population, for example, expectation of employment or the presence of relatives in the new locality. Family mobility between states is normal, although it sometimes causes individual and family problems for which public welfare must assume some responsibility.

Old concerns about "the poor moving in" reemerged in 1989 when the governor of Wisconsin proposed a "two-tiered public aid system" that would reduce benefits by 25 percent for three months for poor people who moved into Wisconsin from other states. In the preceding three years, 21,000 poor families, mostly from inner-city neighborhoods of Chicago, had moved to Wisconsin, a state that ranked ninth in the nation in its level of public assistance benefits—a basic monthly grant of $517 for a family of three in contrast to $342 in Illinois. In that same period, and despite the increase in newcomers, the number of people on welfare in Wisconsin (with its relatively sound economy) dropped slightly (Johnson, 1989).

Those who supported the proposal cited their fear of greatly increased social service costs as well as new demands on resources for police and fire departments that would follow the "risk of increased crime." Critics of the plan charged "veiled racism" (the new residents were largely black), and saw it as unconstitutional given the 1969 Supreme Court decision with respect to residence requirements. To become effective the two-tiered proposal would require approval from the U.S. Department of Health and Human Services (Johnson, 1989).

Emphasis on Social Services. Changes in the public assistance provisions of the Social Security Act by the 1962 amendments were heralded as "the most comprehensive and constructive overhauling of Federal legislation relating to public assistance and child welfare services that Congress has ever made" (Cohen & Ball, 1962). The major new policy emphases in relation to AFDC were twofold: to make available a variety of *rehabilitative and social services* to recipients, and to establish or strengthen *training programs* that would prepare staff to perform these new tasks effectively. These amendments were a re-

sult of studies that had identified the limitations of existing welfare programs and outlined plans for improvement (Wickenden & Bell, 1961). On February 1, 1962, President Kennedy sent to Congress the first presidential message ever to be devoted exclusively to public welfare. In it he said:

> Public welfare, in short, must be more than a salvage operation, picking up the debris from the wreckage of human lives. Its emphasis must be directed increasingly toward prevention and rehabilitation—on reducing not only the long-range cost in budgetary terms but the long-range cost in human terms as well. (J. F. Kennedy, 1962)

In spite of the enthusiasm among most social workers that the 1962 amendments engendered, some early doubts were expressed. Social services were being set up as a means of combating poverty even though the causes of poverty were known to be complex, stemming from an interrelationship of social, political, and economic conditions. The idea of combining investigative responsibilities with rehabilitative services—inherently different functions—suggested an inevitable conflict in duties for the social worker and confusion for the client. In addition, the social services the amendments advocated were difficult to deliver successfully, especially to people whose problems were severe and pervasive. For large numbers of AFDC parents and children, innovative social services were needed in addition to or in place of the traditional case approach through a one-to-one relationship. How to teach these new approaches was not equally well worked out everywhere, nor was there always readiness to try changed approaches in helping AFDC recipients. Difficulties were encountered immediately in implementing the provisions for increased staff training when Congress failed to appropriate money for training grants in 1962. Very important, the implementation of the new emphasis depended on state and local initiative, readiness to move in new directions, available staff, and economic resources. In these characteristics there was wide variation from state to state.

The number of recipients and expenditures for AFDC continued to escalate. In Hoshino's view,

> the strategy of the 1962 amendments proved to be a debacle. . . . The responsibility of administering a massive, complex, and controversial aid program overwhelmed attempts to build a viable service component. Few trained social workers could be attracted to the programs, and former staff members who returned after receiving professional training complained that the mass of paperwork, the punitive policies, and an administrative climate that emphasized investigation precluded effective services. . . . In retrospect, the notion that casework could have any substantial effect on the relief rolls was naive. (Hoshino, 1977, p. 1152)

But perhaps the most significant question raised about the 1962 amendments was whether they represented a real change in philosophy and direction, especially since rehabilitative and social services were being attempted without first building a program of adequate income payments to needy people.

As doubts grew about the wisdom and effectiveness of joining the determination of financial eligibility and the provision of social services, the question of separation of the two functions became a keen issue. A serious danger was cited—that of imposing services on a population of parents who were captive in the sense that they were dependent on a welfare worker for a determination of continuing eligibility for financial aid. Furthermore, the investigative tasks involved in determining eligibility for a regular money grant were very different from those involved in developing an array of effective social services and building professional worker-client relationships.

In 1972 federal regulations mandated the separation of aid and services, with separate eli-

gibility and service staffs, and separate supervisory, administrative, and accounting systems.

Title XX followed, giving authority to the states to develop social services, with wide discretion as to what social services they would offer to low-income families.

Work Requirements.   With a stated purpose of reversing the trend toward ever-higher AFDC expenditures, Congress in 1967 legislated additions to the Social Security Act, which in part represented some constructive forward steps and in certain other significant aspects were regarded by many social welfare professionals as restrictive and highly controversial.

Generally approved was a step bringing the administration of child welfare services and AFDC into a single organizational unit at both the state and county levels, a move intended to increase coordinated planning and delivery of services for children and their families. The provision of social services was also broadened with a focus given to "family services."

More controversial were the provisions for a Work Incentive Now (WIN) program to which caretakers in AFDC families would be referred as a requirement for continued assistance. The ultimate objective was to place as many AFDC parents as possible in regular employment by referral to the state employment office.

As more women from the population generally entered the labor market, many of them mothers with young children, public assistance agencies had already begun to assess the feasibility of AFDC mothers working outside the home as a means of reducing program costs and, in some instances, of helping female heads of families achieve more independence and sense of family responsibility. But what many social workers found objectionable in the work training program legislated in the 1967 amendments was the aspect of compulsory participation; referral for work or training was to be mandatory as a condition for continuing to receive assistance. There appeared to be insufficient protection for AFDC mothers to make their own decisions as to whether their employment outside their homes or alternative plans of child care during the day would be contrary to the welfare of their families. Further, with ill-defined criteria for assessing what constitutes "suitable" work, the door was left open for racial discrimination and poor labor conditions for AFDC parents. Other questions were raised about the feasibility of finding available jobs in the open labor market after AFDC parents had completed work training, in view of already prevailing rates of unemployment among persons with low-level skills. Many social workers believed that efforts might be better expended in increasing the maternal and homemaking skills of AFDC mothers as a means of raising the level of child care for large numbers of dependent children.

Studies of the outcome of the WIN program have yielded substantial evidence that the program has not attained its goal of helping people attain economic independence. Throughout the WIN experience, there have been problems. Weaver summarized them thus:

> Recipients and their sympathizers have objected to the element of compulsion; social services, especially day care, have not been widely available; collaboration between the federal departments and the state welfare and employment agencies has not been adequate; available jobs have often lacked dignity and sufficient earning power; and, most important, the demand for training and work slots has exceeded the supply. (Weaver, 1977, p. 1134)

Nevertheless, given the inherited values and attitudes toward work and economic independence in this country, the issue of work requirements and incentives as policy and procedure in AFDC remained very live, one that inevitably became central to the provisions of the 1988 Family Support Act.

Fragmentation of Social Services. With the passage of Title XX and the use of block grants to channel federal funds to the states for social services, the active role of the federal government in social welfare planning was diminished. Title XX of the Social Security Act allowed significant diversity in the kinds of services states could offer, and in the absence of a clear conceptual framework for a system of social services, considerable fragmentation of services became evident. In an approach to understanding the mental health problems of AFDC parents and the kinds of social services they needed, Wiltse carried out a project in the San Francisco Department of Public Welfare in which social workers carried a small caseload of AFDC families, thus permitting intensive study. Wiltse found a pattern of psychological functioning and social behavior he identified as "pseudo-depression syndrome," characteristic of many of the parents in varying degrees of severity. He termed the condition "pseudodepression" to distinguish it from the clinically recognized depression of psychiatric literature. The term does not imply, however, that the symptoms were affected or consciously assumed; rather the symptoms appear to be "a reasonable response to the buffetings of a series of singularly destructive environmental experiences, coming on the heels of poor ego formation." Symptoms took the form of "immobilization with regard to effective activity, isolation from social relationships, depressed appearance, weight loss, poor appetite and chronic health problems." Among the factors underlying these conditions were (1) the necessity of being "on relief" in a society where that often is equated with inadequacy, immorality, and worthlessness; (2) inadequate money income, leading to below-minimum standards of living; (3) a feeling of vulnerability to the structure of society in which AFDC parents felt themselves to be pawns of the agencies of the community and of the authorities in those agencies, that is, the public welfare agency, the county hospital, social workers, doctors, the police department, and the court; and (4) the necessity of coping with the implications of their own obvious failures (Wiltse, 1963).

McCabe's (1967) in-depth study of a group of families most assailable—fatherless families made so by desertion, separation, or illegitimacy—yielded a vivid and poignant picture. The mothers were found to be clear about their responsibility to give the children care, to feed, clothe, and house them; they used their energies and monies for the children's physical care. By and large, however, the portrait of the AFDC mothers was consistent with that of Wiltse's, illustrated by the mothers' pervasive depressive features, reflecting their experiences of extreme poverty, frequent separation from their own parents in their early childhood, limited education, thwarted desires to establish a home through marriage, and desertion and incompatibility brought on by poor social judgment and chronic unmet dependency needs. Their participation in community groups was low, restricted mostly to church and school contacts related to what they saw as benefits for their children. They felt powerless to effect change in the community and did not belong to civic groups.

Effectiveness of Social Services. The new emphasis on social services to AFDC families inevitably raised questions about the usefulness of the services offered. Social workers were challenged to prove the effectiveness of their traditionally most favored helping method—social casework. In addition, the challenge of accountability in social service delivery was given impetus by public concern over the rising costs of public welfare programs and was reflected by legislators and other policy makers in requirements for receiving public funds for social services.

In an attempt to examine casework effectiveness in a way that recognized the profession's commitment to the scientific method and to serving clients well, Fischer (1973) reviewed the findings of eleven major studies of casework outcomes that had used an experimental treatment group and some form of control group. Several of the studies reviewed were of services to low-income clients. One was a sample of

"multiproblem" families who suffered a variety of health and welfare problems and chronic dependence on community services. Fifty such families receiving AFDC were given intensive social casework by social workers with M.S.W. degrees who were carrying reduced caseloads. A control group of fifty similar families was given the usual public assistance services without reduced caseloads or other opportunities for intensive service giving. After thirty-one months no significant differences were found between the two groups (Brown, 1968).

In a similar study Mullen, Chazin, and Feldstein (1970) randomly assigned new public assistance clients to an experimental and a control group, with the experimental group receiving intensive casework services intended to decrease rates of family disorganization. Control groups received the usual public assistance services. After two years of service, no significant differences in family functioning were found.

In view of the goal of social services as intended by Congress—getting people off welfare—some studies focused on the question of how effective social services were in reducing dependency by helping AFDC recipients to achieve self-support. One such study was based on analyses of 750 cases from two randomly sampled AFDC caseloads in each of five urban areas (Comptroller, 1973). For purposes of the study social services were classified as *developmental* services, designed to give direct assistance in achieving self-support, such as job counseling, job training, or job placement; and *maintenance* services, designed to help recipients sustain or strengthen the quality of family life.

Although some families were helped to find employment and some were helped to cope with and overcome their day-to-day problems, overall, "social services had only a minor impact on directly helping recipients to develop and use the skills necessary to achieve reduced dependency or self-support" (Comptroller, 1973, p. 2). Most AFDC recipients who left the rolls did so because they no longer needed the grant—they had remarried, or no longer had an eligible child, or had moved to another jurisdiction. Of those who left the rolls because they had obtained employment, most had done so on their own initiative; social services had little or no direct impact.

Partial explanations for these disappointing findings were offered in the report: (1) Not all AFDC recipients have the potential for self-support or reduced dependency, and local welfare departments lack adequate objective means to assess the potential of individual recipients and select appropriate services to offer them; (2) barriers inside and outside the public assistance program significantly affect whether AFDC recipients achieve self-support, for example, limited training resources and employment opportunities, shortages of child care facilities in low-income areas, increasing caseloads, poor health facilities and educational systems, and substandard housing. Given the current stage of development of social services, the method of determining who should receive what services, and economic conditions including a high rate of unemployment, it appeared unrealistic to assume that social services could play a larger role in helping AFDC recipients attain self-support.

Similar findings emerged from other studies (Marin, 1969). It appeared important to differentiate individuals on AFDC whose rehabilitative potential was more promising so that appropriate services could be offered to them. For various reasons problems of some segments of the population do not yield to intensive social casework or other forms of counseling. However, there are indications that when AFDC recipients who have more recognizable capacity for rehabilitation and self-help are identified and offered appropriate services, they can effectively reduce their dependency.

One such indication came from a study of AFDC mothers in California (called Aid to Needy Children, or ANC, in that state) (Rudoff & Piliavin, 1969). With the use of an experimental design, three areas were studied: the development of a typology of ANC mothers; the effect of intensive special services on the personality and the termination and employment rates of a random sample of ANC mothers; and the effect of special services on the termination and employment rates of a purposive sample of ANC mothers judged to be employable, using such criteria as good health, motivation for employment, age between eighteen and fifty, at least some high school education, and children either in school or for whom there were suitable day care facilities.

At the conclusion of the study, comparisons between the randomly selected experimental and control groups of mothers showed that in matters of termination from rolls, finding employment, and improving family functioning, experienced public assistance workers with reduced caseloads and professionally trained supervision had been unable to achieve clearly better results than workers carrying normal large-agency caseloads. However, when special services were offered to ANC mothers previously identified as employable, more mothers who had received intensive services were able to find employment than those who had received the usual services.

These findings strongly suggest that when individuals with employment potential are located in agency caseloads, as they can be, and given intensive service, employment rates can be significantly improved. AFDC mothers are not all of one type, and intensive services do not bring successful results with random samples. To give one kind of service to all AFDC mothers reveals two invalid assumptions—that all clients need the same kind of service, and that all clients will profit from the same service. Intensive casework may be effective in bringing about change in some types of clients, while other clients will require different forms of help, and others may be resistant to any of the social services as currently developed. The researchers in this study thus underscored the importance of developing sound client classification systems and offering social services differentially if effectiveness of services is to be improved (Rudoff & Piliavin, 1969).

Generally AFDC parents have indicated that they consider casework services less meaningful than large cash allowances or commodity services that supply food, medical care, and clothing—a reminder to planners and other professionals that social services cannot substitute for an adequate and reliable income.

The Need for a New Program.   From the late 1960s to the end of the 1980s, there was agreement among national leaders of various political and social beliefs that the existing public assistance programs in this country should be extensively revised or replaced. The Advisory Council on Public Welfare (1966) took note of the inadequacies of the public assistance grants, the inequities in eligibility requirements, and the exclusion of large segments of the needy by the categorical separation of eligibility requirements. Its recommendations to the Secretary of Health, Education, and Welfare included the establishment of a minimum standard for public assistance below which no state would be allowed to fall; a nationwide comprehensive program of public assistance based on only one eligibility requirement—need—which would eliminate the partial and categorical approach to insufficient income; a formula for more adequate and equitable sharing of costs between levels of government; and an expansion in public welfare social and medical services (Advisory Council on Public Welfare, 1966). In a widely read study of civil disorders, attention was given to the public assistance program on the basis that an adequate welfare system is one of the necessary conditions for achieving racial equality and integration in the cities. A number of specific recommendations were made (Kerner, 1968).

Other factors began to coalesce to produce a strong claim for change—including escalating caseloads and costs, obvious inequities from state to state in the level of AFDC grants and in eligibility requirements, new awareness of uninsured risks to individuals and families under the social insurance system, the negative public image the AFDC program had taken on, the emergence in the late 1960s of a visible Welfare Rights Organization, and increased difficulty and stress between federal and state governments in the complex negotiations and compromises that the shared AFDC program demanded. Yet no significant basic changes in the public assistance system followed these studies or other various proposals put forward.

When a consensus finally did develop in the late 1980s to end "maintaining poor children and their parents above starvation but in dependency," the action was heralded as "a revision of the social contract between the nation and the needy" ("Real welfare reform," 1988).

THE FAMILY SUPPORT ACT OF 1988

Factors That Influenced the New Welfare Consensus

A convergence of political, economic, and social forces influenced lawmakers and others concerned with social policy toward agreement on long-awaited welfare changes. One such political development was the emergence in 1987 of the states' governors as a critical political force for welfare revision. They had not so functioned in earlier years, but as the federal government under the Reagan presidency moved away from social policy development, various states began to experiment with ways to break the dependency cycle of welfare. Concern was high that the existing AFDC program inadvertently supplied incentives to avoid work and to subsist on welfare payments. Although it was acknowledged that at least half of all AFDC recipients remain on welfare only temporarily following some unexpected inability to work or find other means of supporting their children, fear was great that the other half were caught in a pattern of continuing dependency, and that their children too would grow up without ability to become self-sufficient workers. In their efforts to find a means to break this cycle, several states carried out demonstrations of varied work programs. The common element was large-scale education and job training with targeted groups of teenage mothers, all young families, and others vulnerable to long-term welfare dependence. New Jersey's program, for example, used a written contract between the state and the welfare recipient who agreed to get a job, train for a job, or go to school. In return the state provided child care, health care, and transportation. Studies of several state programs carried out by the Demonstration Research Corporation, a private concern in New York City that conducts independent research on social policy issues, showed a promising level of success and some degree of reason to believe that such programs benefited welfare recipients and that the programs could eventually pay for themselves (Stevens, 1988).

A compelling economic factor also influenced the achievement of a Congressional welfare consensus. Welfare costs had long been deplored as too heavy a drain on tax resources. A more convincing argument had emerged from various projections of serious labor shortages by the mid-1990s, and the conviction that in the 1990s and beyond, the economy would require all or more than the available trained workers.

A social factor that contributed heavily to the new consensus on welfare was the high increase in single-parent families. Women, single or married, for some time had been entering the work force for economic reasons of family support and well-being. Clear evidence existed that quality child care during a parent's working day does not harm children; rather, they benefit from it. A new norm of family life was in place, leaving mothers and their children dependent on welfare for long periods of time in an out-of-date system (Stevens, 1988).

Basic Provisions

The intent of the new legislation, simply stated, was to enable the states to help poor families get off welfare and become self-sufficient. The means employed was to require AFDC recipients to participate in education, job training and work programs.

The Act's provisions for child support and establishment of paternity were discussed earlier in this chapter. A second major provision was the Job Opportunities and Basic Skills (JOBS) program that replaced the outworn Work Incentive (WIN) program and required each of the states to develop and implement statewide education, training, and work opportunities for welfare recipients.

Under the act, with certain exceptions all welfare recipients must participate in the JOBS program if they are to continue to receive financial assistance. Individuals exempted from the compulsory clause include (1) persons who are ill, incapacitated, or of an advanced age; (2) persons needed at home because of illness or incapacity of another member of the family; (3) parents who are providing care for a child under age three (or at state option under age one); (4) persons already working thirty or more hours a week; (5) children less than sixteen years or full-time in elementary, secondary, or vocational school; (6) women in the second trimester or later of pregnancy; (7) persons living in an area where the program is not available.

Certain high-risk populations were targeted for early inclusion in the program: (1) young parents who are under twenty-four years old, have not completed high school or are not enrolled, or have had little or no work experience in the past year; (2) families where the youngest child is within less than two years of reaching the age of ineligibility for AFDC; (3) families who have received AFDC for more than twenty-six months during the past sixty months.

Recipients who volunteer to participate were to be given first consideration. If the state failed to spend 55 percent of its allocated funds on the targeted families, the federal financial match would be reduced.

As part of the JOBS program, each state must provide a range of educational activities (for example, to gain literacy, proficiency in English, job skills and job placement services). In addition the state must develop a range of supportive services, including (1) guaranteed child care for AFDC parents who are working or participating in education or training (as lack of child care constitutes good cause for not participating in the JOBS program); (2) provision to parents of information on accessible child care and when indicated, help to them in selecting appropriate care that meets state and local standards of basic health and safety; (3) establishment of a grant program to improve the regulation and monitoring of child care providers for AFDC families; and (4) provision of transitional child care and Medicaid for 12 months after an AFDC recipient leaves the rolls because of employment and increased earnings.

A long-due provision was the requirement that all states install coverage of two-parent families where the primary earner is unemployed (the AFDC Unemployed Parent—AFDC-UP—program). Formerly only twenty-six states had used the federal option to offer AFDC to poor families where the second parent (usually the father) was at home and unemployed. However, this new provision was weakened by a clause that allowed states that had previously not chosen to use the option to provide AFDC-UP for only six months of a year.

A controversial inclusion in the Act was a compulsory condition of receiving AFDC-UP benefits: At least one parent must participate for at least sixteen hours per week in unpaid Community Work Experience Programs (CWEP) or other forms of work supplementation or on-the-job training. Single parents on welfare with children three years old or older would be required to participate in employment and training programs. Teen-age parents who

had not graduated from high school would have to return to school or seek an equivalent degree. In addition, as a condition for receiving AFDC payments, states were allowed to require minor unmarried parents to live with their parents, other relatives, or in an adult-supervised setting.

In recognition of the new and demanding tasks the states would face in implementing the act, and in order to ensure that its provisions were carried out in an orderly and monitored way, a time schedule was included for phasing in the new program—minimum monthly participation standards that the states must meet. Seven percent of nonexempt AFDC recipients must be enrolled in 1990 and 1991; 11 percent in 1992 and 1993; 15 percent in 1994; and 20 percent in 1995.

One early and innovative JOBS program, subjected to rigorous study, concluded that "while states can save significant amounts of money by requiring welfare recipients to work, the incomes and living standards of the poor may not improve." In San Diego, 4,552 welfare recipients were divided into two nearly equal and randomly selected groups, with one group required to work. The intent was to determine the extent to which the program could bring about increased movement away from welfare rolls and into productive jobs. Close contact by program caseworkers was found necessary to ensure that half of the eligible AFDC recipients would participate in the work program. Many had legitimate reasons for not doing so. The study, conducted by the Manpower Demonstration Research Corporation, termed the outcome as the most encouraging to date in efforts to help a wide range of welfare recipients get jobs. Findings showed that for each dollar spent on the JOBS program, government saved $3.00. For AFDC participants, the outcomes were less positive; those who moved into part-time or full-time jobs earned no more than their welfare checks and benefits had brought, and, in some cases, less. Welfare mothers who went to work increased their income by only $8 to $30 a year;

fathers in two-parent families found that they lost $7 to $13 annually. The basis for judgment of success appeared to depend on whether one "takes the perspective of the tax-payer or the welfare recipient," leading to criticism that the program simply replaced one source of poverty-level earnings with another source (Mathews, 1990).

How well the "welfare reform" legislation will enable families to leave the rolls of public assistance and become economically independent, even for extended but temporary periods of time, is not yet proved. Much depends on the actions of individual states, among whom there has always been wide variation with respect to public assistance.

TRENDS AND ISSUES

Pre- and post-enactment comment on the provisions of the Family Support Act made it clear that although most observers recognized some significant improvements achieved, by no means was there agreement that as a "revision of the social contract between the nation and the needy" the act was a proper one. Commentary was reflected in a continuum of approval/disapproval and a middle-ground position of acceptance with reservations. Common ground within the debate was that individual self-sufficiency should be a major strategy in welfare reform.

On the right were approving conservative proponents who termed the legislation a historical change away from families' living unproductive lives on the "dole" and who strongly believed that mandatory work requirements were needed, given individual characteristics that were the cause of an individual's poverty. On the left were opposing liberal proponents of the post–World War II philosophy and principles of a "welfare state" who, historically, had stood for governmental guarantees of a minimum income for all families and an eventual elimina-

tion of poverty through changes in social and economic direction of society. In the center were those who saw the legislation as "the best that could be done at the time."

The middle point of acceptance was set forth by Senator Daniel Patrick Moynihan, who shepherded the bill through congressional pitfalls. In response to criticism that the bill being considered was only "half a policy" because of a "conspicuous absence of a national minimum benefit," Moynihan responded:

> We are trying to redefine a program that began as a widow's pension, pending the maturing of survivor's insurance under Social Security. What we must work with today is a wholly different population of dependent mothers with dependent children who receive virtually no child support and who are virtually all unemployed. . . . We seek to establish a new social contract; parental responsibility in return for community involvement and concern. . . . How soon might we expect to see social change? Not soon. . . . In the early years we would expect that at most 75,000 of the 3.8 million adult welfare recipients could be served each year by the job training and placement program we propose. Just so. We would establish for the first time, open-ended Federal funding for job training and placement. The Congressional Budget Office estimates that, given the best will in the world, that is all the states will be able to do. These are not fiscal limits, but the limits of a new desperate social reality. If we can get started, and show a little success, that reality might just begin to yield. (1987, p. 22)

The provisions in the new legislation that received widespread support were the extensions of child care and Medicaid for a year after a parent enters the workforce, and the inclusion of second-parent, unemployed families as eligible for AFDC in all states. Beyond these achievements, the legislation has prompted critical analysis.

One of the most serious criticisms of the Family Support Act of 1988 is that the legislation "is linked only tenuously to the economic reality of American society" grounded as it is on the premise that "the private sector has the capacity to absorb those persons currently dependent on AFDC." The relatively low current unemployment rates nationally disguise the fact that almost half of the new jobs of the 1980s were part-time, service sector jobs with no career mobility, few or no benefits, and little chance of moving upward from a place among the "working poor" (Karger & Stoesz, 1989, p. 25). The structure of the labor market has changed in the direction of "high-tech" industry with growth at two work levels: professional-technical levels that require advanced education and skills, and a service level of clerical jobs that pay low wages with limited opportunity to advance without education and training beyond what states will be able to provide in their workfare programs. In addition, geographic redistribution of jobs has occurred with industries moving away from central cities where the poor live and into areas where wages traditionally are below average (Nichols-Casebolt & McClure, 1989).

If we allow the occupational and income structure to remain as it is . . . our present trends toward a separate but unequal society will become institutionalized. (Harrington, 1987, p. 3)

Critics also have asserted that the lawmakers ignored marked differences among the states with respect to factors that will critically influence how well a given state can implement the new legislation: (1) financial resources, (2) variation in the rate of employment, (3) distribution of available jobs and skills required, and (4) a capacity to develop appropriate supportive services.

Concern has been expressed as well about "compulsory" aspects of the new programs. The mandatory nature of the work require-

ments—a "work-or-go-hungry measure" in the view of Bertram Beck, "caters to the erroneous belief that most welfare recipients are lazy and won't work unless compelled." Beck cites the successful welfare-to-work programs in Massachusetts that are voluntary and found to be a more humane, supportive, and cost effective approach than mandatory systems. Furthermore, Beck cited a "fatal error of assuming commonality among welfare recipients" (Beck, 1987).

The provision that states must give first consideration to AFDC recipients who volunteer to enter a work program is sound; motivation is a central part of success in the new work and training opportunities. It is well established, however, that some AFDC families, having experienced long deprivation, are disorganized, headed by a parent without coping skills, lacking in self-esteem and sometimes seriously depressed. These are parents who are least likely to comply and at greatest risk of losing their meager support payments given the mandatory work requirement.

Beck also makes a case for an element of choice by some single parents who believe that "remaining at home and caring for children even on an Aid to Families with Dependent Children grant is the preferred course of action. The alternative could be a minimum-wage job, child care of questionable quality and exposing children to the dangers of the neighborhood as they go to and from school. The decision of a parent to remain at home might be in the interest of children and society. In such instances, it should be allowed" (Beck, 1987).

A significant factor in the extent to which the Family Support Act reaches its goals is how well the separate states can develop and offer appropriate supportive services to the AFDC family population. As has been discussed earlier in this chapter, effective services for these families have not been clearly conceptualized and tested. Effectiveness of services will also be conditioned by the level of professional training of the staff who deliver the services. Undoubtedly there will be wide variation among the states in the nature and effectiveness of available supportive services.

As the states began to wrestle with the challenges the federal government has set and the still-open policy choices, the Children's Defense Fund warned against the risk of "hasty, ill-thought out, or punitive state programs." It was noted that many states were scrambling to begin implementation earlier than required, making them eligible for new streams of federal funds. Advocates, it was counseled, should urge states to "proceed with caution," perhaps starting small in a limited number of counties and doing "careful demographic research" before launching a massive statewide program. The extent of a state's child care capabilities, accurate data, available jobs, the quality of services provided versus boosting quantity to meet arbitrary quotas were sure to be critical (*CDF Reports,* 1989a, April).

The situation in this country has been tragic for children of the poor. Speaking for the Carnegie Council of Children, Kenneth Keniston illustrated the relationship between family income and the children's welfare most tellingly and in so doing emphasized the need for effective assistance programs:

> The single most important factor that stacks the deck against tens of millions of American children is poverty. Other things being equal, the best way to ensure that a child has a fair chance at the satisfactions and fulfillments of adult life is to ensure that the child is born into a family with a decent income. . . .
>
> This is not to say that improving the economic status of low-income families is going to solve all the problems of children. It will not obviate the need to improve health care for children and pregnant mothers; it will not eliminate the need for a well-financed responsive child-care network or solve the problems of unwanted children; it will not put an end to the psychological and social pressures of our high-powered, urban, industrialized, corporation-based society which place extraordinary strains on families. Nor will it end the virulent racial discrimination that remains the ugliest blemish on our society. But the evidence indicates overwhelmingly that improving the economic status of low-income families is the most crucial step for bringing American social practice into line with American ideals. (1977, pp. 83, 118)

FOR STUDY AND DISCUSSION

1. Review the historical development of our governmental income maintenance programs. Trace and evaluate recurring themes still evident in present-day policy and practice.
2. Identify and illustrate the major principles and policies on which social insurance programs in this country are based.
3. What are the principal uninsured risks to income security that enforce hardship on many children and their families?
4. What were the principal concerns in the formulation of the Social Security Act? How did these influence the programs for children that were included or omitted?
5. Review the chapter for evidence of a trend toward more restrictive policies in the AFDC program. Discuss these policies with respect to the effects on children, parents, and all citizens.
6. "With few exceptions, the welfare reform produced at the end of the Reagan administration should be recognized as the most punitive and inadequate addition to American welfare since the workhouse" (Karger & Stoesz, 1989, p. 23). Take a position for or against this statement and document your point of view.
7. Take a stand on this statement: "If we allow the occupational and income structure to remain as it is . . . our present trends toward a separate but unequal society will become institutionalized" (Harrington, 1987, p. 3).

FOR ADDITIONAL STUDY

Axinn, J., & Stern, M. J. (1988). *Dependency and poverty. Old problems in a new world.* Lexington, MA: D. C. Heath.

CDF Reports. Monthly newsletter of the Children's Defense Fund. Washington, DC: Children's Defense Fund.

Kahn, A. J., & Kamerman, S. B. (1988). *Child support. From debt collection to social policy.* Newbury Park, CA: Sage.

Karger, J. J., & Stoesz, D. (1989). Welfare reform: Maximum feasible exaggeration. *Tikkun, 4*(2), 22–25, 118–122.

Kozol, J. (1988, Jan. 25, Feb. 1). A reporter at large. The homeless and their children. Parts I and II. *New Yorker,* pp. 65–84, 36–67.

Schorr, L. B. (1988). *Within our reach. Breaking the cycle of disadvantage.* New York: Anchor Press.

CHAPTER 7

Children's Daytime Care and Development

There was a child went forth every day,
And the first object he look'd on, that object he became,
And that object became part of him for the day or a certain part of the day,
Or for many years or stretching cycles of years.

Walt Whitman

Chapter Outline

"Child care" is a term that encompasses a wide variety of arrangements that parents make for their children's daytime care and development. From her study of working mothers and their solutions in trying to cope with their children's needs and their own work lives, Sheila B. Kamerman concluded in 1980 that "despite the rhetoric in the United States that emphasized concern for children and families," parenting was in fact being carried on in "an unresponsive society" (Kamerman, 1980, p. 122).

By 1988, however, a variety of advocacy groups had continued to press for an effective national child care policy and had achieved a congruence of interests. In a new assessment, Kamerman stated that child care as never before had emerged as "a viable issue in the national public agenda . . . a mainstream family issue" (*CDF Reports,* 1988b, pp. 1, 6–7). Child care was no longer perceived as a service mainly for poor mothers, disorganized families or for children with special needs. Parents from all regions and levels of income had expressed concern about child care and were demanding not only programs that offered nurturance, safety, and affordability, but also experiences that would advance early childhood education.

With wide public support, legislation late in 1988-addressed the necessity for new child care policy and moved through Congress almost to enactment (Act for Better Child Services). Despite the bill's narrow defeat in the closing days of the congressional session, the bill was perceived generally as the best approach yet to improved family options for child care. Advocates were confident that child care had become an issue that inevitably would result in an improved public policy.

FACTORS AFFECTING NEED FOR CHILD CARE

Various factors in contemporary society have contributed to extensive change in family forms, child-rearing patterns, and the necessity for daytime child-care arrangements outside of the "traditional" family. A major factor has been the accelerated entry of women into the labor force even when they have young children at home, a pattern that has occurred in all the advanced industrial countries of the world. In the United States, "as of 1987, over half of all mothers with children under six and nearly 70 percent of mothers with children between six and seventeen were working or looking for work outside the home" (William T. Grant Foundation Commission, 1988, p. 41). A major growth in female-headed families (see Chapter 5) has made it even more likely that a child will have a working mother. Whatever the family composition, as in other industrialized societies, for children born in the last quarter of the twentieth century, "being reared and cared for in a family in which both parents or the sole parent work will be the normal experience" (Kamerman, 1980, p. 8).

A second factor that has increased support for child care programs is the growing consensus that welfare recipients with young children should be given training and find employment, a goal that for success requires access to child care.

Another influence is the increased understanding of the potential benefits for children of socialization and readiness for school that can result from group experiences in early childhood education, whether or not their mothers work (Schorr, 1988, p. 180).

The explosion in women's employment has fundamentally changed the politics of child care. (Schorr, 1988, p. 212)

Yet another significant factor in the widespread support for child care programs is found in the feminist connotations that the term "child care" reflects. Publicly supported child care, as Sonya Michel observes, "is a type of social service that enables women with small children to enter the labor market and compete with men on an equal footing. By shifting at least part of the responsibility for early childrearing from the private to the public sphere—from individual women to public institutions, child care deconstructs women's supposedly 'natural' role as mothers and undermines an ideology which has, historically, severely restricted women's labor force participation. From a feminist perspective, publicly supported child care is inextricably linked to women's full labor force participation—and thus to more general goals of gender equality" (Michel, 1988, pp. 1–2).

The lives of working parents are complicated and demanding, a now common life-style. In a society that requires women to work and recruits them into the labor force but has not established a national policy of child care, finding and maintaining an adequate arrangement for children's care is a central problem for working parents and can become a constant source of tension. Because of the fragmented and uncoordinated patterns of day care provision, working parents usually must rely on multiple arrangements even within the same day. This is often a

package of some in-family care, some out-of-home family care and some group center care, all of which require multiple coping strategies for both children and parents. "Although there are probably more child care services available at present than ever before" (Kamerman & Kahn, 1988, p. 198), many are of poor quality or are more expensive than parents can afford. Locating and maintaining child care arrangements that are geographically convenient, reasonably priced and of satisfactory quality constitute a high priority among all working parents.

Regardless of terminology, auspices, the perceived need prompting some part of the community to offer a child care service, or parents' reasons for using a particular kind of arrangement, all programs of child care should contain all these elements: an understanding of a child's individual needs and stages of growth; consistent nurture; supportive emotional response; attention to the child's health and physical progress; and a variety of stimulating experiences that contribute to the child's cognitive and social development. In other words, child care should deal with the whole child in a well-rounded program. Children are not well cared for and protected if their need and capacity to learn and acquire competence are not given careful attention. Similarly, their success in learning, even in carefully devised educational programs, is hampered if there is not appropriate response to their feelings and emotions. Neither their education nor their welfare can be well looked after if they have unmet health needs, untended handicaps, or insufficient food and rest.

AUSPICES

A variety of sponsoring groups (public, private-nonprofit, and private-for-profit) administer child care programs in family or group settings.

Some of these programs are under the direction and control of state or local public welfare agencies and frequently are designed for children of low-income parents. Relatively small numbers of children are served by public health departments or teaching hospitals who accept children with special health problems, and by compensatory education programs sponsored by colleges and universities or other centers for the study of child development. A growing number of public schools have begun to develop and administer out-of-school hour programs for "latch-key" children who otherwise would be unsupervised during their parents' early morning or late afternoon work hours.

A large and poorly regulated system of child care under public auspices is found in programs conducted on military bases. The professional literature addressed to this phenomenon is meager, but that which does exist strongly suggests that military day care programs are financed and organized in such a way as to encourage institutional neglect of children (Spendlove, 1978; Bowen, 1987, p. 343).

In addition to publicly supported and sponsored child care facilities, voluntary family and children's social agencies provide child care programs. These frequently rest on a combination of financial resources, such as voluntary contributions, public funds through a purchase of care arrangements, and parents' fees. Churches very often provide voluntary sponsorship and space for child care. Cooperative groups of parents who want additional opportunities outside their homes for their children's development may choose to operate nursery schools.

Despite the congruence in objectives of child care services and other family-based social work services, a very limited percentage of child care programs are under the aegis of social work agencies.

Very large numbers of children receive care under proprietary auspices in day care centers operated as a business venture or in day care homes where a woman takes one child or more into her home during the day for pay. A relatively small number of franchised businesses and a larger number of "chain" commercial en-

terprises have developed child care centers on a regional or national basis. Through a company of stockholders, the intent has been to develop more extensive operations than the family or individual owner is able to do, and to operate on a contract basis with industry, labor, and public welfare.

Other types of commercial child care exist. As a response to the rise in the number of dual-career families and single working parents, employer-supported child care has increased dramatically. Between 1978 and 1982 the number of companies with child care programs grew by 395 percent. By 1984 the number had expanded again by 50 percent, with further expansion widely predicted (Burud et al., 1984, pp. 5–7). Care child centers at the parents' work site appear to some to be "the best answer to America's child care problem." The Children's Defense Fund (CDF) points out, however, that such centers often have few openings, employers sometimes give preferential treatment, and tend to establish centers at the industry's headquarters rather than factories, leaving lower-paid employees without access to the benefit. Out of six million employers, the CDF records, only 3,500 provide any child care help, leaving child care as the least often available employee benefit (Children's Defense Fund, 1987a, p. 11).

Where employer-supported child care is offered, working parents gain, especially when they are offered a flexible child care benefit package to choose from. Companies gain as well, often in ways that exceed program expense. Employer-supported child care (responding to federal tax incentives) has lessened employee absenteeism and turnover, served as an effective recruitment tool and a positive influence on employee morale, increased quality of the workforce, heightened productivity, and enhanced the company's public image (Burud et al., 1984).

Employer-supported child care is usually perceived as a recent innovation. Sonya Michel has established that the need was identified and responded to as early as 1798 in Philadelphia. A group of Quaker women, concerned about the poor widows of men who had died in a yellow fever epidemic, undertook to visit them, provide some needed material goods, and also give them paid work to be done at home—spinning. The philanthropists soon noted that the women's productivity was limited by the small, poorly heated space in their homes and the numerous distractions from work that their children posed. The solution agreed on was to set up a "spinning room" where the female workers could come, be fed and warmed, and work more efficiently. To correct the mothers' "pre-industrial practice of repeatedly interrupting their sewing or spinning to attend to the wants of the children," a "charitable nursery" was set up where the children could be supervised in a room separate from the "spinning room," where they could also learn "habits and virtues that would prevent them from following their parents down the road to poverty." While respecting the spinners' maternal affection and recognizing their apprehension about giving over their children's care to strangers, the arrangement was clearly intended to draw the mothers into the "steady rhythm of the modern factory" and increase productivity (Michel, 1988, p. 7).

FUNDING

The federal role with respect to funding and regulation of child care changed drastically in the 1980s under initiatives of the Reagan administration. The Omnibus Budget Reconciliation Act of 1981 (OBRA) "amended Title XX of the Social Security Act by creating the Social Services Block Grant, cut Title XX's appropriations by one-fifth, and eliminated the separately funded training program from Title XX. The child care food program, which had helped meet center and family day care meal costs, was drastically cut and only raised several years later. CETA's [Comprehensive Employment and

Training Act] public service employment, which had helped to staff centers, was ended. The child care allowance under AFDC (Title IV-A) was capped at $160 per month, and other restrictions were placed on allowable work expenses for employed AFDC mothers. In effect, direct federal funding for child care services was sharply reduced, and the requirement of a state-match of 25 percent was eliminated, potentially further decreasing available resources" (see Table 7.1).

The Title XX changes also ended a requirement for systematic state planning and filing of reports of expenditures and service statistics. Federally defined regulations for minimum child care standards were eliminated. The guiding principles for federal child care policy became decentralization, privatization, and deregulation (Kahn & Kamerman, 1987).

At the end of 1988 no single federal agency had the power to assign economic resources to or coordinate the myriad child care programs or enforce standards of quality. Only very limited federal funding addressed the problem of child care costs to parents. Most of the child care costs were being met by parents or by private funds.

Other than the provision in the Family Support Act of 1988 that allows one year of transitional child care for families leaving the AFDC rolls for employment (Chapter 6), the primary public sources of child care currently are Title XX Social Services Block Grants, Head Start, and the federal income tax system.

Title XX provides money to states to apply to the costs of a variety of social services for low and moderate income persons. The states vary considerably in the types of programs they finance and the level of support offered. The Children's Defense Fund reported in 1987 that on the average states awarded about 18 percent of their Title XX money to child care programs. The need for child care assistance to low- and moderate-income parents continued to grow even as Title XX was becoming "a shrinking pie—sliced in half over the past decade by bud-

TABLE 7.1. Federal Expenditures for Child Care, Fiscal Years 1980 and 1986

Programs	Expenditure in Millions of Dollars	
	1980	1986
Title XX (SSBG)	$ 600[a]	$ 387[a]
Head Start	$ 769[b]	$1,040
AFDC Disregard (Title IV-A)	$ 120[c]	$ 35
Child Care Food Program	$ 239[a]	$ 501[a]
Title IV-C (WIN)	$ 115[d]	-0-
ARC (Appalachian Regional Commission) Child Development	$ 11[b]	$ 1
Employer Provided Child Care	-0-	$ 110[e]
Dependent Care Tax Credit	$ 956[a]	$3,410[a]
Total	$2,807	$5,484
Total without tax credit	$1,851	$2,074[f]

[a]ACYF estimate provided by Patricia Divine Hawkins.
[b]Testimony, Jo Ann Casper, Deputy Assistant Secretary for Social Services, *Child Care: Beginning a National Initiative* (Washington, DC: Government Printing Office, 1984).
[c]E. Duval et al., "AFDC: Characteristics of Recipients in 1979," *Social Security Bulletin*, 45(4), 4–19.
[d]Congressional Budget Office (CBO).
[e]CBO, based on Joint Tax Committee estimates.
[f]Since the inflation rate was 31 percent between 1980 and 1985, according to CBO, this total would have had to be $2,425 to sustain the 1980 direct expenditure level.
Note: State and local education and social service expenditure not included in table. (*Source:* A. J. Kahn and S. B. Kamerman. [1987]. *Child Care: Facing the Hard Choices.* Dover, MA: Auburn House, p. 19. Reprinted by permission.)

get cuts and inflations." A result: "Twenty-eight states spent less money for Title XX child care programs in 1987 than in 1981, even though the numbers of low-income working families had increased significantly" (Children's Defense Fund, 1987a, pp. 7–9).

Over 2,000 locally administered Head Start programs of varying quality receive federal monies. Head Start, since its inception in 1965, has remained a popular program, one that President Reagan and the Congress were willing to protect in the wave of social program cuts in the 1980s. By 1985, Head Start enrolled 450,000 children (largely minority children, reflecting the poverty statistics in the United States) with yearly expenses over $1 billion. Even so, Head Start was able to serve less than 20 percent of eligible families (Zigler, 1985, pp. 604, 608).

The largest federal effort to help parents with child care costs is centered in the federal in-

come tax system. The "dependent care tax credit" permits parents to deduct from their federal income taxes between 20 and 30 percent (depending on their income level) of their yearly child care expenses, up to $2,400 for one child and $4,800 for two or more. In 1984, 7.5 million families benefited from the child care tax deductions, which added up to just over $2.6 billion. The tax credit provision is a significant help for parents who earn enough to owe substantial tax sums. Practically, however, families living below or near the poverty level have such low tax liabilities that "a tax break is no break at all" (Children's Defense Fund, 1987a, pp. 8–9).

A second tax subsidy plan, "the flexible benefit plan," permits parents in higher tax brackets and who work for a participating employer, to reduce their taxable income up to $5,000 to pay the costs of child care, the money being held in a special account to be used against

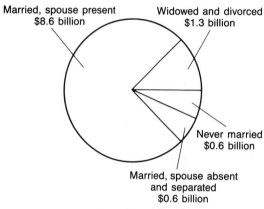

Figure 7.1. Amount Spent Annually on Child Care Arrangements, by Marital Status of Working Women. (*Source:* U.S. Department of Commerce, Bureau of the Census. [1987]. Current Population Reports, Series P-70, No. 9. *Who's Minding the Kids? Child Care Arrangements, Winter 1984–1985.* Washington, DC: U.S. Government Printing Office, p. 11.)

the employee's child care costs. Neither of the two federal tax credits are useful to low-income families in meeting the costs of child care that in turn would enable them to stay in the labor market (Children's Defense Fund, 1987a). It should be acknowledged as well that a tax deduction for middle- or upper-class parents does not necessarily create accessible, affordable and high-quality child care for their children (see Figure 7.1).

CHILDREN FOR WHOM CARE IS NEEDED

Children of Working Mothers

Children need child care for a variety of reasons. The most frequent and urgent one is that their mothers work, usually in paid employment

(and less often as unpaid employees in relation to a family business or farm).

The older the children are, the more likely it is that their mothers are employed. Nevertheless, most of the increase in the last four decades in the numbers of working mothers has been among women with preschool children. The trend is expected to continue, from 7.5 million in 1980 to nearly 15 million in 1995 (two-thirds of all preschool children). In that same year, 1995, four out of five school-age children will have working mothers (Children's Defense Fund, 1987a). (See Figure 7.2.)

An even more problematic change is that in 1987 half of all new mothers (53 percent of black new mothers, 51 percent of white, and 36 percent of Hispanic) were in the workforce within the first year of an infant's life. These percentages loom large in view of the scarcity and uncertain quality of child care facilities that will accept infants ("A threshold is crossed," 1988, June 16, p. 12).

The problem of before and after school care remains critical. Parents most often must

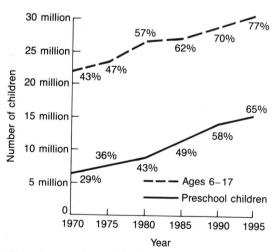

Figure 7.2. Children with Mothers in the Labor Force. (*Source:* Children's Defense Fund. [1987]. *Child Care: The Time Is Now.* Washington, DC: Children's Defense Fund, p. 2.)

leave for work before their children leave for school and are unable to return until after the child's school day has ended. Five-year-old children in half-day kindergartens make up a vulnerable group between preschool and first grade who need thoughtfully worked out child care arrangements to supplement their short kindergarten day. The number of schools offering some form of program for children outside of regular school hours—most often supervised recreation, art and crafts, and other programs of varied enriching value—is increasing. Yet 2.3 million of vulnerable nine- to thirteen-year-olds go home to an empty house or to an older sibling (Children's Defense Fund, 1987b).

In exploring what working mothers considered to be major gaps in community services that could help them with their child care needs, Kamerman found these critical lacks: (1) too short a day in prekindergarten and kindergarten programs and uncoordinated schedules that made it especially difficult for families with two or more children; (2) too rigid school hours; (3) inadequate numbers of after-school programs for preschool and primary school-age children; (4) inadequate summer facilities and activities for children when schools are closed (Kamerman, 1980, pp. 116–117).

Children with Special Needs

Other groups of children may need child care. *Physically handicapped* children frequently need more than the usual opportunity for stimulation, training, and socialization as part of their treatment and rehabilitation. Similarly, *mentally retarded* children often need child care—preschool programs, after-school recreational services, and occupational day centers for older youth.

Many children with *serious emotional problems* have parents who can continue to care for them in their homes if proper therapy is provided. Child care treatment centers for emotionally disturbed children are a useful alternative to outpatient therapy or full-time residential treatment.

Children of migrant farm workers are vulnerable to serious physical, social, and emotional deprivation. Because their parents have no way of caring for them while they are working in the fields, these children may spend their days in hazardous conditions of care. Sometimes they stay in parked cars or buses near the fields with only very occasional attention from adults, or they may be left in the camps under the supervision of an elderly, incapacitated member of the family or with the oldest child—perhaps only six or seven years of age. Even where community child care centers have been established to care for migrant preschool and school-age children, infants and toddlers often have no formal arrangements made for them and go unattended for long hours.

Many families of varying class and characteristics choose group child care for their preschool children as an aid in preparing them for school—intellectually, socially, and in self-perception and identity.

In summary, programs for children's daytime care and development are appropriate for a wide range of children with differing needs, capacities, and family circumstances. If these programs are planned creatively and administered flexibly, child care services are a valuable supplement to family life among all socioeconomic groups.

FACTORS RELATED TO MATERNAL EMPLOYMENT

Why Mothers Work

Working mothers are not new in America. Well before the Industrial Revolution, mothers worked many hours a day in their homes and on farms to produce goods and services that supplemented their husbands' income and supplied a significant part of their families' consumptive needs. This essential work often resulted in as much divided attention to children as occurs now among many mothers employed more formally outside their homes. Viewed against this background, the high rate of maternal employment today is not a radically new phenomenon, but an old one modified by new occupations and changed work locale, relationships, and rewards.

The most urgent reason that women have entered the labor force in the past and continue to do so today is that like men, they feel a strong pressure to earn. Women who enter the labor force almost universally do so out of necessity of one kind or another, and although the pattern is changing, they still bear most of the responsibility for housework and child care. In a study of the employment of women over time, Lynn Weiner identified two persistent themes: (1) the problem of child care for young children, and (2) the question of structural change in the workplace (Weiner, 1985, p. 141). Since women first entered into industrial work more than a century ago, the way in which work is organized has been a "stress factor" in family life. In this highly competitive urban age, family life will require a reorganization of the world of work—not only at home where the tasks of confirming equality at home and in the workplace are unfinished, but also in (1) shorter work weeks for both men and women, (2) provisions for maternal and paternal leave when children are born, or are ill and need a parent's care, and (3) the provision of affordable, flexible child care programs during parents' working hours.

For increasing numbers of women, an equally compelling reason for working is that, just as in the case of men, work is central to their identities. More women than ever before subscribe to and take for granted the aims and principles of the organized women's movement—women as individual human beings, rather than persons treated collectively without recognition of their individual interests and capabilities (Chavez, 1987, July 17). Despite the fact that

women receive 68 percent of the average wage earned by men, women are entering and deriving satisfaction from a wide range of jobs at all levels of occupations previously viewed as suitable only for men.

At the center of the ambivalence in many quarters about the accelerated rate of mothers in the workforce is the tenacity, despite sweeping change, with which many citizens hold to an emotional and nostalgic view of what the structure of the family should be and the roles that men and women should play in it. Throughout the history of America, unyielding fear of change in the traditional concept of the family has been inherent in organized opposition to the rights of women. Yet neither the state nor the economy has ever supported the somewhat romantic traditional concept of the family except for a brief time in the nineteenth century for a select group of upper- and middle-class women. Opponents of the women's movement have tended to ignore or minimize the family's need for the mother's earnings and to perceive the accelerated entry of women into the labor force as a dangerous consequence of "feminist thinking." Lillian Rubin has responded to that view thus: "When over fifty percent of all married women with young children are in the labor force, it's time to stop blaming the feminists for destroying the family. Whatever personal satisfactions these women may find at work, the cold hard fact of American family life today is that it takes two incomes to live decently and still pay the bills" (1987, p. 90).

Dated and unrealistic expectations for girls would only be of historical interest if they had not continued in new ways, despite vast changes in social mores and economic realities. The steady increase in working mothers, their new aspirations, and the necessity for self-support do not fit neatly into the traditional patterns set by private charity or public welfare. (Polier, 1989, p. 104)

Other Forces That over Time Have Influenced Mothers to Work

A variety of other complex factors have combined to effect the present high rate of maternal employment. Perhaps the most influential of these have been *advances in science and technology,* which have brought about an unprecedented growth and change in the national economy. The shift from an agricultural to an industrial society, and the resulting expansion of the urban population, brought changes in the nature of jobs (for example, lessened requirements for physical labor) and greatly expanded job opportunities for women. At the same time, as the goods and services mothers had once produced in their homes were produced by industry, and therefore obtained outside the home, the costs of these essentials and luxuries of living were transferred to fathers, who often found themselves unable to earn enough without outside earnings from their wives. As industry has made more and more goods and services available, families have become increasingly desirous of a higher standard of living, increasing the likelihood that mothers will take advantage of job opportunities to help achieve it.

National crises in the twentieth century have provided opportunities for women to work and impelled them to do so. In the Depression of the 1930s, women sometimes could obtain work when men could not, and the pressing need for family income made it necessary that mothers work if they could. Wars and the burgeoning need for labor in defense industries gave opportunities and social approval for new kinds of employment.

As women have acquired more *education,* and as this education has become more like that of men in content and quality, women have become eligible for a greater variety of jobs and have wanted to use their increased education to continue an involvement with intellectual or social activity outside their homes to which education exposed them.

Changed *patterns of marriage and child-* *bearing* and increased *life expectancy* in the twentieth century have influenced mothers to work, and in turn have been influenced by women's opportunities and desire for employment. They complete their families in a shorter time. They have fewer children; restricting the size of the family through contraceptive methods and abortion is more usual and acceptable now than formerly. With improved obstetrical care and a greater chance of successfully completing pregnancies, the children the mother does have can be spaced over a small interval. The resulting reduction in the period of time in which a family can be completed, combined with the rise in average life expectancy, means that, after all their children are in school, women have increased time in their lives for employment.

As family *ideology* has become more *equalitarian,* there is less support for the idea that the husband, as the dominant family member, must earn all the income and the mother perform all the daily child-rearing responsibilities. Changes in social values and attitudes about women's rights, and new divisions of responsibilities within the family, have led to, and been influenced by, a greater acceptance of working mothers.

Even though working mothers do not arouse the alarmed opposition that they did in the late nineteenth century, concern still is expressed about the employment of mothers, particularly those with young children. What, then, can be learned from research findings about the effects of maternal employment on family life and the behavior of children?

Maternal Employment and Family Life: Early Research

In the 1960s societal concern about working mothers intensified as it became apparent that many women who had been recruited into employment during World War II had remained in the workforce after its end. Researchers began to pursue insights into the phenomenon of "women in the labor force" and its effects on family life. Interest in such investigation was prompted by societal fear about the future of the traditional family structure if women's entry into the labor force continued to accelerate. Implicit in much of the research were questions that focused on mothers' characteristics and personalities: Why did some mothers choose to work outside the home while others did not? How were mothers who chose to work different from other mothers?

Much of the research did not give sufficient attention to adequate sampling techniques, precise criteria for designating a mother as employed or not employed, or control of related variables. Taking these limitations into account, Siegel and Haas evaluated reviews of studies on working mothers in the United States and summarized their findings about certain aspects of family life. "The contrasts between working mothers and those who stay at home are scarcely astonishing. Working mothers' husbands are more favorable toward maternal employment than other husbands; mothers' principal reasons for work are financial need and motivations for achievement through work. . . . With the exception of the difference in family size, the differences which have been found between working mothers and others are not extreme or dramatic" (Siegel & Haas, 1963, pp. 126–166).

In a somewhat later study Ruderman studied working mothers and nonworking mothers and affirmed that in America at least, working mothers and nonworking mothers as generally defined were not two distinct groups. The lines separating working mothers from the nonworking ones were fluid, with some mothers working at the time but planning to stop soon, and others not working but looking for work or planning to work in the years ahead. For purposes of definition and classification, it was not possible to draw a hard-and-fast line between the two groups of mothers. There was no conclusive evidence that problems occurred more frequently among working mother families than among other families of the same class level, leading Ruderman to conclude that maternal employ-

ment should not be equated with any form of pathology (Ruderman, 1968, pp. 461–462).

Research findings about the effect of maternal employment on children were also inconclusive. In a review of the evidence, Stolz concluded: "Children of employed mothers are not all alike. Some of them are delinquent, some are not, some show symptoms of maladjustment, some are quite well-adjusted; some do well in school, some have a difficult time; some are self-reliant, some overly-dependent. . . . The fact of the mother being employed or staying at home is not such an important factor in determining the behavior of the child as we have been led to think" (Stolz, 1960, p. 779).

As it became ever clearer that working mothers were here to stay and that family life had survived and even been strengthened by the mother's labor status and earnings, interest waned in differentiating working mothers from nonworking mothers. Researchers turned to empirical studies of the effects on children of various forms of child care.

Effects on Infants of Out-of-Home Child Care

Economic and social changes in the past several decades have influenced "a phenomenon that can only be termed a new social form"—the placement of infants as young as three weeks into out-of-home care. In percentage increase, child care for infants is currently the fastest growing type of out-of-home care. Most of it takes place in family day care homes, largely unregulated and unobserved (Gamble & Zigler, 1986, p. 26).

In testimony before a United States Senate hearing on child care, Edward Zigler characterized the question of the developmental effects on children who experience out-of-home care during infancy as "the hottest debate going on among child development experts in the United States" ("Hearings before the Sub-committee on Children," 1987, June 11, p. 79). Some researchers have emphasized its "potentially damaging effects" and others have maintained that such care is "essentially benign" (Gamble & Zigler, 1986, p. 1).

A fundamental question about the effects of infant day care has been whether such early care by persons other than the infant's parents can interfere with the development of an affective bond between infant and parents, or redirect the primary attachment from the parents to substitute caretakers. Research has shown that children who experience early out-of-home child care "form their primary bonds with their parents, just as home-reared children do." Further, there is no evidence that child care weakens attachment bonds that have been previously established, a finding that holds across cultures (Farber & Egeland, 1982, p. 105).

In their review of research on the effects of infant child care, Gamble and Zigler identified a common conclusion: There were "no strikingly negative psychological consequences accruing to infants who experience regular nonparental care." However, they cautioned that most of the studies had been of stable middle-class families using high-quality facilities, thus precluding generalizations to the situations most infants in out-of-home care actually experience (Gamble & Zigler, 1986, p. 27; Silverstein, 1981).

Sampling limitations in most of the studies of infant child care raise another problem: Under what conditions might out-of-home child care affect the *quality* of infant–mother attachment? To address this question Farber and Egeland investigated out-of-home care for infants in a low-income population (1982, pp. 102–125). A sample of working mothers who had returned to work or school prior to their infants' first birthday was drawn from a maternal and child care clinic serving families of lower socioeconomic backgrounds. Most of the mothers were single and dependent on public assistance at the time of their infants' birth. These mothers differed markedly from those who had been studied in most infant child care investigations. The type of child care provided was different as well, taking place in varied community-based arrangements of poor quality, including frequent changes in caretakers. From the same low-income clinic population, a control group of mothers was drawn, ones who had not used out-of-home care during their infants' first twenty-four months. Using a wide variety of maternal and infant measures—demographic and observational data, infant tests, measures of the mother's personality, knowledge and attitude—no pre–day care differences emerged between the mothers who had returned to work and those who had not.

Mother–infant attachment was assessed at twelve, eighteen, and twenty-four months for both groups. At twenty-four months the infants' problem-solving behavior in frustrating situations was measured. Infants who were in out-of-home care before their first birthday were found to be more likely to show anxious-avoidant attachments with their mothers. These same infants also displayed less enthusiasm and less adequate skills to cope with frustrating problem-solving situations. Given the absence of significant differences between the working and nonworking mothers, it was concluded that the out-of-home care had caused the anxious attachments; they were not attributable to characteristics of the mothers.

Knowing that poor-quality infant care is most often all that is available to economically disadvantaged mothers, policy makers are faced with the problem of how to provide out-of-home care arrangements that will foster infant development and are yet affordable and feasible. Until this question is addressed, poor children will continue to be at greatest risk of adverse developmental outcomes.

The extensive variations among the states in licensing requirements with respect to critical aspects of out-of-home child care and the scarcity and high cost of quality care adds force to the warning that "the phenomenon of infant day care is simply too new, and the stakes too high, for either layman or scientist to risk premature conclusions about its effect" (Gamble & Zigler, 1986, p. 27).

Child Care and Effects on Preschoolers

In the late 1970s and through the 1980s, child care programs for preschool children three to five years old expanded significantly. Two factors influenced this development—the accelerated numbers of working women with young children, and new awareness by researchers and parents of benefits for children who experience high quality preschool child care. The most commonly cited benefits are interpersonal socialization and cognitive gains, both of which increase readiness for regular school.

In light of a relatively long experience of researchers and parents with preschool child care, a commonly shared conclusion is that "the effects of out-of-home care for children above the age of three years are not particularly worrisome" (Gamble & Zigler, 1986, p. 1). However, Michael Rutter has concluded that although some of the more alarming stereotypes about child care for preschoolers can be rejected, there is still a distance to go to learn what type of care is most suitable for each type of child.

> There are indications that day care influences to some extent the form of children's social behavior (in ways that may be either helpful or deleterious). Further, there are indications that the ways in which it does so may be determined by the specific characteristics of the day care and by its quality; . . . by the age and other characteristics of the child, and by the characteristics of the family (including the meaning of maternal employment and the meaning of day care for the parents). It would be wrong to conclude that day care, any more than home care, is without effects, and it would be misleading to assume that it carries no risks (even though these have been greatly exaggerated in the past). What is now needed is research that moves beyond the crude day care versus home care comparison in order to determine the specific effects of the various aspects of care in specific circumstances. (Rutter, 1982, pp. 22–23)

Various studies have identified contemporaneous effects on preschoolers that flow from differences in quality among child care programs. Poor physical facilities, fewer language experiences, inadequate staff-child ratios, less teacher training, higher staff turnover, large class size—all are factors that have been shown to affect children negatively in language development, social development, ability to persist in assigned tasks, and performance on kindergarten and first-grade reading tests (Vandell et al., 1988a).

To address the possibility that negative effects of poor-quality child care may be short-lived with no long-term negative consequences for children, Vandell and coworkers carried out a longitudinal assessment of children with child care experiences of varying quality. Children were first studied at four years of age. One group attended "well-equipped, spacious centers with good adult–child ratios, well-trained teachers and small classes." The other group attended "large centers that were crowded, poorly equipped, and had poor adult–child ratios, untrained teachers and large classes." Children in the better quality preschool programs showed more positive interactions with their teachers, while children in poorer quality programs spent more time in unoccupied behaviors and in solitary play.

The two groups of children were restudied when they were eight years old. The children who had had more positive interactions with teachers when they were four years old were found at eight to be "more socially competent, peer accepted, empathic, capable of negotiating conflicts, and less impulsive." The eight year olds who had experienced poorer quality care at age four years were found to have ratings negatively correlated with "social competence, peer acceptance, conflict negotiations and handling frustrations" (Vandell et al., 1988b, pp. 1287, 1290).

The study clearly suggested that day care quality can play an important role in subsequent development. The researchers pointed out, however, that the sample had been small ($N = 20$) and that it was not known what family factors

> *The nation's provisions for the care and education of children under five cannot long survive in their present neglected and chaotic state. (Schorr, 1988, p. 179)*

or other unmeasured differences in the children's lives between age four and eight may have mediated the relations between their children's early day care and later outcomes.

Head Start has been a major source of child care for many preschool children. Outcomes of this program will be reported later in this chapter.

Effects on Children in Self-Care

The phenomenon of children going home after school to an empty house is now widespread. Estimates of the number of elementary school "latchkey" children who let themselves into their homes to await the return of a parent from work range from two million to ten million. Most researchers believe the lower figures are artificially low, stemming perhaps from guilt felt by parents who leave children alone, as well as concern about their children's safety if they let it be known they are unsupervised at certain times. The School-Age Child-Care program at Wellesley College has said that about 15 percent of children aged six to nine years come home after school with no parent or other adult present, with the rate increasing to 45 percent among children nine to eleven (U.S. Department of Commerce, 1987a; Gray & Coolsen, 1987; Goleman, 1988).

The subject of children in self-care generates controversy and tends to polarize people, perhaps because it reflects the difficult choice that so many parents have to make—working to support the family versus providing conventional supervision of their children after school (Gray & Coolsen, 1987).

Early research on the effects of child self-care showed mixed results, leaving uncertainty as to whether latchkey children are subject to positive or negative consequences (Long & Long, 1983). Findings of recent studies, within limits, are generally reassuring.

In a study of fourth and seventh graders in self-care compared with counterpart children in adult care, Rodman and coworkers found no differences in measures of self-esteem, sense of control over their own lives, and social skills between those in self-care and those supervised by parents (Rodman et al., 1985).

In a study of white, predominantly middle-class third graders from a suburban school system, Vandell and coworkers compared three groups of children of diverse social class: (1) those who returned home to be alone or with siblings, (2) those who returned home to their mothers, and (3) those who attended after-school day care centers. No differences were found between mother-care and latchkey children in "classroom sociometric nominations, academic grades, standardized test scores, conduct grades, self-reports of self-competence, or parent and teacher ratings of the children." The outcomes held in both divorced and intact families (Vandell & Corasaniti, 1988, p. 868).

In contrast, when the same measures were applied to the group of children who stayed at child care centers after school, problems were found. However, the quality of many of the center programs was questionable, and were designed for preschoolers, not school-age children. Furthermore, informal talks with teachers and parents suggested a stigma associated with these particular after-school programs. "The 'day-care kids' were picked up after school by vans bearing the day-care centers' logos, and all the teachers and classmates knew who the day-care children were. Returning home alone or to a sitter was a much less visible form of alternative care." Different results might have emerged if the children had gone to high quality after-school centers, or programs at their own public schools that served many of their schoolmates (Vandell & Corasaniti, 1988, p. 875).

In a study of a heterogeneous sample of young adolescents in grades five to nine,

Steinberg also found no significant differences in social, emotional, and academic well-being of latchkey children versus those who were supervised by parents at home. However, he questioned whether "a convincing theoretical argument" could be made for linking elements of personality such as self-esteem, locus of control, and social competence with patterns of after-school care. He noted that these were not the real concerns of the public and parents about children's self-care; rather they were more worried about fears of children alone, the dangers they might encounter, and especially for children nearing adolescence, the "undesirable behaviors that they might not engage in if adults were nearby" (Steinberg, 1986, p. 433).

Steinberg was interested in latchkey young adolescents and the role played by "susceptibility to peer pressure." To explore this factor he used measures that would allow for differences among latchkey *situations,* with respect to (1) variations in the settings in which their self-care takes place and their actual after-school activities, and (2) how they are or are not supervised by their parents *in absentia*. He found that "adolescents who are more removed from adult supervision (either proximal or distal) are more susceptible to pressure from their friends to engage in antisocial activity. . . . Boys and girls who are at home alone are less susceptible than adolescents who are at a friend's house after school; and the latter are, in turn, less susceptible than adolescents who describe themselves as hanging out" (Steinberg, 1986, p. 438). A significant variable in diluting potential ill effects for children in self-care appears to be the extent to which a parent is readily available by telephone, and is monitoring the child's after-school activity. Whether someone is there when a child arrives home may be less important than the psychological connection with the parent that gives the child a sense of parental supervision until the parents arrive home and can further bolster a sense of involvement and genuine parental interest and concern.

The essential importance of a connection between latchkey children and their parents at work, and what some children really feel when they are home alone was suggested by experience with a self-care curriculum—five sessions—to help both parents and children develop necessary skills for safety and success in self-care settings. Although both groups gained in confidence in the self-care arrangements with respect to such matters as children being frightened by noise, or worrying about having to deal with someone on the telephone or at the door, lack of security felt by children was reflected in a sentence-completion exercise by the children. The aim had been to learn what specific information or instructions they wished their parents would give them. In responding to the incomplete sentence, "When I am home alone, I wish Mom and Dad . . . ," over 80 percent of the children responded that they wished their parents "would come home," or "would call me" (Gray & Coolsen, 1987, p. 32).

Given that many working parents will continue to use self-care for their school-age children, Steinberg's conclusions as to what the focus of continuing research should be are of interest: "Variations within the latchkey population, . . . in the settings in which self-care takes place, . . . in the extent to which absent parents maintain distal supervision of their children, and . . . variations in patterns of child rearing—are more important than are variations between adult care and self-care broadly defined" (Steinberg, 1986, p. 438).

To learn more about characteristics in the latchkey environment that affect personal and social developments researchers are also emphasizing the need to explore systematically children's response to self-care in different commu-

---

Researchers can neither assign children randomly to child care nor assign parents to varying employment patterns. As a consequence, efforts to decipher the "effects" of child care are a methodological conundrum. Pre-existing family differences—in background, traits, and beliefs—are confounded with child care arrangements. (Scarr et al., 1990, p. 31)

nity contexts—relatively crime-free rural areas, urban neighborhoods that are cohesive and supportive, and mobile and alienated inner city neighborhoods (Galambos & Garbarino, 1983).

WORKING PARENTS' CHILD CARE ARRANGEMENTS

Supplementary care for children of employed parents is most often an informal arrangement between private individuals with no organized community involvement or sanction. Licensed family day care homes, day care centers, nursery schools, and organized after-school programs under any auspices play a lesser role in providing care for children of working parents. How then are the nation's children of working parents distributed among the different child care arrangements?

Researchers and governmental committees have called attention to the lack of a national database of child care statistics. A major problem has been that data have not been collected regularly, systematically, and by the same office. Definitions used for "child care" and "child care facilities" have varied from one time to another, as have ages of children within groups for which data are recorded. Below are listed some principal findings of a Census Bureau study of child care arrangements in the winter of 1984–1985 (U.S. Department of Commerce, 1987b).

1. Of the 8.2 million preschool children of working mothers, 23 percent were attending day care centers or preschools most of the time their mothers were at work. The remainder were primarily in supervised care in their own home (31 percent) or in someone else's home (37 percent) or cared for by the mother herself while at work (8 percent).

2. The use by employed women of group care centers or preschools for their youngest child under five years increased from 16 percent in 1982 to 25 percent in 1984–1985.

3. Preschoolers of full-time working mothers were less likely to be cared for at home (24 percent) than were children of part-time working mothers (42 percent). Child care by fathers was less frequent if women worked full time.

4. The principal difference between preschool child care arrangements used by married women and unmarried women appeared to depend on the availability of the child's father to provide child care. The percentage of preschoolers cared for by their father while their mother worked was 19 percent among married women in contrast with 2 percent among unmarried women.

5. Almost one-half of all women who had a birth in the twelve-month period preceding the survey were in the labor force—either looking for work, on layoff, or currently employed.

6. Seventy-eight percent of infants were cared for in the child's home or in another home. Another 14 percent were cared for in organized child care facilities, a substantial increase over the 5 percent of 1982.

7. From infancy to school age, children of working women may experience considerable change in type of child care.

8. Among women who had only one child and who used only one type of child care, work disruptions resulting from failures in child care arrangements affected 5.5 percent of those 2.6 million working women.

9. Twenty-five percent of working women who had a child under five years old used some type of organized child care facility for their youngest child compared with 16 percent in 1982.

10. Enrollment of children in programs providing educational enrichment appeared to be growing among women, regardless of their labor force status. (For further data on employed mothers' child care arrangements, see Tables 7.2 and 7.3.)

Although the trend appears to be shifting, at present and in view of the child care arrangements that working parents make, it appears that they prefer care in their own home or informal market care (licensed or unlicensed family

TABLE 7.2. Primary Child Care Arrangements for Children under Fifteen, by Age (Winter 1984-1985; numbers in thousands)

Type of Child Care Arrangement	Total		Under Five Years		Five to Fourteen Years	
	Number	Percentage	Number	Percentage	Number	Percentage
Number of children	26,455	100.0	8,168	100.0	18,287	100.0
Care in child's home	4,699	17.8	2,535	31.0	2,164	11.8
By father	2,496	9.4	1,282	15.7	1,214	6.6
By grandparent	712	2.7	468	5.7	244	1.3
By other relative	804	3.0	306	3.7	498	2.7
By nonrelative	687	2.6	479	5.9	208	1.1
Care in another home	3,801	14.4	3,019	37.0	782	4.3
By grandparent	1,138	4.3	833	10.2	305	1.7
By other relative	467	1.8	367	4.5	100	0.5
By nonrelative	2,196	8.3	1,819	22.3	377	2.1
Organized child care facilities	2,411	9.1	1,888	23.1	523	2.8
Day/group care center	1,440	5.4	1,142	14.0	298	1.6
Nursery school/preschool	971	3.7	746	9.1	225	1.2
Kindergarten/grade school	13,815	52.2	62	0.8	13,753	75.2
Child cares for self	488	1.8	—	—	488	2.7
Parent cares for child[1]	1,245	4.7	664	8.1	581	3.2

[1]Includes mothers working at home or away from home. (*Source:* U.S. Department of Commerce, Bureau of the Census. [1987]. Current Population Reports, Series P-70, No. 9. *Who's Minding the Kids? Child Care Arrangements, Winter 1984-1985.* Washington, DC: U.S. Government Printing Office, p. 3.)

TABLE 7.3. Primary Child Care Arrangements Used by Employed Mothers for Their Children under Five, by Age (Winter 1984–1985; numbers in thousands)

Type of Child Care Arrangement	Total		Age of Child					
			Under One Year		One and Two Years		Three and Four Years	
	Number	Percentage	Number	Percentage	Number	Percentage	Number	Percentage
Number of children	8,168	100.0	1,385	100.0	3,267	100.0	3,516	100.0
Care in child's home	2,534	31.0	516	37.3	1,068	32.7	950	27.0
By father	1,282	15.7	252	18.2	528	16.2	502	14.3
By grandparent	467	5.7	102	7.4	208	6.4	157	4.5
By other relative	306	3.7	44	3.2	147	4.5	115	3.3
By nonrelative	479	5.9	118	8.5	185	5.7	176	5.0
Care in another home	3,020	37.0	563	40.6	1,368	41.9	1,089	31.0
By grandparent	833	10.2	174	12.6	361	11.0	298	8.5
By other relative	368	4.5	70	5.1	130	4.0	167	4.7
By nonrelative	1,819	22.3	319	23.0	877	26.8	624	17.7
Organized child care facilities	1,888	23.1	195	14.1	563	17.2	1,131	32.2
Day/group care center	1,142	14.0	116	8.4	401	12.3	625	17.8
Nursery school/preschool	746	9.1	79	5.7	162	5.0	506	14.4
Kindergarten/grade school	61	0.7	—	—	—	—	61	1.7
Parent cares for child[1]	663	8.1	112	8.1	267	8.2	285	8.1

[1]Includes mothers working at home or away from home. (*Source:* U.S. Department of Commerce, Bureau of the Census. [1987]. Current Population Reports, Series P–70, No. 9. *Who's Minding the Kids? Child Care Arrangements, Winter 1984–1985.* Washington, DC: U.S. Government Printing Office, p. 5.)

day care homes). How these preferences are formed is less clear, except for the fact that in-home care and informal market care are appealing for economically rational reasons. Although studies indicate that employed mothers profess to be satisfied with the child care arrangements that they have made, the way in which the survey questions are often stated may invite self-serving answers.

Family Child Care

Made up of many different arrangements between parents and the caretakers of their children, family child care is the largest and most complex system of child care in this country.

For over 5 million children (almost half of all children in some form of child care), going to someone else's home to be cared for is an integral part of their daily lives.

Family day care falls into three major categories, differing in regulatory and administrative structure (see Figure 7.3). The largest category is unregulated family day care, constituting 94 percent of all family day care. These caregivers operate informally and independently of any regulatory agency, even though they may be subject to licensing or registration under the child care statute of the state in which they live. The second category consists of caregivers who are in compliance with state and/or federal regulatory requirements and who are subject to reg-

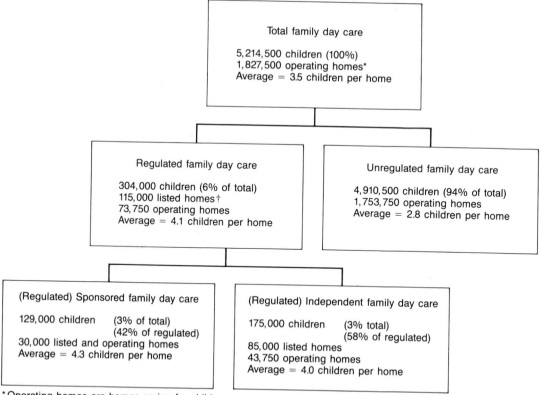

*Operating homes are homes caring for children.
†Listed homes are homes appearing on licensing lists but not necessarily caring for children.

Figure 7.3. Family Day Care, 10 Hours a Week or More. (*Source:* Children at the Center. [1979]. *Final Report of the National Day Care Home Study. Family Day Care in the United States: Executive Summary.* Cambridge, MA: Abt Associates, p. 5.)

ulatory supervision if complaints about the care they give come from parents or the community, but who otherwise also operate quite independently. The smallest group of caregivers (although one growing in importance) is made up of regulated homes functioning as part of a child care system or network under the auspices of an umbrella sponsoring organization.

Few systematically gathered data have been available about family day care until a 1977–1978 National Day Care Home Study was completed, sponsored by the Department of Health and Human Services (DHHS). This study represented a large-scale attempt over a four-year period to provide a comprehensive and detailed account of this very important but little studied day care form. The study was conducted in three urban sites—Los Angeles, Philadelphia, and San Antonio—which were selected for geographic, socioeconomic, ethnic, and regulatory diversity. The research examined the nature of day care in different types of settings and for children of different ages, the daily experiences of children and caregivers, parental preferences and satisfactions, costs, structure of the day care market, and cultural patterns. Selected findings are discussed below (Divine-Hawkins, 1981).

Characteristics of Family Day Care Providers

Most family day care providers who participated in the study were women who were motivated to give care in their homes to other people's children for these reasons: they liked children and liked to be with them and to work or play with them; they wanted to earn some money; and they preferred to do so in some way within their own homes.

The caregivers fell into three groups: (1) young white mothers in their late twenties or in their thirties with young children of their own to care for at home; (2) women in their forties or fifties of different races or ethnic groups who, in addition to the nonrelative children they accepted for day care, had at least one relative's child, often a grandchild; (3) women in their thirties to fifties who had no relative's child to care for, but accepted children for care from friends, neighbors, or others in the community.

The first two groups tended to operate without a license or other form of regulation; the third group made up a large proportion of family day care providers who are either licensed or registered or operating under the aegis of a sponsoring organization (in a family day care system).

Parents often find that family day care costs claim a significant portion of their income, particularly when they have more than one child in child care. For the caretakers, however, the earnings are small. For many their earnings are below the poverty level despite their working long hours, usually without paid sick leave or vacation days. New caregivers frequently give up their enterprise in its first year.

In choosing care for their children, parents usually preferred the more experienced caregiver, other things being equal. Yet upon examination, caregiver experience usually consisted only of having had children of one's own and not being new to the role of family day care provider. Relatively few caregivers had worked in a child care center or in preschool or elementary school programs. It was clear, however, that parents preferred caregivers who were "experienced," that is, who were themselves parents.

Concern has been expressed from time to time that day care providers are socially isolated, unconnected to the child care community, and lacking in adult contacts. Thus it is interesting to note that the caregivers themselves in the national study did not reflect this feeling of isolation and indicated that they had enough contacts with other adults. Interactions with parents of the children in care, during which mutual concerns about the child's welfare were shared, provided one meaningful source of adult contact.

Group Composition in Family Day Care

On the average, family day care providers had 3.5 children to care for, not counting the caregiver's own children who were home all day. Overall, 90 percent of providers cared for 6 or fewer children; 50 percent cared for 3 or fewer.

The family day care providers did not usually take children of widely varying ages, although sometimes a school-age sibling of a younger child would be taken care of before and after school hours. Eighty percent of the children were of the same race or ethnicity as the caregiver. Seventy percent of the children were in full-time care, that is, for thirty or more hours per week.

Parents of the Children in Care

Parents with a child under one year of age preferred making some arrangements for their children to be cared for within their own homes. Family day care was often preferred for one- to three-year-olds, and the more structured environment of a preschool for older preschoolers.

Overall, parents expressed considerable satisfaction with family child care. One-half of them indicated that they had the type of care they wanted. Over 60 percent were pleased that they were able to satisfy their wish for their children to have the company of other children. The homelike atmosphere was satisfying to many parents. And in addition, three-fourths of them reported that their children held loving or friendly feelings toward their caregivers.

Parents had concerns, however. Twenty percent of them said they would prefer a greater emphasis on cognitive development. In addition, it appeared that family day care homes were not as flexible as had been assumed in making special services available—evening and weekend care or care for a sick child. Food was the problem mentioned most often, with many parents stating that the caregivers served many inappropriate foods, specifically "junk foods." About 10 percent of the parents admitted to a "bad experience" with a family day care home—injury to the child, inadequate supervision, the child left unattended, and physical abuse.

Other Views of Family Day Care

As a form of day care in the United States, private family care "has consistently been either ignored or maligned" by many professionals (Sale, 1973, p. 37). One reason for this attitude may be the fact that most of it is unlicensed and informal, implying standards of care below those in regulated child care. Some other professionals view family child care as a useful and necessary alternative to center care for many children. From his studies of family child care, Emlen has maintained that family day care generally compares favorably with the quality of life in the United States and is of higher quality than many professionals have been willing to admit (Emlen, 1973). Wattenberg offered a useful distinction between (1) the "traditional" day care provider who relies on intuition and already formed preferences in her decisions about how to care for children generally, and (2) "the modernized" provider who pursues training and a clearer role as a professional (Wattenberg, 1977, 1980).

DAY CARE SYSTEMS

The organization of family day care homes into "day care systems" is a relatively recent development that has significant implications for child care planning and programming. The National Day Care Home Study carried out between 1974 and 1978 (Divine-Hawkins, 1981) found 30,000 "sponsored" family day care homes in this country, which at the time of the study was only 2 percent of all family day care homes, but representative of a growing trend more important than their numbers suggest. Most family day care funded under Title XX of the Social Security Act (the major source of day care subsidy) is provided through day care sys-

tems. Few spaces in nonsponsored homes are publicly funded. Furthermore, the Child Care Food Program of the U.S. Department of Agriculture (USDA) requires an umbrella sponsor in order for day care homes to benefit from its subsidies for food served to the children. Thus Title XX and the USDA Child Care Food Program are a source of great pressure for the development of family day care systems.

Sponsors of day care systems may be private social service agencies, religious organizations, or agencies of state and local governments. The growth of systems has been encouraged by both federal and state governments to facilitate day care funding and reduce the management tasks of state and local governments. Beyond acting as a conduit for Title XX funds and the USDA Child Care Food Program, the sponsoring system performs other functions, including (1) determining families' eligibility in relation to income levels for free or reduced-fee care, (2) setting the fees to be paid by parents, (3) billing the government for reimbursement, (4) selecting caregivers, (5) supplying training to them, (6) maintaining desirable enrollment levels, (7) monitoring for regulatory compliance, (8) offering a vehicle for parent involvement, and (9) providing supplementary social services and technical assistance, which previously have been largely confined to day care centers.

Sponsored caregivers in a day care system usually had some kind of training in child care (almost three-fourths of them). Those who had received training appeared to offer more structured teaching, language and information activities, music, dramatic play, and comforting. These characteristics were less common among all other family day care providers.

The National Day Care Home Study recommended that strong efforts be made to promote the further development of day care systems in view of the advantages for each of the participants, which were summed up thus:

The [government agency that subsidizes or regulates the care] benefits because the system becomes administratively responsible for regulating the care given, monitoring the quality of care, providing supplementary services and handling the complex issues of reimbursement. The caregiver benefits because the system refers children, provides her with assistance in handling administrative responsibilities, pays her on a regular basis, and provides her with the training and technical assistance needed to improve her caregiving skills. The parent benefits by having the agency help in finding an appropriate home for the child, provide substitute caregivers in case of illness, and arrange for a variety of supplemental services to the family. The child benefits from appropriate placement, from improved nutrition in programs subsidized under the Child Care Food Program, and from the skilled care of a trained caregiver. Finally, an increased emphasis on the development of family day care systems will help reduce the isolation of family day care from the rest of the day care community, thereby increasing its overall visibility and accessibility, particularly for families needing subsidized care. (Divine-Hawkins, 1981)

DAY CARE CENTERS

Care of children in groups was one of the early philanthropic efforts to oversee young children of working women, mainly the children of poor women. Different forms of care emerged— group nurseries, as a response to the need of impoverished women for care of their newborn infants; nursery "schools" that offered some training and supervision; preschools that manifested concern for children's learning; and kindergartens, perceived as an important step for children entering the formal system of public or private school education.

At different points in history, day care centers of different kinds became more numerous and grew in importance for different groups of parents. Many came to prefer this form of out-of-home care for their young children.

A National Day Care Study (NDCS) initiated by the Department of Health, Education, and Welfare and carried out between 1974 and 1978 found that there were 18,307 day care "centers" in the United States (*Children at the center,* 1979). By 1986, a survey of the individual state licensing authorities found a total of 62,988 child care centers, a figure that suggested the licensed centers and their capacity had more than doubled in the last decade (Hofferth & Phillips, 1987).

After-school programs have been developed in many school systems. However, despite the interest shown by public education representatives about school-age child care, Hofferth and Phillips found "no national data on the extent to which day care programs are being provided by public schools." Private schools, in contrast, had moved ahead in providing extended day programs. From a 1983 survey of private schools in seven cities, one-third were operating programs and another third was planning to do so (Hofferth & Phillips, 1987, p. 566).

In the National Day Care Study, the majority of child care centers (59 percent) were nonprofit enterprises. What was astonishing to many observers who were interested in child development was that more than 40 percent (and the numbers were still growing) were profit-making centers. Middle-class parents appeared to be the largest group of consumers of for-profit child care. Profit-making child care tends to be regarded with suspicion, which is, perhaps, a healthy attitude given the demands in providing essential aspects of good child care and the obstacles to translating child care into economic benefits.

Proprietary Centers

Profit-making centers differ among themselves in significant ways (Kagan & Glennon, 1982). Some of these for-profit centers (approximately 86 percent) are independently owned and operated, most often by a husband–wife team. Not only are these small enterprises more numerous; they also are the most varied. Some of them pro-

vide a rich and diversified experience for children; some others provide at best only custodial care.

The other 14 percent of proprietary centers are either chains or franchised operations. Kinder-Care offers an example of a chain of centers. This corporation serves more than 700 centers in thirty-six states and Canada with a clientele of children from infants to twelve-year-olds, although mostly the children are three to five years old. Kinder-Care advertises care from 7:00 A.M. to 6:00 P.M., including before- and after-school care. In the printed matter distributed to applicants, parents are assured of a staff-child ratio of one to ten as well as "colorful toys instead of junk food and TV."

Standardization of care has advantages to the chain provider such as bulk buying of goods used by centers, and money saved and plowed back into the corporation for new profit-making centers. National chains can also store capital to buy new centers and to advertise, a source of controversy among day care advocates who hold that any profits or savings should be turned into the development of better programs and opportunities for children. Major chains also can add on other money-making products—T-shirts, tote bags, and even child life insurance.

The "Quality" Component

In all center-provided day care, a major consumer issue is how quality of care can be assured and enhanced and programs be shaped in ways that will guarantee a better than even chance for the new generation of children requiring care outside their own homes.

The NDCS investigated quality and cost in center-based day care for preschool children. The study was undertaken to ascertain what features of centers were important to quality care, what costs were necessary to maintain different levels of care, and whether regulation of day care centers affected the quality of care received by children. Those kinds of evidence were needed by federal policy makers concerned about setting appropriate requirements for day care subsidy by federal funds. Studies of three sets of center characteristics—classroom composition, caregiver–child ratio, and caregiver qualifications—produced findings of significant interest with respect to three-, four-, and five-year-old children (*Children at the center,* 1979).

Classroom Composition.   Group size showed a consistently strong relationship to measures of quality. In all study sites, smaller groups were associated with better care, more socially active children, and higher gains on developmental tests. At the same time, variations in group size affected center costs only slightly.

Caregiver–Child Ratio.   There was a relationship between staff–child ratios and the interaction between caregivers and children, although no strong or consistent gain was measured for centers with a one to five, as compared to a one to ten, staff–child ratio. At the same time, the staff–child ratio is the strongest determinant of center costs. Fewer children per staff member increase costs rapidly.

Caregiver Qualifications.   Those persons with education or training related to young children provided better care, with somewhat higher developmental effects for children. At the same time, using caregivers with child-related training bore little relationship to center cost. They did not receive higher wages than caregivers without such training or education.

What are the implications of these findings? In smaller groups of children, staff engage in more social interaction with children, rather than passive watching. Especially when smaller groups are supervised by lead teachers with child-related training, an atmosphere of activity and harmony is more likely. Children have more opportunity to engage in learning and to develop ways of getting along with others. In smaller groups, as contrasted with larger groups, children show more cooperation, more verbal initiative, and more reflective and innovative behavior. Less hostility and conflict emerge, and there is reduced likelihood of children's being uninvolved, wandering aimlessly in the group. With fewer children per caregiver, the staff spend less time managing children, that is, commanding or correcting them. Larger groups, especially those supervised by staff without child-related education or training, invite caregivers to fall into a passive mode, monitoring the behavior of many children at once without interaction with individual children.

In summary, factors that were found to be associated with quality care of children relate to characteristics of day care centers that can be regulated. The ceiling on the number of children permitted in each group should be reduced, and these classroom composition requirements should be enforced as requirements, rather than seen as goals. At the same time the requirements governing the staff–child ratio can be relaxed somewhat. A staff qualification requirement should call for child-related training or education. The NDCS recommended that the staff-child ratio requirement for three-, four-, and five-year-old children should be no more stringent than one to seven and the group size requirement no more lenient than eighteen per group. For easier compliance, a preferred policy would be group size less than or equal to fourteen children and a staff–child ratio of one to seven (*Children at the center,* 1979).

HISTORICAL DEVELOPMENT OF DAY CARE

A review of the development of *day nurseries* and *nursery schools* casts light on some of the problems in evolving a comprehensive approach to programs for children's daytime care and development. Formally organized daytime programs have existed in two parts—child care as a philanthropic undertaking, chiefly under social work auspices, and nursery schools as a form of preschool education. Despite their common elements, these two institutional approaches generally developed quite separately and have served different groups and classes of children.

Child Welfare Day Care

The Early Day Nurseries.   For information on the history of early day nurseries, see Forest (1927), Beer (1938), Lundberg (1947), and Fleiss (1962). The first program for the daytime care of young children in this country began in Philadelphia in 1798. This first "charitable nursery" was sponsored by a group of Quaker women and, as was noted earlier in this chapter, its initial goal was to increase productivity of working mothers in the "spinning room" (Michel, 1986). Another goal soon emerged—to attend to the education and welfare of the children. Until Michel's work, the earliest cited charitable nursery was the Nursery for Children of Poor Women, established in 1854 in New York City. This and other early day nurseries were modeled on the French crèche, a form of care for children of working mothers founded in Paris in 1844. The crèche was a response to the rapidly expanding employment of women in factories. In addition, in France, it was used as a weapon against the problem of infant mortality. Mothers of infants nursed their babies in the factory crèches and were taught methods of hygienic child care. French crèches were considered important enough to receive official recognition by an imperial decree in 1862. Regulations were issued to specify the conditions under which they could open and the standards that had to be met to receive a government subsidy.

The early day nurseries in America lacked this kind of official attention. They were usually sponsored by a church, a settlement house, or sometimes a voluntary social agency. Their purposes were to prevent child neglect during a mother's working hours and to eliminate the need to place children of destitute parents in institutions. They served an underprivileged group, handicapped by family problems. The emphasis was on physical care.

Even well into the twentieth century, many of the nurseries were poorly financed and substandard. Children were only fed, often inadequately, and guarded from the most obvious dangers. Provision for cleanliness and medical care was a common lack. The public generally was unconcerned about the nurseries.

Some more progressive nurseries under enlightened leadership developed better programs of health care and incorporated a program of nursery school training during part of the day. A National Federation of Day Nurseries, founded in 1898, and other day nursery associations attempted to demonstrate the value of day care and to encourage maintenance of better standards in relation to health, programs, and personnel.

For the most part, however, the importance of the day nursery was not recognized in America. Gesell wrote in 1923:

> There is as yet in America no solid body of opinion regarding the functions and the future of the day nursery. Social workers, parents, educators, and physicians have numerous and divergent views on the subject; standards are very uneven in different communities and often in the same community, and too often standards do not appear to exist at all. The nursery never comes under educational supervision, and only sometimes under compulsory medical supervision. Only in a few States are nurseries controlled through licenses and inspection. In short, the day nursery is far from being a commonly accepted official agency of child hygiene in this country. (1923b, pp. 41–42)

Day Care Service.   By the 1930s the social work profession seemed somewhat more agreed that day care, although still very insufficiently provided, was an essential part of a child welfare program. Emphasis was placed on social casework as a means of strengthening family life for the child in day care. Some persons cautioned that the conception of child welfare day care was limited by the fact that it was defined as a philanthropic activity and as such served only the economically unfortunate. To become a valuable agency for the care and development of the preschool child, day care sponsors and staff would have to solve problems of integration with the health and education fields.

Efforts were made to differentiate day care, as a child welfare service, from nursery schools, as a form of preschool education. By 1960 it was held that "this purpose [care and protection], the reasons for which a child and family may need it, and the responsibility shared with parents, distinguish a day care service from education programs (Child Welfare League of America, 1960, p. 2). It was believed that the primary purpose of day care is "the care and protection" of children, and that the child who needs day care "has a family problem which makes it impossible for his parents to fulfill their parental responsibilities without supplementary help" (U.S. Department of Health, Education, and Welfare, 1963, p. 2). Day care was regarded as a sharing of child-rearing responsibilities with parents, a way of keeping families together or helping them to maintain an adequate level of child care. Consequently, day care agencies usually applied some test of economic or social need before making the service available to parents.

Preschool Education

The Nursery School Movement. For information on the history of the nursery school movement, see Townshend (1909), Forest (1927), McMillan (1919), and Whipple (1929). The American nursery school is a product of the twentieth century, although its roots can be traced to the early infant schools in England and continental Europe. In the eighteenth century, Jean Frederic Oberlin, a Lutheran minister, established an infant school in France. It was a philanthropic venture, designed to give religious and moral training to young children as a means of substituting for their poor home care. At about the same time a contemporary of Oberlin, Johann Heinrich Pestalozzi, was working in Switzerland to improve conditions of the poor through education. His belief that children learn best by using their own senses and discovering things for themselves was discernible in preschools of later years. In the nineteenth century Friedrich Froebel founded the kindergarten and developed a philosophy and procedures in relation to preschool education.

The English nursery schools, first established by Rachel and Margaret McMillan in 1909, brought together a variety of educational forces and provided a background for the nursery school in America. Like the infant schools, the early nursery schools in London were not for children belonging to prosperous or educated families, but were intended to make up for some of the inadequacies in the lives of children of the poor. Particular emphasis was placed on improving the health and physical care of children who, because of their environment, were suffering from health problems and diseases for which treatment was known. An attempt was also made to improve the standard of family care by insisting on cooperation between the nursery school and the home so that the mother, as well as the child, could be educated.

Another aim in the early English nursery schools was "to provide a suitable environment for the child's growing mind" (Forest, 1927, p. 269). Nursery education was intended to be a part of a child's total education. Methods were concentrated on such activities as enjoyable and rewarding use of voice and language, experiences with nature, teaching of color and form, work formation, dramatic play, handwork, and other self-directed "constructive" activities, and social training through participation in simple and practical life activities. Stress was placed on the benefits of group associations. Attention was given as well to the theory of Maria Montessori and the didactic materials she had developed.

Nursery schools in the United States differed in that they were usually not designed for philanthropic purposes. They were, instead, more directly an outgrowth of early twentieth century progress in such fields as biology, medicine, psychology, and psychiatry, which led to scientific interest in early childhood and a new awareness of the importance of the preschool years. The early American nursery schools were developed for such purposes as these: (1) to conduct research in educational curricula and methods, for example a nursery school at Columbia University Teachers College in 1921; (2) to conduct research in child development, for example, a nursery school organized at the University of Iowa's Child Welfare Research Station in 1921; (3) to serve as a laboratory for the education of students in child care, for example, the Merrill-Palmer School of Homemaking in Detroit in 1922 and, following this, similar laboratories for child study as part of a child development curriculum in many home economics departments of land grant colleges; (4) to serve as centers for the training of nursery school teachers; (5) to offer the opportunity for parents to provide wholesome play for their children, further understanding of them, and released time from personal child care, for example, the Chicago Cooperative Nursery School, initiated in 1915 by a small group of wives of faculty members of the University of Chicago; and (6) to provide a supplement to psychiatric clinics, for example, the Play School for Habit Training, established in Boston in 1922.

As a consequence of the nature of these early experiments in preschool education, the nursery school developed as a "normal" service to be used without stigma even though, like day care, it was conceived as an educational and social supplement to the home. Undoubtedly the fact that nursery schools in America were developed from the beginning as a resource for middle- and upper-class families has contributed to their acceptance and perceived desirability.

The Modern Nursery School. Some persons interested in the care and development of the young child saw very early that there were advantages to be obtained through cooperation between the day nursery and the nursery school, and suggested that the nursery school concept was highly compatible with an "ideal" day nursery. Others believed that, even though a day nursery might incorporate suitable educational activities and trained personnel, the educational value to children would still be greater in a nursery school, since even a progressive day nursery was intended, in the minds of many, to furnish a shelter for the children of unfortunate parents and thus would have difficulties in extending its services outward to other economic strata. A nursery school, they said, was designed to serve children regardless of the economic status of their homes; nursery schools, as a part of the public schools, could reach preschool populations that a philanthropic day nursery could never reach.

Preschool educators historically were willing to leave formulations of the nature of "day care" to social work. They were not professionally concerned with the components of "care and supervision" in all-day centers. They were influenced by the view that the day care center was for a dependent or troubled population, and was appropriate, therefore, as a social work service. Also, considerations of status played a part.

Hunt has suggested a further explanation for the failure of nursery school education to involve itself more directly in the educational needs of young children from very poor families. Because of a traditional belief that class differences in ability were the inevitable consequence of heredity, Americans generally were little inclined to provide nursery schools for children of the poor. As a result, nursery schools were adapted to the needs of middle-class children. Consequently, when projects were launched in the 1960s to improve the future academic success of children of the poor, there was no tested technology of compensatory early childhood education at hand that could be counted on to foster in children of the poor those abilities that underlie competence in the dominant society (Hunt, 1969, pp. 20–21).

Considerable disagreement among professional groups resulted as to what should be the major emphasis of contemporary nursery school programs. The most evident difference has been between those who emphasize personal-social adjustment through group games, free play, unstructured field trips, and similar activities, and others who emphasize cognitive development through structured lessons and activities that attempt to develop language, fine motor skills, conceptual thinking, and positive learning sets (Hodges & Spicker, 1967).

Assumption of Public Responsibility

The WPA Program. There was a major expansion in day care during the Depression of the 1930s, when the federal government made funds available to the states for the establishment of nursery schools for the children of low-income parents. This action was part of the Works Progress Administration (WPA) program, and its immediate purpose was to provide employment for unemployed teachers, nurses, nutritionists, clerical workers, cooks, and janitors. At the same time, the development of nursery school projects represented

> the first official recognition by the federal and state governments that the education and guidance of children from two to five years of age is a responsibility warranting the expenditure of public funds. (Meek, 1937, p. 346)

Federal funds were made available to state departments of education, and the nursery schools were administered by local boards and usually located in public school buildings. For the most part, however, nutritional and health services were stressed rather than educational activities. Children were given daily health inspections and any necessary medical care. In addition they were given well-balanced meals, play, and rest

in an environment conducive to normal development.

Attendance in a one-month period in 1937 was 40,000 young children, and in 1942 about 35,000.

> These nursery schools everywhere demonstrated their value as an efficient and beneficial mode of child care and caused widespread hopes that nursery schools could be incorporated generally into the public school system for the benefit of all children. (U.S. Federal Works Agency, 1943, p. 62)

The Lanham Act. As economic conditions improved, and fewer teachers were unemployed, it appeared that the public day care program would be ended. But as the United States became involved in World War II, defense industries mushroomed. Many children were exposed to instability in family and community life as their parents moved to overcrowded or new communities, where they were attracted by wartime employment. Reports began to be received by the Children's Bureau about various communities with a concentration of defense industries in which children were left alone, locked in parked cars, or expected to shift for themselves or adjust to other unsatisfactory child care arrangements while their mothers worked.

Pressure mounted for a continuation of public financing for day care, this time for children whose mothers were being drawn into the national defense effort. Under the Lanham Act of 1941, federal funds were made available to the states on a matching basis for the conversion of WPA facilities or the establishment of new day care centers and nursery schools to serve children of working mothers in war-impacted communities. The United States Office of Education was given responsibility for developing the nursery school program in cooperation with local schools, and the Children's Bureau was given similar responsibility for day care centers sponsored by agencies that were not part of a school system.

The attitude of the Children's Bureau . . . was that mothers of preschool children should not be encouraged to work; but if they did indeed work, the community had an obligation to provide services to help parents care for their children, with state and local governments assuming the responsibility for supervising and maintaining adequate standards. Thus, the approach of the Children's Bureau towards the Lanham Act day care program was at best ambivalent. Some within the Bureau looked with misgiving on what they feared would be interpreted as a public sanction of the employment of women. They were joined by some social work leaders who were concerned that the federal stimulus to day care would in the long run be destructive of the family and contrary to basic American values. However, as it became clear that the emergency situation had first priority, the Bureau undertook the stimulation of counseling services in support of day care and developed a comprehensive set of standards for the guidance of communities. (Mayer, 1965, p. 27)

At the peak of the program in 1944, from 105,000 to 129,000 children were enrolled in nursery schools and day care centers receiving federal funds, most of them sponsored by schools and school people (Pedgeon, 1953; Farmer, 1969). When the war ended, federal funds were withdrawn in 1946, with resulting difficulties for many families.

The Children's Bureau pointed out that twice there had been public assumption of responsibility for daytime programs for children—in the Depression years, to provide employment for adults; and in wartime, to get women into jobs. Perhaps now the problem could be dealt with in terms of the welfare of children. Communities and states were urged to set up representative planning bodies to deal with the question of day care on a long-range, not an emergency, basis (Bradbury et al., 1962, p. 62).

Nevertheless, most programs disappeared. Some people believed that maternal employ-

ment would cease to exist on any substantial scale with the end of the war. In some communities the expanding school population required all the available classroom space and other educational resources. And there was undermining disagreement or confusion as to whether daytime programs were a continuing responsibility of welfare or education. The largest program to be continued was in California, where the legislature authorized the establishment of a statewide program under the State Department of Education and local school districts, with a fee for services at a level intended to make it possible for low-income families to use the centers (Children's Bureau, 1964).

The loss in public day care facilities following the end of World War II was serious. For example, although Chicago had had twenty-three centers operating during the war, there were no programs of public day care early in 1965. The same was true of Detroit, although during World War II there had been eighty centers in that city supported by Lanham Act funds (Fleiss, 1962).

Heightened Interest and Support for Child Care in the 1960s.

Various social, economic, and political forces in the 1960s removed day care from the periphery of social services for children. For example, scientific interest in how a child's intelligence develops and in the social and psychological factors in the intellectual functioning of poor children led to research into preschool curriculum development and evaluation. As a result, enriched experimental nursery school programs were developed as university researchers investigated the area of early childhood education in search of reliable methods of compensatory training.

In addition, the 1960s generally were prosperous, and high levels of employment made industry's recruitment of women into the labor force more visible. Many of these new employees had difficulties on the job because they lacked reliable child care arrangements during their working hours.

Other forces were significant influences in the development of more day care resources and in shaping the form they were to take, for example, (1) citizen concern for the children of the poor and their right to an opportunity for early learning, (2) the belief that low-income parents should and can be direct participants in planning and carrying out programs for their children's daytime care and development, and (3) interest in providing parents receiving Aid to Families with Dependent Children (AFDC) with an opportunity to receive job training and a work role in society. Work programs for AFDC parents were supported by different people for varying reasons, for example, concern over the sense of hopelessness experienced by many assistance recipients, or alarm over the ever-increasing annual governmental expenditures for assistance payments. But, in any case, if welfare mothers were to take advantage of training and employment opportunities or any other major social, educational, and health services designed to improve their family life, child care programs would have to be considerably expanded.

The heightened support for and interest in child care led many states to reconsider and improve their mandatory licensing standards for day care facilities. Federal agencies—the Department of Health, Education, and Welfare, the Office of Economic Opportunity, and the Department of Labor—joined together to issue a common set of standards and regulations that day care programs under their jurisdiction must meet if they were to receive federal funds (U.S. Department of Health, Education, and Welfare et al., 1968).

Provisions in the Social Security Act.   By a series of amendments to Title V of the Social Security Act in 1962, day care was defined for the first time as a public child welfare service. The goal of day care, as stated in the new legislation, was

to provide adequately for the care and protection of children whose parents are, for part of the day, working or seeking work, or otherwise absent from the home or unable for other reasons to provide parental supervision. (Cohen & Ball, 1962, p. 16)

Funds had to be administered by a public child welfare agency. Congress appropriated only $8 million before a new funding pattern was legislated in 1965. Much of this appropriation was spent on the extension or improvement of licensing activities and not on the development of new day care services (Lewis, 1974, p. 429).

In the 1965 amendments to the Social Security Act, the special section on day care was taken out of Title V. However, day care was defined again as an appropriate child welfare service, one that states could choose to develop under the same state-local matching formula as was applied to other basic services under the Child Welfare Services program. Congressional appropriations for Child Welfare Services rose very slowly, however, and as a consequence day care services expanded slowly as well.

In an analysis of day care under the Social Security Act, Lewis concluded that even where expansion of day care within Child Welfare Services did occur, the approach "appeared to be heavily influenced by the older goals and attitudes of traditional child welfare work." Day care was used largely in cases of neglect or abuse to prevent placement of children outside their own homes.

In statements about day care standards emanating from the Child Welfare League of America and from the U.S. Children's Bureau, the working mother was lumped together with a variety of pathological conditions and defined as a problem. In those statements day care was never discussed as a service for normal children from normal homes. The social work profession . . . seemed committed more to enabling mothers to stay home with their children than to enabling them to work. (Lewis, 1974, pp. 429–430)

With the intent to restore family self-sufficiency and reduce the size of the public assistance caseloads, the 1967 amendments to the Social Security Act introduced a coercive tone and, for the first time, defined day care as an essential element of public assistance. A new program—Work Incentive Now (WIN)—required states to intensify efforts toward job training and employment of welfare recipients. Individuals receiving AFDC were to be furnished with incentives, opportunities, and services, such as day care and family planning, necessary to attain economic independence. In addition, states were permitted to provide day care services, not only for persons certified as eligible on an individual basis, but also for target groups, such as residents of a specified neighborhood, or other groups of children reasonably classified as having common problems or common service needs, including AFDC parents not enrolled in WIN and former or potential AFDC recipients. These criteria conceivably could bring about day care for most poor children in this country.

The WIN program faced serious difficulties. There was objection to the provision that a mother caring for dependent children could be required to seek a job outside her home or lose financial support. Frequently, when mothers had been successfully referred and entered into a training program, they then found no employment in the overpopulated jobs requiring their still-limited skills. Appropriate referrals of mothers to the WIN program sometimes had to be restricted because of the unavailability of suitable child care arrangements. There was objection to the quality of the child care provided, which often seemed to be primarily focused on supervision of children and their physical environment—essential elements, but far short of the instruction, stimulating experiences, and health services many AFDC children need to overcome their deprived early years.

A significant aspect of the 1967 amendments was the provision of new funds made available under Title IV-A and channeled through the large state public assistance depart-

ments. The funding formula was one favorable to the states, with the federal government's share at 75 percent. Another feature that was favorable to the states allowed a state to use privately donated funds as its matching share. One result was an increase in the purchase of day care service for low-income children in settings that served children other than public assistance recipients, with a resultant greater socioeconomic mix of children in some day care centers.

The 1967 amendments continued the option by which states could expand day care as part of their basic child welfare services. The funding formula was less favorable than earlier, however. As a consequence, the expansion of day care services under the 1967 amendments was largely for the children of the working poor. Most of the funding of day care that had originated under Child Welfare Services legislation was transferred to the more generous funding stream of Title IV-A. The entire program of Child Welfare Services day care "became virtually embedded in public assistance" (U.S. Department of Health, Education, and Welfare, 1978, p. II–7).

In 1975, amendments to the Social Security Act added a new Title XX, authorizing grants to the states for a range of social services including day care for children. Low-income families and the prevention of dependence remained the focus. Children other than those from AFDC families could receive day care according to an income-related fee schedule established by each state.

Child care under Title XX resulted in a much higher percentage of care in centers and family day care homes and a much lower percentage receiving care in their own homes. "The differences . . . may reflect more the choices made by the agencies which *purchase* the care." Most Title XX payments for child care go directly from the agency to the provider; the parent usually is not involved in the transaction. Social workers who determine that a child needs day care may refer the family directly to a center or family day care home under contract to the agency. Parental choice in the form of care may be minimal (U.S. Department of Health, Education, and Welfare, 1978, p. II–7).

CHILDREN WHO LIVE IN POVERTY

Basic Learning in Family Life

Children who are born to poor parents and live in poverty during their preschool years are vulnerable to certain kinds of disadvantages that keep them from making normal progress in their learning after entering school. Their academic problems are traceable in large part to their home situations, which did not provide the experiences necessary for adequate development of their intellectual potential and did not transmit the social and cultural patterns that are required in the kinds of learning found in school and in the larger society.

Whatever provisions are made by the nation, the states, or localities to increase access to a more orderly and higher-quality system of child care and preschool education, it is children of disadvantaged families who have both the most to lose and the most to gain. (Schorr, 1988, pp. 181–182)

Many of these children come from homes where poverty and slum conditions have denied them adequate nutrition, clothing, medical care—even sleep and rest. These obvious deficiencies in physical environment diminish children's energy and endurance, force them to be preoccupied with immediate goals related to physical discomforts and demands in their living situation, and generate attitudes of passivity and defeatism toward life. But the problem is not just the physical deprivation characteristic of poverty neighborhoods. Although meeting children's physical needs is an essential first step in preparing the way for effective attention to their learning problems, this alone cannot com-

pensate fully for the deprivation they have experienced.

There are additional critical factors in children's home environments affecting the level of their measured intelligence and success in school. Bloom et al. identified them as involving (1) provisions for general learning, (2) models and help in language development, and (3) parental stimulation and concern for achievement and learning on the part of the child.

Beginning very early, . . . [children come] to perceive many aspects in the world about . . . [them]. This perceptual development takes place through the sensory modalities such as vision, hearing, touch, and even taste and smell. . . . Perceptual development is stimulated by environments which are rich in the range of experiences available; which make use of games, toys, and many objects for manipulation; and in which there is frequent interaction between the child and adults at meals, playtimes, and throughout the day. . . . Linked to this perceptual development . . . [of children] is . . . [their] linguistic development. As . . . [children come] to perceive the world about . . . [them, they are] able to "fix" or hold particular objects and events in . . . [their minds] . . . as [they are] given words or other symbols to "attach" to them. . . . The adults in middle-class homes characteristically tend to use words so freely and easily that they teach them to . . . [their children] at almost every opportunity. They encourage . . . [them] to say the word aloud, correct . . . [them when they] say it incorrectly or . . . [apply] it to the wrong objects or event, and . . . reward [them] when . . . [they use] the word or symbol correctly. . . .

In . . . [disadvantaged] homes, the parent is more likely to respond to the child with a monosyllable or to nod the head without using any words. . . .

Put in other terms, . . . [children] in many middle-class . . . homes . . . [are] given a great deal of instruction about the world in which . . . [they] . . . live, to use language to fix aspects of this world in . . . [their memory,] and to think about similarities, differences, and relationships in this very complex environment. While all of this is not absent in the . . . [disadvantaged] home, it does not play such a central role in child rearing in such homes. The size of the family, the concern of the parents with the basic necessities of life, the low level of educational development of the parents, the frequent absence of a male parent, and the lack of a great deal of interaction between children and adults all conspire to reduce the stimulation, language development, and intellectual development of such children. (Bloom et al., 1965, pp. 13–15)

During the 1960s a high degree of concern was expressed about the number of children who were unprepared for the learning tasks of first grade because of the handicaps imposed by continued poverty. One proposed solution was to intervene in behalf of vulnerable young children by providing preschool programs for their daytime care that would foster their intellectual development and their future educability, or, as Hunt described them:

settings where children . . . [disadvantaged] by accident of the social class of their parents can be supplied with a set of encounters with circumstances which will provide an antidote for what they may have missed. (Hunt, 1964, p. 236)

Factors That Have Focused Attention on Learning Handicaps

A number of forces have contributed to concern about the learning handicaps of poor children. Highly significant are the rapid changes in the economic system and a greatly enlarged reliance upon technology. As more and more jobs are replaced by automated operations, there are fewer positions for persons with little education and no work skills. Personnel must have proficiency in the use of language and mathematics, and in methods of problem solving. If a trained labor force is to be supplied for the jobs of the nation, ways are needed not only to change and improve education but also to prevent the early onset of intellectual deficits which result from poverty-induced deprivation in the lives of infants and young children.

The civil rights movement of the 1960s gave impetus to the need to find ways to equalize opportunities for children to develop their intellectual capacities. An equal chance to attend school, as was intended by our early system of free public education and compulsory attendance laws, was not enough. New services for the daytime care and development of young socially disadvantaged children were needed, programs providing compensatory education to prevent or overcome difficulties in the intellectual development of each child.

Much of the impetus, then, for attention to the learning needs of poor children grew out of social forces and changes in society. However, psychological theory and changes in conceptions of human nature and development provided the basis for a reasonable expectation that preschool services could deal with the disadvantages of poor children in a way that would increase substantially the average level of their intellectual capacity. Hunt identified a number of changed beliefs about the development of an individual's intellectual functions and showed their significant implications for combating the effects of poverty on young children's intellectual development (Hunt, 1964, pp. 209–248).

1. The belief in fixed intelligence is no longer tenable. The conception of intelligence as an unchanging characteristic determined by genetic endowment has given way to the idea that, generally, young children's intellectual potentialities have wide boundaries, and that, while heredity plays a part in the development of intelligence, equally or more important are the kinds of experiences children encounter in the very early years of their lives.

2. Development can no longer be viewed as "predetermined." Like fixed intelligence, the belief in predetermined development has historical roots in Darwin's theory of evolution. It also had an empirical basis in evidence from studies of lower animals that led to the idea that behavior unfolds automatically as the anatomi-

cal basis for behavior matures. However, recent animal studies of rearing under conditions of sensory deprivation have yielded accumulating evidence that even the anatomical structures of the central nervous system are affected in their development by experience.

3. Formerly it was believed that the intellectual processes in the brain's functioning could be compared to those of the static switchboard of the telephone—the notion of reflexes forming stimulus-response chains. Newer thinking sees these processes as more comparable to the active information processes programmed into electronic computers to enable them to solve problems. On the basis of findings from neuropsychological studies of the brain, Hunt concluded:

> From such studies one can readily conceive the function of early experience to be one of "programming" these intrinsic portions of the cerebrum so that they can later function effectively in learning and problem-solving. (Hunt, 1964, p. 220)

4. Since experience is the "programmer" of the human brain, early experiences of young children, even before the development of speech, are highly important for the perceptual, cognitive, and intellectual functions. Changes in the conception of the relative importance of motor and sensory experiences in learning, and an accumulation of evidence that the basis for primary learning may be chiefly sensory, suggest that infants and young children need, for their intellectual development, a variety of experiences in which they can listen, look, feel, manipulate, and respond.

5. Learning is not motivated only by painful stimulation, homeostatic need, or the acquired drives based on these. There is, as well, a kind of intrinsic motivation inherent in information processing and action. Piaget's statement "The more objects a child sees, the more new ones he wishes to see" (Piaget, 1952, p. 277) suggests how this intrinsic motivation

develops. In accordance with this viewpoint, Hunt concluded that the greater the variety in visual and auditory stimuli young children encounter, the more of them they will come to recognize with interest; and the more they recognize with interest, the more of them will offer novel characteristics to stimulate further learning (Hunt, 1964).

All of these changed beliefs showed the feasibility of manipulating the environment of children who were being reared in circumstances of poverty and disadvantage, not only through broad social change and welfare provisions, but also through daytime programs that would utilize an understanding of the importance of early experiences as a means of programming for later effective learning and problem solving.

Project Head Start

A major assumption of public responsibility for children's daytime programs came about through Project Head Start (U.S. Office of Education and Office of Economic Opportunity, 1966; U.S. Office of Economic Opportunity, March 1968; August 1968). This program was an outgrowth of scientific knowledge about how a child's intelligence develops and the findings of the President's Panel on Mental Retardation, which had revealed the magnitude of the problems of inadequate early childhood experiences and had recommended preventive steps. Head Start was intended to give preschool children from economically disadvantaged backgrounds a comprehensive, multidisciplinary program of education, medical care, social services, and nutritional help. Emphasis was placed on working constructively with all aspects of a child's environment, including the family and the community, as well as the classroom.

In an analysis of public social policy for children, Steiner (1976) discussed some of the interacting forces that led to the Head Start program. As noted earlier, the scientific findings of psychologists about how a child's intelligence develops were an important contributor. But there were other factors as well, and without them, in Steiner's view, the scientists' conclusions might have lain dormant for an indefinite time. A critical factor was the development of a "war on poverty" in the administration of Lyndon Johnson. Thus, an environment for creating Head Start came about, one that required a comprehensive program with the potential for wide acceptance and quick results. A shared interest in early childhood development on the part of members of the Kennedy family and Dr. Robert E. Cooke, a professor of pediatrics, made preschool development an item on the political agenda. The conceptualization of Head Start provided the needed vehicle to launch a community action program for low-income groups and to implement some of the findings of psychologists as well.

Head Start has centered on such goals as improving children's physical health and abilities through medical assessment and remedial health programs (many of the eligible children have lacked health evaluations and services since infancy); helping with their emotional and social development by encouraging qualities such as self-confidence, expectation of success, spontaneity, curiosity, and self-discipline; improving their mental processes with particular attention to conceptual and verbal skills; and strengthening the child-parent relationship.

Program guidelines have stressed that even though children of the poor share the disadvantage of not having the kinds of experiences and opportunities available to more affluent families, they do not necessarily represent a homogeneous group. They show diverse patterns of strengths and weaknesses and require an individualization of their special needs. For example, see Figure 7.4 for racial diversity.

The initial summer program of Head Start in 1965 involved more than 560,000 children in 2,400 communities throughout the country. By 1969, 220,000 children were enrolled in year-round programs, and 417,000 not enrolled on a year-round basis had participated in training during the previous summer.

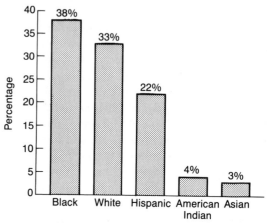

Figure 7.4. The Children in Head Start by Race. (*Source:* U.S. Department of Health and Human Services. [1989, January]. *The Program Head Start Statistical Fact Sheet. Fiscal Year 1988.*)

There has been considerable variation from one project to the next, reflecting communities' differences in leadership, values, material resources, and use of professional consultation. Generally, however, activities have been stressed that can be carried out in small groups—four or five children—oriented to the needs of the individual child. Each child is provided with at least one full meal a day. Teachers make extensive use of speech and conversation with the children. Sometimes children play with telephones to stimulate talk, or speak into tape recorders and then enjoy hearing their words played back. They are taught to name colors, foods, and animals. They play with puzzles and geometric blocks to help them learn sizes and shapes. They are taken on trips to museums, stores, construction projects, libraries, parks, farms, and factories to acquaint them with aspects of the world of work and play.

Parents are encouraged to participate in every phase of developing and administering the program. Many work as teachers' aides and in other nonprofessional capacities. Special courses for parents have been held in such subjects as food budgeting and purchase, child care, and ways to improve the home environment and help young children "learn to learn" at home. Parent involvement was seen as necessary for the parents' benefit as well as that of the children. It is apparent that many have deep feelings of concern and aspiration for their children that can be capitalized on in the program.

In view of the relatively small number of health, social service, and educational personnel trained to work with disadvantaged young children, personnel recruitment and training posed an immediate problem. The Office of Economic Opportunity arranged training courses, published informational materials, and encouraged the provision of assistance by universities, medical centers, and other qualified organizations to communities where the need was great.

With federal funds covering up to 80 percent of the cost, programs have been organized and administered by local communities. Sponsors have been community action agencies, institutes of higher education, schools, voluntary agencies, local governmental bodies, and other nonprofit, nonpolitical organizations.

The Head Start program was put together with remarkable speed. Although it succeeded in generating a wider interest in preschool education, it did not become an appropriate model for a universal program for early childhood development. A large-scale evaluation of Head Start was completed in 1969 (Westinghouse Learning Corporation, 1969). A sample of children from 104 Head Start centers across the country who had gone on into the local public schools was matched with a control group of children from the same elementary grades who had not attended Head Start. The basic question studied was this: "To what extent are the children now in the first, second, and third grades who attended Head Start Programs different in their intellectual and social-personal development from comparable children who did not attend?" Children from the Head Start group and the control group were administered a series of tests covering various aspects of cognitive and social-personal development. Parents were interviewed, and a broad range of attitudinal and

socioeconomic data were collected. In addition, primary-grade teachers rated the children on achievement motivation and gave a description of the intellectual and emotional environment of their elementary schools.

The results were disappointing, leading to these major conclusions: (1) Summer programs appeared to be ineffective in producing gains in cognitive and affective development that persist into the elementary grades. (2) Full-year programs appeared to be somewhat effective, but Head Start children, whether from summer or full-year programs, still appeared to be in a disadvantaged position with respect to national norms for the standardized tests of language development and scholastic achievement. (3) Parents of Head Start children were strongly in favor of the program (Westinghouse Learning Corporation, 1969).

In other words, Head Start children were not found to be appreciably different from their peers who had not attended Head Start. Proponents of Head Start pointed out that the results of the evaluation were hardly surprising. This project had been authorized and initiated on a large scale within a few months. It was a popular undertaking, and expectations were high. While a scientific basis for conceptualizing the project existed, in the field of early childhood education there was a lack of demonstrated and tested curriculum with specific learning objectives for deprived children. Under the pressure of mounting the programs quickly,

> all too often, the Head Start programs . . . merely supported poor children with an opportunity to play in traditional nursery schools that were designed chiefly to exercise large muscles and to enable middle class children to escape from their overly strict and solicitous mothers. Such opportunities are unlikely to be very effective in overcoming the deficient skills and motives to be found in the children of the poor. (Hunt, 1969, p. 20)

Some investigators questioned the design of the research and the interpretation of the data. Head Start was not and is not a single program. Rather, it is a diversity of programs. Evaluation of its effectiveness would depend on a careful analysis of its separate components, for example, curriculum, teachers, and goals. Others pointed out that the possibility still existed that Head Start had made an impact that was negated by poor teaching later on, or that because children in lower-class environments have been badly damaged in infancy, interventive programs must come much earlier than age four or even three years (Farber, 1969; Kihss, 1969; Herbers, 1969).

In any case, in the absence of allegations of negative consequences from the Head Start program, and in view of the high degree of public interest and approval that Head Start had captured, Congress did not find it advisable to make any significant changes in Head Start. But agreement is general that Head Start in its present form is not an effective antidote to disadvantaged preschool children's learning deficits. This is not to say that Head Start may not have other benefits, for example, increased parental involvement in a child's growth and development, improvement in the morale and attitudes of children while they are in the program, or a stimulating impact on the school and community. A report on evaluation studies of Head Start had this to say:

> The assumptions on which Head Start was based are still tenable; that from birth through six years of age are important years in human development; that children of the poor generally have not had the experiences and opportunities that support maximum development during this period; that effective programs for these children must be comprehensive including health, nutrition, social services and education; that for their own and their children's benefit, parents should be deeply involved in the design and implementation of local programs; and that a national child development program can focus attention on the needs of preschool and elementary school children from low-income families, and, through continued review of program effectiveness, stimulate local institutions to do a better job of meeting these needs. (Datta, 1969, p. 16)

Publicity attending the release of the Head Start evaluation influenced Richard Nixon to veto the 1971 Comprehensive Child Care Act, using as justification the opposition to day care as an intrusion of the state into the family. The veto dealt a heavy blow to the bipartisan coalition of child care advocates. The resultant loss of strength relegated their effort in behalf of Head Start to "a holding action"—keeping the program stable while waiting for a political climate more favorable to new child development legislation (Steiner, 1976, p. 90). In the meantime Head Start programs, emphasizing that they were local programs striving to remain flexible and responsive to local needs, suffered as a whole from problems of quality control (Zigler & Valentine, 1979).

In the years following, researchers continued their interest in the hypothesis that young children's intelligence and ability to succeed in school could be improved by high quality preschool programs. The Perry Preschool Project is of particular significance. The project, part of a group of studies begun early in the 1960s, was a longitudinal study of 123 black youths from low socioeconomic-status families, who were at risk of failure in school. The focus was on long-term effects of participation versus nonparticipation in a *high-quality* early educational program. At ages three and four, children were drawn from a single school attendance area and randomly divided into an experimental group (to participate in the preschool program) and a control group that received no preschool program. Annually at ages three to eleven, and again at ages fourteen, fifteen, and nineteen, data were collected with respect to "family demographics; child abilities, attitudes, and scholastic accomplishments; and involvement in delinquent and criminal behavior, use of welfare assistance, and employment" (Berreuta-Clement et al., 1984, p. 1).

At age nineteen, findings indicated "lasting

beneficial effects of preschool education in improving cognitive performance during early childhood; in improving scholastic placement and advancement during the school years; in decreasing delinquency and crime, the use of welfare assistance, and the incidence of teenage pregnancy; and increasing high school graduation rates and the frequency of enrollment in postsecondary programs and employment. . . ." The researchers also evaluated the findings of seven studies of early intervention, including the Perry Project, and emphasized that "only early childhood programs of high quality produce long-term beneficial effects" (Berreuta-Clement et al., 1984, pp. 1, 109).

TRENDS AND ISSUES

Quality versus Cost

Zigler and Gordon encapsulated an urgent problem thus: "By far the thorniest issue in day care . . . is the fundamental issue of quality versus cost. While research indicates that quality makes a difference, most parents can neither afford to stay home to deliver the care themselves nor can they earn enough to purchase quality care if they work" (Zigler & Gordon, 1982, p. vii).

The cost to the economy and thus to government is also evident when parents who cannot afford day care either do not work or else quit work. As a consequence, "unaffordable care has a direct impact upon welfare costs as well as on the family's ability to support government through the payment of sales, property, income, and social security taxes which could

---

Child care is now as essential to family life as the automobile and the refrigerator. . . . Yet most families find it far easier to purchase quality cars and refrigerators than to buy good care for their children. (Scarr et al., 1990, p. 26)

---

significantly offset the cost of their child care subsidies" (Winget, 1982, p. 356).

Research in the past two decades or more has brought gains in being able to define quality day care and in knowing how to deliver it. But questions remain: Who is to pay the cost? What mechanisms of government participation are most appropriate and politically feasible? And what controls will assure that governmental subsidies are not used to maintain unvarying, mediocre programs for children's daytime care and development—programs that fail to utilize rapidly developing knowledge in the area of early childhood education or to offer parents an opportunity for sharing responsibility in program planning and implementation?

The Status of Women in the Provision of Day Care

The issue of quality versus cost is encompassing, and it cloaks other matters of portent. One of the most significant of these has to do with the status and roles of women in the provision of day care. Women constitute virtually all the caregiving personnel in the day care industry in this country. As a class of essential workers, they are grossly underpaid and have access to few government work benefits taken for granted by other wage earners.

Thus we find a large labor force of women who are essential to the economy as well as to the families of working parents. Yet these caregivers are grossly underpaid and denied benefits common to other workers. Furthermore, the fact that additional training in child-related fields and experience in child care brings no rewards in earnings suggests that the government and the public still subscribe to the sexist notion that "since child care is women's work it is not worth paying for" (*Children at the center,* 1979, pp. 21–22).

The devalued perception of child care staff with its low pay and demanding working conditions has led to high rates of turnover at child care centers, increasing from 15 percent in the year 1977 to 41 percent in 1989. It has long been held that staff are a key component of good child care. A study based on classroom observations and testing of children at over 200 child care centers in five geographically dispersed metropolitan areas established that link. Children in centers with persistently high rates of turnover among caregivers, when compared with children at centers with low rates of staff turnover, were found to be less competent in language and social development. The high rates of turnover were found to be directly related to pay and working conditions (Lewin, 1989, p. 9).

What must not be overlooked is that the lack of government subsidies for child care maintains the existence of an exploited underclass of women performing child care work that is essential to the economy and to the well-being of the nation's families. The lack of public attention to this injustice unfairly places two groups of women with opposing needs in confrontation with each other. Working mothers who must pay for day care usually feel financial pressures, as do their caretaking substitutes. If problems of the women purchasing care are lessened by lowering prices, the caregiving women suffer. On the other hand, if the caregivers are paid at higher levels, mothers in the labor force may find it no longer feasible to continue to work outside their homes. Responsibility for this dilemma does not belong to either set of working women. Instead it reflects a vacuum of leadership at the national level in efforts to develop a more effective and fair resolution of the issue of day care cost.

Proposals for a National Child Care Policy

By late 1987, it was apparent that a convergence of social, political, and demographic forces was pushing the issue of child care to a more visible place in the nation's agenda after a long hiatus in federal leadership. A broad-based national coalition had arisen and had set about to organize support for major new legislation to meet the country's growing child care needs. More than seventy national organizations and grass root groups joined together to seek passage of an Act for Better Child Care Services. The act was intended to make the federal government an active partner with states by investing $2.5 billion in improving the supply, quality, and affordability of child care (CDF Reports, 1987b; 1988b; Kahn, 1988).

The child care bill was joined with another proposal to guarantee parental leave for workers, an issue that drew support from persons concerned about the growing use of day care for infants and the possibility of long-term unfavorable effects. The proposal for infant care policy emerged in a congressional bill that would require employers with more than fifty workers to give parents the right to take at least ten weeks of job-protected unpaid leave after the birth or adoption of a child, or to care for seriously ill children.

The United States, lacking a national infant care policy, lags far behind more than 100 other countries that provide a paid, job-protected maternity leave. In European countries, women have access to a five- to six-month paid leave as well as an additional year of unpaid but job-protected parental leave. In many countries, fathers too are entitled to some paid leave and in most instances to an unpaid leave as well (Kahn & Kamerman, 1987, p. 265).

The legislation affecting both the provision of child care and of infant care/parental leave was stalled in Congress by a filibuster. Advocates in both houses of Congress and among citizen advocacy groups regarded the effort as a model for a new legislative initiative in the next session of Congress.

The Act for Better Child Care Services (ABC) was lost largely through philosophical and political differences that pushed aside the demand for affordable and reliable child care. Among these conflicts were (1) the role to be played in the federal subsidy system by church-based programs that account for nearly a third of all child-care slots, and the problem of adequate separation of church and state; (2) whether federal licensing standards would take over state prerogatives and add prohibitively to costs; (3) the preference in some quarters for helping families with tax credits for child care as an alternative to a comprehensive and adequate child care measure, and (4) the long-time objection on the part of proponents of the traditional family in any form of governmental intervention into family life (Greenhouse, 1988a; 1988b; Kahn, 1988).

ABC legislation was again introduced into Congress in 1990, this time under the title of the Early Childhood Education and Development Act. Support for its passage was strong, but in the face of budget issues, and other legislative, financing, and political obstacles, by the time Congress adjourned on August 7, 1990, the House and the Senate had not yet fully reconciled differences in their bills, leaving the legislation not yet brought to the full Congress for a vote.

Parental Involvement in Children's Day Care

An expectation for some kind of partnership between parents and their children's day caretakers has been expressed thus:

> Our society's child-development experts have developed a conventional wisdom which asserts that it is in the interest of the child for parents and nonparental caretakers to form a close relation so that a true partnership will develop in the rearing of the child. A corollary of this assertion is that any sociopsychological discontinuities that are created between home and day care center operate to the detriment of the child. (Zigler & Gordon, 1982, p. vii)

Joffe found the issue of the proper role of parents in child care programming to be one of the most troublesome day care problems. In large part this may be because "parental involvement" is so poorly defined, especially from the parents' point of view. "Because of tremendous cultural hesitations about childcare—especially about its problematic relationship to 'family life'—virtually all publicly funded programs, and many private ones as well, have a rhetorical commitment to 'parental involvement.' But there is little agreement as to what, in fact, 'parental involvement' actually means" (Joffe, 1977, pp. 16–17). Parents need to be consulted on less of a pro forma basis about what involvement they want in their children's out-of-home day care. More creative thinking needs to be brought to bear on the objectives of participation of parents in the day-to-day conduct of the child care arrangements they make. New strategies based on a sounder database are required to secure and utilize effective parent involvement in day care planning and service delivery.

Given the conditions of their jobs and the demands on them in other sectors of their lives, working parents have limited time to spend in their children's place of day care. Operators of child care centers, in turn, do not always welcome parental involvement, even though they may have given lip service to the concept.

The Role of Social Work in Child Care

With evidence of a promising interest in new federal legislation that would advance child care policy for this country, the question arises: What should be the role for social work in developing appropriate, reliable, and affordable child care for a significant portion of America's children? Although the social work profession has endorsed the need for federal legislation, the reality of current social work practice reflects only minimal participation in the planning and delivery of child care services.

On the face of it, this omission is somewhat puzzling given successful efforts of early philanthropists in establishing "charitable nurseries" and the later involvement of child welfare representatives at both the national and local levels in the federal WPA and Lanham Act programs. What then led social work to gradually withdraw from child care issues and service delivery, even as early childhood educators were developing new concepts of preschool programming?

Greenblatt has supplied a historical perspective to the question. With the entry of the federal government into child care–nursery school development during the Depression of the 1930s, which was then extended to meet the wartime need for women to enter the labor market, bureaucratic doctrinal dissension arose between the Office of Education and the Children's Bureau as educators and social workers attempted to define "child care" and the roles of each profession in the new programs. In doing so, Greenblatt concludes, they only reinforced the old conceptual distinction between day care and nursery school in terms of relief versus education (1977, pp. 79–107).

The day care and child welfare literature, Greenblatt has stated, "vibrates" with subtle but significant distinctions among terms such as "supporting," "supplementing," and "supplanting" family functions. However, the wide demand for child care under the wartime Lanham Act demonstrated "no obvious relation to adequacy or inadequacy of the parent," thus putting into question the relevance of casework in day care. In response, new usages for casework were defined—"to prepare the child for entry into day care and to serve as a liaison, to exchange information about the child between mother and day care center." In recent years, at least, such activity has been minimal, although the ideology persists (Greenblatt, 1977, pp. 117–119).

To what extent should the child welfare system be more responsive to the development and delivery of child care? An entry back into the world of child care offers an opportunity to collaborate with child and family advocates in the health, education, welfare, and recreation systems. That kind of cooperation might well be a means of supplying support for mainstream families and bringing their needs to the attention of legislators and other policy makers.

FOR STUDY AND DISCUSSION

1. Discuss why child care personnel remain so poorly paid although they are essential to the economy and to family life. What values within the economy and the status of women come together to maintain this inequity?

2. Look further into the concept of "day care systems." Are there any in your community? Identify the benefits and problems to be derived from this form of organization.

3. What have been some of the effects or influences of the historical separation between day nurseries and nursery schools? What were the positive accomplishments of public nursery school and day care programs under WPA and the Lanham Act? What explanation can you advance for the failure of these two large public programs to lead to a comprehensive provision of programs for the daytime care and development of children?

4. Propose a variety of arrangements that could be made to serve school-age "self-care" children who need outside-of-school supervision and guidance. Look into the Phone-Friend system. Is there such a service in your community? Could you bring one about?

5. Visit a child care center in your community to learn its purpose, the population of children that it serves, its means of financing its operations, its staffing pattern, and the focus of its programs. What evidence is there that the program plays a responsible role in a community network of quality daytime programs?

6. How do you account for the significant differences between this country and European countries with respect to attitudes toward child care and governmental policy?

FOR ADDITIONAL STUDY

Belsky, J. (1986). Infant day care: A cause for concern? *Zero to Three* (Bulletin of the National Center for Clinical Infant Programs), *6*(5), 1–7.

Berreuta-Clement, J. R., Schweinhart, L. J., Barnett, W. S., Epstein, A. S., & Weskart, D. P. (1984). *Changed lives. The effects of the Perry Preschool Program on youths through age 17.* Ypsilanti, MI: High/Scope Press.

Burud, S. L., Aschbacher, P. R., & McCroskey, J. (1984). *Employer-supported child care. Investing in human resources.* Boston: Auburn House.

Greenblatt, B. (1977). *Responsibility for child care.* San Francisco: Jossey-Bass.

Kahn, A. J., & Kamerman, S. B. (1987). *Child care: Facing the hard choices.* Dover, MA: Auburn House.

Seligson, M. & Fink, D. B. (1989). *An action agenda for school-age child care.* Wellesley, MA: School-Age Child Care Project, Wellesley College Center for Research on Women.

Silverstein, L. (1981). A critical review of current research on infant day care. In S. B. Kamerman & A. J. Kahn. *Child care, family benefits, and working parents. A study in comparative policy.* New York: Columbia University Press. Appendix A, pp. 265–313.

Zigler, E. F., & Frank, M. (1988). *The parental leave crisis. Toward a national policy.* New Haven: Yale University Press.

CHAPTER 8

School and Employment: Protection and Opportunity

Far and away the best prize that life offers is the chance to work hard at work worth doing.

Theodore Roosevelt

Chapter Outline

Early school experiences and work are among the most fundamental and pervasive aspects of human activity. Throughout American history persistent questions have been raised about the meaning and importance of work in the development of children. Recent studies show the sig- nificance of children's early socialization to work and its relationship to their later occupational choices, work satisfaction, and acquisition of an enduring sense of competence and self-esteem. "By the time a human being has reached the age of four or five, he [or she] has been conditioned to work. To be sure, child labor is outlawed in most countries, but learning the fundamentals of being a person . . . creates the habit of work. . . . Work is an extension of personality. It is achievement. It is one of the ways in which a person defines himself or herself, measures his [or her] worth and . . . humanity'' (Goldstein & Oldham, 1979, p. 1).

The Protestant ethic as it emerged in the early days of this country was a work ethic, a recognition of the importance and dignity of human labor. But today there are threats to the social meaning of work. A combination of factors have made it harder for children and young adolescents to learn work habits and to have confidence-building experiences with work and, in addition, have effectively blocked access to the world of work for thousands of youths sixteen to twenty-one years old. These adverse factors are found in homes where for a variety of reasons parents do not demonstrate for their children the constructive and satisfying nature of work; in public schools where teachers and administrators do not effectively teach children and youth the knowledge and skills that are basic to entry into the labor market at any level; and in increasingly information-oriented employment situations where highly developed technology has made a large human workforce unnecessary.

To be effective, social services with older adolescents must differ substantially from those offered younger children. Older adolescents want and need job training, work placement, and independent living. Useful and profitable work is essential to a mature and constructive entrance into the mainstream of the life of a community. Yet most of them lack necessary skills and experience to be self-supporting.

Some states are beginning to attack the chronic youth employment problem with a variety of school-to-work transition programs and other opportunities for out-of-school learning, which hopefully will lay the groundwork for a more comprehensive youth employment system. Such efforts hold the promise of strengthening

the basic academic skills of young people and of forging a new community ethic of learning (Lacy & Johnson, 1989).

THE EARLY CHILD LABOR MOVEMENT

Ever since the founding of this country, there have been conflicting interests and wide differences in public opinion concerning the employment of children. The range of these interests can be illustrated by the following sample beliefs discussed more fully below: (1) Parents and society have a duty to train children for work. (2) Parents and society have a right to the fruits of children's labors. (3) Children have a right to education and to protection against exploitation in employment situations. (4) All youth have a right to employment opportunities, and society has an obligation to provide these opportunities.

The Industrial Revolution made possible widespread exploitation of young children in work situations. Although great gains have been made through state and federal legislation, serious pockets of such exploitation remain; in addition there are pressing modern problems regarding the quantity and quality of opportunity for many young people. The history of the child labor movement is linked to the history of public education. The urgent problems and inadequacies of the public school system today actively contribute to the lack of opportunity for useful and satisfying work on the part of large numbers of the nation's young people.

The Duty of Parents and Society to Train Children for Work

In colonial days parents and influential citizens of the community felt an obligation to prevent idleness not only among able-bodied adults but among children as well. This obligation was prompted by religious and moral belief, combined with an urgent need for all able-bodied persons to work together for mutual survival. It was believed that all children should be taught habits of work at an early age as a necessary discipline that would stand them in good stead in the face of natural slothful inclinations and would also prepare them for the demands of a hard life.

An order of the "Great and General Court of Massachusetts" in 1640 stated the obligation of parents and other adult caretakers as follows:

> It is desired and will be expected that all masters of families should see that their children and servants should be industriously implied so as the mornings and evenings and other seasons may not bee lost as they formerly have bene. (E. Abbott, 1910, p. 328)

This official expression represented a serious attempt to prevent idleness among children since idleness, even in a small child, was seen as a neglect of duty by the parent. "There was sympathy for the children, but the dull routine was thought a preparation of the poor for a life of toil" (G. Abbott, 1938, Vol. 1, p. 260).

While it was considered a public duty to provide for the training of children, this training was not only so that children might learn, but also so that they might learn particular kinds of work that would be profitable to the town and colonies. Alexander Hamilton, in 1791, urged that the new industry of spinning cotton "performed by means of machines, which are put in motion by water, and attended chiefly by women and children" be encouraged. He noted that this new industry had the dual advantage of serving as a means "by which manufacturing institutions contribute to augment the general stock of industry and production" and of giving employment to persons "who would otherwise be idle, and in many cases, a burthen on the community, either from the bias of temper, habit, infirmity of body, or some other cause, in disposing or disqualifying them for the toils of the country" (Hamilton, 1791).

In commenting on the transition into the period that saw widespread exploitation of children, Edith Abbott (1910) observed that "the point which is to be emphasized is that child labor was believed in as a righteous institution, and when the transition to the factory system was made it was almost inevitable that this attitude toward children's work should be carried over without any question as to whether circumstances might not have changed" (p. 271).

Reinforcing this tendency to use children was the strong inclination to hire women and children because they could be employed for cheaper wages than men.

The Rights of Parents and Society to the Profits of Children's Work

Although it was the growth of mechanized industry that gave the greatest impetus to employment of children, the need for their labor and a claim to profits from it were present in the earliest colonial settlements. Black children on the coast of Africa were stolen from their parents for the slave trade, which provided labor for the southern plantations. Municipal authorities of England who had responsibility for the care of orphaned and abandoned children cooperated with merchants and shipowners whose agents—"spirits"—supplied children (sometimes by kidnapping or other forms of coercion) to be sent to America to serve as apprentices (Bremner, 1970, pp. 5–23). When they arrived in this country, the African children could look forward only to a lifetime of slavery. The white children, although indentured to a master, were given their freedom when they reached legal maturity.

As industry expanded and became mechanized in the nineteenth century, larger and larger numbers of children were employed, especially at spinning and carding in the textile mills. Children as young as seven were included, and for all children the hours were long and confining, often fourteen to sixteen hours a day. Many worked long into the evening. There was little in the way of safety protection; accidents were common. Corporal punishment was frequently used if children were lax at their work, as they frequently were, as a result of immaturity, fatigue, and general poor health. The children were often poorly clad, undersized, and ignorant of simple academic skills, such as reading or writing their own names. Parents received the meager wages of the children. One early report of an investigation of employed children in "manufactories" contained testimony of adults who had been working in the mills since childhood:

The children are tired when they leave the factory; . . . [they] sleep in corners and other places, before leaving the factory, from fatigue. The younger children are generally very much fatigued, particularly those under twelve years of age; . . . [they] go to sleep on arriving at home, *before* taking supper; [the witness] has known great difficulty in keeping children awake at their work; [the witness] has known them to be struck to keep them awake. (Journal of the Senate, 1837–1838)

During the latter part of the nineteenth and the early twentieth century, extensive investigations of child labor were made by both federal and state governments. For example, the United States Children's Bureau made a study in 1919 of the conditions of child labor in shrimp and oyster canneries in nine communities on the Gulf Coast in three states—Mississippi, Louisiana, and Florida. In the families visited, 544 children under sixteen years of age were employed in the canneries, usually as oyster shuckers or shrimp peelers. Of these, 334 were under fourteen years of age, one being four years and another five years of age. The Children's Bureau report described the conditions of their work as follows:

Oyster canning. The cannery is usually a more or less open shed built near the shore end of a long pier which extends out into the water. The schooners dock at the end of this pier, and a mechanical shovel on a crane hoists the oysters from the schooners into cars which stand on tracks on the pier. When the cars are full they are pushed along the tracks into the steam box, which is usually located near the entrance to the shed—sometimes just inside, sometimes just outside. The cars, loaded with oysters, remain in the steam box a few minutes, where the steam partly cooks the oysters and partly opens the shells. From the steam box the cars run on tracks into the shed. Here the shuckers take their places at the sides of the cars and attach containers, which they call their cups, to the sides of the car. The shucker takes from the car a cluster of oysters, breaks the cluster apart, with a knife opens the shell of each oyster, which the steaming process has partly opened, and removes the oyster meat, cutting it out so that the eye is left in the shell. The empty shells drop to the floor. No seats are provided for the workers. The women and children stand at these cars, swaying back and forth as they work, and bending over farther and farther to reach the oysters as they empty the cars. As the shells accumulate on the floor standing becomes more and more uncomfortable and bending to get the oysters more arduous. . . .

The most common injuries were cuts from the oyster shells, sore hands from the shrimp acid, and sores resulting from running shrimp thorns into the hands. These injuries and physical ills, being directly related to work, occur, of course, more frequently than accidents such as those resulting from falls upon a wet, slippery floor or from being run over by oyster cars. (Paradise, 1922, pp. 371–372, 374)

Another Children's Bureau study in 1922 focused on the problems of children, thirteen to sixteen years of age, employed in anthracite coal mining in the Shenandoah district. The way in which children were located for the study is representative of the thorough, person-by-person search often found in the early studies of the Children's Bureau:

[A] preliminary canvass was made of every house and apartment in the area studied, and the name and age of every child in the family, together with other identifying data, were noted. . . . Altogether schedules were secured for 3,136 children, between 13 and 16 years of age. (Children's Bureau, 1922, pp. 377–378)

The following excerpt graphically describes the work of the young boys engaged in coal mining:

The kind of work these children did was largely determined by the industrial character of the district. The life of the district revolves around the mines and for the boys more than for their fathers their place of employment was the mines. . . . The breakers offered opportunities of profitable employment of young boys. . . .

These breakers which tower above the town of Shenandoah . . . are great barn-like structures filled with chutes, sliding belts, and great crushing and sorting machines. Around these machines a scaffolding was built on which the workers stand or sit. The coal is raised from the mine to the top of the breaker and dumped down the chute into a crushing machine, which breaks it into somewhat smaller lumps. These are carried along a moving belt or gravity incline on each side of which men and boys stand or sit picking out pieces of slate and any coal which has slate mixed with it. . . .

The boys worked in the constant roar which the coal makes as it rushes down the chute, is broken in the crushing machines, or sorted in the shakers. Black coal dust is everywhere, covering the windows and filling the air and the lungs of the workers. . . .

The boys who turned by hand the ventilating fans frequently worked on the dangerous robbing sections where the last remaining coal is being cut away from pillars and walls and where, in consequence, the roof sometimes falls in or the section is filled with a waste material known as slush. . . .

Accidents that had occurred to boys in the breakers as well as underground were recounted to the Children's Bureau agents. One boy told of a friend who had dropped a new cap in the rollers and how in trying to pull it out his arm was caught, crushed, and twisted. . . . One boy told of the death of another while watching the dam beneath the breaker. He and some of the other breaker boys had helped to extricate the muti-

lated body from the wheels in which their companion was caught; he himself had held the bag into which the recovered parts of the dead boy were put. (Children's Bureau, 1922, pp. 379–381)

Perhaps the exploitation of children that was most tenacious and difficult to control was "homework," that is, work sent out by manufacturers to children in their tenement homes, which then became a kind of annex to the factory. Employers sought homeworkers to save space in the factory and to save money, since tenement workers would accept lower wages than "inside" help. Because children could perform the kind of tasks sent to homes, parents who needed their children's scant wages often kept them out of school to help.

To the reformers child labor in the tenements was the most heartbreaking of all. No other form of labor sapped the strength and spirits of children in quite so pervasive a fashion, for tenement work combined the evils of long hours in a filthy, badly ventilated, overcrowded room with those of neglected education and shattered health. The factory child, at least, went home to a different environment at night—the young tenement worker was already home. (Felt, 1965, p. 140)

Sometimes immigrant families worked fourteen to twenty hours a day in their tenement sweatshops. Large numbers of children were employed in the home manufacture of cigars, "a practice that was having a disastrous effect on the wage level of union cigar makers . . . and frustrated the attempts of the Cigarmakers' Union to control the trade" (Felt, 1965, p. 10). Hazards to the health of children in homework were extensive. There were hazards as well for the consumers of children's homework, as a report by a representative of the Child Labor Committee in New York illustrates:

I have seen a girl in the desquamating stage of scarlet fever (when her throat was so bad that

she could not speak above a whisper) tying os-
trich feathers in the Italian district . . . for one of
the biggest feather factories in the lower part of
the city. . . . Men, women, and children suffering with tuberculosis and attending tuberculosis
clinics were found picking nuts and working on
feathers and doll clothes. . . . In another case, a
child eight years of age, sent home from school
because of active tuberculosis, was later found
working at willow plumes in a room lighted by
gas in the daytime. (New York State, 1912,
pp. 362–363)

The Right of Children to
Education and Protection against
Exploitation in Employment

Gradually the demand grew for the years of
childhood to be given to training and development rather than work in tenement homes,
mines, mills, and factories. The health hazards
to children resulting from premature employment were frequently cited as a telling argument
in favor of child labor legislation. But probably
the earliest and the most persuasive argument by
child labor reformers was that education was
necessary in a democracy and that children who
were working were deprived of an education.
The battle within the states for compulsory
school attendance for all children became a potent force in the companion movement for legislation to protect children in labor situations.

It was shocking to concerned citizens that
factory inspectors, who often had been inclined
to gloss over abuses by industrial employers,
began to report that working children who had
been born in the United States could not read or
write. No longer could this condition be attributed principally to the influx of immigrant children. Attention focused on equality of opportunity as a principle of democracy and on the
child's right to at least a minimum of education
and the state's responsibility to secure this right
for all children.

The way in which various social institutions
and provisions of society interlock was clearly

illustrated by the necessity for concurrent progress in securing child labor legislation and compulsory school attendance statutes. For example, children could scarcely realize the benefits
of child labor legislation if they were not enabled or required to go to school and were only
turned out of the factories into the streets, nor
could they be effectively required to go to school
if the law permitted them to work.

Concern over the uneducated class of children influenced twenty-eight states to pass compulsory education laws in the latter part of the
nineteenth century. But to secure legislation was
not enough; enforcement was crucial to attaining the intended goals for children. Not all parents understood and accepted the importance of
education for their children as provided in new
legislation. Lack of sufficiently high wages for
adults in a family increased the wish of parents
for their children to be old enough to become
wage earners. Without an adequate system of
public assistance and without compulsory birth
registration to make children's ages a matter of
public record, it was easy for children to claim
their "working papers" before they were legally
of age to do so, or their "poverty permits" to
serve as an exemption from compulsory school
attendance, and it was common for children to
speak of their "real age" and their "working
age." Poor enforcement of compulsory school
attendance statutes was also aggravated by the
lack of sufficient school accommodations in
many cities and the existence of "waiting lists."
Florence Kelley, in her capacity as chief factory
inspector in Illinois, documented in her annual
report of 1895 the failure of school authorities
in some places to supply facilities for children
who were "ready and willing to go to school."
For example, "in Alton, while 200 children
under 14 years of age were at work in the glass
works, there were on the list of applicants for
admission to the schools 240 children in excess
of the seats provided" (Kelley, 1895, p. 423).

The lack of effective enforcement of school
attendance laws led to such studies as Edith Abbott and Sophonisba P. Breckinridge's on non-

attendance problems in the Chicago schools. This study caused them to argue a need for school attendance officers. They held that these should be social workers, since the reasons for nonattendance were interwoven with the social ills of the community, such as poverty, lack of adequate adult wage levels, illiteracy, and ill health—conditions that existed in many families not known to any social agency and only in contact with the school (Abbott & Breckinridge, 1917, p. 241).

By the beginning of the twentieth century most of the progressive states had enacted some kind of legislation as a protection to children against exploitation in certain work situations, for example, setting minimum ages for employment and maximum hours of child work. However, since this was true mainly of northern states, resistance to enforcement was strong.

A number of factors contributed to opposition to the passage of child labor laws and to the poor enforcement of those that were passed. Employers claimed that industries in states without such laws had an unfair advantage. In addition, since large numbers of children were employed, they feared a reduction of children's hours would lead to the necessity of considering the same reduction for men and women employees. The absence of adequate provision for public assistance, coupled with the poverty of some parents, made it necessary that children work.

Courts were often uncooperative in the enforcement of these new laws, especially while their constitutionality was not firmly established. Some public schools did not want or were unprepared for an influx of immigrant children. Enforcement was sometimes assigned to health departments, who ineffectively met that responsibility, lacking adequate leadership, authority, and financial resources. There were often discrepancies between a state's compulsory education and child labor laws, which confused the basis for enforcement and diffused the authority of inspectors. The early trade unions had mixed interests; while they opposed child labor because it depressed adult wages and could not be unionized, at the same time some trade unionists, like much of the general public, regarded child labor regulation as an interference with parental rights—some of their own children worked. Also, child labor in some aspects was an interstate problem.

> For example, Ohio in 1913 prohibited boys and girls from working in that state until they were fifteen or sixteen years of age, and they walked across the bridge at Wheeling, West Virginia, and found employment readily. (G. Abbott, 1938, Vol. 1, p. 465)

The conflict grew, often stemming from the social reform and child welfare movements of the early twentieth century. Public leaders such as Jane Addams of Hull-House; Florence Kelley, the first factory inspector in Illinois; and A. J. McKelway of the National Child Labor Committee were not easily put aside. For example, James Weber Linn reported an offer in 1903 to Jane Addams of $50,000 for Hull House if she would give up her advocacy of a child labor law then being considered in Illinois (1935, p. 183). Many of the nation's leaders, supported by the Progressive Party in 1912, believed that the evils of child labor could be cured only by a national law. But in spite of national interest, the battle continued to be heavy. From 1890 to 1916 when the first federal child labor act was passed, public opinion divided as sharply and bitterly over the issue of child labor as it did in 1937 over governmental provision of the right of workers to organize (G. Abbott, 1938, Vol. 1, p. 265).

The Path to Federal Legislation

The first federal legislation was proposed during 1906, when Theodore Roosevelt was President. Two bills were introduced into Congress, one "to prevent the employment of children in factories and mines," and the other "to prohibit the employment of children in the manufacture or production of articles intended for interstate commerce." During the ten years that followed, other bills introduced were killed in committee, or reported out but not brought to a vote, or passed by only one house of Congress. The objective was to give protection to children fourteen years of age or under; this had been the age generally adopted in the laws passed by northern states. Conditions in some southern states, especially North Carolina and South Carolina, furnished strong evidence of the need for a federal law.

> The employment of large numbers of young children in the South led to national and even international criticism in the twentieth century. . . . In the textile states legal standards were low and generally disregarded. . . . But southern manufacturers demanded the same freedom in the exploitation of children that the millowners of England and New England had had a century earlier and denounced the movement for federal legislation as the effort of the northern agitators to kill the infant industries of the South. . . . They argued before Congressional committees that the children had to learn to spin when they were young to provide a skilled labor supply and that they were better off in the mills than they had been on the mountain farms from which they and their parents had been brought by the millowners.
>
> When the Democratic party came into power in 1912, the South was in a strong position in both Houses of Congress and was successful for a time in blocking the child labor bill. Finally, however, with a presidential election pending, President Wilson demanded the passage of the child labor bill. (G. Abbott, 1938, Vol. 1 pp. 461–462)

As a result, almost ten years after the first introduction of a bill, a child labor law was adopted on September 1, 1916, to become operative one year later.

In passing the bill Congress had acted under its power to regulate interstate and foreign commerce. The intent was to close the channels of interstate and foreign commerce to the products of child labor. Three days before the law was to go into effect, the United States

district attorney in North Carolina was enjoined from enforcing it as a result of a suit brought by Roland H. Dagenhart, father of a fourteen-year-old son and a twelve-year-old son, each of whom worked in a cotton mill. The United States Supreme Court later upheld this judgment, and the law was termed unconstitutional on the basis that it was not a legitimate exercise of Congress's power to regulate interstate commerce (*Hammer v. Dagenhart,* 1918).

Although the first federal child labor law had been declared unconstitutional, another attempt to control child labor followed. President Wilson asked for, and Congress passed, a law using the taxing power to eliminate child labor. As a part of the Revenue Act of 1918, a tax of 10 percent was levied on the annual net profits of industries employing children in violation of the wage and hour standards of the bill. This law became operative in 1919; in 1922 the United States Supreme Court held this law unconstitutional also, on the basis that it was an improper use of Congress's power to lay and collect taxes (*Bailey v. Drexel,* 1922). By that time seventeen states had child labor laws with standards that equaled or exceeded those set by the two unsuccessful federal laws (Children's Bureau, 1921).

The second Supreme Court decision brought a general demand from supporters of child labor legislation for an amendment to the Constitution specifically authorizing Congress to enact child labor legislation. Most interested persons and groups banded together in support of such legislation, and an amendment was adopted by both houses of Congress and submitted to the states for ratification in 1924.

The bill as finally adopted had passed by very large margins in both houses. By then it was not seen as a partisan measure. But

> the amendment encountered unexpected opposition which misrepresented its history, its authors and its supporters, its terms and its objectives. . . . No other important national labor program was under discussion in 1924, and thus manufacturers' associations were free to devote

themselves to an extensive and aggressive campaign against the amendment. . . . With very limited financial resources, the supporters of the amendment were unable to meet the barrage of misrepresentation which appeared in city and county newspapers. (G. Abbott, 1938, Vol. 1, p. 467)

By 1931 only six states had ratified this amendment.

By 1933, in the depths of the Depression, the public generally was looking to Washington for more guidance. President Roosevelt urged ratification of the amendment and its old supporters rallied their efforts again. But with improved economic conditions, opposition to "federal control" set in. The old characterization of the child labor amendment as a communistic youth-control measure was renewed and listened to (G. Abbott, 1938, Vol. 1, p. 468). Also business people feared that it might lead to the passage of more federal labor legislation. The Roman Catholic segment of the population, generally, suspected that the amendment might be construed as giving Congress power to regulate parochial schools and, in addition, was mindful of the increased financial demands on parishes if children stayed in school longer. Some newspapers opposed the amendment because they resisted any move toward stricter control of newsboys. Farmers, as a large and unregulated employer group, opposed it. Some resistance came about fortuitously because of doubt over constitutional change in the era of the Prohibition amendment. And, of course, the principle of states' rights was cited by some as a reason to oppose the amendment. By 1938, twenty-eight states (not enough for its adoption) had ratified the amendment. But the attention to the issue had done much to alert the public to the problem, and as a result the child labor laws in some states were strengthened or better enforced.

In the early 1930s, when unemployment among all workers spread like wildfire, employed children were also laid off. But children could be hired for the lowest possible wages, and employers began to take advantage of the cheapness of children's labor and employ them in preference to their parents.

With the worker—and the responsible businessman—thus at the mercy of the greedy, desperate or doctrinaire competitor, standards of wages and hours, attained after so many years of battle and negotiation, began to crumble away. No state laws existed to provide effective protection for wages; and, where laws regulated working hours, no state had a weekly limit as low as 44 hours even for women. Sweatshops were springing up on every side. Child labor was coming back. . . . At the same time, the work week in some states was lengthening to sixty, sixty-five, even seventy hours. There stretched ahead only the prospect of longer, grimmer work days and thinner pay envelopes. (Schlesinger, 1959, p. 90)

The regression toward the old abuses of children was checked by the administration of the National Recovery Act (NRA) in 1933. Under this act various industries were brought under a code by which, in return for certain concessions and protections, the industry then pledged itself to shorter hours, higher wages, better trade practices, and better labor relations. The first code was adopted in the cotton textile industry and contained an express denunciation of child labor:

The industry at first demurred, arguing that in practice the minimum-wage provisions would bring child labor to an end. But Johnson [NRA administrator] insisted; and, after an emergency meeting, the cotton textile people agreed to outlaw child labor by name—a decision which produced roars of applause when announced in the hearing room and instantly caught the imagination of the country. . . . By ending child labor in the cotton mills, NRA secured overnight what decades of reform agitation had failed to achieve. . . . Roosevelt said of child-labor abolition, "That makes me personally happier than any other one thing which I have been connected with since I came to Washington." (Schlesinger, 1959, p. 111)

But the National Recovery Act was declared unconstitutional by a decision of the Supreme Court in 1935 (*Schechter,* 1935). By 1936 there was a marked increase in the number of working children.

Nevertheless, the forces were strong to provide for the protection of children in any major labor legislation that was being considered. By now the general public expected that children would be protected, and it was clearly to the advantage of adult workers to secure prohibitions against the use of cheap child labor. A federal wage and hour law, the Fair Labor Standards Act, was passed in 1938. In addition to its basic minimum wage and overtime provisions, which applied to workers of all ages, it contained provisions related especially to child labor.

CURRENT PROTECTIVE LEGISLATION

Every state has a child labor law, although these laws vary widely in the standards and the range of occupations prescribed for the employment of boys and girls. Even within a state, children are not treated equally in relation to employment conditions; exemptions or lowered standards for particular occupations are common, for example, agriculture, domestic service, and the sale and distribution of newspapers or magazines.

Under the federal wage and hour law—The Fair Labor Standards Act of 1938—employers are prohibited from the use of "any oppressive child labor," which is defined further as children under the age of sixteen in any occupation, or under the age of eighteen in certain occupations found by the Secretary of Labor to be hazardous or detrimental to the health or well-being of young persons. Examples of hazardous occupations are the manufacturing or storage of ex-

plosives, coal mining, logging, the operation of sawmills, motor vehicle driving, occupations involving exposure to radioactive substances, and the operation of different kinds of power-driven machines. The clause that makes mandatory the exclusion of persons under eighteen in certain hazardous occupations is an important one, since these occupations are often not covered in the child labor laws of most states.

Exceptions to the sixteen-year minimum age for work are (1) children employed by a parent in an occupation other than manufacturing, mining, or one defined as hazardous; (2) children employed as actors or other performers; (3) children engaged in the delivery of newspapers to the consumer; and (4) children over twelve years of age working outside of school hours on farms. Children of fourteen and fifteen years of age working in a limited number of nonfactory and nonmining occupations may be employed legally, but only outside of school hours and under certain specified conditions of work. The provision affecting the work of children on farms was made by a 1974 amendment to the Fair Labor Standards Act and constitutes a recognition by the federal government of child labor in commercial agriculture and an intent to regulate it. Prior to this amendment, children of any age could work legally in the agricultural industry outside of school hours.

Effects of Legislation

The passage of the Fair Labor Standards Act clearly repudiated the influence of the decision in *Hammer v. Dagenhart.* Abuses in the employment of children became much less of a problem. This has not been a result of federal and state legislation alone. Other reasons for the decline in abuses are found in the activities of citizens' groups and labor unions, and enlightened management. And, significantly, changes in the economy have reduced the need of industry for unskilled youth. Most employers tend to require that new employees have a high school education; consequently, most young people do not enter the labor market until after sixteen years of age—a higher age than is set by the law.

Even so, there are many exceptions, inside and outside the law. The U.S. Department of Labor each year finds a substantial number of violations of the child labor provisions of the Fair Labor Standards Act. Reliable figures on the total number of violations are not available, particularly in commercial agriculture, since in practice the regulatory agencies (Department of Labor and state employment commissions) do not initiate field visits on their own. The reasons given for this failure to adequately supervise compliance are shortages of personnel and large geographic areas to cover.

The child labor regulations under the Fair Labor Standards Act of 1938 were widely approved for four decades as public policy designed to protect children and young adolescents from the penalties of premature employment. Then, in the summer of 1982, the Reagan administration proposed to expand the type and hours of jobs that children fourteen and fifteen years old can work. The proposal called for increasing the maximum daily hours of employment for that age group from three hours daily to four hours daily and the maximum weekly hours of work from eighteen hours to twenty-four hours. Such youths would also be allowed to work up to a maximum of thirty-six hours during any week that school was not in session for at least five days because of holidays or vacation periods. In addition, these young adolescents could work as late as 9 P.M. instead of 7 P.M. on school nights and on other days until 10 P.M. instead of 9 P.M. Under the proposed regulations, youth could work for 85 percent of the minimum wage in an expanded range of tasks, for example, doing kitchen work in fast-food restaurants; tending machines in self-service laundries; doing office and sales work in dry cleaning establishments; dispensing fuel and oil in cars and trucks; monitoring office machines and automatic data processing equipment, dishwashers, and dumbwaiters; working as window

shade cutters; and other similar kinds of tasks (Department of Labor, 1982).

The Reagan administration proposal, in the view of one observer, highlighted "a conflict between two cherished values in American society: the concept that children ought to be protected from the hazards and pressures of the workplace and the well-loved image of young people earning their way through school . . ." (Shribman, 1982a).

The proponents of the changes maintained that they would enable youth to acquire healthy attitudes toward work. Furthermore, the revised rules would make the child labor standards more reasonable in view of industrial changes such as an enormous expansion of fast-food restaurants and advances in data processing that have made it easier to perform sophisticated clerical tasks.

Vigorous opposition came immediately from organized labor, educators, and specialists in adolescent development who claimed that labor organizations, parent groups, and school administrators had not been consulted before the new regulations were introduced. Arguments against the changes were of this order (Shribman, 1982b; 1982c):

1. At a time when schools are under pressure to educate children more effectively for an increasingly information-oriented society, it is hardly in the best interests of children or in the national interest to set up conditions that divert these children's commitment to pursuing an education. Although some children may benefit from early work experiences, such as through an increased feeling of responsibility and competence, on the average those who work long hours spend less time on their studies, are absent from school more often, get lower grades, and are less involved with their classmates and extracurricular school activities. In addition, longer working hours diminish the time young adolescents can spend with their families, thus affecting the quantity and quality of American family life, already a matter of national concern. Findings also indicated that on the average, tenth

graders working fifteen hours or more per week show increased use of cigarettes, alcohol, and marijuana, not only because they have more money to buy them, but because they often work at low wages in stressful, impersonal conditions, frequently under an autocratic supervisor, performing tasks that appear meaningless to them.

2. At a time of very high rates of unemployment throughout society, to create a pool of cheap, part-time child labor would serve neither the health and educational needs of young adolescents, nor the interests of their unemployed sixteen- to nineteen-year-old brothers and sisters who cannot find work and whose slim job opportunities would be further lessened by employers' increased access to cheap labor.

3. Permitting young adolescents who are not old enough to drive to work late at night, when they must walk home or wait in the dark for buses or rides, exposes them to a range of potential harms and negative influences.

The proposed changes immediately became so controversial that the Labor Department found it necessary to extend the time for public comment from thirty days to five months and then to set aside the proposals for the time being.

WORKING CHILDREN

Who are the working children today who still experience exploitation and deprivation? And who are the unemployed youth whose lives are distorted and restricted by lack of opportunity for work? What are the school conditions today that lead into or intensify this lack of protection and opportunity for some children and young persons? These are the questions we shall examine next.

Violation of Child Labor Laws in Cities Today

Child labor in cities is more prevalent than it may seem. Some of these working children are twelve-year-olds or younger who get up at the break of day and work before going to school. Some paste labels in small businesses, sweep up in barber shops, sand cars in auto body shops, or climb high on building scaffolds. Sometimes these boys and girls like what they do—it may have elements of pleasure and play. But more often it is a very serious matter, one of economic necessity, and the work tends to restrict them from normal, maturing experiences, teach them that people cannot be trusted, and condition their life-long aspirations to low-level routines. In fact, "adults who live in cities are so used to seeing children at work that they have begun not to notice them" (Engel et al., 1968).

Currently, more than fifty years after the Federal Fair Labor Standards Act was passed, illegal child labor has become widespread in garment factories, fast-food chains, and supermarkets. The Department of Labor found the rate of violations in 1989 to be the highest since the law was enacted, and twice the number that had occurred in 1982. Some of the children working illegally are as young as ten and eleven years; employers also frequently ignore regulations with respect to times of day and the maximum number of hours sixteen- and seventeen-year-olds are permitted to work. The most flagrant violations in New York City occur in some of the 7,000 garment factories. Not only are the children absent from school; they are also subject to health hazards—harsh fluorescent lights, odors of caustic chemicals, cramped space, and injuries from machines and other prohibited equipment that they are too young to operate safely (Freitag, 1990).

Investigators who are responsible for reporting violations of the child labor laws say that they have all they can do to enforce the minimum wage law and pay standards for Federal contractors, leaving them little time to investigate child labor violations unless they are reported by a parent or a teacher. Traditional opponents of child labor regulation argue that "working at legitimate jobs teaches children free enterprise and provides an alternative to selling drugs." Many others, including educators, say "working long hours tires children too much for their studies and thwarts their progress toward better jobs when they are older" (Kilborn, 1990).

The Migrant Child

Among all the child workers, children of migratory farm workers are most vulnerable to exploitation and harmful conditions. This form of exploitation was vividly apparent during extended cold weather in the South in late 1989 and early 1990 when freezing temperatures threatened substantial portions of the orange crop in Florida. Farmers were challenged to pick the oranges immediately and rush the crop to juice processing plants. Grove owners not only called on adult migrant farmworkers; they demanded that their underage children work as well. Thousands of children, four to twelve years old, went into the groves, even though their schools were open. Their experience was described thus: "Often working from 6 in the morning to 6 at night, they are on ladders, near and even on heavy machinery, lifting 40- and 50-pound crates, using substandard sanitary facilities, breathing pesticides and chemicals and generally risking their future health and well-being" (Newman, 1990, p. 23).

Children have no choice in these circumstances. Their parents are desperate for work, powerless to prevent their own exploitation, and now that of their children's. The executive director of the National Child Labor Committee, an advocacy organization, stated that "these days, strict enforcement of child labor laws is the exception rather than the rule" (Newman, 1990, p. 23).

The families of migrant agricultural workers are beset by many severe problems and the children experience deprivation by the nature of their parents' occupation and conditions of employment. In addition, they may themselves be exploited through long hours of hard, demanding work in the fields with little personal reward.

Investigations of child labor abuses on farms have found significant problems of unregulated child labor, with children "stooping and crawling" in intense heat for as much as ten hours a day. Because many such working children never appear on school census reports or employment records, the exact number of child laborers on industrialized farms is unknown; estimates run as high as 300,000. In one instance, in Willamette Valley of Oregon (the third largest user of migrant and seasonal farm labor), it was estimated that 75 percent of the seasonal workforce harvesting beans and strawberries were children. Shaking potatoes out from the earth in Maine after the mechanical potato digger has gone down the rows turning over the plants; using a sharp forked knife to cut the asparagus stalks out of the ground in Washington and Oregon, and trimming them to a prescribed length; working under pressure to pick berries and fill as many crates as possible before the heat of the day stops further harvesting, by squatting, hunching along the rows on their knees, or bending from the waist—children perform all these tasks for long hours in the hot sun or damp cold. The result is reminiscent of that which followed an earlier era of child labor in tenement sweatshops and factories—children deprived of a normal period of growth and education by too little food, too little rest, and too much work at too young an age (American Friends, 1976).

Domestic migrants are found in almost all the states at some time during the year. Their problems are national in scope. They are largely from minority groups—Chicano, black, Puerto Rican, Native American, Mexican, Filipino. For half or more of these families, farm work is their only source of income except for some in-kind aids such as food stamps. Even those who are able to earn additionally from nonfarm work still have incomes that leave them the lowest paid working families in America. Hunger is common and the work of children becomes necessary for a family's survival (Pollack, 1981). In the view of the American Friends Service Committee, "the fact that such families can only survive by putting their children to work in the fields is no argument in favor of child labor. It is the exposure of an evil system'' (1976, p. 29).

The migrant family experiences special and serious problems in the level of income, housing, sanitation, education, health, child care, leisure time, protected play space, hazardous transportation from one place of work to another, danger from contact with crops that have been treated with pesticides (a risk for their parents as well, but intensified for children of light body weight), and isolation from community life.

Migrant children are among the most educationally deprived of all the nation's children. Most are in need of bilingual education. Their school enrollment is frequently interrupted, and when they are finally able to reenter, they have difficulties in becoming integrated with the permanent students. Not surprisingly, most migrant children are below grade level in school, with the gap between them and other children growing wider as they move through their insufficient periods of schooling. These are serious limitations in view of the fact that this generation of migrant children will need education and technical training even more than their parents did, given the increasing mechanization in agriculture, the declining need for migratory farm workers, and the demand many of the children will face to work ''outside the stream.''

The needs of migrant children have a demanding seasonal impact on rural educational systems with limited staffs, facilities, and financial resources. In 1966 Congress amended Title I of the Elementary and Secondary Education Act to provide special educational services for migrant children. Yet analyses of the programs have shown federal, state, and local failures in the identification of migrant children, in the design and evaluation of projects, and in the administration of the programs at all levels, leaving many children continuing to receive a ''haphazard and disjointed'' education. Despite some gains, migrant children have generally continued in a pattern of lower-level functioning. These findings are especially significant since similar findings appeared in earlier studies as far back as 1954 (Masurofsky, 1975; Stockburger, 1976).

In 1983 the Reagan administration proposed a revised and more stringent definition of ''currently migratory child'' that would exclude significant numbers of migrant children from eligibility for the special education services. The proposal relied on the claim that not all migrant children served by the programs are ''continuously on the move and frequently miss school.'' A Comptroller General study of six selected school districts in Texas, California, and Florida found that about 40 percent of the migrant student population has a ''continuous school experience, generally within a single school district, and migrating only during the summer, over holiday breaks, or before initial school enrollment.'' Congress passed legislation to preclude the new definition; President Reagan vetoed the legislation after Congress had adjourned (Comptroller General, 1983, p. 19).

Migrant Child Welfare Services

There is a critical shortage of data on the availability and use of social services for migrants. It is clear, however, that services are rarely provided to them in the same measure that they are to other populations.

A twelve-state study of services for migrant children yielded an analysis of services in the largest migrant concentrations. Findings are discussed below (Cavanaugh et al., 1977).

1. The life-style, culture, and mobility of the migrant family operate to exclude migrants from eligibility for many family services. Their transiency restricts their familiarity with programs in each locality they go to, and this lack of familiarity is affected further by lack of transportation, community attitudes, and language barriers. Most of the programs for migrant children that exist are administered by the states rather than the federal government, making recertification necessary each time a family crosses a state line, often many times a year.

2. Migrant children seldom receive traditional child welfare services such as in-home services, provision of a foster home, or institutional placement. In addition, they are often ineligible for AFDC and excluded from Medicaid. The food stamp program was found to be the only social program in which migrant families were significantly represented.

3. Child care for migrant children is a critical problem everywhere. Migrant parents have many fewer options than do all other working parents. Conventional informal arrangements, such as relying on a neighbor or relative, are seldom an alternative to taking children to the fields. In the twelve states studied, preschool care was provided to 29,855 young children. Over half of these were served by Title I Migrant Education programs under the Elementary and Secondary Education Act (ESEA), where younger siblings of school-age children were given day care using the same schools and transportation as the older children. The lack of funding for the preschool programs, which is separate from that for the Title I regular school programs, and stringent licensing requirements lessened the availability of these critically needed child care services.

In contrast to the other funded services, Migrant Head Start programs make day care a priority. The use of the Head Start curriculum, extended hours, bilingual/bicultural staff, and the provision of infant care results in programs attractive to parents. However, finding qualified full-time staff is often difficult because the program lasts for less than five months each year. Day care under Title XX, as a local option, results in widely varying availability and eligibility.

4. Parents indicated considerable concern about education for their school-age children. At the time of the twelve-state survey, approximately 200,000 migrant children in the states and an estimated 400,000 nationwide were served by the ESEA Title I program. Summer programs tended to be most effective because of the dearth of other programs during the summer session.

Migrant youths have higher rates of school dropout at the secondary school level; they must earn, and most schools do not meet their present learning, vocational, and earning needs. In turn, schools are hesitant to offer secondary programs for transient youths.

5. The most commonly provided health service for migrant children included physical examination and immunization, nutrition programs (in nine states), programs for women, infants, and children (WIC), and dental care (in all states). In the survey states, teenagers who were out of school and up to 75,000 preschoolers without any day care were not served by these programs. Health education is one of the most effective forms of preventive care. Yet only two of the survey states provided programs of high quality, despite the fact that the health of migrant children is severely threatened by housing conditions and work in the field (Cavanaugh et al., 1977).

UNEMPLOYED YOUTH

Incidence and Contributing Factors

In contrast to the struggles of the early reformers in this century to end the evils of child labor, and the continuing concern today about the exploitation of certain groups of working children, a central objective currently is to create job opportunities for young people. *The unavailability of work opportunities* falls with disproportionate weight on the youthful population, and more especially on young persons who are disadvantaged by lack of sufficient education and skills, and racial discrimination.

A serious problem exists in the numbers of out-of-school, unemployed youth sixteen years of age and over who have been unable to make and sustain a constructive entrance into the labor market and the mainstream of society.

Nationwide unemployment among youths is pervasive and universally high. In 1982 unemployment was high for all groups of workers—9.8 percent in July, a post–World War II record. For youth sixteen to nineteen years, however, the rate was 24.1 percent. For black teenagers, the rate was twice that of their white counterparts—50 percent—more than five times that of all persons in the civilian labor force (U.S. Department of Labor, 1982, August, p. 30).

The unemployment of sixteen- to nineteen-year-olds is highest in the central cities, reflecting the loss of large numbers of jobs rather than lack of desire on the part of teenagers to work. "Of the 4 million young high school dropouts in 1986, one in 6 was unemployed; many were not in the labor force at all, and those who were, faced strong competition from high school graduates for limited job opportunities." In 1987, an average of 1,347,000 persons sixteen to nineteen years old were unemployed—732,000 males, and 615,000 females (Markey, 1988, p. 31). By October 1988, within the total pool of sixteen- to nineteen-year-old high school dropouts and graduates not going on to college, less than half held full-time jobs (Lacy et al., 1989, p. 2).

One of the greatest contributors to these rates of joblessness among youth is the *low level of basic academic skills and cognitive abilities* among a wide range of young people. This is evident most clearly among disadvantaged youth. Today strong basic academic skills are the foundation for entering and competing in a changing labor market where employers expect their employees to be able to learn new skills and adapt rapidly to altered job requirements.

To illustrate the deteriorating job prospects for youth who lack basic academic skills, consider the plight of high school dropouts. Full-time year-round employment for them has "virtually disappeared." In 1968 one-half of male dropouts and more than one-fifth of female dropouts younger than twenty years were employed full time. In 1986 only one in three male dropouts and one in seven female dropouts worked full time. More than 30 percent of all dropouts between twenty and twenty-four years had no earnings whatsoever. Non-college-bound high school graduates have also been affected. In the late 1960s more than two-thirds of all high school graduates younger than twenty years and not enrolled in college held full-time jobs. By 1986, this was true for less than half of such non-college-bound high school graduates (Lacy & Johnson, 1989, p. 4).

What the inner-city ghetto youth sees is that even if you graduate from high school you're still going to be standing on the street corner without a job. (Wilson, 1988, p. 4)

A changing economy and new labor market demands constitute a significant influence on the problems of youth with respect to school and employment. The "lack of strong basic skills poses increasing problems for today's young workers because the skill demands of the job market are ratcheting upward faster than their skill levels" (Lacy & Johnson, 1989, p. 3). A shortage of skilled workers in new fields has emerged as a critical barrier to overall economic progress—a problem that requires attention if a viable labor force is to be at hand as the country moves into the twenty-first century. Recognition of the critical need for a new generation of competent and innovative workers who can satisfy the labor demands of growing "high-tech" industries has emerged as a potent influence toward educational reform. It has become clear that the national economy can no longer afford to neglect the educational problems of youth.

Effects of Unemployment among Youth

From a study of schools in metropolitan areas in the early 1960s, James Conant gave a prescient warning of the "social dynamite" contained in widespread unemployment among black ghetto youth.

> The building up of a mass of unemployed and frustrated Negro youth in congested areas of a city is a social phenomenon that may be compared to the piling up of inflammable material in an empty building in a city block. Potentialities for trouble—indeed possibilities of disaster—are surely there. . . . Unemployment is bad anywhere. Adult unemployment is grievous because it usually involves the loss of support for an entire family. In such cases, one might say that solving the unemployment of adults has the top priority. But in the slums of the largest cities, the reverse is true. The great need is for reduction of unemployment of male youth under twenty-one. . . . One often finds a vicious circle of lack of jobs and lack of ambition; one leads to the other. It is my contention that the circle must be broken both by upgrading the educational and vocational aspirations of slum youth and, even more important, by finding employment opportunity for them, particularly for high school graduates. It does no good whatever to prepare boys and girls for nonexistent jobs. (Conant, 1961, pp. 54–55)

By the end of the decade of the sixties the National Advisory Commission on Civil Disorders had reported that the pervasive effect of unemployment and underemployment was "inextricably linked" to the problem of civil disorder. In addition, there was evidence of the relationship of school conditions and educational practices to the high incidence of riot participation by ghetto youth who had not completed high school. The schools' failure to provide educational experiences to children of the ghetto that could help to overcome the effects of discrimination and deprivation was cited as a cause of persistent grievance and resentment among the black community (Kerner, 1968).

The extensive looting and burning that followed the blackout in New York City in the summer of 1977 was tragic documentation that problems made apparent by the riots of the 1960s had not been solved. The problems were of greater depth and complexity than were once recognized, but the high rate of youth unemployment remains a central causal factor.

In the late years of the twentieth century, other deleterious effects of unemployment among youth stand out clearly. When young men and women are not able to become self-supporting, costs of public assistance, social services, and Medicaid go up at both the federal and state level. The same effect is seen in higher costs for prosecution of delinquency and crime and maintenance of prisons. Unemployment of young men and women also affects the formation of young families. Without adequate earnings and regular employment, young men particularly are less likely to be seen as potential marriage partners. The Children's Defense Fund has found that declining earnings of young men accounts for one-third to one-half of the drop in marriage rates. The resultant increase in single-parent families when the mother is young adds to the hazard of poverty and the likelihood that children will grow up outside of positive paternal influences. Not to be underestimated in the cost of joblessness is the loss of hope for a productive and self-sufficient future. For such youth, job hunting is a depressing and frustrating venture that pushes them farther from accomplishment and increases apathy, suspicion of authority, and reluctance to try again (Lacy & Johnson, 1989).

We may either smother the divine fire of youth or we may feed it. We may either stand stupidly staring as it sinks into a murky fire of crime and flares into the intermittent blaze of folly or we may tend it into a lambent flame with power to make clean and bright our dingy city streets. (Jane Addams, 1909, pp. 161–162)

Governmental Programs

In an attempt to respond to widespread concern about youth out of school and out of work and to meet some of their complex and diversified needs, the federal government tried a variety of approaches during the 1960s and 1970s. Among these programs were vocational training under the Manpower Development and Training Act for some youth who sought jobs but lacked occupational skills; the Job Corps, providing counseling, education, work experience, and occupational training in a residential program for some of the very disadvantaged male and female unemployed youth below the age of twenty-two; and the Neighborhood Youth Corps, a work-training program for disadvantaged young people who needed income to continue their education or who were out of school and lacked job disciplines and skills. Another attempt to help young persons was through Youth Opportunity Centers attached to federal-state employment service systems in major metropolitan areas and designed to find and serve disadvantaged young persons. Indigenous youth advisers, counseling, medical services, and referral to training programs were used, with emphasis on finding the young people who needed help, clearing away their misunderstandings or suspicions, and engaging their interest in participating in the program. In the 1970s, the Comprehensive Employment and Training Act (CETA) became the primary tool for helping young would-be entrants into the labor market by means of training, work experience, and creating public service jobs.

The original purpose of the relatively small CETA program was to provide job training for disadvantaged persons. However, by 1981 it was largely a public service employment program, paying wages to persons employed in subsidized jobs in not-for-profit public and private agencies. CETA's chief limitation was its inability to merge the employment needs of business and industry and the training needs of unemployed and disadvantaged youth, most of whom have few or only obsolete skills.

CETA's minimal effectiveness was conditioned as well by its policy of bypassing state governments to channel training funds directly to local communities. Because states had no substantial role in the federal-local partnership, they in turn had little incentive to take an interest in youth employment. CETA was replaced by the Job Training Partnership Act (JTPA) in 1982. Its greater role for the states in planning and administering federally funded services for unemployed youth has prompted more interest on the part of state government in programs that can address the need of young people for strong academic and vocational skills (Lacy & Johnson, 1989, p. 1).

Well-planned and administered education and job training programs carry potential for gains to society as well as the individual youth. In addition to savings in public money, such programs can restore hope for young jobless persons and help to provide motivation to delay having children. Especially do single-parent families headed by young women desperately need help in obtaining education and work-related experiences. Such programs offer change in their daily surroundings and patterns in positive ways, for example in their readiness to delay second and third pregnancies. Perhaps most important, successful job training programs and work placement add to the individual's self-esteem, and can enable her or him to face future responsibilities of life with confidence and self-sufficiency (Lacy & Johnson, 1989).

SCHOOL CONDITIONS AND PRACTICES

Criticisms of the Public Schools

For more than two decades the public schools have been the focus of extensive criticism. Professional journals and books, literary journals of opinion, and newspapers have carried a profusion of articles questioning the quality of public school education and its appropriateness in the face of serious social problems. Ways in which the family may contribute to a child's poor scholastic performance had been generally recognized, but unsatisfactory school conditions and practices were now cited as significant causal factors for the large numbers of children who do not master the basic academic skills of reading, writing, and computation, who drop out of school, or who graduate from high school poorly prepared for an effective transition into either higher education or employment. In addition, concern for children's schooling has been coupled with an emphasis on the value to the individual of the capacity for learning, not only to provide tools for future learning, or skills to use in earning a living, but also as an essential ingredient of mental health. Escalona stated the position thus:

> One of the primary ego functions that sustain adaptation, and that provide means of coping with stress and of overcoming obstacles, is the capacity for formal structured learning. . . . The experience of learning, and the perception of the self as one who *can* learn, generates a sense of the self as an active being, and a sense of the self as a carrier of power and competence. It also makes available a source of pleasure and of satisfaction that is not directly dependent upon the quality of interpersonal relationships. Last, not least, each instance of successful learning makes the world more intelligible. (1967, p. 2)

Early critical appraisal of the public schools came from the President's Commission on Law Enforcement and Administration of Justice. Consultants to this commission asserted that the schools had not adequately adjusted to present-day social and economic conditions and that the resulting shortcomings had contributed to heightened delinquency (President's Commission, 1967).

Continuing Concern about Quality of Education

Widespread dissatisfaction with the quality of education in America has persisted. In some contrast to the President's Commission of 1967,

which had focused much of its concern on the relationship between inadequate schooling and juvenile delinquency, in the 1980s the issue was redefined as one of misfit between the quality of education and the growing demands for a technologically trained labor force. In late 1981, the Secretary of Education created a National Commission on Excellence in Education, charged to assess the quality of teaching and learning in the nation's schools (public and private), colleges, and universities, and to define the problems that must be overcome. Of interest here is the attention given by the Commission to the formative years children spend in elementary schools, as well as to high-school teenagers, who were targeted for particular attention (National Commission, 1983).

The National Commission report revealed America as "a nation at risk" of losing its "once unchallenged preeminence in commerce, industry, science and technological innovation"; other countries had begun to match or surpass America's educational attainment (p. 5). The Commission was concerned with the essential meaning of education to a free, democratic society and the importance of education if citizens are to reach some common understanding of complex issues. To illustrate the long held value attached to learning in a democracy, the Commission quoted the famous dictum of Thomas Jefferson:

> I know no safe depository of the ultimate powers of the society but the people themselves; and if we think them not enlightened enough to exercise their control with a wholesome discretion, the remedy is not to take it from them but to inform their discretion. (p. 7)

The National Commission's wide search for information uncovered a diversity of opinion about the condition of American education and conflicting views as to what should be done. From the array of data, the Commission identified a number of indicators of "a nation at risk.'' Among these indicators were the following:

1. Some 23 million American adults were found to be functionally illiterate by the simplest tests of everyday reading, writing, and comprehension.
2. About 13 percent of all seventeen-year-olds in the United States were termed ''functionally illiterate.'' Among minority youth the rate was as high as 40 percent.
3. Average achievement of high school students on most standardized tests was lower than twenty-six years previously when the Soviet Union launched Sputnik and triggered new attention in America to the quality of its educational systems.
4. Over half of the population of gifted students were not matching their tested ability with comparable achievement in school.
5. Many seventeen-year-olds lacked ''higher order'' intellectual skills. Nearly 40 percent could not draw inferences from written material; only one-fifth could write a persuasive essay; and only one-third could solve a mathematics problem requiring several steps.
6. Business and military leaders complained that they were required to spend millions of dollars on costly remedial education and training programs in such basic skills as reading, writing, spelling, and computation. One-quarter of the recent recruits to the Department of the Navy read at the ninth-grade level, the minimum needed simply to understand written safety instructions (National Commission, 1983, pp. 8–9).

All these deficiencies were magnified by the accelerating demand for highly skilled workers in new fields. Despite findings that confirmed the vitality of notable schools and programs,

their distinction was in sharp contrast to the of academic and vocational achievement for the majority of students (p. 15).

"Each generation of Americans has outstripped its parents in education, in literacy, and in economic attainment. For the first time in the history of our country, the educational skills of one generation will not surpass, will not equal, will not even approach, those of their parents." (National Commission, 1983, p. 11, quoting Paul Copperman)

A significant factor that contributed to this state of affairs, the National Commission stated, was that secondary school curricula had been ''homogenized, diluted, and diffused to the point that they no longer have a central purpose.'' Students had moved away from vocational and college preparatory programs to enroll in ''general track'' courses. The Commission recommended that state and local high school requirements be strengthened by more rigorous and measurable levels of attainment on the part of all graduating high school students. Such reform would mean a curricular foundation in five basic areas: English, mathematics, science, social studies, and computer science (p. 24). The new standards would require more time spent in learning these basics. This could be accomplished by more effective use of the existing school day, a longer school day, or a lengthened school year (p. 29).

The Commission also recommended changes in the preparation of teachers to make teaching a more rewarding and respected profession (p. 30). All of the Commission's recommendations required increased leadership and fiscal support.

Limitations conditioning the extent to which the reforms recommended by the Commission are implemented, and at what pace, are evident in its statement that ''state and local officials, including school board members, governors and legislators have *the primary responsibility* for financing and governing the schools, and should incorporate the reforms we pose in their educational policies and fiscal planning" (p. 32). Federal government would cooperate with state and local school systems to help meet the needs of certain "special needs" groups of students—gifted and talented, the socioeconomically disadvantaged, minority, students with limited English proficiency, and the handicapped.

The recommendations of the Commission were couched more in the context of goals than concrete steps to take to reach those goals. The significant differences among state and local school systems with respect to leadership, money for fiscal planning, and severity of the educational problems to be solved inevitably will condition the extent and pace of reform among the separate states. For many children and youth, inequality of education will persist.

Classification and Placement

One of the shortcomings alleged to be present in many school systems is the still widespread acceptance of the stereotyped view that most lower-income and nonwhite pupils have limited capabilities, that most are "slow learners," and that therefore not too much can be accomplished with them. As a consequence of this belief in the limited potential of disadvantaged pupils, which is usually coupled with an expectation that certain school programs and services will be used by certain groups of students, these pupils frequently are not encouraged to learn very much; academic goals are lowered because it is assumed that they are not interested in learning, and the children and youth, responding to this negative perception on the part of school staff, fulfill the substandard performance expected of them. The labeling of students who underachieve or misbehave in school is frequent and serves to reinforce the expectation of the staff and the pupil that such behavior

patterns will continue. Some of this labeling is in the form of informal exchanges among staff, leading to "reputation diffusion." It is also found in official cumulative records alerting school staff to "trouble," sometimes even before the pupil has appeared, so that underachievement or misbehavior is then anticipated and suspicions are easily confirmed (Schafer & Polk, 1967; Vinter & Sarri, 1965).

Related to this belief in the limited potential of disadvantaged pupils is the use made in some schools of ability and achievement tests. When these are used as though they were stable measures of innate potentiality, without regard for the extent to which they reflect past learning opportunities and experiences, and familiarity with the kind of task and situation required, then a particular child's abilities may be underestimated and the expectation for his or her performance lowered. In recent years psychological assessment procedures became a civil rights issue when attention was directed to the child's right to be evaluated for educational planning within a culturally appropriate normative framework. As a result, new assessment practices include not only measurement of a child's intelligence quotient (IQ) on a standardized psychological test, but also systematic assessment of the child's adaptive behavior, that is, her or his ability to perform complex nonacademic tasks at home and within the neighborhood and community (Mercer, 1974). Social workers, as part of their long-standing role in home-school liaison, often make these assessments of adaptive behavior. Using scales developed and tested for that purpose, they record specific behaviors of the child that are reported by a parent or other primary caretaker and that they verify through their own observations of the child.

Concern about such school practices pointed up a major issue of school policy that has interdisciplinary dimensions—the question of a child's right to an appropriate education—a program and course of study matched to the child's characteristics and educational needs. Among the controversial aspects of this issue are the practices of classification, tracking, and placement into special-education programs.

Proponents of these practices say that classification is necessary to enable the schools to cope with the almost bewildering array of talent and interests that children and young persons bring to school. Further, differences between children clearly exist and cannot be ignored. To treat everyone alike benefits no one; there must be varied curricula for pupils of varying ability. Proponents of classification also say that it eases the tasks of teachers and administrators. School officials point out that demand has increased for schools to be businesslike and efficiently organized, and that classification and systematic placement are a means to achieve that kind of organizational efficiency. In addition, they say, the economy demands a variety of skills that a standard curriculum does not provide. And federal and state programs of supplementary financial support make special programs attractive to school boards (Kirp, 1974).

Opponents to the practices of classification, tracking, and special-education programs argue that curriculum slots are unequal in that they serve to reward some pupils and punish others. The pupils who feel the punishment are those who are classified and placed in lower-level tracks or special-education rooms with the concomitant stigma that affects their self-perception. Further, opponents say, special programs for such pupils are often unstimulating, and the difficulties are formidable and often defeat their being able to move out of the special program and back into the mainstream of the school's services. Opponents also call attention to the hazards of misclassification and inappropriate placement. Another objection is the charge that, as currently used, classification and special placement do not advance individual pupil learning; instead they separate pupils along racial and social-class lines. Minority pupils repeatedly are found to be enrolled in special-education classes far beyond their proportion in the school population (Kirp, 1974; Children's Defense Fund, 1974).

Serious methodological problems with respect to research on internal school classification complicate an accurate answer to questions about its effects on children. Yet, based on an analysis of the better pieces of research, Kirp states that the consistency of findings is impressive: Most school classification systems have marginal and sometimes adverse impact on a pupil's achievement and psychological development (Kirp, 1974, pp. 19–21). This finding holds true particularly for the educable mentally retarded, the mildly emotionally disturbed, and the perceptually handicapped. In the case of severely handicapped children, special programs do appear to be of benefit. But in the case of the marginally retarded and emotionally disturbed, special classes do not seem to serve children better than regular classroom placement. Neither do they markedly impair academic performance. In fact, they have little measurable effect on academic achievement.

Concern about classification and curriculum tracking has focused attention on the need for due process procedures in the decision making that commits a child to a single and likely closed educational track. Due process would include communication in the native language of the pupil and parent, stated time limits for reevaluation, and explanation of a child's and the parent's right to the child's school records as provided in the Family Educational Rights and Privacy Act of 1974.

School Discipline

The behavior of pupils who violate school rules and in doing so disrupt the learning process for other children is another major concern of school personnel and citizens. During the 1970s the general public, by means of the Gallup poll, consistently rated "lack of discipline" as a major problem in education. Such a persistent and widespread attitude about order and control in school inevitably affects pupils' rights, either positively or negatively. School staff members traditionally have relied on suspensions and expulsions to maintain discipline. The pupil may be excluded from the classroom, suspended from attendance for a stated period, or denied privileges involving extracurricular activities. But do these practices help children? A comprehensive report based on an analysis of suspension data in nine states and the District of Columbia, using interviews and surveys with children, parents, school officials, community leaders and families, provides these findings (Children's Defense Fund, 1975):

1.   The use of suspensions in the public schools was of mammoth proportions. School districts serving a little over half of the total school-age population in the school year 1972–1973 suspended over 1 million pupils, representing a loss of 4 million school days.

2.   Most suspensions were for offenses that were not dangerous or violent or did not seriously disrupt the educational process, for example, truancy, tardiness, minor violations of dress codes, and failure to purchase required materials or equipment. Only 3 percent of the suspensions were for the destruction of property, the use of drugs or alcohol, or other delinquent activity.

3.   Fighting made up one-third of the offenses leading to suspension, but the great majority of cases concerned fighting among pupils rather than acts of violence against teachers or other school personnel.

4.   Black students were suspended at twice the rate of other groups. The largest number of suspended children were white, but a disproportionate number of suspensions involved the black, poor, male pupil.

5.   The grounds for suspension, the procedures used, and the frequency and length of suspensions varied widely among schools within the same district and between school districts.

A major conclusion of the study was that suspensions do not serve any demonstrated valid interests of children or schools. Instead, they are harmful in that they jeopardize chances for children to secure a useful education.

In two companion cases in 1975, the United States Supreme Court found public school students entitled to due process safeguards prior to being suspended (*Goss v. Lopez,* 1975; *Wood v. Strickland,* 1975). Such procedures of due process must precede a suspension, irrespective of its length. The only exceptions are those instances in which the pupil's behavior poses a continuing danger to persons or property, or an ongoing disruption of the educational process. Otherwise, even in a simple short-term suspension, a pupil is now entitled to written or oral "effective notice of the charges," an explanation of the evidence that supported the charges, and an opportunity to present his or her side of the case. Further, school board members can be sued for damages if they violate a student's constitutional rights in the use of suspensions.

For those more serious infractions against school rules (involving a relatively small percentage of children and young persons at school) in which pupils are a danger to themselves or others, or are clearly destructive of school property, or have committed other crimes, suspension may still be used, although not without a hearing, and the duration of the suspension should not be longer than necessary.

In 1988, the Supreme Court clarified the rights of disabled students (particularly emotionally disabled students) under the Education for Handicapped Act (*Honig v. Doe*). The ruling focused on a provision of EHA that a disabled student shall remain in his or her current educational placement pending completion of any review proceedings, unless the parent and state and local school district agree otherwise. The case had arisen because of the attempt to expel indefinitely two emotionally disturbed pupils enrolled in special education because of "dangerous and disruptive behavior" clearly related to their handicapping conditions. In the majority opinion, Justice Brennan stated that the language of the so-called "stay-put" provision is unequivocal. No emergency exception for a disruptive or dangerous student had been intended. The legislative history of the EHA clearly reflects that the intent of Congress was to provide education for all disabled children, even those with severe behavioral problems. "We think it clear," Justice Brennan stated, "that Congress very much meant to strip schools of the unilateral authority they had traditionally employed to exclude disabled students, particularly emotionally disturbed students from school" (at 604). However, the Court did say that the decision does not preclude the school from using normal procedures for dealing with behaviorally disturbed children who are endangering themselves or others. This procedure the Court identified as use of study carrels, time-outs, detention, or restriction of privileges. Further, a student who appears to be an immediate threat of injury to self or others may be temporarily suspended up to ten days, allowing time for school officials to initiate an Individualized Education Plan (IEP) review and ask for parental consent to an interim placement. In very serious instances, school officials can seek injunctive relief from an appropriate court. Such cases carry a presumption in favor of the child's current placement (Center for Law, 1988, pp. 1, 4).

The use of corporal punishment in schools is further evidence not only of national concern about lack of school discipline, but also of the unfortunate acceptance in our society of physical force as a legitimate child-rearing practice. The Supreme Court in 1975 (*Baker v. Owen*) placed some restrictions on the use of corporal punishment in schools (except in instances where the misbehavior was "so disruptive as to shock the conscience") by specifying certain procedures to be followed—a warning, a hearing, and another teacher as witness to the physical punishment.

Two years later the Supreme Court retreated from its advance toward protection of children from unreasonable punishment by holding that corporal punishment in school does not violate the Eighth Amendment stipulations against "cruel and unusual punishment" and that prior notice and hearing are not necessary before such punishment is inflicted (*Ingraham v. Wright,* 1977).

On the more positive side it should be noted that the Court decision does not prohibit states or individual school systems from banning corporal punishment. New Jersey was the first state to do so in 1867. Other states were slow to follow. In recent years, however, with more public attention to child abuse, legal banishment of corporal punishment in schools has grown. Fourteen states now prohibit it as do a number of large urban school districts in other states, including Saint Louis, Atlanta, New Orleans, and Minneapolis (National Committee for Prevention, 1989). (See Figure 8.1.)

School–Community Distance

Among the school's problems in finding better ways to deal with deviant behavior is the task of coordinating the point of view and the actions of the various professionals, inside and outside the school, who deal with pupils in trouble:

> The psychologist, the speech therapist, the social worker, the attendance officer, the counselor, the principal, and the classroom teacher all tend to view the problems of students, education, and misbehavior from different perspectives. Hence, they seek out different types of information and follow varying courses of action. The result is frequent "atomization" of the school's response to students in trouble. (Schafer & Polk, 1967, p. 256)

The responsibility for students in trouble may be pushed off from the school to community youth-serving agencies, with insufficient communication between the school and the community agency, and lack of attention to the adaptations that might be made within the school system itself—adaptations that could help the pupil, and others in similar situations, to perform more successfully.

Lack of communication between the school and the community it serves, and between the school and the homes of its pupils, is another deleterious condition increasing the probability of school failure for many children, especially

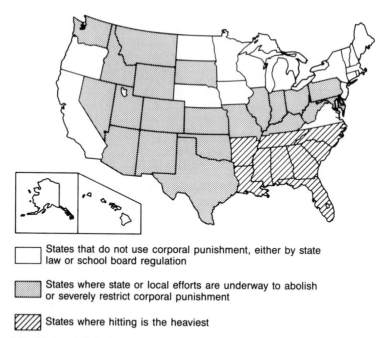

Figure 8.1. Corporal Punishment in Schools, 1989. (*Source:* Committee to End Violence against the Next Generation, Inc., *Network for Public Schools, 15*[1], p. 3.)

those from low-income or minority group homes. Middle-class parents, ready to speak for themselves and generally supportive of education, are more often in reasonably comfortable communication with school personnel. But it is difficult for the parents of poor children. Even though studies show that most low-income and minority group parents place a high value on school achievement for their children (Riessman, 1962, p. 10; Cloward & Jones, 1963, p. 203; Coleman, 1966, p. 192), they often are less able to communicate easily or effectively with school personnel or to offer active support to school activities. Many schools make insufficient attempts to understand poor children's surroundings and their experiences, and then to use this information as a baseline to extend the horizons of these children.

Aspects of school–community distance may be reflected in inappropriate instructional methods and teaching materials that intensify children's feelings of alienation from school and society. Too frequently classroom discussions are held to neutral matters, with an avoidance of the pressing real-life problems and controversies greatly concerning children and youth. For many secondary level pupils, especially the non-college-bound, the irrelevancy of their educational experiences to real life is manifested further by the difficulties they encounter when there are no occupational placement and follow-up services to aid them in the transition from school to the changing world of work.

PUBLIC POLICY GAINS IN EDUCATION

Education for Handicapped Children

A far-reaching step in offering children equal opportunity for an appropriate education was taken with the passage of P.L. 94–142, the Education for All Handicapped Children Act of

1975 (EHA) and implemented in 1977. This significant social policy legislation required states to (1) offer programs for the full education of handicapped children between the ages of three to eighteen, (2) develop strategies for locating such children, (3) use intelligence testing that does not discriminate against the child racially or culturally, (4) develop an IEP for each child, and (5) offer learning opportunities in *the least restrictive educational environment* possible, with an emphasis on mainstreaming—integrating handicapped children into regular classrooms.

Special education for handicapped children was not new when the act was passed. Some states, often at the urging of child advocates as well as parents of handicapped children, had already installed special education programs in their public schools and demonstrated their value for children. By the time the EHA went into effect, 179,000 special education teachers provided special education to a total of 3.7 million elementary and secondary children and youth. The federal government was contributing $252 million in aid to special education programs (Singer & Butler, 1987, p. 129).

However, there were disparities among the established programs in coverage and levels of effectiveness. In other school districts, many handicapped children were simply excluded from school for lack of appropriate educational offerings, left languishing at home, often poorly cared for, and isolated from the normal experiences of other children at school. Some states still maintained residential state schools for deaf, blind, or mentally retarded children. These institutions had been established in the late nineteenth century during a time of expanded professional interest in developing teaching methods for handicapped children. However benevolently inspired, when children were educated in these institutions they were of necessity separated from their parents, siblings, and community for nine months of the year. This type of institution was administered more as a school than as a child-caring institution; attention to emotional nurturance for children was secondary and often lacking.

Given the inequality across the states of education for many handicapped children, the EHA provided a major impetus for the expansion of special education. By 1986, "the number of children served had increased by 17 percent to 4.3 million, the number of teachers had increased by 54 percent to 275,000, and federal assistance had increased by 155 percent (in constant dollars) to $1.16 billion." It should be noted, however, that "the increase in federal contribution has lagged far behind program growth, so that it still represents less than 12 percent of excess expenditure on special education" (Singer & Butler, 1987, p. 129).

The EHA was recognized as a much-needed but complex federal effort to influence education at the state and local levels. Federal requirements were extensive, but limited federal dollars were offered to the states. To implement the act effectively, active involvement would be essential from a range of participants, not only special education teachers, but also principals, other school administrators, school personnel such as psychologists, social workers, and curriculum consultants, parents, advocacy groups, and public and private community social and medical agencies. The act had been modeled from preceding civil rights legislation, rather than from a focus on special education curricula and measurement of benefits to children. As the implementation of this new public educational policy got underway across the country in the late 1970s, it was clear that the impact on educational programs, distribution of resources, professional roles, and school-community-pupil relations would be significant and would require study and evaluation (Singer & Butler, 1987).

A study of interest of the act's implementation was conducted during the fifth and through the eighth year of the legislation. Termed the Collaborative Study of Children with Special Needs—1982–1985, the research was carried out in five metropolitan school systems. The five were selected for geographic, socioeconmic, and ethnic diversity. Each had a sizable enrollment. For each school system, stratified random samples of the pupils in special education were selected. Each child's school record was reviewed. Parents and teachers were interviewed. In addition, to shed light on school system dynamics and circumstances and to establish a qualitatively informed base, school superintendents, principals, special education and regular teachers, union representatives, parents, leaders of local advocacy groups, relevant health care and social service personnel within the district, and board members were interviewed (Singer & Butler, 1987).

In the evaluation of extensive data, the researchers addressed this major question: Had an effective balance been achieved between (1) the detailed demands of the federal regulations designed to standardize compliance, and (2) the capacity of states and local school districts to respond affirmatively? Stated somewhat differently: How well had the states been able to function as agents of social reform?

In the five major metropolitan schools studied, EHA had indeed been "an effective instrument of social reform through its direct influence on local special education programs. Despite severe budgetary and logistical constraints, school systems have managed to comply with EHA's regulations, and local special education directors have managed to negotiate with a wide range of competing interest groups to ensure implementation of the law's guarantees" (Singer & Butler, 1987, p. 126). Favorable acceptance of the legislation was indicated when the Reagan administration proposed revisions in the regulations that would have weakened the educational guarantees of the act; the proposals were dropped promptly in the face of overwhelmingly negative responses from the public.

A second and essential question was addressed: Granting that the study had identified a successful demonstration of compliance with the act's provisions, what was the program's impact on children? For what children had EHA made a difference? Here the results were less

clear, partly because of the difficulties in evaluating program impact when instruction was guided by each child's indivdualized educational plan and learning goals. Measurable outcomes suggested that the EHA had benefited some children more than others. For whom, then, did EHA make a difference? Did children cluster in particular disability categories or socioeconomic groups? (Singer & Butler, 1987).

Greatest benefits were experienced by two groups of children who formerly had been denied free public special education and related services—those the most handicapped and those the least handicapped. Enrollment by these two groups of children increased substantially after passage of the EHA.

The first group includes children with severe cognitive, emotional or physical disabilities. Some were children with hearing or seeing disabilities or were mentally handicapped who had heretofore been consigned to state schools far from home. Some are children who are mobility impaired, chronically ill, emotionally disturbed, or have behavior disorders—a range of conditions that previously had left children in home care without any educational opportunity.

The second group with lesser disabilities includes children and youth classified as learning disabled. Numbers so classified have grown dramatically—from 1.8 percent in 1976-1977 to 4.7 percent in 1985-1986 (Singer & Butler, 1987, p. 133). Contributing to the growth in numbers is increased awareness of the sometimes subtle differences in learning disabilities and the use of reclassification to reduce the risk of stigmatizing children with more traditional labels, such as mentally retarded or seriously emotionally disturbed. Reclassification also can serve as a means to obtain supplemental services for children in the face of reduced funds for other entitlements such as Title I and bilingual education. New eligibility for services led Singer & Butler to suggest that the two groups of "winners" under the EHA—the most and the least disabled—have benefited "more than the traditional special education constituency, for whom schooling may have changed only marginally'' (1987, p. 144).

In assessing gains for children under the EHA, it must be noted that some children are at greater risk of failure to benefit from special education regardless of the severity of their disability or degree of functional limitation. Children in special education programs reflect wide differences in areas such as family background, their parents' income levels and educational levels, the presence of family disorganization or persistent stress within the family, the readiness or ability of parents to participate in the process of arriving at or reassessing their child's Individual Educational Plan. Many children in special education are at levels of socioeconomic risk or experience other family problems that preclude the possibility of their receiving full benefit from school, regardless of its quality. For many special needs children, their handicap is clearly not the most significant deterrent to their success in life. In consideration of the inequities in our society that affect a child's education, Singer and Butler observed that ''a program that gained enormous political support on the grounds that it was an entitlement for all rather than a means-tested program for the neediest few, has conferred predictably different entitlements on middle-class and on low-income children'' (1987, p. 146).

Diverse views about the success of the EHA are common. Yet despite its problems and unequal benefits to children and the difficulties in measuring its results, the Act has brought benefits to many groups of children who formerly were grievously neglected in public education and has demonstrated for society a positive set of attitudes with respect to handicapped children. Public acceptance of the rightness of new social entitlements for handicapped children is reflected in an addition in 1986 to the EHA. In implementing the EHA it was discovered that many handicapped children had never been identified in their community or offered special services of any kind prior to entering school.

Congress added a new Part H to the Act, P.L. 99–457, authorizing the provision of family-based services to families of *infants and toddlers* with handicaps.

The entitlement to the basic provisions of the EHA has not been uniform for all handicapped children; there are great differences among school districts in expenditures, services, and personnel. There are also serious inequities throughout society that schools alone cannot overcome. Nevertheless the EHA stands as a distinctly notable piece of social legislation benefiting children and youth.

Other Educational Gains for Children

Another highly significant advance in public education policy for children came with a decision of the United States Supreme Court—*Plyer et al. v. J. and R. Doe et al.* (1982). The case reached the Supreme Court from Texas where a state statute had authorized the withholding of state funds to local school districts for the education of children who were not ''legally admitted'' into the United States. The suit was a class action one on behalf of school-age children of Mexican origin whose alien parents lacked evidence of legal admission to the United States. The court ruled that excluding such children from enrollment in local public schools violated the equal protection clause of the Fourteenth Amendment, which provides that no state shall ''deny to any person within its jurisdiction equal protection of the laws.'' Whatever a child's status under the immigration laws, the court said, an alien is a person in any ordinary sense of that term and is entitled to due process protections.

In reaching its decision the court also took note of ''the importance of education in maintaining our basic institutions, and the lasting impact of its deprivation on the life of the child. . . . Illiteracy is an enduring disability. . . . By depriving children of any disfavored group of an education, we foreclose the means by which that group might raise the level of esteem in which it is held by the majority'' and heighten the probability that these children, "already disadvantaged as a result of poverty, lack of English-speaking ability, and undeniable racial prejudices . . . will become permanently locked into the lowest socio-economic class." The decision was a clear victory for human rights and for child rights in particular.

Another issue that has been addressed in recent years is the increased expectation that school districts will provide *bilingual/bicultural education* to non-English-speaking students. This expectation has come from court order, federal and state legislation, and community pressure. The federal Bilingual Education Act of 1965 and of 1973 provided some federal financing for instruction to enable children of limited English-speaking ability to progress through the educational system. Programs have varied widely. Some are conceptualized with a compensatory aim of helping children acquire English language skills as rapidly as possible in order to become assimilated into the classroom. Other programs are developed with a greater appreciation for the historical, literary, and cultural traditions of particular groups of non-English-speaking children. Pupils who enter school without effective communication skills in English are a special concern for social workers who have a long-standing commitment to facilitating a constructive communication link between a child's school experiences and her or his parents and home environment.

The *sex-role culture* of the public schools is a force that conditions boys' and girls' expectations and significantly affects their individual aspirations and opportunities. Title IX of the federal Educational Amendments of 1972 specifically forbids using gender as a basis for excluding some children from participating in selected educational programs. Some schools have made substantial gains in removing the more overt forms of sex stereotyping from curriculum materials. School social workers have a responsibility to help ensure that children have equal access to traditionally sex-typed educational re-

sources and experiences. Toward this end, school social workers sometimes have conducted in-service training sessions for teachers or other school personnel, or have consulted directly with individual teachers about the "hidden curriculum" reflected in teacher expectations of boy–girl roles. Social workers have also worked in group sessions with pupils to help them recognize the more subtle ways that role expectations are conditioned and restricted by stereotyped notions of sex-related abilities and legitimate aspirations.

SOCIAL WORK IN THE SCHOOLS

Children Who Can Benefit from School Social Work Services

All children in school encounter stress at various stages of the "pupil life cycle," that is, at one or more of the normal points of progression through the system of education. Most children and young persons can do what is required at school without excessive stress. But others cannot because of varying kinds of conflicts between their needs and the demands of the school, home, or community. These are the children who can benefit from school social work services.

Some children lack an adequate capacity for effective social functioning in relation to pupil life tasks and the requirements of their environment. They may have entered school with inadequate coping behavior and maladaptive patterns of social interaction, which then become exacerbated by the demands of the school environment. For some children inordinate stress at school is prompted by a specific traumatic event or an unbalanced combination of stressful conditions, such as the loss through death or divorce of a parent whom a child has relied on for support in his or her school life or an episode of violence at school that causes a group of children to fear the school setting.

Some other children and young persons experience subtle but powerful community forces that depress their coping capacity and increase the demands on them at school. Common examples may be found in an idiosyncratic philosophy of a juvenile court judge, a malfunctioning foster care system in which a child may be adrift, an ineffective application of health care policy, and prejudiced sociocultural attitudes toward delinquency, mental retardation, race, and sex.

Some children enter school already in a disadvantaged position because they lack earlier experiences that might have expanded the parameters of their developing intelligence and prepared them for the learning expectations of teachers. For children from low-income areas, poverty often severely affects their patterns of school attendance and achievement. Handicapped children, even with the provision of federal legislation for their education, are not yet fully assured that an appropriate individualized educational plan will be implemented. Some children lack access to resources to meet their needs. For example, special educational plans for intellectually gifted children are in short supply, with a resultant significant loss in achievement and development of intellectual resources that the nation will need in the future. Children of migratory agricultural workers and children from other non-English-speaking environments are at special risk of discrimination in access to equal educational opportunities. Neglected and abused children have intensified needs for protective and caring relationships in their school environment. School-age pregnant girls and school-age parents, predelinquent and delinquent children, and young drug and alcohol users—all are at risk of loss of educational opportunity and lack of preparation for adult roles. Children who are frequently absent or truant are especially vulnerable to underachievement. Indeed, children of all classes who for whatever reasons do not learn and achieve their potential in school are children about whom school social workers should be concerned. A

primary task is to bring about an understanding of these children's characteristics in interaction with the demands and conditions of their school-home-community environment.

Organization and Support

School social workers usually are employed by and accountable to local school districts. For the most part local schools make the critical decisions in relation to numbers of social workers to be hired, the size and composition of the student body the social work staff is expected to serve, lines of accountability, and other aspects of the school social work service.

Beginning in the 1960s, state departments of education assumed more responsibility for coordinating or supervising a range of pupil services in the public schools (for example, guidance, psychology, social work, health, attendance, and speech) through a section typically entitled "pupil personnel services" or sometimes "special services."

Almost uniformly school social workers are a group of mature, full-time, professionally educated (with a master's degree) social workers employed by a dominant institution of the community. They are at least equally and sometimes favorably situated compared with teachers with respect to salaries, office space, tenure rights, and collective bargaining.

Furthermore, from the perspective of state departments of education, school social workers are accepted and integrated into the system of pupil specialists. Only guidance counselors are found in schools in more states. In addition, social workers as pupil specialists compare well with the other pupil services in relation to program funding, salaries, and certification requirements (National Association, 1976).

Natural Links between Child Welfare and School Social Work

Social workers employed as staff members in the public schools occupy a pivotal position of leadership between the institutions of public education and public welfare. Some of social work's early leaders were keenly aware of the strategic location the school occupies among a community's institutions and were impressed by the opportunities presented to the school. For example, Sophonisba Breckinridge, addressing the National Education Association in 1914, spoke of the magnitude of the schools' task and the extent to which its importance had gripped the conscience of the community.

> To the social worker the school appears as an instrument of almost unlimited possibilities, not only for passing on to the next generation the culture and wisdom of the past, but for testing present social relationships and for securing improvements in social conditions. (p. 45)

Her plea was for a closer study of failures of the school and the consequent loss to the nation in social well-being. At about the same time that Breckinridge spoke, other social workers in settlement houses were recognizing the need for the school to relate itself closely to the present and future lives of its children. For example, Lillian Wald wrote:

> Intelligent social workers seize opportunities for observation, and almost unconsciously develop methods to meet needs. They see conditions as they are, and become critical of systems as they act and react upon the child or fail to reach him at all.
>
> Where the school fails, it appears to the social workers to do so because it makes education a thing apart,—because it separates its work from all that makes up the child's life outside the classroom. (1915, p. 106)

Unfortunately, for far too many children in school today, education has become "a thing apart," separate from the vital concerns of young people. Despite the statement of Julius Oppenheimer in 1924 that the school is the "strategic center of child welfare work" (1925, p. 28), by the late 1960s there appeared to exist

an undesirable degree of professional separatism between the two fields of social work practice—child welfare and school social work—in terms of communication, joint planning, and cooperative progress toward common goals.

This phenomenon is a reflection of stated and unstated boundaries around institutional and agency functions, special fields of social work practice, funding patterns, and other organizational and system characteristics, rather than a reflection of the needs of the whole child.

In the consideration of certain problems of child welfare we are apt to forget or to undervalue the importance of our public school system. Our vast aggregation of elementary schools ought to be regarded, however, as our largest and, in a sense, our most legitimate child welfare agency. (Arnold Gesell, 1923a)

An effective model of school social work as well as a child welfare system recognizes the interdependent relationship of the schools to the community's other social institutions and functions—the family when it is characterized by instability, the public assistance system, the juvenile court, and the labor market in relation to low-income youth. School social work services are best defined as a response to the most pressing problems of the school's pupils and to underlying conditions both inside and outside the school system that impinge on large numbers of children and youth. In designing the social work service, the purpose of the school must be kept clearly in mind—a life setting for children and youth where learning is possible and competence can be acquired.

The problems of youth's schooling and employment today are complex ones, different from those of a time when the primary need was to protect young children from oppressive and exploitive labor. But the responsibility of society is no less clear. Youth has a right to meaningful education of high quality and to opportunity for constructive and satisfying work;

society, in turn, has an obligation to assure that opportunity is present and in a form that all young people can grasp and use.

TRENDS AND ISSUES

Children's Early Socialization to Work

Although work does not occupy the central position in a child's world that it does generally in the world of an adult, an orientation to work begins in early childhood. Given the requirements for work placed on adults by the economy, and the relationship of satisfying work experiences to ongoing mental health, it is important to give attention to children's early predispositions toward attitudes and behaviors that will enable them to develop a commitment to the social institution of work.

There are fewer informal opportunities than once existed in a simpler society for children to "learn to work," and for some youth these opportunities are virtually nonexistent. Instructional and curricular deficiencies in many schools have also meant that many youth leave school without having acquired the basic academic skills that are essential for them to work successfully in any kind of stable employment. The issue emerges as to how to institutionalize work for children and youth in some manner without exposing them to exploitation through premature employment and without creating an underclass of cheap child labor.

A conviction that better preparation of young people for work is needed must be translated into practical programs. If most of a child's developing work orientation is well under way by the end of elementary school, as research suggests that it is, then curricular revisions and allocation of resources for the purpose of influencing children's occupational orientations are needed during their early years. To wait longer means an eventual development of more costly remedial programs, applied belatedly to extraordinarily high dropout rates from

school and inadequate transitional school-to-work services.

Education in the 1990s

The report of the National Commission on Excellence in Education, *A Nation at Risk* (1983), was widely distributed. With the hope that it would be read widely among the citizenry, over 200,000 copies were distributed by the federal government and 5 to 6 million more reached the public by way of reprinting in newspapers and other periodicals. The report was kept to only thirty-five pages and offered to the public as an "open letter to the people" (Fiske, 1988).

The extent to which the document would be a significant influence in future development of education was problematic. Critics charged that it did not reflect originality, that it was not different from a tide of previous and continuing reports on education. They also noted the Commission's failure to acknowledge that states had already begun school improvement programs, that standardized test scores had been rising for several years and that many of the recommendations for change that appeared in *A Nation at Risk* were already under way. Because of an early statement in the report—"If an unfriendly foreign power had attempted to impose on America the mediocre educational performance that exists today, we might have used it as an act of war"—the document was said to be "full of apocalyptic rhetoric and military analogies." Presidential aides were disappointed with the report because it did not address the Reagan administration priorities—abolishing the Department of Education, permission for organized prayer in schools, and adoption of tuition tax credits (Fiske, 1988).

It was generally expected that interest in the report would fade rapidly as new pressing issues came forward. Unexpectedly, the report caught the interest of American people and became a symbol of the need many felt to improve education for the nation's children and youth. As a result, states began to raise graduation requirements, strengthen curricula, adopt comprehensive educational packages with varied steps such as higher salaries for teachers, new disciplinary codes, competency tests for teachers, and new financial resources from state legislatures.

As changes have been made in education, new questions have arisen. For example, just how do better-paid teachers help students meet new standards? How can the teaching and learning process itself be improved? Some allege that school improvements most help students who were already doing well, leaving the question of how to help those who *need* it most—children from low-income and minority families. These and other questions have led to lessened interest in model schools, demonstration projects, and incremental changes in school structure, and some readiness to focus on broad strategies for systematic change in the educational system (Fiske, 1988).

One such model to protect every child's right to a good education is strongly endorsed by the Council of Chief State School Officers—legislation to create entitlement to preschool programs for at-risk three- and four-year-olds. Their position is that given what we know about how intelligence develops in young children and the proved benefits of early childhood education, "it is economic stupidity and a moral blunder for any state in the nation not to provide pre-kindergarten programs to—at the very least—all its disadvantaged youngsters. Yet not a single state in our nation has achieved that limited goal" (Children's Defense Fund, 1989, August, p. 1).

Another significant report for strengthening education for children contains recommendations from a Task Force of the Carnegie Corporation. The study addresses the early adolescent years (ages ten to fifteen) "as a pivotal time in the lives of the nation's young people—a time fraught with opportunities for success and growth as well as such risks as school failure and exposure to drugs" (Children's Defense Fund, 1989, August, p. 2). The study focus is the potential of middle grade schools, junior high, in-

termediate, and middle schools as a powerful force to reach millions of youth adrift and help them thrive during early adolescence. Recommended modifications in school practice to reach this goal include: (1) creating small communities for learning with a curriculum that includes not only academic skills, but health management, ethics, citizenship; (2) eliminating tracking of children by achievement level and adjusting school resources for a better fit to the students there; (3) giving teachers more power over what they teach, and more opportunity to help run the schools; (4) placing a health coordinator in the school and offering health care and counseling services; (5) providing community outreach to connect children and youth with health and social services, and after-school activities including opportunities for service (Children's Defense Fund, 1989, p. 2).

Another issue of great importance is the significance of racism in American education. Schools play a critical role in shaping attitudes toward racism. In 1985, the editors of the *Harvard Educational Review* addressed a matter of deep concern to them:

> We are experiencing a new strain of racism, coded in new ways, couched in a different language. The foundation is being laid for racism to be fashionable again. We hear talk about taking schools "back to the basics" and fundamentalists restoring the "traditional values," slogans that express a desire to take our society back to where it was, say, in the 1950s. In the effort to find simple solutions and in the wishful avoidance of issues of racism, even people with seemingly innocent intentions are contributing to racial tension and division. (p. vii)

Four years later, the editors again expressed concern that since their earlier statement, the pervasiveness and resilience of racism and its corrosive effects remained evident within a climate of inattention to it (*Harvard Educational Review,* 1989). They suggested that racism today is in a mutated form under an assumption that institutional racism is safely behind us. Yet racially motivated attacks continue, not only in slum streets, but on American campuses and in public schools. The issue they defined is the sensitive and "critical role of schooling in shaping attitudes among both the perpetrators and victims of racism." That many individuals—teachers, school children and youth, parents—treat others fairly and with courtesy does not correct structural injustices that racism breeds. Race is "embedded in our institutions, our class structure, and in the daily efforts of people and groups to protect what they have" (p. viii). More affirmative action must be taken to denounce and eliminate racism in our schools and in all other institutions in our society.

FOR STUDY AND DISCUSSION

1. What forces and diverse interests in this country have influenced the place of work in the lives of children and youth?
2. Compare the lines of reasoning that supported the employment of children in textile mills and mines with the present-day defense of children in commercial agriculture.
3. Look further into the "literacy problem" in your state and community. What programs exist for helping unemployed youth gain basic academic skills and job training? To what extent do these programs appear to be realistically prepared to make an impact on the youth labor force?
4. Discuss and define an effective role for the public schools with respect to teenage pregnancy, drug use, and development of life goals.
5. From your study in this and other courses, identify similarities and differences in the school system and the child welfare system.
6. Identify as many points as you can where the interests of child welfare workers and school social workers intersect. What kinds of collaboration are indicated?

FOR ADDITIONAL STUDY

Addams, J. (1909). *The spirit of youth and the city streets.* New York: Macmillan.

Coles, R. (1971). *Children of crisis: Vol. 2. Migrants, sharecroppers, mountaineers.* Boston: Little, Brown.

Freeman, E. M., & Pennekamp, M. (1988). *Social work practice. Toward a child, family, school, community perspective.* Springfield, IL: Charles C Thomas.

Gallant, C. B. (1982). *Mediation in special education disputes.* Washington, DC: National Association of Social Workers.

Goldstein, B., & Oldham, J. (1979). *Children and work. A study of socialization.* New Brunswick, NJ: Transaction Books.

Salomone, R. C. (1989). Children versus the state: The status of students' constitutional rights. *Caring for America's children. Proceedings of the Academy of Political Science, 37*(2), 182–200.

Zelizer, V. A. (1985). *Pricing the priceless child. The changing social value of children.* New York: Basic Books.

CHAPTER 9

Protecting Children from Neglect and Abuse

In the little world in which children have their existence, whosoever brings them up, there is nothing so finely perceived and so finely felt, as injustice.

Charles Dickens

Chapter Outline

In child welfare and perhaps in all of social services, there is no situation that instigates such concern or outrage as the neglect, abuse, or exploitation of children by parents or others responsible for their care. Fueled by media coverage of sensational instances of abuse and by considerable research and other scholarly attention, the last twenty-five years have witnessed a dramatic new concern for these child victims.

INCIDENCE

No fully accurate figures are available to judge the incidence and prevalence of child neglect and abuse. Estimates have come from three principal sources: (1) the 1975 and 1985 national surveys of family violence (Straus et al., 1980; Straus & Gelles, 1986); (2) the 1980 and 1986 national studies of the incidence of child abuse and neglect (*Study Findings,* 1979, 1988); and (3) the studies that the American Humane Association has produced annually since 1976 on official reporting of child abuse and neglect in each state (American Association, 1986). These studies are not directly comparable with one another, since each measures a somewhat different subset of the total population of abused and neglected children in the United States.

The 1985 national survey of family violence (Straus & Gelles, 1986) measured physical child abuse only, excluding sexual and emotional abuse and all forms of neglect. The study's national probability sample consisted of 1,428 households, with at least one child between ages three and seventeen, and with two caretakers present. The telephone interviews with these caretakers resulted in an 84 percent response rate. The study defined child abuse as acts with a relatively high probability of causing an injury, which the parent used at least once during the study year. These acts were: "kicked, bit, punched, beat up, threatened with a knife or gun, and used a knife or gun" (Straus & Gelles, 1986, p. 468).

The study found that about 1 million children, or 19 for every 1,000 children in the United States, suffered child abuse as defined by the study. This estimate of the incidence of physical child abuse excluded the following acts of parental violence: "pushed, grabbed, or shoved; slapped or spanked; hit or tried to hit with something," and burned or scalded (Straus & Gelles, 1986, p. 467). When the incidence of all these acts were combined with those included in the study's definition of child abuse, the rate of overall violence toward children rose to 620 for every 1,000 children in the United States. All of these figures probably underestimate the actual incidence of violent acts, since the study excluded children from birth to age two and those living in one-parent households, and because those interviewed may have been reluctant to admit committing these acts, although the survey was conducted anonymously over the telephone. The advantage of this study is that it measures acts of violence whether or not they came to the attention of human service professionals, so the estimates may come closer than other studies to measuring the actual incidence of physical child abuse (Straus & Gelles, 1986).

The most comprehensive surveys are the 1980 and 1986 national studies of the incidence of child abuse and neglect (U.S. Department of Health and Human Services, 1979, 1988). The 1986 version defined and measured the incidence of six types of maltreatment: physical, sexual, and emotional abuse; and physical, emotional, and educational neglect. The study also measured the severity of maltreatment, and included children considered seriously endangered because of the parent's abusive or neglectful behavior, though the children had not yet been injured or impaired.

The data consist of cases of child maltreatment that were recognized and reported to the study by "community professionals" in a national probability sample of twenty-nine counties in the United States. The community professionals included personnel in schools, hospitals, police departments, juvenile probation departments, day care centers, mental health agencies, and public welfare and other similar agencies. All cases known to Child Protective Services in the study counties were also included. Cases from all these sources were assessed for conformity to study definitions of abuse and neglect, to arrive at a core estimate of the incidence of maltreatment.

The results of the study, shown in Table 9.1, indicate that 1,584,700 children were maltreated in 1986, for an overall maltreatment rate of 25.2 per 1,000 children. The majority of cases (63 percent) involved neglect, while fewer than half (43 percent) involved abuse. On the severity-endangerment scale, which measured the injury or impairment suffered by the child, moderate injuries predominated (those persisting in

observable form for at least forty-eight hours), which occurred in 60 percent of the cases. These "were followed in frequency by children believed to be endangered by the maltreatment they experienced (19%), then by probable injuries (11%), serious injuries (10%), and fatalities (0.1%)" (U.S. Department of Health and Human Services, 1988, p. xxi). The estimates of the incidence of child abuse and neglect generated by this study probably reflect less than the actual incidence of child maltreatment, since they include only those cases that came to the attention of child protective services or other community professionals. Despite this limitation, this study provides the most comprehensive picture of the extent of various types of child abuse and neglect in the United States. Unless otherwise noted, definitions of maltreatment, abuse, neglect, and the various subcategories of abuse and neglect and corresponding incidence rates reported in this text are from the 1986 National Incidence Study (U.S. Department of Health and Human Services, 1988).

The American Humane Association has been responsible for collecting information on official reports of abuse and neglect made to Child Protective Services agencies in each state since 1976 (American Association, 1986). Their figures indicate the following:

Total 1976 reports	669,000 children
Total 1977 reports	838,000 children
Total 1978 reports	836,000 children
Total 1979 reports	988,000 children
Total 1980 reports	1,154,000 children
Total 1981 reports	1,225,000 children
Total 1982 reports	1,262,000 children
Total 1983 reports	1,477,000 children
Total 1984 reports	1,727,000 children
Percentage change 1976–1984	158%

The national average for confirmed cases from all reports is 42 percent, meaning that in 1984, there were 725,000 confirmed cases. These data must be taken with "a grain of salt." They are subject to idiosyncratic state reporting laws

TABLE 9.1. National Incidence of Child Maltreatment, 1986

Category	1986 Rate[a]	1986 Number of Children	1980–1986 Increase Rate[b]
All maltreatment	25.2	1,584,700[c]	6.5
All abuse	10.7	675,000[c]	3.9
Physical abuse	5.7	358,300	1.8
Sexual abuse	2.5	155,900	1.5
Emotional abuse	3.4	211,100	0.7
All neglect	15.9	1,003,600[c]	3.0
Physical neglect	9.1	571,600	1.3
Emotional neglect	3.5	233,100	−0.1
Educational neglect	4.6	292,100	1.9
Severity-endangerment			
Fatal	0.02	1,100	0.0
Serious	2.5	160,000	0.4
Moderate	15.1	952,600	5.5
Probable	2.8	173,700	0.5
Endangered	4.7	297,200	N/A[d]

[a]Per 1,000 children in population in the United States.
[b]Difference in rate of maltreatment between the 1980 and the 1986 surveys.
[c]Cases involving both abuse and neglect are counted in both categories, so the *All abuse* and *All neglect* categories sum to more than the *All maltreatment* category. Because a case could be included in more than one of the subcategories, the subcategories total to more than the corresponding category total.
[d]Data not collected in 1980.
(*Source:* U.S. Department of Health and Human Services, National Center on Child Abuse and Neglect. [1988]. *Study Findings, Study of National Incidence and Prevalence of Child Abuse and Neglect.* Washington, DC: Government Printing Office.)

and generally involve only cases reported to the state child protection agency. A count of reported cases is a serious underestimate of the actual incidence of child abuse, particularly of the "hidden" abuse that results in mild or moderate injury and goes unreported. Schene (1987) estimated that only about one child had been reported to Child Protective Services for every seven identified as abused in the Family Violence Study. Only 46 percent of the maltreated children identified by community professionals in the National Incidence Study were reported to Child Protective Services (U.S. Department of Health and Human Services, 1988). The confirmation rate, based heavily on legal standards, is also an underestimate. The advantages of the American Humane studies are that they are produced annually, they are the only series to include cases reported by neighbors and other nonprofessionals, and they provide information on family and child characteristics of cases in

the public child protective system. Trends suggested by data from each of these studies will be discussed in the Trends and Issues section at the end of this chapter.

Behind each statistic is a child, a child whose immediate safety, comfort, welfare, and future development are jeopardized or whose very life may be at stake. Parents also exist behind these numbers, parents who may have their child removed from their care or at least have their autonomy as parents eroded. For society, the costs are similarly high. Balancing society's desire to maintain and support the integrity of the family while protecting the welfare of its children is a complicated proposition demanding clarification of our national values. The care and protection of these children consumes large amounts of money. Research suggesting that child maltreatment is linked to future delinquency and crime indicates that the indirect costs to society may be much higher than the direct costs (Polansky et al., 1981, pp. 120–121; Sandberg, 1989).

AIMS AND SPECIAL ATTRIBUTES OF PROTECTIVE SERVICES

Child protective services are intended to guard children from further detrimental experiences or conditions in their immediate situations, bring under control and reduce the risks to their safety or well-being, prevent further neglect or abuse, and restore adequate parental functioning whenever possible or, if necessary, take steps to remove children from their own homes and establish them in foster situations in which they will receive more adequate care. Synonyms for the term "protective," such as "sheltering," "saving," "covering," "defending," and "harboring," all suggest some identifiable risk and emphasize the protective purposes of the social services.

Protective services today reflect the convictions that among parents whose level of child care is unacceptably poor, many can be reached in behalf of their children and can be helped to improve their parental functioning. The focus of child protective services is on both the investigation of reported maltreatment that initiates agency responsibility and on stabilizing and improving the children's own homes by helping parents to perform more responsibly in relation to their children's care. Protective services also are concerned with social planning to organize and coordinate collaborative efforts among community agencies involved in the child protection system (Carroll & Haase, 1987).

Child protective services are characterized by certain distinctive features: (1) the way in which service is initiated; (2) the increased agency responsibility that accompanies work with parents of children at risk; (3) the kind of agency sanction, or community authorization; and (4) the balance required in the use of authority in relation to the rights of parent, child, and society.

1. *Child protective services are authoritative.* The protective agency initiates the service by approaching the parents about a complaint from some element of the community, for example, police, schools, public health nurses, neighbors, or relatives. Since the protective service is involuntary, the situation that justifies an agency's "intruding" into family life must strongly suggest that parents are not providing the love or basic care a child needs for healthy growth and development.

2. *Child protective services carry increased social agency responsibility, since they are directed toward families where there are children at risk.* Children are highly vulnerable when their homes lack normal levels of care or protection. Children cannot make effective claims by themselves for the enforcement of their rights. If just and quick initiation of services does not follow a complaint from the community, lasting harm may result for a child who is experiencing physical abuse or neglect.

Social workers in the protective agency must act promptly; their decisions about the nature or seriousness of the complaint and the action to be taken must be based on accurate fact-finding. Moreover, the social agency cannot withdraw from the situation if it finds the parents uncooperative or resistant to taking help, as it may in situations where individuals have voluntarily sought help. Once protective service has been initiated, the agency can responsibly withdraw only when the level of child care in the home has improved to acceptable levels, or when satisfactory care has been arranged elsewhere, as in a relative's home or in foster care.

The protective agency, then, has a high degree of responsibility to the child at risk; to the child's parents, who are usually found to be experiencing great stress; and to the community, which charges the agency to act for it in the provision of child protection.

3. *Child protective services involve agency sanction from the community.* A child protective agency has been delegated responsibility by statute or by charter to receive reports

about instances of unacceptable child care, to investigate them, and if necessary to initiate service to the family even though the parents have not requested help. Other social agencies expect and look to the child protection agency to act. Having one agency in the community providing protective service to all who need it is an advantage "so that there is no confusion as to where to refer cases and the community can have a concentrated focus on protective service. What is 'everybody's business' tends to be 'nobody's business'" (Child Welfare League, 1960b, p. 42).

The provision of child protective services is regarded as a fundamental public agency responsibility. Norris Class (1963) has pointed out that the provision of protection is as basic and essential for children as the provision of education, a governmental responsibility. Voluntary agencies were pioneers in establishing child protective services, but the trend has been for the public sector to take exclusive responsibility. By the 1970s, protective services under public welfare auspices were present in all states, the District of Columbia, Puerto Rico, the Virgin Islands, and Guam (Hildenbrand et al., 1979). Concern about child neglect and abuse has spread throughout the country, and public agencies in all the states have attempted to strengthen and extend their services more effectively.

4. *Child protective services require a crucial balance in the use of the agency's authority.* Child neglect or abuse is both a social and a legal problem. The fact that the agency approaches a family about its problems without a request from the family itself denotes some invasion of privacy, however well motivated the services may be. Furthermore, an integral part of the protective agency's methods is to reserve the right to invoke the authority of the court by filing a petition alleging parental neglect or abuse if the parents do not improve their level of care. This "threat," implied or acknowledged, is recognized by the family and may be perceived as either subtle or overt coercion—pressure to cooperate or conform to other ways of child care. The protective agency has the difficult task of maintaining a just and effective balance in its use of authority in relation to the child at risk, whose rights and protection depend on other persons; to parents, whose right to rear their children without outside intervention is being questioned; and to society, which has delegated a responsibility for the protection of children from neglect or abuse.

These four attributes of child protective services will assume fuller meaning as we consider the specific social services which are extended and the issues involved in doing so. But first it is important to look at the origins and subsequent growth of the protective service idea.

HISTORICAL DEVELOPMENT OF PROTECTIVE SERVICES

Early Attitudes toward the Treatment of Children

Accepted ideas on ways to rear children have undergone many changes through the centuries. We tend to lose sight of how recently the general public has strongly objected to indifferent parental care or to aggressive actions toward children by other members of society.

For many hundreds of years, history has recorded mistreatment of children. The Bible contains examples of cruelty to children, including Herod's order to slay "all the children that were in Bethlehem, and in all the coasts thereof, from two years old and under" (Matthew 2:16). Infanticide by different means was carried out in a number of societies to assure that only strong, healthy infants would survive who could become able to serve the state in combat and to rid oneself of "undesirable" offspring—females, or out-of-wedlock children, or any infant who did not seem to be a promising child. Parents who were poor sometimes put children out, exposed to weather and hunger, to escape the burdens of rearing them; richer parents often did the same to avoid dividing property into too small parts. Even in the Roman family, children were the father's property, and he had absolute power over them, including the privilege of ordering their death, selling them, or offering them in sacrifice. Speculators mutilated or maimed children before setting them up as beggars so that their injuries would arouse pity and increase their rewards from begging.

Violence toward children and youth has been expressed in endless ways in the history of this country. Deeply rooted in many places, it has been resistant to control. Indifference and inaction in the face of violence to children was hardest to identify when it occurred within the family. It was also difficult to uncover or to challenge when practiced by social institutions. (Polier, 1989, p. 27)

During colonial times and even later, parents often enforced absolute obedience to the demands of adults or emphasized breaking the children's will to free them from the evil disposition with which they supposedly had been born. Drugs, particularly laudanum (a form of opium), were given by parents or servants "almost indiscriminately" to infants to stop their crying. Inquests made in the years 1837 and 1838 show that 52 infants were included in a total of 186 deaths due to opium (Sunley, 1963, pp. 155–160). Flogging and caning were used extensively and brutally by schoolmasters. In 1861 Halliday reported his personal discovery of many instances of cruelty to children by their parents in New York City. He recorded this situation, which parallels in certain respects cases of today's "battered child":

In the corner of a room where a German shoemaker is at work, is a large wood trunk or chest, such as is seen in numbers conveyed from every vessel bringing German immigrants to our port. Seated on the floor, with its back against the chest, is a child twenty months old. The woman at the wash-tub is the shoemaker's wife, and the babe is her child by a previous husband. She has two older children, who make themselves useful in gathering fuel, and in other ways. For *these* the shoe-making step-father appears to have some fondness; but for the poor little thing sitting on the floor, only hate. From others we learned that he abused it daily and envied it the little bread it ate. If the child cried, he would beat it cruelly; and so long had he continued this, that no noise of any kind would come from the child's lips from morning until night. He would not allow the mother to show the child any attentions, and from want and neglect it had become a mere skeleton.

Its place was always in the corner on the floor leaning against the old ship chest, with not a particle of anything between it and the hard boards; and when the little creature was taken to the Home for the Friendless, its bones in several places were worn through the skin, forming sores. The mother had a mother's feelings, but dared not express them in the presence of this fiendish brute. The terrible suffering and neglect of this little thing resulted in its death, a few weeks after it was taken to the institution. (Halliday, 1861, pp. 102–106)

As we saw in Chapter 8, incredible exploitation of children in employment situations persisted well into the twentieth century, again demonstrating how recently a fuller measure of attention has been given to the rights of children and the necessity for their protection from unscrupulous, uncaring adults.

Beginnings of Care for Neglected Children

An unusual statute marked a beginning of legislated assumption of responsibility for neglected children. It was passed in Massachusetts in 1735 for the city of Boston because that town had "grown considerably populous and the idle and poor much increased among them." The statute provided that when persons

were unable, or neglected to provide necessaries for the sustenance and support of their children,

. . . and where persons bring up their children in such gross ignorance that they do not know, or are not able to distinguish, the alphabet, or twenty-four letters, at the age of six years, the overseers might bind out such children to good families for a decent and christian education. (Folks, 1911, pp. 167–168)

Various states passed legislation from 1790 to 1825 that recognized the needs of neglected children to the extent of authorizing the binding out, or commitment to almshouses, of children who were found begging on the street or whose parents were beggars. Homer Folks cited the year 1825 as the beginning of more general recognition and application of the principle that public authorities have a right and duty to intervene in cases of parental cruelty or gross neglect of children and "to remove the children by force if necessary, and place them under surroundings more favorable for their development" (Folks, 1911, pp. 168–169).

Before the end of the nineteenth century, special laws were passed in nearly all states to provide for the protection of children from neglect or ill-treatment by authorizing the courts to remove them from parents or guardians and commit them to some proper place of care.

Societies for the Prevention of Cruelty to Children

The new laws provided a legal basis for acting in behalf of neglected or abused children if they became objects of attention by a child-saving agency or a children's institution, or if the police chose to bring the situation to the attention of the court. However, there were no clear lines of responsibility among agencies or officials for *finding* neglected and abused children unless families were already requiring support from public or voluntary relief funds. Organizations were needed to bring about the enforcement of existing laws for the "rescue" of neglected children. As a consequence, voluntary societies for the prevention of cruelty to children (SPCCs)

were established, the first in New York City in 1875.

Examining the circumstances under which the first SPCC came into existence provides an aid to understanding the purposes and focus of the early societies and the means by which some late-nineteenth-century reformers attempted to act as child advocates. Late in the year 1873, Etta Wheeler, a church worker visiting tenement homes in New York City to try to relieve the suffering of sick and lonely people, heard the story of a nine-year-old girl who for two years had been cruelly whipped and frequently left alone, locked in an inner room during a long day. The thin partitions between the tenement apartments let other occupants hear the child's cries and other evidence of the cruel treatment inflicted on her by the man and woman with whom she lived. They had obtained the child from an institution at two years of age, but no inquiry about her well-being had been made by institution personnel during the intervening seven years. Concerned occupants of the house had not known to whom to complain or how to get help for the child. The tenement visitor went to great lengths to investigate the report and establish evidence of the abuse and neglect. Then, when she sought advice as to how to obtain protection for the child, no one seemed to know of any legal means to "rescue" the child. Up to that time the legal removal of children from cruel or neglectful parents was rare if not impossible. Finally, the tenement visitor took her report to Henry Bergh, who had founded the New York Society for the Prevention of Cruelty to Animals. The popular version of the case has been that, when Mrs. Wheeler approached Bergh, he readily responded that the child as a member of the animal kingdom was entitled to protection under the laws against animal cruelty and the aegis of the animal protection society.

Two legendary aspects of the Mary Ellen story—that the child was rescued as a member of the animal kingdom, and that the chance discovery of her cruel treatment and her rescue led directly and promptly to the beginning of a widespread child protection movement—have been accepted as fact even into contemporary social welfare history (Payne, 1916; Coleman, 1924; Lundberg, 1947; Allen & Morton, 1961; Mulford, 1971; Lystad, 1979; DeFrancis, 1987). However, the rescue of Mary Ellen was not accomplished so readily as has been recorded (Costin, n.d.). Well before the Mary Ellen case, Bergh had been urged to interest his society in the all too evident instances of cruelty to children. These appeals he had ignored or resisted on the basis that cruelty to children was entirely out of his sphere of influence. His philanthropic interests were invested in the New York Society for the Prevention of Cruelty to Animals, which he had founded in 1866, and he was reluctant to be diverted from his crusade for animal protection (Steele, 1942). However, for a constellation of reasons, the Mary Ellen case was difficult for him to ignore. Consequently, he instructed his society's counsel, Elbridge T. Gerry, to look into the matter and if warranted, to file a petition to have the child removed from her present custodians and placed with persons who would treat her more kindly. However, Bergh stated clearly that he was acting only as a humane citizen, and in no sense in his official capacity as President of the Society for the Prevention of Cruelty to Animals. The abusing foster mother was sentenced to prison and Mary Ellen eventually gained loving parents. In 1875 the New York Society for the Prevention of Cruelty to Children was established and Elbridge Gerry became its president.

In a study of political agenda setting for social problems, Barbara Nelson noted that "a single incident, however momentous, does not guarantee that concerned individuals will view the event as an example of a larger problem, and organize to solve it" (1984, p. 5). Large social movements rarely, if ever, are traceable to accidental causal beginnings. The Mary Ellen instance of private violence becoming "public property" is best explained by a fortuitous coming together and fusing of varying and sometimes competing factors. Among such factors were these: (1) the wide and often lurid publicity given the Mary Ellen case; (2) Mary Ellen was an "illegitimate" child and beaten by someone other than her natural parents, a circumstance that muted the old precept of a parent's right to determine the nature and severity of a child's punishment; (3) awakened public awareness of the plight of children in a system of child-saving where public authority added to the neglect of children by failing to set standards and supervise child placement activities; (4) the women's rights movement of the 1870s and its overarching influence on various thrusts toward social justice, one of which was reform toward child care and child nurture that emphasized the ideal of "protected childhood" and fostered cultural rejection of child abuse and punitive corporal punishment (Costin, n.d.).

In a study of the politics and history of family violence, Linda Gordon observed that the child protection movement closely integrated gender, class, religious, and ethnic goals. "It never represented the interests of a single homogeneous dominant group." Among an array of influences, she credited the women's rights movement of the 1870s with being "most influential in confronting, publicizing, and demanding action against family violence," first acknowledged as cruelty to children, and later as violence toward women and other family members (1988, pp. 57–64).

Another significant influence on the movement to prevent cruelty to children was a publicly perceived link between characteristics of children and animals. An affinity between animals and children is ancient, illustrated in Aesop's *Fables,* animal stories told to illustrate human faults and virtues. Even before the Mary Ellen story became public, the press had alluded to children as "human animals" who were as worthy of protection from cruelty as were horses, cattle, and dogs. The humane literature of the time also added to this perception by references to children as "little animals" and emphasis on the common defenselessness of animals and children and their shared right to protection (Costin, n.d.).

The formation of the New York Society for the Prevention of Cruelty to Children (SPCC) triggered a rapid growth of other child cruelty societies. By 1898 more than 200 SPCCs had come into existence in the United States, with the model being put into place in foreign countries as well (*New York Times,* 1898, Feb. 20, p. 2). Some were established societies for the prevention of cruelty to animals where the function of preventing cruelty to children was simply added on in the title—thereafter referred to as Societies for the Prevention of Cruelty to Animals and Children, another reinforcement of the idea of commonalities.

Whatever the effects of a publicly perceived link between animals and children, the most powerful influence of the animal societies on the "discovery" of cruelty to children and the child protection movement that followed was this: The animal organizations offered a tested model of a carefully circumscribed organizational purpose, policy, and strategies of intervention into instances of cruel treatment. The animal movement also supplied another essential ingredient—a proved and impassioned leader, Elbridge T. Gerry, who had emerged from the Mary Ellen case as the recognized authority who could lead and expand the child rescue movement. The new wave of support for the prevention of cruelty to children offered Gerry an attractive opportunity, one that he welcomed and was eminently qualified for—the development and application of law that would expand judicial power in the area of domestic governance, a form of "judicial patriarchy" that in the name of reform would still maintain male supremacy in decisions about parental rights and definitions of acceptable parental care (Costin, n.d.).

The primary function of the new societies was to investigate cases of alleged cruelty or neglect, present the facts to the courts, and assist the police and public prosecutors in bringing to justice the adults who were responsible for crimes against children. Although these societies were largely private bodies, agents were sometimes given police powers.

These new societies sponsored the passage of child protective or "wrongs-to-children" laws. In New York the SPCC drafted an act to prevent the establishment or spread of the scandalous "baby farms." In addition, action was directed against the *padrone* system of importing children who had been sold by their parents in Italy, against abuses in the employment of children in theatrical and acrobatic performances, and against other similar practices that endangered child life. An amendment to the New York State Penal Code in 1892, brought about through the efforts of the New York SPCC, prohibited children who had been brought to court from mingling with adult criminals—a step toward the children's court later to be established (Lundberg, 1947, p. 104).

Some of the SPCCs came to exercise a high degree of control over the disposition of all classes of children coming before the courts (Folks, 1911, p. 175). "Cruelty agents" began to investigate all cases involving children, not just those of neglected or abused children. They assumed an advisory role to the court magistrates, recommending whether a commitment should be made and to what particular institution a child should be sent.

Folks cited additional significant influences of the societies. Although first supported wholly by private funds, they generally came to require aid from public tax sources, thus extending the subsidy system. Also, their single-minded and vigorous approach to the enforcement of laws to protect children and prosecute parents substantially increased the numbers of children becoming wards of public or private charity. Because the societies saw their overriding purpose to be the *rescue* of children, they displayed little or no interest in helping parents to reestablish a home for the return of the children, or in placing children in foster homes.

Usually they have not cooperated to any extent with placing-out societies, . . . but have rather become the feeders of institutions, both reformatory and charitable. . . . Without detracting from the great credit due to such societies for the rescue of children from cruel parents or immoral surroundings, . . . their influence in the upbuilding of very large institutions, and their very general failure to urge the benefits of adoption for young children, have been unfortunate. (Folks, 1911, pp. 176–177)

Folks believed the most favorable influence of the societies had been as a moral restraint on parents "who would be cruel if they dared."

Probably their greatest beneficence has been, not to the children who have come under their care, but to the vastly larger number whose parents have restrained angry tempers and vicious impulses through fear of "the Cruelty." (Folks, 1911, p. 177)

A Shifting Philosophy in Protective Work

"Vital and fundamental" differences in viewpoints were found among some of the early SPCCs as to the basic purpose and role of protective work. For example, the New York SPCC embodied a primary focus on child rescue—ferreting out and investigating cases of alleged cruelty or neglect and presenting facts to the court—and stood aloof from other children's agencies. In contrast, the Massachusetts SPCC saw the tendency of anticruelty societies to become arms of the police to be a dangerous direction and maintained that the need for prosecution of parents was "a diminishing phase" of protective work. This SPCC gave greater recognition to the importance of unity in all work with children on the basis that protective work was but one part of a broader responsibility for improving conditions surrounding child life. It held that preventive and remedial measures were needed to use in behalf of children and their parents (McCrea, 1910, p. 142).

This latter viewpoint has prevailed since the passage of the first statutes in behalf of neglected and abused children and the formation of the child-saving and anticruelty societies. The foremost aim of protective service today is to strengthen the child's family so that she or he can remain in the care of her or his own parents. To achieve their goals, child protective services must be planned and administered as one of a number of essential social welfare measures.

Recent Antecedents: Federal Legislation

In 1974, under the sponsorship of Senator Walter Mondale, the Child Abuse Prevention and Treatment Act was passed. This act required the Department of Health and Human Services to establish a National Center on Child Abuse and Neglect, which would be a clearinghouse for the development and transmittal of information on research and demonstration programs in child protection. The Center was authorized also to make small grants to states for innovative programs.

In order to receive funds, states had to meet certain eligibility requirements. Only three states met these requirements initially, but remarkably over the next six years most states made the changes needed to qualify for federal aid. Eligibility requirements included: a law giving immunity from prosecution to those reporting instances of child abuse and neglect; mandatory reporting laws, which require certain categories of professionals to report suspected abuse and neglect, and encourage nonprofessionals to do so; and provisions for dissemination of information to the general public on prevention and treatment of child maltreatment (Besharov, 1985). Although funding of this act has been meager, ranging from $19 million in 1975 to nearly $30 million in 1986, it has greatly affected Child Protective Services in the states through its requirement that states pass reporting laws (Besharov, 1985; *Abused Children,* 1987).

In 1975, President Ford signed into law Title XX of the Social Security Act. One of the provisions of the Act was that protective services were mandatory for states wanting to claim federal dollars. Title XX is the largest source of federal funds available to states for child protection. Its effect has been weakened by the Omnibus Reconciliation Act of 1981, which cut the total annual appropriation by 21 percent and eliminated requirements on how the money was to be spent. The $2.6 million appropriated in 1986 was spent by states on a variety of social service programs, and most states have experienced a substantial loss of resources for child protection and child welfare (*Abused Children,* 1987).

THE DEFINITIONAL DILEMMA

There is no consensual definition of either child abuse or neglect. The type of extreme cases most frequently reported by the media offer few problems, but such cases are relatively rare. The great majority of cases fall into more ambiguous categories in which complex sets of factors must be taken into account. The difficulty and the importance of developing clear definitions can be understood if viewed as a society's attempt to establish minimum standards for the care of children. "At the very foundation of research, treatment, prevention, or legislative and judicial decision-making lies the question of what constitutes child abuse and neglect. In a large, pluralistic nation, the answer may be an impossible dream" (Giovannoni & Becerra, 1979).

Child neglect and abuse are related, and elements of each may be present in a situation requiring protective services. The term "child maltreatment" combines abuse and neglect, and refers to both types of situations. Maltreatment may be defined as a situation in which "through purposive acts or marked inattention to the child's basic needs, behavior of a parent, parent-substitute or other adult caretaker caused foreseeable and avoidable injury or impairment to a child or materially contributed to unreasonable prolongation or worsening of an existing injury or impairment" (U.S. Department of Health and Human Services, 1979, pp. 39, 42). However, many people believe that abuse and neglect are quite different from one another and should be studied as separate entities.

Any conclusions about who *abuses and* how much *they abuse depend upon a culturally validated definition of what abuse is. (Garbarino & Ebata, 1983, p. 773)*

In general, abuse is thought of as "any nonaccidental physical injury inflicted on a child by a parent or other caretaker deliberately or in anger" (Justice & Justice, 1976). Abuse is therefore an act of commission. Types of abuse would include physical abuse (battered child), sexual abuse, and emotional abuse.

Polansky and coworkers have offered the following definition of neglect:

> Child neglect may be defined as a condition in which a caretaker responsible for the child either deliberately or by extraordinary inattentiveness permits the child to experience avoidable present suffering and/or fails to provide one or more of the ingredients generally deemed essential for developing a person's physical, intellectual and emotional capacities.

Neglect is often viewed as an act of omission rather than an act of commission. This definition is in line with current social work thinking in recognizing that (1) a neglectful caretaker may be someone other than a parent; (2) the neglect many not be consciously motivated; (3) allowing the child to experience suffering that could have been avoided can be considered neglect even though there may be no certain, long-term damaging effects; (4) neglect, like abuse, may have serious, even lethal, effects; and (5) the definition can be expected to change and become less ambiguous as knowledge about the phenomenon becomes more certain (Polansky et al., 1975, pp. 3–5).

These definitions of abuse and neglect are not without problems. The first problem is distinguishing between acts of abuse that are deliberate or intentional and those that are not. Many times child abuse reflects a mixture of intentional and chance elements, as for example, when harm to the child results from parental discipline. Some unintentional accidents may be the result of neglecting the supervision or physical care of a child. Specifying intentions or motivations is hazardous at best.

A second problem is distinguishing less than optimal care from that which is actually harmful. It is this problem that confounds protective service workers and juvenile justice officials. Both Meier (1964) and Polansky et al. (1975) discuss child neglect as falling somewhere along a continuum of child care—from adequate care, through cause for grave concern, to neglect. Delaney, a juvenile and family court judge, also uses the idea of a continuum of child care in relation to abuse, with gradations of mistreatment at one end "ranging from the grossest, most obvious physical injury to subtle, intangible, emotional deprivation" (1976, p. 344).

The 1986 version of the National Incidence Study addressed this problem by establishing two sets of definitions: one requires that children have suffered demonstrable harm (injury or impairment); the other also includes situations where the child's health and safety are seriously endangered by abusive or neglectful treatment, even though no injury has yet occurred (U.S. Department of Health and Human Services, 1988, pp. 2–6, 2–7).

Factors Influencing Definitions

The definitions of abuse and neglect vary on the basis of (1) a state's legal provisions, (2) attitudes toward the family and child-rearing behaviors held by individual communities, and (3) the professional decisions social workers make

about extending protective services beyond a preliminary investigation (Valentine et al., 1984).

The Legal Provisions.   In every state, people, through their legislators, have provided a legal framework for society's intervention into family life when parental care appears to be neglectful, abusive, or cruel, or in some way dangerously inadequate. Legal provisions are contained in the criminal law, juvenile court acts, and child abuse reporting laws (Paulsen, 1974).

In the criminal code of every state there are punishable crimes, including murder, assault, and sexual exploitation, for example, that can be applied to parents who inflict injury on their children. Often, criminal prosecution is an undesirable response to abuse and neglect. Imprisonment divides the family, and the hostility engendered by the adversarial proceedings can make it impossible to establish a therapeutic casework relationship with the family (Paulsen, 1974). On the other hand, sometimes arrest and criminal prosecution are appropriate. Jailing the perpetrator can solve the immediate problem of protecting the child by getting the adult out of the house. If the adult is not detained, the child may have to go through the additional trauma of being removed from home and placed in foster care. Some policy makers believe that criminal prosecution in some cases reaffirms community standards on what constitutes unacceptable domestic behavior. The Attorney General's Task Force (1984) recommended that "family violence should be recognized and responded to as a criminal activity," and that law enforcement agencies should "presume that arrest, consistent with state law, is the appropriate response to situations of serious injury to the victim . . . or other imminent danger to the victim" (pp. 10, 17).

Juvenile court statutes in all the states, with their varying definitions of neglect and abuse, also serve as a determinant of the conditions under which intervention into family life is justified in behalf of children. The differences in statutory language indicate what evidence is necessary to sustain a charge of neglect. In some, there must be evidence of direct parental involvement in a child's neglected or abused condition, while in others, an inference of parental responsibility may be sufficient, as in the case of an infant severely malnourished or repeatedly injured, who is in the custody of his or her parents and cared for most of the time by them.

In 1977, the Juvenile Justice Standards Project proposed new standards for governing child neglect proceedings. The report reflects a trend in judicial thinking that argues for a curtailment of judicial discretion by setting more specific and more stringent criteria for state intervention into family life. The proposed standards require that the child must have suffered or is likely to suffer some specific harm and that there is reason to believe that state intervention will benefit the child (Institute of Judicial Administration, 1977).

Child abuse reporting laws are a third kind of legislative provision reflecting a community's unwillingness to countenance serious injury inflicted on children. When children are neglected or abused, they can scarcely receive protection unless their condition becomes known to a social agency or the courts. Reporting statutes are designed to increase the probability that children injured through mistreatment will be identified and brought to the attention of a protective social agency and/or a law enforcement authority. A child abuse reporting statute, in effect, is a casefinding technique.

Prior to the passage of these laws, cases of serious abuse frequently were not brought to public knowledge. The abuse occurred within the privacy of the child's own home; he or she was usually too young to speak out. Neighbors, relatives, teachers, and other persons in the community were reluctant to become involved or to believe that certain parents could be so harmful to their children. With new knowledge and diagnostic skills in pediatric medicine, physicians became able to detect with far greater certainty that particular children had been deliberately injured by another person. Even so, they frequently were unwilling to report such cases because of fear of litigation against them by angry parents, or reluctance to divulge what they considered to be confidential information between themselves and their patients, or lack of knowledge or confidence about whom to report the situation to, so that prompt and constructive help would be given.

In the deluge of interest and publicity—in medical and social work literature, and in newspapers, magazines, and television programs—which followed the identification of the battered child syndrome by Kempe et al. in 1962, it became apparent that physicians had a special responsibility for reporting instances of child abuse, since they have the particular skills to detect inflicted injury and the opportunity to see a child in a setting that permits a thorough examination and diagnosis (Kempe et al., 1962). If physicians were to be required to report such cases uniformly, they would have to be given immunity from resultant legal action.

The American Academy of Pediatrics supported mandatory reporting legislation. The Children's Bureau and the American Humane Association each published guidelines for model legislation in 1963 as a way of assisting states to draft effective reporting laws. In the following several years, child abuse legislation was passed by the individual states with almost unprecedented speed (Children's Bureau, 1963; American Humane Association, 1963). The 1974 Child Abuse Prevention and Treatment Act (P.L. 93–247) gave further impetus to passage of uniform laws.

All states now have some kind of child abuse reporting statutes. All give immunity to physicians against litigation for having reported, and most of them make it compulsory to report. In addition to physicians, hospitals are usually required to report instances of child abuse. In some states, other professional persons, such as teachers, social workers, nurses, and day care personnel, and in a few instances anyone who suspects a case of child abuse, are covered by the statute.

Problems Associated with Reporting.   The last fifteen years have witnessed radically improved performance in the reporting of suspected child maltreatment. Much of the increase in the number of reports can be attributed to improved reporting, rather than to an actual increase in the incidence of abuse and neglect. Before the reporting laws were enacted, responsibility for investigating reports of abuse and neglect was fragmented among various agencies, such as the courts, the police, welfare, and child protection agencies. Now a system has been created in which child protection agencies are expected to take major responsibility for investigating reports of abuse and neglect. The reporting process is strengthened by publicity campaigns, twenty-four-hour hot-lines, and administrative linkages between agencies likely to report, such as schools, welfare, and visiting nurses, and the legally mandated child protection agency in the community. Recognition of abuse and neglect is improving among those mandated to report, and this results in increased reporting.

In spite of these improvements, many problems remain. The plight of many vulnerable children continues to go unreported. Although legally mandated to do so, many professionals do not report cases in which they suspect child maltreatment. Reasons for this reluctance include lack of clarity on which situations require reporting, concern about confidentiality and the effect of reporting on the therapeutic relationship, concern about lawsuits or reprisals from clients, reluctance to become involved, and a belief that reporting won't help the situation. Most professionals who do report are in the public sector; perhaps as few as 5 percent of all reports are made by private practitioners such as physicians and psychologists (Stein, 1984). Lack of definitional clarity may be the most serious obstacle to improved reporting by professionals.

An ambitious study done by Giovannoni and Becerra found that professionals vary considerably both on the types of behavior labeled neglectful or abusive and on the severity of the behavior warranting some action (1979).

A second problem is the large number of reports that, upon investigation, are found to be without enough basis to warrant further action. These "unfounded" or "unsubstantiated" reports constitute about three-fifths of all reports made to child protection agencies (American Association, 1986). One troublesome aspect of the large number of unfounded reports is that agency resources are necessarily deployed to investigate reports while children already identified as abused are insufficiently served by the agency. The large increase in reports of child maltreatment has not been accompanied by an increase in appropriations for child protection agencies, so staff must spend time investigating new cases rather than treating families already known to them.

The large number of unfounded reports also affects the credibility of the agency. If those reporting begin to perceive that their reports are likely to be unfounded, or the family is not helped as a result of the report, they may lose confidence in the system and be less likely to report suspected cases (Schene, 1987).

Unfounded reports are of concern also because of the possible conflict between a family's right to privacy and the state's interest in protecting children who may be abused or maltreated. A protective service investigation is intrusive. Workers must inquire into intimate details of family life. The children usually must be questioned, and also friends, school personnel, day care workers, clergy, and others who know the family. The fact of the investigation is stigmatizing, even if the report is later unfounded. Justice Hugo Black pointed out that the parent "is charged with conduct—failure to care properly for her children—which may be viewed as reprehensible and morally wrong by a majority of society" (*Carter v. Kaufman,* 1971, p. 959). Critics question a system that infringes on the family's right to privacy without giving much assurance that the lives of children will be improved as a result of this infringement (Stein, 1984; Besharov, 1985).

Community Attitudes.   One of the forces shaping a community's prevailing definition of neglect and abuse is the kind of attitudes toward family life and child-rearing behaviors held by its members. These attitudes are reflected in the types of situations that persons select to refer to a protective agency. By such choices, a community

> sets up the boundaries within which protective action can take place and establishes a culturally sanctioned definition for neglect that expresses community values, norms, and assumption of responsibility. (Boehm, 1964, p. 454)

When Katz et al. analyzed the child neglect and abuse laws in America, they concluded, broadly speaking, that

> child neglect occurs when the dominant expectations for parenthood are not met—when a parent fails to provide for a child's needs according to the preferred values of the community. . . . Primarily, neglect denotes conduct in conflict with the child-rearing standards of the dominant culture and determination of neglect is based on social as well as legal judgements. (Katz et al., 1976, p. 5)

Analyses of sources of reports to child protective agencies have found that community people are the source of about half the reports, a rather high percentage considering that they are not required to report. However, their reports are more likely to be unfounded after investigation than are those of professionally mandated reporters (American Association, 1986). These findings support those of Giovannoni and Becerra (1979) and Rose (1989), whose studies revealed that community lay people, in general, view child mistreatment as more serious than do professionals and are less likely to make fine distinctions with regard to the seriousness of the cases.

Because a disproportionate number of those reported for abuse and neglect are poor (Russell & Trainor, 1984), the question arises as to whether poor people have different standards for acceptable ways of rearing children than does the middle class. There is also the question of whether social workers and courts try to impose middle-class standards of child rearing on poor people. Polansky and Williams (1978) studied attitudes toward neglect of lower- and middle-class Caucasian mothers. The researchers designed a series of vignettes on child rearing at home and asked respondents to rate them. They found an impressive level of agreement among the two groups of mothers in judging situations as neglectful. Where a difference existed, working-class mothers tended to place more emphasis on physical care and less on cognitive/emotional aspects of child rearing than did middle-class mothers. The authors concluded that "with respect to the evaluation of elements essential in child care, opinion in our society is surprisingly unified. . . . Therefore, parents who have low standards of child care are probably demonstrating individual incapacity to provide better care rather than following norms sanctioned by some reference group" (p. 400).

Do different ethnic and racial groups vary in their attitudes toward child maltreatment? This question has just begun to receive attention. Giovannoni and Becerra (1979), studying attitudinal differences toward child maltreatment among Hispanics, blacks, and whites in Los Angeles, and Rose (1989), studying these same ethnic groups in Chicago, found similar results. Overall, attitudes and values about abuse and neglect did not differ for different ethnic groups. Where a difference existed, blacks and Hispanics rated maltreatment vignettes as more serious than did whites.

Much remains to be learned about differences among ethnic and racial groups in defining what constitutes child maltreatment. Garbarino and Ebata (1983) have raised key issues. (1) A major difficulty is to separate the effects of socioeconomic status from those of ethnicity. "When class and ethnicity are confounded, we always run the risk of confusing legitimate ethnic differences in style with the deleterious effects of socioeconomic deprivation" (Garbarino & Ebata, 1983, p. 774). (2) Level of acculturation into dominant American society may make a difference; isolated ethnic enclaves may have culturally specific attitudes toward maltreatment that are no longer shared by assimilated members of this same ethnic group. (3) Ethnic groups may vary in attitude toward specific types of maltreatment, or other situationally specific factors: for example, the abuser's relationship to the child; chemical dependency of the abuser; child characteristics, such as handicapped, born out of wedlock (Long, 1986; Korbin, 1987). (4) Cultural factors may bear indirectly on child maltreatment, such as: the embeddedness of child rearing in extended family contexts; cultural value placed on children; cultural coping mechanisms that deflect stress and frustration away from the child; ease or difficulty of acculturation into dominant society (Korbin, 1987).

While cultures differ in their definitions of child maltreatment, all societies have criteria for behaviors that fall outside the realm of acceptability. (Korbin, 1987, p. 26)

Social Work Decisions to Extend Protective Services. Social workers in protective agencies contribute to a prevailing definition of neglect and abuse by the decisions they make in selecting those families for whom full-scale protective service is considered necessary and those for whom no further action is planned after the preliminary investigation. These key gatekeeping decisions help determine who will be released from the system and who will be retained. Those retained will have access to services available only to families identified as abusive or neglectful, but also will be subject to possibly involuntary agency surveillance of family life. Because these decisions are so important, investigators have tried to ascertain the extent to which workers use a consistent set of criteria in making them. Craft and colleagues (1980) studied factors that influence protective service workers to recommend court involvement in abuse cases. They identified the following as influential: (1) severity of injury; (2) explanations of how the injury was sustained (consistent or not consistent with the type and location of the injury); (3) the presence or absence of prior reports; and (4) parental conduct at the time of the report (positive or negative). In a somewhat analogous study, Alter (1985) studied factors used by workers to substantiate allegations of neglect. Factors identified include (1) severity of harm the child suffered; (2) whether or not the behavior of the parent was willful; (3) assessment of the parent–child relationship; (4) level of parental deviance; and (5) whether or not parents indicated a desire to change their behavior.

Other factors also influence worker decisions to confirm reports. Wolock (1982) found that judgments made by protective service workers on the severity of child abuse and neglect cases varied according to economic conditions in the area. Workers in economically depressed areas carrying more serious cases tended to rate vignettes as less serious than did workers in more prosperous areas with better functioning families on their caseloads. A decision to confirm a maltreatment report may depend somewhat on the availability of services. If the service system is already overstrained, workers may be reluctant to confirm additional cases that, they believe, the system cannot help.

Because specific criteria for decision making are lacking, workers must also make decisions based on personal judgments. Stein's and Rzepnicki's (1984) review of the literature led them to conclude that "personal values and idiosyncratic judgements exert a strong influence on decision making" (p. 11). They warn that decisions made from personal bias are difficult to justify to courts and legislators, and they point out that "professional ethics and social work's long-standing commitment to client self-determination demand a more rational, less subjective approach to selecting the options which have strong and enduring effects on the lives of the clients that are served" (p. 31).

A consensus has not yet emerged on definitions of abuse and neglect. Two characteristics that appear important to all observers are first, clear and identifiable harm or injury to the child, and second, evidence of intent of the caregiver to inflict the harm or injury. There also appears to be a trend to acknowledge the need for different kinds of definitions to be used for different purposes. Narrow definitions may be valuable to guide and perhaps retard legal decisions on state intervention into private family life and termination of parental rights. Broad, inclusive definitions may be useful for case management decisions and determination of ·eligibility for voluntary services (Valentine et al., 1984).

CAUSES AND CORRELATES OF CHILD MALTREATMENT

Conditions leading to the neglect or abuse of children cannot be defined in simple, discrete terms. Multiple causes and conditions interact, reinforce each other, and generate new influences that lead toward family malfunctioning (Belsky, 1980). In general, child maltreatment results from the interaction of (1) environmental stress, (2) personality traits of the parent, and (3) characteristics of the child that make him or her vulnerable.

Poverty

The relation of poverty to child maltreatment is dramatically illustrated in the differences in maltreatment rates between high- and low-income families (*Study Findings,* 1988). As Table 9.2 shows, maltreatment was about seven times more likely to occur in families with incomes under $15,000 than in high-income families; 54

low-income children per 1,000 were mistreated compared to 8 high-income children per 1,000. Poor children were more likely to experience each of the types of abuse and neglect than were better-off children. There was a difference between low- and high-income children in what kind of maltreatment they were most likely to experience. Children in low-income families were more likely to suffer neglect (36.8 per 1,000) than abuse (19.9 per 1,000), whereas children in high-income families were about equally likely to suffer either neglect (4.1 per 1,000) or abuse (4.4 per 1,000). Low-income children experienced more severe maltreatment than the high-income children; they had higher rates of fatal, serious, and moderate injuries, and they were much more likely to be considered by reporting professionals as "endangered" (U.S. Department of Health and Human Services, 1988).

As Table 9.2 shows, child abuse and neglect occur at all socioeconomic levels. To some ex-

TABLE 9.2. Difference in Maltreatment Rates Based on Family Income (per 1,000 Children from Families in That Income Category in the Population)

Category	Less than $15,000	$15,000 or more
All maltreatment	54.0	7.9
All abuse	19.9	4.4
Physical abuse	10.2	2.5
Sexual abuse	4.8	1.1
Emotional abuse	6.1	1.2
All neglect	36.8	4.1
Physical neglect	22.6	1.9
Educational neglect	10.1	1.3
Emotional neglect	6.9	1.5
Fatal injury/impairment	0.03	0.01
Serious injury/impairment	6.0	0.9
Moderate injury/impairment	30.9	5.5
Probable injury/impairment	5.4	0.9
Severity-endangered	11.7	0.6

(*Source:* U.S. Department of Health and Human Services, National Center on Child Abuse and Neglect. [1988]. *Study Findings, Study of National Incidence and Prevalence of Child Abuse and Neglect.* Washington, DC: U.S. Government Printing Office.)

tent, the differences in rates between income groups may reflect differences in recognition of maltreatment rather than differences in occurrence. Deviant forms of child treatment are more easily concealed in families of higher social status. However, the magnitude and consistency of the difference in rates between the two income groups suggest that family income is a powerful predictor of child maltreatment and of maltreatment-related injuries (U.S. Department of Health and Human Services, 1988). It seems possible that poorly educated people at the bottom of the social and economic ladder express their abuse more readily in direct, aggressive actions, whereas those in higher income groups may resort to other means, such as verbal attacks or withdrawals of affection. Gil (1981) argues that abuse is probably more prevalent among the poor because

> poverty is a major source of insecurity, frustration, and stress, and . . . poor parents have fewer options than affluent ones for dealing with insecurity, frustration, and stress and for making alternative child care arrangements. Poor households also have less space, a circumstance which may increase tensions in interactions with children (p. 300).

Social Support

In addition to income level, another relevant aspect of the environment is the extent to which parents can mobilize outside support to help the family. Such compensation may be extra financial resources making relief possible when pressures are great (through vacations, evenings out, and the help of housekeepers and babysitters), reliable relatives to assist with homemaking and child care at crucial times, and status-producing and satisfying work (Polansky et al., 1985).

Sociological explanations of maltreatment related to the nuclear family emphasize the role played by stress on parents in a period of rapid social change, and by isolation from other families in similar situations and from relatives who,

in other circumstances, might give emotional support and concrete aid (Tracy & Whittaker, 1987).

Garbarino and Sherman (1980) studied the social environment of neighborhoods in relation to the incidence of child maltreatment. They compared two communities that had similar socioeconomic profiles; in each, about 70 percent of the families had low incomes and all of the residents were white. However, the two neighborhoods had very different maltreatment rates: 130 maltreatment cases per 1,000 families for the "high-risk" neighborhood; 16 per 1,000 families for the "low-risk" neighborhood. The researchers interviewed community residents to develop a profile of each neighborhood's social support system. The findings revealed that residents of the low-risk neighborhood were relatively "free from drain." They looked after their children and took care of their houses adequately, and seemed to have spare energy to help out neighbors through informal exchanges of babysitting and other support. In contrast, the residents of the high-risk neighborhood were both more socially needy and less helpful to one another. They rated the neighborhood less positively as an environment for child and family development and revealed a general pattern of social impoverishment, in comparison to families in the low-risk neighborhood. The researchers suggest that neighborhood cohesiveness, independently of the general socioeconomic level of its residents, can affect the likelihood of child maltreatment.

Community Deficits

Environmental conditions that contribute to child neglect and abuse often can be identified within a community's system of social services. There can be lack of early casefinding techniques, resulting in a pattern of providing social services only after a child is observed to be in an already dangerous situation, or when the care he or she is receiving finally reaches such a low level that it defies what a neighborhood or community can tolerate. A deficiency in "case accountability" is another factor, reflected in such practices as (1) giving inadequate or incomplete services, (2) failing to follow through on referrals for another service, (3) setting up barriers of communication or bureaucratic procedures that cut off some people from asking for or receiving help, (4) showing concern only about fragments of family life that present symptoms troublesome to the community, and (5) failing to develop an agency function that is an active part of a communitywide program of services. Preventive services may be unavailable to avert the onset of family problems through easily available aids for families to use as they need them at normal transitional points of family life, for example, marriage, pregnancy and childbirth, early infancy, and school entrance, and at other times of peak demand upon family functioning.

Serious social problems abound in our communities today, and all of these, directly or indirectly, tend to increase the incidence of child neglect and abuse. Some of the most pressing social problems are a large-scale incidence of mental ill health; escalating health costs and unequal medical services; poverty in the midst of affluence; lack of jobs for youth and heads of families; deplorable housing for large numbers of the population; high rates of delinquency; inadequate and irrelevant education for much of the nation's youth, with a lack of preparation for jobs, higher education, parenthood, and other aspects of adult responsibility; and a pervading sense that individuals lack the power of self-direction and are subject to the restrictive rules of bureaucracies or intangible outside forces that limit daily experiences for them and their children.

Poverty, lack of social support, and impoverished communities are related to maltreatment generally. Other related factors, including characteristics of the parents and the children, will be discussed separately for abuse and neglect.

CHILD NEGLECT

Physical neglect is the predominant form of child maltreatment in the United States; the National Incidence Study reported that 571,600 children, or 9 for every 1,000 children in the United States, suffered physical neglect in 1986. These figures include children who suffered moderate and severe injury or impairment, as well as those who were unharmed but whose health or well-being were thought to be seriously endangered. Specific types of physical neglect are: "conspicuous inattention to avoidable hazards in the home"; "inadequate nutrition, clothing, or hygiene, and other forms of reckless disregard of the child's safety and welfare"; "inadequate supervision"; "abandonment"; "expulsion of a child from the home without adequate arrangement for care by others"; and "refusal of health care" or "failure to seek timely and appropriate medical care for a serious health problem" (U.S. Department of Health and Human Services, 1988, pp. 4–11, 4–12).

Children in neglecting families in 1984 had an average age of 6, and were about equally divided between males and females. Sixty-three percent of the families were white, 23 percent were black, and 13 percent were Hispanic. The neglecting families had on average more children than other families in the United States. Forty-three percent of the caretakers were unemployed, and slightly over half of the families were headed by a single parent. Nearly two-thirds of neglecting families were receiving public assistance (American Association, 1986).

Cycle of Neglect

Polansky and coworkers cite cultural influences as operative in some child neglect among isolated, extended families in which child-rearing standards border on neglectful and act to perpetuate a *cycle of neglect*. The parents in such families often have been reared in similar situations where meaningful standards were lacking as to how children should be treated (Polansky et al., 1975; 1981).

The idea of a generation-to-generation cycle of neglect that Polansky et al. have derived from some neglect situations is in contrast to the conclusions of Giovannoni and Billingsley, who interviewed 186 low-income mothers from three ethnic groups in order to gain insight into "the ways in which poor families who do not neglect their children differ from those who do." Factors associated with neglect included having more children than nonneglecting mothers, being without a husband or experiencing recent marital disruption, being less able to accept and meet the dependency needs of very young children, having impoverished relationships with extended kin, and living at a level of poverty even lower than that of nonneglecting mothers in the study. The social and familial background factors of neglecting mothers were not significantly different from those of nonneglecting mothers—a finding leading these researchers to emphasize as a primary cause of neglect current environmental and situational stress coinciding with fewer resources and supports for coping, rather than personality traits stemming from the effects of early life (Giovannoni & Billingsley, 1970).

However, the concept proposed by Polansky et al. of an intergenerational cycle of neglect in some of the incidence of child neglect is supported by other investigations of seriously socially disorganized families (Young, 1964; Pavenstedt, 1967; Minuchin et al., 1967; Polansky et al., 1972; Geismar, 1973; Sullivan et al., 1975).

> All researchers who had continuing contacts with families studied—so that life histories could be known with reasonable certainty—have been impressed with the degree to which current family disorganization and neglect seem rooted in the families of origin. . . . The pointing up of inter-generational cycles does not dis-count the impact of current life stress, as emphasized by Giovannoni and Billingsley. But it does imply that earlier deprivations leave marks on one's personality which make the person less capable of adequate parenting. Since these marks are old and go deep, they will not be reversed by superficial measures; nor will they respond reliably to environmental manipulations. From their own hard lives, many neglecting parents have emerged isolated and cold, narcissistic and basically depressed. (Polansky et al., 1975, p. 17)

Parental Illness

Personality and health problems of parents are associated in varying degrees with child neglect. Some mothers are borderine psychotic. For many mothers of young children, life is a chronic experience of depression. Many are physically ill, often with chronic health problems, including gynecological issues, nutritional deficiencies, hypertension, and obesity (Helfer, 1987). Fathers, too, contribute heavily to child neglect by failing to provide support for family life and child care. Fathers, like mothers, may be alcoholic, psychotic, mentally retarded, or drug addicted. Society, in deinstitutionalizing the mentally retarded, did not plan for the children born to mentally retarded adults after they were returned to the community. These mothers and their children are often on their own, with no supervision from human service professionals (Helfer, 1987).

Severe immaturity in a large segment of neglecting parents is common. They show dependent and infantile characteristics. The youngest baby may be used by such mothers to ward off their pervasive loneliness and anxiety; older children are thrust into maternal responsibilities for their young siblings. Among these parents, inner controls are lacking. Judgment is poor, and indifference to their children is evident. Parents' needs take precedence over those of their children (Polansky et al., 1975; 1981).

Symptoms of Child Neglect

We have seen that the label "neglect" is commonly attached to those symptoms denoting parental failure to adequately perform essential child care tasks, or parental failure to perform certain duties at all. Some of these symptoms are observable in children's personal appearance or behavior. For example, they may be poorly fed, with the result being lack of proper growth, a low energy level, apathy, restlessness, or susceptibility to chronic infections. They may be shabbily clothed or not dressed for protection against extreme weather conditions. They are often dirty or show other signs of faulty parental care in their personal appearance. Sometimes the neglect involves failure or refusal to obtain essential medical care. Frequent and persistent absence from school may be a symptom of parental failure to get children up on time in the mornings, to start them off feeling prepared for the day's demands, or to support them in their school life with interest and approval. Preschool children who belong to multiproblem, disorganized families often show distinctive and handicapping deviations in their psychological development. Some infants and young children show a general failure to thrive even when no organic basis can be established for their lack of healthy growth and development. Children of all ages may reveal parental neglect by a range of maladjusted behaviors and emotional disorders (Felt, 1983).

Children's neglect may be directly observable in home conditions that affect them adversely, including dilapidated housing without the essential material equipment for normal family life, overcrowding, and lack of privacy. Children may experience eviction and homelessness. A mother may maintain such low housekeeping standards that her family lives in squalor. Children may not have an adequate place to sleep. Young children may be left alone in the house or be very poorly attended when their parents are away. The home may contain physical hazards, such as poisons within reach of a young child, or unsafe heating equipment, or unprotected stairways. Children may experience unwholesome or demoralizing circumstances at home—violence, excessive quarreling, parental dishonesty, defiance of proper authority in society, or lack of love or concern for each other's welfare among family members (Helfer, 1987).

Child Neglect in the "Problem" Family

Various terms have been used to characterize families who live in conditions that give rise to persistent community concern about the care of the children—"problem" families, "hard-to-reach" families, "socially disorganized" families, "multiproblem" families, "hard-core" families, and "socially delinquent" families.

Problem families are not simply all those who are poor. In characterizing the "culture of poverty," Oscar Lewis made it clear that only about 20 percent of all persons or families officially designated as poor in the United States displayed the traits he described—traits often associated with, or contributing to, child neglect. Some families have many more serious problems than others, but are not necessarily reduced to a state of family disorganization (Lewis, 1966).

Although problem families have common features, and can be distinguished from more stable and normal families, various investigators have stressed that such households do not reflect an abrupt transition into family inadequacy, but display a level of functioning at the lower end of a downward slope (Hall et al., 1984). There is not one distinguishing characteristic making a family a problem family rather than a stable or normal one; problem families constitute a wide spectrum, exhibiting a range of disorganization, pathology, and personality types rather than forming one homogeneous group or single family type (Helfer, 1987).

Aspects of problem family life have been noted consistently by social workers who have tried to understand and help problem family members. Two main themes exist. First, *the problem family has failed to attain certain generally accepted minimum social standards*—a condition repeatedly recorded in these areas of social functioning: (1) general disorder in living patterns, with failure to perform adequately certain essential tasks of family life (money management, controlling the number of pregnancies, health care, food preparation, and housekeeping); (2) demanding, personal needs of parents, often growing out of their own early lives of deprivation, which interfere with the care they give their own children; (3) disorganization and instability in the family members' interpersonal relationships, seen in constant dissension, absence of affection and trust, or extreme marital discord; (4) isolated and anomic relationships to neighborhood and community; and (5) certain prevalent tendencies in the behavior of children of seriously disorganized problem families (shyness, avoidance of adults, low self-esteem, a general withdrawal from relationships, and impulsive acting-out behavior) (Jackson, 1984).

Second, *the problem family has not benefited from social services* although it has repeatedly come to the attention of the community through contacts (predominantly negative ones) with community organizations and authorities. Agencies report that problem families make multiple requests for service but do not follow through, and frequently show an aggressive, demanding attitude or an extreme apathy toward suggested courses of action. Their chronic need is aggravated by inconsistent responses and hostility, and by the accumulating discouragement with which agency personnel approach them (Jackson, 1984). Overall, the problem family

> takes more than its proportionate share of welfare funds, services, and supplies, and contributes more than its share of juvenile delinquency, neglect cases, alcoholism, and other types of adult deviant behavior. (Geismar & LaSorte, 1964, p. 34)

The disproportion between numbers of problem families and the amount of social services directed toward them makes it difficult to escape the conclusion that existing services are ineffective with most of them.

Young described the following situation, which illustrates some of the symptoms of severe neglect and some of the characteristics of parents observed frequently in child protective services:

> A baby lies on a filthy, sodden mattress. There are no sheets or blankets, though the room is chilly and the cold drafts seep along the floor. Sometimes the baby cries wearily, but more often lies in dull silence. . . . He looks ageless, with his shrunken body and his distant stare. Actually, he has lived in this less than perfect world for only one year.
>
> He was the fifth child born to the Lake family. The seven Lakes live in a three-room apartment which had been dirty and deteriorating to begin with and has not improved with the occupancy of the Lakes. . . . The floor is littered with dirty clothes, decaying garbage, broken bits of old toys, papers and boxes and rags. The children, nearly as dirty as the floor, squabble and scream over a bag of potato chips and a half-empty bottle of soda pop. . . .
>
> The oldest of the five is Shirley, now seven. She has successfully appropriated the bag of potato chips and is doling them out one by one to the frantic smaller children, each time popping one into her own mouth. All of them ignore the baby, silent in his crib. They also ignore the inert woman, sitting in a chair from which broken springs and bits of wadding protrude. The woman yells at them now and then, but mostly she stares blankly at the stained wall.
>
> Mrs. Lake is not mean to the children. If you ask her, she will tell you that of course she loves them. If you talk more, she will also tell you, "If only they wouldn't fight so much. Then I get sick of them. They never pay any attention to me. . . ."
>
> If you remark that the children are thin and seem hungry and that they might quarrel less if they were fed and cleaned up, Mrs. Lake might stir to a petulant defense. "I do try to clean them

up, but they get dirty right away. I tell them to stay off the floor but they're right back there soon as I look the other way." Again the note of complaint is strong in her voice. As for food, she puts some on the table. They can eat when they want. You look at the table with its crumbs of bread and cake, at the dregs of coffee in a battered cup, at the two year old girl who would have to climb to reach the table top, at the baby who cannot even climb.

Mrs. Lake sees your look and again she comes to her own defense. "I do the best I can. If my husband brought his money home the way he should, if he'd help me with all these kids. But he says that's a woman's job and he works all day and he shouldn't have to help at home. He says he earns the money. . . ." Caught up in her grievances, Mrs. Lake forgets both you and the children. There is an expression almost of pleasure on her face already aged ten years beyond its actual twenty-six. The children pay no attention. They have heard it all many times. The baby continues to stare at nothing and now and then to give a small, despairing wail which no one hears.

Nothing changes when Mr. Lake walks in. The children continue with their own affairs and after one brief glance ignore their father. He does not speak to them. His whole attention is riveted upon his wife's recital of complaints. Angrily he interrupts. "If she'd clean up this place and take care of the kids, there wouldn't be any trouble. I give her money and what does she do? . . . She goes next door and drinks beer all day. She goes down to the bar and talks to the bums that hang around there. I work all day. . . ." Mr. Lake is thin and short. His body is tense and his movements jerky. Like his wife his face looks older than his twenty-seven years, and like her, his face has the crumpled look of a petulant child.

Mrs. Lake answers her husband's accusations eagerly, reiterating what he has done to her, what he continues to do to her. His retorts follow the same theme, what his wife does or fails to do for him. Neither of them talk to the children although each accuses the other of neglecting them. . . . Two of the children are crying but neither parent notices. Deep in their quarrel now, their voices grow shrill, and they search the past for more evidence to support the theme of their ever-recurrent exploitation. (Young, 1964, pp. 11–13)

Fortunately, some instances of neglect can be viewed more optimistically. Some families show a higher degree of organization—for example, one parent can make decisions, some degree of family routine is present, or there is less "running away" by a parent (Young, 1964).

Lack of Supervision

Lack of supervision (LOS) refers to situations in which children are without a caretaker or the caretaker is inattentive or unsuitable, and therefore the children are in danger of harming themselves or possibly others (American Humane Association, 1984, p. 83). Also included are situations in which children are allowed to remain away from home overnight without the parents' knowing or attempting to find out the child's whereabouts, expulsion from home or refusal to allow the child to return home, and abandonment. The National Incidence Study estimated that about 192,100 children experience inadequate supervision during a year's time, 45,300 are expelled from home, and 17,100 are abandoned. LOS is a common form of child neglect, involved in over a third of all physical neglect situations (U.S. Department of Health and Human Services, 1988). The consequences can be quite serious, including severe injury or death (U.S. Department of Health and Human Services, 1979).

In a study of 375 LOS cases in New York State, Jones (1987) identified five types of supervision problems: (1) "child left unattended"; (2) "child left in care of unsuitable substitute caretaker," such as a slightly older sibling; (3) "child left in the care of a suitable substitute caretaker, but without proper planning or consent" (for example, the mother tells the caretaker she will be right back but doesn't return for days); (4) "caretaker inadequately supervising child" (for example, parent or other caretaker is either sleeping or under the influence of chemicals); (5) "child permitted, encouraged, or forced to engage or not restrained from engaging in harmful or potentially harmful activity" (for example, child is locked out of the house or permitted to engage in prostitution or drug use).

The study found a variety of LOS patterns. The most frequent LOS situation was the first, "children left unattended," which accounted for 72 percent of all study cases. Jones estimated that in about half of all the families studied, the parent's absence was due to some essential activity, such as school, work, or errands. The remaining parents were socializing, engaged in illegal or irresponsible activity, or were hospitalized or incarcerated. Analysis of the parents' explanations for leaving their children unsupervised indicated that about 40 percent believed that there was nothing wrong with what had happened. For example, a parent who left a child with a slightly older sibling may be convinced that the caretaker was competent. In most other cases, the parent did acknowledge a supervision problem but blamed someone else or said it was unavoidable.

Social workers attributed the LOS problem to parents' "lack of knowledge or poor judgment re: abilities or needs of children of a given age" in 40 percent of the cases, and to "physical or mental impairment of the caretaker, including impairment due to alcohol or drug abuse" in another 33 percent. Other reasons cited were parents' attitude toward the child, cultural norms of child rearing, and personality problems of the parent.

In estimating what kinds of services would have helped these families to improve their level of child care, Jones concluded that about half of the families could have been helped with regular day care or as-needed babysitting. The other half of the cases were thought to need "supplementary child care . . . to shore up, stabilize, or enhance the caretaker's child care functioning," such as homemaker service, respite care, or foster care (Jones, 1987, p. 29). A correlation was found between the child care services needed and the type of LOS situation. For two-thirds of the cases in which children had been left unattended or left with an unsuitable person, the families needed only regular day care or occasional babysitting. Most of the rest of the cases in all categories were thought to require supplementary child care services to improve the parent's functioning. Providing only day care or babysitting would have been insufficient to ensure the child's safety.

These service needs as identified by the researcher stand in marked contrast to the services actually provided to the families. In three-fifths of the cases, the family received no service beyond the Child Protective Services investigation, because either services were not offered, or the family refused them. Of the families who did receive some service, 8 percent were provided day care and another 8 percent received homemaker service. Twenty-five percent were provided foster care, and the rest received a limited amount of counseling, preventive, or mental health services.

The study findings confirmed that harm and injury often befall children in LOS families. In about two-thirds of the cases, an injury was reported, including:

> a death due to falling out of a window; a skull fracture; attempted suffocation; attempted strangulation; burns—some deliberately inflicted, others not; sexual abuse; smoke inhalation, drug withdrawal; and aspirin overdose. (Jones, 1987, p. 46)

Most of these incidents were due to parental abuse or neglect, though not all were directly related to the incident that initiated the protective services investigation.

Lack of supervision, as a child maltreatment concept, raises difficult definitional issues. American society has not reached a consensus on what constitutes lack of supervision. One ambiguous area is the minimum qualifications of the caretaker. At what age may children reasonably be left unattended? At what age is a child competent to look after a slightly younger sibling? What level of competence should be expected minimally of the ill, mentally retarded, or chemically dependent parent? Should an infant be removed from an incompetent parent at birth, or should nothing be done until the child is harmed? (Jones, 1987).

Another area of ambiguity is minimum level of surveillance. Even conscientious parents are not always watchful. Accidents happen. To what extent are parents culpable of lack of supervision because they had the misfortune of having their child harmed while they were inattentive? (Jones, 1987).

An obstacle to developing a consensus on minimum standards of supervision is the relationship of lack of supervision to poverty, inadequate housing, and dangerous neighborhoods. Families with better houses in safer neighborhoods may need to provide less supervision to keep their children safe than do those residing in poor areas. Further, families that are better off financially can obtain babysitters and day care providers and have more resources to compensate for incompetence. Because of resource inequities, policy makers may face the dilemma of setting standards too stringent for poor people to reach or setting the standards so low as to be meaningless (Jones, 1987).

Clearly, a solution is to increase the day care and babysitting services available to poor families, so that children are supervised while parents need to be away. A more modest but useful goal would be to increase public awareness and educational activities so parents understand minimally acceptable levels of supervision. Jones has two innovative suggestions: establishing a task force of child development specialists and low-income mothers to arrive at reasonable standards for minimally adequate supervision; and requiring parenting classes for certain targeted families who fail repeatedly to supervise their children, in the same spirit that the Department of Motor Vehicles requires driver's education of traffic violators (Jones, 1987).

Expelled and Runaway Youth

Adolescents told to leave home by a parent who has made no adequate arrangement for their care by others and who refuses to accept the youth's return may be labeled as expelled or "throwaway" youth. "Runaways" are adolescents who have left home with or without permission for an extended period of time. Although the circumstances of their departures vary, these teenagers may comprise one homogeneous group who are characterized primarily by having extensive problems at home. A recent national survey estimated that there are about 500,000 expelled and runaway youth yearly under age eighteen and that 150,000 youth are homeless during a year, with "homeless" defined as "without a safe place to sleep" (Barden, 1990). Other estimates of the number of children who are outside the care and protection of nurturing adults or child welfare agencies are much higher. A national survey of shelters reported turning away 3,000 young people a year for lack of space (Barden, 1990).

Because of their transiency, little is known about this population of young people. Studies of youth in shelters and those at home but "at risk" of departure suggest that most have experienced maltreatment. Three patterns exist. Most commonly, maltreatment starts in childhood and continues uninterruptedly into adolescence. Some children experience an abusive period in childhood, followed by a reprieve, and then the maltreatment recurs when they become teenagers. For still other children, the maltreatment starts in adolescence. Many suffer from more than one type of abuse or neglect (Berdie & Wexler, 1984).

The families of runaway adolescents show characteristics common to maltreating families: chemical abuse, psychopathology, family system dysfunction, and attitudes favoring violence and coercion. Garbarino and coworkers (1984) found that a disproportionate number of families at high risk for adolescent abuse were stepparent families, who apparently had failed to create a well-functioning, cohesive social context for raising children. These families seemed to have a formidable array of interpersonal difficulties making them particularly vulnerable to the stress created in family life by a developing adolescent. Difficult behavior in the adolescent may "present acute challenges that push many of these families past the threshold at which maltreatment precipitates" (Garbarino et al., 1984, p. 177).

A runaway who has been maltreated since childhood may represent the failure of several service systems. In one study, only 40 percent of the youth surveyed at shelters who had experienced maltreatment since childhood had ever been reported to child protective services. Neglected children were most likely to have been reported, while the situations of only about a quarter of those suffering other maltreatment had been known to protective services. Many had received services in childhood and in adolescence from other social agencies, including the juvenile court, and mental health, special education, and substance abuse programs. However, these services do not appear to have resolved the young person's problems in the family. Many shelter residents believed that they had filled the family role of "scapegoat," "target," or "outsider," which suggests that their departure from home during adolescence continued a family process of exclusion that had started long before (Berdie & Wexler, 1984).

The following example shows the multiple deprivations and chaotic life events that seem to characterize the life experiences of many runaway and expelled youth.

> The 13-year-old girl seemed relaxed and fairly happy at the shelter run by the Centers for Youth and Families in Little Rock, Ark., because she was safely away from her father's beatings. She had been at the shelter for three weeks, brought by the police.
>
> Her only worry was that her 6-month-old son was with her parents, who had adopted the girl and a boy her same age when they were small children.

> She was beaten with switches and belts, the girl said, because "sometimes I did something wrong, but sometimes my brother would say I did something wrong when I didn't do anything."
>
> The authorities first entered the case more than a year ago when the girl went to the school nurse. "I was hurting and she took off my blouse and saw where I had been beaten," she said, "I wouldn't tell them what happened but the principal came and they figured it out. They took pictures of me and took me to a hospital for treatment. Family services took me over and put me in a foster home with seven other kids."
>
> It was in the foster home, where she spent only a month, that the girl became pregnant by one of the boys there, she said. She returned home when her parents agreed to family counseling.
>
> After her mother discovered that the girl was pregnant, she moved into a home for pregnant teen-agers. "I first said I would put the baby up for adoption then changed my mind," she said. "I don't know why I changed my mind."
>
> The girl had been living at home with the baby until another beating by her father. "I don't want to go back home and I don't want my baby there," she said.
>
> Within a month the girl went to a foster home. Her baby remained with her parents. (Barden, 1990, p. B7)

Emotional Neglect

It is apparent that the quality of the relationship between parent and child and the quantity of its reciprocal emotional sustenance are critical factors in a young child's physical growth and personality development. This is true not only for infants and young children; the nature of the emotional care in a family continues to be a discriminating element in the growth and well-being of older children and young persons as well.

Compared with the number of years in which the community has been concerned about the physical care of children, concern about their emotional care is new. Only recently has inadequate emotional care come to be considered as neglect.

The emotional care provided within a family involves a range of parental responses to a child's behavior. Guidelines for assessing adequacy in the emotional climate of a home have included such criteria as the extent to which parental responses to a child are recognizable as supportive and valuing, rather than discouraging or demeaning; whether the parents show concern about the child instead of a noncaring indifference; whether they treat the child with the respect another individual merits; whether they postpone gratification of their own needs in favor of meeting the child's dependency needs, and gear their expectations for behavior to his or her individual level of readiness to perform adequately. These and other criteria are relied on by social workers in determining whether a child is neglected. For emotional neglect, social work services will include attention to alleviating or correcting or compensating for the lack of parental emotional nurturance.

Emotional neglect, however, has not been incorporated generally into legal definitions of neglect, and even when it has, it has proved difficult to use in legal actions. The following case is illustrative:

> Eleanor, ten years old at the time of her referral to the Massachusetts SPCC, was an adopted child whose parents later had several other children. She was referred to us as an emotionally deprived child, completely rejected and suffering from malnutrition, although the parents were able and willing to provide adequate food, clothing and shelter. There was no evidence of physical neglect, but Eleanor would not eat and was gradually losing weight to the point where the psychiatric clinic, to which the protective service agency referred her, felt that placement was necessary. Both the clinic and the protective agency tried to help the parents accept placement, but without success. The mother, who was completely rejecting, was an unhappy, unstable person not amenable to treatment. The father, who had some warmth for the child, was

not strong enough to assert himself and meet Eleanor's emotional needs. There was little evidence on a physical level for court action. Conferences with lawyers and even with the juvenile court judge resulted in the decision that successful court action could not be sustained to remove the child, and unsuccessful court action probably would block subsequent efforts to work with the family. (Mulford, 1958, p. 22)

Allegations of emotional neglect usually constitute sufficient grounds for modification of parental rights only when they are linked to evidence of physical neglect as well. Social workers have disagreed as to whether emotional neglect should be given greater weight in legal actions. Some place emphasis on the importance of a child's emotional care and the necessity for society to intervene when children are poorly cared for in relation to their emotional needs, just as it does when physical needs are ignored or insufficiently attended to. Others oppose using emotional neglect as a basis for modification of parental rights on the basis that lags in the development of knowledge in the behavioral sciences lead experts to disagree about the nature of adequate emotional care and the effects on a child of various differences in parental approaches to emotional nurturing. One usually cannot introduce evidence of emotional neglect that would unquestionably justify a modification of parental rights. Furthermore, there is no assurance that a child placed in foster care will receive more *effective* attention to emotional needs than the child would with his or her own parents. Because a child carries the impact of earlier experiences, a change of environment does not automatically bring about desired changes. Corrective emotional care usually is more complex than is the provision of corrective physical care.

"Failure to Thrive" as Neglect

Failure to thrive (FTT) refers to chronic, severe, undernutrition of an infant. Medical staff may diagnose FTT if the infant's weight is 20 percent below the ideal weight for the infant's height. Poor weight gain over time is another indicator of FTT. Thirty percent of FTT cases have an organic cause, 50 percent are due to extreme neglect and dysfunctional mothering, and the rest are caused by errors in formula preparation or breast-feeding problems. Infants are thin with prominent ribs and wasted buttocks. If their condition is due to neglect, they may also show poor hygienic care, such as diaper rash, untreated impetigo, uncut nails, and dirty clothes. These babies may also show signs of abuse and of dehydration. When offered food, underfed babies will often eat voraciously. FTT infants have stunted development, and show delays in social interaction and speech. They may avoid eye contact and resist cuddling. Mothers are observed to interact very little with their infants during feeding, and may act angry at the child (Schmitt, 1988a).

FTT appears to be the result of insufficient attachment between the mother and the baby. Explanations for the lack of bonding include early deprivation of the mother during her own childhood, difficulties during the pregnancy or childbirth resulting in prematurity or congenital defects, acute illness of mother or baby, and stressful current life events (Mayhall & Norgard, 1983).

Parents of children who fail to thrive for reasons other than organic causes do not neglect their children in the usual meaning of neglect, that is, failing "to do" for them. Instead, there is some failing or disorder in the mothering figure, so that there are serious consequences in her manner of caring for her child. Neglect reflected in a baby's or young child's failure to thrive rests on an assessment of maternal care going beyond a determination as to whether food and shelter were provided or child-caring tasks were carried out. It involves the quality of the mothering process, the nature of the mother-child relationship, and intimate relationships between an infant's physical and emotional needs (Bullard et al., 1967).

Results of FTT can be serious. If untreated

it can result in permanent retardation. It is possible that this experience can lead these infants, when older, to feel chronic dissatisfaction with themselves and their life circumstances (Mayhall & Norgard, 1983).

In extreme cases, the infant must be hospitalized and possibly later placed in foster care until the medical condition is alleviated. In most cases, however, the infant and mother are treated at home. Skill and effort are required to establish the exact nature of the failure to thrive and its causes. A team of professional workers may be needed not only to diagnose but also to treat the ailment and manage the case situation at physiological, social, and psychological levels.

Medically Fragile Children

Disregard for Fetal Development. Although it has been known for many years that pregnant women sometimes behave in ways that may harm a growing fetus, only recently have some of these behaviors been categorized as fetal abuse or neglect and come to the attention of child welfare agencies. Neglecting to get prenatal care and not acting on sound medical advice are ways that pregnant women might show insufficient care for the developing fetus. Reasons for maternal medical neglect include mental illness, mental retardation, and addiction to chemicals. Maternal substance abuse places the fetus in double jeopardy, because it not only causes women to neglect prenatal medical care but also greatly increases the chances that the developing fetus will be born permanently damaged (Rosenberg, 1988). Fetal alcohol syndrome, caused by maternal ingestion of alcohol during pregnancy, is one of the three leading causes of mental retardation in this country. Pregnant women who abuse tobacco, alcohol, cocaine, or other addictive drugs increase the chances that they will have health problems during pregnancy, and give birth to babies with low birth weight and developmental abnormalities. These infants are more likely than others to die during their first year (Chasnoff et al., 1985; Belsky, 1987; Nieburg et al., 1985). Infants who became addicted to their mother's drugs before birth may suffer a painful withdrawal.

Scientific advances have made it possible to monitor fetal development, to identify maternal behaviors that are likely to seriously injure the fetus, and even to intervene medically to promote fetal health and prevent permanent disabilities. However, coercive interventions undertaken to protect the fetus may violate the mother's right to privacy and the principle of bodily integrity and autonomy. The question of "fetal rights" also raises issues that affect the right of women to choose abortion. The courts have not yet given unambiguous guidance on these issues (Landwirth, 1987). In deciding whether or not to intervene in cases of disregard for fetal development, factors to be considered for both the fetus and the pregnant woman include: the severity of the consequences if the problem is left untreated; the likelihood that the problem will occur; the likelihood that intervention will be successful; and the alternatives to intervention (Rosenberg, 1988). Counseling and educational programs should always be available to gain the mother's voluntary compliance with medical recommendations.

The dearth of accessible, low-cost, prenatal medical care in the United States exacerbates the consequences to infants of their mother's careless life-style. About 15 million American women of child-bearing age do not have medical insurance that covers prenatal care, although many of them are working or are married to workers. One-third of pregnant women receive inadequate or no prenatal care. More than 11 million children are without medical insurance. Medicaid now extends only to about half of America's poor children. Yet lack of prenatal care is a leading cause of low birth-weight, which in turn leads to increased risk of infant mortality and a range of serious developmental disabilities (Rowe, 1989). Similarly, a great lack of drug treatment facilities hinders the recovery of pregnant women who wish to stop their ad-

diction. Advocacy efforts for infant and fetal health can be directed profitably to the official neglect of federal and state governments that fail to ensure that adequate maternal and infant health care is available, as well as to the harmful behaviors of individual mothers.

Children with AIDS. By early 1988, a total of 839 children below the age of twelve and 226 adolescents aged thirteen to nineteen had been diagnosed as having AIDS. Over half of the children in the younger group had died. The Public Health Service predicts that by 1991 some 3,000 children will have full-blown AIDS and estimates that, for every child with AIDS, another 2 or 3 will be at earlier stages of the disease, testing positive for HIV infection or manifesting symptoms of ARC (AIDS-Related Complex). Many of the parents of these children are poor, of minority ethnicity, lack medical insurance and health care, and are in ill health themselves (Hutchings, 1988).

AIDS is transmitted to children in several ways. Infected mothers transmit the disease to their children in utero, during labor and delivery, or postnatally through breast-feeding. Seventy-three percent of those who become infected prenatally have mothers who are intravenous drug users or are sexual partners of intravenous drug users. Children can become infected from blood transfusions, a particular risk if they have hemophilia. Adolescents are at risk for infection through sexual contact and intravenous drug use.

Not all infants of infected mothers contract the disease. Most of those who do will develop full-blown AIDS before their third birthday. As with adults, treatment with AZT or intravenous gamma globulin has promise to alleviate symptoms and side effects of the disease (Hutchings, 1988).

Infants with AIDS whose parents are drug users are very likely to require state intervention and have become a focus of child welfare programs. Some can be adequately cared for at home with persistent, intensive in-home services. A prerequisite for placement at home is that the parent must be seriously engaged in a drug recovery program. Treatment with these families is a long, slow process, and only small gains can be expected (Woodruff & Sterzin, 1988).

CHILD ABUSE

Between 5 and 6 children out of every 1,000 suffer physical abuse each year, according to the National Incidence Study (U.S. Department of Health and Human Services, 1988), though it is likely that the actual incidence is much higher (Straus & Gelles, 1986). After physical neglect, it is the most common type of child maltreatment. Girls and boys are about equally likely to be physically abused. Children from birth to age two are less likely to be physically abused than are older children; however, when infants and toddlers are physically assaulted, it is likely to be more injurious (U.S. Department of Health and Human Services, 1988). In comparison with all maltreating families, those who physically abuse their children are more likely to have two parents in the home (American Association, 1986).

Cultural Attitudes

As with neglect, so it is with child abuse. No one cause can be cited, only the interaction of many different forces. Nor is child abuse a single phenomenon. Symptoms of child abuse may be uniform, but child abuse is a multidimensional phenomenon likely to be diverse in causation. This conceptualization should help to avoid fruitless controversy between those who cite the psychopathology of parents and those who see certain economic, social, and cultural factors as primary in the etiology of child abuse (Gil, 1970; Belsky, 1980).

Gil's public opinion survey illustrates convincingly that a certain degree of physical force in child rearing is accepted by various segments of American society. He concluded that the basic dimension of physical child abuse "upon which all other factors are superimposed is the general, culturally determined permissive attitude toward the use of a measure of physical force in caretaker–child interaction, and the related absence of clear-cut legal prohibitions and sanctions against this particular form of interpersonal violence" (Gil, 1970, p. 135).

Stress and Family Violence

A reminder from a media campaign captures the essence of the widely held belief that parental stress is related to child abuse. "Take time out. Don't take it out on your kid" (Stone & Cohn, 1984). Straus and Kantor (1987) studied this connection using data from a national survey of family violence (Straus et al., 1980). Stress was measured as the number of stressful life events, such as "death of someone close," "serious health or behavior problem of a family member," "troubles with other people at work," or "big increase in hours worked or job responsibilities," experienced by the parent during the past year. Child abuse was measured using the same definition as that of the Family Violence Study (Straus & Gelles, 1986).

Families function as lightning rods for the stresses of everyday life. They serve as settings for uninhibited discharge of feelings of hurt, insult, frustration, anger, and reactive violence, feelings which originate mostly outside the family, but cannot usually be discharged at their place of origin. . . . Releasing these feelings in the privacy of one's home is relatively safe, in that behavior in the private domain is hidden from public view. . . . (Gil, 1985, p. 30)

The analysis revealed different patterns for fathers and mothers. About 18 to 25 children out of every 100 were abused by their mothers; this rate remained about the same for both low-stress and high-stress mothers. For fathers, the relationship between stress and child abuse was quite strong. Only about 9 children out of every 100 with low-stress fathers were abused, whereas the corresponding number for children of high-stress fathers was 35.

The study also made clear that most parents with high stress did not abuse their children. High-stress parents were more likely to be abusers if, in addition to being under great stress, they also had any of the following characteristics: their own fathers were abusive; they approved of slapping family members; their marriages were unsatisfying; they believed in male dominance as a way of organizing power in the family; they were poor; or they were socially isolated.

The authors concluded that parents who abuse their children have learned to cope with stress and family problems by committing acts of violence against family members. Only if parents have a belief system that condones domestic violence will they act abusively during times of stress; without this belief system, parents are unlikely to abuse their children.

Symptoms of Child Abuse

With its connotations of violence and injury "inflicted upon" the child's person, child abuse is a phenomenon of medical, social, and legal significance.

Each year in this country substantial numbers of children are beaten, cut, or burned by their caretakers in circumstances that cannot be explained as accidents. Moreover, their injuries usually result from recurring acts of violence rather than from a single expression of anger or loss of control by the adults who care for them. The severity of such injuries ranges from a mild form of abuse, which may not come to the attention of a doctor or other persons outside the home, to an extreme deviancy in child care resulting in extensive physical damage to the child or even death.

In what way are children abused? They are severely and repeatedly hit with a hand, hair-brush, or fists, or are beaten cruelly with sharp or heavy objects, straps, electric cords, ropes— sometimes baseball bats. They are cut with knives and broken bottles. They are assaulted by adults who sexually molest them, or administer overdoses of drugs to them, or expose them to noxious gases or other toxic substances. Sometimes young children, even infants, are thrown against a wall, or down a flight of stairs, or are held by their legs and shaken hard. Children of all ages may be viciously yanked or shoved. They are burned by having hot coffee thrown at them or scalding water poured on them; their limbs may be held over open flames or pressed against steaming pipes. Sometimes they may be burned systematically by lighted cigarettes (Feldman, 1987; Schmitt, 1988b).

Concern about child abuse increased sharply in the 1960s, when attention was widely focused on "the battered child syndrome," a term that dramatized a clinical condition in young children who had received serious physical abuse. The "battered child" with multiple bone injuries represents an extreme form of deviant child care. The majority of abused children experience less serious maltreatment, or they may be subjected to the same acts of violence by caretakers, but escape injuries or sustain ones that heal without care in a hospital, where a determination of inflicted trauma can be made (Helfer & Kempe, 1987).

The following case illustrates severe abuse that places a child's life in danger as long as that child is in the home:

> Jack Burt, 3 years old, dead on arrival, with continuous welts around both arms, across his back, a large swelling on his head, old burn scars from chest to lower abdomen. As his stepfather carried him in, a nurses' aide heard the man say, "I don't want any more of this; I won't take any more of this. No more." Depositing the boy's body on an examining table, he walked across the room, saying in casual social tones to the aide, "Don't I know you from somewhere? I'm sure I've met you somewhere before."
>
> The physician's question brought, "I just hit

him like I always do when he pees the bed. This time he went and fell on his head. . . .''

Though both Mrs. Burt and her mother knew Jack was being ''punished'' by being placed on a hot gas burner, neither woman had asked for protective placement. Legal charges against the father came with Jack's death. (Morris et al., 1964)

Another situation illustrates abuse that is more moderate in its physical damage, although highly conducive to personality disorder:

The A family consisted of the parents and two children, both daughters—April, age 14 and May, age 13 years. Mother was the abusing parent in this situation. She abused both of her daughters equally. Father is a steady, reliable worker who, though earning a reasonable week's wages, is probably working considerably under his potential. He is an intelligent person with two years of business school training which he has never utilized. He is a very unaggressive man who has a need to have others help him, make his decisions and tell him what to do. . . .

Mrs. A is a woman in her mid-thirties who appears thin and haggard. She is a nervous, high-strung woman, is very controlling, makes the decisions in the home and carries them through. She is a person who appears to be either always angry or always ready to become so. This anger is directed at all things and all people, including the family members. Mother nags father and the two children continuously and always seem to be looking everywhere for attention, affection and recognition. . . .

Both of the children, April and May, give some evidence of personality disorder. This is shown by the difficulty they have in making friends at school and not being able to feel warmth toward their teacher. . . .

The abuse in this situation was inflicted on both girls over a period of time and consisted of severe beatings with such objects as cooking pans, shoes and actually any object at hand. The physical result was severe bruises, lacerations, and, on one occasion, the fracture of several small bones in the hand of one of the girls. The father had shown some concern about the

mother's behavior toward the girls and had attempted to discuss this with her but he had been told by the mother to ''shut up.'' He did shut up and when the mother was particularly angry he would leave the home for a few hours.

The situation was finally referred to the Massachusetts SPCC by school authorities who saw severe bruises on both girls. (Merrill, 1962, pp. 10–11)

Characteristics of Abusing Parents

The research literature reveals these significant points of general agreement in relation to family characteristics of the abused child:

1.   An abused child most often encounters mistreatment while living in his or her own home. Although responsibility for the injury may at first be attributed to someone else, usually the abuse has been inflicted by one of the parents (Steele, 1987). Although more mothers than fathers are reported to be abusers, this finding reflects the fact that a substantial proportion of abused children live in fatherless families. Actually the involvement rate in cases of abuse is higher for fathers and stepfathers than for mothers (Gil, 1970).

2.   The majority of abusive parents often experience severe marital difficulties, with repeated separations; there is a high proportion of stepfather relations. Gil (1970) reported that nearly 20 percent of the families of abused children had a stepfather. Many of these parents married young or were still relatively young at the time the abuse occurred. The parents were not extremely young, however. Less than 10 percent of the mothers and less than 3 percent of the fathers were under twenty years of age. Not infrequently the mistreated child is unwanted in the sense that the pregnancy began before marriage, too soon after marriage, or at some other unwelcome time, intensifying burdens in relation to pregnancy and child rearing.

Recent research suggests that teenage parenthood per se does not increase the risk of child abuse, but that mothers who begin their child bearing at a young age and then go on to have several more children, closely spaced, are at greater risk for becoming abusers (Miller, 1984; Zuravin, 1988).

3. Parents who abuse their children often have experienced defective parental care themselves, frequently having been the victims of abuse in their own childhood. If they were not treated with open cruelty, they commonly experienced rejections, indifference, or other forms of hostility. In addition, they often seemed to be transmitting the same faulty parent-child relationships they had experienced, rearing their children in the same life cycle in which they were reared (Steele, 1987).

4. Parents who suffered massive emotional deprivations and physical abuse in early life often manifest a marked lack of empathy for their children. They seem unaware of and insensitive to their children's affective needs and moods, and are unable to respond appropriately. This deficit may be a precondition for serious deprivations and assaults on children to occur. Particularly when under stress, unempathic parents find the satisfaction of their own needs to be so compelling that they disregard those of the child (Steele, 1987).

5. Many abusing parents appear to have little understanding of normal growth and development of children. They may have unreasonable expectations for compliant behavior. When these expectations are not met, the parent assumes the child is being willful or defiant and lashes out physically. For example, a parent believes that a three-month-old infant who keeps on crying after being told to stop, just "won't mind." It is not unusual for parents to justify their abusive behavior as appropriate punishment.

Some parents have a very limited repertoire of techniques for guiding their children's behavior. They know how to spank a child, but not how to use time-outs, explanations, trades, diversion, and positive reinforcement. Some researchers now believe that lack of knowledge is rarely the whole explanation for inappropriately severe physical discipline. They believe that abu-

sive parents, in addition to lacking parenting skills, are rigid, lack empathy, and believe in authoritarian control (Sussman et al., 1985; Milner & Wimberly, 1980, Steele, 1987).

6. Parents who are at risk for becoming abusive have an impaired ability to form a normal attachment to their newborn infants. This deficit is observable in hospital maternity wards in the first interactions of the parent and child. The mother may seem cold, uninterested, and unwilling to attend to her newborn infant's needs. She may avoid eye or body contact with the child. The ability to form these attachments is thought to depend on the quality of care the parent received as a small child, so failure to bond tends to get transmitted intergenerationally. Attachment disorders can also be observed in fathers and other caretakers (Steele, 1987).

7. Drug and alcohol abuse are associated with higher risk of child maltreatment. Black and Mayer (1980) found that child maltreatment occurred in 41 percent of the drug- and alcohol-addicted families they studied. This relationship occurs in part because chemical substances lower inhibitions; an angry parent, when drunk, may become a physically abusive parent. Many addicted parents who abuse their children have had life experiences related to both the substance abuse and the maltreatment of their children. Stress, poverty, poor health, and depression are often in the backgrounds of both child abusers and those dependent on chemicals (Famularo et al., 1986).

The Abusive Attack. Perceptions of social workers in Gil's investigation of child abuse provided a basis for a factor analysis of the circumstances of 1,380 abusive incidents. The result was a typology of circumstances that tended to precipitate child abuse:

a. Psychological rejection leading to repeated abuse and battering;
b. Disciplinary measures taken in uncontrolled anger;
c. Male babysitter acting out sadistic and sex-

ual impulses in the mother's temporary absence, at times under the influence of alcohol;

d. Mentally or emotionally disturbed caretaker acting under mounting environmental stress;

e. Misconduct and persistent behavioral atypicality of a child leading to his own abuse;

f. Female babysitter abusing child during [the] mother's temporary absence;

g. Quarrel between caretakers, at times under the influence of alcohol. (Gil, 1970, pp. 140–141)

Steele's (1987) identification of factors that, in combination, often precipitate an abusive attack may provide a common base for the abusive incidents in Gil's typology. These preconditions are: (1) the caretaker's predisposition, including deficits in forming an attachment to the child, lack of empathy, excessively high expectations, and his or her own anger, emptiness, and low self-esteem; (2) a crisis, particularly if it involves emotional abandonment, precipitated by an event such as a marital argument; (3) lack of a "lifeline" or source of immediate help in the form of a neighbor or friend who could step in and defuse the situation; and (4) a child who is behaving in a way that is perceived by the caretaker as annoying or purposefully provocative.

Characteristics of the Abused Child

The part played by the child in an unhealthy interaction with his or her parent is not clear. Bryant and coworkers stated: "The behavior of these children seldom provoked or warranted the abuse they received; instead, they seemed like innocent victims of something far more complicated than their own behavior" (1963, p. 129). Nurse's findings were in essential agreement: "parental abuse expressed overdetermined needs of the parent rather than a reality based reaction to a provocative child" (1964, p. 25).

Some consideration has been given, how-

ever, to the individual characteristics that may identify a particular child as "high risk" for abuse. Characteristics that might be factors in instigating abuse include gender (having been born a girl when the parents wanted a boy or vice versa); time of birth (having been the result of an unplanned pregnancy and therefore being perceived by the parent as unwanted and burdensome); and having been born following a difficult pregnancy or delivery. Children with congenital deficiencies, abnormalities, or many perinatal illnesses and hospitalizations are also more likely than other children to suffer abuse. These health conditions increase the amount of personal care required and limit the infant's ability to respond early as a normal, happy baby. Some infants behave in ways that require unusual tolerance from the parents, such as hyperactive, fussy babies with abnormal sleep patterns, who cry excessively and are difficult to console or cuddle (Steele, 1987).

In a survey of parents of 3,334 children, Straus and Gelles (1987) found that abused children had more "special difficulties" than nonabused children, as reported by the parents. As the bar graph in Figure 9.1 shows, abused children were more prone than nonabused children to exhibit a variety of behavior and adjustment problems, including temper tantrums, failing in school, misbehaving and being disobedient at home, and having trouble making friends.

This study and others show that many abused children exhibit more difficult and problematic behavior than other children (Webster-Stratton, 1985; Wolfe, 1985; Martin, 1976). Whether it stems from congenital factors, or from environmental experiences following birth, or from both, this provocative behavior probably contributes to the abuse they experience.

Do abused children inevitably grow up to be abusive parents? As indicated earlier, studies of abusive parents show that many were themselves maltreated as children. However, it also appears that many abused children are able to escape the cycle of intergenerational abuse when

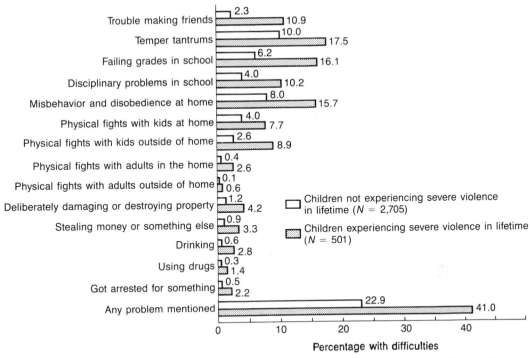

Figure 9.1. Relationship between Experiencing Severe Violence and Special Difficulties of the Child. (*Source:* M. Straus & R. Gelles. [1987]. "The Costs of Family Violence." *Public Health Reports, 102*(6), p. 640.)

they grow up. One estimate is that around 30 percent of abused children become abusive parents. Those who are able to break the pattern and become adequate parents are more likely than repeaters to have had one loving parent or foster parent who provided adequate support and nurture. As adults, they are more likely to have an emotionally satisfying relationship with a lover or spouse, and they tend to have fewer stressful events in their lives (Kaufman & Zigler, 1987).

Sexual Abuse of Children

The National Incidence Study estimates that 155,900 children are sexually abused annually. Nearly 80 percent of these children are girls. Children of any age may experience sexual abuse (U.S. Department of Health and Human Services, 1988). Reports of sexual abuse have increased greatly since 1976, the first year that national statistics were collected (American Association, 1986). This trend probably reflects increased willingness of the public to identify and report sexual abuse, not an increase in incidence (Russell & Trainor, 1984).

Two recent studies have raised public awareness of sexual abuse, as they indicate that it is much more prevalent than was supposed. Finkelhor (1979) surveyed 796 students in New England colleges and found that 19 percent of the women and 9 percent of the men reported that they had been sexually abused as children. In this study noncontact sexual abuse was counted as well as sexual contact. In interviews with over 900 women in the San Francisco area, Russell (1983), found that 38 percent of them reported sexually abusive contact as children.

Sexual abuse has been defined as "any act occurring between people who are at different developmental stages which is for the sexual gratification of the person at the more advanced developmental stage" (Faller, 1988a, p. 11). This definition includes situations where both the perpetrator and the victim are children as long as they are at different developmental stages. For example, an adolescent may abuse a latency-aged or preschool child, or a child may abuse another child of the same age who is retarded. This definition assumes that sexual gratification plays a role in sexually abusive interaction. Even though other motivations may be involved, it is the sexual element that distinguishes this form of abuse from others (Faller, 1988a).

Sexual abuse of children includes various types of sexual behaviors: (1) noncontact behavior such as "sexy talk," perpetrator's exposure of intimate body parts to the victim, and voyeurism; (2) sexual contact that includes touching of intimate body parts such as fondling or masturbating, and penetration; and (3) sexual exploitation in the form of child pornography or child prostitution. Often more than one type of behavior is involved (Faller, 1988a).

Sexual abuse that comes to the attention of child protective services is usually perpetrated by a family member, neighbor, or friend. The police usually handle cases of stranger rape and abuse. Patterns of sexual abuse vary widely. The mean age of the victim at onset of abuse is probably about 10, but infants and preschoolers are not immune. In Faller's (1988a) clinical sample of 148 Michigan cases, on the average a given perpetrator victimized a child 23 times. Sexual contact was the most prevalent type of abuse, with noncontact abuse comprising only 15 percent of the sexual acts. In more than half the cases, some form of force was used by the perpetrator to gain compliance. In cases where force was not used or threatened, the children had a history of deprivation and abuse, and viewed sexual abuse as a way of receiving nurturance. Victims reported the abuse about three months after it began, on average. About half the perpetrators made some kind of admission or confession to the abuse (Faller, 1988a).

Causes of sexual abuse include cultural, individual, and familial factors. Scholars have pointed out that a male-dominated culture implicitly sanctions the sexual abuse of children by men (Wattenberg, 1985). Support for this view comes from the evidence that perpetrators are mostly males and victims are usually female (Russell & Trainor, 1984). Sexual abuse occurs at all socioeconomic levels, though it appears to be more prevalent among the poor. No race is more likely to be involved in sexual abuse than others (U.S. Department of Health and Human Services, 1988). Incestuous families tend to be somewhat socially isolated. Social isolation may contribute to the onset and prolongation of abuse because no one from the outside world is interfering in the family. After the abuse starts, perpetrators often actively work to isolate their families to avoid detection (Conte, 1984).

Perpetrators are characterized by a failure to control their sexual impulses toward children. Studies indicate that they frequently molest children outside as well as inside their own families and may be engaged in a variety of other sexual activities as well (Finkelhor, 1984; Conte, 1984). These offenders frequently have suffered sexual abuse themselves as children (Sebold, 1987). As adults they often have ambivalent or hostile relationships with women, and have limited ability to develop intimate relationships or show affection. They also demonstrate excessive self-centeredness, strong dependency needs, and poor judgment (Bresee et al., 1986; Sahd, 1983). Alcohol and drugs, which act as disinhibitors and also weaken guilt pangs, are frequently used by perpetrators.

Mothers of sexual abuse victims frequently have been abused themselves as children, or they were nonvictimized members of incestuous families. Faller's clinical sample included a fair number of mothers with some incapacity, such as alcoholism, mental illness, mental retardation, multiple sclerosis, or heart conditions, which may have limited their ability to protect their daughters (1988a).

Victims suffer in many different ways from sexual abuse. Sexual behavior is common, manifested by excessive masturbation, sexual play with dolls, sexual statements, or behavior interpreted by others as seductive. These behaviors are the result, not the cause, of the abuse, and they do not imply acceptance of the sexual role by the victim. Nonsexual behaviors include sleep difficulties, enuresis, encopresis, poor school performance, and, in older children, suicide attempts, delinquency, and substance abuse. Damage to children from sexual abuse can be considerable and can last into adulthood (Garbarino & Gilliam, 1980; Faller, 1988a). Health problems include sexually transmitted diseases, pregnancy, and physical injury as a result of the sexual abuse.

Child protective service workers may have great difficulty substantiating allegations of sexual abuse. Physical evidence exists in only a small percentage of cases, and, if present, may not identify the abuser (Rosenberg & Gary, 1988). Corroborating witnesses are a good source of evidence, but they rarely exist since sexual abuse usually takes place in secrecy. Perpetrators are likely to deny that they have engaged in sexual abuse, fearing rejection, shame, and criminal prosecution.

Child abuse thrives in the shadow of secrecy. It lives by inattention. (Bakan, 1979, p. 139)

Children do not often make false allegations or misunderstand innocent behavior (Jones & McGraw, 1987). Interviewing sexual abuse victims requires specialized knowledge and techniques. Children making true allegations can usually give detailed information about the context in which the incidents occurred, and describe the sexual victimization and their own emotional state (Faller, 1988b).

The first goal of intervention is to stop the sexual abuse. Victims need protection not only from further abuse but from retribution from family members for disclosing the sexual abuse. Intervention possibilities include permanently removing the child from the home, criminal prosecution of the perpetrator, permanent exclusion of the perpetrator from the family unit, and reunification. Careful assessment of each parent is needed to guide case planning decisions. Mothers who are financially independent, or are able to become so, and who are loving and protective to their children can fruitfully be involved in a family rehabilitation plan. For perpetrators, key factors are their general level of functioning as providers and family members, the extent to which they acknowledge and feel guilty about the abuse they have inflicted on a child, and the duration, intensity, and frequency of the abuse (Faller, 1988c).

The Child Witness. Legal entities that may intervene in sexual abuse cases include child protective services, law enforcement, the juvenile court, prosecuting attorneys and the criminal courts. These agencies often are not well coordinated. Children who are sexual abuse victims may suffer additional trauma by having to describe the circumstances of their abuse to many investigators. If the case is criminally prosecuted, children face public court appearances, confrontation with their abuser, and cross examination. The process may be even more painful if the accused is a family member than if he is a stranger, since the child and others in the family may have mixed feelings about criminally prosecuting a father or close relative of the child. The child wants the abuse to stop but may not understand the need for legal interventions to stop it (Berliner & Barbieri, 1984).

Decisions on whether or not to prosecute a sex abuse case through the criminal justice system depend on the plan that is developed to protect the child. When the plan requires that the legal system become involved, several innovative techniques and procedures have gained acceptance as ways to reduce trauma to the child during the investigative phase. These are identified by Duquette (1988a, pp. 399–403) as follows:

1. Adopt the federal rule of evidence establishing the presumption that the child witness is competent. This would eliminate the need to have the child's trustworthiness as a witness established, through interviews with judges and court personnel.

2. Reduce the number of interviews and interviewers the child must endure by coordinating the procedures of different agencies. Videotape the initial interview, so that those who need to know the child's story can watch the videotape. Employ "vertical prosecution," in which a single prosecutor is assigned to the case through all stages of juvenile and criminal court proceedings. Videotapes can often substitute for the child's live testimony at preliminary and grand jury hearings.

3. Allow an emotionally supportive adult to accompany the child through all stages of the legal process, such as a relative or a victim/advocate. This escort can make the child much more comfortable as she encounters unfamiliar people and situations.

4. Allow children with limited vocabularies to use anatomically correct dolls and drawings with which they can show interviewers and judges what happened to them.

5. Expedite the legal process.

Two recent U.S. Supreme Court decisions have clarified procedures courts may use to protect child witnesses during a trial of the accused abuser. These clarifications were needed because many states, in order to protect child victims, were permitting closed-circuit television to present the child's testimony to the court, with the child in a separate room from that of the

court. Some states were also allowing as evidence statements children had made to third parties such as physicians or investigators. The use of closed-circuit television and the admission of statements made to third parties raise constitutional issues. The Bill of Rights grants the accused the right "in all criminal prosecutions . . . to be confronted with the witnesses against him." This confrontation does not directly occur if the witness is on closed-circuit television or if her/his statements are reported by a third party.

In *Maryland v. Craig,* by a five-to-four majority, the Supreme Court found that the state has a compelling interest in protecting child victims of sex crimes from further trauma and embarrassment. Therefore, testimony on closed-circuit television was admissible if the trial judge first determined that this procedure was necessary to protect the welfare of the particular child being called to testify. The Court noted that the Maryland law that it upheld ensured that all other elements of confrontation were in place—the oath of the witness, cross-examination, and the opportunity for the Court to observe the demeanor of the witness—even though the child was appearing on closed-circuit television (Greenhouse, 1990b).

In a related case, the Court limited the ability of prosecutors to present as evidence statements the child made to third parties. In *Idaho v. Wright,* an Idaho court had admitted as evidence a pediatrician's testimony about his interview with a three-year-old girl whose mother and a male acquaintance were accused of sexually abusing her. In another five-to-four decision, the Supreme Court ruled that the pediatrician's testimony was not admissible because no evidence had been offered to show that the circumstances of the interview were such as to ensure the reliability of the child's statements to the pediatrician. However, the Court did not spell out how the reliability of a child's statements to a third party is to be established. Nor did the Court give a clear guideline on the use of videotapes of investigative interviews with children as evidence later on in court (Greenhouse, 1990b). These issues await further clarification from the courts.

Cases of child sexual abuse raise particularly difficult issues for professionals in the human services. Many people are bewildered or repelled to learn that adults could have sexual feelings toward children. Discounting or disbelieving the child or rage at the perpetrator are understandable but unhelpful reactions, as are blaming the victim or the mother (Wattenberg, 1987; Faller, 1988a). Another reason that sexual abuse cases are difficult to manage is that they require the specialized knowledge of several disciplines. The medical, legal, mental health, and child welfare fields each contribute needed knowledge to the resolution of sexual abuse cases. Multidisciplinary teams are an effective way for the community to respond to sexual abuse cases. Through a team approach the resources of the community can be effectively coordinated to arrange a case plan that is most likely to assist the victim's recovery (Faller, 1988a).

Preventive Programs for Children

Widespread attention to sexual abuse of children . . . has led to a variety of books, films, and one-to-one or group interventions aimed at teaching children protective behaviors. The intent is to empower children to an extent that will enable them to exercise more control over what happens to them in an often unfriendly world. This development is usually applauded. . . . Children and youth . . . generally receive too little planned instruction about their bodies, their sexuality, and how to handle encounters with the world around them. . . . However, in an enthusiasm for new techniques, we may be expecting children to bear too much of the responsibility to protect themselves from adult behaviors that adults themselves do not understand sufficiently and find abhorrent. With the best of intentions, we may be tampering with some children's already fragile sense of basic trust in the world. . . . Teaching "good touches," "bad touches," "private zones," and skepticism of strangers is a simplistic approach. Most sexual abuse of children goes on in the child's own home and involves someone she or he has been led to trust. . . . Do we not overstate the degree of empowerment that a young child can maintain in such situations and ignore the complexity of the judgments as to when "good touches" that were first introduced gradually within an atmosphere of affection and trust become "bad touches"? (Costin, 1985b, 210–211)

In a study of the effectiveness of preventive sexual abuse programs, Reppucci and Haugaard (1989) examined the context and format of such programs, and evaluated selected programs for effectiveness and the untested assumptions that guide them, most of which have developed from anecdotal clinical information. They found that few, if any, of the prevention programs were comprehensive enough to have a meaningful impact in the complex process a child goes thorough in an attempt to repel an abusive approach or to report the act of abuse. Reppucci and Haugaard concluded that the extent to which the programs are working is unclear, as is whether the programs may be causing more harm than good, for example, the possibility that some children may actually be placed at greater risk for sexual abuse if adults incorrectly assume that children are protected and reduce their vigilance about the problem.

In an enthusiasm for new preventive strategies to confront a highly publicized problem, professionals often tend to break the problem into small parts for treatment, which inadvertently results in neglect of the ubiquitous related problems and the larger societal context.

Child Fatalities

Each year about 1,100 children die from abuse or neglect. Neglect and abuse each account for about half of these deaths. This figure is probably a low estimate. An unknown number of deaths officially labeled as caused by accidents, Sudden Infant Death Syndrome, or child homicide may be more accurately attributed to child maltreatment (Daro & Mitchel, 1989). One study has estimated the number of child maltreatment deaths each year to be 5,000 (Christoffel et al., 1981).

The little research that has been done on the etiology of child maltreatment deaths indicates that only a few factors distinguish fatal from nonfatal abuse. Death is more likely to result from abuse if the child is younger, a father or father-substitute is in the home, a paternal history of drug use and arrests exists, the victim or siblings had been placed out of the home at an earlier time by court order, the maternal grandmother does not live with the family, siblings have medical problems, and the parents are separated or divorced. Fatal cases are more likely to have adolescent parents and two-parent households than are nonfatal cases (Mitchel, 1987).

Between 25 percent and 50 percent of fatal child maltreatment cases are known to child protective services or another community agency before the fatal incident occurs. Policy makers are concerned with how to increase the percentage of potentially lethal family situations that come to the attention of child protective services, and how to prevent the deaths from occurring once the family is linked to the child protective system. Research is needed to develop a more accurate system than now exists for identifying families at high risk for child fatality. This would help protective service workers to spot dangerous situations and offer services, even if no serious incident has yet occurred. Preventing child fatality will also require improved training for caseworkers and manageable caseloads.

Better linkages between service systems would also help to identify and monitor families at risk for child fatality. Some states have established death review boards with representatives from health services, law enforcement, child protective services, the medical examiner's/coroner's office, and the prosecutor's office. These multidisciplinary groups review the circumstances leading to the death, including the extent to which social and health agencies were involved with the family. They also develop and implement policies to improve the response of the community to endangered children. An important function of review boards is to develop more accurate definitions of child maltreatment deaths and to maintain records on these cases (Daro & Mitchel, 1989).

ASPECTS OF PROTECTIVE SERVICES

Nature and Use of Authority

To make effective use of the authority essential to protective services, all those who provide these services must understand its nature and source and convey it clearly and objectively; the parents, in turn, must be able to some degree to accept the authority if their child care and family functioning are to improve.

Authority is a complex phenomenon. Authority is the power to influence or command thought, opinion, or behavior. The key concepts—*power, influence,* and *behavior* appear in other definitions of authority, sometimes used in such a way as to result in a sociolegal emphasis, and in other instances, more focused on the psychological aspects of authority. For example, Parsons defined authority in this way:

> Authority is an institutionally recognized right to influence the action of others, regardless of their immediate personal attitudes to the direction of influence. It is exercised by the incumbent of an office or other socially defined status. (1954, p. 76)

This definition is primarily sociolegal. The power to influence behavior stems from the authority of an office, or designated position, and the possession of this formal power is a legitimate one, a matter of right attached to the person who occupies a specified and socially endorsed position in the institutional structure of a society.

Mencher defined authority as "the power to induce changes in, or to exert control over, the behavior of another. Its influence is dependent upon how it is perceived or accepted by those to whom it is directed (1960, p. 127)." This definition is more focused on the psychological aspects, emphasizing that the power to bring about change, that is, to influence behavior, is subject to another person's perception of authority and readiness to be influenced, directed, or controlled.

Elements of both these definitions are essential when authority is defined in the context of protective services: the sociolegal emphasis on the nature of authority as a legitimate possession of the power and right to influence, traceable to office or other mandate; and the psychological emphasis on factors that enter into all authority relationships and make it necessary for the person who presents the authority to find some degree of acceptance on the part of those over whom this power and right are exercised.

Authority in Child Protective Services. To be effective in protecting children from neglect and abuse, the worker must rely on and use both the sociolegal and the psychological aspects of authority. The worker who extends child protective services is given sociolegal authority by the law authorizing the agency to act in ways that will protect children from neglect and abuse. A caseworker's position and role in a publicly mandated child protective agency, then, embodies a legitimate and formal assignment of authority. This legal aspect of authority in child protection is expressed most centrally in the agency representative's duty to investigate complaints about the care of children, and if substandard care or maltreatment is found, to continue to visit the home until the level of care is improved or until the children are cared for adequately in another setting. Legal authority, then, brings what De Schweinitz and De Schweinitz refer to as the power "to be there" (1964, p. 288).

While legal authority is a necessary element in protective services, it is not sufficient by itself. The power of someone else "to be there" can lead to an oppressive sense of restriction on parents that may only exacerbate their inadequacy and resistance to change. Whether the agency representative who exercises the authority "to be there" can then motivate neglecting or abusing parents to face their need to change—the first step toward improved child care—will depend in large measure on the extent to which the psychological aspect of her authority, that is knowledge and skill in ways of helping people, is developed and used.

What is the nature of this part of the child protective worker's authority that is accorded such a decisive influence in improving the care of neglected and abused children? Some characterize it as a psychological force and cite Fromm's definition: "an interpersonal relation in which one person looks upon another as somebody superior to him" (Fromm, 1941, p. 164). This definition suggests that when the authority of the worker is based on competence, the parent can acknowledge that the worker is superior for the purposes of the problem at hand and can show a readiness to reconsider his or her parental functions (Studt, 1954).

Psychological authority does not imply some intangible quality that a child protective worker may or may not happen to possess; it can be learned through study and experience. It encompasses an understanding of the law and administrative policies that relate to child protection, and of a community's standards in such areas as family life, health, and housing; the capacity to ascertain and evaluate relevant facts; a grasp of the nature of the protective worker's authority and an ability to use it constructively; sound judgment about the capacities of a particular parent; and an ability to develop, interpret, and implement a variety of treatment plans (De Schweinitz & De Schweinitz, 1964).

Use of Authority. Social workers in agencies serving families referred for treatment by child protective services, and others providing ongoing services to confirmed child protective services cases, are vested with both sociolegal and psychological authority. Their authority becomes most clearly evident at these points of service: (1) when services are initiated even though the parents have not asked for them; (2) when parents are confronted with the reality that their care of their children is inadequate, and their basic choice is interpreted to them, that is, either to accept services to improve their level of child care or face the possibility of the children's removal from their home; and (3) in selected situations when it becomes necessary for the social worker to recommend that the child protection agency file a petition in court alleging neglect or abuse.

Authority need not be a necessary but negative part of protective services; it can be utilized as a factor to enable inadequate parents to fulfill their responsibility to their children more satisfactorily. The social worker who presents authority skillfully can use it to create a climate of communication that may motivate resistant parents toward change. As Koerin (1979) notes: "The authority of a caseworker may represent . . . a source of strength to rely on, and may represent a first encounter with consistent expectations and structure."

Certain difficulties commonly occur, however, and the social worker cannot expect parents to be motivated simply because he or she comes to them representing an agency with authority. This very action may tap a variety of negative feelings on the part of parents, who probably already have had harsh and demeaning experiences with persons in an authoritative relationship. Parents who become clients involuntarily respond to the agency's offer to help in varying ways, such as superficial compliance, hostility, passive resistance, and belligerent defiance. Some parents are deeply distrustful of authority, while others may welcome it as a means of escaping their burdens and responsibilities. Whatever the parents' initial response, the social worker attempts to accept with empathy the basis for their feelings, but proceeds to identify objectively the areas of child care that are of concern to the community and tells the parents the first concrete tasks they can perform in using

the service, for example, taking a child to a medical clinic, getting him or her off to school each day, serving food regularly, following through on a search for employment, or applying for assistance.

One of the principal tasks of the social worker is to develop alternatives, or choices of action, for the parents to consider, and to create opportunities for them to use their own initiative to improve their situation. The social worker must convey that their freedom is restricted in only one direction—they are not free to neglect or abuse their children. Furthermore, the community endorses the right of the parents to receive help in improving their level of child care before declaring them neglectful, and the social worker stands ready to try to help them without resorting to legal action; but the community will not cease to be concerned until the level of child care is improved, and the social worker "will not disappear or be denied" (Moss, 1963, p. 388).

The social worker in protective services cannot expect marked improvement immediately. The parents' problems are very great and their capacities are limited, so expectations, although presented consistently, must be reasonable. Encouragement and endorsement of even very minimal achievements toward improved family functioning are necessary.

In extending protective services, especially to very low-income or "problem" families, one of the most difficult matters facing the agency and its staff is the maintenance of proper balance in the use of authority. The families are difficult, often exasperating and defeating. The children are vulnerable and dependent on others for improvement in their care; citizens in the neighborhood and community are affronted by the family and expect the social agency to act and effect improvement in the situation promptly. Under such pressure, administrative actions that dangerously erode the right to direct one's own life may come to be regarded as inevitable.

It is important that administrative and legal

procedures be in place to safeguard the rights of the families or "there is a danger that the rights of the families may be obscured by the urgency and the magnitude of the problems they present to society" (Philp & Timms, 1957, pp. 22–23).

When neglect or abuse of a child continues and parents cannot accept their need to change, or they have disabilities too great to permit sufficient improvement in meeting their parental duties, court action must be sought to clarify the parents' continuing rights and responsibilities, and to determine the future status of the child and a suitable plan of care. When such action is taken, parents are entitled to know from the social worker why the agency is moving in this way, what their part in the procedures will be, and what basic questions will be decided by the court. In addition, they are entitled to present their own point of view before the court and to receive due consideration of their rights.

Rights of Child, Parents, and Society

Child protective services in a democracy must provide safeguards for the rights of the child, the parents, and society; the development of clear standards and rules, as a basis for agency intervention, and the proper observance of legal provisions will help to ensure that decision making is reasonable and based on relevant criteria.

The Need for Objective Criteria. Two key decision points precede the inclusion of a family as a confirmed child protection services case: (1) the decision to accept the report for investigation of alleged abuse or neglect; and (2) the decision to confirm the report after conducting an investigation.

The authority to investigate a complaint about a child's neglect or abuse is made clear in the mandate given to a protective agency by statute or charter. Further, the Child Abuse Prevention and Treatment Act of 1974 requires that, to be eligible for funding, a state must investigate all reports of abuse and neglect. Most state reporting laws are in compliance with this federal requirement (Wells et al., 1989). However, state laws and agency policies may permit initial screening to determine whether or not the referral is a valid report of child abuse and neglect and therefore needs to be investigated.

A recent survey found that child protective services agencies commonly screen reports. The following are criteria agencies may use to screen in reports for investigation, as identified by the survey. (1) The report gives identifying information on the perpetrator. (2) The perpetrator is a legal guardian or regular caretaker of the child. Mistreatment by babysitters, neighbors, and strangers, for example, may be referred to the police in some jurisdictions. (3) A specific act of mistreatment is alleged. Reports of parental substance abuse or other illegal or immoral behavior in and of itself might not be accepted for investigation unless the reporter states that abuse or neglect has occurred. (4) If the problem reported seems to be in the provenance of another agency, the situation may be handled best by referral, not investigation of abuse or neglect (e.g., school truancy, delinquency, family eviction, physical and mental health problems). (5) Reports involving custody disputes and repeated unfounded allegations made by a single reporter on the same family may be screened out prior to investigation (Wells et al., 1989).

Most people who report instances of abuse and neglect to child protective services are motivated by genuine concern about children they know whose care is clearly less than optimal. Relatively few reports are malicious or intentionally frivolous. When concerned persons desire to respond protectively to the plight of a child, understandably they are likely to call child protective services, the most widely publicized and well-known child and family agency in many communities. Yet, as the above list of screening criteria shows, intake workers may sometimes appropriately decline to subject a family to an investigation, if the reported problem is not abuse or neglect. Less serious problems usually can be handled more appropriately by a genuine offer of help from a child and family agency serving clients on a voluntary basis.

Investigating Abuse and Neglect. Once the child protective service agency has accepted a report, it must conduct an investigation. It is not clear, however, which facts must be evident in a particular situation to justify an authoritative offer of the agency's help beyond the preliminary investigation. Traditionally, the decision to continue agency intervention is based on information collected through a social study. Such a study is likely to reflect a broad psychosocial approach to the family's functioning and the child's well-being, rather than an appraisal of the child care situation that is focused on the community's and the statute's definition of neglect and abuse. As a result, decisions on whether or not to substantiate the allegation of abuse or neglect may lack consistency from one worker to another or even within a worker's own caseload. Another problem is that the decisions made, even if consistent, do not necessarily separate out the most serious cases from the less serious ones (Selinske, 1983). The mandate of child protection services to investigate cases without clear, consistent, and valid guidelines for decision making has led to justifiable criticism of the child protection system.

> [It] invests judges and state agency personnel as *parens patriae* with almost limitless discretion in areas generally under the exclusive control of parents. Such legislation is used to justify the *ad hoc* creation of standards of intervention in case-by-case determinations to investigate, supervise, and supervene parental judgments. It invites the exploitation of parents and children by state officials. Acting in accord with their own personal child-rearing preferences, officials have been led to discriminate against poor, minority, and other disfavored families. (Goldstein et al., 1979, p. 17)

Recently, the concept of *risk assessment* has received attention as a way to improve con-

> *As I look at CPS intake services, I think of the Statue of Liberty. CPS stands with arms poised to the community and says, "Give me your tired, your poor, your huddled masses. . . ." Too often it takes in all kinds of cases without clearly defining and discriminating what belongs in child protective services. (Brown, 1987, p. 13)*

sistency in decision making and the identification of serious cases. Risk assessment, like an investigation of a report of abuse or neglect, involves collecting information on the family. The difference is that an investigation is oriented toward the past, to determine whether or not maltreatment has occurred. Risk assessment is oriented toward the future; it attempts to establish the likelihood, or an educated prediction based on a careful examination of the data (Palmer, n.d.), that the child will be maltreated at another time. Child protective services agencies use risk assessment to prioritize cases for investigation and services, and also to help determine the level of service that a family will receive. For example, a family rated as "high risk" would receive immediate and intense interventions, in comparison to a family rated as "low risk."

Items on risk assessment instruments are those that research and practice experience have shown to predict later maltreatment of a child, whether or not maltreatment has already occurred. The following is a list of "risk factors" compiled by the National Association of Public Child Welfare Administrators (1988).

- Impact of parental behavior: CPS intervenes if behavior is serious and harmful even if harm to the child is not easily observed (e.g., emotional maltreatment, sexual abuse)
- Severity of abuse or neglect
- Age, physical and mental ability of the child
- Frequency, recency of alleged abuse or neglect
- Credibility of the reporter

- Location and access of child to perpetrator
- Parental willingness to protect child and cooperate
- Parental ability to protect

Risk assessment instruments are mainly still under development, and have received little validation so far when used under field conditions. Proponents of risk assessment emphasize that they are intended as an aid to worker judgment. They are not yet accurate enough to replace the experienced judgment of seasoned caseworkers, and should not be relied on as the sole basis for case decisions (Miller et al., 1987; Baird & Neuenfeldt, 1988; Magura et al., 1987; Magura & Moses, 1986; Tatara, 1987; Pecora et al., 1986–1987; McDonald et al., 1988).

Risk assessment instruments hold promise of standardizing data collection and helping to make decisions more consistent within an agency, since all workers will collect the same areas of information on families and share, to some extent, a common understanding on how to assess the information collected. However, prediction of human behavior is quite inexact. Helfer, for example, believes that, unless the parent is suffering serious, obvious disability, it is impossible to tell with reliability that the child will be harmed. He concludes that "the ability to separate out a distinct group of parents (or future parents) who will physically abuse or seriously neglect one or more of their children will probably never be possible" (Helfer, 1976).

Because future abuse or neglect is hard to predict in families where it has not yet occurred, a critical issue is whether the absence of an accepted norm of child-rearing behavior, per se, should provide the basis for intervention, or whether intervention should depend on a clear indication that a specific deviation from the norm in parental behavior is producing an adverse effect on a particular child. Besharov took the latter position: "Laws should be redrafted so that child protective intervention is authorized only when the parents have already engaged in abusive or neglectful behavior. . . . Intervention should also be authorized if the parent did something which was capable of causing serious injury" (Besharov, 1985, p. 580).

If this injunction were accepted in setting standards for the provision of protective services, intervention would not be justified on the basis of parental behavior that is contrary to accepted norms, such as excessive use of alcohol or irregularities in sexual behavior, unless it could be shown that the child's physical or mental health is adversely affected. Protective service, in other words, is not "a punitive attempt to reorganize parental behavior for its own sake" (Cheney, 1966, p. 90), but an attempt to protect children from neglect and abuse, and to advance their welfare.

Wald also endorses a narrowing of the scope of coercive state intervention in matters of neglect. He maintains that definitions of parental neglect should be premised on a substantial deference to parental autonomy in child rearing, in recognition of our political commitment to a diversity of life-styles and child-rearing patterns. Further, he contends, neglect statutes should focus on the kinds of harm, specifically defined, from which we wish to protect all children. Wald is influenced toward this view by observations of the difficulties in improving a child's situation through state intervention except in cases involving seriously damaged children. He takes note of the lack of knowledge and public welfare resources to make involuntary intervention effective. He recognizes the correlation between neglect and poverty, and society's failure to provide each family with adequate income to assure basic necessities in housing, nutrition, and health services. But he believes that these large societal problems should be tackled by noncoercive means—ones that reinforce parental autonomy (Wald, 1975).

Goldstein, Freud, and Solnit propose a similar set of rigorous standards before state intervention is warranted. The approach is based on the following beliefs:

When family integrity is broken or weakened by state intrusion, [the child's] needs are thwarted and . . . the effect on the child's developmental progress is invariably detrimental. . . . By its intrusion the state may make a bad situation worse and therefore . . . the law [should] ask in every case whether removal from an unsatisfactory home is the beneficial measure it purports to be. (1979, p. 17)

The authors' advocacy of limiting state intervention is seen as consistent with both legal principles and knowledge of child development.

In commenting on proposals to limit state intrusion, Brieland and Lemmon note that such proposals remind one "of the intent of Gault for delinquency: more care, more specificity, more caution, more attention to parental autonomy and therefore to parental rights" (Brieland & Lemmon, 1977, pp. 205–206).

Approaches to Treatment

Child protective services are initiated with families who have very serious and long-standing problems in different areas of psychosocial functioning. No single treatment method has proved uniformly successful. The family worker is advised to use a broadly based treatment approach, with attention to individual, family, neighborhood, and community interactions. Family workers are often part of multidisciplinary teams, in which case their functions may include coordinating and monitoring the interventions from mental health, legal, medical, family service, and law enforcement agencies. Further, family workers often recruit assistance for the family from community-based agencies, homemaker service, parent-aides, the schools, parent education programs, self-help groups, employment service, housing assistance, welfare, and other services that can bolster the family's ability to maintain the child safely at home. Each component of a carefully designed treatment plan contributes to the family's rehabilitation. They are held together and given

meaning to the family through the relationship the family has with their primary worker.

Establishing a "working agreement" or contract with families is a means for establishing goals, collaborating with the client to define the problem and solutions, defining the responsibilities of each party, and setting time lines and is a basis for monitoring and evaluation (Maluccio & Marlowe, 1974). A contract keeps clearly in front of the parents what the protective services expect the parents to do in order for the child to remain in the home and provides measurable indicators of success. A contract can also help clarify and keep straight the purpose of each of the referrals the worker makes for the family.

An effective protective service will make services easily available to families. For many neglecting and abusing families, help must be located within their own neighborhoods and must be available at night and on weekends. These are people for whom emergencies and crises abound; at such times they lack the capacity to deter their feelings or sustain a modicum of balance until the time for a regular appointment. In addition, the family worker must represent a stable, continuing, and reliable force to the family; on the one hand, he or she makes clear to them in easily grasped language what is not being done for the children and what needs to be done; on the other hand, they can be confident that the family worker will help them or protect the children if they cannot.

Worker–Client Relationship.   The relationship between the social worker and the client is critical to successful service. A study by the Family Service Association of America found that the relationship was by far the strongest predictor of outcome (Beck & Jones, 1973). Similar findings were reported in *A Second Chance for Families* (Jones et al., 1976). A good client-worker relationship helps engage and motivate clients and usually involves agreement on the problems and how to solve them (Jones et al., 1981).

At the beginning of building a trusting relationship with the family, a worker must "manage" any bitter, shocked, or incredulous feelings about parents who hurt their children or who are indifferent to their distress or neglected condition. Management of such feelings includes keeping them subservient to the needs of the victimized child, the parents, and the plan of treatment. Social workers must deal appropriately with varying attitudes on the part of persons in the community—sometimes harsh, punitive reactions toward the parents, and sometimes a reluctance to interfere with parental rights.

One of the realities in child protective services is that clients and social workers often come from different races, genders, and social classes. Davis and Proctor (1989), in their review of the literature, state that research is conclusive that these differences are salient issues in the treatment relationship, a point that many workers know intuitively. Both the social worker and the client may initially feel ill at ease in working with someone whose life experiences and world view are perceived to be different from one's own. Clients confronted with a worker of a different race, gender, or class may have initial concerns relating to: (1) *trust* ("Does this person have my best interests at heart?"); (2) *competence* ("Does the worker have professional expertise or mastery of skills that can resolve my problems?"); or (3) *credibility* ("Does the worker have sufficient understanding of my social reality or my world view?") (Davis & Proctor, 1989, p. ix). These questions are likely to be particularly pressing for clients who are receiving services involuntarily and whose workers embody the legal authority of the state. Workers who are aware of the implications of their own personal demographics for the treatment relationship and have become well informed about client groups with whom they differ can successfully allay initial suspicion and are able to form constructive treatment relationships with their clients (Davis & Proctor, 1989).

Considering the well-entrenched problems

neglecting and abusing parents have, and the heavy losses that they experience daily in their lives, it is not reasonable to expect that they can readily improve their family situations. Just as the involuntary nature of protective service differs from the voluntary request for help characterizing most family services, so does the worker–client interaction differ in the amount of consistent "reaching out" the social worker must do to demonstrate interest, concern, and readiness to help.

Reaching out to involuntary clients entails more than "going out to" them through home visits, or displaying aggressiveness in offering a service. Rather, "it is a frame of mind, a psychological readiness, a determination of the social worker to find a way to help the client" (Haas, 1959, p. 44). This determination has to be strong enough to persist in the face of rebuff and to withstand the "testing out" that the parent carries on before showing some sign of a beginning trust and meaningful involvement with the social worker. "In such testing a parent might hang her head out of a window during the entire interview, or let the television set blare as loudly as possible. (Frequently, reducing the volume of the television set, or finally turning it off, was a barometer of a family's acceptance of the worker.) Often the parents left the room during the interview or even went out of doors, only to return later expecting to find the worker still there. On some occasions a mother would surround herself with friends or relatives. On other occasions she would be rude and take pleasure in the children's overt aggression toward the worker" (Bandler, 1967, pp. 261–262).

To these kinds of behavior, the family worker must respond with firmness, consistent interest, lack of retaliation, and clearly conveyed expectations. To reach out successfully to neglecting and abusing parents, one cannot respond to such rejecting attitudes and behaviors at face value; instead, these must be evaluated and used as diagnostic clues to the parents' experiences with other people in an authoritative position, and to appropriate ways to help them.

Regardless of their initial responses, neglecting and abusing parents need an authoritative structure and someone who approaches them not only with sympathy but also with firm expectations that they will be able to improve their situation. They may come to realize that this kind of aggressive reaching out is "caring about them."

Neglecting and abusing parents generally place their own gratifications ahead of their children's. Because their early needs to be dependent were not fulfilled in a nurturing, growth-producing way, they may still yearn for childhood satisfactions from their own parents. Preoccupied with their own unmet needs, they are often not sensitive to the needs of their infants for soothing, feeding, cuddling, and protection. "An infant may be perceived alternately as a mechanical doll to be fed and changed when convenient or as a demanding, precocious tyrant, scheming how to get his own way at the parents' expense" (Kempe, 1987, p. 361).

An obstacle to teaching such parents how to take better care of their infants is that the worker's concern for the child may rouse the parent's jealousy and anger. Once the rudiments of a trusting relationship have been formed between the worker and the parent, it may be possible to recruit the parent's interest in providing better care. One way to help the parent is to show her how to elicit rewarding behavior from the infant. Learning to make the baby smile can motivate the parent to further efforts. The parent may take pride in showing the worker newly learned competency in feeding the infant, stopping the baby from crying, and soothing him to sleep. As the baby progresses developmentally to locomotion and the beginnings of self-control, the worker may be able to help the parent relinquish the need to control the child's behavior totally. The parent needs to learn that encouraging playfulness and independence are ways to be a "good" parent (Kempe, 1987).

Meeting an inadequate adult's dependency needs, even partially, is demanding and can be draining of one's own strengths, particularly when the inadequacy produces hurt or lonely and uncared-for children. Because neglecting and abusing families are extraordinarily difficult to work with, and because many treatment decisions are critical to the well-being of children, it is important that the responsibility for making decisions be shared, through case review teams, multidisciplinary groups, or other forums. Not only does shared decision-making lessen the burden for the individual family worker, but also it lessens the possibility that decisions will be made from misperceptions or bias. "To make these decisions alone and to have to then handle the potential failures alone, can be devastating to any therapist" (Beezley et al., 1974, p. 170).

Services for Maltreating Families

Coordinated Service Delivery.   Cases of abuse and neglect are complex, often involving multiproblem or severely disorganized families. In such cases, the protective service worker is unable to directly provide the full range of required help. Shapiro's (1979) study of protective service found that families who received several services did better than those who received only one or two.

The Juvenile Protective Association of Chicago carried out an unusual and long-term demonstration of a *comprehensive, readily available range of services* for neglecting families. The demonstration was notable in a number of respects. From one large building complex, the center staff developed and offered to children at risk and their families within a neighborhood these services: casework; group work; day care; homemaker service; temporary foster care; emergency shelter care; pediatric service; education of children in a special school established for children of the neighborhood who had been excluded from public school, or had been excessively truant, or had never enrolled in school; after-school programs; financial aid for special needs essential to rehabilitation; and transportation to and from the center. Having this range of services available under the agency's own administrative control meant that needed services were more easily available and coordinated. A strong effort prevailed in reaching out to parents and their children at risk. The entire staff of the center worked as a team; hierarchical roles and inflexible assignment of staff were avoided (Sullivan et al., 1975).

The following factors have been gleaned from other studies of comprehensive services:

1. An appropriate array of services must be available—not counseling alone or concrete services alone, but a combination.
2. Outreach efforts are essential; merely having the services available is not enough. Clients must be enabled to use these services through such mechanisms as (1) physically bringing the client to the service by providing transportation, escort service, or payment for transportation; (2) advocacy efforts with other institutions to obtain needed services for clients; and (3) skill in case management and resource utilization, since the whole array of needed services is unlikely to be provided by one agency, and workers will have to obtain and coordinate services from many sources (Jones et al., 1981, p. 73).

Help with Reality Problems. For neglecting and abusing parents, actions usually speak louder than words. The disorganized daily living pattern of neglecting families means that family workers must relate directly to everyday problems and behaviors, and give direct help with pressing reality problems. These parents are not ready to deal with introspective questions, as highly motivated and verbal clients tend to be.

As important as these forms of help are, rarely do workers from public protective service agencies have an opportunity to provide such assistance. Large caseloads and high turnover of personnel often prevent any but token efforts. Increasingly, agencies purchase homemaker or parent-aid services from a voluntary agency to fulfill these needs. (See Chapter 1.)

In one innovative program in Detroit, the workers are university students who receive intensive training on offering comprehensive services to families whose children are likely to require foster care if home conditions do not improve. The agency, Parents and Children Together (PACT) each year recruits students interested in graduate study in the human services for a one-year internship as PACT counselors (Van Meter, 1986).

The counselors must be prepared to go into the home and respond to tangible problems and demands the family is unable to cope with. For example, a counselor may need to teach the mother how to shop more economically, perhaps by going to the store with her; it may be necessary to accompany a parent to the legal services office or a medical clinic, or to participate in making a request to a landlord for repairs. PACT has an emergency fund for food, clothing, and shelter.

Sometimes the counselor must help a mother look for new housing, and then help her to move her family and belongings. "Many PACT parents have commented on how important it was to their family functioning to get into decent housing" (Van Meter, 1986 p. 81). Sometimes the counselor must transport children to nursery schools if they are to go; on arriving at the home, the worker may be requested to help dress the children and see that they have breakfast before they leave, until such time as the mother can begin to assume these responsibilities herself.

In all this activity, the counselor is demonstrating how tasks can be done, supporting the parents in their own efforts, and helping them recognize and feel the improvement in the family situation when such tasks are performed.

The aims of a practical approach to everyday problems include helping a family achieve some order in its daily life, reinforcing its developing capacity to deal with its reality problems more effectively, bolstering the self-esteem of individual family members, and changing the parents' isolated way of life. To achieve these aims the counselor sets limits, supervises, reinforces the parents' desire to improve their situation, and teaches by a combination of examples, warm interest, and support for parental efforts.

Emergency Services.   The purpose of these services is to offer families a substitute for the parents for a short period of time, to prevent the need of placing the children in foster care. *Emergency homemakers* are used to prevent sudden foster placement of children who have been left alone. It usually is a traumatic experience for children to be removed from their own homes by strangers in the middle of the night. And even though an investigation may show that foster care is necessary, it is important to delay placement so that children can be helped to understand what is happening, their parents can participate in the removal, and an appropriate placement can be arranged. One "emergency parent" service worked this way: When a complaint was received about children being left alone, the social worker first tried to locate the parent or some responsible adult known to the family. If this effort failed, an emergency parent drove to the home, equipped with an emergency kit (blankets, food, a flashlight, a first-aid kit, light bulbs, candy, disposable diapers, insect spray, and an aluminum folding cot), and took over the care of the children. The emergency parent's function was to perform the normal supervisory tasks of a parent until the child's parents returned or another plan was arranged. The sponsoring agency reported that the emergency parent service completely eliminated nighttime emergency placement of children left alone in their homes (Paget, 1967).

Crisis nurseries provide alternatives to parents when stressful situations threaten to become overwhelming and result in injury to or abandonment of a child. By providing short-term care, the nursery can give a parent time to draw back and consider alternatives to abusive behavior (Beezley et al., 1974).

"Treating Loneliness."   This phrase with respect to neglectful mothers grew out of the observation that "among neglectful parents are many who make their circumstances worse by self-imposed aloneness, and who must thus live with dreadful loneliness" (Polansky et al., 1981, p. 210). Although the roots of this isolation may lie in circumstances of the parent's own childhood, it can to some extent be remedied by providing parents the opportunity to be with other people.

Group treatment of abusing and neglecting parents has been used as a medium for dealing with individual problems, marital problems, and child management techniques (Bean, 1971; Bellucci, 1972; Beezley et al., 1974; Linnell et al., 1984). However, an often overlooked function of these groups, apart from other benefits, is that they give parents an opportunity to socialize with other adults.

Self-help parent groups, usually called "Parents Anonymous," are a source of support to many abusing and neglecting families. The first such organization was founded by Jolly K., who herself had been an abusing mother and repeatedly had found agency protective services not suited to her needs. Members of these self-help groups offer each other a nonjudgmental climate of anonymity in which they can face problems with other persons in similar situations. Telephone numbers are shared for purposes of relief at points of impending crisis. Some protective service agencies have been sufficiently impressed with the strength of these self-help groups that they refer families to them as an additional form of treatment (Beezley et al., 1974). Some parents are able to use the nonthreatening self-help group as a first step toward accepting more intensive interventions, such as individual or family therapy with a mental health practitioner (Fritz, 1986).

Family support programs of all types address the parents' need for companionship along with offering a wide range of other services (Miller & Whitaker, 1988; Zigler & Black, 1989). An Israeli researcher, recognizing the isolation and past deprivation of many abusing parents, tested the idea that mere human contact, not accompanied by any formal treatment, would positively affect parents' behavior. Twenty families whose children had been hospitalized for abuse during the year received social visits from young women who lived in the same neighborhood and were of the same socioeconomic background as the abusive mothers. The assigned visitor spent three hours a day, three days a week, for a period of three months, in the family's home, socializing and doing some housework. Changes in pretest and posttest scores revealed that nine of the mothers altered their abusive behavior, compared to only one in a matched control group. In interviews, the mothers explained why the visits were effective. Some mothers, recognizing that their abusive behavior was wrong, said that they were inhibited from abusing the child since the frequent visits meant that abuse could not be hidden. Mothers also cited the increased attention they received and the easing of burdens as helping them to control their abusive behavior. Significantly, a follow-up three months after the intervention stopped indicated that the effects were not lasting; only one of the mothers had maintained her nonabusive behavior. The author concluded that positive human contact by itself can reduce abusive behavior in parents, but only as long as the intervention continues. The service can be helpful as part of a multifaceted treatment plan, and, because of its low cost, would be feasible for families who need additional social support for a long period of time (Zimrin, 1984).

Self-Management Training. A promising approach to the treatment of abusive parents is the use of behavioral techniques to teach alternative responses to stress situations (Barth et al., 1983). Mastria et al. (1979) report the successful use of videotape, modeling, and feedback to teach (1) how to attend to cooperative behaviors, (2) how to ignore aggressive behavior, (3) how to identify behavioral cues leading to ag-

gressiveness, and (4) how to withdraw physically when the impulse to hit a child becomes great.

For effective treatment of neglecting and abusing families, the community needs to have an overall coordinated set of services to address the kinds of stresses—socioeconomic, psychological, and environmental—that bear upon families, especially single-parent families. Neglectful families, in particular, are subject to the overwhelming problems of poverty, inadequate housing, and social isolation. In planning treatment, attention must be given to the use of all social work methods and to means by which protective social workers can act as catalysts to those agents in the community whose function is primarily to change the pattern of social provisions.

Direct Service to Children. Protective services have focused on casework with the mother. But children in these families may need services directly and are entitled to help in their own right. Frequently, these children experience rejection in their communities and feel considerable pressure within their homes and outside as well. Many desperately need new experiences and opportunities to identify with appropriate older-child and adult role models. In some instances the child may need to be helped to modify the relationship with his or her parents and at the same time to retain what is necessary and constructive in it.

Children, because of their great responsiveness to environmental stimuli, are often able to show tangible improvement in treatment; this responsiveness may seem quite marked when contrasted with the entrenched resistance to change encountered in some of their parents. Workers understandably may be tempted to concentrate on salvaging the child and bypassing the parents, by placing the child in foster care or attempting to treat the child in the home while ignoring the parents. However, exclusive focus on the child ignores the reality that, in the long run, the child's psychological well-being and social adjustment will be influenced by ongoing home conditions. Unless the parents' behavior precludes the possibility, it is likely that the child will remain with or return to the parents. Therefore, child-focused treatment is undertaken most profitably with the participation of parents. Child treatment is particularly helpful if it is part of a comprehensive treatment plan that may include attention to individual family members and to the family as a whole (Kempe, 1987).

Therapeutic day care or preschool may give parents needed respite while permitting the child to spend part of the day in a growth-enhancing environment. Therapeutic preschools that include parents will give them a chance to receive enriching play experiences they missed as children and still need, permit modeling of appropriate child management techniques in a nonthreatening atmosphere by staff, and reduce parental isolation (Fraley, 1984; Welbourn & Mazuryk, 1980). For children, goals include (1) helping them to use words to describe actions and feelings; (2) helping them control impulsivity through offering alternatives to action and improving communication; (3) improving their ability to interact with peers; (4) offering new stimuli as they are able to integrate them; and (5) monitoring their development and home conditions (Seitz et al., 1985; Kempe, 1987).

For school-age children, problems arise in getting the child to treatment if the parents are uncooperative, either because they are uninterested or view the child's need for therapy as a poor reflection on them. Sometimes parents can be encouraged to facilitate treatment if the problem is defined as the child's unacceptable behavior and not as a family problem. The child's problems frequently include poor school performance and disruptive behavior that the parents want changed. Individual or group treatment at school may be feasible, but unfortunately gains will be limited if abuse continues at home (Kempe, 1987).

Adolescents often are referred for treatment because of their own behavior, including delinquency, truancy, substance abuse, suicidal ideas and gestures, school failure, and running away. The maltreatment at home underlying these behaviors is often overlooked. These young people may lack rudimentary ability to recognize, express, or cope with their emotions. They may have few cognitive skills for handling everyday life situations. They often lack self-esteem from years of belittlement and recrimination, and retreat to the margins of school life, where they feel more accepted (Kempe, 1987).

An innovative approach to maltreated adolescents is a self-help program established by Boys Town. The program includes a youth-staffed hot-line, a self-help group for maltreated youth, a pamphlet for youth on guidelines for recognizing maltreatment and taking steps to obtain help, and a public awareness campaign aimed at youth. The project grew out of a belief that such youth were isolated from potent, prosocial support systems. This is especially true in sexual abuse cases (Garbarino & Jacobson, 1978). Other similar programs may also include emergency shelters for youth and opportunities for ongoing family and individual counseling (*Adolescent Maltreatment,* 1984).

For school-age and adolescent children, individual and group treatment usually address the following problems: (1) trust-mistrust ("the therapist is tested constantly as to benevolence, reliability, consistency, and interest"); (2) need for nurturance, including food, attention, and possessions; (3) poor self-esteem and little capacity for pleasure; (4) poor ability to express emotions; and (5) poor cognitive and problem-solving skills (Kempe, 1987, p. 376).

Protecting Children in Their Own Homes

A crucial phase of child protective work is the determination that children can be properly protected within their own home, or that they should be in foster care. In the past, practice in relation to neglected and abused children was heavily weighted toward removing them from their homes, placing them in foster care, and considering the problem solved. Time proved that helping neglected and abused children was far more complex. Social workers today generally hold that it is better to serve children in their own homes, whenever possible, and to extend social work effort to the strengthening of their family situations. Nevertheless, not all children can remain at home, and some must be removed for their own safety and well-being.

Investigators of child abuse agree that parents who inflict serious and extreme assaultive abuse on their children either are not amenable to treatment or require extensive therapy before they can care for their children safely. Consequently, the protective agency must try to remove these severely abused children from their homes in order to prevent further damage (Jones & Alexander, 1987).

For less severe or moderate abuse, empirical evidence or even clear guidelines are lacking as to the conditions under which children should be left in their own homes or placed in foster care. Risk assessment instruments show promise for addressing this difficult problem of prediction, but at their current state of development they are intended to enhance worker judgment, not substitute for it (Baird & Neuenfeldt, 1988; Johnson & L'Esperance, 1984). In view of the shortage of adequate foster placements and the commitment of social workers to help children and their parents to stay together, probably most of the moderately abused children remain at home, with no verified knowledge about the extent to which further abuse has been prevented and family life strengthened for them and other children in these families.

Families that show only moderate child neglect are more hopeful in terms of preserving and strengthening the home as a place for the care of children. Parents in these families often have greater adequacy in their social functioning. They can be expected to respond in greater numbers to a constructive use of agency authority and social work services. Also, if a greater investment of the nation's resources is made to alleviate some of the serious social problems which impinge upon these families, the outlook should be improved very considerably for strengthening not only these homes but also the level of child care so that foster placements need not occur.

Reasonable Efforts.   With the intent to protect children from unnecessary separation from their parents, the Adoption Assistance and Child Welfare Act of 1980 required agencies to make "reasonable efforts" to preserve the family unit before ordering that a child be removed. The legislative purpose was to encourage agencies to work with families in more than a cursory way and ensure that foster placement is used as a last resort. Federal regulations require that in implementing the Act, agency workers integrate their efforts toward family preservation into a written case plan (*Keeping Families,* 1985; Hardin, 1989). Unfortunately, defining "reasonable efforts" was left to state legislatures and the courts, which resulted in much confusion and uncertainty as to what kinds of efforts were required.

To address this problem, advocacy groups have developed guidelines for states to use in developing policy that would ensure compliance with federal requirements for "reasonable efforts." These guidelines have identified a range of essential services—24-hour emergency caretakers, homemaker services, family and individual counseling, home-based family services, and housing, medical, and transportation assistance. The guidelines suggest formats for giving the court documentation of services that have been provided (Ratterman et al., 1987; Alsop, 1989; *Making Reasonable,* n.d.). Perhaps the greatest shortcoming of the Act is that it has not provided sufficient funding to develop a range of quality family preservation services in each community. Without these, all efforts fall short, and children may be "saved" from foster care but harmed at home. With the implementation of the Adoption Assistance and Child Welfare Act, more children are remaining at home who at an earlier time would have been removed from their families. Critics have pointed to cases in which children were left at home although they were not safe, as agencies and courts seemed to bend over backwards to give failing parents chances to improve their level of child care (Dorris & Dorsey, 1989).

That potential hazard led to a decision in early 1989 by the U.S. Supreme Court (*De-Shaney v. Winnebago County*). The question was whether under the due process of law clause of the Constitution public officials have a "duty to rescue" children from child abuse in their own homes. Joshua DeShaney first came to the attention of protective services in Wisconsin when he was two years old because of abuse from his divorced father; Joshua remained on a protective services caseload for two years. In that interval, despite two emergency room visits and the caseworker's observations of other evidence of abuse during her monthly home visits, the agency did not take action to remove Joshua from his father's custody. The Court, however, absolved Winnebago County, indicating that public officials were not obliged to save children from privately inflicted harm.

The DeShaney case has many ramifications beyond the bounds of the decision itself. By the time the Wisconsin case was heard by the Supreme Court, there were some eight other similar cases waiting in reserve, suggesting that the DeShaney case was not the final judicial word on whether the Constitution ever imposes a "duty to rescue." In a very similar case, *Ledbetter v. Taylor,* the Court denied review of a case where a two-year-old girl was abused, not by a parent, but by a foster parent. By denying review, the Court let stand a suit against child welfare officials in the State of Georgia, in effect rejecting the state's argument that it was not constitutionally responsible, suggesting that "the Court holds states to a higher constitutional duty for the foster children in their care

than for children in the care of their own parents" (Greenhouse, 1989a, p. 14).

The Child Protective Services Agency

Public child welfare programs have responsibility for full geographic coverage throughout the state. Child Protective Services (CPS), as one aspect of the state's public child welfare program, are intended to provide short-term, intensive, services throughout the state to protect children and preserve families.

The National Association of Public Child Welfare Administrators (NAPCWA) has issued guidelines for state and local CPS agencies (National Association, 1988). The guidelines emphasize that the purpose of CPS intervention initially is to assure the child's safety, but that "all decisions and activities should be directed toward enhancing the family's functioning and potential for growth. The agency's policies, procedures, and practices should reflect its focus on 'family based' child welfare" (1988, p. 27). The guidelines list four core services that the NAPCWA believes *must* be provided by the public child protective services agency: intake, crisis intervention, case planning and coordination, and discharge. Other child welfare services, under private or public auspices, may be part of a case plan to help families, but the core services should be offered by a single CPS agency.

Intake is the service that receives reports of abuse and neglect. Functions of this service include report taking, screening, investigation, risk assessment, and determination of case disposition. In the case disposition phase, CPS decides that the case is either (1) unsubstantiated ("no credible evidence of abuse or neglect has been identified") or (2) substantiated ("credible evidence has been identified that abuse or neglect has occurred"). In many unsubstantiated cases, the child care is only minimally adequate, and the families should be referred to other agencies to receive services voluntarily. For some of the substantiated cases, the evidence provides a legal basis for initiating court action. In others, services will be offered without court intervention (National Association, 1988, p. 31).

Crisis intervention services should be available from CPS as needed during the time that CPS is engaged with the family, including the intake phase. These services should provide for immediate protection of the child and also help families remain together during short-term emergencies. Crisis nurseries, domestic violence shelters, emergency housing, short-term placement with relatives, removal of the perpetrator, and 24-hour emergency homemakers should be available to help stabilize families during a crisis.

Case planning and coordination services are also the responsibility of CPS. For substantiated cases, the agency workers should design an individualized, goal-oriented case plan that clearly sets out what the agency expects parents to do in order to keep their children in the home. The CPS agency may provide the services listed on the case plan or it may refer families to other service providers through purchase agreements. In either case, the CPS worker stays involved to monitor the parents' progress and coordinate the work of other agencies providing services to the family.

Discharge services are appropriate when the CPS agency determines that one of the following conditions exist: (1) the child is no longer at sufficient risk to warrant CPS involvement; (2) the family is voluntarily receiving services from another agency to strengthen family functioning and CPS involvement is not needed because the child is no longer at risk; or (3) the agency places the child in substitute care (National Association, 1988).

Although this is the model for most CPS agencies, it must be acknowledged that CPS is not always able to carry out these four functions well. CPS suffers from high community expectations combined with insufficient resources. Staffing problems exist, including rapid turnover and low morale. Work with resistant, problem parents, with unsatisfactory care of children the pressing concern, is a heavy responsibility, requiring a range of knowledge and acquired competencies. Increased staff-development programs, lower workloads, improved relationships with the juvenile court, and skilled, available supervision are needed if CPS workers are to meet society's expectations of them.

Other considerations also interfere with the ability of CPS to meet the sometimes unrealistic expectations of society. It must be remembered that the job is complex, and most of the decisions are not clear-cut. Very few of the family situations are of the sort that make headlines; most are in the gray area of marginally adequate child care. Also, there is tremendous variation across jurisdictions in the staffing and organization of CPS. This makes it difficult to gain a consensus on what reforms are needed and what the appropriate focus of CPS should be. A further problem is that there are limits on the knowledge we have about how to intervene effectively in some families. Finally, a major difficulty for CPS is that it operates with conflicting values: on the one hand we are protecting children, but we also believe in the integrity and autonomy of the family. This conflict sometimes leaves CPS workers caught in a double bind, and at best, requires a careful weighing of factors before a decision is reached (Forsythe, 1987).

The Role of a Central Registry

When child abuse emerged in the late 1960s as a major concern countrywide, the establishment of central registries of suspected abuse and neglect cases was proposed and generally endorsed. Proponents expected that central registries would help "track" suspected abusers and neglecters who tended to avoid detection by rotating their use of community emergency wards and other services. It was hoped also that central registries would help monitor case handling and the use of community resources, and provide a statistical database on reported child neglect and abuse and the characteristics of the children's families (Whiting, 1977).

Enthusiasm for central registries was based on assumptions that have not proved reliable. Documentation of the large percentage of reported cases that are unconfirmed after investigation has reduced confidence that reported cases provide valid information on abusive and neglectful families. Registries have not proved helpful in monitoring casework activity, since data are often not entered reliably or in a timely fashion. The justification that registries would help identify service gaps is unwarranted, since "the problem is not lack of knowledge of service gaps; it is lack of money and effort to fill those gaps" (Whiting, 1977, p. 765).

Not only have registries failed to meet the purposes for which they were established, but they have also produced considerable danger to the citizens involved. For example, information stored in central registries has sometimes become accessible to other computers either by plan or error. This is a major threat to tenets of confidentiality for both the reported families and the reporter. In general, central registries have not met their objectives, have not significantly improved the delivery of protective services, have risked usurping the civil liberties of families and children, and have consumed considerable amounts of resources in the process.

Multidisciplinary Teams

An increasingly prevalent model for organizing community professionals in protective services is the multidisciplinary team. A 1983–1984 survey found that every state had at least one multidisciplinary team, with over 900 teams identified nationwide (Kaminer et al., 1988). The development of this approach continues to be characterized by a diversity of forms and purposes with little empirical data attesting to their efficacy. In the 1983–1984 survey, all teams included a social worker; other disciplines identified by at least half the teams were psychologists, nurses, physicians, lawyers, educators,

and law enforcement and public health representatives. Most teams were involved in assessment and case planning, but others were involved in providing crisis service, case management, direct services to the family and child, public education, community organization and program planning, and advocacy. The team can work out of a hospital or be affiliated with a private or public child welfare agency (Kaminer et al., 1988; Bross et al., 1988).

The use of a multidisciplinary team in relation to a particular case provides flexibility in the kinds of arrangements that can be made when family crisis occurs. It helps to prevent a service from becoming wholly commited to traditional methods or narrow professional identifications, because the variations in background, training, and special interests of the team members can be used to foster a climate that will stimulate innovation and response to newly perceived needs of families. It provides an opportunity for mutual support among staff members, which can lessen their need to receive some appreciation from a family or see some sign of progress prematurely. It can spread responsibility for crucial decision making, for example, for deciding when an infant can safely be left in the care of a parent who has injured him or her.

ASPECTS OF COMMUNITY SUPPORT AND INFLUENCE

The way in which a protective agency discharges its responsibilities is influenced not only by the quality of its staff and its organization and structure, but also by factors within a community. Public attitudes and level of community support affect the responses of government, the professions, and voluntary associations to protect children from abuse and neglect.

From the early 1960s to the present, there has been increasing awareness of the problem of abuse and neglect among the public and an increasing commitment to respond to the plight of vulnerable children. Awareness began in the early 1960s with the publication of the "battered child syndrome," a term used by the medical profession to describe seriously abused children seen in hospital emergency wards. Throughout the 1960s and 1970s, as states implemented their mandatory reporting laws, the public became increasingly aware of the extent of child maltreatment. The change in awareness is reflected in contrasting results of two Harris Survey polls. One taken in the early 1970s showed that only about one American in ten was aware of child abuse as a major problem; by the early 1980s, over 90 percent of the American public believed that child abuse was a serious national problem (Schene, 1987).

During the 1980s, various media events further increased public interest in child abuse. In 1982, a group of Kansas citizens initiated "No Hitter Day" to raise people's awareness of child abuse and family violence in their own communities. Linked to a baseball game in many communities during National Child Abuse Prevention Month in April, the day has been successful in mobilizing the electronic and print media to publicize the theme of stopping family violence (Cohn, 1987b).

In 1984, a television network aired the movie, "Something about Amelia," a story of child sexual abuse within a family. This movie evoked tremendous public response; one national child abuse advocacy organization reported receiving over 3,000 letters from adults describing their own childhood experiences as victims of sexual abuse. For most, it was the first time they had ever told anyone about what had happened to them. Senator Paula Hawkins publicly disclosed that she was a survivor of child sexual abuse. Several prominent criminal prosecutions of sexual abuse in day care centers further increased awareness that sexual abuse was more widespread than people had thought. Together, these various events lifted the taboo on public discussion of child sexual abuse. People became aware that sexual abuse could happen within their own neighborhoods and fami-

lies, and interest in prevention began to be mobilized (Cohn, 1987b).

A backlash developed in the formation of a citizen's organization called Victims of Child Abuse Laws (VOCAL), founded by people who stated that they were wrongly accused of abuse, which has lobbied state legislatures to drastically decrease the scope of child protective services investigations. The public also became aware of the possibilities of false accusations and false denials from caretakers, perpetrators, and sometimes children, particularly in the context of child custody disputes. However, these countertrends do not appear to have reduced public interest in reducing child abuse.

Advocacy Groups

The *Children's Trust Fund* provides state revenue to fund programs to prevent child abuse and neglect, bypassing the traditional legislative appropriation process. Kansas was the first state to establish a Trust in 1980; by 1986 the idea had spread and thirty-eight states had established trusts. Revenues for the trust program are raised in various ways in the different states, including surcharges placed on marriage licenses, birth certificates, or divorce decrees, or voluntary check-off plans using state tax refunds. The common feature of these methods is that they are separate from the ordinary state tax and revenue collecting processes, and the money is earmarked especially for child abuse and neglect prevention. Responsibility for administering the trusts rests with community boards made up of public representatives and, in some states, heads of relevant governmental departments. These boards provide small grants to community groups to fund child abuse prevention programs. Among the projects are resource centers for preschoolers and their parents in "high-risk" neighborhoods; parent education programs from pregnancy through the infant's first year; training of volunteers to act as advisers to new parents; and play programs for children of violent homes (Cohn & Birch, 1988). These programs, proponents believe, have given the public a way to respond meaningfully to the child abuse problems in their own communities. So far, the trust programs have not appeared to deflect state legislatures from continuing more substantive funding appropriations for ongoing state programs.

The *National Committee for the Prevention of Child Abuse* was founded in 1972, by Donna J. Stone. This Chicago philanthropist was concerned with the number of infant deaths that appeared to be caused by inflicted injury and believed that a preventive approach was the best way to address the problem. This organization has launched a number of national media campaigns generating between $20 to $40 million worth of free public service adverstising each year in all media. The organization also collects data on child fatalities and disseminates information on child abuse.

The *American Association for Protecting Children,* the children's division of the American Humane Association, was founded over 100 years ago to protect children from abuse and neglect and to ensure that "their interests and well-being are fully, effectively, and humanely guaranteed by an aware and caring society" ("AAPC's Framework," 1988–1989, p. 3). This organization, in addition to publishing annually the aggregated state data on child abuse and neglect reports, also publishes a newsletter, sponsors conferences, gives national recognition to leaders in child protective services, works to improve the operation of child protective services, and in other ways advocates for children at the federal and state levels.

The *National Center for Child Abuse and Neglect* (NCCAN) was established in 1974 with federal funds from the Child Abuse Prevention and Treatment Act. The Child Abuse Prevention and Family Services Act of 1988, the successor to the 1974 legislation, continues and expands the role of NCCAN. With a budget between $16 and $24 million a year, NCCAN gives small grants to state, local, and voluntary

organizations for demonstration projects, research, and training. It disseminates information on abuse and neglect, sponsors conferences, and has funded the two national incidence studies of child abuse and neglect (*Study Findings,* 1988). Three resource centers, for child protective services, clinical practices, and sexual abuse, offer technical assistance and training to agencies around the country.

TRENDS AND ISSUES

Change in Incidence of Physical Child Abuse

Straus and Gelles (1986) have conducted two national surveys of family violence, one in 1975 and one in 1985. Surprisingly, the 1985 survey found that the incidence of physical child abuse, though still high, had declined 47 percent during the ten-year period. This finding has raised the question of whether intrafamilial violence toward children has in fact declined. Straus and Gelles argue that the reported decline is plausible. They point out that demographic changes in the family, including an increase in the average age of having a first child, a decline in the number of children per family, on average, and the wide range of planned parenthood options (including abortion) available to the parents in the 1985 study may have reduced the number of unwanted children and therefore also the rate of violence. They suggest that the increased rates of child abuse reported to the authorities (American Association, 1986) and the increased number of children recognized by professionals as physically abused (U.S. Department of Health and Human Services, 1988) indicate that more families are receiving treatment for physical child abuse, and hypothesize that the increased number of treatment programs available is having the desired effect. Straus and Gelles also speculate that the declining rate reflects a fundamental attitude shift, a "moral passage"

(Gusfield, 1963). According to this view, family violence has become less acceptable than it was formerly; their finding that the incidence of spouse abuse, as reported by the married couples surveyed, declined by 27 percent during this same period, lends support to this interpretation of the findings (Straus & Gelles, 1986).

The study may give grounds for some optimism that the hard work over the past twenty years to reduce physical child abuse is beginning to have some effect (Cohn, 1987a). Schene (1987) on the other hand believes that it is too soon to tell whether or not child abuse is decreasing. She points out that the decline may be accounted for by the increasing reluctance of parents to admit to assaulting their children. She also argues that many "at-risk" children, those under age three and those in one-parent families, were not included in the survey, and therefore it is not known whether violence against these children is decreasing. Further, she reminds us that even if the rate is going down it is still very high (over one million children physically abused in 1985), and that there is still a large gap between the number of children who are subject to family violence and the number receiving official attention. Finally, she points out that the survey did not address sexual abuse or neglect, two categories that have shown large increases in reported rates.

The Neglect of Neglect

Throughout the past twenty-five years of increased public interest in child maltreatment, maltreatment has often been implicitly defined as child abuse. In comparison to neglect, physical child abuse has received a disproportionate share of media attention, research funding, and concern of policy makers. Yet neglect is far more prevalent than abuse. Further, its consequences are equally serious; as many children die each year from neglect as from abuse (Brown, 1987; Wolock & Horowitz, 1984).

A powerful and prestigious group, the medical profession, has focused primarily on physical child abuse. Pediatric radiologists first brought child maltreatment to the attention of the public with their discovery of a new "illness," the "battered child syndrome." The origin of this illness was thought to lie in parental pathology, and its incidence was considered to be at least somewhat independent of socioeconomic status. Primarily, child abuse was considered a mental health problem. However, this preoccupation with the small proportion of maltreating parents who deliberately set out to inflict severe physical injury on their children ignored the many families whose children suffer maltreatment in other ways.

Neglect is clearly closely related to poverty. Solving the problem of child neglect would require large public expenditures to address the social and economic conditions associated with both abuse and neglect: poverty, unemployment, poor housing, poor health, and dangerous neighborhoods. These problems have to be addressed with quality health care, good schools, safe and decent housing, and other material preconditions for living in decency. Material deprivation transforms problems such as mental illness or chemical dependency into situations that are seriously dangerous to children. Supplementing the material deficits of these families would alleviate much child maltreatment and other threats to the child's well-being even if the parent's behavior does not change as much as one would wish.

There is concern that child neglect, in the future, will not move to the forefront of public attention, but instead become further removed from the public eye, since it is most prevalent among poor, powerless families and no powerful segments of society have organized to alleviate the problem (Wolock & Horowitz, 1984).

Due Process for Parents and Children

Another major issue relates to the appropriate scope of state intervention into parental child-rearing practices. On the one hand, some contend that neglect jurisdiction should be narrowed, giving a high degree of recognition to parental autonomy (Besharov, 1985). Wald, for example, cites state statutes that define neglect in such broad, vague language as to invite almost unlimited state intervention. He advocates fuller protection of the rights of parents by drafting statutes that would focus less on parental behavior and more on evidence of specific harm to a child (1975). Current concern about the use of computerized central registries also relates to the issue of fairness and due process, and the right of parents to protection against unwarranted intrusion on their privacy in child rearing.

Others advocate extending the reach of child neglect and abuse laws. For example, the Polanskys (1968) believe that the degree of danger to neglected and abused children is more often underestimated than overestimated by the public. They are skeptical about the potential for change in a large proportion of abusing and neglecting parents, and skeptical as well about the state of the art with respect to known methods of treatment. They endorse a protective service approach in which social, medical, and legal action are "authoritative, intrusive, and insistent."

Many social workers and juvenile court judges take a position somewhere in between the views of Wald and the Polanskys, often with considerable ambivalence. In turn, that ambivalence exacerbates the issue of due process and equal treatment under the law for parents and children involved in neglect and abuse.

Interventions and Evaluation

The principles and practices by which neglecting and abusing parents and their children can be helped are by no means fully developed. Innovative programs are being reported from across the country. Yet they tend to come and go for lack of critical evaluation, revision, and incorporation into ongoing services.

Perhaps the most immediate problem in protecting children from neglect and abuse is the wide gap between the number of cases reported and the level of prompt and intensive service offered. Every state has witnessed an increase in the number of reports, but few have received adequate funding for investigative personnel or for services for confirmed cases. Merely improving the identification and reporting of child maltreatment is an insufficient response to these children.

If children are to be protected from neglect and abuse, a public guarantee is required that parents can provide them with at least a minimum standard of living in terms of income, housing, and medical care.

Help must be made available earlier to families known to be part of a highly vulnerable population. Protective intervention comes very late in a family's problems, after heavy stresses have been borne and neglect or abuse has occurred. Further development of ways to reach out is needed to interpret early to parents the relevance of certain services to the stresses they are experiencing and to enable them to use help voluntarily. A larger volume of auxiliary services is required, such as birth control counseling, day care centers, homemaker service, recreation centers, and family life education. It is noteworthy that increased attention is being paid to prevention of child maltreatment through identification of high-risk families, parenting education, and availability of family support services. Many of these prevention programs, however, will be threatened by reduced levels of governmental funding.

An agency's protective service must be defined and organized in relation to all of a community's social, medical, and legal services, with attention to coordinating these services effectively and continuing sound social planning in behalf of the community's most vulnerable children.

FOR STUDY AND DISCUSSION

1. Discuss the factors contributing to the underreporting of sexual abuse. What steps could be taken to improve the reporting?
2. Explain what you see as the principal causes of child neglect or physical abuse, and what in your point of view is a major direction for treatment.
3. Differentiate between "sociolegal" and "psychological" authority. Enumerate guidelines or ways of presenting and using authority constructively.
4. Social workers in protective agencies are faced with a difficult dilemma: a feeling of urgency in reaching low-income, multiproblem families and assuring that they have access to social services versus the ethical necessity of avoiding unjustified authoritative imposition of services. In view of this dilemma, evaluate the material in this chapter dealing with the need for safeguarding the rights of child, parents, and society during the agency's decision-making processes. Then present your own point of view. Discuss the feasibility of having two levels of definitions: narrow definitions of the various categories of maltreatment for legal purposes; broad definitions for the purpose of determining the need for services. Give examples of narrow and broad definitions for one of the categories of child maltreatment.
5. In view of the characteristics of neglected and abused children as you have come to see them, make suggestions for new treatment approaches in direct work with such children.
6. Draw together what you regard as significant aspects of agency organization and community support if effective protective services are to be provided. Then study the protective service agency in your community in relation to these aspects.
7. Define "lack of supervision." To what extent and in what ways should child protective services be involved with families reported for lack of supervision? What other approaches do you propose to address this category of neglect?

FOR ADDITIONAL STUDY

Besharov, D. J. (1985). "Doing something" about child abuse: The need to narrow the grounds for state intervention. *Harvard Journal of Law and Public Policy, 8*(3), 539–589.

Faller, K. C. (1988a). *Child sexual abuse: An interdisciplinary manual for diagnosis, case management, and treatment.* New York: Columbia University Press.

Folks, H. (1911). *The care of destitute, neglected, and delinquent children.* New York: Macmillan.

Giovannoni, J. M., & Becerra, R. M. (1979). *Defining child abuse.* New York: Free Press.

Helfer, R. E., & Kempe, R. S. (1987). *The battered child,* 4th ed. Chicago: University of Chicago Press.

Polansky, N. A., Chalmers, M. A., Buttenwieser, E., & Williams, D. P. (1981). *Damaged parents: An anatomy of child neglect.* Chicago: University of Chicago Press.

Protecting children. Denver, CO: American Humane Association.

Rothman, J. (1991). *Homeless and runaway youth.* White Plains, N.Y.: Longman Publishing Group.

Straus, M. A., & Gelles, R. J. (1986, August). Societal change and change in family violence from 1975 to 1985 as revealed by two national surveys. *Journal of Marriage and the Family, 48,* 465–479.

U.S. Department of Health and Human Services, National Center on Child Abuse and Neglect. (1988). *Study findings: Study of national incidence and prevalence of child abuse and neglect.* Washington, DC: U.S. Government Printing Office.

CHAPTER 10

Foster Care for Children

Children begin by loving their parents; as they grow older they judge them; sometimes they forgive them.

Oscar Wilde

Chapter Outline

Techniques for Moving Children Out of Foster Care
Case Review
Use of Contracts with Parents
Banished Children—Remedies

Management Information Systems
TRENDS AND ISSUES
FOR STUDY AND DISCUSSION
FOR ADDITIONAL STUDY

A decade of foster care reform was ushered in with the passage of the Adoption Assistance and Child Welfare Act of 1980 (P.L. 96–272), a legislative response to widespread indictments from persons inside and outside the foster care domain. Studies had revealed a phenomenon termed "foster care drift" by which children were allowed to grow older in foster care without the benefits of any long-term planning in their behalf. Recognition of the foster child's need for a permanent living arrangement—"permanency planning"—became the hallmark of the act.

The scope of the act included factors pertaining to the entry and the exit of children into and out of foster care, and the state's responsibilities in that interim. In an effort to ensure that children would no longer be "lost" in foster care, the Act included specific requirements that the states must meet to obtain federal funding. Briefly stated, these are: (1) written case plans for achieving a permanent home for each child; (2) case review every six months, under court auspices or by administrative review; (3) the establishing of statewide information systems containing needed data on children in care; (4) fair hearings on appeal when prescribed benefits or services are denied; (5) incorporating into the foster care system programs of reunification, prevention, and adoption subsidy (Stein, 1987, pp. 644–645). How these requirements have been met in the states will be discussed at more length in this chapter.

The effects of new initiatives stemming from the act are dramatic. New efforts in family reunification, use of transfer of guardianship, and preventive services to children in their homes have reduced the numbers of foster children in care. At the end of March 1977, there were about 500,000 children living in substitute care arrangements as compared with 328,000 on December 31, 1988, a 34.4 percent reduction (Gershenson, 1990).

Despite these reductions, societal changes have brought an upsurge of foster placements and pressure of crisis proportions in existing substitute care systems. Unpredictably large numbers of infants of drug-involved or HIV-infected mothers are coming into care, as well as infants who have been physically or sexually abused, or are on ventilators—all requiring specialized foster care. Foster care systems have not previously accommodated this high proportion of traumatized and medically involved infants. At the other end of the foster care continuum, older children are "aging out" of care but continue to need services. Many are not adequately prepared for independent living or for emancipation. Thus the foster care system is challenged to meet the divergent needs of both its youngest and oldest children.

The foster care system not only continues to serve large numbers of children and families; it also consumes a great amount of money. It has been estimated that foster care spending exceeds $3.5 billion a year (Besharov, 1984, p. 248). This estimate is based on a calculation of a year of foster care costing from $5,000 to $15,000, depending on locale and specialized services. These monies become large, fixed costs for social agencies and impede the development of other services for families in need. Despite the problems of funding, the demand for more foster homes is now national in scope. The recruitment of new foster homes, especially specialized foster homes, is a key priority.

How has a service that affects so many children and that has such a long-established position in child welfare become so burdened with highly complex problems? To shed light on this question, this chapter will trace the history of foster care, identify the components of the foster care system and the processes involved, describe the elements of the controversies, and detail the most promising strategies for improving the delivery of foster care services.

BASIC CHARACTERISTICS

As a child welfare service, foster care has certain distinguishing characteristics: (1) It is arranged by a public or voluntary social agency (although an unknown number of children are living in foster homes or institutions under arrangements made by their parents independently of a social agency). (2) Responsibility for children's daily living usually has been transferred from their biological parents because of some serious situation—a set of interacting conditions or parental characteristics leaving them unable to continue to care for their children and thus necessitating community assumption of responsibility. (3) Foster care is full-time care, twenty-four hours a day, outside the child's own home.

Out-of-home care may be given within a foster family home, an agency group home, or an institution. In contrast to adoption, foster care implies a temporary arrangement—an expectation that the child will be enabled to return to his or her parents' home, be placed for adoption, or be discharged from agency care upon reaching legal maturity. Using social work methods, the agency tries to play a major role in planning and carrying out the child's care. To be effective, this broad child-rearing responsibility has to be shared with parents, the court, and other institutions of the community. Children who enter foster care have had difficult experiences and often have unresolved conflicts in relation to their biological parents, as well as other unmet social, psychological, and physical needs.

As a consequence, effective foster care is not supplied by a change of setting alone. Attention must be given to the child's previous experiences and continuing total development.

Underlying Principles

Certain generalizations or principles underlie foster care practice today. These have been modified somewhat from time to time as new knowledge has been gained or as social work values have shifted, but for most of this century they have remained relatively stable.

1. The parent–child relationship and adequate parenting are of utmost importance to the child. Society's first responsibility is to try to preserve the child's own home.

2. If at least minimally adequate parental care cannot be restored to a level that will protect children, substitute parenting arrangements and the socializing experiences a family normally provides must be furnished until a permanent living arrangement can be achieved for the child.

3. Different foster care settings—foster homes, group homes, and institutions—have different potential capabilities. No one setting is necessarily the best placement for all children needing care. A placement choice is determined not only by a particular child's needs, but by the characteristics of the available settings and their capacities to adapt to the child's needs.

4. The family is the identified client and the service goal is family reunification or an alternative permanent family.

5. The foster caregiver is an integral part of providing services to the foster child and in participating in the forming of a permanency plan. The foster caregiver manages complex roles and relationships between the child and the biological family, serves as a role model to biological parents, and aids in facilitating family reunification.

6. Special consideration must be given to the rights of children when decisions are made that are crucial to their future. At the same time,

a balance is required in attention to rights of children, their parents, the agency, and the foster parents or other caretakers.

Limiting Definitions

The way in which foster care services are defined and the assignment of administrative responsibility for programs may contribute to a lack of professional concern about certain groups of children who live away from their parents. Neglect by professionals has long existed in relation to the care and treatment of young persons in correctional institutions. Many children who live in private boarding schools, such as military academies, are there because of psychosocial problems that have influenced their parents to seek out-of-home care. Yet these situations are not included in traditional definitions of foster care and do not figure in professional child welfare planning.

Professional concern has been minimal in relation to the substantial numbers of American Indian children who must live away from their parents because of critical social and educational factors. In the early 1980s, the Bureau of Indian Affairs operated sixty-three boarding schools with a total enrollment of 14,600 children. An additional 1,792 lived in federal dormitories while attending public schools (American Indian, 1981).

Children are admitted to these institutions on the basis of certain educational and social criteria and include, for example, those who lack access to a day school, those who are retarded scholastically or who have pronounced bilingual difficulties, and those who are "rejected or neglected . . . who belong to large families with no suitable home . . . whose behavior problems are too difficult for solution by their families or through existing community facilities" (*Indian Education,* 1969, p. 209).

Passage of the Indian Child Welfare Act of 1978 is a significant step in guarding the right of Indian children to their own homes within their own culture (see Chapter 3, pp. 78–79).

HISTORICAL DEVELOPMENT

Early Beginnings

According to Slingerland's treatise on foster care, the earliest accounts of legal child placing as a means of caring for dependent children are found in the Old Testament and in the Talmud. Among the peoples of antiquity the Jews made the care of dependent children a special duty under law. Their practice of placing orphans in selected family homes was carried over into the early Christian church, where the necessity to care for many children made dependent by the persecutions by emperors led the church to begin boarding children with "worthy widows," paying for a child's care by collections taken in the various congregations. Slingerland cites this practice as "the real genesis of the boarding-out system, revived, not originated, in the nineteenth century" (1919, p. 29).

Slingerland found no record of formal institutions for dependent children until about the close of the second century. By the fourth century institutions for the poor began to grow in number, among them orphanages and "houses for infant children." Some of these early orphanages were the so-called endowed charities—the first known endowed institutions for children. For a thousand years or more these forms of child care continued with much the same character and methods (1919, p. 30).

In 1663 St. Vincent de Paul founded the Sisters of Charity, who devoted their main energies to the care of unfortunate children in Paris orphanages, many of whom had been made homeless by European wars. Jewish child welfare work continued to place children in families. By the middle of the nineteenth century, Jewish institutions for dependent children were being established in numbers. In England the system of child placing for profit began under a system of indenture given national sanction in 1562. This system was imported into the American colonies, where it left a significant imprint on the development of child placing.

Indenture of Children

Indenture was provided for in the statutes of many states. Under this system, trustees of the poor in the various towns and counties were authorized to "bind out" to a master artisan a poor child, orphan, illegitimate child, or any other destitute child old enough to work. Such children would then become members of their master's household and be taught a craft or trade. In turn, the children were obliged to give their master obedience and labor, which was expected to pay for their keep and training by the time they reached maturity and the end of their indenture.

Indenture was seen in both England and America as having two basic purposes: (1) to fix responsibility for the support and care of a dependent child on some person or family (it was considered important that every person be attached to a family and have legal settlement in some town or place); and (2) to give training for work (it was a period of history when there was much work to be done for survival, and the growth of the country required most persons to acquire some skills or an occupation).

Homer Folks notes that the old-fashioned indenture or apprentice system in this country passed largely into disuse and disrepute by 1875, although there were some instances of indenture into the twentieth century. The system had not been without merit and provided in varying degrees an experience of substitute family life for dependent children. However, changing industrial conditions in the nineteenth century tended to make the relationship of apprentice to master less intimate and kindly. The indenturing of children

> underwent a change for the worse. The value of the instruction received from the "masters" became less, and the value of the services rendered by the children increased. . . . In the early part of the century, however, when learning a trade was of the highest importance, the system was undoubtedly something quite different from what it became in later years. Though there were

> . . . many cases of hardship from exacting or cruel masters, . . . the indentured children, as a whole, were more fortunate than those maintained by public outdoor relief or in almshouses. (Folks, 1911, pp. 41–42)

It was in this sense that Thurston evaluated indenture as "a forward step in child care" (1930, p. 10).

Almshouses

Not all poor children were indentured in the early years of this country. Sometimes "outdoor relief"—material aid supplied by the town to destitute parents in their own homes—preserved a child's own home. But punitive attitudes toward the poor, especially the able-bodied "unworthy poor," made outdoor relief the least accepted form of care. When towns grew large enough to build almshouses, needy children were often sent to live in them. During the early part of the nineteenth century, outdoor relief came in for severe criticism, in large part because of its careless administration and the idea that public relief increased pauperism. The prevailing belief was that outdoor relief was the worst method of giving assistance and that almshouse care was the most desirable and economical. This notion was reinforced by studies such as one directed in 1824 by J. V. N. Yates, then secretary of state in New York. Yates surveyed the condition of paupers in that state and reached conclusions that were highly critical of outdoor relief. He strongly recommended the extension of almshouse care and urged that every county in New York maintain a poorhouse. The children of the pauper inmates were to be educated and at a suitable age sent out for useful labor (*Report*, 1824). Yates's report was favorably received and led to the establishment of the almshouse system in New York, which was then copied generally by the rapidly developing central and western states.

Within thirty years after Yates's enthusiastic report on what the almshouse system would accomplish for children in the way of health, morals, and education, an investigation of the poorhouses found them to be "most disgraceful memorials of the public charity" and "for the young . . . the worst possible nurseries" (*Report of Select,* 1857). Publicity about the poorhouse environment in which children were living led to the conviction that the placement of children there had been a serious mistake. As a result various states began to pass laws to remove children from the almshouses or prohibit their being sent there.

The demand for the removal of childern from almshouses was slow to be implemented, however. States had public funds invested in land and buildings; children could be placed there with "fatal ease"; and new forms of care were not yet fully developed and available for the large numbers of children in almshouses (Abbott, 1938, Vol. 2, p. 7).

The Growth of Children's Institutions

While the controversy was going on about outdoor relief, indenture, and almshouse care, some institutions for children apart from adults were being established. In the nineteenth century, public and private agencies set up institutions for special classes of children—the blind, deaf, mentally deficient, and delinquent—as well as orphanages for dependent children to protect them from neglect and abuse (see Chapter 1). While these institutions appeared to their founders as an improvement over the mixed almshouses (and many were), in some of the large congregate institutions there were problems of inadequate sanitation, poor medical care, inadequate diets, and epidemics of contagious disease from which many children died. The trend toward orphanages grew, however, not only because of continuing dissatisfaction with the public almshouses, but also because of the emerging practice of awarding assistance from the public treasury in the form of subsidies to voluntary agencies. Most of the "orphan asylums" were established under denominational

auspices as various religious groups sought to provide for their own needy children and teach them their faith. Their programs combined religious duty with missionary zeal, lack of individualization of children, hard daily work for the children "to inure [them] to hardship and fatigue," and little chance for enduring individual relationships with particular adults (Thurston, 1930, p. 47). When children were received into care, the usual practice was to require parents to surrender their rights to their children. As they grew older and had been given some education, indenture was the means for moving them back into the community.

Free Foster Homes

Still another approach to the care of dependent children was the free foster home movement, best illustrated by the work of Charles Loring Brace, who in 1853 began the practice of taking needy or homeless children from the city in large parties to a rural locality, where they were placed in the homes of farmers and tradespeople of the area. Brace was concerned about the increasing crime and poverty among the children of New York City and the plight of the many uncared-for, ignorant, and vagrant youth. In his book *The Dangerous Classes of New York,* he wrote that immigration "is pouring in its multitude of poor foreigners, who leave these young outcasts everywhere abandoned in our midst" (Brace, 1872, p. 91). It was to this "class" of children that he turned the energies of the Children's Aid Society, which he had founded. His intent was to give the vagrant children work and bring them under Christian religious influences in the families of respectable persons, thus "relieving the city of its youthful pauperism and suffering" (p. 227).

Brace was cognizant of the demand for labor in the rural areas of the expanding country.

Moreover, the cultivators of the soil are in America our most solid and intelligent class. From the nature of their circumstances, their laborers . . . must be members of their families, and share in their social tone. It is, accordingly, of the utmost importance to them to train up children who shall aid in their work, and be associates of their own children. . . . With their overflowing supply of food also, each new mouth in the household brings no drain on their means. Children are a blessing, and the mere feeding of a young boy or girl is not considered at all. (p. 225)

To stimulate demand for these dependent children of the city, Brace sent notices to rural newspapers in various states. The notices emphasized children's need for homes, but also clearly suggested that children would pay through their work for all that was done for them, thus reflecting a characteristic of the system of indenture. Brace received many applications for the children as a result of his publicity. "At first, we made the effort to meet individual applications by sending just the kind of children wanted; but this soon became impracticable" (p. 227). Brace further described his method as follows:

We formed little companies of emigrants, and, after thoroughly cleaning and clothing them, put them under a competent agent, and, first selecting a village where there was a call . . . for such a party, we dispatched them to the place.

The farming community having been duly notified, there was usually a dense crowd of people at the station, awaiting the arrival of the youthful travelers. The sight of the little company of the children of misfortune always touched the hearts of a population naturally generous. . . . The agent then addressed the assembly, stating the benevolent objects of the Society, and something of the history of the children. The sight of their worn faces was a most pathetic enforcement of his arguments. People who were childless came forward . . . ; others, who had not intended to take any into their families, were induced to apply for them; and many who really wanted the children's labor pressed forward to obtain it. (pp. 231–232)

The placement of children by this means began in the north Atlantic states, then grad-

ually moved westward and southward into Indiana, Illinois, Michigan, Minnesota, Iowa, Missouri, Kansas, Nebraska, Texas, Oklahoma, Arkansas, and other states, following a pattern that probably reflected the shifting frontier of farms and small villages. A study of the Society's records showed that 31,081 children were placed in family homes from 1853 through 1929 (Thurston, 1930, p. 121).

Brace's movement attracted followers. It was bold; many children did get good homes; and it provided a stimulus generally to the placement of children out of almshouses and into families. But there were critics as well.

Some of the child welfare leaders of religious faiths different from Brace's had little enthusiasm for his program. Brace instructed his agents to seek "good Christian homes." The rule followed by those who advocated his placing-out system was later expressed as follows:

All differences of opinion regarding theological and religious belief must be set aside in the endeavor to secure *good* homes in which to place . . . children. The *character* of these homes is to be considered, not the denominational sect of the Christian Church which is attended by the family therein. (Bailey, 1890, p. 207)

As a consequence, there were indignant charges that Brace failed to place children in homes of the same religious faith as their natural parents.

Most of the homes to which children went were Protestant families. In contrast, most of the children came from immigrant families largely Catholic in faith. The tone of much of the opposition to Brace's methods and philosophy is reflected in this excerpt from a lecture given in 1864 in behalf of a newly established Catholic agency:

Efforts well meant, efforts flaming from a desire to do good, often actually do harm, sometimes from ignorance, sometimes from false zeal, sometimes from false principles. . . . Suppose these children [from destitute families] differ from their benefactors in religion? Here a temptation prevails, steps are taken . . . to place a bar between these children and their parents. . . . The yearnings of the mother are stilled by tales of wonderful advantages for her children. . . . Yet all this while they are undergoing a secret process by which, it is hoped, that every trace of their early faith and filial attachment will be rooted out, and, finally, that their transportation to that indefinite region, "the far West," with changed names and lost parentage, will effectually destroy every association [with the] . . . religion of which they have been robbed—the religion of their parents. Here, then, a new principle has been at work; . . . what we had supposed charity turns out to be only sectarian zeal. (Ives, 1864)

Such objections added a significant stimulus to the growth of child care programs under sectarian auspices and to legislating religious matching as one determinant in the choice of foster or adoptive homes. These outcomes are still reflected in today's existing pattern and practice of child welfare.

There were other criticisms of Brace's work. Child welfare leaders were concerned about insufficient investigation of the homes in which children were placed; some believed much more should be known about the motives of the adults who took in children and the quality of care which they would provide. There was objection as well to the lack of follow-up supervision and of accurate record keeping and reporting by Brace's society. States to which children were sent began to consider the necessity for regulating interstate placement of children. By the early twentieth century, the free foster home movement had focused concerned attention on the necessity for safeguards in foster home placements.

What Does the Child Really Need?

By the last quarter of the nineteenth century, two fairly well developed forms of care for dependent children prevailed: foster homes and institutions. As the states grappled with the task of getting children out of almshouses, the merits

of each as a preferable form of care were a controversial issue among child welfare leaders (Wolins & Piliavin, 1964). In general, four principal systems of care were adopted among the states. Typical examples follow.

Massachusetts established a state-supervised system of local foster home care for all the dependent wards of the state. Michigan combined a state school for dependent children (an institution) with a placing-out system from the school and provisions for study and supervision of the child placed in a foster home. In Ohio the legislature authorized and encouraged the establishment of public orphanages in each county. And New York moved into a system of state subsidies to private institutions by the court or local public relief agencies.

Although divisions, disagreement, misunderstandings, suspicions, and heated argument marked progressive child saving, so did a strong sense of being part of a large, united movement. (Ashby, 1984, p. 34)

A philosophy of child care centering on the question "What does the child really need?" began to emerge, exemplified in the work of Charles W. Birtwell, who came to the Boston Children's Aid Society in 1886 with the title of "Outdoor Worker." As Birtwell assumed more responsibilities for the agency, he began to distill from his experiences a child welfare process based on individualization of the child, which he expressed in these words:

The aim will be in each instance to suit action to the real need . . . to study the conditions with a freedom from assumptions, and a directness and freshness of view, as complete as though the case in hand stood absolutely alone. (*Twenty-fourth annual report, 1888,* 1930)

This philosophy was refined and enlarged on in the twentieth century by child welfare leaders intent on securing nurturance and protection for each child who had been deprived of care in his or her own home.

The new century ushered in a period of social reform from which children benefited. The provisions of the Social Security Act made possible a variety of services to children in all parts of the country. Yet one of the most critical conditions at the beginning of the 1970s was a crisis in child care. Once again attention was focused upon an urgent need for improvements in the existing forms of foster care, as well as new social inventions to meet the needs of very large numbers of dependent children.

WHY CHILDREN ARE PLACED IN FOSTER CARE

Problems relating to parental characteristics and social conditions that precede foster care are in most instances very serious ones, not easily corrected by existing services. Although the child welfare concept of foster care emphasizes its temporary nature, foster care often is a long-term experience. Contrary to popular belief, most children in foster care are not orphans; at least they have not lost their parents through death. Foster children usually have living biological parents who may or may not visit them or assume even partial responsibility for them. As a result, children in foster care have been termed "orphans of the living" to emphasize the emotional, social, and legal limbo in which these children frequently live. Too often they are tied to their parents by unmet needs and unresolved conflicts, but they are unable to live with them and for a variety of reasons are trapped into having a future that promises only a succession of foster homes or institutions.

Even though foster care has long been regarded as a primary child welfare service, data are incomplete about the children it serves and their earlier experiences with their parents. Nevertheless, one fact stands out clearly: The primary reason why children come into foster care

is found in family breakdown or incapacity, exacerbated by severe environmental pressures. This breakdown may reflect one or, more frequently, a cluster of critical and visible individual and environmental problems, such as neglect or abuse of children, physical or mental illness of parents, broken homes, unmarried parents, and continuing poverty or marginally low income.

The thread of poverty is woven throughout the foster care system . . . in financial deprivation among families, and in communities who have rarely been willing to appropriate adequate funds for supportive services. Child welfare agencies have thus suffered their own kind of "poverty." (Boehm, 1970, pp. 674, 676)

Family Characteristics

Children who enter foster care, particularly those who then are in danger of growing up in foster care, usually have biological parents who have a configuration of serious personal and environmental problems that have grown over time and who have insufficient support from other adults. Nor have social services been available early enough and in appropriate forms to enable these children to continue to be cared for in their own homes.

Because almost all families whose children enter foster care have multiple problems and needs, it is difficult to identify a single principal reason for each placement. When problems are categorized, overlapping is evident and social workers' judgments inevitably are subjective and imprecise in varying degrees. For example, children's disturbed behavior may stem from situations of serious marital discord, or a neglecting or abusing parent may also be mentally ill. In any case, a series of studies have provided evidence that the major problems bringing children into foster care are not their emotional or behavioral disorders, but *problems related to parental functioning* (Phillips et al., 1971;

Jenkins & Norman, 1972; Phillips et al., 1972; Jones et al., 1976; Vasaly, 1976; Rapp, 1982; Fanshel, 1982; Jones, 1985). For example, Fanshel's review of the family conditions of the 26,865 children in care in New York City on March 31, 1979, found that parental or adult functioning failures accounted for at least 80 percent of the reasons their children were in placement. The resulting distribution of families according to reason for placement is seen in Table 10.1.

The durability of the finding that parental malfunctioning is key to understanding why children come into care was evident again in an examination of national statistics for 1984 with a view to the primary reason for placement. In over three-fourths of the cases, the primary problem was found to lie in some aspect of parental functioning. Of all the known placement reasons, in only 11 percent of cases was the primary problem a child's behavior or condition (Duva & Raley, 1988, p. 13).

Despite the consistency in findings, the search for case characteristics predictive of foster care placement is not fully definitive. The role of various aspects of parental functioning is clear. Less clear is the specific role of environmental factors, although it is recognized that parental characteristics become critical as they interact with an all too often harsh environment.

To obtain documentation about the *onset* of problems that brought about foster placement, Jenkins and Sauber (1966) interviewed 425 families in New York City as soon as possible after their children had entered public foster care for the first time. When parents were asked to tell what happened that brought about their child's foster care, they described a variety of crises.

Physical illness or incapacity of the child-caring person was the major reason in 29 percent of the cases. A Puerto Rican mother, who was separated from her husband eight months prior to her illness, said:

I felt very tired and sick, and I went to a hospital in my neighborhood where they told me I need to be hospitalized immediately since I had hepatitis. I told them I had no one to take care of my children and the doctor took me to Social Service. Social Service called 250 Church Street and the children were placed. I have no friends here in New York and the only one to take care of my children was my mother-in-law and she was in Puerto Rico. (p. 82)

TABLE 10.1. Distribution of Children According to Parent-related Reason for Placement

Reasons for Placement	Number	Percentage of Children in Care
Death	1,281	4.8
Mentally defective	866	3.2
Physically ill	967	3.4
Alcoholic	1,589	5.9
Drug addicted	1,622	6.0
Arrested or in prison	613	2.3
Abandoned child	2,261	8.4
Abused child	1,222	4.5
Neglected child	4,050	15.1
Unable to cope	10,291	38.3
Mentally ill	1,993	7.4
Parental conflict	1,403	5.2
Parent–child conflict	3,065	17.3

(*Source:* D. Fanshel. [1982]. *On the Road to Permanency.* New York: Child Welfare League of America/Columbia University School of Social Work, p. 8.)

The principal cause for placement in 11 percent of the cases was the mental breakdown of the mother. One mother described how she had recognized her incapacity and managed to initiate placement herself:

> I had a nervous breakdown and I knew I was not myself. I asked my neighbor to call the police because I was so nervous and confused. My vision was blurred. I could not touch anything that was not colored blue. I was not paying attention to the baby. I would feel sad for long periods of time. My sister committed suicide four years ago so when I began not to feel myself I got help. The police came for the baby. (pp. 103–104)

Personality or emotional problems of the child were the primary reason for placement in 17 percent of the cases. One woman reported the following about her fourteen-year-old daughter, whose fears and anxieties caused her to remain away from school:

> The last thing that happened was that she was home about four or five months and not going to school. When I asked her why, she said her classmates called her names. She began not to study, did not pick up a book at home, and then complained she did not understand her school work. She started to go around with friends, started smoking. She started going to a woman on the block who has one husband today and another tomorrow. Finally, she stopped going to school and just walked around the neighborhood. One day she left at 2:00 p.m. and did not get home until the next day. . . . The truant officer came and said that if she did not behave better she would have to be placed. Finally, I agreed because I saw there was no other way. I do not know English and there is no man in the house. They took her to an institution on Staten Island. (pp. 125–126)

Children in 10 percent of the families were placed because of neglect and abuse. An aunt of several children placed for this reason reported as follows:

> There was lots of fighting between the parents. The father beat the children in the head. He fought with the mother because she would not clean the house, fix food for the children or generally care for them. She was always out in the streets. (p. 143)

In 33 percent of the families studied by Jenkins and Sauber, a group of factors associated with breakdown in family life and relationships, rather than a single major factor, accounted for the placement of the children. Children had been deserted, left unattended or with irresponsible persons, or abandoned, or there was evidence of parental incompetence and inability to manage. Frequently there were rejecting stepparents, conflicts within the family, arrests, or other symptoms of the unwillingness or inability of a parent to continue to care for the children. One mother of a large family with four of her children under the age of five described the situation thus:

> I went out and planned to be away for about an hour. Before I knew it the time went by, the kids started to cry while I was out, and the neighbors called the police and they took them away. When I came home, I didn't see them. I thought their father had taken them to his house. He did that a couple of times before when he visited and found them alone. I just went to bed and I didn't think about the children any more until the next afternoon; then I heard the police had been there and I went to the police station and they told me where the children were. (p. 159)

When Jenkins and Sauber evaluated the family circumstances that had existed a year before placement actually became necessary, they concluded:

> Although family problems were . . . at a critical phase at the time of placement . . . a year prior . . . these families, by and large, were even then functioning at a marginal level, and . . . had experienced an abundance of problems and difficulties so severe that it might have been anticipated that further stress could not be tolerated. (1966, pp. 179–180)

The consequences for children whose mothers are drug dependent have received relatively little attention in the professional literature until the epidemic of cocaine-addicted or HIV-positive infants occurred. From a major longitudinal study of children who entered foster care in New York City, Fanshel was able to draw out evidence of the fate of a subgroup of children in the study population—children of drug-abusing mothers. Even though, with minor exceptions, all the children in the total study sample reflected family situations of extreme deprivation at the time that foster care became necessary,

> the entrance of these children of drug-abusing mothers into care and their subsequent placement histories were replete with reports of circumstances so stark as to cause the cases to stand out in bold relief.

These mothers were assessed as among the most damaged in the study population. They tended to become unable to care for their children earlier in their maternal careers than did other mothers in the study. Consequently, such children came into care at young ages. Social workers found the drug-abusing mothers to be extremely difficult to involve in meaningful planning for their children's future. Visiting patterns were erratic, and the children could seldom count on sustained parental contact. Although these mothers were almost totally disabled as maternal figures, they were strongly ambivalent in relation to parenthood, showing negative attitudes toward releasing their children for adoption and toward temporary foster care as a resource for their children. Given their critical inability to resume maternal responsibilities, their children became locked into the foster care system in disproportionate numbers (Fanshel, 1975b).

System Variables

The complexity of family situations and the uniqueness of each case makes it difficult for researchers to arrive at only a few predictive variables that link case characteristics with the decision to place. Perhaps other variables are more

powerful indicators. For example, Poertner and Rapp (1980) observed that the problem of "drift" in foster care is more a function of characteristics of the system than of characteristics of the child. Characteristics of the system would include criteria for decision making, amount and quality of services available, caseworker practices focused on maintaining families together, and systematic case review procedures. Emlen found that from 57 to 82 percent of the variance in permanency planning decisions (depending on the subgroup) was predicated by nonclient variables (Emlen, 1978). Another researcher has observed that the number of cases accepted for service is primarily influenced by funds available for service rather than objective (case) factors (Richan, 1978).

Characteristics of the decision maker—particularly the social worker, are among the nonclient variables that have been given research attention. Important case decisions, including whether to place, are being made by social workers with less specialized education and child welfare experience than in the past. Difficult tasks are often performed by persons who do not have the necessary skills and training. A majority lack professional graduate social work education. The situation is exacerbated by staff turnover. A recent appraisal of the situation had this to say: "Obstacles to recruitment and retention of professional social workers exist in many public agencies. Many states have declassified and reclassified social work positions. In these states, applicants for highly sensitive positions are not required to have a BSW or MSW degree. Salaries are low, and caseloads have tripled on the average in the past decade. The standards are not in keeping with those promulgated by the National Association of Social Workers (NASW). Other working conditions—such as lack of adequate clerical assistance, insufficient professional consultation and training opportunities, and excessive paperwork—add to the unattractive nature of the work" (Harris, 1988, pp. 483–484).

The importance of the decision maker as

the processor of information has long been recognized, suggesting that the placement decision may be more a function of the decision maker than of case characteristics. Evidence for this position can be found in the numerous studies of clinical judgments and diagnoses by psychologists and social workers (Stuart, 1977). Meyer concluded that "placement decisions are more than a little subject to the constraints of our limited knowledge, our value preferences and our professional biases" (1972, p. 28), or as stated in another view, "individuals (caseworkers) pursue different bases of inquiry stimulated by different value perspectives and ultimately leading to differing conclusions" (Phillips et al., 1971, p. 42). Some have suggested that child welfare decision making is dominated by middle-class, majority assumptions that perceive pathology in behavior that does not conform (Billingsley & Giovannoni, 1972).

Despite the importance commonly attributed to the decision maker, research findings describing the relationship between the placement decision and the characteristics of the decision maker have failed to produce any reliable predictors. In one of the most complete studies to date, Fanshel and Shinn (1978) found no association between the placement decision and professional experience, agency position, education level, social work training, age, sex, marital status, parenthood, or attitudes toward foster care. These findings are consistent with research focused on other child welfare decisions that find little relationship between decision outcome and characteristics of the decision maker (Brieland, 1959; Briar, 1963; Brown & Brieland, 1975). However, Emlen found that caseworker attitudes are a significant barrier to one part of foster care practice—permanency planning, especially attitudes focused on termination of parental rights (1978).

Professional and personal characteristics have not yet been shown to be highly relevant to placement decisions. Jones did find that child welfare experience resulted in fewer children entering foster care, and that, against prediction, children were more likely to enter care whose families were served by a preventive service worker with an MSW. Explanations that the researcher offered included these: the finding might be spurious due to statistical design and a large share of unexplained variance; the possibility exists that MSW workers are not a good fit in preventive services; or it might be that staff with an MSW exercise greater independence from agency policy. Research randomly assigning cases to MSW and non-MSW workers would be required to resolve some of these uncertainties (Jones, 1985, p. 130).

The placement decision maker operates in an environmental context. The processing of information is influenced by contextual elements such as place, time, and persons involved in the decision making. While the research is limited and clearly not conclusive, some potentially key variables have been identified. For example, the *location* of the decision maker can be a powerful predictor of decision. Emlen found that 39 percent of the variance in permanent plans could be accounted for by knowing the county from which the case comes (Emlen, 1978). The Arizona Social Service Bureau found that the frequency of caseworker contact with natural parents of children in placement was largely determined by the county (Arizona, 1974). Briar reported a statistically significant association between social workers' placement recommendations and the type of agency in which they were employed, and others have found different placement rates for private and public agencies (Briar, 1963; Phillips et al., 1971). These studies indicate the possible existence of decision-making subcultures. The adequacy of training programs, the quality of agency administrative leadership, and the degree of emphasis on supervision have been hypothesized as underlying dimensions to this subculture (Brieland, 1959).

Time is another dimension of the decision-making environment. While the specific effects are unknown, several factors are well-established in practice folklore. For example, large caseloads allegedly contribute to less than adequate service delivery. Child welfare practitioners are forced to operate on a crisis-to-crisis basis, limiting the information collected and time allowed for processing it. This leads to decisions based on expediency and convenience.

The *range of persons involved in the placement decision* is another dimension of the decision environment. Although the principal decision maker usually is the caseworker, the placement decision is rarely made unilaterally. In addition to input from other staff in the child welfare agency, family members and staff of community agencies frequently participate in the decision.

In practice, perhaps many placement decisions are in large measure a codified concurrence in a decision that most participants feel has been made by someone else.

Standards for Decision Making

The decision whether to place a child is influenced not only by the characteristics of the case and the decision-making context, but by the criteria which have been established for such decisions. Public agencies provide about 96 percent of child welfare services, directly or through purchase from voluntary agencies. Standards for public agencies are promulgated through legislation and administrative rule making. All states have statutes authorizing intervention to protect children, but the statutes are broad and generally vague as to specific parental or child behaviors that warrant intervention (Mnookin, 1973; Katz et al., 1975). The Adoption Assistance and Child Welfare Act set a standard that agencies must make "reasonable efforts" to keep children in their homes rather than foster placement. Before placement occurs, *for each case* a judge must determine that reasonable efforts to this end were made by the agency. Without federal criteria for meeting this standard, it is incumbent upon the agency caseworker to document carefully for the court the nature of the preventive services selected, their implementation, and results comprising "reasonable efforts."

Wald's "specific harms" formulation (1976) offers a direction for making criteria for decisions more explicit. An example of its potential is illustrated in these proposed standards for decision making at intake, the point at which permanency planning should begin. Under one or more of the following conditions, out-of-home placement is appropriate (Stein & Rzepnicki, 1983, pp. 60–62):

1. There is no adult willing to care for a child, or the child refuses to stay in the home.
2. There is medical evidence that physical abuse or nutritional neglect is so severe as to be life threatening.
3. There was intent to kill the child, even if injury is not severe. Medical evidence should support a hypothesis of deliberate poisoning, or marks on the child's body should indicate assault with a deadly weapon or repeated beating with a heavy object.
4. There is medical or psychological evidence of abuse or neglect that, without intervention, may threaten the child's life, *and* the parent refuses help.
5. Medical evidence of repeated abuse exists. This reference is to previous untreated injuries, generally identified through X rays, where the location or type of injury suggests prior maltreatment.
6. Severe abuse or neglect recurs after services were offered.
7. There is evidence of extreme emotional disturbance, or withdrawal by the child, *and* the parent rejects the child.
8. Medical or psychological evidence suggests that the parent is incompetent to provide minimum child care and there are no resources (e.g., family, friends, or community services) to help in the home while assessment is under way.
9. A child has been raped by a related adult or a nonrelated adult known to the parent, *and* the parent did not attempt to protect the child.

When given ambiguous decision-making criteria, child welfare workers are reluctant to risk leaving an allegedly abused or neglected child in her or his own home and prefer to err in the direction of diagnosing pathology and prescribing treatment (placement) even when it may not be warranted (Mech, 1970). The lack of professionally defined criteria for placement decisions means that individual social workers are forced to define their own private criteria, leading too often to idiosyncratic decisions and to inequities in the delivery of services. This concern is amplified when one considers that a social worker's decisions on the same case are subject to considerable variation on repeated administration (Fanshel & Shinn, 1978, p. 480).

PLACEMENT PROCESS

When a child is referred to a social agency because placement outside his or her own home is likely to be necessary, the agency must undertake a series of tasks. The use of a systematic placement process helps to assure that the agency meets its responsibilities for (1) trying to maintain or restore the child's own home; (2) selecting an appropriate form of care if placement is decided on; (3) helping the child separate from parents and move into the new child care arrangement; (4) helping foster parents or child care staff to carry out their child care responsibilities successfully; and (5) seeing that a permanent home is provided for the child, either in her or his own restored home with biological parents or relatives, or in a new permanent home through adoption, awards of guardianship, or other forms of planned long-term care.

The Child's Parents

To remove children from their own homes and place them into the foster care system is a very serious step with far-reaching consequences. It cannot be stated too often that it should be undertaken only when it becomes clear that, even with outside help, the children's parents cannot continue to care for them.

To make such a crucial decision, the social worker must reach out to the child's parents and try to understand them—their life experiences, their daily pressures and reality problems, the ambivalent feelings they hold in relation to their child, and their strengths and weaknesses in parenting and how these affect the child.

When the decision is made to move a child into foster care, the social worker attempts to work out realistic plans with the parents about their contributions to the child's support as well as arrangements to visit the child under circumstances that will reinforce their affection and commitment to him or her. In all situations, and especially when guardianship has been transferred to another person, it is essential that parents be helped to understand their continuing rights and responsibilities. Time is a critical factor in determining whether foster children can return to their own homes or move into new permanent homes through adoption. Therefore it is essential that the social worker strive to help parents establish a realistically attainable plan to restore their home, or, if this is not possible, to maintain a constructive tie to their child in foster care, or to release the child for adoption. Because many of the children who enter foster care do not have adoptive homes made available to them, even though they could become legally free for adoption, it is all the more important that whatever is of value in the parent–child relationship be supported.

Considerable attention has been given to the effects on children of maternal deprivation and separation experiences. In contrast, insufficient attention has been given to understanding the experiences of parents when their children enter foster care. Jenkins and Norman term this reciprocal aspect of the placement transaction "filial deprivation." They recognize the likelihood that in a society where the prevailing expectation is that parents themselves will rear their children, failure to do so will have serious consequences for parents whose children are placed away from them. When they interviewed over 400 mothers and fathers about their feelings at the time of placement, parents reported that they had had feelings of such kinds as these: sad, worried, nervous, empty, angry, bitter, thankful, relieved, guilty, ashamed, numb, and paralyzed. If these feelings go unrecognized and unattended, they may generate renewed difficulties for the child during foster care or upon returning home from foster care (Jenkins & Norman, 1972).

Interviews with 160 of these mothers five years later revealed that feelings about foster placement had tended to diminish in intensity.

> Bitterness dropped sharply, and there was a decline of sadness, worry, and nervousness and a rise in relief and thankfulness. The feelings that persisted most strongly over the years were guilt, anger, and shame. (Jenkins & Norman, 1975, p. 133)

Parents whose children enter foster care have very serious problems, and many will have little to offer their children once they are placed unless they are offered services that enable them to strengthen their parenting potential and reassume care of their children. In 1981 Fanshel noted that "we have a long history in the United States of crassly neglecting biological parents and of treating most of them as if they have no value for their offspring. Once the children enter care, the parents are likely to be treated as discardable" (p. 685). The Adoption Assistance and Child Welfare Act's emphasis on family preservation and reunification of families signals an admission of past errors and the intent to rectify the loss of large numbers of biological parents to their children.

Selecting the Placement

Few empirical data exist to support decisions in selecting from a range of foster care facilities. Nevertheless, certain guidelines generally prevail in choosing between a foster home and an institution (see Figure 10.1).

Despite its difficulties, the foster home continues to be preferred for the majority of children if it appears that a child can participate in family life, attend community schools, and live in the community without danger to self or others. Especially for preschool-age children, foster homes are considered almost mandatory except for those with very severe problems requiring a specialized service. This principle remains generally intact in child welfare literature although many infants are, in fact, in institutions and some of them will remain there during the early years of their lives. Guides for the care of infants in institutions have been developed specifying essential elements in caretaking (Provence, 1967).

Adolescents are most often in institutions, not always "community-based" ones. Adolescents may benefit from foster homes if they have not reached the level of personality development that causes them to rebel against paren-

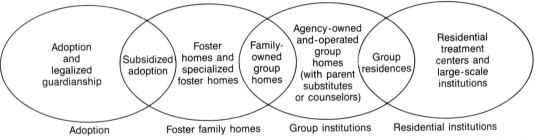

Figure 10.1. Foster Care Continuum for Dependent and Neglected Children. (*Source:* J. Koshel. [1973]. *Deinstitutionalization—Dependent and Neglected Children*. Washington, DC: The Urban Institute.)

tal relationships or if they have special needs that are likely to respond to family influences.

A group of siblings who need to stay together usually find their best opportunity to do so in the foster home, in spite of the difficulties in recruiting foster parents who can accept several children at once. The use of institutions does not necessarily assure that a family of children will share cottage living.

Foster homes are suitable for the emotionally disturbed child or adolescent who is ready for discharge from a residential treatment center after a long period of therapy for emotional problems and who needs the experience of family living as an interim step back into his or her own family or community.

Children who need highly individualized care because of physical conditions or handicaps benefit from foster family homes when they can be found.

Children who cannot make use of family living are usually referred to institutions, for example, troubled adolescents who are trying to free themselves of close family ties and for whom peer influences and group experiences may have greater value than family life. Some children fare better in institutional living if they are restricted in forming relationships with substitute parents because of certain family experiences, for example, if they have reacted negatively to psychological stress in the family or if they are torn in their loyalties to their quarreling parents and interfering relatives. Parents may refuse to accept foster family care for their child because of the meaning it has for them to see other "approved" parents succeed where they could not. Some children have experienced successive failures and replacements in poorly selected foster homes and can use the institution as a stable setting that provides continuity and physical roots and a chance to seek out a few accepting or "safe" adults with whom to try to form ties.

Children and young persons who act out in aggressive ways dangerous to themselves or others or who display other behavior that the family or community will seldom tolerate are usually served in an institution. Many children are cared for in institutions because their communities lack appropriate educational, medical, or psychiatric resources that they need.

Despite these guidelines, decisions as to the choice of foster care facility are often determined by practical realities such as what is available, proximity of the facility, cost constraints, placement patterns, and existing agency contracts in particular agencies (Stein & Rzepnicki, 1984; Briar, 1963; Fanshel, 1963).

Helping the Child Use Foster Care

Separation Experiences. Children who leave their own homes and enter foster care have experienced varying kinds and degrees of deviation in parental care. They are highly vulnerable to a stressful separation from their parents and familiar surroundings. (Strangely, very limited attention has been directed toward children's loss by separation from siblings—see Ward, 1984.) Social workers have given considerable attention to assessing the likely long-term effects on children of poor parental care, particularly poor mothers, and to finding ways to help children with the distress they feel at separating from their parents, even neglectful or rejecting ones.

Child welfare workers were very strongly influenced by the publication of Bowlby's *Maternal Care and Mental Health* (1951) and other reports in the literature that had described deviating patterns of maternal care, labeled "maternal deprivation," which were thought to be associated with later disturbances in intellectual and social functioning (Lowrey, 1940; Goldfarb, 1945; Spitz, 1945).

One outcome of this influence was that child welfare personnel became more cautious about admitting children into foster care and less optimistic about the gains they expected for them in their new foster care situations.

Later analysis of the early research on maternal deprivation brought a more hopeful outlook (Bowlby, 1961; Yarrow, 1961; Ainsworth, 1962; Rose, 1962). It became apparent that a range of deviations and conditions of infant care had been subsumed under the label "maternal deprivation"—institutionalization, separation from the mother, multiple mothering, and distortions in quality of mothering. While it could be *generally* concluded that these deviations tended to be associated with later disturbances in the child, the effects were not necessarily irreversible nor as adverse as had been thought. It was recognized that maternal deprivation and separation are not synonymous and that children do not react in uniform ways to separation from parents. Different types of separation have different long-range and short-range effects. Important variables include the child's age at the time of separation, the impact of early learning experiences, varying constitutional sensitivities, the characteristics of the mother from whom the child had been separated, and the amount, quality, and consistency of mothering provided by the mother substitute.

Of interest is a follow-up study undertaken to clarify some aspects of the assumption that the preschool child who is separated from his or her parents and placed in any group-care residence suffers irreversible psychosocial damage. Maas studied twenty young adults who had been separated during childhood from intact families and later returned to them after a stay of at least one year in a British wartime residential nursery. Most gave no evidence in young adulthood of any significant personality damage, attesting to the resiliency of the human personality. Maas concluded that at least from about age two, early childhood separation and residential care "are not themselves sufficient antecedents to a seriously troubled . . . young adulthood" (Maas, 1963, pp. 57–72).

Even though the long-term effects of separation from parents need not be as damaging to children as once thought, the social worker who is responsible for helping children move into foster care should be highly cognizant that separation is a stressful experience for children. Al-though each child's reaction to separation from biological parents is unique, certain painful feelings are common to the placement process. Children may be torn between conflicting feelings of love and hate for the parents. Yet no matter how appalling their homes appear to others, it is something children know and with which they have developed ways of coping. In these situations children know that they have no control and almost inevitably feel that being taken away from parents is something "done to me." They feel abandonment, rejection, helplessness, and worthlessness. They may feel shame or guilt about their "terrible" behavior that caused their parents to give them up. These feelings can affect the child's self-concept and sense of reality and distort the child's interpretation of old and new environments (Freud, 1955; Littner, 1978).

In a study of factors associated with successful foster placements, using a sample of children who had experienced at least one failure in a foster home, Trasler (1960, pp. 43–46) described some of the traits and attitudes that emerged among children as a reaction to separation from their parents. Because they could not understand that their parents were overwhelmed by circumstances beyond their control, they tended to interpret separation as the withdrawal of their parents' affections. Children often responded with alarm, unhappiness, or bewilderment. Some others, particularly those who had suffered previous rejections, showed no initial overt symptoms of distress. In either instance, the initial reactions usually subsided, and their substitute parents might report that the child "soon settled down and forgot all about his mother." However, with more time, the children tended to develop other traits and attitudes that contributed to failure of the foster placement. For example, sometimes a child displayed hostility toward parents who had been "rejecting" by separating themselves from adults. Children who might have repressed this hostility or who feared repeated harm in a hostile world began to display fear and anxiety, reflected in tenseness, restlessness, nervous habits, or somatic reactions. Still other children showed fear of being rejected again by an unwillingness to risk establishing a new trusting relationship, so that they withheld themselves from affection and response. And last, some children reflected their anxiety by alternating between reaching out and withdrawing, which made their behavior appear to foster parents as unpredictable and inconsistent.

The Foster Child's Identity.   At the time that children move into foster care and in the months or years that follow, many show an intense need to understand the circumstances of their separation from their parents. Their feelings tend to be most accessible early in foster care, offering the social worker an opportunity to help them talk about their experiences and begin to understand and accept them. Leaving the child alone with feelings of rejection and confusion over what has taken place, or avoiding stressful feelings by giving the child too ready reassurance about the future, fails to alleviate the child's real suffering. Furthermore, the social worker is apt to lose a critical opportunity to forestall the hazards of denial, fantasy, and repression on the part of the child.

The need to help children connect their present life in foster care to their past experiences with their own parents has not always been recognized in practice. In earlier years, most agencies sought to break as completely as possible all continuity with a former home when a child for any reason was moved into a new foster home. This policy was based on the assumption that the child would adapt more completely in a new home if he or she did not remember and yearn for people and conditions in a former home. The following letters in the files of a childplacing agency are illustrative of practice in the 1930s (Cowan & Stout, 1939, pp. 330–331). The first is a letter written by a social worker to a new foster mother. The foster child was twelve years old when she was taken from her own mother.

Dear Mrs. C _____:
    I am just in receipt of the letter which Betty has written to her mother and former friends. I forgot to tell you that from this time on, Betty must not write her mother nor these friends who would tell her mother where she is. You have taken Betty now to be your little girl, and she cannot come to the point of loving you and your family if she is permitted to hold on to her former family. . . . This will perhaps make her feel badly and out of sorts for a while but it is our rule for every child who comes into our care.
                    Miss B _____, Caseworker

That such a policy was favored by foster parents as well as social workers is illustrated by this letter from a new foster mother to a social worker.

My Dear Miss N _____:
    Your letter of January 2 and enclosures received and would like to talk to you instead of writing but am not sure I can see you soon. . . .
    We have felt from the first that a gradual forgetting would be best for Mary and the sooner those memories are dimmed the more she will conform to her new life. . . .
    Now, as to Ruth. Her letter contained so much news of the very things Mary is determined to forget so I did not give her the letter from Ruth.
                                Mrs. J. W.

Having become aware of such agency policies, Cowan and Stout studied the possibility of a relationship between certain kinds of behavior problems among foster children seen at a child guidance clinic and the degree of contact maintained with their old environment. The results indicated that a partial break in the environmental continuity in the life of a child was less likely to be followed by behavior indicating insecurity than was a complete environmental break (pp. 337–338).

In discussing the fact that physical separation of a parent and child does not necessarily interrupt the influence of the parent on the child, Jolowicz offered further insights into some effects of the concealment of the parents' life upon the child's use of a foster home.

> The child continues to maintain some kind of relationship to his parents long after separation from them has taken place. This relationship may be one that exists entirely in the child's inner life, with no counterpart in reality. It may be built on fantasy that is both rose-tinted and poignant, on unexpressed hopes, or unfulfilled yearnings. In it may mingle love, anger, disappointment. Whatever these feelings are, part of their power over the child's behavior comes from the fact that they are hidden. (Jolowicz, 1946)

It appears that children can modify their relationships to parents more effectively if their parents are not denied to them and if they are not expected to abandon them completely. For the significant persons in the foster care system not to talk to a child about former experiences with parents is a form of denying their existence and increased confusion about the child's own identity.

To understand more about the identity problem of children in foster care, Weinstein (1960) interviewed sixty-one children under the care of one agency who were five years of age or older and who had been in placement for at least one year. The interview consisted of twenty open-ended questions in relation to children's conception of their situations vis-à-vis their biological family and their foster family, their concepts of the role of the agency, and their patterns of identification with their biological or foster parents. The findings were as follows:

1. Continuing contact with the biological parents is important for the child's adjustment in placement and tends to have an ameliorative effect on the otherwise detrimental consequences of long-term foster care.

2. The child's predominant family identification is an important factor in his or her well-being in placement. On the average, children who identified predominantly with their biological parents had the highest ratings of well-being

of any group in the study. Children who identified predominantly with the foster parent or who had mixed identifications were significantly lower. Interestingly, children whose biological parents visited them regularly but who also tended to identify with their foster parents got along much better than children who had similar identification patterns but whose parents did not visit them. The two most problematic groups were those children with mixed identification and those with foster parent identification whose biological parents did not visit them.

3. Adequate conceptions of the meaning of foster status and of the role of the agency are important for the child's well-being. While child welfare workers tend to identify more strongly with children than with the other parties in the foster care system, this overt relationship with the child may be relatively minimal, ordinarily one of clarification and interpretation only in times of crisis or imminent change. A more direct relationship between agency and child may be desirable, one that would give the child more interpretation of the placement situation and a fuller notion of the agency's responsibility (Weinstein, 1960, p. 39).

Helping the Foster Child's Caretakers

Being a foster parent is a demanding and often intense experience. It carries enormous pressures and expectations, not only for the foster parents themselves, but also for the community. Despite the critical role foster parents play in the child welfare system, they are frequently neglected by agencies and their social workers. The neglect contributes significantly to the high turnover rate among foster parents. The neglect can assume different forms.

First, payments to foster parents have traditionally been low, especially in view of the essential and demanding service they provide. Most states pay only enough to cover the actual costs of a child's care. Typical monthly board payments in 1988 (American Public Welfare Association—APWA) were:

Colorado	$244–$327
	(depending on age)
Hawaii	$194–$233
Nebraska	$222
Oregon	$204–$322
Rhode Island	$243–$281
Texas	$330

In addition to the monthly board payment, agencies provide the additional costs of medical and dental care, clothing, and some other incidental expenses. In an attempt to increase the availability of well-qualified foster homes and highlight the importance of the foster parents' service to the agency and the community, some agencies pay a service fee in addition to the usual board rate. However, most foster parents are inadequately compensated for the services they provide. Prompt reimbursement of costs and fees to foster parents is "an essential part of the agency's plan of care for the child and an investment in both the child and society. The agency also should acknowledge that there are children with special needs regardless of age and establish a cost schedule accordingly" (National Association of Social Workers, 1987, p. 3).

Salaries for foster parents providing specialized treatment-oriented care may be the future of foster payment. A salary rather than a board rate may be a promising solution to attracting skilled professional care-givers. Full-time foster family-based treatment would become feasible with a foster salary "commensurate with the employment market" (Duva & Raley, 1988, p. 63).

A second aspect of the neglect of foster parents is the feeling that they do not receive the help they need from agencies and social workers. Rising caseloads and high staff turnover lead to reduced levels of contact with foster parents. The expectation that social workers will commit additional time to biological parents as a means of returning a child home sometimes further reduces agency activities with foster families.

A third form of neglect of foster parents is nonexistent or insufficient preparation to assume their new role. Many new foster parents undertake their responsibilities without any special training. Most states do not require it, and with limited funds, the training which is provided is often inadequate. At the least, new foster parents need information on their legal rights and responsibilities, as well as aspects of child development and behavior management.

The value of systematic training for foster parents is well established. As examples: A thirty-two week training project compared twenty-four foster parents who completed the course with fifty-four foster parents who did not have the training. The experimental group showed significant differences in their relationships to the agency, in understanding of the growth needs of children and in their ability to respond appropriately in their relationships with biological parents (Soffen, 1962). Foster parent training has been shown to have the potential for reducing the incidence of failed placements, increasing the probability of desirable placement outcomes, and encouraging foster parents to remain licensed (Boyd & Perry, 1978). In a demonstration of joint training of foster parents and caseworkers, attitudes of both groups were significantly strengthened with respect to a teamwork approach to case planning and management. A common definition of the foster parent role was achieved—that of a specialized professional who provides temporary, not long-term, care for children (Fimmen & Mietus, 1988).

There are a number of fully developed foster parent training curricula, with one of the more publicized being the Eastern Michigan University project. This particular package contains nineteen training modules twenty hours in length that are usually delivered through community colleges. In general, the training is based on the principles of adult learning with its emphasis on self-directed learning and considerable input into the design of the training program by the foster parents themselves (Jacobs, 1980; Noble & Euster, 1981).

The Model Approach to Partnerships in Parenting (MAPP) is a foster home selection and training program used in many states. It includes ten three-hour group meetings and several home visits led by a team of two licensing workers and a seasoned foster parent. The program combines take-home study and meetings to teach the team approach to permanency planning and problem solving in foster care. Foster parent candidates explore their experiences and perspectives with the training team in a mutual assessment of their readiness and commitment to foster parenting (Anderson, 1988).

Foster Parent Organizations. In the past two decades foster parents have organized themselves into groups for the purpose of effecting change in the foster care system. Social workers have served as organizers, consultants, and as agency liaisons to foster parent associations. Although some foster parent organizations existed earlier, many more were formed between 1968 and 1970, and were followed by a first National Foster Parents' Conference in 1971. Memberships in the associations across the country vary from a small number of foster parents to as many as 3,000. Objectives have focused on (1) better remuneration and fringe benefits for their service to the community; (2) training programs, information exchanges, and other kinds of educational programs for new foster parents; (3) more clearly defined roles for foster parents and more participation in foster care decisions; (4) increased reliability in foster parents' relationships with agency social workers and administrators, with evidence of trust and mutual help in regard to the problems of children in foster care; and (5) legislation to improve the foster care system. It seems generally agreed that foster parent associations are exerting a significant influence inside and outside the foster care system and are an important resource in improving services to children.

Social Work Service to Foster Parents. The social agency or institution staff responsible for the child in foster care has a continuing obligation to supervise the placement situation to see that proper care and treatment are given, and to consult with the foster parents or child care staff to help them perform their roles as effectively as possible. The team approach to foster care in many communities is changing the nature of the social worker's supervision with tasks being carried out more frequently in a setting with foster parents as team members in a collegial relationship. Ultimately, responsibility is shared by all team members to help one another oversee child placement (Fimmen & Mietus, 1988). The social worker uses agency-constituted authority as well as the inherent authority that derives from knowledge and competence to further role performance by foster parents. Consultation is performed by teaching the foster mother or child care worker within a relationship of supporting trust and shared responsibility for the child.

The child welfare literature reflects general agreement that foster parents and child care staff are not "clients" to whom the social worker gives treatment. They have not come forward to seek help with a personal problem but to offer a service, so they become extensions of the professional staff with their own appropriate status and a share in planning for the child. How this role becomes operational has not been adequately demonstrated. There is, instead, some indication of confusion in role perceptions (Fimmen & Mietus, 1988, pp. 21–26).

What kinds of problems arise in foster care to which attention must be given by the foster parent and social worker together? Problems may range from concern about the behavior of the child that the foster family cannot tolerate to complaints about agency policy on matters of board payment. Timms has grouped them as *problems of adequacy, problems of rivalry,* and *problems of control* (1962, p. 101).

When foster parents offer to give care to children, they are presenting a part of themselves that they view as capable and affectionate. But in undertaking foster care, they risk failure and a challenge to their adequacy. Difficult behavior on the part of the child may make them feel threatened lest it be perceived as failure by the social worker or by friends, neighbors, or relatives. Threats to adequacy usually cannot be met fully by the social worker's reassurance or simple explanations of the child's behavior.

Rivalry and jealousy can easily arise in a foster situation when the child's biological parents visit. Comparisons may be made between the foster parents' biological child and the foster child. Foster care places increased demands on all members of the foster family to share relationships and possessions.

Controlling children other than one's own is apt to produce special problems, especially if their behavior is demanding, aggressive, or otherwise troublesome. Foster parents may find themselves plagued by doubts about their usual methods of discipline and uncertain about action to take in behavior control. Frequently, problems of adequacy, rivalry, and control appear together in complicated forms.

A study of 145 new foster parents provides important leads into the ways in which workers can be most helpful (Cautley, 1980).

1. In predicting a successful placement, the extent of preparation by the social worker in terms of length and frequency of contacts and the inclusion of the foster father was critical. In general, a social worker with at least two years of experience can help mitigate the detrimental effects of abrupt placements.

2. The most frequent criticism of the social worker by foster fathers was his or her relative unavailability when information or help was needed.

3. After six months of placement, the foster parents whose social workers had responded to their requests for help were clearly more satisfied. In particular, the social worker needs to help the foster parents understand their relationship with the biological parents and the changes the child may be going through with the end of

the "honeymoon period" in the new foster home arrangement.

4. After one year of foster care experience, foster parents reassess their situation in terms of the rewards for their investment. If affection from the child or a belief that the child is improving is not present, the social worker needs to provide support, reassurance, and encouragement.

FOSTER HOME CARE: A SOCIAL SYSTEM

Foster home care is a system with its own set of component parts and relationships among these parts. The foster child, the biological parents, the foster parents, the biological siblings, the foster siblings, the agency social worker, the court-appointed guardian—each party is an integral element of the whole and is bound together with others and interacts with others in the foster care system. As a system, foster home care is in continuous change, and no part of it can be affected without affecting the whole.

The foster care system has an environment, or set of external influences. These influences include such institutions or forces as the placing agency's supervisory and administrative structure and policies, the court, the child's school, the agency that applies mandatory standards to the foster home for purposes of licensing, individual community child care norms, and treatment agencies within the community, for example, mental health clinics (see Figure 10.2).

The Jewish Child Care Association of New York carried out a study to learn more about the interactions of the participants in the foster home care system and how these interactions were perceived and valued by the participants (Gottesfeld, 1970). It was assumed that if each participant in the system held divergent views as to the values of the different elements of agency service and the interpersonal relationships between the parties, then the likely result would be disharmony that would impede the child's suc-

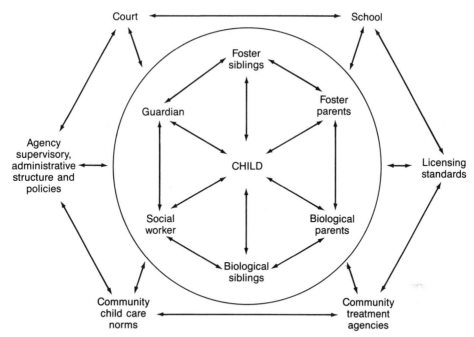

Figure 10.2. Foster Care System

cessful use of foster home care. If the views of the various parties in the system were harmonious, then the more likely results would be cooperation, effective use of services, and successful adjustment on the part of the foster child.

The research involved seventy-six foster children. Each of these children had lived in his or her foster home for at least a year and had at least one biological parent available to participate in the study. In addition to the foster children and biological parents, foster parents, foster siblings, and agency social workers also participated in the study. The findings highlighted a number of conflict areas that erode the successful use of foster home care.

1. Conflict of interest was especially evident between foster parents and biological parents. Parents on both sides wished to be viewed as occupying the major parental role and indicated that what was important for the foster child was that their role be emphasized and the other parents' role deemphasized.

2. The conflictual nature of foster home care took its toll emotionally on the foster children. To protect themselves from the conflict, foster children were likely to withhold commitment to either set of parents, thus intensifying their own problems of identity.

3. Social workers were not always neutral arbiters in the conflict over the child. Expected to implement an agency policy that circumscribes the role of the biological parents in the foster care situation, the social workers tended to give greater emphasis to the role of the foster parents.

4 In general, foster children did not perceive the social workers as persons who could help them to deal with the problems and conflicts in their foster status. The children mentioned that there was limited contact with the social workers and frequent turnover, and that social workers were too problem-oriented in their approach to them.

5. Social workers were of the firm opin-

ion that the agency's role and services were very important for the well-being of the foster child. Only about half of the foster parents agreed; the other half wanted a more nearly exclusive relationship with the foster child and minimal intervention by the biological parents and the agency.

6.   The adjustment of the foster child was related to the degree of agreement among all participants in the foster care system as to what the various parties thought should be done for him or her.

Such conflicting interests and perceptions of the foster care system on the part of foster parents, biological parents, social workers, and children in care critically affect constructive relationships among them and the ability of the foster care system to meet its goals of family preservation and permanency in living arrangements for children. The study reported above illustrates the conflictual nature of the foster care system, which long prevailed. Findings such as the ones described were influential in bringing about the current reconceptualization of foster care and redefinitions of primary roles in the provision of out-of-home care for children.

FOSTER CARE FACILITIES

Foster Family Homes

Because of the value attached to the family in our culture and its potential for supplying the child with social and emotional experiences essential for development, the foster home for some time has been regarded as the preferred form of care when children cannot live with their natural parents. Most children who require foster family care live in homes, once called "boarding homes," a term brought into use early in the foster home movement to distinguish those homes (where a regular "board payment" was given by the agency) from free homes and from work and wage homes.

Some Characteristics.   Foster homes may provide temporary shelter for children who need protective care pending social study and determination of their best interests. Although children's agencies must have access to temporary shelter homes, emergency placement should not be used routinely when children are referred because of some crisis situation. Assessment of children's need for placement can be made more reliably when they are still in their own homes, rather than after they are abruptly separated from parents and placed in an unfamiliar temporary situation.

Long-term foster homes are sought for children who have no chance to return to their natural parents, who need permanent family living, and who are denied guardianship or adoption because of the shortages of guardians or adoptive parents for certain groups of children. For various reasons foster parents may not want to assume the responsibility of guardianship or adoptive parenthood but are willing to give a particular child a stable environment and an assurance of lasting relationships with them as substitute parental figures.

Specialized foster family homes are used by some agencies for children who can profit from family living although they have severe emotional problems and show seriously disturbed behavior. Increasingly, specialized foster homes are being used for developmentally disabled children. In such instances, foster parents are sought who have special qualities of personality (especially a substantial level of tolerance for the child's particular behavior and special needs) that will enable them to collaborate with the social agency in a plan of therapy and schooling for the disturbed or disabled child. Remuneration is higher than in the usual foster home arrangement, and the foster parents are included as part of the treatment team.

Growing use is made of specialized foster homes for infants born with fetal alcohol syndrome or with cocaine addiction. Other medically dependent children in specialized care include youngsters with respirator-assisted breathing. The development of AIDS-specialized foster family homes began in New York. They are now found in at least five states, and sixteen states are writing policy on the foster care of AIDS children (Gurdin & Anderson, 1987; Tourse & Gundersen, 1988, p. 16).

Treatment foster care (also called therapeutic foster care) is implemented in most states. In-home treatment affords the special needs child a family setting that is less restrictive than group or institutional treatment. In this type of care, family life offers a normalizing and socialization experience for the child. A designated foster family member acts as the principal *treatment agent* for the foster child. The intensive services provided in-home by the agency distinguishes treatment foster care from regular foster care. Treatment families are specially trained. In addition they are given a coordinated program of agency staff support and technical assistance. Staff support enables treatment families to gain and maintain a balanced perspective of their stressful work and provides the family with the sense of shared commitment. The agency provides crisis intervention, respite care when required, and acts as advocate for the child within the family and community. In turn, the foster family is held accountable for meeting written and measurable treatment goals for the child.

Selection of Foster Parents. Foster parents are selected by means of a social study from persons in the community who apply to give care to children. In selecting persons to serve as foster parents, the standards the agency applies beyond the mandatory licensing standards, and the decisions it makes in choosing a particular home for a particular child will depend largely on the availability of families most likely to succeed with the types of children for whom the agency must arrange care.

Recruitment that is specifically targeted to finding families for the kinds of children the agency is placing is more productive of suitable families than is a generalized campaign to interest as many families as possible. Targeted recruitment emphasizes the need for foster families to provide *temporary* care for children while working as part of a *team* to serve children *and their families*. This message, along with selecting current foster families for retraining in new roles, maximizes agency development of specialized homes (Ryan, 1987).

Agencies recruit new foster parents through newspaper publicity, radio, and television announcements. Media and marketing consultants bring a new approach to foster recruitment campaigns. Some agencies have contracted for or have been recipients of donated foster recruitment campaigns by public-spirited advertising firms. Speeches to community groups and consultation with community leaders may encourage persons from the groups they represent to apply. This means of recruitment is vital to more vigorous recruiting of foster parents from minority, racial and ethnic groups so that children can be placed in families similar to their own in background. Foster parents who have had satisfying experiences in their child care service often interest their friends and relatives.

Nevertheless, the literature on foster parenting yields evidence of a diminishing supply of foster homes at a time of increased demand (Duva & Raley, 1988, p. 39). Various factors contribute to this imbalance: the "aging out" of foster parents, competing occupational opportunities for women, smaller houses and greater family mobility, lack of knowledge within the community about foster care programs, inadequate compensation for the exacting service expected, confused perceptions of the rights and responsibilities contained in the foster parent role, and foster parent attrition.

With attrition as high as 60 percent in the first year, retaining foster homes is as important as new recruitment (Ryan, 1987, p. 1). A good working relationship between foster parent and worker and foster parent support group attendance are two of the strongest predictors of foster care retention. When former foster parents were asked what could have been done to prevent their leaving the foster care system, the most frequently stated response was improvement of their relationship with their social worker. Among participants in foster parent organizations or other support groups, 82 percent remained active foster parents for two or more years (Anderson, 1988, pp. 11, 4).

Factors Predictive of Foster Parent Success. Predicting the success of foster families has been a recurring theme in the research literature. Such predictive power continues to elude the field, but a recent study by Cautley is suggestive. Eight factors were found to be most predictive of success.

1. Experience with children as a parent or older sibling
2. Having grown up with parents who provided good parenting models
3. Willingness to work with the social worker and the agency (acceptance of visits)
4. Parenting skills in handling specific behavior incidents
5. Parenting skill in responding to a "difficult" child
6. Democratic decision making by the couple
7. Parenting attitudes (sensitivity of foster father, degree of differentiation, and the foster father's extent of child-centeredness)
8. Older mothers up to 45 years old (Cautley, 1980).

Finding a foster home today is both similar to and different from what it was in the past.

Originally homefinding was dominated by a moralistic philosophy. The unspoken assumption was that foster homes were either good or bad and the workers were responsible for measuring goodness and badness. These were the days when one descended unannounced, catching prospective foster parents off their guard, and measured goodness by respectability, morality, and cleanliness. . . . This early era of homefinding coincided with the popular belief that children could be redeemed by an environment unblemished by dirt and distinguished by correct deportment. . . . The selected home was always right, and the child won or lost it according to his ability to throw off old habits and take on the new ones of the foster parents. . . . Later, case workers became more closely identified with the foster child . . . and as a result more particular about foster homes, even to the point of demanding of them an unreal and conventional perfection. (Hutchinson, 1943, pp. 3–4)

Topical outlines were carefully followed in collecting detailed information. This procedure often produced only a static picture of the foster parents without evidence of how they could function in relation to the kinds of children who needed family care.

Motivation of foster parent applicants was also emphasized on the assumption that there was a relationship between "acceptable" motivation and successful parenting. Various motives (or satisfactions that foster parents expect to derive) have been identified: a liking for children and a desire for their companionship, a desire to secure a playmate for a child of their own, loneliness and lack of satisfaction in other relationships, a desire to give better care to a child than they received in their own childhoods, identification with neglected or unhappy children, a wish to provide a community service, and a need to supplement family income.

Foster parents often reveal multiple reasons for wanting to give foster care. Even though some motives appear promising and some suspect, seldom can expressed motives be evaluated as clearly acceptable or unacceptable. Rather, it is necessary to evaluate the mode of expression the foster parents can be expected to use in fulfilling their expressed needs through child care.

Nor is it certain that strength of motivation, as it is expressed by initiating an application to become foster parents, is necessarily a determining factor in successful foster parenting. Stanton found no significant difference in child care provided by families who initiated their own application and invested considerable effort in becoming foster parents and those who responded to a visit from a social worker seeking homes for babies compelled to stay on in hospital care because the agency's usual recruitment system had not produced homes for them (Stanton, 1956).

Fanshel (1961a, 1961b) carried out investigation that supported the feasibility of "matching" to increase the chance of success in foster parenting. By means of structured interviews with foster mothers and fathers in 101 families who made up one agency's active roster of foster parents, an attitude scale administered to foster mothers, and ratings by social workers, Fanshel studied some of the satisfactions and special abilities and preferences of foster parents. He found a dichotomy between foster parents who cared primarily for infants and those who cared for older children. Those caring for infants were oriented more to private gratifications (for example, "[enjoying] a cuddly baby"); in contrast, foster parents caring for older children derived more social gratifications (for example, "knowing I am doing something useful for the community"). In examining specializations among foster parents who care for "acting-out" and handicapped children, he found that foster parents who had had children of their own appeared best suited to care for "acting-out" children and physically handicapped children. Those who were democratically oriented appeared more successful with aggressive children. Those especially responsive to dependency needs in children fared better with the physically handicapped and mentally retarded child. And foster parents from clan-type families showed a greater readiness to accept the physically handicapped and mentally retarded child.

Colvin offered evidence that foster parents showing specific needs do relatively well or poorly with children of different temperaments. For example, mothers showing a high need for *play* (to relax, amuse oneself, laugh, and avoid serious tension) did best with children of low impulse control. Mothers with a high need for *order* (to arrange, organize, put away objects, and be scrupulously precise) did best with children showing high withdrawal. And mothers with a high need *for play and for nurturance* (to nourish, aid, protect, and express sympathy) did best with children showing a low degree of withdrawal (Colvin, 1962, pp. 45–46).

Successful matching requires the identification of relevant variables in a more systematic and tested way than has yet occurred. For the most part the foster care literature continues to reflect a reliance on basically similar qualities when foster parents are selected to give care—whether for dependent, neglected, handicapped, or emotionally disturbed children.

Characteristics of Foster Parents. Although most children's agencies can cite gratifying examples of effective, reliable foster care, the professional literature suggests that these are not the norm. A wide gap is often apparent between what social workers state should be provided and what they recruit and approve for use.

Early indication of this dichotomy came from studies in the 1960s (Eisenberg, 1962; De Fries et al., 1965; Taylor & Starr, 1967; Fanshel, 1970). Foster parents were recruited generally from lower socioeconomic groups who had minimal education, were older than the foster children's biological parents, and often lived in rural or suburban areas quite a distance from the social and health resources of metropolitan communities. They frequently showed strikingly ambivalent attitudes toward the disturbed children they cared for. Some foster parents were found to be more authoritarian in child-rearing than was desirable. Their lack of empathy with or understanding of the problems of their foster children often retarded or prevented successful therapeutic efforts in their behalf.

These foster parents frequently were unable to follow through on recommendations of a child guidance service. Most were particularly unable to withstand the impact of impulsive, aggressive children, who made up a large proportion of the children needing care. As a group, they showed lack of clarity about their role and a paucity of knowledge about child behavior. They lacked constructive techniques to use in child rearing.

More recently, in a study of a random sample of foster children served by thirty-three different agencies, Fanshel assessed characteristics of foster parents (1982, p. 227). The children in the study had been in their foster homes for a year or more and were held to be representative of a much larger number of children in the foster care system. Characteristics of the foster parents reflected in the data were these: (1) the foster parents were mostly in their middle years with an average age in the late forties; (2) they had been with the agency for an average of six years and had cared for an average of 4.7 foster children; (3) they were heavily recruited from minority groups; black families made up more than half of the sample; (4) almost three-fourths of the foster parents owned their own homes; 13 percent rented apartments in public housing projects, and 8 percent rented apartments in privately owned buildings; (5) they were largely of high school education, had mostly average incomes with the foster fathers concentrated in unskilled labor and service occupations.

Fanshel's studies (1982) also included an assessment of the foster families by their social workers. The ratings were made separately for the foster mothers and the foster fathers. Taken together, they were designed to portray the "ability of foster parents to meet the emotional needs of the children placed in their homes" (p. 264). Rating scales gauged foster parents on (1) degree of affection shown the child, (2) understanding of and rapport with the child, (3) capacity to intellectually stimulate the child, (4) stability of personality, (5) parental competence, (6) quality of discipline, and (7) coordination of household. These measures were used in conjunction with a rating scale on the adjustment of the child in the foster home. For the most part, foster parents were judged positively in the way they related to the children placed in their care. Only rarely did any given scale show more than 10 percent of the foster parents showing qualities that cast doubt on their ability to provide sound care (p. 276). The picture that emerged from the social workers' ratings provided "a counterbalance" to the sobering picture of the biological families and their widespread loss of contact with their children. Many of the children appeared to have compensated for their loss of family by taking on the foster families as their own. "Almost 53 percent of the children were rated as being deeply integrated within the foster families, and 26 percent were rated as quite strongly identified" (p. 303). It should be noted that these were children that on the average had been with their foster families for considerable periods. More differentiation would be expected in ratings for groups of children who had been in care for a shorter time. Further, the findings depended on a single informant—the child's social worker (pp. 303, 304).

Amid obstacles, foster parents give an increasing amount of essential child care service. One of the obstacles is the difficulties agencies have in recruiting enough qualified applicants for a position that is poorly compensated and inadequately supported with agency service and other rewards. In addition, the increasing number of children who need foster care influences the agency to yield to pressures of supply and demand. Also, a tendency to hold to a romanticized view of the foster home (the "room for one more" concept) inhibits a full exposure of its weaknesses and lack of suitability for many children who enter care today.

Fanshel has suggested a further complication in trying to recruit better homes. Foster parenthood in the United States is regarded as a lower-class phenomenon, having a status on a level with that of a service occupation, such as a waiter, a custodian, or a domestic worker (1970, p. 234). Undoubtedly this view of it gives it less appeal to persons who hold the needed qualifications than it would have if it were projected as an essential child care occupation for which the community requires education and skill, and that it rewards with status and adequate financial payment.

Residential Group Care

The Child Welfare League of America characterizes residential group care as "a child welfare service that provides 24-hour care for a child in a residential facility designed as a therapeutic environment" (Child Welfare League of America, 1982a, p. 15). Varying types of residential group care facilities share a common goal— "for every child to return to life in the community with improved ability to cope and succeed, whether with his or her own family or a substitute family, in another type of group care (for example, a group home), or for older youth, through independent living" (Whittaker, 1987, p. 673).

Kinds of Group Care Facilities and Their Populations. Although all "institutions" have common characteristics, different types have been established to deal with particular sets of problems and serve distinct categories of children. These facilities maybe under public or voluntary auspices and be administered by persons with a primary orientation to social welfare, education, medicine, psychiatry, or juvenile corrections.

There are (1) residential group facilities for the care and protection of dependent and neglected children, including temporary shelters; (2) correctional institutions for delinquent and predelinquent young persons, including training schools, detention homes, and diagnostic reception centers; (3) treatment facilities for the emotionally disturbed, including psychiatric inpatient children's units, residential centers, and mental hospitals; (4) residential drug and alcohol programs; (5) facilities for developmentally disabled children and youth; (6) private board-

ing schools; (7) boarding schools under the federal Bureau of Indian Affairs; and (8) private boarding schools.

Wherever children are cared for, some degree of restrictiveness in the environment exists. Proch and Taber (1987, p. 9) offer this ranking of types of placements with rank 1 being least restrictive and 9 most restrictive:

> Home of parent, 1
> Home of relative, 2
> Foster family home, 3
> Specialized foster family home, 4
> Group home, 5
> Private child welfare institution, 6
> Shelter, 7
> Mental health facility, 8
> Correctional facility, 9

Drawing from a series of systematic and comprehensive surveys of children and youth in group residential care, Whittaker states that more than 125,000 children and youth were living in 3,900 residential group care facilities in 1981. This is in contrast to 155,000 children in 2,300 facilities in 1965. These figures reflect a decline not only in actual placements but in the rate of group care placements as well—from 19.9 per 10,000 youths in 1965 to 17.3 per 10,000 youths in 1981. Despite the decline of population in residential group care, the number of such facilities increased markedly after 1966, a growth that was concentrated largely in juvenile facilities for status offenders, delinquent youth and those needing mental health treatment. However, all types of residential care have declined in size. In 1966 less than 50 percent of facilities had fewer than 26 children in care; by 1982 the majority of residential group care facilities were of this size (Whittaker, 1987, pp. 675–676).

Most of the children's "institutions" caring for children today were established either before 1920 or after 1945. Institutions were less favored as a form of care in the 1920s, 1930s, and early 1940s, and few were established then. The earlier period was an era that gave rise to institutions for neglected and dependent children. In contrast, the most recent period has produced a growth in facilities for emotionally disturbed and delinquent children and youth.

The trend toward more facilities for emotionally disturbed children illustrates a shifting pattern in the primary function of the older institutions for neglected and dependent children. Many of today's facilities for the emotionally disturbed are older institutions that adjusted their primary function when they recognized that children being referred for admission required not only nurturance, education, and kindly supervision, but also special help to improve their psychosocial functioning as a necessary step toward returning to their communities. From the data in a national survey of children's institutions, three-fourths of the children in institutions of all types throughout the country in 1966 were judged to be emotionally disturbed or to exhibit disordered behavior, a finding reinforced in a later study that found that far and away the predominant reason for institutional referrals was the "emotional problem" of the child (Pappenfort & Kilpatrick, 1969, pp. 449–450). In contrast to foster family care, where the principal determinant of placement seems to be the degree of family functioning, institutional care appears to occur when the locus of the problem is attributed to the child.

Special Attributes. Certain characteristics of the group residential care setting can be specifically useful in helping some disturbed children and young persons. These characteristics, which are different from those of the family home, in principle permit a controlled living process and a consciously designed therapeutic environment that can be varied to meet the needs of a particular group of children.

The institution can free a child from an obligation to form close personal relationships. The nature of a family home setting implies some expectation that the foster child will not only receive some satisfactions but also give

some to others in the family group. In institutional group living, the troubled child can keep relationships with others diluted so that there is less need to persist in old ways of reacting. Thus, energy the child might have to expend in giving love and satisfaction to parents can be channeled into new learning processes.

The group residential facility can allow greater variation in behavior than can the smaller, more compact family unit. The impact of difficult behavior—perhaps acting out or excessive withdrawal—may be less because it is diffused among a series of adults who can anticipate relief after their work hours from the stress the behavior produces.

A child in an institution has opportunity for a variety of interpersonal relationships and subgroup patterns of behavior since the child has access to more adults with whom he or she can identify and can establish friendships and other supportive relationships. This wider choice can permit the child to return to relationships which are rewarding and supportive, and remain relatively detached from those that are undesirably disturbing.

The peer group in institutional living is an important resource that can be molded to be a catalyst for constructive change. It offers the child an opportunity for interaction with others who share his or her experiences day by day—the successes and failures in learning, in games, in relationships with parents and other family members, and in responses to the institutional controls.

Special resources can be obtained and combined for a group of children with similar or special needs. Generally, a greater range of remedial and therapeutic programs and group activities can be brought together in an institution and made available in planning children's daily living experiences.

The accessibility of the child to the institutional staff facilitates diagnosis, observation, and treatment. Therapy for emotional problems and remedial programs for learning problems can be brought together and related directly to the child's daily life.

An institution's consistent and regular routine may contribute to a disturbed child's sense of continuity, regularity, and stability. Many children who require care outside their own homes have come from disorganized environments and need a routinized structure to facilitate impulse control. A child's environment can be consistent and regulated without its being attributed to one individual's controlling decisions, as a similar structure in a foster home may be.

Institutional staff members, by accepting formal employment conditions, assume an obligation for professional functioning and can be readily accessible to regular inservice training and supervision.

These attributes, which permit the institution to serve particular children effectively, are not self-fulfilling. The same factors can be barriers to treatment if they are not used with professional skill. It may be very difficult to individualize the child in group care. Depersonalizing influences, which under certain circumstances are therapeutic, can also penalize the child who needs intimate, personal attention as an individual outside a group. Children may be denied privacy in group living. Opportunities may be lost to them to learn how to make decisions and sound personal choices. Some children are overstimulated by the variety of relationships and activities in group care.

Although institutional staffs are increasingly cognizant of the need to involve children whenever possible in the mainstream of community life through relationships to persons outside the institution and the use of services off campus, many are still unnecessarily isolated from outside individuals, groups, and community influences to which they must eventually learn to adjust.

Children may be visited by their parents less often than other foster children if their parents live a considerable distance away or perceive the institution as impersonally inaccessi-

ble. The staff, in turn, may tend to be removed from the children's parents and handicapped in supporting the positive elements in their relationship with their children.

For a rehabilitative environment, children to be served must be selected by a particular institution in relation to its resources and the kinds of problems and child characteristics with which it can be expected to succeed. But admitting and then grouping children for successful living is made difficult by the urgency of referrals from social agencies and courts, the lack of carefully prepared social studies, and incomplete knowledge about principles of grouping, particularly in facilities that have statutory responsibilities for accepting a diverse population of children subsumed under such categories as dependent and neglected, delinquent, or mentally handicapped.

An institutional staff may rely on individual psychotherapy as the primary focus of treatment and neglect to develop other beneficial programs, for example, therapeutically planned recreation. Or the psychotherapy may be unrelated to the social and cultural processes of daily life in the institution, so that the children are not treated in their total living experiences.

In a study of the social system of cottage life in a treatment institution for disturbed and delinquent children, Polsky documented some of the main patterns of interaction and the presence of an effective peer social organization within the separate cottages. As a participant-observer, Polsky found older youth, or at least those who had acquired most power and status in the peer group, vying with the staff as the major socializing influence. Peer influences can constitute a deviant subculture within the cottage that takes precedence over, or comes into sharp conflict with, the values being promoted by the professional staff. Cottage parents who have predisposing personality traits, or who are isolated from the professional staff and immersed in intense interaction with the disturbed children, may reinforce the deviancy in the subculture, which then further separates daily living within the cottage group from the therapeutic influences within the rest of the institution (Polsky, 1962).

Methods and Results. The range of specific approaches to a planned therapeutic residential environment includes individualized psychotherapy, behavior modification, play therapy, milieu therapy, group work, and positive peer culture. Individual psychotherapy, although dominant in earlier times, has largely been replaced by behavior modification and various forms of group work as the preferred models of treatment. In all such approaches, the attempt is to use the everyday living environment as a therapeutic tool rather than isolating therapy as something distinct from the other 23 hours.

Group work approaches have emphasized social and peer supports and sanctions as a means of establishing new patterns of behavior. Youths are given selected responsibilities for the day-to-day operation of the unit and for governing their own and each other's behavior. The youth group assigns, schedules, and monitors the necessary chores, other activities, and privileges. The staff act as facilitators or guides and enforce minimum institutional standards.

A dominant treatment approach in children's institutions is behavior modification (Whittaker, 1977, p. 172). This approach is based on the idea that behavior is learned and is largely under the control of the consequences elicited by a given behavior. The task for the institutional staff is to make the desired behavior as well as the consequences explicit to the residents and then to arrange a system of rewards and punishments to support and give authority to the expectations. Familiar techniques include the use of tokens or point systems, levels of privileges, and behavioral contracting.

Do institutional care and treatment work well for children and youth? The answer is important for two reasons. First, institutional care is the most intrusive form of care. It removes the child from one world and places him or her in another, often located a significant distance from the child's own home. Institutions bring varying degrees of loss of liberty. Contact with community activities and resources is often limited or nonexistent. The child often goes to school on the institution grounds and is dependent on the institution environs for all of her or his recreation. Parental visits may be restricted to institution offices or grounds. By design, institutions are commonly the most restrictive environment to which a child may be referred for foster care.

Second, institutional treatment consumes a large amount of child welfare dollars for proportionately few children. The annual cost for each of these children ranges from $8,000 to at least $40,000 (Whittaker, 1977, p. 172).

Evaluating the outcomes of institutional care and treatment is fraught with difficulties. As Whittaker has noted:

> Typically, studies are conducted without benefit of controls, and although in many instances it is clear that a change occurred, it is almost impossible to specify the precise nature or number of independent variables responsible for the change. Service units are poorly conceptualized and extremely difficult to quantify. For example, virtually all residential services now classify themselves as "treatment" centers, even though the differences among these services are often greater than the ways they are similar. (1977, p. 172)

Others have pointed to the diversity of outcomes used, which makes generalization difficult. Many studies also lack follow-up data.

With these constraints in mind, a few generalizations can be made. First, there is considerable evidence that behavior modification techniques with a variety of populations are effective in developing new patterns of acceptable behavior (Davidson & Seidman, 1974). Second, these same studies fail to prove that the behavior learned and performed in the residential setting generalizes once the child moves to another setting (Davidson & Wolfred, 1977). Third, there are a number of studies that do claim significant positive outcomes, but their inability to isolate the critical variable involved makes replication difficult (Maluccio & Marlow, 1972). Fourth, from a study of thirty-six institutions for dependent and neglected children, it appears that "by and large the institutional experience does not prove to be potent enough to produce gross deviations in child development for good or ill" (Thomas, 1975).

From an analysis of follow-up studies of children and youth who had lived in residential group care and then had been discharged back to their families or communities, Whittaker (1987) identified a cluster of common findings with respect to their postdischarge well-being:

1. Whatever definition is given to success in residential care, and irrespective of gains made while in the residential program, "ecological factors," that is, "supports available in the post-treatment community environment" are critical.

2. Contact between the children and their biological parents, as full partners in the helping process, from the time of a child's entrance into group care is a vital component of treatment.

3. Constructive "linkages between the neighborhood, the peer group, the world of work, and other potential sources of support in the environment" are imperative for postplacement well-being. Without these supports, in a stressful family or community situation, gains made by youth during residential care and treatment are likely to erode.

4. Social work can and should assume a role, not only in the design and implementation of services within the residential unit, but also in postdischarge services—parenting education, family support groups, community liaison work, and consultation with informal helping networks.

Without attention to these findings, Whittaker concludes, "it is doubtful that any model of residential treatment . . . can improve on the meager results emerging from outcome studies with respect to ultimate community reintegration" (p. 680).

Agency Group Homes

Many children who need foster care have characteristics that make them unsuited to either foster homes or institutions. Adolescents—even young adolescents—frequently fall in this group. They may have serious unresolved conflicts in relation to their parents, making it difficult for them to accept the traditional foster family setting. Yet they need an opportunity for more informal living and casual community experiences than available institutions permit. Or they may have lived in an institution but now need a transitional experience to test their readiness to move successfully back into their own homes and communities.

The majority of residents in agency group homes are teenagers with some type of emotional problem. A study of group care of 2,844 youth in the custody of the California Department of Social Services between 1982–1984 showed their physical and psychological conditions ranging from withdrawal, depression, and bizarre behavior to extreme dependence, hyperactivity, and eating disorders (Duva & Raley, 1988, p. 16).

Agency-operated group homes showed the largest relative growth between 1961 and March 1977—from fewer than 1,000 children to over 35,000 (Shyne, 1980).

The Uniqueness of the Group Home. The agency-operated group home has special usefulness to the needs of different kinds of children, although it has been used mostly for adolescents. The group home is usually a single dwelling or apartment, owned or rented by an agency, institution, or other organization, and located in a residential area of the community. Its architecture is usually very much like that of other homes and apartments in the neighborhood. It cares for about four to twelve children. Child care staff members are viewed as counselors rather than as foster parents. Other professional personnel serve the group home regularly—social workers, a psychiatric consultant, a psychologist, and perhaps others. The parent agency or institution has administrative and supervisory responsibility for the service provided. However, the group home reaches out to the community for many activities (Gula, 1964, p. 2).

Herstein has examined the characteristics of the group home in relation to four dimensions of foster care structure: (1) the nature of the caretaking matrix, (2) the nature of social agency control, (3) the extent of small-group autonomy, and (4) the degree of community permeability (Herstein, 1964).

The family and the artificial group make up contrasting models of the *caretaking matrix* in forms of foster care. Foster homes rely on the family model, utilizing already existing relationships and established rules, expectations, and prescriptions for living that have been worked out, often unconsciously, by family members. Communication within the family is highly informal. The institution relies on the artificial group model. The child care staff members are salaried employees without previous relationships to each other, and they work designated hours and alternate their responsibilities with relief staff. Communication between staff members tends to be planned and formal. Even though group homes may emphasize family features in certain living situations, Herstein classified them as modeled primarily on the image of the artificial group.

The group home is also more like the institution in regard to the second dimension—the nature of *social agency control*. The foster family home retains a high degree of control. Although the agency attempts to help the foster parents find ways to give effective care to a child, they make many decisions alone and rely largely on their own inclinations in methods of child rearing. Furthermore, if they find the experience unsatisfactory, they can request that the child be removed, leaving the agency no alternative but to find another placement. In the group home, as in the institution, agency control is paramount in planning and directing the child's treatment.

In the extent of *small-group autonomy,* however, the group home is more like the foster home with its small, relatively intimate group and its high degree of self-containment in the major tasks of living. The cottages of an institution, although having some of these family characteristics, are still dependent in large measure upon the structure of the institution for many of the tasks of daily living and other aspects of program and activities.

A group home's degree of *community permeability* appears to be in between that of the foster home and that of the institution. Foster homes have relatively low visibility in the community. A foster home makes it possible for children to participate in the community's educational, social, and religious activities with relative ease. They can usually form friendships and visit quite freely in the neighborhood. An institution, on the other hand, must give more conscious planning to interaction between its children and the community, so children's experiences in relation to the community tend to be more structured, and their differences are more likely to be visible to outside persons. The degree of community permeability of the group home will vary, depending on the characteristics of the community, particularly the neighborhood where the group home is located, and the extent to which children in the community have characteristics similar to those of the children in the group home.

In summary, Herstein (1964) concluded that the group home is more like the foster family in the extent of small-group autonomy, more like the institution in its caretaking matrix and degree of agency control, and in between the foster home and the institution in the degree of community permeability.

Certain problems are typical of group homes. One is resistance from neighborhood people that halts or delays many attempts at establishing new group homes. "Home owners, concerned about property values and the effects foster children will have on their children, quickly organize to prevent foster group homes from being established in their communities"

(Pierce & Hauck, 1981, p. 477). Strategies for overcoming this opposition may be low-profile or high-profile efforts. Low-profile strategies eschew neighborhood education and assume the right to locate a group home in that location. The high-profile strategy involves considerable effort to educate and involve the community in each stage of the planning process. The literature provides successful examples of both approaches (Weber, 1978).

Meeting the expectations of multiple constituencies is another problem for group homes. The constituencies include schools, police, the children's parents, and neighbors. Since group homes are an open system, interaction with these groups is frequent. The rather rapid turnover of residents exacerbates the difficulty of managing these relationships.

Independent Living Services

Unanticipated increases in the number of adolescents in foster care triggered a new challenge to the child welfare system—the necessity to prepare large numbers of at-risk foster adolescents for independent living. Traditionally, children who have remained in foster care until they are the age of majority (or the age at which laws of the state allow agencies to discontinue services) have been discharged into the community with the expectation that they could assume responsibility for themselves. Today many of these youth "aging out" of the foster care system are seriously unprepared to achieve economic and sociopersonal self-sufficiency with its demands that "each will work, find a place to live, be able to budget and manage money, pay bills, prepare meals, and in general be able to meet the responsibilities of being on one's own" (Mech, 1988c, p. 489).

Despite already heavy demands, the child welfare field has responded by accepting the necessity of developing a variety of programs to enable these foster youth to live outside the foster care system. By 1988 several hundred programs existed to provide independent living programs for adolescents near exit from out-of-

home care and the numbers were expected to grow (Mech, 1988c, p. 487).

Problems of Youth at Discharge from Foster Care.   In an effort to establish the need for and the dimensions of transition programs, the New Jersey Division of Youth and Family Services (DYFS) carried out a study of 357 youths, randomly selected, aged sixteen to twenty-one and served by the DYFS. The sample was drawn from urban, suburban, and rural counties. Data were collected from case records to provide a profile of characteristics of these youth and an assessment of their needs (Wood et al., 1989).

The profile showed that many of these foster adolescents had serious behavioral and emotional problems requiring an array of services ranging from intensive mental health care to education and training in survivor skills. A relatively small group had developmental disabilities that limited their ability to function independently. Sixty percent belonged to racial minorities. A "substantial" number had been placed in foster care from four to nine times. For over 70 percent, the record showed incidents of maltreatment that had been confirmed by the foster care agency (Wood et al., 1989).

Educational deficits and lack of readiness for employment were present for a large majority of the New Jersey sample, an especially troubling finding given projections of labor shortages in the 1990s related to lack of skills rather than to lack of jobs. Other researchers also have warned about the unmet educational needs of foster children (Fanshel & Shinn, 1978; Barth, 1986b; Gershenson & Kresh, 1986; Westat, Inc., 1986) leading Mech to conclude that "the interaction between foster placement and educational deficits is of such a magnitude that it cannot be ignored" (1988c, p. 489).

They should have demanded more of me. . . . I was capable of doing much better in school, but no one seemed to care much about that. (Festinger, 1983, p. 114)

The need was confirmed as well in Festinger's follow-up study of young adults who had been former foster children (1983). The youths were each asked how much on the whole the foster care agency had prepared them "to go out on their own." Twenty-five percent said they had been prepared "a lot"; 23 percent replied "some"; slightly more than 9 percent said "a little"; and 43 percent said "very little" or "not at all" (p. 64). These indicated that they had wanted more preparation. When asked what areas of preparation before discharge were most needed, two areas stood out—education and work (p. 290). Learning problems at the time of their discharge from care had affected their employment and work confidence.

Program Elements. In addition to education and work, the respondents in Festinger's study, looking back and now adult, named other major areas in which they wished their agency had offered them preparation for independent living; financial planning; housing; family planning and parenthood; legal information and insurance matters; personal relations and marriage; health and nutrition. In addition they wanted to have been able to return to the agency for advice or wished that the agency had reached out to them after discharge (1983, pp. 289–290).

In a two-year study of operating independent living programs in the United States and Canada, Stone (1987) identified and ranked elements that staff members and youths from the programs thought to be common to successful programs. Among ten most frequently selected elements thought to be needed, six were selected by all the respondents as essential: financial management; finding housing; accepting responsibilities; medical care/basic health; decision making; and developing a support system.

Regardless of variation in programs, Stone (1987) identified three basic principles that should be common in all:

1. "The developmental tasks of adolescence are the priorities in the lives of adolescents regardless of their situations or problems. Separating from parents, developing peer and adult relations, discovering their identity, defining a place outside the home in society, and entering the world of work are necessary life tasks at this time and therefore become the basic areas for learning and support in any Independent Living program";

2. the Program "needs to be integrated into the total agency program, not operated as an extra service that is somehow tacked onto current workloads. . . . Policies and practices that create opportunities for increasing self-reliance—for sharing household tasks, for decision making or risk taking, for accepting consequences of behavior—are essential to all phases of agency programming for children in foster care";

3. "for those youths . . . who have not learned the appropriate developmental tasks of childhood and preadolescence . . . the program must take on a remedial character . . . and do so at an accelerated pace prior to age 18" (pp. 41–42).

In many jurisdictions, foster parents are being trained to teach their foster children the needed life skills for independence. Some universities in extramural programs prepare foster parents to be primary teachers of independent living skills for children in their homes (Independent Living, 1987, p. 1).

Creating support networks of former foster parents, birth parents, volunteers, organizations, and church groups is part of independent living services offered by the Los Angeles county Independent Living program. A first-year assessment found that youths who participated in the program showed desired behavior gains over those who had not participated (Waldinger, 1988).

Other program initiatives include supervised group homes, independent living subsidy, scholarship programs, and other types of postcare services (Barth, 1986b; Sims, 1988).

The impact of the need for independent living programs was illustrated in the New Jersey study when the researchers concluded that in their state 2,769 seventeen-year-olds would require services at different levels. The cost of such services, although expected to be substantial, was considered relatively small compared to that involved in maintaining the youths as adults by publicly funded programs—on welfare, in shelters for the homeless, in prisons, or as parents unable to care for their children (Wood et al., 1989).

Federal Legislation.   The growing proportion of adolescents in foster care arrangements at the end of 1984 (46 percent of the children in foster care) did not go unaddressed by child advocates who took their concerns about problems facing youth who were aging out of the foster care system directly to Congress and its House and Senate committees. The advocacy witnesses provided evidence of the youths' low levels of self-esteem; that former children were becoming a dangerous part of the homeless (for example, half of the young people who came to New York City shelters had previously been in foster care); that foster children displayed more deviant behavior, including more arrests for serious crimes; and that many youths leaving foster care ended up on the roles of Assistance to Families with Dependent Children, or other forms of public relief (Allen et al., 1988, pp. 515–516).

As a result, Congress authorized the Independent-Living Initiative by amendment to Title IV-E of the Social Security Act—P.L. 96–272. States were thereby allowed to a share of $45 million for each fiscal year 1987 and 1988. The funds were to be used for a broad range of services for youth over sixteen and for whom Title IV-E foster care maintenance payments were being made, that is, youth who were placed in foster care from eligible AFDC families. The legislative intent was to enable such youths to seek a high school diploma or its equivalent or participate in vocational training, enroll in a program for learning daily living skills as well as individual or group counseling, integrate and coordinate all other services available to these youth, establish programs for outreach to eligible youth, and provide each participant an individualized written independent-living case plan (Allen et al., 1988).

Federal participation was provided only for fiscal years 1987 and 1988. The individual states were required to document the effectiveness of their program. In addition, Congress contracted with Westat, Inc. to carry out a national evaluation of the impact of the federal initiative on policies, extent of funding provided by foster care agencies, and the benefits for the youths who received services (Allen et al., 1988). Congress reauthorized the expiring Foster Care Independent-Living initiative for a third year. Additional changes were proposed for consideration: An extension of the program through September 30, 1992; an increase in federal funds from $45 million to $60 million; and extension of services to youths up to one year instead of the original provision of six months.

The Casey Family Program.   Within the past two decades a significant new program has been addressing the need to enable foster children to make a successful entrance into independent living when they reach the age of emancipation. The Casey Family Program, a privately endowed social service agency, was founded in 1966 and now has divisions in Washington, Idaho, Montana, Colorado, and Oregon. From the beginning, the intent has been to provide long-term quality foster care to children who present complex problems that the majority of foster parents cannot tolerate—distressed children with unstable life histories and associated problematic behaviors. These are children who are very unlikely to be reunited with their parents or to be offered an adoptive home. A common pattern is a history of multiple placements in both foster homes and group care facilities. These are children who are also at high risk of being economically dependent all their lives, or becoming involved in crime or other deviant careers. Highly significant in this uniquely funded voluntary agency's success is its capacity to mobilize resources as needed for the long-term care of difficult and virtually homeless children in the foster care system (Fanshel et al., 1989a; 1989b).

Fanshel and his associates studied the modes and conditions of exit of 585 youth who had entered and then left the Casey program at some time between its founding in 1966 and the end of the year 1984. Using the method of content analysis, four competent clinical social workers extracted data from the case records of these youth. The researchers also studied the personal and social functioning of a subset of 196 of these youth by interviews with them seven years after their departure from the program.

"What was the most gratifying experience while you were in foster care in The Casey Family Program?"

"That I finally belonged somewhere. I went through many homes before coming to Casey and after. What was important to me was that no matter where I went, I knew I was a Casey Family Program kid. It gave me a positive identity. . . . Casey did a lot for me but this simple fact, that I belonged, was the most healing. It may not sound like much, but when one grows up in a world of continual crisis and disorganization, it means everything. That I had a chance. They gave me an opportunity to change my life. They gave me hope." (Fanshel et al., 1989b, p. 477, quoting a Casey Family Program child)

Almost three in five of these troubled children were enabled to remain in the program until emancipation and to leave care in relatively good condition, an indication of noteworthy success for the program in view of the children's history of early severe deprivation and instability. One in five returned to his or her own parent. One in four was a "failed placement," that is the youth had run away or had been returned to the court because it was no longer possible to continue to serve that child in the Casey Family program (Fanshel et al., 1989a and 1989b).

Youths who stayed in the Casey program

and then were emancipated at the age of eighteen showed an adjustment significantly better than that of any other group. Those who had been emancipated under the age of eighteen showed the next best condition upon departure, followed by children returned to a parent. Not surprisingly, the runaways and the children who had to be returned to the court or a public social agency had the poorest adjustment scores at time of exit from care.

Conditions associated with poorer adjustment at exit from the Casey program reflected past deprivations, such as a greater degree of conflict with biological parents, more impermanent living arrangements even before separation from biological parents, physical abuse before entry into care (particularly true for boys), and hostile and negativistic attitudes on the part of the youth. Fanshel and coworkers (1989b) identified a sequence of variables that conditioned the child's eventual ability to leave the program and live independently in the society:

The extent of the child's hostility at entry was the best explanatory variable of the child's adaptation to foster care, and the child's adaptation to foster care was the best explanatory variable of the child's condition at exit. . . . The data from the follow-up survey showed that the child's condition at exit from the program was the best explanatory variable for the child's subsequent adjustment as an adult. . . . When a successful intervention occurred so that a child's oppositional behavior was overcome and the child led to a good adjustment, the effects of this good adjustment to foster care continued to a better condition at exit and greater financial security and conventional success in living as an independent adult free of antisocial behavioral tendencies. . . . The payoff from an investment of program resources in improving the adaptation of a foster child thus was like a continuing set of dividends in the form of better condition at exit and a more successful adult life. (Fanshel et al., 1989b, pp. 470–471)

As others have found in studies of youths' success in independent living after termination of care (Festinger, 1983; Mech, 1988c), Fanshel and his associates identified educational deficits among the children they studied. Children in the Casey Program who were behind their age-appropriate grade levels at school when they entered care, tended to remain at that level of underachievement. In the follow-up interviews with Casey youth, now living independently, three-fifths identified problems that had prevented them from achieving their best academic performance. Two-thirds of them expressed regret for their underachievement in school (Fanshel et al., 1989b). Clearly, more attention should be given to foster children's educational needs.

THE PERMANENT PLANNING REVOLUTION

Foster care historically has been viewed as the *temporary* care of children who are unable to remain at home. Several decades of research have clearly demonstrated that foster care has not been temporary for many children, but that once in the system, they have tended to remain in care for indeterminant and protracted periods of time. How to decrease the numbers of these "orphans of the living" became a challenge recognized throughout child welfare practice. Yet despite some gains, the central problems are still prevalent.

What is meant by "permanent care" as a goal for children who require foster care at some stage of their lives? Emlen (1978) defined the quality of "permanence" that is so often missing from foster care:

1. First of all, "permanent" describes *intent*. A permanent home is not one that is certain to last forever, but one that is *intended* to last indefinitely. Permanent planning means clarifying the intent of placement, and, during temporary care, keeping alive a plan for permanency. . . .

2. Secondly, permanence means commitment and continuity in the child's relation-

ships. . . . Disruption of a foster care placement entails discontinuity in those relationships that sustain a child's nurture and learning. . . . Whether the child is with his original parents or with adoptive parents, a permanent family means assuming that one shares a common future. . . . It is no derogation of the love and commitment of foster parents to say that their role, the expectations of the agency, and legal authority do not permit the kind of commitment and continuity of which permanence is made.

3. A permanent family also is one in which the sense of belonging is rooted in cultural norms and has definitive legal status. In American society, the customary way in which children's rights, welfare, and interests are protected is by those adults the law holds to be their parents, either biological or adoptive. . . .

4. Finally, permanence means a respected social status. Temporary placements can avoid stigma because they have an acceptable temporary purpose. Prolonged placement, however, reveals the second-class status that foster care has. (pp. 10–11)

The significance of intent of permanence as well as perception of permanence was a finding of the Oregon Project, an effort to accelerate the movement of children from foster care to permanent arrangements. The perception of permanence on the part of the child, foster parents, and agency representatives was found to be one of the best predictors of a child's adjustment. "Whether the child was in a legally permanent placement, adoption or returned home, or was in legally temporary foster care made very little difference in . . . level of adjustment and health at the time of the interview. Perception of permanence was the key" (Lahti, et al., 1978, p. 93).

Examples were given from the everyday life of foster children to show some of the negative aspects of foster care status:

Foster families often ask that the foster child be removed when a crisis occurs, even if the child has been there a long time—for instance, when the foster father dies or is laid off, or the foster mother becomes pregnant; she's tired and the extra room is needed.

If a child changes families and schools during primary school years . . . reading disabilities or poor vision may go unidentified and untreated. . . .

Not all doctors wish to participate in the public medical assistance programs so foster children often go to a different doctor from the rest of the family.

A foster child may not know until the last minute where he will spend important anniversaries or holidays. A foster boy soon to be five years old, on being told that he would be adopted by his foster parents, said, "Oh, now I know where I'll be on my birthday."

Foster children always have a different name from the family and other children they live with, for which they have no simple explanation. (Emlen, 1978, p. 12)

Background to the Permanent Home Movement

The foster care controversy began in 1959 with the publication of *Children in Need of Parents,* Maas and Engler's study of foster care practices affecting 551 foster children in nine communities across the nation using random community samples. On the basis of how frequently parents visited their children and the plans they had made with the agency regarding them, Maas and Engler (1959) predicted that better than half of the children were likely to live a major part of their childhoods in foster homes and institutions and that some among them were likely to leave care only after they had come of age and had had numerous homes, none their own, for ten years or so.

A follow-up study ten years later of 422 of these children is of interest. Maas (1969, pp. 331–334) found that more than half of the children spent six years or longer in foster care; almost one-third of the 422 were in care ten or more years. Children in long-term care were distinguished by below-average intelligence, non-

white status, and religion (they had a greater likelihood of being Catholic and a lesser likelihood of being of undesignated religion). They were less likely than other children in foster care to have an affectionate relationship with their parents. Their families were more likely to be very poor.

Children were not kept in long-term care because they were engaged in intensive treatment; there was no evidence of uniqueness in the level of agency service. More of the parents of children in long-term care had had little or no agency contact or treatment.

> Most of the children in long-term care, thus, seem to have remained in care while their parents and the child welfare agencies were not in contact with one another, and alternative dispositions to the children's returning home (e.g., adoption) were not considered possible. (Maas, 1969, p. 331)

The extent to which concern about instability and impermanence in foster care captured professional and public attention is reflected in testimony that David Fanshel gave before the United States Senate Subcommittee on Children and Youth:

> The notion that all children should be living with their biological families or adoptive families and that foster care should not be a permanent status has taken on such force in recent years that we face the prospect of a small revolution in child welfare as a result. The first revolution in child welfare was the closing down of the mass congregate institutions and the development of foster family care as a major alternative living arrangement. The second revolution may soon be upon us: a massive effort to make the foster care status a time-limited one. (U.S. Senate Subcommittee on Children and Youth, 1975)

Length of Time in Placement

In their landmark study, Maas and Engler (1959) warned that if a child remained in care beyond eighteen months, the chances of that child's being adopted or returned home were greatly diminished. A series of cross-sectional studies that followed found large proportions of children who had remained in foster care for extended periods—from 39 percent to 68 percent generally, with average time in care about five years (Bryce & Ehlert, 1971; Wiltse & Gambrill, 1974; Rothchild, 1974; Vasaly, 1976; Stein, 1976). A commonly accepted conclusion was that "the majority of children who enter foster care are likely to spend their growing-up years there . . . indicating the extent to which the foster family care program has assumed the character of a publicly subsidized alternative to adoption" (Wiltse & Gambrill, 1974).

In a study of 1,238 children in foster care provided by twenty agencies in New York City, Fanshel (1982) found that the average time in care was seven years. (Children who had been in care for less than one year were not included in the study, which boosted the length of time in care by two years.) While an unidentified number of children had come and gone, many had remained as long-term wards of the foster care system, leaving the issue of case planning for permanency of home for each child highly pertinent.

Cross-sectional sampling of a population of children in foster homes at one period of time, such as the studies referred to above, are informative and useful. However, they have the limitation of biasing the findings in the direction of a disproportionate high percentage of children in long-term care (Kadushin, 1978b, p. 98; Fanshel, 1982, p. 100). Longitudinal studies of children over an extended period of time give a clearer picture of the movement of children in and out of the foster care system.

Fanshel and Shinn's longitudinal study (1978) of 624 children (aged birth to twelve years) found that five years after entry into foster care, some 36 percent of the children were still in care; 56 percent had been discharged (most of them to their own homes); another 5 percent had been placed in adoptive homes;

about 3 percent of the children had been transferred to state institutions (mental hospitals, institutions for the retarded, or state training schools for delinquent children) (pp. 115–116). Discharge rates had dropped rapidly after two years of stay in foster care. A degree of optimism was shown, however, in the fact that at each of the time intervals of the five-year study, some children did leave foster care. They were not without exception locked into long-term care, even though the chance for the child to have his or her own permanent home seriously erodes with the passage of time.

In a longitudinal study of all children ($N = 185$) placed into foster care with the Children's Aid Society of Pennsylvania from June 1, 1978, through May 31, 1979, Lawder and coworkers (1986) arrived at findings similar to those of other studies. Five years after the children's placement in foster care, case records were read by a team of experienced social workers who then completed structured case summary forms on each child. Limitations of the study were acknowledged: As examples, use of case records rather than data directly from the children or families; variation in quality of the case records; and lack of follow-up data after the children were discharged from care that would have shed light on the success of reunification or a later reentry into foster care. The majority of children had returned to their parents' homes within a "relatively short time."

About 70 percent of the children were in care two years or less. (Thirty-four percent had left care within three months.) Five years after placement, 61.7 percent of the children had been discharged from foster care, most of them returned to parents or extended family members. Sixteen percent were in adoptive homes. Six children had been transferred to other agencies. Three children had died, and one had been emancipated. Eighteen percent were still in the agency's care.

Overall, Lawder and coworkers concluded that "the foster care experience is a relatively stable one for children" (p. 250). Because of the severity of their problems or those of their parents, some children required continuing care. They formed an accumulative core-group of children that accounted in cross-sectional studies for the high percentage of children in care for extended periods.

Instability of Placements

In addition to the risk of foster care being prolonged throughout much of a child's growing up years, many of these children lack continuity of environment and relationships because of transfers between agencies, transfers within an agency, or return to foster care after having been discharged. Fanshel and Shinn (1978) analyzed the number of placements experienced by the 624 children in their longitudinal study of foster placement. Three or more placements were termed "excessive." Almost 42 percent of the children experienced only one placement. Almost 30 percent experienced two. Slightly more than 18 percent had three placements, and 10 percent had four or more. These findings were comparable to those of Jeter's earlier survey of child welfare agencies (1963, pp. 81–82).

Each move leaves its own scar. After a while, the children become more insecure about their lives, and each succeeding move feeds this feeling. We found that children who were exposed to more changes in life situations before coming into the agency's care appeared more hostile and oppositional at intake. (Fanshel et al., 1989b, p. 470)

Fanshel and Shinn found the length of time spent in foster care to be the best predictor of the number of placements; that is, the longer children are in care, the more vulnerable they are to the possibility of a series of placements. Of children discharged from foster care during the first year, only a little over 2 percent had three or more placements. The proportion of placements rose, however, during each successive year that children remained in care—19 per-

cent of second-year discharges, over 35 percent of fourth-year discharges, and 42.5 percent of fifth-year discharges experienced three or more placements. Of the children remaining in care longer than five years, almost 46 percent lived in three or more foster homes (1978, pp. 139–140).

Jewish children experienced the fewest placements, most of them having gone directly into long-term residential treatment. More black and Puerto Rican children had three or more placements, reflecting the likelihood that minority children will remain in care longer than white children (Fanshel & Shinn, 1978, pp. 140–141).

When the number of placements was examined according to the primary reason for placement, children who had behavior disorders and whose parents were unwilling to care for them experienced fewer placements. However, children whose behavior was considered to be defiant and hostile tended to have more placements than other children. Children who entered care because of family dysfunction and because of neglect, abuse, or abandonment also showed a relatively high number of placements. Fewer placements were experienced by children who went directly into foster family home care instead of going first into congregate shelter care. And finally, children whose parents visited less frequently suffered fewer placements—a fact suggesting that the more the biological parents are out of the picture, the fewer the placements for children (Fanshel & Shinn, 1978, pp. 141–143).

Proch and Taber (1987) analyzed the placement histories of eighty-seven adolescents who had experienced two or more placement disruptions and had been referred by their caseworkers for specialized services. "Disruption" was defined as "an unplanned change in foster placement made in response to a demand for replacement by a child's caregiver" (p. 9). The children were from eleven years of age to nineteen years with a mean of sixteen years. These eighty-seven children had experienced a total of 746 placements since coming into agency care. Individually the children had been in 3 to 27 placements with a mean of 9 and a median of 8 placements. The statistical analysis focused on patterns of movements in care and characteristics of living situations rather than number of placements and length of time in care.

Findings included these: The older the child, the shorter the length of time he or she remained in a placement. The length of time in a placement usually became shorter with each placement. Placement changes occurred more frequently over time and in the direction of more restrictive settings. Children who had been in care for an extended time did not move at regular intervals. Rather, when they were younger they had had one or two placements of relatively long duration; then at adolescence they moved with increasing frequency.

Explanations for the disruptions of placements focused on the youth's behavior and the interaction between the child and caregiver when the youth refused to obey household rules or was aggressive verbally or physically. The researchers concluded that the explanation of the disrupted placement lay in a struggle for control that becomes more central at adolescence. More often than not, the caregiver's role in the conflict was not acknowledged. The youth was blamed by the caregiver and also by the caseworker.

For the group of children in extended care and multiple placements, Proch and Taber reconceptualized placement disruption as "a pattern of moves in care reflecting alienation, and eventually mutual rejection, between children and caregivers" (p. 9).

The challenge of adult authority and the need to become independent are common to adolescents, and perhaps more acutely characteristic of youths who have lived away from the care of their own parents. The role of caregivers and caseworkers in this conflict requires early agency attention to help caregivers understand more fully the challenge to adolescents of adult authority, and if not addressed, the risk of placement disruption.

The Outcome of Placements

Although the number of foster care placements each year far exceeds the number of adoptive placements, follow-up studies to evaluate the outcome of placements have been less frequent for foster care. Sophie van Senden Theis carried out a unique study in 1924 of 910 children who had been placed in foster homes by the New York State Charities Aid Association between 1898 and 1922. Those selected for study were all who had reached the age of eighteen by the time of the study. The results were generally positive.

Over 77 percent were judged to be "capable" persons—"able to manage their affairs with average good sense and who live in accordance with good standards in their communities." Another 11 percent were "harmless . . . not clearly a burden nor . . . in any obvious way an asset to society." The other 12 percent were "at odds with society" or still needing protection or training (Theis, 1924, p. 161).

More recent studies have relied on smaller samples, pursued different questions, and used varying procedures. These factors make it difficult to generalize from the findings.

Meier interviewed sixty-one adult men and women who had spent at least five years in foster homes in Minnesota without ever having been returned to their own homes. As far as possible, information was obtained in relation to marriage, children, housing, employment, and social relationships. The results showed that these former foster children had been very successfully compared with their biological parents; the majority were self-supporting and had found a place in their communities. There was, however, some impaired sense of well-being—a higher incidence of marital breakdown and a higher proportion of nonmarital births than among the general population (Meier, 1965, pp. 196–206).

Believing that agencies should have routine procedures for continuous evaluation of the effectiveness of their services, Gil (1964) demonstrated a method agencies might use for examining postplacement functioning. He held that a follow-up procedure, to be meaningful for child welfare practice, should examine postplacement functioning in relation to preplacement circumstances and the child's developmental potential, rather than to normal levels of functioning in their communities. Among twenty-five children discharged from foster care by one agency in 1956, about half had realized their potential to a considerable extent and the other half only to a limited extent.

Some studies have dealt with factors that bear on success in residential treatment. Of interest is a follow-up study of fifty boys who had left Bellefaire—a residential treatment institution in Cleveland—two years before the study. Success was relatively high both within Bellefaire and in the community on discharge, considering the severity of the disorders the boys had manifested. However, positive adaptation to the institution could not be taken as sufficient reason to expect adequacy in the community environment on discharge. The circumstances the boys encountered after discharge were highly important, as well as how aftercare plans were implemented. An internally oriented approach to the child was deemed insufficient. Children must be prepared to return to their communities by accelerated exposures to community experiences (Allerhand et al., 1966).

Festinger (1983) studied 277 young adults who had entered foster care as young children and had been discharged at eighteen to twenty-one years of age after having been in care for at least five years. Thirty child-placing agencies cooperated in the study—small and large agencies, voluntary agencies and public foster home divisions. Data were derived from agency records and from a carefully designed two-hour interview with each of the 277 young adults. Findings with respect to the former foster youth were compared with data from several national surveys of young adults in the same age range.

How did the former foster children fare when compared with other young adults in society? Festinger's reply was this: "There is no one

simple answer unless one is willing to be trapped into a 'good–bad' dichotomy. Rather, there is a continuum of 'faring.' Some fare a little better, some a little worse, but most are functioning in society in about the same way as others their age" (p. 252). Ninety-four percent of the females and 91 percent of the males said that the statement "all in all I was lucky to be placed in foster care" was "very true" or "pretty true" for them. Percentages were somewhat lower for those whose foster care had been in residential group facilities (p. 258). The self-assessment of the respondents on the whole was one of satisfaction with life. In general, "these young adults were managing their lives adequately and feeling quite satisfied with their physical, social, and psychological environments" (p. 133). Yet, 10.5 percent indicated some feeling of isolation within society by saying that the statement "no one cares much what happens to me" was "very true" or "pretty true" for them (p. 125).

The four principal reasons for entry into foster care were neglect, mental illness of the primary care person, inability or unwillingness to cope with child rearing, and abandonment. Festinger found that "those who were placed because of neglect or abandonment, or because their caretakers could not or would no longer cope ultimately had a poorer sense of themselves and their lives than those who were placed for reasons that were more apt to have been seen as beyond immediate parental control (such as death, physical illness, or imprisonment). Those who were placed because of mental illness were in between" (p. 46). Festinger emphasized throughout the findings that overall the former foster children, now adults, were coping with the realities of life and were reasonably optimistic about achieving their goals in the future—testimony to the strength and resilience of children.

It is of interest that when Fanshel and Shinn (1978) compared foster children who had remained in extended care with those who had returned home, they did not find that the experience of living in foster care, by and large, had been destructive. Apparently extended care had not brought problems of personal and social adjustments clearly linked to being in foster care. Also, no great benefits to children had resulted. The need for foster care had been related to the needs of the parents rather than to any therapeutic impact on the children. Although their data did not support the view that foster children were necessarily faring poorly, Fanshel and Shinn said:

> We are not completely sure that continued tenure in foster care over extended periods is not in itself harmful to children. On the level at which we were able to measure the adjustment of the children we could find no such negative effect. However, . . . we are not sure that our procedures have captured the potential feelings of pain and impaired self-image that can be created by impermanent status in foster care. (1978, pp. 479, 490–495)

The significance of that concern was reflected in a survey (Rest & Watson, 1984) of a sample of adults who had come into foster care provided by a voluntary multiple-service child welfare agency that served an inner-city population. The research examined current functioning, the significance of the foster care experience during childhood and in present life, and the subjects' conclusions about their experiences. Twenty-two potential subjects were identified; thirteen participated in the study. Each had come into agency care as a young child, had reached adulthood and been discharged as an "independently functioning adult." During their years in foster care, the agency had provided supportive counseling and other therapeutic services aimed at helping them cope with the impact of being foster children. (The study is limited by its very small sample, but is of interest in view of the range of services provided the children during their stay in foster care.)

Rest and Watson's findings were consistent with those of other studies in this sense: the experience of "impermanence" did not appear to have impaired their abilities "to live independent, outwardly satisfactory lives" (p. 291). However, they tended to compare themselves with "an idealized self who would exist now had they been reared by their biological families" (p. 293). Unpleasant facts about the separation from biological parents were forgotten or rationalized in some way to make it acceptable. As an example of the "casework scenario endlessly repeated with minor variation throughout agency records" the researchers cited this instance: "A social worker recorded considerable efforts to help a 15-year-old youngster to locate his biological mother. After seeing her, the young man acknowledged to the worker that, although he had been thinking about going to live with her, he now realized it was not possible. 'That lady can't even take care of herself, so I know that she can't take care of me.' He also sought his mother again at age 21, shortly after his foster mother died, and finding that contact unsatisfactory, he has made no further efforts in the past 7 years. Yet when interviewed for the present study, he said that he had come into care only because his mother did not have the money to take care of him" (pp. 303–304).

Rest and Watson concluded that despite their outwardly satisfactory lives the young adults had been left "at risk of an impaired self-image from a deeply felt stigma of foster care, a difficulty in establishing emotional intimacy, and an unresolved sense of loss" (p. 291).

Despite the lack of firm evidence that long-term foster care is harmful to children, child welfare professionals continue to view such a situation as undesirable. They base this opinion on the belief that the anomalous status of a child in foster care is harmful, that conflicting expectations and loyalties affect a child's capacity for effective relationships, and that no child can grow emotionally as long as he or she never belongs to a parent except on a temporary or ambiguous basis.

If foster care is often unstable, how do so-called permanent arrangements fare? The research in this area is relatively recent. Adoption has a strong record in terms of the stability of placements. Returning children to their biological parents seems more problematic. Block (1981) found that 28 percent of children discharged to parents had returned to care. There is little solid and consistent evidence that long-term foster care is detrimental to a child's general well-being and adjustment, or that it hinders future success as young adults. The research suggests that the quality of the living arrangement is critical to future adjustment. Returning children to biological parents who have not been able to improve their circumstances and their level of child care sufficiently may not be a solution to continuing tenure in foster care, leaving adoption as a more appropriate alternative to be considered.

Parent Problems after Foster Placement

Does foster care help parents to resolve some of the serious problems that made it necessary for their children to have care away from them? Five years after placement Jenkins and Norman (1975) assessed the circumstances of mothers whose children had been returned to them. The fact that the majority of these children had eventually gone home suggests that to some extent mothers had been able to renew their child-caring capacities. But what about the basic family problems that had resulted in entrance into foster care? Five years after the placement of their children the mothers were in somewhat worse financial situations. There were more of them receiving public assistance and more of them living below the poverty level than there had been when their children had come into care. As to housing, they had moved far oftener than the general population. Two-thirds of the mothers were in the same marital status as at the beginning of the study, but there had been many changes of relationships and they had continued to have children in spite of their earlier child-rearing problems. The percentage of households headed by single women had risen as subfamilies moved out from extended family households to establish independent units.

Jenkins and Norman (1975) concluded that foster care had been helpful when parents had been unable or unwilling to perform their expected roles, but only partially helpful. Basic family problems had not been solved as a result of placement. The foster care system had not prevented further out-of-home care or resolved the problems that had brought children into care.

Many agency services for restoration of family life are of insufficient strength and direction to have a sustained impact. Elements of more effective programs that are emerging include (1) a wide variety of helping options; (2) a primary and continuing social workers' or staff team; (3) small caseloads; (4) crisis intervention services around the clock; (5) making use of natural helping resources in the neighborhood and community; (6) intensive counseling services; (7) provision of transportation, health services, respite care, and child care payments (Pecora et al., 1985; Berry, 1988; Ten Broeck & Barth, 1986).

Barriers to Planning Permanent Care

Characteristics of the parents and the child, as well as characteristics of the service delivery system, can act as barriers to permanent homes for children.

Child and Family Characteristics. Fanshel and Shinn (1978) identified certain child and family variables that influence the length of a child's stay in foster care. One is the age of the child: younger children tend to stay in foster care in greater proportions than older ones. Minority children and those born outside a marriage are more likely to have longer stays in the foster care system. Abandoned children and those who come into care because of neglect and abuse also face greater obstacles in finding permanent homes either through return to parents or through adoption.

Characteristics of the mother (as assessed by caseworkers) may constitute a barrier to a permanent home, particularly characteristics that would affect her ability to care for her child adequately, such as mental illness and the degree of her disturbance, serious problems in the parent–child relationship, harmful child-rearing/child care practices, the outlook for working with her, and predictions of whether she will withdraw from the use of services (Fanshel & Shinn, 1978; Fanshel, 1982).

When Jenkins and Norman (1975) studied reasons for foster placement, they noted that certain reasons tended to group together as "socially approved" reasons, for example, physical or mental illness, emotional disturbance of a child, and unwillingness or inability of a mother to assume care of an out-of-wedlock infant. Quite different reasons for placement were grouped under the label "socially unacceptable," for example, abandonment, severe neglect or abuse, and family dysfunction as seen in alcoholism, drug addition, retardation, imprisonment, and unwillingness or inability to continue a legitimate child's care. When children classified according to the two groups of reasons were compared, the socially unacceptable group of reasons emerged as barriers to permanent homes. It was also found that mothers whose reasons for foster placement were socially unacceptable felt angry about their child's placement; evaluated the foster situation negatively; perceived the social workers as less interested, understanding, and helpful; had more problems in visiting their children; and were far less likely to use community services.

Parental Visiting. The visiting of foster children by their natural parents is a second factor that powerfully affects rates of discharge from care. The issue of unvisited children was first established by Maas and Engler (1959) and confirmed by subsequent studies.

Fanshel and Shinn's five-year longitudinal study (1978) revealed that the frequency of contact between the biological mother and the foster child showed a strong, statistically significant relationship to the child's return to the parental home. Parents who visited the child regularly and took full advantage of all opportunities to do so were able to effect the child's discharge in 73 percent of the cases during the first year and 64 percent during the second year. In contrast, 66 percent of those children who were not visited during the first year were still in foster care five years later (Fanshel, 1975a).

Earlier studies showed that in practice, regular parental visiting occurred in considerably less than half of foster care placements. An Iowa study showed that 53 percent of the children for whom the degree of parental contact was known were visited less than once every six months (Iowa Department, 1973, p. 17). Similar studies in California and Massachusetts found that only 30 percent of the children were visited (Children waiting, 1972, p. 9; Gruber, 1973, p. 18). Only 16 percent of foster children were visited by their fathers and only 28 percent by their mothers during a fifteen-month period in Illinois (Hartman et al., 1971). A more recent study shows a higher proportion of parental visiting, perhaps due to greater emphasis on visiting by the child welfare system. Forty-six percent of 1,200 foster children in New York City saw at least one parent during the prior six-month period (Fanshel, 1982, p. 99). Of children not freed for adoption, 69 percent were visited. Although unvisited children remain "worrisome," their numbers are "on a smaller scale than originally presented" (Fanshel, 1982, p. 100).

Visiting by biological parents is discouraged by a number of conditions. When Jenkins and Norman (1975) queried mothers with children in foster care, only one-quarter reported that there was "no problem" in visiting. Of the mothers with problems visiting their children, the following reasons were given: illness of the mother, 50 percent; distance and lack of travel money, 33 percent; inconvenient visiting times set by the agency, 20 percent; visiting made difficult by foster parents, 11 percent; visit emotionally upsetting to the mother, 33 percent; and visit emotionally upsetting to the child, 25 percent. (Percentages add up to over 100 percent because some respondents listed more than one difficulty.) Interestingly, 73 percent of the mothers said that their children wanted more visiting. The respondents noted that if agencies had placed their children closer to home and made visiting times more convenient, their visiting frequency would have increased.

Fanshel and Shinn (1978) concluded that, with a few exceptions, parental visiting is linked to discharge from foster care, and that this holds across ethnic and religious groups and is persistent over time. Visiting patterns of biological parents—whether they visit and how often they visit their children in foster care—were found in their work to be the strongest correlate of discharge from foster care. Other studies also have affirmed continuing visits by biological parents as central to family reunification (Weinstein, 1960; Fanshel, 1975a; Mech, 1985; Milner, 1987). Clearly, motivating and assisting parents to visit their children is a major responsibility of foster care agencies.

To test the extent to which established knowledge about the importance of parental visiting is reflected in agency policy and practice, Proch and Howard (1986) reviewed 256 randomly selected case records of children in foster care in Illinois. This research led to the conclusion that despite the recognition of the importance of parental visitation to the well-being of children and in maintaining attachment and achieving family reunification, "knowledge and policy about visitation are not fully integrated into current child welfare practice" (p. 178). Specific findings included these: (1) most parents who were scheduled to visit did so, and most visited in compliance with the schedule specified in the case plan; (2) parents who did not have a visiting schedule or who were told to request a visit when they wanted one did not visit; (3) visiting plans were seldom individualized in matters such as age of the child, the place of scheduled visits, and attempts to involve fathers in the visitation; (4) office visits were the most common plan even when the goal was reunification; (5) in approximately 30 percent of cases for which reunification was the goal, there were no visiting plans in the record; (6) overall, visiting plans had little direct connection to the needs of individual children. Rather, they seemed to be a function of the social worker's particular style or standard practice in an agency (pp. 180–181).

It is of interest here that in Festinger's study (1983) of young adults formerly in foster care, looking back, these young people felt that they should have been consulted along the way as to what they wanted or needed, particularly about "the atmosphere surrounding visits, about timing and about whom they saw or did not see" (p. 96).

Caseworker Practices. As can be seen from the discussion above, not all barriers to permanent homes for children can be credited to child- and family-centered characteristics. The child welfare system of services often acts as a barrier to better ways of meeting children's needs for consistent nurturance.

A significant barrier to planning permanent care for children is "drift as a mode of practice," characterized by social workers' indecisiveness about goals and pessimistic attitudes toward certain children, their parents, their experiences and their future (Emlen, 1978). Child welfare workers who make effective decisions provide services as soon as possible following a child's entry into foster care; keep frequent contact with parents; encourage them to visit their children; clearly define case objectives; and choose services directly related to reaching a decision concerning the child in care (Gambrill & Stein, 1981, p. 110). Failure to set goals for action at key decision points makes it more difficult to monitor the foster care system and accentuates "drift" for children.

Given the importance of the social worker's evaluation of the mother as a predictor of discharge, and workers' difficulties in assessing maternal adequacy, pessimistic attitudes about families whose children require foster care can act as a barrier to planning permanent care, particularly in regard to planning children's return to their own families (Shapiro, 1976).

Some agency directors and social workers hold negative or ambivalent attitudes about legal termination of parental rights when children remain in foster care and are unvisited or in other ways are unattended by their biological parents.

Casework behaviors that tend to lead to early discharge from foster care include higher frequency of caseworker contact with the biological parents while a child is in foster care. This in turn increases parental visiting, and both factors together increase the probability of discharge (Fanshel, 1975a). A high frequency of caseworker contact increases discharges during the first year of placement, but the impact diminishes after that, suggesting that intensity of casework contact is at least as critical as frequency of contact, and that "intensity of effort in a short period may be more productive than a diffuse effort over a long period" (Shapiro, 1976).

The experience and training of the caseworker is vital. Shapiro found that the proportion of children awaiting permanent care in the caseloads of the least-experienced workers was more than three times as high as for the most-experienced. The proportion of children that returned home was also considerably higher for the most-experienced (1976).

Although frequency and intensity of service are important, contact alone is rarely enough; goal-directed and coordinated services to the biological parents are essential (Stein, 1976). Various tasks are performed by caseworkers with families of foster children. As a *catalyst,* the worker uses community resources, stimulates new ones and identifies natural networks useful to families (Maluccio & Sinanoglu, 1981). Caseworkers act as an *initiator* of parent–child contact and other services and as a *broker* for the family to reduce isolation and stressors. The worker becomes a *mediator* "between the parent–child relationship and the ex-

ternal forces that affect the relationship. In the process, duration of foster care is directly affected" (Milner, 1987, p. 121). The social worker is also a *teacher and model* of child management skills during parent–child visits (Blumenthal & Weinberg, 1983, p. 376).

When a child comes into foster placement, too often most agency services are turned in the direction of foster parents and the foster child to help maintain the foster care relationship, rather than in the direction of the biological parents to help them reunite their families or surrender legal rights to enable the child to have a permanent home through adoption. Studies in Illinois, New York, and Arizona provide evidence of this phenomenon, clearly a barrier to a child's being able to move out of foster care and into a permanent home (Vasaly, 1976).

Lack of service to biological parents occurs very often because of limited agency resources and high caseloads, leading to patterns of crisis-based intervention. "In agency after agency, the pattern is often one of handling emergencies rather than providing systematic services and support to children and their parents." When social workers who are actively dissatisfied with this mode of practice are willing to go beyond formal regulations and use informal procedures, they can sometimes increase the chances that children will not remain in foster care. As Shapiro found in a study of eighty-four agencies, social workers who were dissatisfied with the foster care system tended to increase their service to families and children, thus significantly enhancing the chances that children would move out of foster care (1976).

Multiple placements of children in the foster care system and the lack of continuity and security that results are exacerbated by the turnover of caseworkers. In the national study of child welfare service, Shyne reported:

The number of caseworkers to whom the child had been assigned rose steadily with the length of time in foster care. For example, 48 percent of those in care for two years or longer had had at least four caseworkers, compared with 9 percent of the children who had been in foster care for less than two years. The instability of placements and the changing of worker's assignments underscore the importance of concentrated efforts to effect the early return of children to their parents or relatives or the incorporation of the children in a new family by adoption. (Shyne, 1980, p. 30)

While there is little doubt that more services to families can prevent or shorten many placements, caseworkers may not necessarily use additional services in this way. Rapp (1982) found that often workers with extensive service alternatives were as likely to place the same children as did workers with less service resources available. Simple ignorance of available planning options, as Emlen noted (1978) sometimes closes the exits from foster care. So may the lack of training in means to work effectively with parents of children in foster care. The responsibility of the agency to provide inservice training for social work staff is reflected in this conclusion of Stein and Gambrill: "Skill deficits may be a crucial dimension in explaining the absence of services to biological parents" (1977, p. 510).

Despite these problems, it appears that many states and the federal government have shifted emphasis to support and preventive services. "There has been a conscious departure from efforts that centered on removing mistreated or neglected children from their natural homes" (Harris, 1988, p. 483). At the same time, while there is little doubt that more services to families can prevent or shorten many placements, it is evident that caseworkers may need additional training to use additional services effectively.

Other Delivery System Barriers to Permanent Homes. Children's agencies that maintain a foster care program not linked to preventive supplementary services and alternatives to foster care increase the likelihood that the court and the placement agency will develop maladap-

tive ways of meeting their shared responsibility for children. In such instances the child welfare agency may become quite dependent on the local juvenile court judges in decisions concerning the placement of the child, a return home, or termination of parental rights. Some judges become locked into a pattern of ordering foster placement as an almost exclusive solution to family problems. Some are reluctant to fully terminate parental rights and thus free a child for adoption, even when the parents demonstrate only the most minimal involvement with their child in placement, and even this on an unplanned and sporadic basis.

Another organizational obstacle to permanent homes for children in foster care can occur when very large agencies specialize staff functions through separate divisions and separate staff for intake tasks, protective services, foster home supervision, adoption, and service to biological families. Such a structure allows three to five different persons to be involved in a single case over the course of a few months; it also invites ineffective communication between the various staff members, as well as the need to invest time in coordinating the different parts of the service delivery time needed for direct services.

Studies of social work behaviors clearly suggest that the timeliness of service delivery, the skills of the worker, and the intensity of investment are influential in securing the early discharge of children from care. More carefully planned use of staff resources is indicated. Those features that social work has traditionally considered good do in fact make a difference, especially in the early stages of foster care (Shapiro, 1976).

Techniques for Moving Children Out of Foster Care

Case Review. Many children remain in foster care for extended periods for no reason other than that no one in the agency reviews the cases. Decision points in many cases simply pass by without any action being taken. Systematic and regular case review procedures are essential to clarify mutual expectations of parents and caseworker within a time frame in moving toward permanent placement for the child. The purpose of subsequent review is to determine whether a specific child should be returned to parents, continued in foster care, or freed for adoption and, if adoption is chosen, to identify an adoptive home and carry out placement. All successful permanency planning projects, according to one researcher, contain, as one element, a review system (M. L. Jones, 1978).

All states now have either a full court review, a citizens' board review, or a full agency review system. Court review is the most authoritative. It can be a social worker's report to the judge or a full evidentiary trial (Dodson, 1983, p. 86). Review boards are operated by three to five citizen volunteers. Agency or administrative reviews by the agency that holds custody of the foster child are often made even where judicial reviews take place. Within each method there are variations from state to state. Periodic reviews every six months is a minimum frequency required by the Adoption Assistance and Child Welfare Act of 1980.

Festinger (1975) studied the New York court review process in 392 cases to determine how effective it had been. Focusing on the actions of agencies to free children for adoption, she compared cases that had been reviewed by the court with cases that had not been reviewed. She concluded that the process had indeed spurred agencies to take steps needed to free children for adoption and had stimulated agency personnel themselves to review cases more carefully and develop and implement appropriate plans for children. In a follow-up to this study, Festinger (1976) again found that court reviews had facilitated movement of children out of foster care. Furthermore, this movement was occurring at a somewhat faster rate than at the time of the first study, despite the fact that subsidies had been available during both periods and that children by the time of the

second study were older and had been in care longer.

Subsequently, the Oregon Permanent Planning Project showed that closely supervised cases result in more permanent plans (Emlen, 1978). Fanshel and Shinn's longitudinal study suggested that monitoring caseworker investment and parental contact increased permanent planning (1978). South Carolina's system of review is based on the use of citizen boards. Within eighteen months of its establishment, the number of children in foster care was reduced from 4,000 to about 3,300 and adoptions had increased by 44 percent (Chappell, 1975). An administrative case review system in Illinois also was found to reduce the foster care population (Poertner & Rapp, 1980).

Although some studies have shown review systems to be limited in their usefulness (Calburn & Magura, 1978), on balance they appear to be an effective strategy for moving children out of foster placement and into permanent arrangements. Disparate findings are sometimes explained by noting that case review systems vary considerably in their design; their particular characteristics may be critical. These critical differences may be the use of staff training before installing a case review system, explicitly stated goals to provide permanent homes for children, clearly defined procedures to follow, and effective leadership.

Use of Contracts with Parents. In California, Stein, Gambrill, and Wiltse (1974) reported an interesting and successful experiment in working with parents whose children are in foster care. Treatment included the use of "hard" services, such as housing and financial assistance as well as direct counseling. The aim of the project was "to introduce an intensive relationship which will help to rebuild the parent's sense of parenthood and sense of authority to make the decision about his or her children." Possible decisions were to return the child from foster care; to terminate parental rights, with adoptive placement following in most instances; and to continue foster care, usually with a guardianship arrangement or a long-term foster care agreement. Intensive casework services were offered to the biological parents, and contracts with them were used as a tool to encourage parental participation in planning and decision making and as a means to prevent or interrupt drift in foster care.

Contracts were written documents that specified particular agreements between the project director, the social worker, and the client. They provided a focus for services by explicating long-range goals for children, problems that required remedies, the treatment method to be used, alternative consequences of parental participation, and time limits for accomplishing goals.

The social workers assumed an active role, making clear the range of alternatives for the child's future as well as the consequences if parents did not participate. In addition, in view of Fanshel's evidence of parental visiting as a predictor of the fate of foster children (1975), social workers took a firm stand that parents should visit and often provided them with transportation.

Parents almost uniformly were positive about the use of a contract, often indicating that it was the first clear direction they had received as to what must be done in order to move toward the return of their children. Court judges also reacted positively to the contracts because they found the specificity, as well as the minimum conditions set forth for the return of a child, useful, particularly when termination of parental rights was pursued.

At the end of two years, the results were significantly different ($p < .001$) between 148 experimental and 148 control children. Specifically, 41 percent of the cases in the experimental group and 25 percent of those in the control group were closed after restoration of children to their parents or after completed adoption or guardianship actions. In addition, 35 percent of children in the experimental group and 15 percent of those in the control group were on their way out of foster home care. Only 21 percent of the children in the experimental group versus 60 percent of those in the control group were reported as needing long-term placement (Stein & Gambrill, 1977, p. 505).

Banished Children—Remedies. In the early 1970s the widespread practice of out-of-state placement of certain kinds of children came under scrutiny. Frequently the children were sent to states far removed geographically from their homes and those of their parents. Justine Wise Polier, a former New York family court judge, was foremost among those who called attention to the phenomenon. She labeled these children "banished children" to emphasize the punitive effects of sending children whom nobody wanted to states remote from their homes and past experiences. Polier's investigation disclosed that not only delinquent children but also neglected and dependent children, children in need of supervision, and children with mental or emotional disabilities were being placed in facilities (sometimes unlicensed) in other states rather than being provided with appropriate facilities created for them in their home states. For example, hundreds of so-called hard-to-place children in Illinois were, as Polier termed it, "exiled" into proprietary institutions in Texas until their mistreatment was exposed after a girl's death. American Indian children from Florida were being sent to southwestern states. Retarded and disturbed children in Alaska in need of long-term treatment were being sent to institutions in Colorado and California. Banishment also came to light in other states, and there was a strong suggestion that this practice was disproportionately used with poor and nonwhite children (Polier, 1974).

The Children's Defense Fund's nationwide study of children in placement found that in 1976, 4,491 children were placed out of their own state. The estimated figure was closer to 10,000. The states sending the largest number of children out of state were New Jersey (735), Louisiana (715), Virginia (436), Indiana (329), and Iowa (207). Seven states and the District of Columbia did not know how many children had been placed out of state. The testimony in *Gary W. v. Cherry* involving Louisiana children placed in Texas vividly depicts the process:

> State neglect and abuse were even more likely for children placed out of state than those placed in the state. It showed that Louisiana parents were forced to agree to out-of-state placements; offered no options; and told if they did not accept this "help" they would receive no help at all. The state provided no funds for parents to visit the children . . . few parents received any information about their children's progress. . . . Perhaps most tragic, once the children were placed, the state made no efforts to bring them back to Louisiana or ensure their placement in the least restrictive setting. (*Children without,* 1978, pp. 61–64)

Following the exposure of this unfortunate placement method, efforts were made to bring out-of-state placement under control. A first reaction was to try to reduce the number of such placements by returning children to their home states whenever suitable services could be found or developed. For example, by 1976 only 75 children under Illinois guardianship were out of state, compared with 785 children in such arrangements four years earlier (DCFS, 1976, p. 3).

But a variety of circumstances make it essential that child placement services and supervision not be restricted to the territory of a single state. The number of children requiring foster or adoptive placement and the resources within a state to meet individual needs of children are seldom if ever in complete balance. Awareness of the need for selective and regulated out-of-state placement led to the Interstate Compact on the Placement of Children (American Public Welfare Association, 1973).

It is of interest to remember that interstate placement of children and legislation to regulate it were matters for concern as early as 1895. In that year Michigan passed the first law regulating interstate placements, with the practice widely copied by other states in the next fifteen years. However, the early concern was not related to the exile or banishment of children, but "was due to the desire of the states to protect themselves against the burden of dependency and delinquency which they considered originated outside their boundaries and was therefore not their responsibility." The regulation did not come during the period when Charles Loring Brace and the New York Children's Aid Society were directing a stream of children into the Midwest, but came "after the states had become populous, had their own problems of child dependency, and were no longer welcoming all settlers young or old." The concern clearly was to provide protection for a state from the responsibility to provide care for children from other states. Concern for the exported child was minimal and by 1938 was included in protective legislation in only seven states (Abbott, 1938, Vol. 2, pp. 133–135).

But proper investigation and supervision of out-of-state placement at a great distance became costly, and the numbers of children placed in other than adjoining states became very much reduced. Concern about out-of-state placement gradually became minimal until the 1970s, when knowledge about the tragic plight of large numbers of banished children came before the public.

In brief, the present Interstate Compact on the Placement of Children requires notice and determination of the suitability of a placement *before* it is made and explication of the specific legal and administrative responsibility during the continuance of an interstate placement. It also provides a basis for enforcement of rights and responsibilities among the participating states. By 1973 the compact had been enacted in seventeen states, and by 1990 forty-nine states had become compact members. But enacting the compact seems not to be enough. The Children's Defense Fund study concluded that:

> participation in the Compact appeared to have had little impact on the knowledge of state offi-

cials about children out of their own state, or on state efforts to protect such children more effectively. (*Children without,* 1978, p. 71)

Recommendations emanating from this study included the development of in-state alternatives, stronger procedural protections for the placement and monitoring of children, and more careful review procedures.

Management Information Systems. Systematically recorded information about the characteristics of children in foster care, the services offered to them and their families, and changes in their situations is a means of providing a rational basis for the provision of child welfare services and eliminating drift in foster care. Yet accurate and significant data to use in child and family policy formulation have been in short supply. Administrators and program planners in large child welfare systems have turned to development of computerized information systems as a means to monitor services and progress toward goals and to modify services. However, although computerized information systems proved capable of collecting a vast amount of data, they often lacked the analytic capability to do anything meaningful with what had been collected. "It is one order of activity to *collect* data about thousands of children, it is yet another task to distil useful information from this effort. It is no easy undertaking to organize data so that they are comprehensible and truly contributory to enhanced understanding of the phenomenon under scrutiny" (Fanshel & Grundy, 1975, p. 1).

Long familiarity with child welfare data and extensive experience in analyzing such data during a five-year longitudinal study of foster children enabled Fanshel and Grundy to develop a Child Welfare Information System (CWIS) covering all children in foster care in New York City, which was based on conceptions drawn from past research efforts dealing with a range of variables in foster care services. One example of benefits derived from the system relates to the very high cost of foster care and the importance of reliable and valid data on which legislators and other policy makers can rely in reaching decisions about allocation of funds. The information system was able to calculate the total per diem payment made by the city for each child in foster care, thus providing a conservative estimate of costs for the entire sample of foster children under study.

> We came up with some findings which, when published in a monograph, created great interest in governmental circles and influenced the U.S. Senate Finance Committee in recommending greater funding for child welfare services with an emphasis to be placed upon services geared towards the prevention of need for foster care placement or early termination of the arrangement after a child enters care. (Fanshel, 1976, p. 11; *Social Security,* 1972)

The Adoption Assistance and Child Welfare Act of 1980 was an impetus to better data collection in that it mandated permanent statewide management information systems. Administrators and program planners of child welfare systems in forty-two states have developed automated foster care information systems to monitor services and improve the performance of the foster care and adoption system. "A more active way in which findings can be exploited beyond simply reporting them is to use findings as the basis for organizing a 'decision support system' that could improve the performance of the foster care system on a child by child basis" (Fanshel et al., 1987, p. 51).

Most foster care databases collect cross-sectional, or one-point-in-time information that is aggregated, limiting capability for identifying trends or for tracking children over time. Some researchers consider longitudinal tracking of individual children and families to be the most useful organization of a foster care database. "The fruit . . . would be information and research findings that had a life course perspective leading to understanding about the development of a child while in foster care and the operation of the foster care system from a child's admission to an agency to the implications of the child's treatment while in foster care or the child's subsequent experience as an adult" (Fanshel et al., 1987, pp. 24–26).

Other prototype foster care information systems have special capabilities. The Child and Youth Interagency Management Information System (CYIMIS) is distinguished from the CWIS for its *interagency focus* and its capacity to track children over time (Fanshel et al., 1987, p. 42). It aggregates statistics from five New York state agencies that are most active in child placement and shows the movement of foster children among placements. A milestone in the development of a *national* foster care database is the Voluntary Cooperative Information System (VCIS) initiated in 1982 and administered by the American Public Welfare Association. Reports generated from state child welfare departments provide national scope, somewhat offset by differing state definitions and methods. Further, its aggregate data format limits calculation of some rates of foster care phenomena. At present, then, the development of a national system of foster care information that meets the intentions of the Adoption Assistance and Child Welfare Act remains an "elusive goal" (Fanshel et al., 1987, p. 4).

TRENDS AND ISSUES

This chapter opened with recognition of the gains for children that were anticipated with the passage of the Adoption Assistance and Child Welfare Act of 1980 and the new initiatives stemming from the act. Subsequent efforts in family reunification and preventive services to children in their own homes have been a factor in the reduction of the numbers of children in foster care. However, other forces have been at work and have placed new and heavy responsibilities on the foster care system.

Unpredicted large numbers of infants now require specialized foster care; adolescents aging out of foster care require the development of a new set of services to enable them to live independently in our society. Increases in crime, a heavy increase in the reporting of physical and sexual abuse, the diminished number of women for whom foster care is an attractive employment option—these and other societal factors have added to difficulties in the foster care system.

In the midst of these demands the foster care system has come under strong criticism from the general public and the social work profession itself. In some states, legal action has occurred in charges of mismanagement and neglect of children in the foster care system. One result has been a loss of status for the entire field of child welfare, and particularly for foster care, the oldest service within the social work profession.

In the nineteenth century, "child-saving" efforts were dominant in the deliberations of the National Conference of Charities and Correction. The Settlement movement spoke out for social reform and public responsibility for child and family services. The U.S. Children's Bureau, from its founding in 1913 to the 1950s and the 1960s, set the pace for standards in child welfare and research. Its postwar program of stipends to students to pursue a graduate degree in social work with a specialization in child welfare brought professional social workers into the public child welfare system as never before. Research in child welfare, much of it related to foster care, burgeoned and in the main has been exemplary.

Then why has the foster care system fallen into such disapproval in many quarters? Multiple factors are involved. For one, public policy with respect to the social and legal rights of children and parents has always aroused controversy and ambivalence, particularly in relation to the scope of state intervention and the allocation of child-rearing responsibilities between parents and the state. The thrust of child advocacy is aimed at the need to change the discriminatory status of children and make the child's needs primary. At the same time there is a strong desire by many in this country to assure parental autonomy and privacy in child rearing to the fullest extent possible, except in instances where children are clearly and seriously harmed by their parents' child-rearing preferences and practices. In addition, even with new legislation, our society and its legislators have paid only limited attention to the problems of all families that merit a range of preventive social services. Further, public attention to reports of extreme or criminal abuse of children has damped recognition of the everyday complexity of the foster care system. Far too little analysis has been directed to the ambiguity in the placement process, which, in turn, has perpetuated what Carol Meyer has termed "the triangulated conflict among parents, children, and foster parents" (1984, p. 499).

Another factor is the widespread reclassification of previously defined social work positions in the child welfare system that has led many qualified professional social workers to move away from the once envied child welfare arena and opened the door to untrained "social workers." Still another influence has been a combination of demographic and legal factors that have come to dominate and curtail child welfare practice. In the view of some observers, legislative concepts, increased regulations, monitoring, and preparation of reports control child welfare practice (Lawder et al., 1986, p. 252).

Reliance on untrained social workers who are assigned some of the most complex tasks in all of the social services without adequate preparation and support from the social work profession has increased the role of the judiciary and an imbalance in the rights of parent-child-state.

Declassification is likely to continue, and the emerging legal framework is apt to grow. Admonishing agencies to hire professionally trained social workers is not likely to change hiring practices. Schools of social work must identify the skills required by public agency practice, and they must teach those skills. . . . (Stein, 1987, p. 648)

In the midst of it all, Meyer maintains, "child welfare is still the centerpiece of social services—a legitimate social service that probably always will be necessary in a modern world" (1984, p. 499).

Instead of denigration of a service essential to many children and their parents, a variety of modifications within the complex foster care system should be emphasized, including professional training for child welfare staff, smaller caseloads, and more frequent visits to children in care by both biological parents and foster care staff, all combined with greater effort to keep children at home while working to assist the parents to improve their level of child care.

FOR STUDY AND DISCUSSION

1. Identify positive and negative vestiges of the historical development of foster care that exist in current child welfare practice.
2. Identify the barriers to planning for the permanent care of children who come into the foster care system. Discuss ways to overcome these barriers.
3. Consider the proposed standards for decision making formulated by Stein and Rzepnicki.

How would you go about determining whether one or more of these conditions existed?
4. Devise a plan for effective agency recruitment and study of foster parents. What factors in your plan suggest that it will appeal to adults with adequate child care capabilities?
5. Talk with a staff worker in a child-placing agency of your community. What kinds of foster care facilities are available? What criteria are

applied in selecting a placement for a particular child?

6. Seek out some additional reading about the characteristics and living conditions of Ameri-can Indian families. What factors contribute to their children's need for foster care? What programs could be developed to enable these children to remain within their own homes?

FOR ADDITIONAL STUDY

Balcerzak, E. A. (1990). *Group care of children: Toward the year 2000.* Washington, DC: Child Welfare League of America.

Child Welfare League of America, Inc. (1989). *Report of the CWLA task force on children and HIV infection.* Author.

CWLA standards for independent living. (1989). Silver Spring, MD: Child Welfare League of America.

Fanshel, D. (1982). *On the road to permanency: An expanded data base for service to children in foster care.* New York: Child Welfare League of America/Columbia University School of Social Work.

Festinger, T. (1983). *No one ever asked us . . . A postscript to foster care.* New York: Columbia University Press.

Kadushin, A. (1978). Children in foster families and institutions. In H. S. Maas, *Social service research review of studies,* pp. 90–148. Washington, DC: National Association of Social Workers.

Maluccio, A. N., & Sinanoglu, P. A. (Eds.). (1981). *The challenge of partnership: Working with parents of children in foster care.* New York: Child Welfare League of America.

Mech, E. V. (Ed.). (1988). Independent-living services for at-risk adolescents [Special issue]. *Child Welfare, 62*(6).

Stone, H. D. (1987). *Ready, set, go: An agency guide to independent living.* Washington, DC: Child Welfare League of America.

Ward, M. (1984). Sibling ties in foster care and adoption planning. *Child Welfare, 63*(4), 321–332.

Whittaker, J. K., Overstreet, E. J., Grasso, A., Tripodi, T., & Boylan, F. (1988). Multiple indicators of success in residential youth care and treatment. *American Journal of Orthopsychiatry, 58*(1), 143–147.

Wolins, M., & Piliavin, I. (1964). *Institution or foster family: A century of debate.* New York: Child Welfare League of America.

CHAPTER 11

Families by Adoption

In every child who is born, under no matter what circumstances, and of no matter what parents, the potentiality of the human race is born again and in him, too, once more, and each of us, our terrific responsibility towards human life.

James Agee

Chapter Outline

Open Adoption Controversy
Independent Adoptions
Transracial Adoptions

FOR STUDY AND DISCUSSION
FOR ADDITIONAL STUDY

Adoption is a social and a legal process whereby the parent–child relationship is established between persons not so related by birth. By this means a child born to one set of parents becomes, legally and socially, the child of other parents and a member of another family, and assumes the same rights and duties as those that obtain between children and their biological parents. Adoption is a life-long process of benefits to and adjustments by all members of the adoptive triad—the adopted person, the birth parents, and adoptive parents.

Adoption practices continue to evolve as the needs and attitudes of society change. Today adoption services are in the forefront of permanency planning for children who have been in long-term foster care and who cannot return to their families of origin, children who once stayed "adrift" in foster care until they reached maturity. Changed attitudes toward adoption are reflected with respect to "openness" in the adoptive process. In contrast to the years when contact between biological and adopting parents was discouraged, today many agencies are facilitating varying levels of personal contact or information exchanges between the two sets of parents. In addition, there has developed a nationwide thrust by agencies to institute postlegal adoption services to all members of the adoptive triad, on either a service-upon-request basis or as an integral part of agency adoption work. These new practices are in contrast to the older assumption that after a child's adoption was legalized, the adoptive family would have no need of services specifically related to the adoption process.

Adoption serves a variety of purposes. Its most socially approved purpose is to enable children to have permanent homes and enduring, constructive family ties they would lack otherwise. Adoption is also a means by which infer-

tile couples can become parents, or persons with children of their own can satisfy other needs and capacities for nurturance. Adoption provides a means for continuing a family name and for directing inheritances. When adoptive placement exists as an alternative for parents who are unable or unwilling to care for their children, it provides a means through which they can responsibly discharge their duty for their children's long-term care.

A child regarded as "adoptable" is one who would not otherwise have a permanent home, who can benefit from family life, and who either is or can be made legally free for adoption. Such a definition precludes denying a child an adoptive home because of age, race, religion, and most physical or mental handicaps. Current adoptive practice emphasizes the needs of children and the tasks in providing fit parents for children who need permanent homes. This is a different focus from an older one of providing acceptable children for would-be adopters.

Adoption is of considerable interest to a variety of professional and academic disciplines. Persons in the fields of social work, law, religion, psychology, sociology, psychiatry, genetics, and medicine have found it to be a significant field for the application of their knowledge and the testing of hypotheses. Adoption also identifies and perpetuates the values of community institutions, for example, governmental institutions at all levels, individual families, communication media, and health and religious organizations.

Adoption is a matter for public concern. The reorganization of a family and the establishment of new and permanent parent-child relationships are of serious consequence for society as well as the private parties involved. Community decision makers need to assess continually whether existing adoption practice provides sufficient protection for the children and other persons.

HISTORICAL DEVELOPMENT

Adoption as an Ancient Practice

The adoption of children dates back to antiquity. Its purpose has varied considerably by country and by period of time, for example, to make possible the continuance of family religious traditions or ancestor worship; to provide an heir; to overcome difficulties in recognizing an out-of-wedlock child; or, more recently, to provide needed homes for homeless children (Schapiro, 1956, p. 14).

Roman adoption was formalized by a judicial hearing. The primary adoptive purpose was to assure the continuity of the male line and the family's political power. A man without sons, but with property and family traditions regarded as worth passing on, adopted boys who became his direct heirs. Adoption was undertaken primarily to strengthen the adopter's position, not to advance the welfare of the child. Female children could not be adopted, nor could women adopt. The Romans believed that adoption should imitate nature. Consequently, the law provided that an adopter be at least fifteen years older than the child adopted (Infausto, 1969, p. 3).

Roman law influenced the origins of adoption in France found in Napoleon's Civil Code, which in turn influenced law in the states in this country that had a French or Spanish colonial background. The emphasis on the adopted person as heir was perpetuated.

Early Development in the United States

While legislation in some states was based on the civil code of Europe, most of the new states in this country patterned their law on the common law of England, and adoption was unknown in common law. In fact, England did not pass adoptive legislation until 1926, because of such factors as the closely guarded rights and duties of parents, the governance by law of the inheritance of real property, the maintenance of class lines based on blood and the passing on of property ownership within a family, and the association of the idea of adoption with nonmarital children and the low social status they had been thought to represent.

The nature and social purpose of adoption as it is conceived today in many countries began to emerge in the United States during the latter part of the nineteenth century. Up to that time, inheritance had run through the history of adoptions so much more prominently than any other factor that its importance can hardly be overestimated (Witmer et al., 1963). Indeed, the first adoption statute in this country, passed in Texas in 1850, by providing for adoption by "deed" (a legal means to transfer property), reflected the association of a child's adoption and property interests. Although that law might be perceived as an improvement over the old practice of indenture, it still affirmed the child as property to be exchanged (Cole, 1987). But gradually adoption with a more recognizable social welfare purpose was provided for in some of the states.

Massachusetts in 1851 was the first to enact an adoptive statute in line with present concepts of the purpose of adoption. This act served as a model for legislation in other states. The Massachusetts law required

> a joint petition by the adopting parents to the probate judge and the written consent of the child's parents, if living, or of his guardian or next friend if the parents were deceased. The judge if satisfied that the adoption was "fit and proper" was to enter the adoption decree. (Abbott, 1938, Vol. 2, pp. 164–165)

The passage of new adoption laws did not reflect a great issue of the day. More likely, as Witmer and coworkers (1963) observe, these new statutes were regarded as an approved and logical next stage in a development already taking place. Chief among the social and legislative factors in the background of adoption statutes were (1) certain special acts by some state legislatures and (2) a growing body of court opinion in cases involving a child's custody and parental relinquishment.

By the middle of the nineteenth century, it was not uncommon for a state legislature to pass a special act authorizing the adoption of a particular child by a particular adult. Adoption statutes, then, in a sense simply made general and open to all a practice that was already being opened to some.

"De facto adoption" existed in some states prior to the passage of general adoption legislation through informal agreements between parents and "adopters," or sometimes through a contract that set forth the willingness of the parent to relinquish a child and the adopter to assume custody, and perhaps even eventually to share an estate with the child. A legal contest would sometimes arise when a parent sought to regain custody, usually through habeas corpus proceedings. Witmer has cited early court cases to show that courts were inclined to take advantage of the flexibility habeas corpus offers and to shape their judgments to fit the needs of the situations presented. In other words, judges were not deciding contests of relinquishment through contract on the basis of property alone, but on considerations of the best interests of the minor (Witmer et al., 1963).

The states' new adoption statutes contained standards similar to those being developed in court opinion. In addition, they put adoptive status on a firmer legal ground by giving a state some control in adoptive situations before a contest arose, and they secured permanent status for the child in a new family as well as a right to an equitable share of the adoptive parent's estate.

The early American statutes differed generally among the states in the varying provisions for public inquiry and control over proposed adoptions. Some of these statutes were intended only to require evidence and a public record of the legal transfer of a child through private agreement, with little or no inquiry into the suitability of the arrangement for the minor. In other states, a more explicit recognition of the social welfare purpose of adoption law and the interest of the state in ensuring successful placement of the children was reflected in varying provisions for judicial determination to ensure that the best interests of the child would be served by the proposed adoption. For example, Michigan's statute of 1891 required that judges make an investigation before entering a decree of adoption. However, there were no standards to guide them or directions for the investigation. Sometimes they requested a county welfare agency or a probation officer to investigate. Minnesota went further in 1917 and amended its adoptive statute to provide for a more comprehensive plan of investigation and control. Before an adoptive petition could be reviewed by the court, a social investigation must have been done by the state welfare department, a licensed children's agency, a social worker approved by the court, or some other competent person. The legislation provided for other protections for the child, such as a trial period before the final decree was entered, adoptive records kept from public inspection, changes in birth certificates, and restraints on advertising as a means of soliciting adoptions.

Adoption as a Professional Social Work Service

The advancement of American adoptive practice has been furthered significantly in this century by the development of professional adoption agencies and by the standard-setting activities of such agencies as the United States Children's Bureau and the Child Welfare League of America (CWLA).

As a professional social service for children, requiring the collaboration of social workers, psychologists, lawyers, and physicians, adoption lagged behind the development of other professional social work services. The early adoption agencies were founded by laypersons, and even into the twentieth century several new and influential adoption agencies were formed and staffed by laypersons (Lawder, 1969). Well-meaning as these efforts were, professional standards and legal controls were lacking.

Evidence of beginning assumption of professional responsibility occurred in 1921, when Sophie van Senden Theis of the New York School of Philanthropy (now the School of Social Work of Columbia University) developed a manual of professional principles for adoption practices, with attention focused on the study and selection of the adoptive family, the role of the natural parents, and agency responsibility for placement and supervision of the child. (Schapiro, 1956).

Another important landmark event occurred in 1938, when the CWLA undertook a study of adoptive practice that led to the publication of its first statement of professional standards for the guidance of adoptive agencies (*Minimum safeguards,* 1938). An additional significant factor in the growth of professional adoptive practice and the assumption of public responsibility for it was the influence of the Children's Bureau through its role, stated in the provisions of the Social Security Act, in stimulating and providing resources for programs of child welfare services in state and local public welfare departments.

The end of World War II made visible the needs of large numbers of homeless children. Many couples indicated their readiness to care for children through adoption. The increased demand on adoption agencies brought into the open certain of their outmoded requirements and cumbersome decision-making practices. Independent adoptions, that is, placements arranged by individuals other than representatives of licensed child-placing agencies, increased rapidly, promoting public doubt about the necessity of a professional adoption service.

Children's agencies responded by assessing their practice through individual agency study and national conferences. Problems became ap-

parent: lack of professional adoption service in many areas of the United States; lack of knowledge or insufficient application of existing knowledge as a basis for professional practice; and, above all, inadequate or nonexistent placement resources for minority children or sibling groups needing adoptive homes. Since these shortcomings in professional adoption practice became apparent, the social work profession has worked actively to strengthen the knowledge needed as a basis for practice through research and to serve more adequately all the community's children who need permanent homes through adoption. The extent of progress and the still unresolved problems in removing deterrents to children in having their own permanent homes through adoption will be examined later in this chapter.

SOME ADOPTION FACTS AND PATTERNS

Problems in Collection of National Data

There is no aspect of child welfare practice where over time accurate statistics have been in such short supply as in adoption. In 1944 the National Center for Social Statistics (NCSS) was charged to develop annual national statistics on adoption. These data were to focus on adopted children, adoptive parents, and the legal aspects of adoption as found in court records in states that cooperated with the federal agency. Data collection began in 1951 and ended in 1975 when the NCSS was disbanded. Despite instruction by Congress in 1978 that the Department of Health and Human Services (DHHS) resume adoption data collection, this did not happen. Only limited data on adoption were included in two surveys of the substitute care population—Maximus, Inc. in 1977, and the DHHS Office of Civil Rights in 1980. To address the critical need for national adoption statistics, the American Public Welfare Association in 1983 established a Voluntary Cooperative Information System (VCIS), a significant undertaking but limited by the fact that data were provided only by states that chose to cooperate and for adoptions made by public agencies, which constitute only about one-third of all unrelated adoptions. Planning groups within DHHS continued to develop a design for collection of national adoption statistics, but no accepted plan or national statistics emerged (National Committee for Adoption, 1989).

To demonstrate that national adoption statistics could be assembled without exorbitant cost and to meet the serious need for such data on the part of policy makers, adoption agencies, social workers, attorneys, researchers, and others, in 1983–1984 the National Committee for Adoption (NCFA) designed and carried out a national survey of data existing in state departments of social services, adoption agencies, and vital statistics offices (National Committee for Adoption, 1985). In the late 1980's, with no clear evidence as to when the collection of adoption statistics would be resumed by a federal effort, the NCFA in 1988 again conducted a national adoption study with 1986 as the base data year (the most recent base year, given time lags in state data processing). Their findings in 1989 (the most recent state and national adoption data available) are discussed here (National Committee for Adoption, 1989).

Adoptions in 1986. There were 104,088 domestic adoptions of children already living in the United States in 1986. Of these, 52,931 (50.9 percent) were adopted by stepparents or other relatives; 51,157 (49.1 percent) were adopted by nonrelatives. In addition, 10,109 children brought in from foreign countries were adopted in this country, making a total of 61,176 domestic and foreign unrelated adoptions, with foreign adoptions constituting one-sixth of all unrelated adoptions (National Committee for Adoption, 1989).

Among the unrelated domestic adoptions, almost half of the children were infants, numbering 24,589, and making up only 0.7 percent

of 1986 live births and 2.8 percent of births to unmarried women, findings that underscore the prevailing choice among unwed mothers to keep and parent their babies (National Committee for Adoption, 1989).

Special needs children (infants and older children) composed almost one-fourth of the unrelated domestic adoptions. When compared with the 1982 data of the NCFA, special needs children in 1986 had continued to be a relatively constant share of adopted children (National Committee for Adoptions, 1989).

Of the nonrelated domestic adoptions, 68 percent were placed by social agencies (39.2 percent by public agencies and 29.4 by voluntary agencies). The remaining 31.4 percent were arranged independently by private individuals, chiefly by attorneys (National Committee for Adoption, 1989).

By comparing the 1982 and 1986 data of the NCFA, we find that the numbers of related domestic adoptions have dropped—91,141 in 1982 to 52,931 in 1986. Because related adoptions are most often stepparent adoptions, the decline in remarriage rates in the 1980s may have influenced that drop. Other factors noted by the NCFA (1989) include changes in state and federal support benefits, court awards of support payments by the noncustodial parent in divorce, and more feasibility in the collection of support payments in recent years.

In summary, the NCFA cited these national trends in related and unrelated adoptions between 1951 and 1986: Adoptions increased from 72,000 in 1951 to a peak of 175,000 in 1970, then declined to 104,088 in 1986. Unrelated adoptions increased from 33,800 in 1951 to a peak of 89,200 in 1970, then fell substantially in the early 1970s, and remained relatively constant at about 50,000 per year in 1974, 1975, 1982, and 1986. Unrelated adoptions as a percentage of total adoptions have constituted less than half of all adoptions since 1971 (National Committee for Adoption, 1989).

The number of children adopted annually is far from the number for whom adoption would be desirable. Gershenson and coworkers (1983–1984) summarized data from a 1982 national survey of child welfare agencies and estimated that 50,000 children were awaiting adoption. These included minority children, severely disabled children, more boys than girls, children over eleven years of age, and children who had been in foster care longer than four years (Gershenson, 1990). A 1989 CWLA study found 34,000 children waiting for adoption who had already waited an average of two years (Child Welfare League, 1989b).

Agency Placements and the Children Needing Homes

In the earlier years of adoption as a social service, voluntary agencies arranged the majority of agency adoptions. This pattern has changed. As the NCFA (1989) data showed, public agencies placed 39.2 percent of the nonrelated domestic adoptions, as compared to 29.4 percent by voluntary agencies (see Figure 11.1). Placements by private individuals, termed independent adoptions, made up 31.4 percent, surpass-

ing the numbers placed by the more traditional voluntary agency pattern.

As public agencies have assumed increasing responsibility for social services to children, public welfare departments have substantially extended their adoption services, particularly for children with special needs—those with physical or mental handicaps, adjustment problems due to abuse, older children and sibling groups, and minority children. These are children for whom there are grossly insufficient numbers of adoptive homes.

In general, the characteristics of children that decrease the likelihood of a permanent home through adoption are still those identified thirty years ago in a comparison of two groups of thirty children without parental ties—children placed in adoption and children left in foster care. Boehm found that children who had remained in foster care differed significantly from those who had moved into adoptive homes, and that these differences operated as deterrents to adoption placement (Boehm, 1958). Five critical characteristics were identified: age, race, health, intelligence, and emotional adjustment. Her

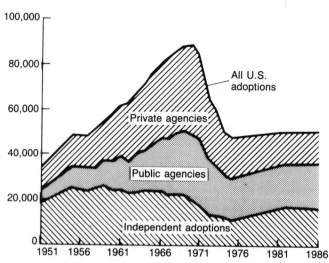

Figure 11.1. Who Arranges Adoptions?(*Source: "Who Arranges Adoptions?" N. Y. Times,* Oct. 5, 1989. Copyright © 1989 by The New York Times Company. Reprinted by permission.)

findings showed, for example, that the age of a child was the most extensive deterrent, particularly age beyond one year; in fact, the likelihood of adoptive placement of a child of four was very slight. There were twelve black children in the foster care group of thirty children, but only two black children in the same-size adoptive group. There were seven children in each group who deviated in intelligence from the normal range, but those in the adoption group deviated upward, and those in the foster care group deviated downward. Children in the adoption group were in excellent health; those in foster care had only adequate or average health. The greatest difference between the two groups was in emotional adjustment. Foster children, far more often than adopted children, evidenced behavior problems, conflict about parental relationships, and confused feelings of identity—differences seen as a product of age and extended foster care status.

Boehm's finding of five characteristics that acted as deterrents to a child's adoption—age, race, health, intelligence, and emotional adjustment—has been borne out in contemporary research. In his extensive studies Fanshel (1982) also found *age,* and its relation to length of foster care placement, to be a deterrent to early adoption. *Race* continues as a deterrent; minority children average two and one-half years longer in foster care after being freed for adoption than do white children (Olsen, 1982). Level of *intelligence* acts as a deterrent; developmentally delayed children of all races are found to be the least likely to be adopted (Kadushin, 1984). *Health* is a barrier to adoption when some long-term foster parents are reluctant to consider adoption because of the child's medical condition or physical disabilities (Fanshel, 1982). Problems of *emotional adjustment* due to abuse or neglect is a frequent reason given by some long-term foster parents for not considering adoption (Fanshel, 1982).

The most disturbing finding of Boehm's 1958 study and other investigations (Child Adoption Service, 1960; Fanshel, 1982) is related to the factor of time and the importance of early planning for children who come into agency care. The adoptability of children changes during their years of foster placement. The longer the time spent in care, the more likely it is that adoption will eventually be identified by the social worker as the needed plan for discharge. Fanshel (1982) found that for children in care two to five years, adoption was the discharge plan for about 50 percent; and for those in care six to nine years, adoption was seen as the desirable plan for 67 percent. Such children in the past have been labeled "hard-to-place," a term that suggests an expectation of failure in a search for adoptive homes. Now it is recognized that many of these children who have special needs would have been adoptable when they first became known to the court or social agency if there had been a more realistic evaluation made of their family situation, immediate casework attention given to the best ultimate planning for their future lives, and aggressive steps taken to find suitable adoptive homes. Today when there is systematic and optimistic reevaluation of their capacity for family life, more children who formerly would be adrift in foster care until they reached maturity are being recognized as adoptable.

Evidence of the current dichotomy between available children and families asking for children to adopt comes from data of the Illinois Adoption Exchange. While nearly 80 percent of the children listed as ready for placement were black, the largest group of families (70 percent) were requesting white children. Of these, almost half indicated that they would accept only a white child between six and ten years with a "mild" disability, while children in this age group were only four percent of the total, and tended to have "moderate" disabilities (A. M. Smith, 1989). Unfortunately, this pattern of mismatch is not atypical of situations found in other states.

Information compiled by agencies may underestimate the number of children who need adoptive homes. No central reporting system exists to record the exact number of children available for adoption, and social agencies define "available" children in varying ways.

Independent Placements

In this chapter we are primarily concerned with agency placements of children whose new parents were previously unrelated to them. That is not to say that concern is lacking for children placed independently for adoption without the protections offered by the special study process of an authorized adoption agency, especially those children who are subject to "baby selling" in the black market.

Not all of the 31.4 percent of nonrelated domestic adoptions who were placed independently of adoption agencies (National Committee for Adoption, 1989) involved risk as great as that implied in the term "baby selling." Independent adoptions are of three types. *Direct placements* made by legal parents to someone known to them are among these. Sometimes parents may gradually and informally relinquish more and more of their responsibilities for a child to a family friend or neighbor, and eventually adoption takes place. These placements are arranged within the state's legal framework and tend to work out satisfactorily for the child. Direct placements of this kind are legal except in three states.

Intermediary placements not for profit are those arranged by a third person who is usually not seeking profit and may be well-intentioned. Usually the adopting parents are unknown to the biological parents. An exchange of money may take place, for example a standard fee for legal services or payment of the mother's medical or other living expenses during pregnancy. Because the money exchanged is not disproportionate to real expenses and the placement is not motivated by a desire for profit, placements like these are often referred to as "gray-market" adoptions. Such adoptions are legal in all but

three states. A danger in this kind of independent placement is that the dividing line between paying legitimate expenses and paying for a child may be hard to distinguish and may facilitate black market adoption (U.S. Senate Committee on Children and Youth, 1975; Hardin & Shalleck, 1984).

Intermediary placements for profit put children at great risk. These children are sold for adoption on the black market, that is, children moved for profit, often across state lines. The intermediary in these instances usually charges what the traffic will bear. Sometimes these operations are carried out in connection with abortion counseling services where vulnerable women or young adolescents are identified—those ambivalent about abortion or too far along in pregnancy for termination, or those who appear likely to give up the idea of abortion for an assurance of profit. In all instances of black market placement, the best interests of the child are given little or no consideration; the profit motive is primary. By a conservative estimate, at least one-third of the independent (nonagency) adoptions are black market adoptions (Baker, 1978). However, since such placements are illegal in all states, it is difficult to obtain accurate figures on the incidence. Reports suggest that such illegal placements are increasing because of the current shortage of white infants for adoption, a shortage caused in turn by more effective use of contraception, increased readiness on the part of single mothers to keep their babies, and easier access to abortion. Declining fertility rates, impatience with adoption agency process, adopters' desire for more background information, and more openness in adoption also play a part (Wingard, 1987).

Some states have sought additional safeguards for reducing the known risk of independent adoption. The most extensive protections are in the five states of Delaware, Connecticut, Massachusetts, Minnesota, and Michigan where all nonrelative types of independent adoption are illegal (Cole, 1987).

THE AGENCY ADOPTIVE PROCESS

In recent years major changes of great significance have entered into the social agency adoptive process. The issues involved are usually couched in terms of "open versus closed" adoptions and the controversy surrounding the rightness of "sealed versus open" adoption records. There are numerous and varied opinions about the merits of the traditional promise of confidentiality in adoption to protect all members of the adoptive triad, in contrast to the current thrust toward more openness in carrying out the steps in the adoptive process through mutual participation of biological parents, adopting parents, and the child to be adopted. Limited research has been done on the merits of open versus closed adoptions or variations within each practice. Definitions of openness in the agency process vary. At one end of a continuum is a definition that calls for completely open arrangements in which biological and adoptive parents meet together and continue to have access to one another over the years. At the other end are cautious definitions that seek to protect the traditional position of confidentiality—the exchange of identifying information, or giving the child an explanation of why the birth mother had placed her child for adoption (McRoy et al., 1988a, pp. 19–20).

The differing values and attitudes toward adoption contained in this issue and the changes it has brought to agency practice will be discussed more fully in later sections of this chapter. But first it is important to consider other basic aspects of the adoptive process that have evolved over the years of agency adoption practice and that remain relevant to contemporary adoption issues.

Underlying Principles

The social work profession relies on certain principles or generalizations in planning and extending adoption service. These are similar to guidelines for foster care, but reflect greater attention to the permanency in the new parent–child relationship.

1.   If a child has no long-term home and is legally free of parental ties (or could become so), society bears responsibility for action in his or her behalf; it is not a private matter. The formation of a new family unit, once an original one is broken, carries social responsibility and requires social and legal safeguards.

2.   In most instances such homeless children should be provided with family life. Children of all ages need affection, security, continuity in relationships, and other kinds of care and guidance that are most feasibly and effectively provided within the family setting.

3.   When adoption is contemplated, society has responsibility to give protection and service to three parties: the child, the biological parents, and the adopting parents.

The child must be guarded against unnecessary loss of the biological parents and protected by the selection of new parents who give evidence that they can reasonably be expected to fulfill parental responsibilities. The child's first parents merit society's early help so that they can utilize their strengths to establish and maintain a satisfactory home. When they cannot do so, they require protection from hurried decisions made under duress and sympathetic attention as individuals facing a critical life experience. Adoptive parents are entitled to counseling or guidance that may enhance the formation of a healthy parent–child relationship and an adequate assumption of parental duties.

4.   Early placement of children who need adoption is desirable. Earlier placements generally are less complicated to carry out and offer a greater chance for success.

5.   Adoptive parents must be selected with care; their personal qualities and the kind of home they create are of first importance to the child. The social worker's primary task is to assess and enhance the applicants' capacities for parenthood, and enable them to assess and un-

derstand their own readiness to be parents. (There has been only limited research to establish the qualities needed for parenthood and the ways by which the capacity for parenthood can be appraised critically. Criteria and techniques vary among agencies as well as among staff members within agencies.)

6. Despite the many basic similarities between biological parenthood and adoptive parenthood, and the fundamental needs shared by all children, adopting is different from having children of one's own. Adoptive families are a minority group, and they experience certain differences. For example, some adopting parents have been unable to have children biologically and lack the experience of pregnancy and childbirth. All adoptive parents face the necessity of accepting the child's background, and the adopted child's curiosity about her or his origins.

7. For the safe development of their identity, children must be told that they are adopted and be helped to understand the concept of adoption. This prescription is universally endorsed by social agencies.

8. Children lacking their own permanent homes constitute the primary service group in an adoption program. Although understanding help is offered to birth parents and adoptive applicants, children and their need for family must be paramount in planning and extending adoption services. Social workers are increasingly committed to children who need permanent homes but who are denied them because they have certain less "marketable" characteristics.

9. Adoption services must be linked to other community social services and offered in ways that reflect cognizance of community attitudes and resources.

Adoptive Process in Relation to Other Social Work Processes

The creation of a satisfactory family unit through adoption embodies many subtle complexities. Because systematic investigation of the adoptive process is sparse and the findings are often inconclusive and contradictory, social workers may have difficulty in separating out their private and idiosyncratic criteria for the judgments and decisions they must make. They are assisted to a more objective and uniform selection process by recommended professional standards developed and revised periodically by the Child Welfare League of America.

Adoption is one of the oldest of child welfare services. It began as a basic gatekeeping process and evolved into a much more extensive process. (To some extent it has become so extensive as to lead some commentators to call for simplified procedures given the high success rate of adoption.) The agency process began with a reliance on social casework skills with a focus on particular attention to the developmental needs of children and the social and psychological adjustments required of the parties to the adoption. Group work methods began to be used at the point of intake and in the study of applicants' qualifications. More recently individual or group postadoption counseling is offered as well as teaching adoptive parenting skills and promoting the bonding of children and adoptive parents as they form new families. All of these tasks are linked to an identification of the children who need adoptive homes and to ongoing study of them to understand their individual characteristics and the parenting capacities that will be needed for them.

Biological Parents

Society generally tends to regard the unmarried mother's decision to place her child for adoption with acceptance and approval. Further, society seems inclined to favor adoptive placement for children of married parents where there is a pattern of neglect, desertion, or profound family deterioration. However, for parents with less obviously serious problems who voluntarily seek adoptive planning for their children born in wedlock, attitudes of social workers and of the community are apt to be less accepting.

Some are young couples who married hastily after pregnancy was discovered and find themselves unready to meet the responsibilities of parenthood. They may have married to make the child's birth legitimate, with the expectation of divorce and adoptive placement of the child. Some have other children, and another would upset the tenuous balance in their family life and jeopardize their marriage. The expected child may have been fathered by someone other than the husband, with the likelihood of continuing rejection of the child by one or both parents.

Although statistics have not been gathered systematically, only a small number of married parents voluntarily seek to surrender a child for adoption. Of these, only a small percentage actually make a decision to give up their child (Heller, 1966; Bachrach, 1986). Nevertheless, the nature of their request merits an accepting climate and help in examining their situations, considering alternative actions, and arriving at a decision they can sustain responsibly.

The importance of an environment in which parents can make a voluntary and informed choice on whether to transfer their parental rights was reflected in studies of postbirth experiences of parents who had surrendered their children for adoption. Among 125 self-identified birth fathers, many indicated that even years after transferring their parental rights for adoption, their action remained conflictual, particularly for those who cited external pressures as the reason for the adoption decision (Deykin et al., 1988). Fathers who later sought contact with their children, now adopted, wanted to find a way to take back their children. In contrast, birth-mothers who sought contact reflected a need to reduce guilt through knowing their children were alive and well (Deykin et al., 1984). These studies are not representative of all birth parents. They do, however, poignantly illustrate that to be effective, services to birth parents must be noncoercive and allow for grief counseling and other kinds of help whenever requested. A continuum of agency services may provide intermediary aids such as exchange of updated information with the adoptive family, open-ended support group meetings, counseling and go-between services in the event that contact of birth parent and child comes about through "search," and individual or family problem-solving counseling (Spencer, 1987).

Agency Requirements

Through individual interviews or group meetings with adoptive applicants, visits to their homes, and sometimes consultation with persons named as references, social workers attempt to determine the qualifications of persons who have indicated their desire to create or add to their family by adoption. Agencies usually seek information about certain aspects of the applicants' personalities and social situations to use in determining if they meet agency requirements earlier agreed upon by staff, advisory boards, and other policy-making persons.

The *age* of the persons who wish to adopt is of concern to the agency as it seeks to ensure as fully as possible that parents will remain young enough during their child's growing-up years to meet their responsibilities with the vitality to which young persons respond. In general, adoptive children should have parents selected for them who are in an age range similar to that of their biological parents. Some agencies have upper age limits, often about forty years. Yet life expectancy at age fifty is generally sufficiently long to permit adults to complete the rearing of a child. And while age may bring greater likelihood of reduced stamina, patience, and flexibility, older persons may be free of financial struggle and have more time than younger couples to devote to a child. Much depends on the reasons for an older couple's application at that particular time in their lives, their previous experience with children, and their capacity for rearing a growing, developing child (Fellner, 1968; Brieland, 1984).

Social agencies seek to know the state of *physical health* of adoptive applicants. Reports of current medical examinations are usually asked for to protect the child against the loss of a parent through death and to avoid a marked lessening of parental capabilities because of the emergence of serious parental health problems.

Agencies are concerned, too, with *emotional health,* often a difficult area to assess reliably. Nevertheless, through interviews with applicants, social workers attempt to establish evidence that the potential adopters are mature, sufficiently flexible to respond to changing times and the changing needs of children, and capable of postponing their own immediate gratifications in order to respond to the more urgent needs of a child. Applicants are favored who possess a sense of their own identity as individuals, with sufficient self-confidence to convey consistent expectations and offer guidance to a child; who are able to allow a child individuality and aspects of a life apart from theirs; and who are able to form and sustain close personal relationships, with satisfactions from a variety of adult roles and a degree of optimism toward life and its demands.

Closely allied to an assessment of the applicants' emotional health is their *motivation* for adoption. Just as with foster parents and other persons engaging in child care, motives are varied and are not necessarily acceptable or unacceptable in and of themselves. A stated motivation may require exploration before it can be evaluated. The reasons people give for wanting to adopt are varied: They cannot have children of their own but feel that marriage and life are not complete without the experience of parenthood. They are aware of the needs of homeless children and want to help them by providing them with security, love, and a family. They come from large families and miss the presence of children and the companionship and love that children bring—it is lonesome without children. They believe they can help children learn about life and work, and guide them in meeting life's responsibilities. They feel that life is more interesting and vital with children to look after and to watch develop—children help them to remain young and flexible and close to life. They feel more capable and more fortunate than many in today's world—adopting is a way of meeting responsibility and contributing to a better society.

The crucial element is not the expressed motive, but the actions it will lead to in relation to children. More important than establishing the motivation of individuals wanting to adopt and assessing its worth is encouraging them to recognize and understand their reasons for undertaking adoption and the way in which their motivation is likely to influence them to behave toward a child.

The *marital adjustment* of persons seeking adoption has been used as an indicator of potential success in adoptive parenthood. Because many problems of children grow out of marital discord between their parents, social agencies have attempted to rule out of adoption those couples who appear to have a less than satisfactory marital relationship and more than usual problems in meeting their responsibilities to each other. The social worker assesses the concern each shows for the welfare of the other, and the strength of the agreement about the decision to seek adoption. Parenthood brings rewards and new enriching experiences that can strengthen a marital relationship; it also brings demands and responsibilities that may tip the balance in an already precarious marriage.

Because time for adjustment in marriage is desirable before the advent of children, and marriages fail oftener in the early years, agencies sometimes apply requirements about length of marriage; for example, applicants must have been married at least three, four, or perhaps five years to be considered. Such an arbitrary requirement does not permit sufficient individual evaluation of a particular couple's capabilities. It is illustrative of the kind of rigid requirements being questioned and modified in current practice.

When foster parents seek to adopt children in their care, considerable weight is given to the extent to which they have come to feel and act as *psychological parents* to the child and are in turn regarded with love and trust by the child who needs a permanent home through adoption.

Even in subsidized adoption, some degree of *financial stability* is important in selecting adoptive homes. More important than the amount of income is the extent to which money can be managed and income can be relied on to provide a basic family security.

Agencies consider factors related to a prospective *parent's employment* on the basis that the stability of his or her employment and the degree of satisfaction derived from it will strengthen parental capabilities.

Traditionally, agencies denied adoption to women who intended to continue their employment. As *working mothers* became the majority of mothers and demonstrated their capacities for combining child rearing and employment, and as the need for adoptive homes became urgent, this requirement has been modified in most agencies.

The ability of applicants to have their own children has been a factor in denying applications for adoption. When agencies received more applications to adopt than they had children to place, a requirement that applicants provide some evidence of *infertility* was little questioned. If applicants had not sought medical assistance in understanding and correcting their infertility, then they were usually required to do so before an application would be taken up for study. The policy carried an unfortunate implication: requiring proof of infertility subtly implies to applicants and to the community that "adoption is second best—it is better that you have your own children if you can." Today such requirements about infertility or sterility are less rigidly applied.

As agencies responded to a changed definition of "adoptable child," many more special-needs children entered into the pool of children needing permanent homes. The social worker's task of arriving at a long-term prediction of successful parenting for children became more difficult, particularly with respect to applicants who are childless couples or single persons. Simplifying home studies by placing children with applicants who already have children, and selectively using others—childless couples or single persons—may be a developing trend (Brieland, 1984). Increasingly, in addition to adoptive applicants' predicted capacity for child rearing is the issue of the extent to which they can value as their own a child without denying its birth to other parents.

Fees for adoption service are charged by most voluntary and some public agencies. Justification for this practice is offered in terms such as these: Adoption planning is a professional service worth paying for. Just as attorneys and physicians charge a fee for their services where an adopted child is concerned, social agencies should expect to receive a fee for their professional service. Biological parents have medical and other expenses for childbirth, and agencies also encounter expenses in providing professional staff, medical care for unmarried mothers, and care for children while they await adoptive placement—adoptive parents should rightfully expect to share these costs. Furthermore, paying a fee may enhance adoptive parents' feeling of "entitlement" to a child born to others and thereby strengthen the new parent–child relationship. If a sliding fee scale is applied, depending on ability to pay, no one need be denied adoption because of the fee, and it can always be waived.

Certain questions about application of adoption fees have not yet been answered. Does charging a fee, particularly if it is applied to adopters of white infants but not to adopters of nonwhite, handicapped, or older children, reinforce undesirable connotations of a "market situation" in adoptive services? Is an image of "second-class child" perpetuated in relation to certain children who are waiting for an adoptive home? Even though agencies may waive fees for persons who apply but are unable to pay, how do we know that other homes for children are not lost because persons who cannot pay a fee never apply at all? Brieland (1984) suggests that ideally fees should not be charged, thus removing barriers to recruiting families for older children and eliminating any possible influence of income in adoptive applicant selections. Watson (1987) sees the adoption process as too expensive. Maternity and birth expenses should not be charged to adoptive parents. Rather they should be a public expense borne by the government in its responsibility for dependent children. Stated another way, given that a successful adoptive placement saves taxpayers and voluntary contributors to agencies substantial sums of money over the years, should an assumption of responsibility for rearing an adoptive child be regarded more as a service to society than as a privilege for which one should pay?

A barrier to adoption that has been removed in some areas is the requirement that adopters and the child to be adopted must be of the same *race*. As it became apparent that Asian, American Indian, and black children and children of mixed racial background can be successfully integrated into white families, the practice of transracial adoption became more common. This interesting development and the controversy about it will be discussed more fully later in this chapter.

Religious Factors

Adoption practice is influenced significantly by state statutory provisions as these refer to religion and child placement. Legislation in virtually all states provides that the religion of children and their parents must be considered in the selection and approval of adoptive homes. In some states, the legislation specifies only that the religion of the child and the adopters shall be noted on the petition for adoption. Some others authorize or require a report to the court prior to the adoptive hearing that sets forth the religious background of the child and that of the adoptive parents; then religion must be taken into account as one factor when the court decision is made to approve or disapprove an adoption. Some statutes provide that religious fac-

tors are to be substantially determining factors in the placement and the issuance of an adoption decree. These latter stipulations are generally to the effect that whenever "possible" or whenever "practicable" children must be placed with persons of the same religious faith as that of their biological parents. When such provisions are interpreted as absolutely binding on agencies and without latitude for discretionary judgments by courts, they restrict the flexible selection of adoptive parents and the assumption of broad responsibility for finding adoptive homes for children with varying characteristics. In addition, they pose constitutional issues relative to the separation of church and state.

Paulsen stated this perspective to the issue of religion in adoption: "In respecting the natural parents' wishes the state does not violate the separation principle but merely reinforces the already accepted fundamental proposition that parents primarily control the religion of the young" (1965, p. 138).

The influence of religious factors in adoptive practice is evident in that agency staffs, boards, and court personnel have tended to rely on "religious matching" in selecting homes for adoptive placement and have ignored the flexibility that may be permitted in the law. The church as a whole has traditionally shown a concern for sound policy and practice in relation to child adoption, emphasizing that adoption is a means to meet the need of a child for a home, not to seek special advantage for a particular religious group or to increase the membership strength of the institutional churches (National Council of the Churches, 1965). Yet sectarian agencies have traditionally served children and parents of their sponsoring faith. Generally, Catholic-sponsored agencies recruit Catholic applicants for Catholic children, and Protestant and Jewish agencies act similarly in relation to Protestant and Jewish populations. This practice discourages broad recruitment of adoptive parents and assumptions of responsibility for finding homes for children with special needs (Sachdev, 1984, p. 288).

Determining the religion of a particular child can be difficult. Agencies generally rely on these means:

1. The biological mother is asked to specify the religion in which she wants her child reared, and her decision is accepted. But on what legal or ethical basis does the biological mother retain the right to choose her child's religion for the future when all other rights (to determine place of abode, education, and other crucial aspects of child rearing) are given up when a court fully terminates parental rights for the purposes of adoption?

2. If the biological mother does not want her child placed in a home of her own religious faith or does not have a preference, she (and the father of her legitimate children) may be asked to sign a waiver of religious preference that gives the agency power to make a decision. While this power of decision might be used by an agency to favor a particular religious identification in its choice of homes, it can also be used as the basis for choosing the best available home for a child without regard to religious affiliation.

3. A child's religion may be decided on the basis of baptism or participation in some other religious ceremony that usually has been arranged by biological parents or other caretakers. If the religious ceremony took place when the child was very young, the question arises whether religious affiliation can be absolutely assigned to a child who is not yet old enough to understand and accept special religious doctrines. Is the religion of children necessarily that of their parents, or do they have their own rights in the matter?

A further question concerns the relationship between legal factors and religious practices and the propriety of "legally imputing religion to the child on the basis of what is deemed by a church to fix a child's religion" (Ramsey, 1959, p. 672).

The question must be faced as to whether it is good public policy to place the force of law behind every method of initiation or entrance into a religion practiced by all the many different religious faith groups in this country. (National Council of the Churches, 1965)

4. Abandoned children, or foundlings, present still different problems in assigning religion since the parents may be unknown and unavailable to give information or state a religious preference. In some cities (for example, in New York City as late as 1967), an agreed-upon rotational system was used by court and social agencies—one abandoned child was designated as Protestant, the next Roman Catholic, and the third Jewish, and then the rotation was repeated. Such a system assumes erroneously that a population is divided equally among these three particular affiliations, and it ignores other religious groups as well as persons who hold to no religious belief.

5. Older children are more apt to be accorded an element of choice about their religious identification along with other aspects of their move into adoption. With the increasing number of older children being placed, further attention is needed to unanswered questions: At what age should a child be given choice in the matter? Are all children of a certain age able to exercise such choice? What help could be given to children to enable them to express their own wishes in a meaningful way?

In discussing problems in utilizing religious factors in adoptive placement, and whether a religious test in adoption matters violates the principle of church-state separation, Paulsen took the position that since the state cannot prefer one religion over another, even for the purpose of acting as a parent, the state has two choices under the Constitution in regard to the designation of a religion for its ward: it may ignore the religious factor altogether and make a placement in the best available home without regard to religious upbringing; or it may accept someone else's determination in regard to religious training. He cites Delaware's adoption statute as clearly expressing these choices (Paulsen, 1965, p. 138):

No child born out of wedlock shall be placed for adoption unless at least one of the prospective adopting parents shall be of the same religion as the natural mother or of the religion in which she had reared the child or allowed it to be reared. . . .

Should the natural mother in a notarized statement made prior to the placement for adoption declare that she is indifferent to the religion in which the child shall be reared, or if the religion of the mother is not known, or there is none, then the authorized agency may make placement without regard to religion. (Delaware, 1953, p. 911)

Given the extensive attention long given to religious factors in adoption and the inherent presumption that all adoptive applicants will state a religious affiliation, the CWLA's endorsed position is of interest: "Lack of religious faith or affiliation should not prevent consideration of applicants for adoption nor should a mixed faith marriage (Child Welfare League, 1988b).

COURT ACTION IN RELATION TO ADOPTION

Depending on the legislation in a particular state, jurisdiction over adoption may be vested in juvenile courts, probate courts, or family courts within a district or circuit court system. Most desirably these courts are in the county or district where the adopting parents live and also have jurisdiction over other family matters closely related to adoption: guardianship, custody, termination of parental rights, divorce, support, and paternity.

Adoption statutes vary considerably among the states in the safeguards that are provided for children, their biological parents, and their adoptive parents. The following conditions are generally acknowledged as essential to the best interests of the child (Children's Bureau, 1961).

1. *The consent of the biological parents to the adoption or a judicial termination of par-*

ental rights so that the child is legally free for adoption. To avoid problems in the matter of required content, procedures for two groups of adoptive petitioners are recommended. In adoptions by close relatives, consent to a child's adoption should be required from the biological parent(s), or the guardian of person if there is no parent. If the child's mother is a minor, then her parents or court-appointed guardian of person should be expected to concur in her consent. In all other adoptions, that is, all nonrelative adoptions, a hearing and a decree of termination of parental rights should precede court action for adoption. This procedure is highly preferable to relinquishment directly to a social agency, which leaves aspects of the child's status open to question. When there has been judicial termination of parental rights and responsibilities, the guardian of person named in that decree is in a clear position to file with the court his or her consent to the adoption and evidence of authority to give such consent.

Under certain conditions putative fathers of children being placed for adoption are entitled to a court hearing before they can be denied custody of their children. (See Chapter 2 for discussion of *Stanley v. Illinois* and *Quillon v. Walcott.*)

Frequently a state statute specifies that when children to be adopted are of a certain age, perhaps ten, twelve, or fourteen, their consent must also be given to the adoption. Children even younger than this age should have the opportunity to express their wishes and experience a sense of participation in the final steps to adoption.

2. *Placement of the child in a proposed adoptive home by a social welfare agency except in adoptions by close relatives.* As indicated earlier in this chapter, it is of current concern that the proportion of nonrelative adoptions arranged independently of a licensed child-placing agency has increased. State legislation to control the exploitation of children that takes place in "black-market adoptions"—those arranged for profit by an otherwise uninterested party—is a sign of progress. But even where statutes have

outlawed placement for profit, a "gray market" often operates through provisions allowing a mother to place her child directly with adoptive parents, thus leaving the door open for unscrupulous or misguided third parties to cooperate with or influence a mother to place her child for adoption. The third party may be a lawyer who stands to profit through a fee for legal adoption services at the same time as he technically stands free of the charge of procuring an adoption for profit. Physicians, nurses, clergy, or other persons in contact with unwed mothers also may participate in gray-market placements by arranging a well-intentioned but ill-advised meeting between an unwed mother and a childless couple.

3. *A mandatory social study to be submitted to the court prior to judgment on the adoption petition.* As in other judicial actions involving children, a social study by an agency authorized to work with the adoption of children and the judge's consideration of it are essential to adoption practice. The report should include a summary and evaluation of the social data relevant to the pending adoption and a written recommendation regarding the suitability of the proposed adoption. Such a study and report should be required for adoptions by both relatives and nonrelatives. Not all adoptions by relatives are compatible with the child's welfare. For example, when a child of divorced parents is to be adopted by a stepparent, the child's best interests in relation to the other biological parent require attention.

4. *A period of time for the child to live within the proposed adoptive home under the guidance of a social welfare agency before the adoption is finalized.* In some states the required period of residence is 6 months; in others, 12. Waiver provisions give flexibility so that the court can shorten the time if doing so is in the best interests of the child.

5. *Issuance of new birth certificates following adoption decrees.* This is usually accomplished by requiring the court to forward a report on the adoption to the registrar of vital statistics in the state where the child was born.

6. *Authority of the court to take various actions in relation to children found in unsuitable proposed adoptive homes.* For the protection of the child, the court must be empowered to remove a child from the home of an adoptive petitioner if doing so is in the child's best interests. In such instances the court should vest legal custody in an authorized agency, fix responsibility for the child's support, or certify the case to an appropriate court for any further action needed.

7. *Confidentiality of records.* The files of the court on an adoption proceeding should be kept separate and withheld from public inspection. Persons and agencies having a legitimate interest in the case should be able to have access to them by court order or legislation. The adoptive hearing should be informal, and only those persons should attend whom the court recognizes as having some direct interest in the adoption.

If the court's decision is to approve the adoption, entry of its decree should endow the child and the adopting parents with all the legal rights and obligations that exist between a child and his or her biological parents. (Citizenship is not transferred to the child, however. This factor requires special attention in intercountry adoptions.)

THE DECISION-MAKING PROCESS IN PARENT SELECTION

The early history of placement of children in homes other than their own (whether for foster care or adoption) illustrates the extent to which social norms have had a distinctive impact on decisions about the kind of foster or adoptive parents that could be entrusted with a child and the criteria that should determine the characteristics of children to be "placed out." Reviewing that history also illustrates outmoded answers over the years to the question "Who is the primary beneficiary of this service?" (Hartman, 1979, p. 13). Clearly the child has not always been that primary beneficiary.

Whatever can be said about the system of indenture (Chapter 10) and its link to homes for children is overshadowed by the larger purpose of training children for the kinds of work the labor-short society of the times required with the master tradesman or craftsman being reimbursed by the apprentice's free labor for a considerable number of her or his growing-up years. Similarly, although some children, by no means all, in Charles Loring Brace's large child placing program (Chapter 10) acquired nurturing permanent homes, the value premises inherent in that enterprise reflected the projected gains to the larger society—to the city when vagabond children of "the dangerous classes" were shipped away from the city and into the rural Midwest to be given to farm families where the children's work was needed. The children thus served by Brace's new program were to be benefited by the virtues of an agrarian life; they also lost their parents, their familiar environment, and in large measure their religion.

In the latter part of the nineteenth century, charity workers engaged in a long debate about the merits of the institution versus foster home as best for a child needing care (Wolins & Piliavan, 1964). When Birtwell raised the question, "What does the child really need?" (Chapter 10) the beginning of formal foster home investigation emerged. This was a turning point in organized formal attention on the part of charity workers to the need for a child welfare process based on individualization of the child. Birtwell developed "a detailed and comprehensive list" of questions to be answered by the adoptive applicants. In addition, he noted that "it is . . . futile to think that one can surely get an inner view of a family by a visit; if there is a 'skeleton in the closet,' it will be concealed at such a time." The investigation was then supplemented by information from "persons known . . . to be people of character, intelligence, and standing in the community who have had constant communication with and opportunities to judge the applicants as fellow-townsmen or neighbors year after year" (Thurston, 1930, p. 189).

Hartman has noted that not only were families "investigated," but the notion of "matching" began to appear. As illustration she cited this statement from the Proceedings of the National Conference of Charities and Correction of 1884:

> In all cases where adoption of a child is sought by childless parents, too much care cannot be taken by the visitor to consider the personal equation. . . . It is of real value to fit the right peg in the right hole. A child that may be a torment in one family would be a blessing in another. And for children of promise, promising parents should be sought. (Hartman, 1979, p. 19)

Hartman identified from this evidence a new value-related principle that long dominated adoptive practice. "The effort became one of finding a child for a family that was as close as possible to the child the couple might have had were they the biological parents. The notion of family building as a service to childless couples began to be entrenched in adoption practice." The model adoptive couple had become the primary beneficiary of adoption; the emphasis was on ideal families versus meeting the needs of children (Hartman, 1979, p. 19).

As early social work began to emerge as a profession in the late nineteenth and early twentieth centuries, adoption services were identified as a developing professionalized specialization within the field of child welfare. Of necessity the characteristics of the "ideal" home had to be defined. Slingerland (1919) suggested these basic principles to apply to homefinding:

1. Are the applicants conscientious, personally suitable and well qualified to assume the care of a child now their own?
2. Are the home and its finances proper and adequate for all the ordinary needs of the family including such a child?
3. Is the environment, including school and church privileges such as is likely to allow the child to grow up healthy and happy and to develop into a good citizen? (p. 122)

Perhaps no area of adoption practice has been more obviously an expression of the value positions of the time than the assessment process or "the home study." (Hartman, 1979, p. 17)

Although Slingerland's principles appeared sound, the social work profession was moving into a period in which its members were deeply interested in psychoanalytic principles and the increased understanding of personality that they offered. Assessment of adoptive applicants now included learning about the applicants through their past experiences and relationships. This exploration, however, "often took the worker and applicant far afield from the purpose of the home study, and while it revealed many areas wherein the applicant might need help . . . it did not necessarily reveal how the applicant might serve as a parent for the child the agency placed" (Lerman et al., 1943, p. 9).

Dorothy Hutchinson, a highly respected figure in the field of child welfare, reflected the need for improved methods of assessment of prospective adoptive parents. She rejected the early methods of investigation in these words: "Homefinding practice has suffered from a large amount of artificial pumping for information and a rigid faith in outline forms. . . . The major skill in homefinding is to know what to look for. After all, the crux of the matter is to select normal families." She acknowledged that "normality is something that is hard to define," and then added, "but easy to feel and see" (1943, pp. 51–52), a statement that left open the possibility of hidden criteria that could allow the application of values related to the adoptive workers' personal biases and family experiences or perhaps the kind of socialization process that they had experienced in their professional study.

From a sample of 184 professional social workers in twenty-eight agencies in thirteen states, Brieland (1959) investigated the degree of agreement among social workers in evaluating the intake study as to the acceptability of particular couples for continued study. Although the overall agreement among the social workers was statistically significant, there was considerable disagreement among specific couples and among workers within some agencies, leading Brieland to recommend that social workers give more attention to specifying the hidden criteria that apparently were operating in the decision-making process of rejecting or accepting a couple's application for an adoptive child. Brieland's study was replicated later (Brown, 1970). A similar overall pattern of worker decisions to accept or reject the couples emerged; consensus between the two studies was generally high. Fanshel (1966) was led to comment that "it would appear . . . that the matter of whether or not they [adoption applicants] would be accepted by the agency for home study would depend on which caseworker was assigned to interview them" (1966, p. 130).

In a study of social workers' perceptions of adoptive applicants, Bradley (1967) sought to discover implicit perceptual dimensions underlying social workers' assessment of candidates for adoption. Data were collected by questionnaire assessments of 398 adoptive applicant couples in eight agencies, selected because they carried the bulk of adoptive practice in a large eastern metropolitan community. The results showed that although social workers were discriminating in their judgments, they kept within a narrow range. Bradley speculated that perhaps social workers in the adoption field had been expected to process information into unrealistically fine judgments and that a deemphasis on social workers' screening ability might be more attuned to the realities of assessment capacities.

Bradley also found two alternative routes that led social workers to evaluate applicants positively—seeing the "better" couple as suitable for the "better" child, and assessing the marginal couple as more suitable for the "different" child. Her findings were similar to those in Maas's earlier study (1960) of adoptive parents selected by agencies in which he found certain characteristics more related to the placement of a child other than the "normal" child. For example, adoptive parents of children who were physically, ethnically, or psychologically different, tended to be older, married longer, and of lower educational and occupational status.

Related findings were found as well in Kadushin's study based on a review of case records of ninety-one adoptive parent couples with whom children with special needs had been placed—that is, children over six years of age, children with mental or physical handicaps, or children of mixed racial background placed with white parents. This study led to a description of the "process of accommodation which takes place between the adoptive applicant who fails to meet some of the generally acceptable eligibility requirements, and the social worker who is attempting to place a child with special needs." Kadushin concluded that, when measured against a standard of preferred attributes, the applicant who is offered and accepts the child with special needs is very likely to be the one with marginal eligibility as an adoptive parent *in the traditional sense* (1962, pp. 227–233, emphasis added).

With today's new thrust to find adoptive homes for older children in foster care, social workers have been compelled to reassess and modify their previous pattern of perceptions and evaluation of applicants for adoption. A less rigid set of requirements exists, partly because of the difficulties in finding enough homes for children with special needs, clearly a market factor, but also because social workers came to recognize and value particular characteristics (previously termed marginal for purposes of adoption) that enable selected adults to succeed in providing safe and caring family experiences for children with special needs.

The Adoptable Child: Outmoded Practices

With limitations on funds and staff, and against the background of the nature-nurture controversy of earlier years, social workers, supported by physicians, defined an "adoptable" child as one who was nearly perfect in health and development and, as far as could be determined by extended observation and examination, one who posed minimal risk to the adopting adults.

Well into the middle of the twentieth century, infants released for adoption by their biological mothers did not go immediately after birth to adoptive parents. Even when the delivery of the baby was a normal one and there were no danger signals of poor development, the newborn infant was usually placed first with a "boarding home" mother whose "wisdom gained from her broad experience in caring for different babies with different personalities would contribute to the study of the child" (Costin, 1953), a study process commonly lasting from three to six months. Physicians also contributed to the baby's developing capacity for adoption.

In a further effort to understand a child's potentiality before selecting a permanent home, most agencies relied also on a psychologist's evaluation of the baby's performance on one of the infant intelligence scales—more correctly termed infant developmental scales (Costin, 1953). Adoption workers were in the peculiar position of attaching far greater significance to and making more far-reaching predictions from the test than would a psychologist informed and skilled in infant testing. Many social workers made fine distinctions from the psychological report as to whether a baby should be placed with a "good" family or an "average" family, meaning a family where intellectual achievement was valued and sought, or one where there was less emphasis on such successes. Eventually it was acknowledged that a careful "matching" of intellectual abilities between parents and children, even were this possible, was no guarantee that a child would be enabled to use her or his intellectual abilities. Of critical importance were the qualities in parents of warmth, flexibility, understanding, enjoyment of living, and other components of emotional maturity. Gradually these improper uses of infant tests were eliminated from adoption practice. Newborn infants became eligible for adoptive placement without the losses to adoptive parents and children through delayed formation of relationships.

Another outmoded practice that has been replaced by the current "openness" in adoption policies is the step referred to as "history giving," a term used for that part of the placement process in which prospective parents were given selected information about the child they were soon to see and consider for adoption. No clear guidance was at hand for this interview with the adopting parents at the point when they had been offered a child. Little was known as to what background information most adoptive parents wanted to know or what use they would make of it. In the absence of clear criteria, usually information was provided that attempted to answer questions the adopters raised or that offered them an opportunity for a positive identification with the child. Generally, the social worker presented a rather benign picture of the child's experiences at birth and since, gave any pertinent facts about the child's medical needs, and other selected information about the child's development that would enable the adoptive parents to accept the child readily and integrate him or her into the family (Costin, 1954).

Regardless of what the adopting parents might have wanted to know, a study's findings of what they did know about their children's biological background is of interest. Adoptive parents were asked about the kinds of information they had been given in this matter. Responses indicated that most of them knew very little about their children's biological parents— their education, their intelligence, the nature of their relationships with their children, or other information about their social characteristics (Jaffe & Fanshel, 1970).

Outmoded definitions of "adoptable" children and the responsibility to select and in a sense "certify" a child as adoptable in those terms meant that agencies were faced with having many more adoptive parent applicants than children to offer, a condition that influenced them to develop procedures to restrict the num-

ber of applicants. Such a prevailing situation in the late 1940s, and perhaps a forecast of developments to come, especially in relation to children with special needs, is illustrated in this excerpt from a discussion of the rejection of adoption applicants:

> The agency is forced, by the extreme disproportion between the numbers of children available for adoption and the numbers of families wanting to adopt, to refuse children to many who would probably do at least as good a job with a child as the majority of biological parents in the community, and who would qualify if the problem were that of finding adequate homes for large numbers of homeless children. . . . If there were several times as many children, it would be appropriate to explore the nature and extent of the actual risk in the patterns and attitudes the latter group present because they often have many positive things to offer a child. (Michaels, 1947, pp. 370–371)

The latter half of the twentieth century brought pressure for more equitable distribution of social welfare programs and services. As part of this movement, concern grew among leaders in adoption about children who needed permanent homes and were denied them because of instabilities within the foster care system and the limitations and restrictions of adoption services. Attention turned to searching out factors that led some children to be termed unadoptable and to discovering if there were adoptive applicants who would accept these children.

Gains made in finding adoptive homes for children were dramatic during the 1960s, especially among departments of public welfare where staff workers were increasingly resourceful in placing children who only a few years previously would have been considered unadoptable. Yet despite the gains derived from a more liberal definition of "adoptability" and "suitable adoptive parents," agency efforts to find adoptive homes for children with special needs are not yet sufficient.

CHANGING PRACTICES IN ADOPTION

Open Adoption

In the last three decades, significant changes in methods of adoptive study and placement have been incorporated into agency policy and practices. Interest in revised methods of adoptive study was given impetus by findings that adoptive applicants were accepting of physical and psychological differences among children more often than agencies were taking into consideration in placing children with special needs (Maas, 1960). Many social workers became convinced that, given the numbers of children today who need adoptive homes, agencies could not afford to eliminate any applicants unnecessarily. "The responsibility of not accepting a possible home is just as great as the responsibility of placing a child in a home" (Hagen, 1965).

Such concerns led to a greater reliance on factors such as these: (1) applicants' abilities to participate in the study process and to evaluate their own capacities to be adopting parents; (2) the fact that before most adoptive couples approach an agency, they already have thoughtfully considered their motives and other aspects of their desire to seek adoption; (3) the readiness of many adoptive applicants to accept "aspects of parenthood" once regarded as "unjustifiable risks"; (4) open acknowledgment by the agency of its hope that the applicants will be able to receive a child, rather than projection of a more guarded attitude associated with "screening out"; (5) interviews for the purpose of helping applicants achieve satisfaction in their forthcoming adoptive parenthood, with less emphasis on information gathering per se and judging that information.

Continuing readiness for change in the late 1970s and 1980s led to a significantly greater distinction in adoption policy and practices, one that centers on the merits of traditional practice, termed "closed" (or "confidential") adoption versus a new "open" (or "cooperative") adoption model. The changes in policy and practice, although taking varying forms among agencies, center on these issues: (1) a relinquishment of much of the decision-making control that agencies have traditionally maintained and a granting to birth parents and adoptive parents the right to make decisions that they see as most appropriate to their needs; (2) a more significant role for the birth mother in the selection of adoptive parents; (3) a more extensive exchange of information between birth parents and adoptive parents; and (4) the possibility of a continuing role for birth mothers in the life of the adopted child and the adoptive family (McRoy et al., 1988a).

Whatever form adoption may take, the skill and knowledge of the social work professional will continue to be necessary to enhance the process and to safeguard the rights and welfare of children. (Cole, 1987, p. 74)

Many adoption agencies today have revised their traditional practices toward varying degrees of "openness" in the adoptive process. These changes take the form of planned communication between the adoptive parents and the biological parents prior to finalization of the adoption. They may have face-to-face meetings before the birth of the child, at agreement for placement, or at various times after the birth of the child. At such meetings the birth mother and the adopting parents may share first names, photographs, addresses, letters, or phone numbers. The range of information that is exchanged may include ethnic and religious backgrounds, level of education, aspects of personality and interests, physical characteristics, genetic background, or other matters of common interest. These options are arrived at when birth parent and adoptive parents with the help of an agency social worker have agreed on the extent of "openness" in the present and future. Some agencies may be more specific about the possibility of a continuing relationship after legal adoption with the birth parent playing an active role in the adoptive family life (McRoy et al., 1988a; Pannor & Barran, 1984).

Adoption Resource Exchanges

A development in adoption practice designed to increase the likelihood of permanent homes for children who need them is that of national "clearinghouses" by which agencies can cooperate more effectively in the location and use of adoption resources. Agencies having few contacts outside their own locality tend to be limited in the range of prospective adopters and children to be adopted. If agencies can be helped to communicate effectively, regional prejudices that prevent homeless children from being adopted can sometimes be surmounted.

In 1967 the CWLA formed the Adoption Resource Exchange of North America (ARENA), designed to serve agencies in the United States and Canada. Prior to that event, some states had set up their own adoption resource exchanges, Ohio being the first to do so in 1948. By 1989, there were fifty-one such exchanges in the two countries. The primary purpose of ARENA was to mobilize national efforts to find more homes for children with special needs, particularly those who were physically or mentally disabled or who belonged to minority groups or were of mixed racial background. ARENA provided a model for developing and publicizing a large-scale picture of the needs of the adoption field, that is, an identification of regions and localities where there was a surplus or shortage of homes and of children, the kind of homes available, and the kinds of children waiting for homes. Additional efforts were directed toward promoting better interagency relationships, raising adoption standards and practices among agencies, and identifying and breaking down agency and state barriers to adoption, for example, state laws blocking or hindering interstate placements. By the end of 1977 ARENA had facilitated the placement of over 1,800 children, all of whom were ones for whom homes could not be found in their own states (Buzawa, 1977).

Exchange functions are now performed by the federally sponsored National Adoption Exchange based in Philadelphia and administered by the National Adoption Center. In its "match-referral" service, the Exchange coordinators search the computerized national registry to identify families who have expressed interest in adopting the kinds of children registered. Among the criteria used to determine appropriate match-referrals are the age of the child, sex, race, sibling status, and type of disability. Based on a review of this information, referrals are made to agencies and families. In 1988, which marked the completion of a full-scale network of all states, the Exchange facilitated eighty-two special needs adoptions (Lawrence, 1989). This number appears small unless one considers the highly significant individual and collective benefits of a permanent home to each child and to society.

SPECIAL KINDS OF ADOPTIONS

Intercountry Adoptions

Since World War II there has been a substantial movement into the United States of children who are adopted across national boundaries. During 1987, 10,097 such children found adoptive homes in this country, the largest number in the last fifteen years. Over half of these children (7,614) came from Asia with the largest proportion from Korea (5,910), India (807), and the Philippines (634). Slightly over 2,000 came from South and Central America. Only 122 adoptees came from Europe and only 22 from Africa. Other countries as well sent small numbers of adoptees (National Committee for Adoption, 1989, p. 101).

Eleven states received more than 300 children each and together made up more than half of the foreign adoptees. These large population states with a relatively high demand for adoption were New York, Minnesota, California, Michigan, New Jersey, Pennsylvania, Washington, Illinois, Massachusetts, Maryland, and Wisconsin (National Committee for Adoption, 1989, p. 72).

Agency reports have suggested that to some extent "surplus" white homes were being used for the placement of children from other countries. The problem of a surplus of white homes in the United States was matched by a corresponding problem of orphaned nonmarital children in Asian countries—out-of-wedlock children of mixed race as a result of the continuing population of Americans in Asia since World War II (Haring, 1976). For example, in Korea children born outside of marriage and having one American and one Korean parent (termed "Amerasian" children) are "virtually unadoptable within Korean society because of certain Korean cultural and moral factors." One such factor is the Korean cultural ideal of ethnic homogeneity and the rejection of children who are products of admixture with other races or nations, even in the midst of foreign occupation. Another factor is the strong disapproval of promiscuous sexual relationships in Korea, as well as legislation that discriminates against those classified as "illegitimate." In addition, historically, adoption in Korean family life has served mainly to facilitate inheritance and establish a lineal relationship with a male offspring of a relative in the adoptive parents' maternal or paternal line (Kim & Carroll, 1975). Eventually Korea hopes to develop a strong domestic adoption program that would enable it to end international placements. At the present time, however, foreign adoption is "a solution with mutual benefits for all concerned" (National Committee for Adoption, 1989, p. 73).

Factors contributing to intercountry adoptions include the mobility of families around the world; the increase in international marriages; the greater ease of communication between countries; the continuing large numbers of American servicemen stationed abroad, many of whom seek to adopt children during their residence in another country or who father children out-of-wedlock with no means to care for them; and a humanitarian concern by many persons for the plight of refugee and other homeless children, many of whom are grossly neglected or discriminated against in their own country because of illegitimacy or mixed racial background.

Persons in this country become interested in adopting a child from another country in various ways. Often they are related to the child whom they want to bring to this country. Sometimes they seek to adopt a child with an ethnic background and cultural ties like their own. In some instances they have met a child during a temporary stay abroad and want to adopt him or her.

Temporary immigration legislation after World War II, later incorporated into the Immigration and Naturalization Act, permitted a limited number of orphans or abandoned children to enter the United States without the usual quota restrictions. The legal adoption of children from other countries requires the cooperation of social agencies in two or more countries. International Social Service, American Branch, a voluntary nonsectarian organization, is the principal agency recognized by the United States government to assist in the immigration and adoption by United States citizens of children from other countries. There are some sectarian agencies as well. The cooperation of child welfare agencies at state and local levels is also required.

Geographical distances and national boundaries create additional hazards to an adoption service:

> Because there are few adoption or other social service agencies in the countries with children needing homes—whether Korea, Southeast Asia, India or Latin America—it is difficult to have the same assurances, as an adoptive parent, as one would have with an adoption arranged within the United States.

First, since there are frequently no medical or other records on the child, it is difficult to know how old or how sick the child is.

In addition, due to the extreme poverty of some families, as well as because of the social disruptions taking place, it is difficult to be sure that the child is legally free for adoption. Sometimes a child is abandoned—but sometimes, as press reports from Colombia have shown, children are stolen for "adoption" in other countries. Traffic in children, according to many reports, has become a massive, lucrative, illegal activity—just like traffic in narcotics. (National Committee for Adoption, 1982, pp. 2–3)

A sound intercountry adoption plan requires collaboration between child welfare agencies in both countries. CWLA standards state that intercountry adoption of children should be considered only when suitable arrangements cannot be made in their own country. When family or ethnic-cultural background prevent their acceptance and optimum care in their native land, international adoption should be considered. In all instances, parents should be helped to consider alternatives within their own country and to understand the finality of the adoption process (Child Welfare League of America, 1988b).

The same safeguards should apply in intercountry adoption plans as exist in this country for native-born adopted children. Observing this standard requires pertinent information about the child's background and development, active involvement of older children in the planning and preparation for their new relationships and way of life, a study of the adoptive parents' suitability, and counseling with them about the needs of the particular child they are receiving, including what it means to a child to leave a familiar environment and enter a new culture. The agency is responsible for postplacement supervision until the adoption is legally finalized and for supplying postlegal adoption services when they are requested (Child Welfare League of America, 1988b).

Sociolegal aspects of intercountry adop-

tions require special attention to parental consent (Bell, 1985), the child's status in matters of guardianship (Epstein, 1982), citizenship, birth certificate, and assurance that the adoption is legally valid in both countries.

The realization that international adoptions could be successful and the demonstration of adaptive capacities of both adopting parents and children appear to have been factors in influencing agencies in this country toward more flexibility in procedures and requirements, such as adoption with working mothers, single parents, and older persons (Rathbun et al., 1964; Welter, 1965; Sokoloff et al., 1984; Weil, 1984).

Transracial Adoptions

Another development in adoption is the placement of children across racial lines. The term "transracial" as applied to adoptive families is attached to a variety of parent-child characteristics. Most often, however, it refers to a family constellation in which a child with mixed racial background (most usually a child with one white parent and one Asian, American Indian, black, or Puerto Rican parent) is adopted by a white couple. An adoption of a child of mixed racial background by a nonwhite couple usually is not considered transracial.

Transracial adoptions began within the intercountry adoption movement involving children with mixed racial background from Europe and Asia after World War II, Korean-American children after the Korean war, and refugee Chinese children in Hong Kong, some of whom were placed with white couples in this country. Finding adoptive homes for American Indian children followed; the movement to place black children with white families is most recent.

Canadian agencies provided significant leadership in transracial placements of Asian, American Indian, and black children. In Alaska a considerable proportion of adoptions by white couples are of children with Indian parentage. Participation in the Indian Adoption Project (to be described) has involved other states. A number of agencies in various cities have been conducting very active and innovative programs to place children with mixed racial background in white homes. One of the early projects was in Minnesota, where private child-placing agencies cooperated with the state department of social welfare and some of the county departments to recruit homes for nonwhite children.

Many transracial adopters wanted to reach other persons who might be interested in adopting children of another race. They formed organizations to encourage acceptance of children of minority races, promote the legal adoption of such children, and cooperate with adoptive agencies toward these goals. Examples are the Open Door Society in Montreal; the Council on Adoptable Children in Ann Arbor, Michigan; Families for Interracial Adoption in Boston; and Transracial Adoptive Parents in Chicago.

In a review of accumulated experience from the relatively small practice of transracial adoption, Billingsley and Giovannoni noted the large numbers of variations and complexities in the policies of agencies, as well as in the attitudes of social workers, all of which reflected variation in the prevailing social norms about interracial contact at the family level. They cited the higher volume and longer history of placement of Asian children with whites and indicated that "the resistance to interracial adoption probably follows a continuum based on skin color, reflecting the situation in the larger society (1972, p. 65).

The Child Welfare League of America Standards for Adoption (1968) stated that "racial background in itself should not determine the selection of the home for a child. It should not be assumed . . . that difficulties will necessarily arise if adoptive parents are of different racial origin" (p. 34). In 1972, the standard was amended to "it is preferable to place children in families of their own racial background." In 1988, the standards were again amended in an effort to recognize both the preference of minorities for inracial placements and the need for decisions that will not deny a child an adoptive home when one is needed. "Children in need of adoption have a right to be placed into a family that reflects their ethnicity or race. Children should not have their adoption denied or significantly delayed, however, when adoptive parents of other ethnic or racial groups are available (Child Welfare League of America, 1988b, p. 34).

Early systematic investigations of transracial adoption were extremely limited and precluded any firm conclusions in view of the variations in the groups used for study and the questions asked. Tentative studies and observations within agencies (Falk, 1970) suggested that couples who adopted transracially showed some characteristics different from those who adopted within their race. They appeared to be of relatively high socioeconomic status in terms of security of income and levels of education and occupation. They frequently had natural-born children or previously adopted children. They were sometimes more distant geographically and socially from relatives. They often impressed agency social workers with their confidence and independence and apparent resources to cope with stress. Frequently they approached an agency with an already-formed preference for a child racially different from themselves. They often appeared to be motivated by ethical and moral values, and indicated awareness and appreciation of cultural and individual differences.

Studies of American Indian Children.
Fanshel carried out a descriptive investigation of ninety-six families in which white couples had adopted American Indian children as part of the Indian Adoption Project of the CWLA. The study involved repeated observations and interviews of adoptive families over a five-year period (Fanshel, 1972).

The adoptive parents were not a strongly homogeneous group. Instead they seemed to represent a cross section of attitudes of Americans. These adopters were about equally divided between those who held conservative and liberal political views. However, when they were compared to a sample of parents who had adopted white children, a significant difference emerged in attitudes toward the importance of civil liberties. The adopting parents of Indian children evidenced a stronger civil libertarian point of view. Whether this attitude existed before an Indian child entered the home or developed afterward was not established. Overall, the study showed that a broad range of social types had undertaken adoption of American Indian children. Little relationship emerged between the adjustment of the adopted children and their parents' liberal or conservative political orientations. Although these adoptive parents were not seen as nonconformists, data from some 435 interviews by caseworkers revealed a certain "independence of mind" on the part of the adopting parents that may have enabled them to accept children who, by entering their homes, caused them to be viewed as different from other families (Fanshel, 1972, pp. 321–322).

At the end of the study it appeared that the children were doing "remarkably well" as a group. This evaluation held true in terms of physical growth and development, intellectual and cognitive competence, and, to a somewhat lesser extent, personality and behavior patterns. The children appeared to be "well imbedded within the adoptive family" and to have relationships "as close and devoted as one would find in other kinds of adoptive families or in biological family units" (Fanshel, 1972, pp. 322–323). Overall, the success in adjustment closely approximated the rate of success that Kadushin found from a summary of the results of a large number of studies involving over 2,000 adoptions (1970, pp. 64–69).

Because the children were young at the time of Fanshel's study, it was not possible to be sure how they had integrated an awareness of a racial background different from that of their parents. From the perception of their parents, however, there was little evidence that the children felt uncomfortable about their racial difference. As to the way in which the adoptive parents had dealt with the Indianness of their children, Fanshel concluded that, overall, the parents had become quite comfortable with the Indian characteristics and that, for most, these characteristics had taken on a quite positive quality.

Nevertheless, the motivation of these transracial adopters sprang not so much from social consciousness and a humanitarian concern for the minority child as it did from a straightforward desire for a child. Their acceptance of an Indian child did not carry over to a generalized acceptance of minority group children; a large majority held reservations about adopting a black child (Kadushin, 1970). Another study of willingness to adopt atypical children strongly suggested that determination of such willingness on the part of potential adopters requires an individually focused appraisal and depends on the type of attribute of a child in question rather than a general readiness to consider all children with atypical attributes (Chambers, 1970). This selective readiness of adopters to accept children different from themselves was also reflected in a study of the adoption of black children by white parents. Most indicated they would have accepted a child of any racial background. They were less ready, however, to adopt an older, handicapped, or retarded child (Grow & Shapiro, 1974).

Studies of Korean Children.   A study of Korean children adopted by white Americans examined the long-term results for more than 400 adolescents from twelve to seventeen years of age who had been in their adoptive homes for at least one full year (Kim, 1977). For purposes of this study, the children were classified into two almost equal-sized groups—an "early group," who had been placed in their adoptive homes before they were one year of age; and a "later group," who were at least six years of age at the time of placement. The average length of time in placement was almost five years for the later group and almost fourteen years for the early group. The families were residents of thirty-eight states. Children and parents each completed questionnaires. Some supplemental interviews were carried out. The general purpose of the study was to assess the self-concept of these transracially adopted children during adolescence.

Among the interesting findings were these:

1.   Socialization processes appeared to be positive and healthy. Overall, these adolescents reported themselves to be generally contented with their adoptive home life—a state of affairs that matched the adoptive parents' perceptions of their children's moods.

2.   Academic performance was rated at least average for the "Later Group" and better than average for the "Early Group." The aspirations of the children included college and professional careers.

3.   The adopted Korean children retained relatively little Korean identity. Even those placed at school age in American homes seemed to have lost aspects of Korean culture and to view themselves as Americans, or more frequently as Korean-Americans. Overall, the children's self-concept was very similar to that of a normal group of other American teenagers. Even though the Korean-American children had had some initial difficulties, at the time of the study they were doing as well as, and sometimes better than, others.

4.   Children from the "Later Group" fared almost as well as those adopted at earlier ages. They seemed only to need a sufficient period of time in which to adjust.

5.   A supportive family climate was of fundamental importance. This climate was marked by somewhat disciplined parental attitudes as well as open interaction with the children—qualities associated with a generally good "parenting capacity." The researcher was led to say that "this not too surprising truth should be reinforced in all home studies and placement decision making" (Kim, 1977, p. 6).

Studies of Black Children.   Grow and Shapiro (1974) carried out a descriptive study of transra-

cial adoption of black or part-black children by white parents. The 125 children (almost equally boys and girls) were all at least six years of age and had been in their adoptive homes at least three years, a period deemed long enough for initial adjustments to have been made. Parents were interviewed individually and jointly at the beginning of the study and a year later. Parents also completed a questionnaire. The California Test of Personality was administered to each child. Data also included teachers' judgments of children's academic work and classroom behavior. A wide range of topics was given attention: the general family situation, the neighborhood, the family's leisure activity, the parents' social and racial attitudes, their contacts with blacks and black culture, their attitudes toward child rearing, the reactions of family and friends to the adoption, and the degree of parental satisfaction with the adoption. A major focus was the child's behavior and adjustment with attention to his or her racial awareness and identity.

Of the children studied, 77 percent were judged as successful adoptions—a success rate typical of conventional as well as less usual adoption studies. Two statistically significant relationships were found between the summary success scores and variables describing the family and child. Children in the largest family units (five or more children) and children perceived by their parents as obviously black were more likely to have high summary success scores—high to an extent that could be regarded as highly predictive of success in adoption. The positive influence attached to perceiving children as obviously black suggests that less "well-matched" children are more advantaged than are "better-matched" ones for whom it is easier to deny a difference between parent and child. In turn, the researchers observed, it may mean that

parents who acknowledge openly the child's difference may also have the ego strength to deal competently with the problems of child rearing in general. Conversely, parents who deny the child's difference may also tend to use this defense mechanism more generally and with negative consequences. (Grow & Shapiro, 1974, pp. 225, 236)

Scarr and Weinberg (1976) studied 130 black or part-black children adopted by socially advantaged white families. The average age at placement in the adoptive home was twenty-two months; however, the majority of the children (111) were placed during the first year of life. The biological parents of the adoptees were "educationally average." Testing of the children's IQs and educational achievement (no children were tested below the age of four years) showed them to be above the IQ and school achievement means of the white population. Their scores represented higher performances than would have been predicted if the children had remained in their own homes, given the fact that IQ and educational achievement scores are, on the average nationally, lower for black children than for white children.

The authors concluded that the transracial adoption of these children enhanced their intellectual and educational achievement. However, they were careful to point out that they did not endorse as a general social policy the adoption of black children by white families. First of all, they emphasized, only a small proportion of black children would ever be available for adoption. Secondly, many would or should be adopted by black families. What they did endorse was that

> *if* higher IQ scores are considered important for educational and occupational success, then there is need for social action that will provide black children with home environments that facilitate the acquisition of intellectual skills tapped by IQ measures. (p. 738)

The widespread interest in transracial adoption is evident in another study of racial awareness, racial preferences, and self-identity among white and adopted nonwhite children (Simon & Alstein, 1977). Parents in 204 families in the midwest were interviewed. Almost all the parents had white children born to them or adopted, as well as at least one nonwhite adopted child. In addition, the 366 study children (199 adopted; 167 born into the family) between the ages of three and eight years were interviewed with the use of various projective tests using dolls, pictures, and puzzles. The major finding was that black children reared in the special setting of transracial families had not taken on the ambivalence toward their own race that had been previously reported among other groups of black children. Furthermore, white children in the study preferred "white" to other groups to a lesser degree than other white children. It appeared, the authors concluded, that the practice of transracial adoption is having "a significant . . . impact on the racial identities and attitudes of young black and white children."

A follow-up study of 71 percent of the original sample in the Simon and Alstein study (those who could be located seven years later) solicited demographic data for a family update, the children's performance in school and their relationships with peers and teachers, relationships with the larger family, and any changes in the nature of the relationship between spouses. Parents were also asked to anticipate the kind of community their adopted children were likely to live in. The data for the follow-up study came only from the parents; children were not interviewed. The researchers concluded that the majority of parents were well satisfied with the adopted children and expected a bright future for them. However, something less than a fourth of the parents indicated that "the problems have been greater than they had anticipated, and bitterness and disillusionment had become everyday emotions (Simon & Alstein, 1981, p. 5).

In a third wave of data, the researchers again studied 89 of the families with black adopted children, now adolescent. They reported that the parents and their children felt good about themselves and their relationships with each other, and continued to hold accurate racial identities. Despite these overall conclusions, the authors took the position that inracial placement is preferable; transracial adoption is a viable alternative for black children that should be examined on a case-by-case basis. Less emphasized was the finding that 11 percent of the transracial adoptees indicated that they preferred to be white and that 27 percent of the adoptive parents thought their black/white children held white identities.

Shireman and Johnson (1986) undertook a longitudinal study of black children placed for adoption. Three almost equal samples of children have been under study since 1972 when the children were less than three years old. The three groups included black children placed with single parents; black children placed transracially into white homes; and, for comparison purposes, black children placed traditionally with black couples. Reports were published on the children and families soon after placement when the children were three to four years, and again at age eight years (Shireman & Johnson, 1975; 1976; 1980; 1986). Special attention has been given to racial preference and racial identity of the children.

At age four years, the transracially adopted children had had minimum experience with other black persons, but knew that they were black and reflected a greater black preference than did the children in black homes, a finding taken as some indication that their white parents were helping their black children to form a positive and accurate beginning identity. At age eight years, the transracial group had maintained their positive conception of blackness.

At age four years, the black children placed traditionally with black families had a high mean score for white preference. By age eight, however, these children showed a marked reversal to a very low white preference, lower than those of the transracial group.

The measure of racial identity also showed the same pattern. At age four, 71 percent in the transracial group and only 53 percent of the tra-

ditional group identified themselves as black. By age eight, the two groups were identical in this matter. In other words, the transracially adopted children were maintaining but not intensifying their early good sense of racial identity, as had the children in black homes. Data will be gathered again when the children are age twelve (Shireman & Johnson, 1986).

In another study of transracial and inracial adoptees, McRoy and Zurcher (1983) studied the experience of black adolescents who had been adopted at very young ages, thirty children in white homes, and thirty in black homes. By use of questionnaires and interview data, the researchers sought the perspective of both adoptive parents and the adolescent adoptees with respect to relationships with parents, extended family, siblings, peers, school and community, as well as perceptions of racial identity and aspirations for the future. Both groups of adoptees were found to be "physically healthy and exhibited typical adolescent relationships with their parents, siblings, teachers and peers. Similarly, regardless of the race of their adoptive parents, they reflected positive feelings of self-regard" (p. 138). Although the transracial adoptive parents had experienced some challenges that were different from those of inracial adoptive parents, they had handled the challenges well. A significant conclusion was that "the quality of parenting is more important than whether the black child has been inracially or transracially adopted" (p. 138).

A major distinction found between the two groups of adoptees was the social psychological context that influenced their socialization with respect to ethnicity and perceptions of and attitudes toward their racial identity. The transracial adoptees living in white neighborhoods and acculturated by the white society tended to "disregard or dismiss observable racial differences between themselves and their adoptive parents." In addition their white peers tended to view them as being "different from their stereotypes of other blacks." The transracial adoptees who had been growing up in integrated neigh-

borhoods and who, with their parents, had had frequent contact with black families "seemed more flexible in their racial self-perceptions and were less likely to exhibit wholly white oriented attitudes and behaviors" (McRoy & Zurcher, 1983, p. 139).

The Controversy. A nationwide survey on transracial adoption in 1972 indicated that since 1967, when agencies had begun to increase substantially their efforts to make such placements, about 10,000 black children had been placed in white homes across the country. Figures for 1971 were then incomplete but were expected to be similar to those for 1970, when more than one-third of the adopted black children went into white homes (Klemesrud, 1972). Social workers, although not unanimous in their approval, for the most part seemed to endorse the practice as a means to provide homes for children who were otherwise likely to grow up in foster homes and institutions.

In the early 1970s, however, the climate of opinion about the appropriateness of transracial adoption began to change sharply as minority groups stressed the fostering of racial and cultural identity. At their 1972 meeting, the National Association of Black Social Workers came out "in vehement opposition" to the practice of placing black children with white families and called on the public and voluntary agencies to "cease and desist" transracial placements, which were termed "a growing threat to the preservation of the black family." The association directed much of its attack toward the CWLA for sanctioning placement of children across racial lines in its standards and for undertaking research on transracial adoption (Fraser, 1972).

The position taken stirred heated responses from professionals and parents involved with the relatively recent development of transracial adoptions. It was apparent that even among black social workers, opinion was divided as to whether transracial placements should be eliminated completely or continued and used under

the direction of a black social worker as an available alternative for children who might otherwise grow up without a permanent home.

The publication of the study by Grow and Shapiro restimulated the controversy. Chimezie (1977) attacked the study on the basis of its design, subjects, and measurement. In particular he stated:

> The most serious methodological fault of the study is the use of white adoptive parents—a group that is biased in favor of transracial adoption—to evaluate transracial adoption and its effects on the black adoptees' identity.

He also criticized the study because it was not focused directly on the adoptees' black identity. Grow and Shapiro responded that the study was focused on child development, not racial identity (1977).

In any case, the practice of transracial placement of black children and of American Indian children fell off sharply and in some agencies virtually ended. A renewed effort was made to recruit more black and Indian adoptive homes. Given the lack of clear and mandatory reporting of adoptions, precise data on which to judge the results were lacking.

In the absence of recent and convincing evidence that permanent black or American Indian homes are being recruited in sufficient numbers, and in view of the positive findings about the well-being of children who have been placed across racial lines, the question remains whether transracial placement should be an alternative practice. In evaluating transracial adoption Billingsley and Giovannoni have stressed the need to see the practice in the context of the total need for homes and an entire array of child welfare services for the increasing number of minority children who need care and protection (1970, p. 71). They observed that although transracial adoption is an eminently worthwhile undertaking in the enrichment of individual family life, as well as a reflection of social change in intergroup relations in the larger society, it is "a minuscule effort" against the magnitude of the problem of nonwhite children needing care and protection—"virtually not a solution." The urgency of the problem demands that transracial adoption be seen as one alternative, along with a variety of other adoption alternatives and child care arrangements.

In addressing the question of whether the adoption of Indian children by white parents should be continued, Fanshel noted the changing climate of opinion on such placements and made this observation:

> It seems clear that the fate of most Indian children is tied to the struggle of Indian people in the United States for survival and social justice. . . . Whether adoption by white parents of the children who are in the most extreme jeopardy in the current period . . . can be tolerated by Indian organizations is a moot question. . . . Reading a report such as this one, Indian leaders may decide that some children may have to be saved through adoption even though the symbolic significance of such placements is painful for a proud people to bear. On the other hand, even with the benign outcomes reported here, it may be that Indian leaders would rather see their children share the fate of their fellow Indians than lose them in the white world. It is for the Indian people to decide. (1972, pp. 341–342)

The passage of the Indian Child Welfare Act of 1978 reaffirmed the right of tribal courts to assume jurisdiction over the placement of Native American children. Its intent is to reduce the number of Indian children placed in non-Indian homes as a means to preserve cultural and racial identity. Preferences that must be given in adoptive placements are listed in section 105 of the act: (1) a member of the child's extended family; (2) other members of the Indian child's tribe; (3) other Indian families. Adherence to these preferences for adoptive placements is high according to a federally commissioned survey of the implementation of the act (Plantz et al., 1989). Compliance appears to be enhanced by employment of Native American staff in child welfare programs. Staff serving Native American children in foster care are more likely to see returning children home or arranging care by other relatives as the appropriate plan rather than adoption.

Subsidized Adoptions

One development designed to expand adoption resources is the practice of subsidized adoption, an arrangement by which a social agency makes financial payments to a set of adoptive parents beyond the point of their legal consummation of the adoption. Many agencies have children in foster care who would be adopted if the agency payment to the foster family could be continued. The need for adoption subsidies was underscored by Shyne and Schroeder's nationwide survey of children receiving public child welfare services (1978). They estimated that there were 102,000 children who were legally free for adoption but that one-third would require a subsidy if they were to be placed.

Subsidies are of three general types: (1) those for specific services, such as medical care, legal services or special education; (2) time-limited subsidies, to be agreed on by the family and the agency, to help absorb the costs of transition into a family with an additional member; and (3) long-term subsidies in the form of monthly payments until the child is grown (Freeman, 1984).

Subsidies have several advantages: (1) They can open up new possibilities for children who have handicaps or medical problems, those who are "older," and those who are black or have mixed racial parentage, for whom the prospects for attaining a permanent home through traditional forms of adoption have been bleak; (2) they can obtain greater security, continuity of care, and clearer status for children with close ties to foster parents who have all the essential qualifications for adoptive parenthood except an adequate financial base; (3) they have the potential for providing considerable financial saving in comparison with the costs of long-term foster care. As a general rule, adoptive subsidies must be lower in amount than the monthly foster care payment rate.

Income supplementation as a means of reaching new groups of potential adoptive parents was suggested by the CWLA in the early 1960s, but agencies were slow to respond. Such a service in a Pennsylvania voluntary agency was reported in 1969 (Lawder), where it was termed "quasi-adoption." Other agencies experimented with subsidized adoption, but only to a limited extent, probably because it required a commitment of funds over a long period of time. The idea of adoption by foster parents was little explored even after foster parents had shown their commitment to a child and an ability to provide a reliable and caring home. For example, in a study of 377 cases representative of a much larger group of potentially adoptable children, primarily black and Hispanic, under the care of thirty-three children's agencies, it was found that the possibility of foster parents' becoming adoptive parents had been discussed only after the children had been in care for six to seven years (Fanshel, 1982). But with the demonstrated success of other nontraditional adoptive arrangements, the merging of foster and adoptive parent roles, and the new availability of subsidies, agencies have turned predominantly to foster parents to secure legal adoptions for children with special needs (Shapiro, 1984). Fully 90 percent of subsidized adoptions are with foster parents for whom subsidy has enabled adoption of children with whom they have established a relationship (Cole, 1987).

Subsidized adoptions and long-term foster care arrangements have tended to blur the once-clear distinctions between foster family care and adoption. (Kadushin, 1977, p. 124)

Subsidized adoption programs are most feasible for public welfare departments. New York in 1968 became the first state to enact subsidized adoption legislation. Illinois, California, Minnesota, and Maryland followed in 1969. Currently all fifty states and the District of Columbia have such legislation for special needs children. However, not all states have implemented the legislation or used it to develop a program fully. As of early 1982, there were approximately 19,000 children receiving adoption subsidies nationally (Waldinger, 1982).

Legislation varies widely from state to state. Some of it is complex and restrictive. For these reasons, the CWLA, at the request of the Children's Bureau, developed a Model State Subsidized Adoption Act (U.S. Dept. of HEW, 1975; 1976). The emphasis was on facilitating the adoption of children with special needs. Through Title XX of the Social Security Act, federal matching funds for the first time were authorized to be used for adoption. The federal Adoption Assistance and Child Welfare Act of 1980 allows some federal funding for adoption subsidies through Aid to Dependent Children in Foster Care (ADC-FC) and Medicaid. Consistent and adequate funding is needed if the legislation is to have its intended impact. Nevertheless, foster parents are increasingly being viewed as potential adopters by law and agency policy. Proch found that preference is given to foster parents by law in nine of forty-six states and the District of Columbia, by written agency policy in fifteen states, and in practice in nineteen states. The Model Statute for Termination of Parental Rights and the Model Adoption Act also indicate that foster parents are to be given particular consideration as adoptive parents (Proch, 1981).

Have adoption subsidies worked? Most indications are that they have, and most importantly, they seem to succeed with special needs children. As an example, a program in Ohio reported the adoption of 291 children through the use of subsidies. The average age of the children was eleven, 72 percent were black, one-third were severely emotionally disturbed, and one-third were functioning with low intelligence quotients. The group included children with "cerebral palsy syndrome, prune belly syndrome, Down's syndrome, curvature of the spine, deafness, glycogen storage disease, dwarfism, severe retardation," and nonambulatory children (O'Bryne & Bellucci, 1982, p. 177). Reports from other states further testify to the power of subsidies on making adoptive placements for older children, minority children, and handicapped children (Dall, 1977; Jones, 1975).

The state of Illinois has used the subsidized adoption alternative extensively. Its program was assessed as successful in that a large number of children viewed as "unadoptable" found permanent adoptive homes, including children who were physically or mentally handicapped and had been in foster care five or more years. Many of them had already experienced relatively stable relationships with foster parents, who were now enabled to adopt them (Shaffer, 1977). A survey of adoptive parents receiving subsidies in California found high levels of satisfaction with the program, and 90 percent of the respondents indicated that they would definitely encourage suitable friends to participate in the program. The major complaint was that the parents had to be annually recertified as needing the grant. The potential for savings in costs through the use of subsidized adoption was supported. An average savings of just under $3,000 per child was achieved by placing a child in a subsidized adoption home rather than keeping that child in foster care until the age of eighteen (Waldinger, 1982). For the sample of children Shaffer studied in Illinois, numbering 287, the savings were expected to be $853,260. This estimate was a conservative one because additional thousands are saved by reducing the agency's overhead costs, social workers' salaries, and educational and vocational costs (1977). Currently, eleven states report an average savings of 44 percent by substituting subsidized adoptive payments for foster care payments (Interagency Task, 1988).

The subsidized adoption program is not a cure-all for the problems of children in substitute care. Shaffer (1977) found that the need continued for supportive services and for the development of new ones. Some of the same problems of the foster care system plagued the best use of subsidized adoption. The length of time children spent in foster care had not been reduced by the use of subsidy. To have done so would have required more effective monitoring of the foster care system as well as more intensive staff development programs. The use of subsidies had been primarily a means to turn longtime foster care into adoption. Few new homes for children with special needs had been found, and recruitment from a new pool of potential adopters had not been emphasized. The implications of the policy of limiting subsidies to families with low or very moderate incomes also needed examination.

Not surprisingly, the subsidized adoptive families had different characteristics from those of families recruited under more traditional practices. For the most part they fit the description of applicants viewed as "marginal" and identified in other studies as suitable for the child with special needs. Subsidized adoption had changed children's legal status, but little was known about any concomitant psychological changes.

Foster parent adoptions are a relatively new phenomenon and research is therefore limited. One survey of foster parents who adopted found the following:

1. The fifty-six children studied were all defined as hard-to-place (80 percent were minorities; 66 percent were over five years of age; and 29 percent had chronic physical or psychological problems requiring special services).
2. Forty percent of the parents originally took the child with no intention of adopting, but decided to adopt later after becoming attached to the child.
3. Almost one-third wanted to keep the child without adopting him or her but

were afraid the child would be removed if they did not.

4. Most of the children knew of no other home, so the adoption had little or no significance.

5. Children who remembered living in other foster homes distinguished between foster care and adoption in terms of permanence.

6. Parents and children received little preparation for adoption.

7. Only 25 percent of the parents attributed changes in their child's behavior to adoption, but all were positive changes. Only 20 percent indicated that their parent–child relationship had improved.

8. The overwhelming response to the question "If you knew at the beginning what you know now, would you do it again?" was "Yes, definitely" (Proch, 1980, p. 14).

The relationship between the social worker and foster parent is critical to the decision to adopt. In a study of adopters and nonadopters conducted in one large public and three voluntary child welfare agencies, continuity and quality of the relationship with the social workers constituted an important discriminator between the two groups:

> Adopting families perceived their relationship with their workers as more open than their non-adopting counterparts. They felt free to talk with their workers and to share their concerns, hopes and fears with them. They also felt that their workers knew them well and were concerned about them. The findings confirm the need for a "partnership" relationship between worker and family. Such a partnership means mutual respect and sharing of ideas and information. (Meezan & Shireman, 1985, p. 216)

The large need for permanent adoptive homes, especially for special needs children, increasing attention to the concept of "psycholog-

ical parents," the potential for cost savings, and the apparent positive results all augur for a continued expansion of this form of adoption.

Legal-Risk Adoptions

Children who are not legally free for adoption are sometimes placed with families committed to permanent placement as foster parents or as adoptive parents in the event of termination of biological parental rights. Legal-risk adoption differs from foster parent adoption since the commitment to permanency takes place before placement rather than after a long-term relationship with the child has been formed. In that respect, legal-risk adoption varies from traditional adoption in that adoption is not the sole goal of the prospective parents, nor is there any certainty that the child will become legally available for adoption. Such families are assessed as "potential adoptive families, as well as for their ability to tolerate short-term care and separation from the child under agency supervision, if adoption does not eventuate" (Proch, 1981, p. 623). This form of adoption provides another alternative in planning permanency for neglected/abused children who are at risk of multiple foster placements. A ten-year program of legal-risk adoptions in Illinois served 265 children, of whom 167 were freed for adoption. The program showed the importance of proper selection and preparation of families interested in this specific type of placement. From the Illinois experience, social workers and lawyers developed categories for identifying children appropriate for legal-risk adoption: (1) the child has been relinquished by the mother and the identity of the father is unknown; (2) the child has been relinquished by one parent and a diligent search has been made in an attempt to locate the absent parent; (3) the child has been relinquished by one parent and the identity and whereabouts of the other parent are known and it appears that this parent might also relinquish the child; (4) the child has been abandoned in circumstances in which there was indication of the parents' intent to give up the child permanently, and the identity and whereabouts of the parents are unknown; (5) termination of parental rights has been granted by the trial court but the case is on appeal to a higher court; (6) other children in the family have been freed for adoption and it seems feasible that adoption may become the eventual plan for this child; (7) a child lives in a state where courts formally or informally require that the child be in an adoptive family before considering a petition for involuntary termination of parental rights; (8) the parent is mentally ill or developmentally disabled and unlikely to ever be able to parent the child (Gill & Amadio, 1983).

Single-Parent Adoptions

In the search for permanent homes for children, legal adoption by single parents (unmarried, widowed, or divorced) has gained ground—further evidence of the dearth of foster homes or two-parent adoptive homes for certain groups of children and a greater readiness by social workers and the public to question old practices and discard artificial barriers keeping children from having their "own homes."

In the late 1960s, the practice of single-parent adoption was given considerable publicity in newspapers and popular magazines through appealing photographs and stories of successful adoptions. No laws in any state prohibit adoption by single adults.

Social workers have reported instances in which they have been highly impressed by the positive development of children placed with single mothers and the recognizable "good parenting" that followed placement. Placements with single males also have been made, but more rarely.

Certain safeguards are observed in an attempt to make sure that a single-parent adoption is the best alternative to the agency's inability to provide a child with both a mother and a father. If the adoptive mother is employed, and she usually is, careful evaluation is made of her plan for the child's care during her working hours to ensure, not only that the care provided is good care, but also that the plan has some probability of permanence. Sometimes the arrangement is with a long-standing friend of the mother, or a neighbor, or sometimes a relative living in the home. In addition, applicants are more likely to be favored when the single adult has relatives who can provide close ties and family support for the child as well as concrete help in the event of crisis. Value is placed on opportunities for the child to have meaningful relationships with both sexes, either in the extended family or among friends, particularly couples who have children. In assessing a single adult's motivation to adopt a child, attention is given to the readiness to bring love and companionship to a relationship with a child without the need to be overpossessive or to keep him or her from social contacts and normal activities.

The strength of the belief that adoption by a married couple is more desirable than by a single adult is evident in the amendment of the California adoption law to permit single-parent adoption; single adults "may be accepted only when a two-parent family has not been found because of a child's special needs." However, persons who approve of single-parent adoptions hold that social conditions make it highly unlikely that more traditionally qualified homes for these children can be found. Therefore, it is unfair to children to deny them the love and security of their own permanent home with one parent when a two-parent adoptive home cannot be found.

Some take an opposing view, or at least a more cautious one: Flexibility and innovation in social work practice may obscure the undeveloped potentialities in traditional forms of service for children who need long-term care, and inhibit other provisions which would lessen the number of children who need adoption, for example, improvements in foster care, greater use of private guardianship, wider availability of daytime programs for children's care and development, and forms of subsidization of a child's home, as in a family allowance.

There is also the charge that the practice of adoption by single adults reflects a double standard—a complete family for nonhandicapped white infants, but single parents for children who are older or nonwhite, or who have special characteristics that need the best that a home and parents can provide. Persons who hold this view usually deplore an adoption "market" in which applicants not meeting the usual eligibility requirements can draw a social agency into departing from an ideal standard. Proponents of the new practice counter, however, that it is unrealistic and scarcely humanitarian to hold to an ideal while a child grows older without a permanent home and the chances for one diminish each year.

Single-parent adoptions account for relatively few adoptive arrangements. Documented practice is scarce. In two large Chicago multiservice voluntary agencies, adoptions by single persons numbered only thirty-one during a two-year period (Shireman & Johnson, 1976). In California where single-parent adoption pioneered, such placements made up 1 percent of private agency, and 10 percent of nonrelative independent adoptions in 1981–1982 (Wingard, 1987).

Kadushin studied the problems and disadvantages of single-parent adoption by means of a review of relevant research on single-parent families. Herzog and Sudia did the same through an analysis of studies of fatherless families. Both reviews were informative but gave no clear direction beyond a cautious yet generally positive endorsement of this innovative approach to finding homes for children (Kadushin, 1970; Herzog & Sudia, 1968).

A central question is whether single parents can provide adequate homes for those children for whom homes are most scarce—older children and handicapped children.

Feigelman and Silverman (1977), by means of mailed questionnaires, collected a large sample of data about single parent adoptions. In general, findings reflected parental satisfaction with their adopted children, and they were managing adequately the complex tasks of combining child care and work.

Shireman and Johnson (1976) embarked on a longitudinal study of single parents who had adopted black children during a two-year period (1970–1972) from either of two well-established Chicago voluntary child welfare agencies. They set out to describe the experiences of single parents who adopted black children under the age of three years as part of a larger ongoing study of black children adopted at less than three years of age by black couples, white couples, and single persons. At approximately four-year intervals, interviews were carried out to compare these types of families and to assess the overall development of the children and the problems and rewards for the families. A major focus was the children's handling of identity.

Thirty-one single parents were included in this study sample. These single parents appeared to be highly suitable for adoption in terms of their interest in adoption and their capacity to handle life experiences and become adequate parents. Their most evident risks were low income and reliance upon the employment of a single female parent. The closeness and interdependence of an extended family was seen as a compensating factor. At the time of the second follow-up, when the children were about four years of age, the adoptive parents seemed to be strong, healthy, educated people with jobs. Many were following a family model that they had experienced, having grown up with only one parent.

Although these applicants had been flexible in their stated preferences about the kind of child they could accept, the children placed with them were those considered to be relatively low-risk children. They were young and healthy, with "good" family histories; they had had care in one foster home prior to adoptive placement.

Apparently in this new venture these agencies had considered it advisable to make the "safest" placement rather than to place older or handicapped children.

In some contrast to the experiences of the two voluntary Illinois agencies, Shaffer found that the Illinois statewide public children's agency had accepted single parents for subsidized adoption from the beginning of the program and had given them children with special needs (Shaffer, 1977). Over 14 percent of the subsidized adopters between 1970 and 1976 were single parents. Compared with couples in subsidized families, the single parents typically were older, black, Protestant, and widowed, and had other children of their own in their care. Their incomes were quite low—only half the mean income of subsidized adopting couples whose incomes were also generally low. The children placed for the most part were adolescent and nonwhite, and had special needs. This fact raised questions about the basis on which children had been selected for this particular group of single parents and the impact that adoption would have on these children's relationships and opportunities.

If new practices in adoption are to be fully successful for children, clearly they must be based on careful evaluation of children's needs, attention to equitable distribution of resources for children, and explicit hypotheses that can be tested through follow-up studies or comparative studies of family life.

ADOPTABLE CHILDREN DENIED ADOPTION

Much progress has been made in gaining adoptive homes for children previously considered "unadoptable." A variety of strategies have been described that have increased the range of people considered suitable as adoptive parents. Despite this progress, there remain groups of children for which an adoptive home is unlikely. The number of older children, handicapped children, and children of color who are freed for adoption greatly exceeds the number of adoptive homes available. More aggressive agency action and community support are needed.

The Older Child

Being beyond infancy, and particularly beyond school age, has been identified repeatedly in social work literature as a handicap to being given an adoptive home. Moreover, the condition of being an "older" child is often linked to other deterrents to adoption, especially nonwhite status and medical conditions.

While progress has been made, older children still are highly likely to be passed over in adoptive practice. At each stage in the adoptive process, additional agency services are required to place older children in adoption. Such placements are therefore more costly than the placement of infants. Of course, the successful placement of an older child in an adoptive home brings long-term savings in costs of foster care and other aspects of the child's maintenance and nurture, as well as in social costs that occur when children who lack permanent homes become emotionally disturbed or develop maladaptive behavior patterns. Nevertheless, if an adoption agency is focused narrowly on its immediate access to staff and funds and those demands for adoptive service that are most readily dealt with, it may turn away from a challenge to respond to the needs of older children and ignore the evidence provided by more innovative agencies that such children can be successfully placed.

Despite difficulties, social agencies have demonstrated the process by which older children can be given permanent homes through adoption. Kadushin's investigation (1970) into the outcome of placements of older children provided evidence of a level of success nearly parallel to that for infants placed in adoption. He studied ninety-one children, almost equally divided between boys and girls, placed for adoption when they were at least five years of age. At the time of the study they were in early adolescence. These children had suffered considerable trauma at an early age—a prolonged period of social deprivation, poverty, substandard housing, parental personal pathology, and marital conflict. Court action had terminated parental rights because of their neglect and/or abuse. The researcher's intent was to determine the extent of success in the placements and to assess whether the emotional damage the children had sustained had been reversed after a period of living in an adoptive home.

The criteria of success focused on the parents' satisfactions and dissatisfactions with adoption, the problems they encountered, and the adaptations they made. Tape-recorded interviews were conducted jointly with each set of adoptive parents. The ratio of satisfactions to dissatisfactions expressed by parents showed 73 percent of the adoptions successful, 18 percent unsuccessful, and 9 percent indeterminate. The investigator compared these results with other adoption outcome studies in which most of the subjects were placed in adoption as infants and found that placements of the older group were only slightly less successful.

In view of the conditions under which these children lived during their critical early years, how can the generally favorable outcome of these adoptive placements be explained? A more detailed contrast within the study sample favored subgroups of children who had experienced a relatively more benign environment prior to adoptive placement. The findings do not mean, then, that neglect and physical deprivation are not harmful. As an explanation for the overall favorable outcome, Kadushin cited a biological factor—children's constitutional resilience in recovering from deprivation—and a sociological factor—upward displacement, which reinforces self-acceptance. Supporting these two factors was the provision of a therapeutic milieu, the adoptive home, which provided an opportunity for the child to learn new, more adaptive modes of behavior and a new view of parental figures.

The living experience teaches new ways of relating to people and new ways of perceiving oneself. In this sense, life is therapeutic. It acts as a large-scale conditioning matrix which stimulates and supports changes in the child's feeling and behavior. (Kadushin, 1970, p. 228)

But the transition from foster care to an adoptive home for an older child can be difficult. As Boyne describes it:

In addition to the task of adjusting to a new family, the vast majority of older adoptees have to contend with a difficult and lengthy grief over losses in their past. One of the most common ways of anesthetizing the pain is to develop certain character traits. Not infrequently, that means a shallow, manipulative approach to relationships, evasion and escape as primary means for handling frustration (e.g., by getting the caseworker to move you), mistrust, a view of persons as interchangeable, etc. The dynamic may be grief, but the form may well be in characterological symptoms. (1978, p. 197)

This situation has led Jones to conclude:

The development of an adoptive relationship for children who have been in the limbo of foster care is a continuous process. It is unrealistic to expect these families to live happily ever after. Agencies must begin developing regular services to meet the special needs of the families being created. (1979, p. 34)

Adoption of older children is far more than an answer to the question of how to reduce the foster care census. Indeed, adoption is only a partial answer to that narrow question. Older child adoption is a far better, but not perfect, answer to the larger question of how to improve the lives of children in foster care. (Barth & Berry, 1988, p. xi)

Children with Medical Impairments

As long as the definition of an adoptable child was focused on favorable heredity and good physical development, children with various mental or physical handicaps were viewed as unwarranted risks for successful adoption. Children with somewhat below-average intelligence usually were denied adoptive homes, and children with only minor medical conditions were not placed until the defects were improved or corrected. Children with severe defects were clearly seen as unsuitable for adoption. However, the growing flexibility of both public and voluntary agency practice brought progress in the placement of children with physical handicaps.

Franklin and Massarik (1969) reported a study of the outcome of adoptive placements of 314 children with diagnosed medical impairments. A control group of adopted children without medical conditions was included. The intent of the investigation was to learn how well the traditional objectives of adoption had been reached with these medically impaired children and how well their adopting parents had coped with the additional stress of the child's physical condition and its social consequences.

A medical panel assessed the severity and correctability of the children's impairments and classified them into three main types. "Severes" included children with such defects as blindness, deafness, cleft palate, incorrectable skeletal deformity, and other congenital anomalies. "Moderates" included children with such conditions as congenital cataract, hearing impairment, and urogenital defect. "Minors" consisted of children with inguinal hernias, minimal clubfoot, hydroceles, and a variety of skin disfigurements.

Joint interviews were held with the adoptive parents of all the "severes" and all the "moderates," and with reduced samples of the "minors" and "controls." An observation period with each child was requested to note behavior in the home, the salience of any residual medical condition, and its effect on the child's functioning.

The major conclusions were these:

1.   Children with medical conditions of all degrees of severity and correctability can be suc-cessfully placed and reared in adoptive homes. A global rating of the interview data, to determine the degree of satisfaction and role fulfillment which had been achieved by the families, indicated that more than three-fourths had developed strong, satisfying, and resilient relationships. The child's medical condition was not viewed as a principal stressful problem. Parents of almost all the "minors," 92 percent of the "moderates," and 71 percent of the "severes" maintained that the defect had not adversely affected them or restricted family life. They emphasized the general normality of their lives and reported satisfaction with their child's social functioning as well as with her or his school achievement.

2.   A broadened concept of "adoptable child" and "adoptive parent capability" was confirmed. Adoptive parents and children evidenced a fundamental adaptive capacity; the parents accepted full responsibility for parenthood and showed a readiness to accept risks, and great strength and resourcefulness.

3.   Delay in permanent placement of children with medical impairments until a prognosis is established or corrective treatment begun is not justified. The effect of such delays was to deny many of the study children the consistent care of the same parents from their earliest months. Interview data suggested that many of the adopting parents would have preferred to accept the child at a younger age and see him or her through corrective treatment from the beginning.

Today's effort to find adoptive homes for children with medical conditions is affected by the high costs of health care. Prospective adoptive parents are aware that health care costs for such children will exceed those of most children. Under state and federal law, Medicaid can help with these expenses. "A child who is covered by an adoption assistance agreement and who has a pre-existing medical condition is entitled to Medicaid regardless of the financial standing of the adoptive parents" (Secretariat, 1988, p. 1).

Racial Minorities

Proportions of children of racial minorities who need permanent homes through adoption are high. Social agencies, both public and voluntary, for at least the past three decades have engaged in special efforts to recruit adoptive homes for them. Agencies in various cities have joined forces to coordinate their homefinding efforts. Interested citizens have been organized to give publicity to the need for homes. Agencies have held discussions among groups of successful adopters of nonwhite children to find ways to generate interest among prospective parents. Mass communication media have been used to impart information about the need for homes and the adaptations that could be expected in agency requirements. For example, minority children of varying characteristics who have needed homes have been shown on television to attract applicants.

The CWLA and the United States Bureau of Indian Affairs cooperated in a nationwide endeavor to place American Indian children in adoptive homes (Fanshel, 1972). The concerted efforts of family and child-placing agencies in Chicago helped to alleviate the shortage of black adoptive homes (Dukette & Thompson, 1959). Special projects in other major cities as well have been regarded as successful in advancing some aspect of adoption practice, but all have fallen far short of needs in terms of the numbers of children to be placed and the homes found.

In addition to special recruitment and placement measures, systematic inquiries have been made to uncover factors that hinder or otherwise affect the placement of black children. The Chicago project referred to above found conditions restricting the number of black applicants to be (1) limited income and inadequate housing; (2) a general lack of knowledge and understanding among blacks about adoption service; (3) doubts and suspicions they held about black children who were uncared for by their own family, relatives, or friends and therefore

available for adoption; and (4) the fear of rejection, which is disturbing to most couples and especially so to blacks who had already experienced rejection by the white community and its institutions.

Fanshel studied the outcome of adoption applications in one large family agency (1957). In comparison with white applicants, black applicants had lower income (although they had higher income when compared with the general black population), less education, and a higher rejection rate because of social breakdown associated with low-income status. They were also older. Similar findings resulted from other studies (Woods & Lancaster, 1962, pp. 14–21). Fanshel cited the withdrawal of promising applicants as a phenomenon that merited careful attention by agencies. He recommended more flexibility in procedural regulations that jeopardized rapport between the social worker and black applicants.

Deasy and Quinn (1962) carried out an interview survey in Washington, D.C., and Baltimore to inquire into the apparent lack of interest in adoption among a sample of 484 urban blacks, all of whom had intact marriages, lived in good neighborhoods, and were generally upwardly mobile. It was not ignorance about adoption or overt disapproval that prevented this group of black couples from adopting in greater numbers. Instead, the researchers concluded, the insecurity of the future for middle-class blacks in cities tended to make them unwilling to raise families.

Bradley, like Fanshel, found that black adoptive applicants who were judged good prospects for adoptive parenthood withdrew at a higher rate than similar white couples. Forty percent of the black applicants "decided to adopt privately." Among comparable white applicants, 39 percent withdrew because the woman became pregnant (Bradley, 1966, p. 436).

Billingsley and Giovannoni cited indications of a high correlation between percentages of independent adopters and percentages of nonwhite adoptions, and the fact that the relaxation of agency restrictions and policies regarding acceptance of applicants had not been far-reaching enough to increase the number of black adoptive parents. They observed that the children needing adoption were increasingly black children. Yet the agencies continued to be mainly white-dominated institutions. They called for "basic changes in both agency policy and structure." More black social workers were needed as well as black lay representation at the policymaking level (1972, p. 74).

Although there are varying reasons—some obvious, others subtle, and most insufficiently documented—that influence black couples not to apply to white agencies today, the major and overriding reason why they do not seek adoption in greater numbers appears to be socioeconomic. Studies show that nonwhite couples who are financially able to adopt do so at as high a rate as, or a higher rate than, white couples. This fact challenges an assumption that black couples in a position to adopt are less ready to do so than white couples (Riday, 1969). Large numbers of black families who might otherwise adopt lack reliable income, stability in employment, better job opportunity, adequate housing, or general good health—deficiencies that tend to rule them out of an adoption program and leave large numbers of vulnerable children without permanent homes of their own. In recent years subsidized adoption has helped to remove such barriers to adoption of minority youngsters. Nevertheless, serious problems remain in finding good homes for all black children who need them.

ASSESSMENT OF ADOPTION

Major Directions of Adoption Research

Compared with other social services for children, adoption has been the object of considerable interest on the part of researchers. However, adoption presents many complexities to the systematic investigator. As a result, findings reflect serious limitations in sources of data, tools used for data gathering, samples studied, and control of the multiple sources of variance that exist in the adoptive situation.

Much of the interest of social workers in assessing adoption practice has turned toward investigations to establish the validity of their work—studies of how adoptions have turned out. Van Senden Theis's significant study of children placed in foster care included 269 persons who had been legally adopted as children. Follow-up information was available for 235 of them. Evaluations were made by interviews with these adults and their adoptive parents. The intent was to

> find out what kind of people our placed out children had grown to be, "what education they had had, how they were maintaining themselves socially and economically, what their standards of conduct were and what their general place is in their own communities." (Theis, 1924, p. 10)

Each placement was evaluated in terms of whether the subject was "capable" or "incapable" of managing his or her life with ordinary prudence. Criteria of the adoptee's capability included such factors as school record, reputation in the community, and the extent to which he or she was law-abiding, managed daily affairs sensibly, and was adequately self-supporting. The rate of success was high: 88.1 percent of the adoptees were rated "capable" (p. 122).

In later studies of outcome, a frequent criterion of success has been the level of satisfaction or dissatisfaction expressed by parents at some selected point in the postadoptive family life experience (Morrison, 1950; Nieden, 1951; Kadushin, 1970). Alternative criteria have included parental assessment of the child's functioning in those life tasks of the latency-age child (Ripple, 1968); an assessment of the parents' characteristics, behavior, and attitudes toward the child (Brenner, 1951; Witmer et al. 1963); and factors associated with disruption or stability in adoptive placements (Barth & Berry, 1988).

Success of adoptive placement has also been evaluated in terms of the extent to which babies placed under three months of age progress satisfactorily (Fairweather, 1952); the intellectual development of adopted children in relation to what would have been predicted from the intellectual, educational, and socioeconomic level of the biological parents (Skeels, 1965); the success of placement of children with possible racial admixture and the accuracy of genetic predictions about their future appearance (Nordlie & Reed, 1962); and the results of adoptive placement of children with medical impairments (Franklin & Massarik, 1969).

Limitations in the sources of available data and the multiple interrelated variables in adoption research present formidable obstacles to an attempt to "cull the factors associated with varying degree of success in adoption." As a result, "it is not possible to state with assurance what the actual predictive factors are and what relationship each bears to adoption outcome. However, certain findings can be organized into a series of propositions for which there is considerable supporting evidence" (Mech, 1965, p. 28).

Rate of Success

The percentage of adoptive placements deemed satisfactory is high. Kadushin summarized findings of eleven outcome studies, using only those in which the source of data and the criteria were indicated and the results statistically stated. Out of 2,236 placements, 74 percent had been judged "unequivocably successful"; 11 percent were "intermediate" or "fairly successful"; and 15 percent were "unsatisfactory" or "poor" (Kadushin, 1970, pp. 63–71). Furthermore, as we have reviewed earlier, research findings show that not only the very young child can receive a satisfactory home through adoption; so can the older child, the one with medical impairments, and the one moving from one country and culture to another.

Despite [the lack of] universality of criteria for outcome, variations in data-collection procedures, and differences in populations, the findings confirm what practitioners already believe—that adoption is a highly desirable placement choice for many children in need of homes and may be of particular benefit to children who have been exposed to difficult life experiences prior to permanent placement. (Mech, 1965, p. 19)

Social workers find it gratifying that adoptions generally turn out well, especially since children waiting for adoptive homes are considered to be more vulnerable than children who remain in their own homes. Pringle raises the interesting question, however, of whether it may not be a fallacy to attempt to establish an overall adoption success rate.

This question is rarely asked about biological families nor, indeed, do generally acceptable criteria exist according to which judgments could be made. And it is not only appropriate criteria which are lacking, but also techniques, tests, and other measuring devices. Similarly, the prevalence of emotional maladjustment among children at various ages and stages of development is not known. Is it not then a fallacy to expect to be able to answer these questions with regard to adopted children? (Pringle, 1967, p. 26)

Emotional Disturbance among Adopted Children

Although the claim has been made that adopted children are more prone to emotional disturbance than nonadopted children living with their own parents, studies so far have not clearly established a higher than usual incidence of maladjustment or emotional disturbance in adopted children.

In the early 1960s considerable interest in this question arose when several psychoanalytically oriented therapists reported that adopted children were coming to the attention of their treatment agencies at a rate very much higher than their proportion in the general population. Schechter reported that over 13 percent of the 120 children whom he saw in his private practice were adopted children (1960, pp. 21–32). Toussieng reported that over 10 percent of the 357 children seen at Menninger Clinic's Children's Service over a five-year period were adopted (1962, pp. 59–65). Similar findings, although with lower percentages, were reported by others (Sweeny et al., 1963, pp. 345–349).

The claim that adopted children experience more emotional problems than nonadopted children has been questioned. The U.S. Children's Bureau called attention to the selective factors in the makeup of treatment agency caseloads and the usual predominance of middle-income groups among patients (1964, pp. 137–139). Madison rejected the claim on this basis:

> In making comparisons with non-adopted children, the wrong population base is used; no allowance is made for race or for urban residence, although it is well known that clinics are largely situated in cities in certain parts of the country; no heed is paid to economic status, although the adoptive parents described obviously had money enough (which is not always the case) to obtain psychiatric help. That adopted parents might have less hesitance about seeking psychiatric help than natural parents is not taken into account. (Madison, 1966, p. 257)

Borgatta and Fanshel undertook a study of adoption status and the use of treatment agencies as part of an investigation of behavioral characteristics of children coming to psychiatric outpatient clinics. They concluded that although the question of incidence of behavior disorders and appearance at community agencies is very complex,

> a higher agency arrival rate does exist for adopted children than might be expected for the general child population. The rate is . . . not as extraordinarily excessive as was originally suggested by Schechter. If even relatively simple things such as the selective factors of race, social class, and prior contact with agencies are taken into account, the apparent difference becomes of questionable significance. (Borgotta & Fanshel, 1965, p. 3)

From his extensive review of adoption research, Kadushin concluded that "interest in . . . the question of the number of adoptive children referred for treatment of emotional disturbance has fallen off" (1978a, p. 60).

Importance of Adoptive Parents' Personal Qualities

A most important variable in the outcome of adoptive placements is the attitudes and behavior of adoptive parents. As stated by Pringle:

> Perhaps the main point that emerges from the research work of the past sixteen years is a commonsense one: that no other circumstances of adoption . . . are as important as the kind of people the adopters are and the kind of home they create. (Pringle, 1967, p. 28)

Of particular interest is a finding from Jaffee and Fanshel's follow-up study of the life adjustment of 100 adult adoptees. The great majority of parents reported that they had never at any time experienced problems they thought were connected with being *adoptive* parents. Even in regard to the least well-adjusted third of the adoptees, parents of three-fifths of them did not believe that the fact of adoption per se had been a particular source of difficulty for their children (Jaffee & Fanshel, 1970, p. 393).

Numerous overt, easily recognized characteristics of adopters have been found to have only chance relationship to placement outcomes, for example, age of the adoptive parents, length of marriage, education of the parents, reason for childlessness, sex preferences, reaction to first sight of the child, socioeconomic status, presence of other children in the home, religion, and marital status (except when both adopting parents had been divorced previously) (Brenner, 1951; Witmer et al., 1963). The arrival of other biological or adopted children coming into the adoptee's home after his or her placement has been shown to be unrelated to adoptee adjustment. Adoptees who entered families with one or more children already there tended to fare better than adoptees placed with childless couples (Jaffee & Fanshel, 1970).

Less tangible characteristics appear to be related to placement outcome, but these qualities are difficult to assess with certainty during a social investigation. Witmer and coworkers (1963) specified some of these more elusive variables to be general climate of the home, quality of the marriage, and personalities of the adopting parents. In a report on a study of postplacement functioning of 200 adoptive families, Lawder et al. (1969) found several parental factors to be indicative of outcome: presence of warmth and affection toward the child, acceptance of the adoptive role, and satisfaction in the parental role. The researchers identified the overriding conclusion to be "the unmistakable predominance of parent characteristics, attitudes and behavior over child factors as determinants of later adoption functioning" (pp. 121–122).

Preplacement Factors Have Less Importance

Certain relationships between children's background and the outcome of their adoptions are apparently not significant. For example, such factors as age of the child at adoption, number of placements prior to adoption, psychological evaluations, and ratings of emotional deprivation showed practically no relationship to later functioning of the family, the parents, or the children (Lawder et al., 1969, p. 104). Wittenborn's follow-up study of infants found that the results of the Yale Developmental Examination had no useful predictive validity (1957). Skeels (1965) found adults who had been adopted as children achieving at levels consistently higher than would have been predicted from the intellectual, educational, and socioeconomic levels of the biological parents. Ripple found a surprising lack of significant association between the adopted child's adjustment at follow-up and "the age at which he or she was placed in an adoptive home, the number of preadoptive placements, the apparent quality of care in those placements, or the early behavior of the child" (Ripple, 1968, p. 485). Furthermore, for the white subsample, "matching" of the child to the adoptive parent, by coloring—hair, eyes, complexion—and ethnic background, was not a factor in the outcome, although matching had been regarded by social workers as a practice important to the establishment of the identity as a family.

Age at Placement

There is consensus on the desirability of placement of children at a young age, but strong evidence that early placement portends more successful outcome is lacking.

Early placement of infants increased in practice as a result of such factors as (1) research on maternal deprivation and the efficacy of continuity in mothering; (2) evidence from a number of follow-up studies of adoption which had been in favor of the earlier placed children (Pringle, 1967); (3) the low predictive validity of infant developmental tests, as a result of which it was no longer regarded as worth delaying a child's placement in order to match parent and child; (4) similar difficulties experienced by physicians in detecting developmental pathology in children at a very young age; (5) the expressed wish of many adoptive applicants to receive an infant or very young child; and (6) savings in agency administrative costs when children are placed early after coming into care.

Although early placements are seen as desirable, "late" and "early" have been defined differently in different studies; and late groups often contain children who have had multiple foster placements or other harmful life experiences prior to adoption. The findings of the Witmer et al. study suggested that "other things being equal—the outcome prospects are slightly more promising if the child is placed before he or she is a month old." But the researchers go on to point out:

> The fact that the association is relatively low, however, also means that other more important factors, favorable or unfavorable, are operating simultaneously and could either reinforce or nullify the effect of this one. (Witmer et al., 1963, p. 344)

Further research is needed to establish whether it is primarily the child's age at placement that is crucial, or the likelihood in later placements of deprivation, multiple placements, or other deleterious experiences prior to adoption, as well as an increased probability under those conditions of a less favorable adoptive home.

Capacity to Predict Parental Potential

Increasing evidence indicates that social workers in adoptive practice are expected to make too many judgments of attitudes and other inferential material related to adoptive applicants' capabilities. Brieland's early study on the selection of adoptive parents stated: "Perhaps adoption agencies have been pushed into trying to achieve more diagnostic skill than is realistically possible at our present state of knowledge" (1959, p. 59). Bradley's later study on caseworkers' perceptions of adoptive applicants produced findings that

> made us wonder whether in the adoption field we have at times made the error of endowing caseworkers with the task of making judgments about parental potential, when such a magical capacity should not be the expectation. (1966, p. 187)

Evidence that "good" adoptive parenting cannot be predicted with confidence came from Ripple's (1968) study of preadoptive evaluations and selected aspects of postadoptive experiences of 160 children seven through ten years of age at the time of the follow-up study. The data consisted of the record of the original adoption study and supervisory period, follow-up interviews with the adoptive mother and the father, and observation of the child for about half an hour, usually after he or she returned from school. Attention in assessments was directed toward those life tasks whose mastery is the primary job of the latency-age child.

The findings produced little evidence of association between the assessment of the parents'

attitudes and behavior at the follow-up and the assessment of those same qualities based on the case record of the original adoptive investigation. In general, associations that did emerge were between "negative" factors and "unfavorable" outcome, rather than between "positive" factors and "favorable" outcome. These findings led to the conclusion that while potential for "good" parenting cannot be assessed with certainty, a few major indicators of "bad" parenting can be identified. The implications of this study for practice were these: Since social workers know considerably more about the elements of bad parenting and have considerable skill in identifying these elements, they should move early in the adoptive study to identify the possible presence of known negative factors—a fairly small number—believed to present the greatest potential risk to adequate parenthood and to be the least amenable to modification, for example, uncertainties relevant to motivation and acceptance of adoption, and low health and energy of the adopting mother. If negative factors are not found, the "exploration" should end and attention should be turned to the placement process (Ripple, 1968).

Telling a Child about Adoption

Social workers are agreed that for healthy development of identity, children must be helped to know about and understand their adoptive status. There is relatively little documentation about how parents have gone about accomplishing this goal or the experiences children and parents are apt to have in doing so.

Social workers have stressed that children should know about their adoption as early as possible and should learn about it from their adoptive parents. In addition, they have tended to believe that if the adoptive parent–child relationship is a happy one, children will reflect less curiosity about their origins and will experience minimal conflict about their adoptive status. No body of knowledge from adoptive research clearly supports this notion. Rather, many adoptive parents have indicated that the telling process is a difficult assignment about which they would like more knowledge from professionals or other adoptive parents (Brenner, 1951; Witmer et al., 1963). This appears to apply to families who adopt infants as well as those who adopt older children. In both instances, Raynor (1980) found that less than one-third of the parents were at ease in discussing their child's background.

Social workers have usually advised adoptive parents to begin using the word "adoption" in the child's earliest years. Yet adoption is a complex concept for preschool children to understand. However, even though they cannot grasp the significance of the differences inherent in adoptive status, it appears that telling children in their preschool years carries less risk than waiting (Brodzinsky et al., 1984).

Because adoption has different meanings to a child at different stages of life, social workers urge that the telling be a gradual and progressive sharing of information throughout childhood and adolescence. Meaningful explanations of adoption must be linked to answers to a child's questions about the birth process. One study demonstrated that adoptive parents who performed less well in the telling process were unable to recognize that their child had any sexual curiosity. Areas of discomfort in the telling process were identified as: the reason for the surrender of the child, the biological parents, and the adoptive parents' childlessness (Baumann, 1963). Discussing the circumstances of the child's birth was also troublesome for many adopters.

Most adopted children probably deal with the fact of adoption throughout their lives. A follow-up study suggested that an adopted child needs to communicate openly about her or his status, background, and feelings about being adopted, during various states of development (Elonen & Schwartz, 1969).

Jaffee and Fanshel (1970) studied the life adjustment of 100 adult adoptees as perceived and reported by their parents. One area of ex-ploration was the possible relationships between the adoptees' adjustment over the years and the particulars of how they were informed of their adoptive status. No significant associations were found between adult adjustment and the source, the timing, or the circumstances of the initial "telling"; the frequency with which the subject of adoption had been dicussed over the years; or whether or not the adoptive parents had tended to make the fact of adoption visible to others.

Only one aspect of revelation was definitely associated with life adjustment of adoptees. There was a tendency for various kinds of adjustment problems to occur in those adoptees who had shown marked interest in their biological past and who had not received sufficient information to satisfy their curiosity. These two factors—marked interest and insufficient information—tended to influence the adoptees to ask their adoptive parents, or the placing agency, for more information than parents had or were willing to share. Jaffee and Fanshel saw this finding as difficult to interpret with certainty, given the absence of other related and rigorous research on this aspect of adoption. Perhaps, they suggested, the decisive factor in the impact of the revelation is the degree of ease and the absence of anxiety that parents feel in telling the child about adoption—the extent to which the stance they assume is congenial to their own emotional and psychological makeup. It is of interest that 100 sets of adoptive parents perceived the "telling" of the facts of adoption to have been largely unconnected with the nature of the life adjustment of their adopted children (Jaffee & Fanshel, 1970).

In their examination of the ways in which parents had told children about their adoptive status, Jaffee and Fanshel discovered that parents had dealt with the revelation in a way that reflected their basic underlying orientation to child rearing generally.

Families which tended to take a sheltering approach to the general upbringing of their children . . . tended to postpone revelation, to give minimal information about the child's biological background, to decrease the visibility of the adoptive status and, in effect, to simulate a biological parent-child relationship. On the other hand, parents with a less protective orientation toward the rearing of children were likely also to be more "open" about adoption, to reveal more information about natural parents, and to acknowledge freely the nonbiological nature of their relationship with the adoptee. (pp. 311–312)

In any case, the prevailing pattern had been to withhold most or all information about the biological parents and circumstances of the adoption. Only 12 percent of the parents had given their children all the facts they knew.

Although surveys of adopted adults tend to report that they want more information about their birth parents than they have been given, it is not universal. Raynor's work (1980) with adoptees found that one-third of her sample indicated they were satisfied with the information they had, even when it was minimal. Another third wanted to know somewhat more. The remainder wished for more information, particularly the reason why they had been given up for adoption and what the birth mother looked like.

It appears clear that a significant determinant of success in adoption is the extent to which the adoptive parents and the child acknowledge and accept the differences between adoption and building a family biologically (Hartman, 1984). Kirk, who over a period of a decade studied adoption relations among more than 2,000 families, advanced a theory of adoptive relations that has special relevance to the process of revealing the facts of a child's adoption (1964). He focused on the cultural and social meanings of childlessness, the concomitant feelings of deprivation and alienation on the part of the childless couple, and the resulting special nature of adoptive parenthood with its ambiguities and distinctions from biological parenthood. He theorized that childless couples undertaking adoption are confronted with a series of diffi-

culties—a role handicap—with which they must learn to cope. This handicap is frequently reinforced by distorted or insensitive attitudes of other persons in the community at large, the adopters' own parents, or professionals. As a result adoptive parents are faced with certain dilemmas in the course of their child rearing that tend to complicate various phases of adoptive family life. Adoptive parents, Kirk says, employ one of two patterns of coping with their role handicap and consequent feelings of alienation: they may attempt to deny that their situation is different from biological parenthood—"rejection of difference"—or they may act from "acknowledgment of difference." The greater the original feelings of deprivation because of childlessness, the greater the tendency toward coping patterns characterized by a "rejection of difference." In such instances, there is likely to be poor communication with the adopted child and subsequent disruption in the adoptive relationship. In contrast, "acknowledgment of difference" entails a high problem-solving ability, promotes order and dynamic stability in adoptive family life, and enhances parents' readiness and ability to communicate with their adopted child.

Very little is known about the effect on the telling process of having both biological and adopted children within the same family.

The Sealed Adoption Record Controversy

Some of the complex identity problems adopted children must resolve have begun to receive more attention as adult adoptees in greater numbers have sought access to sealed court records or have returned to adoption agencies for information about their origins. When agencies emphasized to adopting parents the importance of telling children they are adopted, they expected that if this revelation were handled evenly and openly in the atmosphere of a loving home, children would accept adoption and integrate that status into their sense of individual identity. Certainly they did not expect that under those conditions of "telling," children would then or later want to meet their biological parents.

To protect the adoption and enhance children's security, public policy found in state adoption statutes has been to terminate biological parents' rights and responsibilities fully and permanently and transfer those rights and responsibilities to the adoptive parents. Adoption practice has included principles addressed to protecting the anonymity of all parties to the adoption, the confidentiality of agency records and court proceedings, and the sealing of the court record and original birth certificates.

> These principles are based on the assumption that intervention of the natural parents after the child's adoption is not conducive to the child's well-being or to development of the new parent-child relationship. They assume also that the natural parents, having relinquished parental rights and responsibilities, should be free to pursue their own lives without fear of intrusion by the relinquished child or the adoptive parents. (Jones, 1976, p. 2)

Minnesota in 1917 was the first state to develop legislation to protect the adoptive process and the adopted child. The protection of court records from public inspection and the revision of birth certificates were part of these early legislated safeguards. Other states began to pass similar measures. Today, adoption records remain confidential in all but three states—Alabama, Alaska, Kansas (Rosenberg & Pierce, 1987). The prevailing pattern is one in which the court hearings on adoption are not open to the public, and papers and records are closed, to be opened only when good cause is shown, sometimes with the requirement of a court order. Access to the original birth certificate is also restricted, and a new one is issued under the child's new name, with the names of the adoptive parents substituted for those of the biological parents.

All fifty states allow the court to release identifying information if "good cause" is shown. This is true even though all affected parties may not have consented (Rosenberg & Pierce, 1987). Adult adoptees have been able to show good cause when need is demonstrated for medical, genetic, and inheritance information or in instances when denial of access to information would cause psychological disturbance. Courts are more likely to open records when there is adoptive parent support for the action.

In actuality it is agency records that have most of the background information about the birth parents and the adopted child of the kind that adult adoptees are seeking. Traditionally, agency records of birth parents have been witheld from the adult adoptee and the parties to the adoption, although in most states there is no legal requirement to do so (Bell, 1978).

In the past, agencies received inquiries from time to time, but these seemed to be only occasional happenings and little attention was given in the literature to adult adoptees' rights to information about their origins. In the past two or three decades, however, a national movement was initiated by adult adoptees that has gained support from many social workers, lawyers, and other professionals. Jean M. Patton, a social worker and adoptee, founded an organization called Orphan Voyage for the purpose of helping adult adoptees who want to learn more about their background and in some instances locate their biological parents (Patton, 1968). Another such organization is the Adoptees' Liberty Movement Association. The new thrust was given additional support by a study of adult adoptees in Scotland who had searched for additional information about themselves or had wanted to meet their biological parents. It is of interest that Scotland gives adopted persons seventeen years of age or older access to an adopted children's register, which in turn provides a link to the registry of births (Triseliotis, 1973). In the United States, twenty states have established Mutual Voluntary Consent Adoption Registries, which supply a means by which birth parents and adult adoptees can register and indicate their wish to meet. In instances when a match appears, identifying information can be released and a meeting can be arranged. Eight more states have procedures that allow the state or a licensed agency to locate the birth parent and ask for consent to release identifying information to an adult adoptee (Rosenberg & Pierce, 1987).

Secrecy about adoption was fostered by societal attitudes about sexuality, which ostracized women who became pregnant outside of marriage and the children so born. The secrecy of adoption began when the pregnant woman hid herself until after her child was born. (Dukette, 1984, p. 236)

Among adult adoptees who embark on a search of their past, some want only information, for example, the personal, social, or physical characteristics of their biological parents. They may believe such information will add to their understanding of themselves and their sense of identity. Practical considerations, such as obtaining security clearance for a job or obtaining medical history, may also cause adopted persons to seek more information about themselves than they have. Some others want to locate their first parents, meet them, and attempt to establish a relationship with them. In an examination of the sealed record controversy, based on reports from CWLA member agencies, Jones concluded that a reasonable guess of the proportion of returning adult adoptees who actually wanted to locate their biological parents was about 60 percent—not 60 percent of all adult adoptees, but 60 percent of the small proportion who returned to an agency or a court for information (Jones, 1976). The number of adult adoptees who return for information with or without an intent to search, has most likely increased in the years since that study.

What changes in public social policy will occur as a result of the sealed record controversy are still unclear. Some adoptees have sought to challenge the "good cause" requirement by asserting that knowledge of one's biological family is a liberty interest, protected by the Fourteenth Amendment's due process clause. This argument has been rejected in at least five state court actions (Rosenberg & Pierce, 1987).

Agencies began by viewing the issue as a major challenge to their practice even though individual social workers were sympathetic to the desire of adult adoptees who wanted to engage in a search for their past. However, more recently agency practices have been reexamined in a number of areas: (1) the strength of the guarantee of confidentiality that can safely be given to biological and adoptive parents and the ethical considerations involved in such an assurance, given the uncertainty of the future; (2) the kind of history that should be obtained from each biological parent when a child is relinquished for adoption and how it should be given; (3) and the particular implications for situations where children in foster care are adopted by their foster parents, who may have met the biological parents and learned a considerable amount of information about them.

Balancing the rights and privileges of adoptees, biological parents, and adoptive parents depends in large measure on how the issue is cast, given that consensus is lacking about the primacy of the best interests of the adoptee for whom adoption exists. One direction taken is that embodied in a Minnesota law passed in 1977 that has been followed by other states. Upon request of an adult adoptee, the state department of public welfare is mandated to perform a six-month search for the biological parents and to notify them of the adoptee's request. The biological parent has four months to file an affidavit of consent or refusal. Without consent, the birth certificate remains sealed. The adoptee retains the right to petition the court when the parent cannot be located, does not file a consent, or refuses. For persons adopted after passage of the act, as part of the termination of parental rights hearing, biological parents are required to sign a consent or refusal statement. This can be altered at any time thereafter. During the first two years of the new law, 679 requests for information were received. Of the adoptees requesting certain types of information, 25 percent obtained birth certificates, 77 percent received genetic histories, and 42 percent received permission to contact biological parents. In all, 58 percent of the biological parents were located (Weidell, 1980).

POSTLEGAL ADOPTION SERVICES

"One of the areas that require the most change in the new conceptualization of adoption practice is the whole area of the postplacement services" (Hartman, 1984, p. 2). Child welfare practice was long in acknowledging that most adoptive families are different from other families in at least three significant ways: Adoptive parents go through a unique process, often without the kinds of supports and sanctions that accrue to biological parents; adopted children come into the family by means of a unique set of circumstances; and family dynamics are affected differently by adoption than by childbirth (Bourguignon & Watson, 1987, p. 3).

Prior to development of openness in adoption, contact between adoptive parents and the placing agency was time-limited, ending when the legal adoption decree was issued. Although termed "postplacement *supervision*," a worker's visits to the home, particularly in infant adoptions, were often superficial with the worker hesitant to appear interfering, and the adoptive parents unable to mention any problems through fear of losing the child. The agency, having done an extensive home study prior to placement, did not expect problems and tended to assume that all would go well. Writing about adoptive placement in the 1940s, a time when many of the principles and practices of closed adoption were developing, Dorothy Hutchinson differentiated adoption from foster care with its continuing supervision by saying that, after legal adoption, the new parents will "walk alone" (1943, p. 42). As adoptive parents

have been given more opportunities to share their experiences, it is apparent that many new adoptive parents felt the home study was "investigative" and stressful, which intensified their need to show themselves as good parents after the placement, thus reducing their readiness to share with the agency any concerns they might have about their new status.

The movement toward openness in adoption prompted the realization that at different times in the developmental cycle of family life, issues related to adoption will emerge, especially with respect to identity formation. In addition, it was recognized that to achieve adoption for special needs children, ones who are older and have had painful life experiences, ongoing help to the child's new parents would be essential. As a result, adoptive agencies have established postadoption services and have encouraged adoptive families to use them.

The purpose and rationale for postlegal adoptions services has been expressed thus: "Adoption is both a legal event that occurs at a particular moment and a lifelong condition with continuing impact on the lives of the individuals involved. Post-legal adoption services are those available to all the participants in the adoption process (adopted persons, adoptive parents, and birth parents) beyond the point when an adoption is legally finalized" (North American, 1984).

Hartman (1984) has identified certain principles or assumptions that apply to successful postadoption services:

1. Postplacement services recognize that normally, adoptive families from time to time will need help with some of the complex changes in their lives. Such difficulties do not represent failure or a serious problem—only an understandable part of a special life situation.
2. The concept of a "probationary" or "supervisory" period following placement is outmoded and renders families reluctant to share concerns.

3. The changed ethos must extend into the home study period. Heavily evaluative studies and judgmental attitudes on the part of the agency are counterproductive to a sharing and helping relationship. Often the result is defensiveness felt by the adoptive parents which can lead them to perceive their difficulties as caused by aspects of the child's special characteristics or behavior.

4. Family assessment during the home study must be an open and sharing decision-making process with active participation by both the agency and the family.

5. The new conceptualization of postplacement services requires that appropriate services be available as needed and desired by the adoptive parents throughout the child's growing-up years. Services may address the development of the parent–child relationship as well as problems inherent in adoption. (Hartman, 1984, pp. 2–3)

Well-directed adoptive postlegal services provide varied functions (Spencer, 1987). They may:

1. offer workshops designed to help adoptive parents keep abreast of changing practices and controversies that apply to adoption, such as "searches" that result in meetings between adopted late adolescents or adults and birth parents.

2. facilitate the sharing of genetic background information and its implications.

3. provide intermediary services to the adoptive triad members for the purpose of obtaining and exchanging non-identifying information.

4. reach out to triad clients to urge them to give current addresses and updated medical and other information that may be of value to one or another.

5. meet with open-ended support groups on a regular basis for birth parents, adopted

persons, or adoptive persons with the purpose of supplying an opportunity to distinguish expectations from realities, identify concerns and productive ways to address them.

6. provide counseling and go-between services at various times after the parties to adoption have established contact.

7. offer other kinds of individual and family problem-solving counseling.

8. teach coping strategies for transcultural and transracial adopted family members (Spencer, 1987, pp. 156–163).

A reflection of the long-held expectation that adoptive parents would cope well without help after a child's placement is found in a review of parent training programs with respect to reunifications, foster care placements, and adoptive parenting (Berry, 1988). Behavioral parent training in adoption was rare. Those that were located were "exclusively didactic in nature and consist of more information than skills training" (p. 320). The groups had appeared to help adoptive parents "feel better about themselves and the placement but have no demonstrated effect on behavior" (p. 320). Potential problems in adoption were sometimes discussed, but although adoptive placement of older children carries a risk of disruption, none of the programs focused on teaching parenting skills.

Clearly recognized in today's practice is that adoption is a family building process. The development of postlegal services simply represents "an orderly extension of the quest to make adoption a positive experience for all those involved, an attempt to meet the needs of the individuals concerned at whatever point in their lives these may occur" (North American, 1984, p. 2).

An unresolved issue remains, however. "Some argue that even if adoptive families need help, this does not mean that adoption agencies should provide that service when the community has other family service and mental health organizations. Are the parenting problems of adoptive parents so unique that they must be dealt with only by an adoption agency?'' (Cole, 1987, p. 74).

ADOPTION DISRUPTION

Although the large majority of adoptive placements prove to be successful for both children and adopted parents, in some instances and for various reasons a particular placement falls short of expectations. Inability to establish stable family relationships then may result in disruption of the placement.

Adoption disruption (a term more useful than the old one—failed adoption) refers to placements that end with the return of the child to the agency before legal finalization has occurred. The extent of current adoption disruption is of concern in view of the inherent risk that accompanies the present-day commitment to find adoptive homes for older and special needs children.

Disruption rates were low in the 1950s and 1960s when most placements were of *white infants or very young children without handicaps.* Kadushin reviewed studies of over 34,499 such children and found an average disruption rate as low as 1.87 percent (see Table 11.1). Similar studies of 4,443 *special needs children* placed for adoption in the 1970s and 1980s showed an average disruption rate of 11.3 percent (see Table 11.2). In view of differences in questions addressed and the particular variables given attention, rates varied among the different studies. Systematic and reliable information about the rate of disruptions continues to require study.

A first step in understanding adoption disruption and finding a means to reduce it is to identify factors that appear to be linked to it. In reviews of previous studies, Festinger (1986) and Barth and Berry (1988) identified some elements that with some consistency appear to be associated with adoption disruption.

Older children—six years or more—are dis-

TABLE 11.1. Adoption Disruptions: Infant Studies

Study	Agency Auspices	Period Covered by Study	Children Placed	Children Returned to Agency	Disruption Rate
Davis & Douck (1955)	Public	3 years (1951–1953)	396	25	6.3%
Calif. Citizens' Adoptions Comm. (1965)	Public-voluntary	1 year (1962)	4,470	85	1.9%
Kornitzer & Rowe (1968)	Voluntary	1 year (1966)	9,614	109	1.1%
Kornitzer (1968)	Public-voluntary	Unclear	664	15	2.2%
Edmonton, Canada (1969)	Public	2 years (1967–1968)	3,086	43	1.4%
L.A. County Dept. Adoption (1967)	Public	2 years (1965–1966)	4,910	129	2.6%
Lefkowitz (1969)	Voluntary	5 years (1965–1969)	8,040	82	1.0%
Kadushin & Seidl (1971)	Public	8 years (1960–1968)	2,945	85	2.8%
Goldring & Tutleman (1970)	Public	1 year (1968–1969)	2,384	75	3.1%
Total			34,499	648	1.87%

(*Source:* Reprinted with permission of Macmillan Publishing Company from *Child Welfare Services, Fourth Edition* by Alfred Kadushin and Judith A. Martin. Copyright © 1988 by Macmillan Publishing Company.)

TABLE 11.2. Adoption Disruptions: Special Needs Children

Study	Children Placed	Children Returned	Disruption Rate
Children's Home Society of North Carolina (U.S. Congress, 1975)	410	24	8%
Spaulding for Children (Unger, Dwarshuis, & Johnson, 1977)	199	21	10.6%
Ohio Adoption Project (U.S. DHHS, 1980a)	59	8	13.6%
Children in Group Care (Borgman, 1981)	20	9	45%
C.S.R. (1983)	263	20	13%
Wolkend & Kozaruk (1983)	84	5	6%
Spaulding for Children (Boyne et al., 1983)	309	66	21%
Tremitiere (1984)	536	72	13%
Coyne & Brown (1985)	1,588	138	8.7%
Festinger (1986)	897	116	13%
Kagan & Reid (1986)	78	23	29%
Total	4,443	502	11.3%

(*Source:* Reprinted with permission of Macmillan Publishing Company from *Child Welfare Services, Fourth Edition* by Alfred Kadushin and Judith A. Martin. Copyright © 1988 by Macmillan Publishing Company.)

proportionately represented among disruptions. Older age at placement also tends to combine with other factors to increase the risk of disruption—factors such as *behavioral and emotional problems,* the experience of *previous multiple placements* (foster or adoptive), and the likelihood that the older child will make more *challenging demands* on the adoptive family.

Given the higher risk of disruption in older-child placements, adolescents have commonly been little considered for adoption. From their larger survey of older-child adoptions in thirteen counties of northern and central California, Berry and Barth (1990) studied a subsample of adoptive placements of adolescents (mean age 13.9 in 1988). Although adolescents were one-third of the foster care population, they were only 11 percent of the older-child adoptions. The adolescent rate (24 percent) was about double that of all other older-child adoptions (11 percent).

Placement of a group of *siblings* into the same adoptive family also appears to predict adoption disruption. Age and sibling status are connected in that siblings are usually older when placement occurs. The risk of disruption is compounded when a sibling group goes into a home with other children.

Physical, emotional, or cognitive *disabilities* of the placed child also act to increase the risk of disruption. One should not conclude, however, that children who are older, in sibling groups, or have some kind of disability cannot have successful adoptive placements. An adoptive disruption does not necessarily result in continuing impermanence for the child. Some of these children are placed later in other adoptive homes. From 45 to 61 percent of such disruptions eventually result in replacements (Barth & Berry, 1988, pp. 211–212).

Various dimensions of adoptive family life can reduce or increase the risk of disruption. Families where the adoptive parents expect and are prepared to accept behavioral and emotional problems resulting from the stress the child has already experienced and who can be flexible in family roles and rules have a better chance to succeed then others. The degree of adequacy in family system supports and the parents' skill in adaptive problem-solving in some instances can be crucial. Unpredicted events in family life can severely affect the chance of disruption, for example, marital stress, financial difficulties, serious illness of an adoptive parent or of another family member that brings long-term demands on the adoptive family. In such instances, if the new family stability has not yet been established or is tentative, the risk of disruption is keen.

In their work Barth and Berry (1988) addressed some of the ways the children's and the parents' experiences in the child welfare system influenced adoptive outcome. Long time lags between entrance into care and a referral for adoption, followed by another long lag between referral and placement were counterproductive to successful adoption. Disrupting families were found to have sought the agency's help later than was true for stable families, leading to services being offered "too little and too late." Adoptive parents were not always given adequate preparation for the changes to come. Children, in turn, were sometimes not allowed a valid opportunity to express their feelings about a continuing desire for reunification with biological parents or to examine the ambivalence they felt. These omissions contributed to failure of child and adoptive parents to develop reciprocal positive personal exchanges.

Barth and Berry (1988) found social worker characteristics to be generally unrelated to the outcome of the placement. Experience of the social worker did appear to make a difference, especially in high-risk cases. However, conventional child welfare services showed only minimal success in preventing disruption. The social work role was assessed as mainly that of an information resource. As in other studies, Barth and Berry could not clearly identify compelling indicators of "good matches" on the basis of parent or child personality, leading them to state that "the way agencies contribute to the matching process has been overestimated as a contributor to disruption or stability" (pp. 167–168).

Barth and Berry (1988) concluded that "postplacement services were few and generally inadequate to the task of preventing disruption" (p. 153). Significantly, however, the benefit of subsidies to the adoptive parents was clear.

Disruption rates were higher for unsubsidized children than for subsidized children. More adequate and uniform provision of subsidies appeared warranted (pp. 216–217).

Festinger (1986) acknowledged that adoption disruption "is a jarring experience for all involved." She observed that many children in foster care move frequently but such moves "are handled with more equanimity." To expect that disruptions in the adoptive placements of special needs children will not sometimes happen, unjustly leaves adoption workers with a sense of failure. Pursuing homes for children through adoption requires that agencies be ready to take risks. Despite delay in permanency for children after a disrupted adoption placement, "in the long run most of these children do get adopted. . . . Giving all children the opportunity to grow up in families they can call their own necessarily involves an element of calculated risk" (p. 44).

The current quest is not to decide whether older child and special-needs adoptions are disruption-prone, but rather, recognizing their central place in permanency planning, to determine what adoption practices reduce this tendency. (Barth & Berry, 1988, p. 77)

TRENDS AND ISSUES

Open Adoption Controversy

The last two decades have seen the emergence of a controversy around the "search" phenomenon and the development of "openness" in present-day adoption practice. One result has been a recognition that the adoption experience has dimensions that were not acknowledged in closed adoption practice. Two main reasons for the growing controversy have been cited: "First, there is no consensus among adoptive professionals as to what openness or open placement means. Second, the practice of open placement is relatively new and its impact on members of the adoptive triad . . . has not been adequately addressed by research'' (McRoy et al., 1988a, p. 18).

The interest in various degrees of openness is in sharp contrast to the traditional viewpoint that normal well-adjusted individuals, although adopted, would not need nor want to know about their birth parents; the adoptive parents, the ones who raised them and brought them to maturity would be sufficient. But we have learned that in addition to satisfying parenting, adoptees may at some point want access to a wider range of information that will give them a better understanding of themselves. These adoptees are not motivated by idle curiosity; they have specific questions related to their personal identity. Most searches stem from a lack of needed information (McRoy et al., 1988a, p. 7).

Kirk (1981) has extended his "shared fate" theory of adoption and applied it to the institutional arrangements of adoption. In doing so, he sheds some light on why the new openness in adoption came into being. He states: "Given that the adoptive situation at the interpersonal level is objectively different from the situation of the family based on consanguinity, the solidarity of the adoptive family's membership is enhanced when their atypical reality is acknowledged in their daily relationship. . . . In addition . . . the institutional arrangements which were intended to create solid and satisfying new family relationships are not without responsibility for the strains inherent in modern adoptive kinship'' (p. xv).

Adoption, Kirk notes, became the professional preserve of social welfare where the larger adoption kinship patterns went unacknowledged. Agencies showed minimal concern for the continuing internal processes in adoption kinship. Little was done to help adopters consider risk-taking tasks within a framework of "loving acknowledgment of difference." He sees these omissions as based on three aspects of professional organization: (1) a sharing by adoption workers of the values that in adoptive parents led to rejection of difference; (2) well-intended agency practices that in fact reinforced adopters' orientation to rejection of difference;

and (3) the psychodynamic viewpoint that slanted the professional education of case workers away from a capacity to think about the dimensions of social structure. Social work staked its professional right to adoption, Kirk maintains, on certain areas of claimed competence that eventually led to a myopia that insulated professionals from an awareness of their mistakes. Compounding this deficiency was a demographic factor: the majority of adopters were highly mobile socially and geographically, a condition that made it less likely that they would consult the original adoption agency when uncertainties arose in their daily adoptive family life. An organization factor also shielded the adoption agency from an awareness of errors. This factor, Kirk says, was a wall of prestigious professionals that the U.S. Children's Bureau and the Child Welfare League of America put around the agency. This behavior reduced the necessity for agencies to see and hear evidence of their mistakes at work among adoptive families. The ideas and practices of a generation ago are still apparent, for example, in sealed records, amended birth certificates, and the disappearance of adoption as a vital statistic. All of these fostered the current social movement of the adopted (Kirk, 1981).

Dukette (1984) identified some of the changing values in the 1960s that influenced adoptees toward searches and made inevitable the expectation of change in adoption policies and practices. (1) As abortion became more widely used, and as marriage was no longer an absolute condition for an out-of-wedlock mother to keep her child, fewer infants became available for adoption. The birth mother found more leverage in the process of relinquishment and preferences about adoptive parents. (2) The civil rights movement of the 1960s brought about openness in varied ways. Access to one's school records, medical records and to information in other institutions was achieved. Secrecy was associated with discrimination: individuals claimed their civil right to know fully about matters concerning them that others knew. "A lack of trust in institutions and a devaluing of expertise became more prevalent'' (p. 237). (3) Individuals who felt different and isolated in their personal life—gay and lesbian individuals, as well as others who struggled with serious problems that were hard to acknowledge such as drug addiction, began to let their situation be known. Assertiveness training and self-help groups became a means to obtain individual rights. Not unexpectedly, some adopted adults felt the increased openness in society that allowed them to seek information about their birth origins. '' 'Entitlement' came to be a word used in private lives as well as in public policy'' (p. 238). (4) In addition, advances in communication technology simplified the task of finding persons in adoptee searches (Dukette, 1984).

There is considerable acknowledgment that for birth parents and adoptive parents who freely and fully agree to ongoing contact, open adoption has the potential to bring about genuinely satisfying relationships for all concerned. At the same time, questions have been raised as to the problems open adoption can bring and the need for various degrees of openness, and for some birth parents and adoptive parents, availability of some degree of closed adoption. Fears about too rapid policy changes include these: Some families have more than one adopted child; what will it mean in family relationships if one has continuing contact with the birth mother and another does not? What of the risk of birth parents dropping out of the child's life after contacts have been in place? Young birth parents, however conscientiously they try to make the right decisions affecting their child at the time of adoptive planning, cannot foresee or judge future demands on their yet undeveloped capacities and the opportunities or disappointments that may follow. How will the task of helping children to understand the concept of adoption be further complicated by an active role of the birth mother in the child's life? Clearly the problem of role ambiguity is a serious and unresolved one in open adoption (McRoy et al., 1988a).

Some professionals have observed that in discussions of open adoption, few benefits to

the adopting parents are mentioned. There are concerns that because of a deeply felt need for a child, and the stated or unstated requirement in open adoption to satisfy the needs of the birth parents, the adoptive applicants may agree too quickly to arrangements that are proposed that may be to the detriment of their own needs and right to privacy. In addition, to the extent that aspects of "openness" affect adoptive parents' decisions about child rearing, to what extent will normal difficulties in parenting be made more complex in serious and subtle ways? (Kraft et al., 1985a; 1985b).

These and other questions require research to assess the effects on adoption and its outcomes for children and families. It is troubling that much of the discussion of open adoption is based on ideology, anecdotes, and untested presumptions. Whatever the shortcomings of the traditional model of adoption with its emphasis on confidentiality and family privacy, several decades of research have found that adoption has been "tremendously advantageous" for children, with benefits to all parties to adoption that should not be lost (Dukette, 1984, p. 241). Admittedly, traditional adoption was faulty in the limited choices it afforded to adoptees who might want to know more about their birth and biological parents, as well as the limitations in the role assigned the birth parents during the adoptive process. However, Dukette warns of "a tendency now to repeat the mistake of a rigid policy that offered few variations by being equally rigid in the opposite direction" (p. 241).

There are repeated suggestions in the literature that adopting parents and birth parents should be allowed to choose participation in either open or closed adoption. The degree of acceptable and workable openness in any adoption plan is a highly individual matter, reason enough for caution about making drastic policy changes before research has been done.

Still untested but of considerable interest is this observation: "Over time and between groups of children placed through open versus closed adoption procedures, there may be no substantive differences in the eventual adjustments of the children. This appears to be the outcome of earlier dialectical arguments such as within-race versus transracial adoption and two-parent versus single-parent adoptions. . . . There may be no single characteristic that predicts success in adoptions" (Curtis, 1986, p. 443).

Independent Adoptions

Whether independent placements provide sufficient protection for children, compared with agency placements, has not yet been fully answered. In the 1950s and 1960s independent adoption became a matter of keen concern in the child welfare community and prompted several follow-up studies. The rate of success among independently arranged adoptions was found to be greater than had been claimed by critics of nonagency placements.

A frequently cited early evaluation found that better homes for adopted children were arranged by social agencies than by independent placements (Amatruda & Baldwin, 1951). However, the lack of clear reporting of the methodology by which social workers evaluated the homes and the development of the children made the findings of doubtful validity.

Wittenborn's study (1957) found a slightly better outcome for independent placements but the data suggested that independently placed children in the study were younger, freer from physical deviations, and more easily placed, while those with illness, injury, or other complicating conditions had been referred to agencies for placement.

A major investigation of the outcome of independent adoptions (Witmer et al., 1963) was based on a study of 477 children whose adoption had been granted in Florida during the period 1944–1947 and who were between the ages of nine and fifteen years at the time of the study. A matched control group of nonadopted children was drawn from the adopted children's classmates. Psychological tests of the children and home interviews with the adoptive mother pro-

vided the data. Over two-thirds of the homes were rated as fair to excellent—a rate higher than was expected by those most doubtful about the outcome of independent placements. All in all, the rate of success compared reasonably well with that found in outcome studies of agency placements. The much-publicized risks to adopting parents—of receiving a handicapped child and of encountering problems with biological parents—did not turn out to provide major arguments against independent placement.

A more recent study by the CWLA found that while most independent adoptions seemed to fare well, there were more risks for the adoptive parents including "the absence of specific background information on the biological mother and the even more marked absence of information on the biological father's background and his legal status. Some adoptive parents reported exceptionally high costs. In the staff's judgment, some of the adoptions also appeared legally questionable (Meezan et al., 1978b, p. 451).

The study also found that biological mothers often did not receive help in deciding whether to relinquish their parental rights, in exploring other alternatives, or in adjusting to the decision once it was made. Among the recommendations were "a call for preplacement investigation in all independent adoptions; the establishment of fee scales for facilitators involved in the adoption; and the strengthening of statutes concerning the sale of children" (Meezan et al., 1978b, p. 452).

New attention to placement of children for adoption that are arranged apart from a recognized public or private adoption agency has accelerated with a claim that independent adoptions have become "part of an increasingly self-protective institution with its own advocacy groups, its own protocol and its own lawyers" (Mansnerus, 1989, p. 1). Children placed in independent adoptions are most often infants who are sought by urban, college-educated couples who are accustomed to directing their own lives. Frequently they have already approached an adoption agency and looked into foreign adoptions. Disappointed by the lack of assurance of a certain and early infant placement, they see advantages associated with bypassing adoption agencies. By going to a lawyer who is known to arrange adoptive placements, they expect to find a more acceptable reception and to avoid rejection and a long waiting list. In addition, lawyers who specialize in helping prospective parents often give clear instructions as to efforts they can make themselves to find a healthy baby—writing and distributing résumés that include descriptions of their characteristics, their interests and values, photographs of themselves and their homes (a practice used often in open adoptions). The lawyer may also provide a list of newspapers across the country that will accept adoption advertising—illegal in nineteen states (Mansnerus, 1989).

Birth mothers may prefer not to work with an agency out of fear of too much questioning. Or they may seek more financial compensation for expenses than they would receive from an agency. Child welfare professionals, in turn, cite the drawbacks for the birth mother in the lack of counseling and other safeguards that agencies provide. The National Committee for Adoption cites the hazards to some children who are "transferred or actually 'sold' for high fees . . . a black market that actually exists" (1989, p. 170).

The opposition to independent adoptions by many social work and legal professionals who seek better protection for children has led to proposals that all nonrelative adoptions, by use of regulatory power, should be processed by licensed adoption agencies or be accredited by the Council on Accreditation for Services to Children and Families (COA). The Child Welfare League of America and the National Committee for Adoption take that position.

Brieland cautions, however, that "before one responds enthusiastically, it is important to be aware that child welfare staffs are already increasingly overburdened as a result of the passage of child abuse statutes in every state and of the increased urgency in investigating neglect. Protective services have a higher priority than the selection of adoptive parents. If all nonrelative adoptions had to be processed by an agency, many placements would still be made in advance of the home study, and lack of adequate staff could easily lead to superficial adoptive studies. To provide advantages over the status quo, mandatory adoptions through agencies must involve more personnel to do the larger job effectively—a requirement that is not feasible in most states" (Brieland, 1984, p. 77).

Transracial Adoptions

The adoption of children by persons outside the child's racial and cultural identity continues to be controversial. This is so despite consistent findings that transracially adopted young children, preadolescents, and adolescents are in large measure developing well. Studies of such children that have focused on racial awareness, identity, and self-esteem have not amassed findings of serious problems in these areas. Given such consistent findings, researchers and others with varying links to the child welfare system "are beginning to raise serious questions about the appropriateness of curtailing these placements" (Feigelman & Silverman, 1984, p. 601). These questions are often asked in the context of the large numbers of minority children waiting for adoption. The issue has been debated in the Senate Labor and Human Resources Committee with witnesses testifying against policies that discourage transracial adoptions, policies that in their view leave many black and biracial children adrift with no permanent home throughout their growing-up years. Other witnesses challenged the claim that more transracial adoptions would address the problem of waiting children. That form of adoption was said to serve mostly healthy infants and to leave other minority children still waiting in foster care. Agency policies were also cited as a deterrent to black families who want to adopt (*CDF Reports,* 1985). The issue is a complex one, particularly because it is debated on both sides by persons who are seriously concerned about the great need to find adoptive homes for large numbers of minority children who need them.

The issue is complicated further—on the one hand by the growing body of positive findings of the benefits to transracially adopted children and, on the other, by the acceptance by social scientists that such judgments should be based on empirical evidence. However, collecting sound data in family research is difficult and when collected, its quality is often poor. Various factors contribute to these limitations. Grotevant (1988) named these: "(a) family research in general is difficult because multiple individuals in each family must agree to participate; (b) access to recruitment of adoptive families is protected by a layer of social service agencies who take their gatekeeping function seriously; (c) the American tradition of family privacy is very strong and limits access by researchers to families; (d) due to ethical considerations, experimental designs, which require random assignment to conditions but permit the drawing of causal inferences, are not possible; and (e) the rudimentary level of theoretical development concerning adoptive family relationships has limited the sophistication of research questions that have been posed" (Grotevant, 1988,

p. 853). Evaluation of transracial placements is hampered further because clear consensus is lacking about the relative weight to be given to different psychosocial outcomes—racial identity, self-esteem, positive family and peer relationships, progress in schooling, and more. If racial identity is preeminent, drawing conclusions is complicated because "there are no commonly accepted psychometrically tested measures of racial identity" (Grotevant, 1988, p. 854).

Social work problems subjected to research usually seek policy-relevant results. The tendency then is to move too unknowingly to a unidimensional answer. With respect to transracial adoption, the questions might well be reframed to move the child welfare field closer to a strong research basis for the critically important social policy issue that transracial adoption presents. Appropriate questions for study might be these: "For what children and what parents, under what immediate living circumstances, and in what community contexts, could transracial adoption be desirable and beneficial? . . . What are the distinctive needs of transracially adopted children at different developmental levels? What is the process of racial identity development in transracially adopted children?" (Grotevant, 1988, p. 854).

FOR STUDY AND DISCUSSION

1. Debate the merits of this recommended CWLA standard: "Lack of religious affiliation should not prevent consideration of applicants for adoption nor should a mixed faith marriage."

2. What special characteristics of the child, the foster family, and the biological parents should be considered before legal-risk adoption is undertaken? In what ways can the child be helped to understand and participate in the decision that is made?

3. With respect to the sealed-record controversy, formulate reasons that justify (a) the "good cause" requirement and/or (b) the claim that

knowledge of one's biological family is a "liberty" interest.

4. Review the section in the chapter on postlegal adoption services and then answer the question posed there: "Are the parenting problems of adoptive parents so unique that they must be dealt with only by an adoption agency?" Explain your reasoning. Did it lead to an "absolute" answer? If so, are there other special conditions that would allow a more flexible policy?

5. Consider the merits of the position taken by the National Committee for Adoption and the one

taken by Brieland with respect to the issue of independent adoptions. Should all nonrelative adoptions be processed by an adoption agency? If so, how could the obstacles to implementing the policy be overcome? If not, how could the risks that are said to attach to independent placements be reduced?

6. What position do you take on the issue of transracial placement as an alternative adoption practice? State your reasoning on the question and compare it with that of others.

7. Consider and debate with others what you see as the benefits and the risks to open adoptions. On the assumption that some degree of "openness" in adoption practice is here to stay, state and describe a flexible policy that could best serve the needs and preferences of the three parties to the adoption triad.

FOR ADDITIONAL STUDY

Dukette, R. (1984). Value issues in present-day adoptions. *Child Welfare, 63*(3), 233–243.

Festinger, T. (1986). *Necessary risk—A study of adoptions and disrupted adoptive placements.* Washington, DC: Child Welfare League of America.

Kirk, H. D. (1981). *Adoptive kinship. A modern institution in need of reform.* Toronto: Butterworths.

McRoy, R. G., Grotevant, H. D., & White, K. L. (1988). *Openness in adoption. New practices, new issues.* New York: Praeger.

National Committee For Adoption. (1989). *Adoption Factbook, 1989.* Washington, DC: Author.

North American Post-Legal Adoption Committee. (1984). *Model statement. Post-legal adoption services.* St. Paul: Author.

Sachdev, P. (Ed.). (1984). *Adoption: Current issues and trends.* Toronto: Butterworths.

Sorosky, A. D., Baran, A., & Pannor, R. (1989). *The adoption triangle: Sealed or opened records: How they affect adoptees, birth parents, and adoptive parents.* San Antonio: Corona Publishing.

CHAPTER 12

Child Advocacy

But the young, young children, O my brothers,
They are weeping bitterly!
They are weeping in the playtime of the others,
In the country of the free.

Elizabeth Barrett Browning

Chapter Outline

Although the practice of child advocacy has taken new forms in recent years, it has its origins in earlier periods of heightened concern about children. Much has been written and said about child advocacy since the concept was highlighted anew in the social reform climate of the late 1960s. At that time, child advocacy was enthusiastically accepted as an attractive concept "because it combined the promise of needed change with a lack of specificity. . . . Thus child advocacy understandably took many forms and had many sponsors—it was a banner behind which to rally, a funding bandwagon on which to ride, and a gimmick to exploit. But it also represented a series of efforts to cope with children's unmet needs in new ways" (Kahn et al., 1972, p. 9).

Current child advocacy reflects the foundation laid in the programs of Mobilization for Youth (MFY), which introduced child advocacy into the social reform climate of the 1960s. Avoiding psychological theories of delinquency, the MFY sought to open opportunities for low-income youth in juvenile justice, employment, education, and other areas as well (Rothman, 1974). This agency spawned numerous conferences, books and articles, "advocacy" programs, position statements by professional organizations, legislation mandating advocacy activities on behalf of specific target populations, and changes in child welfare curricula. For many professionals and involved citizens of that era, the term "child advocacy" continues to conjure up images of excitement, action, and partisan concern for children and youth.

THE NEED FOR CHILD ADVOCACY

We have seen in previous chapters how children in earlier times were considered to be the property of their parents, who had sole power over them. Parental rights were dominant, and no one was entitled to interfere with the parent-child relationship. Gradually, the state assumed authority to intervene in behalf of the child in selected and specific situations. The doctrine of *parens patriae* was developed and extended to children who were thought to require certain kinds of protection by society, for example, children who were in need of guardianship, or those who were neglected, abused, or abandoned. Organizations, programs, and institutions to serve the special needs of children and their families evolved.

As knowledge about the needs of children increased and as the industrial age placed new demands and constraints on family structure and roles, parents became increasingly dependent on resources outside the family in order to cope with their own lives and with the tasks of rearing children. Yet new knowledge about the needs of children and new standards for their care, protection, and education, even when expressed in law, proved to be difficult to implement in an equitable way. Social structures such as health, education, and welfare systems, the courts and correctional systems, and child care agencies tended to become large and awkward. Barriers arose to the effective use of these insti-

tutions by the very persons they were created to serve. This situation made it increasingly difficult for parents, teachers, social workers, and other members of the helping professions to perform effectively in behalf of children.

As growing numbers of public agencies came to have a part to play in the welfare of children, doubts arose as to whether these helping agencies were always benign and effective. Thus, the institutions, organizations, and goals established to serve children were seen as being part of the problems facing children. Advocacy for children appeared to be the essential next step in society's efforts to provide satisfactory conditions for child development. The transition to advocacy was marked by an awareness that "someone had to regulate the regulators (juvenile courts) or monitor the family substitutes (schools)" (Kahn et al., 1972, p. 32).

The kinds of situations that indicate the need for child advocacy have been discussed in each chapter of this book. Poverty, with all its damaging consequences, is a primary concern for child advocacy. The unfavorable influences of poverty on children too often continue throughout their lives, for example, poor nutrition, inadequate housing—even homelessness, and lack of proper health care at so basic a level as immunizations for preventable childhood diseases and early and continuing prenatal care for pregnant adolescents.

Conditions within the public schools and the system of school–pupil–community relations continue to be another major child advocacy target. The use of corporal punishment, the failure to provide educational programs that succeed in preparing young people for the basic skills that are required for entry into the world of work, the lack of appropriate continuing education for pregnant school-age girls—these are examples of situations that are appropriate for child advocacy. The interlocking problems of migrant agricultural workers—problems of health, education, and opportunity—also call out for the attention of child advocates, as do the high rates of unemployment and lack of opportunity among teenage youth that have reached unprecedented levels and retard their movement toward responsible adulthood.

The juvenile court and programs of correction make up another one of society's institutions that has made the need for a child advocacy system highly visible as found in the application of due process guarantees, the definitions of child neglect, the jailing of children, the presence of sexism and racism in the dispositional alternatives used by the court, the provision of legal representation for individual children in adjudications directly affecting them, and in the entire question of the child as a person before the law. The guardianship of thousands of children is an advocacy issue in view of their lack of a personal relationship with their guardians and the fact that decisions affecting their whole lives are made through layers of bureaucratic process.

Suspicious of state paternalism in the person of teachers, social workers and juvenile court judges, the modern child advocate wants to constrain discretionary power . . . [and] does not trust the state to represent children and instead sees state policies as reflecting a welter of interests, many of which are inconsistent, if not irreconcilable, with the interests of the child. (Mnookin, 1985, p. 56)

Attention must also be paid to issues related to the child welfare system such as the continuing problem of children who, despite the efforts toward "permanency," are adrift in foster care or who wait throughout their childhoods for a permanent home through adoption. Awaiting critical analysis and strong advocacy intervention are highly complex issues reflected in the formal structures that have been established to protect children from abuse and neglect.

Advocacy on behalf of children is needed now as much as it has been in the past. The conservative political attack on social welfare programs in the 1980s included the reduction of

Medicaid, school lunch programs, food stamps, the Women, Infants, and Children (WIC) program, and funds for child welfare services. The initiation of block grants gave the states increased discretion to allocate funds and to set policy affecting children. These decisions are made with reduced funds and strong competition from other welfare groups, as well as those who seek funds for highways and other capital improvements.

All of these situations, and others as well, call attention to the necessity of monitoring legislative, administrative and budgetary processes and, at times, the professional behavior of persons charged by society to act in behalf of children.

Child Advocacy Defined

Some confusion continues as to what child advocacy actually is. As Gilbert and Specht noted: "One finds the word advocacy used to describe consumer education, civil rights, and social protest, referral and brokerage activities, and a big brother program for the developmentally disabled" (1976, p. 288). A nationwide survey of child advocacy found that many programs were little more than traditional services under a new banner (Kahn et al., 1972).

Probably most people interested in the concept would agree with this brief definition: "In a real sense, child advocacy is a social movement directed to the rights of children" (Paul, 1977a, p. 8). However, some concerned people seem to refer to any worthy goal in behalf of children as child advocacy. Some other ideas are more definite but still expansive, for example, this one stemming from the influence of the Joint Commission on Mental Health of Children (1970): "Child advocacy is a planning, coordinating, and monitoring system on each level of government to assert priorities on behalf of children." Kahn et al., in search of baseline data about child advocacy, noted that advocacy systems under this definition had been proposed but were "hard to find" (1972, p. 13). Definitions that are too broad and that do not suggest a specific activity usually fail to draw tangible support. Yet definitions that are too limited may be viewed as constraining, and also fail to gain support.

For the purposes of this discussion, the definition developed by Kahn et al. is sound. Child advocacy is "intervention on behalf of children in relation to those services and institutions that impinge on their lives" (1972, p. 13). This definition was given wide circulation in connection with the authors' baseline study of child advocacy and was endorsed by the National Center for Child Advocacy. However, it too has been criticized as allowing any form of intervention to be labeled child advocacy, since almost all services and institutions in society impinge in some negative way on children's lives (Kutchins & Kutchins, 1978).

In 1981 the Child Welfare League of America defined child advocacy as "the process of sensitizing individuals and groups to the unmet needs of children and to society's obligation to provide positive response to these needs" (p. ix). This definition emphasizes the educational role inherent in all advocacy efforts. But the League also recognized the definitional dilemma by stating: "whether one talks in terms of advocacy, or influencing public social policy, or engaging in social action or promoting institutional change makes no essential difference" (p. 1). It is interesting to note that persons who viewed advocacy as a large part of their work defined it as "intervention on behalf of a client or client groups with an unresponsive system" (Epstein, 1981, p. 8). In short, a precise definition with consensual understanding continues to elude the field, but perhaps such clarity is impossible and unnecessary.

Assumptions Underlying the Concept of Child Advocacy

Whatever definition of child advocacy is used, generally the child advocacy field accepts two basic assumptions particular to the status of children. "First, it is assumed that children are in a state of dependency that leaves them vulnerable to abuse by caretakers" whether intentional or not. Second, "the fulfillment of basic needs is important in childhood to enable their self-actualization and future adult functioning" (Melton, 1983, pp. 1–2).

Writing from the perspective of the highly effective advocacy programs of the Children's Defense Fund, Knitzer further identified some underlying assumptions common to all forms of advocacy (1976).

1. *Advocacy assumes that people have, or ought to have, certain basic rights.* The belief that children should have certain legal rights that society is obligated to observe is intrinsic to child advocacy. Traditionally, however, children have not been regarded as persons under the law. Thus a system of child advocacy requires a reassessment of the legal framework of children's affairs. The matter of child rights is complicated by the need to secure for children the rights that reflect their status as children and their special needs for developmental opportunities.

2. *Advocacy assumes that rights are enforceable by statutes, administration, or judicial procedures.* Statements of child rights that cannot be enforced are useful chiefly as a means of setting goals. Enforceable child rights are essential in view of what has been learned about the effects on children when adults make arbitrary interpretations of what is in their best interests.

> For too long and with severe consequences to children and families, we have relied upon the assumption that adults with power to intervene in the child's life care about children and inevitably make the right decision. (Knitzer, 1976, p. 204)

3. *Advocacy efforts are focused on institutional failures that produce or aggravate individual problems.* This assumption is not intended to imply that the characteristics of individual children or families play no part in their problems or that no need exists for a one-

to-one response to individuals. It does mean that successful strategies of advocacy are focused on the barriers that keep people from getting the help they need—barriers that may appear in administrative procedures, statutory or budgetary constraints, stereotyping by professionals, denial of due process, and decision making based on incomplete or inappropriate information.

4. *Advocacy is inherently political.* As Knitzer (1976) points out, efforts to improve conditions for children have too often been tied to the notion that politics should play no part in matters involving children. Therefore, effective sources of leverage were not used in behalf of children, sources such as the authority of the courts, persuasion by lobbyists, and the power derived from access to information or community organizing.

> Yet change for children is as political as change in any other area, with deeply embedded resistances built into professional practices, national priority preferences, and, indeed, basic concepts about the family. (p. 205)

The problem for child advocates is how to find ways to ensure attention to children's needs by policy makers, elected officials, administrators, and others.

5. *Advocacy is most effective when it is focused on specific issues.* Couching advocacy efforts in terms of the needs of *all* children has been defended by calling attention to the many special-interest groups that already exist, for example, groups concerned with handicapped children, migrant children, or the need for day care, and the fact that these special-interest groups often compete for limited resources. Nevertheless, successful child advocacy efforts for the most part have been directed toward special groups. Knitzer emphasizes, however, that orienting advocacy toward specific issues does not mean ignoring larger issues. For example, advocacy by the Children's Defense Fund in behalf of children suspended from schools was part of a larger effort against racism, for suspended children are disproportionately from racial minorities. Similarly, advocacy in behalf of children in mental hospitals provided a means of raising broader questions about children's mental health services generally.

6. *Advocacy is different from the provision of direct services.* Paul views the distinction between advocacy and service delivery as constituting one of the most pervasive conceptual problems of child advocacy. Maintaining a distinction between the two is made difficult by the tendency of professionals and others concerned with children's needs to think more in terms of provision of services than in terms of accountability, that is, to assume the availability and reliability of what is provided. It is the latter factor—accountability—with which advocacy is concerned.

Paul attempts to clarify the boundaries between the institutional service system, advocacy, and the family system in this way:

> One could think about two major systems of influence that have impact on the lives of children. One is the parenting system and the other is the institutional care-taking and service systems. Both include functions such as caring for, protecting, educating, controlling, and correcting. There is a division of labor and a division of responsibility and authority, either legally specified or socially understood, between these two major forces. The advocacy functions are usually grafted onto the boundary area between them. (Paul, 1977a, pp. 139–140)

Child advocacy, then, is primarily concerned with seeing that existing organizations and services work for children rather than with undertaking to provide another special service. In contrast to the professional service role, the role of a child advocate is partisan. The advocate looks primarily at the needs of children or families and stands by them in a partisan way. The advocate is first and foremost for the child. The professional, in contrast, is to a large extent for all the persons concerned with the problem situation—even the target agency, and tries to bring about a constructive balance in the varying and sometimes conflicting characteristics and needs of the different parties. This does not mean that a professional social worker in a children's service agency cannot take an advocacy stance in behalf of children or groups of children and sometimes go beyond role expectations and conventional procedures to enable individual children or families to secure a necessary service or the observance of their rights. In addition, some child welfare services have added an advocacy unit that performs a separate administrative function.

The term "child welfare" used in the sense of "a children's field encompassing broad areas of concern and activity in behalf of children" does include the child advocacy function. But child welfare as a field of social work practice refers to a specific and limited subsector of the children's field, one that includes characteristic methods, such as protective services or the provision of foster care. Although consultants from other disciplines may be used, child welfare services are provided mainly by social workers. Child advocacy is more likely to be an interdisciplinary endeavor and to rely on a larger proportion of paraprofessionals and users of child welfare services. Helping individual children and their families is the major focus of child welfare professional activities. For example, child welfare agencies, by means of child protective services, attempt to advance the welfare of children by intervening in the parent–child relationship and offering social services or substitute parental care—foster care. In contrast, child advocacy intervenes in the "ecology of the child"—overall societal conditions that critically influence what happens to children and their parents—and the institutions that impinge on children's lives (Kahn et al., 1972, pp. 66–69).

By most definitions child advocacy derives from an ecological point of view. Ecological theory is a theory of interaction. It does not rely on static units of human behavior, which are en-compassed in such labels as "status offender," "emotionally disturbed," "neglected child," and "unmarried mother." Instead, ecological theory is concerned with a dynamic interaction of which a child's behavior is but one part (Paul, 1977c).

For too long professionals have been locked into a point of view that tells them that "trouble" or "problems" are the exclusive property of a child or of his or her parents. Far less frequently has attention been given to the social process of interaction between a child and his or her environment. By "environment" is meant the aggregate of external conditions and influences that affect or control a child's life and development. In addition to the family, such determinants include schools, courts, neighborhoods, hospitals and clinics, and the mass media. Advocacy intervention is focused on the events that have taken place or are taking place between the child and his or her environment and are causing trouble—perhaps even to the point of expulsion from the family or peer group. Child advocacy objectives are not attained by defining the job to be done in terms of either problems of children or problems of the environment of children. Instead, advocacy tasks must be defined in terms of problems that are generated by the interaction between children and their environments—in the exchanges or transactions that take place in those interactions (Paul, 1977c).

Child advocacy, then, searches for solutions addressed to the ongoing interplay between children and their environments. It views children and their environments as a single complex system and seeks to locate children's problems at the point of "misfit" between their needs and characteristics and the characteristics and influence of their environments. The transactions between children and their environments are the immediate focus of child advocacy. A major and early task of advocacy is to locate with accuracy the difficulty in the child-environment transaction (Paul, 1977c).

Case and Class Advocacy

The term "child advocacy" has been used to encompass two different approaches to the rights of children: *case advocacy* and *class advocacy*. Case advocacy is focused on an individual child in order to bring about resolution of some barrier to the child's receiving a needed service or concrete benefit. A child may need a service, but none is given. The needed service may not be available in the community, or is in such short supply as to be unavailable to this particular child at the time it is needed. Sometimes the service exists, but parents do not know how to find and use it. And sometimes children are denied service without any defensible rationale. In other instances, services may be given, but in a form that is seriously inadequate or inappropriate. In situations like these, advocacy action is usually initiated by someone directly concerned with the child—a social worker or other professional, or a paraprofessional, such as a health aide or teacher's aide. Pelosi and coworkers described another type of situation that may lead to child advocacy action (1977, pp. 109–110). A child may be receiving a service or some form of "treatment," but persons close to the child do not like that action even though it is quite legal. An example they cited is one that exists in many public schools: The laws and regulations permit corporal punishment of pupils although many parents and other citizens object to the practice; they hold different values about children and the ways in which they should be treated. Many advocacy situations, Pelosi et al. point out, are not clear-cut. They may not rest on the violation of legally established rights, or on negligence or incompetence of service delivery staff persons, or on the unavailability of a service because it does not exist. The problem may be based on a difference in values between groups of people.

Other situations that invite case advocacy are readily illustrated. For example, a child is unfairly detained in jail, or is inappropriately or unfairly placed outside the mainstream of the school learning structure, or is denied an adoptive home because no one in the foster care system has initiated or followed through on a positively oriented review of his or her suitability for adoption, or is repeatedly suspended from school without a hearing by school personnel to determine whether the child is persisting in the offending behavior for reasons over which he or she has little or no control.

Sometimes problems like these are resolved by an advocate on a one-to-one basis as similar situations occur and recur. But with the development of class advocacy, these situations more often lead the advocate to seek change that will advance fair and appropriate treatment for a group of children. For example, the advocate may involve a citizen's group in examining the conditions that lead to children's being held in the community's jails, or with a group of parents the advocate may endeavor to bring change in school practices in relation to suspensions or curriculum placement. These actions may not be adversarial. They may rather be aimed at supporting school or court personnel in the development of corrective measures to advance generally approved goals for children. This approach is intended to "help the system to see how its own purposes are being thwarted by its own policies and practices, and then support the system in developing alternatives that will enhance rather than inhibit achieving the system's own goals" (Riley, 1971, p. 378).

Members of a "class" may sue as representative parties on behalf of all but only if: (1) the class is so numerous that to join all members in the court action is impracticable; (2) the problem common to the class predominates over any problem affecting only individual members; (3) claims of the representative members are typical of the claims of the class; and (4) the representative members will fairly and adequately protect the interests of the class (Black, 1979, p. 226).

By Paul's definition, class advocacy clearly "is issue oriented, not individual oriented. It focuses on a problem, not on a person. It has as its goal a common need, not a unique need; what is similar, not what is different." Further, in considering the differences between case advocacy and class advocacy, Paul takes note of a myth about class advocacy—"the assumption that the individual is represented along with other individuals. The fact is, the individual is represented only in terms of the particular need(s) he or she shares with the class or group" (1977c, p. 28).

Action on behalf of a class of persons is primarily for the purpose of efficiency. Progress on a case-by-case basis takes too long and does not necessarily bring change for others. Nor does case advocacy provide the political leverage that helps to bring change for children generally in related problem areas. Nevertheless, efficiency and political leverage are by no means the central reason for child advocacy. Protecting the rights of the individual child is the central purpose of all child advocacy efforts. Although for child advocacy to be successful, individual needs must often be grouped and classified, the needs and the rights of the individual are the heart of advocacy at any level and for any group of persons. Advocacy of the individual and class advocacy are inseparably related.

BACKGROUND OF THE CURRENT INTEREST IN CHILD ADVOCACY

Influences of the 1960s

Among the forces that helped to produce interest in child advocacy were the new visibility given to poverty and delinquency in the 1960s and the government programs intended to reduce the number of children and families living under seriously inadequate economic conditions. From the Mobilization for Youth project came the concept of "client advocacy," defined as intervention "on behalf of a client with a public agency to secure an entitlement or right which has been obscured or denied" (Cloward & Elman, 1967, p. 267). Mobilization for Youth was an inner-city youth project developed by a multidisciplinary social agency on New York City's Lower East Side. Its focus was on the need for broad social, economic, and institutional reform. Delinquency was viewed as the result of a lack of congruence between a young person's aspirations and opportunities. A range of services was offered—employment, legal, educational, psychological, and social.

The community action programs under the Economic Opportunity Act were largely modeled on the Mobilization for Youth experience. The "War on Poverty" launched by the Economic Opportunity Act produced the principle of "maximum feasible participation" on the part of clients affected by the new antipoverty programs, challenged the conventional and sometimes complacent service delivery methods, and persistently questioned the processes that led to institutional decisions about poor families and children.

Another set of influences that moved the idea of child advocacy forward came from attention to problems in public school education. Under such provocative titles as *Death at an Early Age, How Children Fail,* and *Crisis in the Classroom,* the 1960s brought a stream of studies, evaluations, and opinions about inadequate educational facilities and the failure of the schools to educate children, especially children of the poor and children with special needs, for example, physically and mentally handicapped children and children in need of bilingual education (Holt, 1964; Kozol, 1967; Silberman, 1971). Out of the controversy came attempts to create new approaches to education by modifying school conditions and practices. These modifications included changes in curricula, school decentralization with more community and neighborhood control, performance contracting, the development of free schools and other alternative educational programs from which parents and/or pupils could choose the form of education most acceptable to them, the establishment of pupils' rights and grievance procedures, and mechanisms for moving children out of separate special-education programs into regular school programs.

Successful demonstrations in the late 1960s of the gains to be made for children through the use of the judicial system constituted another influence on the development of the child advocacy movement. The Kent and Gault decisions affirmed due process rights of juveniles alleged to be delinquent and, in doing so, fostered questions still under debate about the rights of neglected and abused children under the law. A significant court case in Pennsylvania questioned the constitutionality of school policies that resulted in the exclusion of handicapped children (Pennsylvania Association, 1971). Similar suits followed and eventually played an important part in congressional enactment of the Education for All Handicapped Children Act of 1975. Another major litigation challenged conditions in juvenile correctional institutions and resulted not only in an order for changes in such institutions but also in the creation of a community-based system of alternative forms of care and treatment (*Morales v. Turman,* 1974). These and other demonstrations of ways in which litigation can be used to advance child rights not only led to change in service procedures and methods but also helped to establish important principles inherent in the concept and practice of child advocacy.

Another development begun in the 1960s was also related to the emergence of interest in child advocacy. Ralph Nader's consumer advocacy efforts have been focused on the obligations of corporations to respond to consumer interests and on the failure of government regulatory authorities to monitor the activities of industry adequately. Knitzer pointed out that, unlike the participatory model of antipoverty activists, Nader's strategies are "overtly elitist, both in choice of staff and in the processes by which issues are selected." Nevertheless, she acknowledged, Nader and his staff have been highly successful in researching and focusing attention on systemic problems—an accomplishment that has not been lost on proponents of child advocacy (Knitzer, 1976, p. 207).

ADVOCACY EXEMPLARS: PAST AND PRESENT

Illustrations of avant-garde child advocacy programs are found in the records of the U.S. Children's Bureau in the years between the Progressive era and the enactment of the Social Security Act in 1935, and in the contemporary Children's Defense Fund. In each instance the successful leadership is credited to far-thinking and daring women committed to social justice for women, children, and young families. Julia Lathrop was the first and Grace Abbott the second chief of the Children's Bureau; Marian Wright Edelman is the founder and president of the Children's Defense Fund. All three have records of effective definition of problems that require social action; development and maintenance of diverse constituencies; building and supporting coalitions; conceptualizing and implementing systematic studies of the problem and the forces affecting it; disseminating findings in strategic forums; astutely recognizing political factors that control the targeted problem; and applying sound judgment as to where and when pressure can be effective.

The Children's Bureau

Advocacy for the right of women to safety in child-bearing and the reduction of infant deaths was one of the first causes that Julia Lathrop addressed when she was appointed by the president as chief of the newly established Children's Bureau in 1913. A major concern that influenced Congress to establish the Children's Bureau was awareness of the very large number of babies who died in their first year of life. To the Progressive reformers, infant deaths represented an enormous and needless loss of human resources and a threat to the value placed on life itself. Yet it was not known just how many infants died each year; the United States, unlike other civilized countries, had no uniform laws for the registration of births and deaths. Investigating infant deaths through field studies across the country and promoting birth registration laws among the states became immediate priorities for the Children's Bureau (Costin, 1983).

With the intent to achieve federal maternity and infancy legislation, Julia Lathrop set about laying a foundation of facts about why so many babies died in their first year and why so many mothers either died in childbirth or suffered long periods of invalidism following it. The continuing health of mothers was critical to the kind of care children received. Given the prevalence of unsafe milk supplies, whether mothers were well enough to breast-feed their infants successfully was often crucial to their survival. Findings from the scientifically based infant mortality studies that Lathrop instigated led her into investigation of maternity and the circumstances under which women in all parts of the country gave birth. The findings were striking.

"Childbirth in 1913 was a greater hazard to the lives of women of childbearing age than any disease except tuberculosis, with a death rate almost twice as high in the black as in the white population. . . . The majority of maternal deaths was caused by puerperal septicemia commonly called childbed fever. By 1875 Joseph Lister's methods of antisepsis were being applied in some hospitals to prevent infections of childbirth, and, where this was accomplished, maternal deaths dropped enormously. Yet across America, where these scientific principles were not known or not applied, women continued to lose their lives to puerperal septicemia well into the twentieth century" (Costin, 1983, p. 131). Studies of the states that had some system of birth registration showed no demonstrable decrease in death rates from childbirth and childbed fever between the years 1900 and 1913—the same years that marked great gains in control of other preventable diseases—typhoid, diptheria, and tuberculosis (Meigs, 1917, p. 7).

"Why were the conditions that led to maternal and infant deaths so generally ignored? From its studies the Children's Bureau concluded that childbirth had been shrouded with an age-long mist of prejudice, ignorance, and fatalism. If a mother or baby died, it was the will of God, or in the eyes of others an unavoidable accident. Principles of proper hygiene during pregnancy and childbirth were not 'public property' but almost exclusively the possession of physicians" (Costin, 1983, p. 132). Yet obstetrics and pediatrics were not well-developed specializations, as reflected in the curricula of many medical schools (Meigs, 1917).

In addition, inaccessibility to safe medical help in many areas of the United states was a strong factor in the low standards of prenatal and early infancy care—for example, in the inner cities, in isolated homes of the mountains of Appalachia, and in the vast stretches of ranch land in the West where a woman ready for labor could rely only on a neighbor or husband and often had to deliver the baby herself, alone. Black midwives in the South and immigrant midwives in the inner cities provided the only care available. In contrast to the European system of licensed midwives educated for their work, most in this country were completely untrained and relied mainly on a range of superstitious practices to aid in the baby's delivery. Significant and troubling as well was the economic factor—poverty and its relationship to the loss of infant life—a finding that appeared in the first studies of the Children's Bureau and was repeatedly identified in successive studies (Costin, 1983).

Wide dissemination of findings of the Children's Bureau studies, combined with women's awareness of their power attested to by the suffrage amendment, made passage of maternity and infancy legislation a central and feasible goal. Jeannette Rankin introduced the first bill into Congress in 1918. A powerful and persistent lobby of women fought for its enactment. In addition, Julia Lathrop's and Grace Abbott's carefully planned and executed regional meetings in eight cities across the country, which constituted the 1919 Conference on Standards of Child Welfare, enlisted active participation of millions of women representing almost all the varied woman's organizations, adding substantially to the formal constituencies on which the Children's Bureau could call. Women deluged Congress with letters and telegrams, not only from organized feminist groups, but also from women acting individually who had become aware and vocal about the oppressed status of their sex in pregnancy and childbirth, and the widespread hazards for their babies. Support also came from influential men who had known Julia Lathrop and Grace Abbott during their former years of residency in Jane Addams' Hull-House and had often facilitated their efforts for various social justice causes.

Open opposition to the bill emerged as well and it continued undiminished and often strident all through the 1920s. The forces against the Sheppard-Towner bill were armed to protect special interests—states' rights, a conservative fiscal policy, anti-woman suffrage, fear of "leftist" ideologies that would destroy the privacy of the family, and the domain of the medical profession. The most dangerous threat to the maternity and infancy legislation came from the Public Health Service, concerned about proper jurisdictional boundaries of health work with the federal government, and from the American Medical Association and state medical societies who feared expanded governmental influence over medical practice—the specter of "socialized medicine."

The Maternity and Infancy Protection legislation (termed the Sheppard-Towner Act) became law in late 1921. By then Grace Abbott was bureau chief and charged with heavy responsibility in administering the act. To move toward the ultimate goal of the new legislation—to reduce the incidence of maternity and infant mortality and to promote the health of mothers and babies—the Sheppard-Towner Act provided for federal matching grants to the states, a daring step in its time, one that rested on a single precedent in the Smith-Lever Act of 1914 for agricul-

tural extension work. Abbott's first task was to secure the cooperation of the states by engaging trust and honest cooperation with state and local officials and helping them with the development of individual "state plans." Despite the diversity among states, all showed an intent to bring about better care for infants by teaching mothers, better care for women by informing them about the need for individual care during pregnancy and childbirth, and more accessible care for women and babies by bringing about more widespread health facilities. As a result prenatal and health conferences conducted by a physician and nurse reached many women in thousands of counties; these were held in churches, schoolrooms, grocery stores or homes—wherever space was available. The Children's Bureau offered the states various innovative ways to reach mothers with simple but scientifically correct instructions about pregnancy, childbirth, the care of the unborn child, and infant care following birth.

The new program did not attempt to provide birth control methods as an essential step for women to gain control of their own bodies. The extent to which societal attitudes constricted the Children's Bureau's maternity and infancy work in matters of contraception was evident in the refusal of some states to show the Children's Bureau film "Well Born" because its general theme was held to be included in those prohibited by the censorship law. Implacable opposition had endangered the enactment of Sheppard-Towner by claiming that it was a measure intended to promote the use of contraception. Julia Lathrop and Grace Abbott were politically astute and knew that it was too early to sustain the principle of public money for birth control (Costin, 1983, p. 176).

When the maternity and infancy legislation came up for extension by Congress in 1926, the constituencies that had grown out of the 1919 Conference fought successfully for it once more, as they did again in 1929. The Act was allowed to lapse in 1929 in the face of President Hoover's preference for voluntary charity and a reluctance to act against the Public Health Service. However, proponents did not relinquish their goal, even as the Great Depression brought many new claims upon revenues. Their continued support was evident in their unyielding support at the 1930 White House Conference on Child Health and Protection for the concept of a "whole program" of child welfare. In 1935 the astute work of Grace Abbott, Katharine Lenroot, and Martha Eliot brought about the inclusion of maternal and child health provisions in the Social Security Act of 1935 (Costin, 1983).

The Children's Defense Fund

Following the new surge of advocacy in the 1960s, attempts were made to develop national child advocacy organizations, most of which had limited success (Steiner, 1976). One that has survived as an effective and dynamic advocacy unit is the Children's Defense Fund, a nonprofit organization that is committed to long-range systematic advocacy to bring about reforms in behalf of children. Marian Wright Edelman, who founded the organization in 1973 and has provided its leadership since then, is recognized as a dynamic and highly effective advocate for children in the complex and competitive arena where social policies and legislation are influenced.

The route to Edelman's involvement in advocacy for children is an interesting one. As a college student in the South, she had planned to continue with graduate work in Russian Studies as preparation for foreign service. In her senior year, however, she became involved in the early 1960s civil rights movement and its student protest actions, which influenced her to change her goal to one of securing a law degree. When her study was completed, she was awarded an internship by the NAACP Legal Defense and Educational Fund, intended to encourage young lawyers to work in the South. She chose to fulfill her internship in Jackson, Mississippi and

opened a legal office there to support civil rights efforts (Tomkins, 1989).

The summer of 1964 brought thousands of white students from northern universities into Mississippi to carry out a black voter registration project throughout the State. Edelman was caught up in using her legal skills to assist those many civil rights workers who were beaten and jailed by the obdurate proponents of the white power structure. It was a highly emotional and physically exhausting time. In retrospect Edelman stated that the experience had required her "to learn how to get my emotions out of the way in order to function more effectively" (Tomkins, 1989, p. 62).

Edelman became interested in community organization as a means to change Mississippi and recognized an opportunity in President Johnson's War on Poverty, specifically in its Head Start program designed to provide education, nutritional, and health services to preschool children from poor families. The State of Mississippi chose not to apply for federal Head Start funds. To make up for the lost opportunity, a small group of public, private and church organizations formed the Child Development Group of Mississippi (CDGM). Edelman was an influential board member. The group applied for and received federal Head Start funds of $1.5 million, which made possible programs for 20,000 children in the first year and created 2,500 jobs. "The program established centers in small communities throughout the state, where local poor people, most of them black . . . were encouraged to elect their own C.D.G.M. representatives, choose the teachers, and have a voice in everything that went on. More than any other Head Start project in the nation, C.D.G.M. changed the expectations of the poor people it served—helped them to feel like active participants in the social contract. In that way, it became a major and somewhat revolutionary agency for social change" (Tomkins, 1989, p. 63).

Edelman recognized the eventual necessity to find a way to affect not only state policy but federal policy as well. She sought and obtained a Field Foundation grant and in 1968 established a Washington, DC, based organization—the Washington Research Project—with an intent to monitor a variety of federal level activities and influence change by research and dissemination of findings. This experience demonstrated the necessity to set priorities and specific goals if one sought the attention of policy makers. "The country was tired of the concerns of the sixties. When you talked about poor people or black people, you faced a shrinking audience" (Tomkins, 1989, p. 67). Carefully defined goals in relation to children and their unmet needs seemed to her an effective focus for broadening the base and building a coalition for social change. She sought to cut through race and class barriers by addressing the needs of children throughout the country. In 1973 she founded the Children's Defense Fund (CDF).

"What scares me is that today people don't have the sense that they can struggle and change things. In the sixties, in Mississippi, it just never occurred to us that we weren't going to win. We always had the feeling that there was something we could do, and that there was hope." (Tomkins, 1989, p. 74, quoting Marian Wright Edelman)

The CDF set out to protect effective programs already in existence and work for new programs that would emphasize parental involvement and community change. The selection of targets for reform activity was made on the premise that effective advocacy must be specialized in contrast to global approaches to change, and that the issues should be ones that affect large numbers of children, that are easily understood by the public, that are subject to attacks at local, state, and federal levels, and that give promise of being affected by a combination of strategies.

The early issues the CDF chose to pursue included: (1) the exclusion of children from school, (2) classification and treatment of children with special needs, (3) the use of children in medical (particularly drug) research and experimentation, (4) the child's right to privacy in the face of computerization and data banks, (5) reform of the juvenile justice system, (6) child development and child care, and (7) children in foster care (Beck & Butler, 1974). As time went on, other concerns have been addressed by investigations of child neglect and abuse, homelessness, and teenage pregnancy and parenting. The wide dissemination of findings from CDF studies by means of publications, testimony before congressional committees, and presentations in a variety of public forums have been highly effective in securing interest and action for change.

Even though the success of the CDF has rested in large measure on the particular talents of Edelman, its staffing pattern and its in-depth strength are also crucial. Staff members from various disciplines have been able to use their specialized knowledge in a unified approach to change. They serve as litigators, researchers, and federal administrative monitors. Community liaison people are also important in maintaining a constituency and in helping to bridge the gap between people in local communities and advocates at the federal level.

On the assumption that some groups who may not support a general effort may come together around a children's issue that affects their special interests, the CDF relies on specialized coalition building as a primary strategy. Issues for reform activity are selected not only for their importance to children and families but also for their potential for building coalitions and constituencies. Other specialized strategies and activities include litigation, drafting and pushing legislation, monitoring administrative agencies, providing public education, and organizing local groups who work with children and offering them technical support (Steiner, 1976).

FUNDAMENTAL COMPONENTS OF CHILD ADVOCACY

Child advocacy projects vary in significant ways. Within the diversity, however, there appear to be features that are fundamental to all projects. The following components will be discussed: auspices, sanction for intervention, target selection, and basic tasks, strategies, and techniques.

Auspices

The question of auspices for a child advocacy program is a significant one. Auspices determine certain basic characteristics of a project: who authorizes it, who pays for it, and who runs it, that is, the balance between citizen and professional participation. Auspices to a large extent determine the "degree of freedom" a child advocate has to take risks and push against resistance to change.

Early debate about who should authorize and fund child advocacy centered on the question of whether child advocacy should be separate from any governmental system to avoid the inhibitions that might result from risks in challenging high-level officials. But private funding can also pose constraints. Consider this example cited by Knitzer—that of a child advocacy program run by a local voluntary agency receiving funds from the United Way: "The child advocates may have difficulty focusing community attention on children excluded from schools if the United Way Board includes several school officials who have publicly denied the problem." In practice, the necessity of locating and competing for funds has meant that both public and private funds have been used for child advocacy projects (Knitzer, 1976, pp. 213–214).

As child advocacy has developed, advocacy projects have come to include these types, classified according to their auspices: (1) projects authorized and paid for by a governmental body, for example, county councils or commissions made up of citizens and mandated by a county government to serve as an adviser on children's needs; (2) projects authorized and operated within a governmental body, often at the state level, with staff members who are employees of government, for example, the South Carolina Office of Child Advocacy, which is responsible to the governor; (3) projects independent of governmental auspices and supported by, and part of, preexisting private organizations, for example, the Child Advocacy Program of the Child and Family Services of New Hampshire, which, as a component of a private child and family agency, serves as a catalyst for change in behalf of children; and (4) projects independent of any government or preexisting private organization and often funded by private foundations, for example, the Children's Defense Fund, or projects funded by memberships or other forms of individual contributions.

The auspices of a project can be a crucial determinant of what can be undertaken and accomplished by child advocacy. But, as Knitzer pointed out, any advocacy effort involves risks, and important as the auspices are, the energy, commitment, and political know-how of the advocates are equally important.

Who Is the Advocate?

The question of "who is best equipped to be an advocate for children" continues to be debated. The last twenty years have witnessed proposals for a wide range of professionals to be involved, including lawyers, social workers, psychologists, physicians, and urban planners. Similar involvement has been advanced by the scientific community for sociologists, anthropologists, community psychologists, and a range of "hard" scientists. The scientist-as-advocate position is based on a belief that science is not a neutral activity and the expertise of such people should be used on behalf of disadvantaged groups (Weber & McCall, 1978).

Others have argued for a more limited role

for professionals. In fact, the renewed interest in child advocacy was largely based on a mistrust of professionals and the organizations they operate. The fear was that professionally directed advocacy efforts would be weighted more toward professional self-interest than toward the needs of children. This has led to a demand for a significant degree of citizen and paraprofessional participation in advocacy projects.

The debate largely centers on the issue of "degrees of freedom" mentioned earlier. In short, the advocate must have a degree of freedom that will not interfere with the commitment to children or make the advocate vulnerable to cooptation or negative sanctions. Professionals are often viewed as having conflicting loyalties which do not allow such freedom. As Davidson and Rapp note:

> One source of restriction is the interaction between formal and informal processes—that is incompatible loyalties; threats of being fired, sanctioned, or not promoted; responses to existing norms, relationships, procedures, channels. Responsibilities to an advocate's career, to his family and friends, limit the commitment and the range of strategies to be considered. In most segments of society, conformity and adherence to established procedures are rewarded. (1976, pp. 225–233)

On the other hand, the degree of freedom possessed by parents, citizens, college students, and older youth acting as their own advocates can be attenuated by a lack of skills and expertise.

In many cases, an effective advocacy effort involves multiple groups of professionals, scholars, citizens, and the youth themselves. Many advocacy efforts are complex, which require a variety of roles to be filled depending on the situation. Successful child advocacy programs have employed, in various configurations, different kinds of personnel, including college students, social scientists, parents, citizens, lawyers, and other professionals. There is obviously not a single answer. What is most clear, however, is that the welfare of children is best served

when increased numbers of people from all stations of life become actively involved.

While much of the literature is devoted to recommendations concerning who *should* be the advocates, little attention has been paid to people who currently *are* advocates. A recent study by Epstein (1981), although not limited to child advocates, found that such people had an unusual degree of commitment that was often based on personal experience, were relatively young (under thirty), and were susceptible to burnout resulting from internal organizational obstacles. The majority of the respondents had not earned a master's degree.

Sanction for the Right to Intervene

Child advocacy requires sanction. Responsible child advocacy means that persons who attempt to intervene in society's institutions must be sure that their assertive or adversarial stance is justified.

In view of all that has been said about the injustice to children and the unmet needs for social services, one may well question why individuals should be required to justify their right to try to improve the status of children. But when an advocacy group decides that an individual agency or institution is not responding adequately to the children for whom it carries responsibility, then that advocacy group is usually attempting to bring about some significant change in an institution or agency, for example, to make the target agency more flexible in its approach to child needs, to increase budget allocations, to undertake new programs, or to reassign control of programs.

> In short, *substantial changes may be sought or demanded* in the way professionals work, resources are deployed, or organizations make their decisions. The child advocate . . . challenges, interferes in, or demands change when—on the face of it—no one is necessarily departing from precedent, standard practice, or mission. Thus the issue of sanction, right to intervene,

and reference points in choosing targets must be faced in child advocacy because a practitioner, a citizen, or an organization (with either public or voluntary funding) is challenging the domain of other practitioners, citizens, and organizations. (Kahn et al., 1972, pp. 69–70)

But on what basis can child advocates establish their right to intervene? Kahn and co-workers (1972) gave the following guidelines for validating the right to advocate (pp. 70–75):

1. A sanction for child advocacy exists when children have justifiable rights, that is, "legislatively specified benefits for which administrative discretion is quite circumscribed and which can be adjudicated in the courts when administrative agencies do not deliver." In such instances there is a clear-cut entitlement to a benefit or a specific service, for example, survivors' benefits under Social Security, or an appropriate educational program in the least restrictive environment for a handicapped child. In such cases, the child advocate's sanction to act is clear-cut.

Other instances in which the right to advocate is easily recognized include those where there is strong indication that some children or families are being treated differently from others in a similar situation, perhaps because agencies and personnel are ignoring their own policies and procedures, or are acting carelessly or in a discriminatory way. For example, the right to advocate is clear if a children's agency mandated by law to receive and investigate all reports of child abuse and neglect attempts to manage a heavy work load by deciding to respond to reports of neglect only when those reports carry an indication of physical abuse as well, or if a juvenile court makes sure that middle- and upper-income parents are present and informed of their right to counsel when hearings affecting them and their children are held, but fails to do the same for parents who are very poor.

2. A sanction for child advocacy exists when the effort is intended to expand the boundaries of legally governed child rights. For example, it is generally held that the parent–child relationship remains intact with parental rights primary unless serious abuse or neglect or unfitness on the part of parents is established. But a question arises as to whether continued state intervention is justified if it is merely an exchange of governmental neglect for parental neglect. If a child's parents make the difficult but often necessary decision to institutionalize their child and then only a simple regime of enforced custodial care is given—not treatment that is appropriate and adequate in light of present knowledge—then the issue of a right to treatment emerges.

In situations like these, advocates for children may choose to work for an extension of child rights beyond what is already clearly established in law. Sometimes the sanction to do so rests on a series of lower court decisions or inconclusive actions, or simply on statements of some authoritative body that has spoken out on the issue.

It lies within our reach, before the end of the twentieth century, dramatically to improve the early lives of several million American children growing up at grave risk. We can substantially improve the odds that they will become healthy, sturdy, and productive adults, participants in a twenty-first century America whose aspiration they will share. The cycle of disadvantage that has seemed so intractable can be broken. (Schorr, 1988, p. 291)

A class action suit—*Wyatt v. Stickney* (1972)—is significant in relation to the question of whether mentally ill or mentally retarded children can be held in institutions where there is continued failure to provide suitable or adequate treatment. The decision, in effect, was on the side of the right to treatment and took the position that a lack of staff or facilities is not a sufficient reason to justify continued institutionalization without adequate and appropriate treatment. A later case heard in the United States Supreme Court did not explicitly state a constitutional right to treatment but did imply that involuntarily committed mental patients who pose no danger to themselves or others have a right to either treatment or release (*O'Connor v. Donaldson,* 1975). In view of the Supreme Court's reluctance to be more explicit, the Wyatt case can be expected to serve as a sanction for advocates to continue to develop a "right to treatment" (Brieland & Lemmon, 1985, p. 523).

3. A sanction for child advocacy may exist even when no specific right or statement of principle appears in law, but in such instances validating the right to intervene is more difficult. Child advocacy in its extralegal forms is most needed "at the cutting edge of the process of evolving and institutionalizing norms and rights" (Kahn et al., 1972, p. 73). Because the issues are likely to be less clear-cut and the proposed solutions less fully demonstrated and evaluated, the advocate is more subject to challenge.

Yet the right to intervene can be validated in a number of ways, which Kahn et al. identified: (1) Available professional knowledge and expertise about dangers to child development may provide backing for child advocacy. (2) The joining of knowledge and values may bring about agreement on a "social minimum" that finds support in professional and community norms and thus gives validity to the child advocacy effort. (3) Sometimes groups such as parents of disadvantaged or handicapped children articulate their own needs, and in doing so provide a sanction for child advocacy. Even though this sanction rests on self-definition and personal experience, it is often enough for advocacy to proceed. (4) Sometimes the view people have of society, social justice, and acceptable priorities in the use of resources leads them to study social indicators of the status of children and to collect data about families and children in relation to such critical factors as school attendance and achievement, health and illness,

and nutrition. Their analysis of such data then becomes a sanction for child advocacy.

Selecting the Target for Advocacy

In some child advocacy projects, the target is only one system, for example, the school system, and the advocacy group attempts to deal with a range of school-related problems, for example, suspension, corporal punishment, education for handicapped children, and the use of drugs for control of pupil behavior. Other projects may at various times attack issues involving a number of agencies or institutions that impinge on children's lives. Often a project that starts out with only one institution as the target begins to uncover negative effects of other institutions on children, and so its advocacy efforts are expanded. For example, dealing with advocacy issues in a public school often raises questions about the mental health system, and attention to the mental health system may lead in turn to concern about the juvenile justice system.

Whether the project takes a single-system or a multiple-system approach requires careful decision making. For geographic areas with dense populations and large numbers of children affected by one system, Knitzer found that

> the realities point to a single system project. This is true because effective advocacy demands in-depth knowledge of the workings of a system. Moreover, an advocacy project directed toward one system provides a visibility that may hasten the process by which the advocate becomes a voice in the formulation of future policies and practices. In contrast, when the abuses to children are spread over several systems, and the children are spread over a wide geographic area, a single system focus will limit the advocate's ability to respond to problems as they surface. (1976, pp. 212–213)

Whatever institution becomes the target for child advocacy, it is seldom that the entire system is the target. Rather, selected aspects of the school, court, mental health, or child welfare system become the target, or "whatever is seen as the central or most accessible locus of decision-making" in relation to the particular problems or issues chosen for advocacy (Kahn et al., 1972, p. 98). As Kahn et al. determined, the target may be any one of the following: policy, administrative procedures, specific personnel, budgets, legislation, and political action (pp. 76–78).

Policy: Class advocacy can focus on a broad category of policy in which the advocate undertakes to change the character of a program, for example, the matter of a fee schedule for service, the question of whether the program is to be segregated by sex or race, or the question of whether foster parents are to be encouraged to adopt children in their care.

Administrative procedures: When the focus is on administrative procedures, it is the way in which policy is carried out that is the focus rather than the overall policy per se. For example, if parents are encouraged to visit their children in foster care, may they do so in a setting of their choosing, or must it be in the foster home or agency office? When it is recognized that isolation from the community is undesirable, will the state agree to close large institutions and place teenagers in community-based residence?

Specific personnel: Sometimes the focus of advocacy is on specific staff members of agencies or institutions when their performance raises questions of professional ethics or general competence.

Budgets: Agency budgets are a significant focus for child advocacy. For example, while Congress may pass legislation for a program favorable to children, advocacy may be needed to obtain an adequate appropriation of funds. Citizens' groups may find it necessary to publicize state and local governmental agency budgets and secure attention to the way in which the allocation of funds affects the welfare of children.

Legislation: Advocates may lobby for or against proposed legislation affecting children, or may initiate a legal challenge of a law or ad-

ministrative practice through a "class action suit." Children's rights have been advanced substantially in some areas by this means.

Political action: When political action is the focus of child advocacy, the ultimate goal is generally the redistribution of power and resources rather than the more limited goal of changing service systems, which Kahn found to be the goal of the majority of child advocacy programs. Political action may be the focus even when the issue is defined somewhat narrowly, for example, day care, school lunch programs, or students' rights.

Tasks, Strategies, and Techniques

Child advocacy sometimes is an adversarial process, but, as Knitzer reminds us, "it is also a problem solving process that requires keen attention to problem definition and analysis" (1976, p. 208). Once a constituency is settled on, whether that constituency be mentally ill children, teenage parents, children adrift in foster care, children waiting throughout their childhood for a permanent home, children given corporal punishment at school, or some other group of special concern, then the advocacy group must turn its energies to *fact-finding*. Both client-centered and institution-centered data that are relevant to the need for advocacy must be collected, organized, studied and assessed—data such as the identified characteristics, needs, and legal rights of clients; societal and institutional perceptions of the client group; the responsibilities and resources of the institution; the location of the sources of power in the institution; and the nature of the decision-making processes in the institution. Gaps in services and obstacles to the utilization of services must be identified, for example, barriers posed by insufficient or inappropriate allocation of staff resources, or failure to develop alternative practices, for example, alternatives to the use of jails for children or to "banishment" into distant states of children in need of foster care. The problem that is causing the trouble—the difficulty in the child-environment transactions—must be documented and analyzed before remedies can be developed and effective intervention can take place. Frequently this procedure requires becoming informed on substantive matters that affect the workings of the target institution, for example, the nature of law and the judicial process, the knowledge about foster care that has been verified through research, the curriculum content of a public school program and what school administrators and teachers consider to be major curriculum issues, or the institution's sources of funding and the legal constraints upon its budgeting processes.

Political factors that affect or control the situation of concern must be assessed, for example, the positions taken earlier by key persons in the institutional target or the points at which pressure is likely to be effective or to intensify resistance.

Once the problem has been defined and analyzed, then comes attention to what Knitzer terms "the heart of advocacy," that is, *the development of strategies and remedies.* "Without attention to strategies and remedies, fact-finding alone would be nothing more than an exposé" (1976, p. 208). The advocate may rely on a single strategy or a range of interventions. The strategy may be adversarial, for example, the use of a class action litigation. Courts are often the target system for advocacy, but they are also important instruments of advocacy. The strategy selected may also be benign, such as one that relies on support from consensus about values or from widely accepted knowledge and ideas about human rights. Whether the strategy is adversarial or benign, the advocate must be a person or group of recognized status and must possess influence that can be expended. Enthusiasm, compassion, and a sense of mission are not enough.

The advocate's influence can derive from coalitions of different groups of people, sometimes quite diverse, who have an interest in the problem or the proposed remedy. Steiner (1976)

has emphasized the significance of involving groups with a self-interest and joining them with social altruists as a driving force in the children's cause. As an example he cites the national school lunch program.

A powerful coalition of political forces came together to produce a greatly expanded national school lunch program. Lobbyists for agricultural interests and congressmen from rural states wanted to maintain an outlet for surplus farm products. Welfare-oriented congressmen were responsive to the nutritional problems of children in poor families. The school lunch program was a convenience for middle-income groups, and the middle-income subsidy it provided was popular with some lawmakers in Washington. Lobbyists for various nutrition groups and others interested in children's learning problems saw hungry children as unable to learn at school. Proponents of the War on Poverty viewed school lunches as an acceptable relief program. The American School Food Services Association, an association that exists in all fifty states, had a self-interest in an expanded universal program rather than one for poor children only. The Association is made up of school lunch directors, supervisors, and line workers, and their organizational intent is to maintain job opportunities and improve wages and working conditions. A group of social altruists—an ad hoc Committee on School Lunch Participation—made up of five women's organizations, each with a religious orientation, set out to find out why relatively few children were participating in the school lunch program and why it was failing to meet the needs of poor children. As a result of their inquiry, they came out on the side of a universal program. An expanded program also had the support of another lobby, the Children's Foundation, an antihunger organization made up of social altruists and functioning independently of governmental funds. The result was a social benefit that is almost universally available in schools. Aside from public education itself, Steiner noted, no social welfare program provides public benefits to more children than the national school lunch program (Steiner, 1976, pp. 176–205).

As important as coalition building is, so is the *maintenance of coalitions.* Keeping a coalition together can be difficult and sometimes impossible, particularly when advocacy efforts at the peak of their consensus and influence meet powerful opposition. The congressional enactment of comprehensive child development legislation in 1971 provides an example. An unusually effective coalition had been put together (despite far from identical goals among the groups) by the advocacy talents of Marian Wright Edelman and her Children's Defense Fund. The coalition reflected the interests of these major segments: (1) professionals and citizens interested in child care for children as a program of care and protection; (2) similar groups whose interest in child care was focused on early childhood education with an emphasis on cognitive development; and (3) activists interested in community change, for example, those in the movement to enlarge the input of parents and citizens into the use of public funds and into program design. Edelman's emphasis was on child development as an instrument for civil rights and community change. She was able to put together a coalition of groups such as the National Association for the Education of Young Children, the League of Women Voters, the AFL-CIO, the Day Care and Child Development Council of America, the National Committee of Negro Women, the National League of Cities, the U.S. Conference of Mayors, and the National Welfare Rights Organization. The appearance of support from organized labor was important. The bill that passed Congress was far from perfect, but it stood as a significant effort in child advocacy. President Nixon's veto, however, halted the drive for child development legislation. The coalition began to weaken as the differences among its three main segments became clearer. Child development as an issue in Congress went into a "holding action"—meaning "maintaining Head Start without growth while waiting for a political climate

more favorable to new legislation" (Steiner, 1976, p. 90).

Supporters of federal legislation for child care began again to rebuild the coalition and succeeded in influencing significantly higher appropriations for Head Start during the Carter administration. With child care becoming a white, middle-class issue, as Edelman went around the country she found growing public support for federal child care legislation. A comprehensive child care bill became the legislative goal of the CDF in 1988. The reconstructed coalition was larger than the one put together in 1971. Outreach to the business community corrected an earlier omission and strengthened the coalition (Tomkins, 1989).

A strategy that has been used successfully by advocacy groups as a way to increase the cadre of advocates and give them a self-interest in bringing about reform is to *reach out to and coopt groups of volunteers.* "The volunteer-as-participant invariably becomes the volunteer-as-partisan" (Steiner, 1976, p. 249). As examples: The Children's Defense Fund organized Junior League members in nine states to look into the circumstances of children held in jails on the assumption that volunteer citizen indignation would do more for reform than protests from known social activists (Children's Defense Fund, 1976). In Mary Keyserling's study of child care, members of the seventy-seven sections of the National Council of Jewish Women (NCJW) were given the responsibility of contributing detailed reports of deficiencies in child care based on their personal observations in day care homes and centers, and on interviews with working mothers (Keyserling, 1972). Steiner commented on this strategy as follows: "If there is to be a drive for improved monitoring of the conditions under which day care is provided, the drive will involve NCJW members who have come to believe that they have a personal stake in reform" (1976, p. 249).

Advocates use the technique of *articulating findings in appropriate forums,* for example, among persons or groups who have potential power to affect the problem—the governor, city councils, school boards, regional and county officials, civic organizations, federal officials, state department heads, or mayors. In such instances advocates must have a repertoire of technical knowledge about government structures, budgeting, legislatures, and official program guidelines, as well as skill in political negotiation. It is not enough to know how to reach and even influence major officials; the advocate must also be well informed on substantive issues.

Child advocacy groups may also engage in *lobbying* in an effort to persuade legislators to introduce certain bills or to influence the passage or defeat of bills under debate.

Advocates use a range of *other specific techniques*—suggestion, negotiation, education, persuasion, pressure, demands, confrontation, and legal action.

Another important part of successful advocacy is *monitoring*—maintaining contact with persons in a position to watch over the conduct of those who serve children. Monitoring, or follow-through, is essential if advocacy is to be more than a one-time exposé. Monitoring is a way to assure continuous community awareness and presence. It is particularly important in class action litigation in order to make sure that the process of implementing court decisions gets under way. It has also been used successfully in assuring that federal agencies implement legislation or that state agencies observe federal program guidelines.

AN INTEGRATED MODEL OF CHILD ADVOCACY

The last two decades have witnessed some advancement in the assumptions, principles, and strategies of child advocacy and the development of coherent frameworks for the practice of child advocacy. One such approach is a multiple-strategy model developed by Davidson and Rapp (1976). The model helps integrate many of the concepts discussed earlier, including concep-

tual foundations, types of advocacy, tactics, targets, and levels of intervention.

The multiple-strategy model is based on a conception of human behavior that has an ecological perspective. This conception holds that human behavior is a function of the resources available to people and groups. It explicitly rejects any focus on individual and environmental deficits and takes the view that, in a pluralistic society, equal access to resources is desired. In this view all children have a right to the resources of society, and the problem for a child advocate is to decide how to assist a given child or group of children in obtaining their rights and resources.

The multiple-strategy model includes the notion of sequential problem solving as a purposeful approach to generating environmental resources. A ten-step problem-solving format is portrayed in Figure 12.1. The steps involved are divided into primary assessment, intervention selection, and implementation, each of which includes a series of discrete tasks (Davidson & Rapp, 1976). In actuality, the ten steps are highly interrelated, and are dependent on information gained from preceding steps and on continual interaction with the specific social environment in which the advocacy effort is taking place.

Primary Assessment

This initial step includes (1) assessing unmet needs, (2) identifying the needed resources, (3) determining who is currently in control of the resources, and (4) assessing the vulnerability of the individual or group currently controlling the resource.

1. The search for *unmet needs* involves an assessment of the child or group of children in terms of the major life domains: education, employment, family life, health, recreation, and legal rights. Examples of cases needing advocacy include a child's having difficulty in keeping up in school, a youth's desiring a summer job, or a toddler who is often ill. Class advocacy

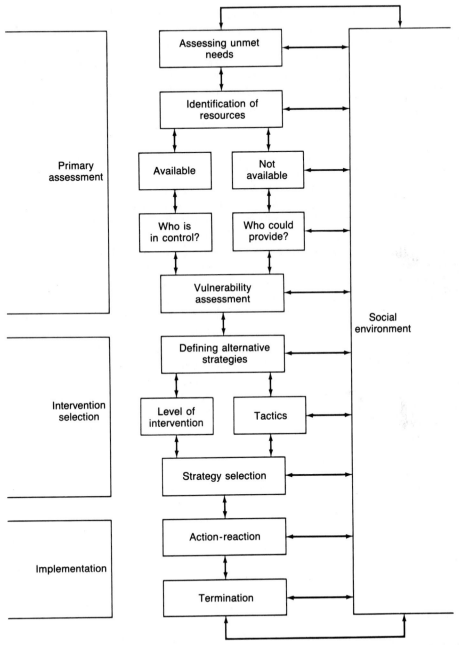

Figure 12.1. Multiple-Strategy Model of Child Advocacy. (*Source:* Reprinted with permission from W.S. Davidson and C. A. Rapp. [1976, May]. "Child Advocacy in the Justice System." *Social Work, 21* [3]. Copyright 1987, National Association of Social Workers, Inc.)

would involve similar situations affecting groups of children, for example, the differential school suspension rate between blacks and whites, the high unemployment rate for youth, or the lack of recreation opportunities for elementary school children.

To the degree possible and appropriate, the advocate should involve the child or youth in the assessment. For very young children, the parent or guardian becomes a major collaborator, although not to the exclusion of other sources, for example, potential employers, teachers, and peers, who might verify the observations and provide other useful information. Knowledge of child development, social science, and law can help to specify areas of need and desirable change.

2.   The next step in primary assessment is to *identify the resources* needed to alleviate the situation considered problematic. The advocate does not place blame or attribute the unmet needs to inadequacies of the child. Whatever the cause of the problem, the solution rests in acquiring resources to remedy the need. For example, a teenager who has dropped out of school, reads poorly, and has been in trouble with the law wants a job. The advocate's task is to help that youth gain a job. Attributing the lack of employment to lack of motivation, job experience, or skills or to poor family life is irrelevant to the advocate's responsibility.

In many cases, the need to identify resources is completely ignored because the advocate comes with his or her favorite remedy and is eager to apply it. However, resources at hand may not include all the possibilities, nor are they often the best options. What is critical is that as many options as possible are generated and their probable outcomes assessed.

3.   The third step is *identifying the controlling individual.* This step involves two sequential elements. The first is to determine whether the needed resource is available. The second stage depends on the outcome of the first: whether the resource is available. When the resource *is* available, the organization or person in control must be specifically identified. When the resource is controlled by an organization, it is particularly critical to identify the individual within the organization who is specifically responsible. When the needed resource is not available, the task becomes one of figuring out a way in which it could be provided. Other individuals or organizations with a related purpose provide a starting point. This step in the assessment process ends with the identification of an individual, group, or organization that can provide the resource in question.

4.   The final step in primary assessment, *vulnerability assessment,* is to establish the conditions under which the individual or organization controlling the needed resource is likely to provide it. Questions to which the advocate seeks answers include: Does the individual or organization have a bias that would encourage or support the request to be made? For example, has the manager of a local business hired teenagers during previous summers? Is there currently any interaction between the target group and the controlling individual? If so, does that individual view the interaction as positive or negative? What are the controlling individual's immediate interests in the matter at hand? And to what official or formal organization is that individual responsible—county supervisor, taxpayers, consumers, legislators, school board? How can the advocate gain personal access to the controlling individual? Who are the potential allies and enemies in the controlling individual's decision making? Sometimes it becomes obvious that the individual identified as critical in providing a particular resource may actually be secondary.

Intervention Selection

The second major component of the multiple-strategy model of advocacy is the selection of a type of intervention, and a determination of the level at which the intervention should be made—through a single individual who appears to control the needed resources, at the administrative level of an agency, or at the policy level where a

political or social system is responsible for the resources that are lacking.

A range of tactics must be considered: (1) at the positive end, attempting to gain the good favor of the person or agency in control of the needed resource; (2) at midpoint, selecting a neutral strategy, often referred to as consultation or joint problem solving, in which information is provided to the critical individual or agency about the area of unmet need; (3) at the negative end, deciding to take direct action against the critical individual or agency. If the needed resource is not provided, threats to take such action may become a major strategy.

To be effective, the intervention selected should be one that offers the highest probability of obtaining the needed resources and that at the same time minimizes potential negative consequences. In general, positive and neutral strategies have little chance of incurring negative consequences. Negative strategies, however, have a high probability of causing backlash or short-range negative consequences. In some cases, such backlash must be risked to ensure that the position of the child is not compromised.

Implementation

The multiple-intervention model has been presented in an orderly, sequential manner. However, actual advocacy efforts are often a series of *actions and reactions*. The goal of maximizing gains while minimizing losses dictates an ongoing interplay of components. For example, the process of assessment continues to take place throughout the advocacy effort.

In addition, initiation of a particular strategy may result in feedback from other individuals, groups, or organizations in the client's environment, which provides information for modifying strategies or selecting new ones. Consider the situation in which an advocate identifies a school district as needing innovative alternative programs for educating youths who are functional dropouts or who have been pushed out of the traditional school system. After care-

ful assessment and selection of interventions, the group attempts to convince the superintendent of schools that an alternative high school is needed. Attention to these efforts by the media stimulates the interest of a group of neighborhood parents who are also working on educational alternatives. However, efforts to convince the school district to include an alternative high school in educational program planning arouse the objections of the local teacher's union. The combination of these developments requires the advocate to incorporate new information into the planning for change. Additional interventions may be selected, other groups recruited to join in the effort, different targets for change identified, or newly available resources located. The complexity of the arena for child advocacy dictates that all options be maintained, that no strategies be arbitrarily discarded, and that the action-reaction cycle be used both for accomplishment and information gathering.

Termination is warranted when the goals of the advocacy effort have been achieved in such a way as to suggest their continued maintenance.

The efficacy of the multiple-strategy model of child advocacy was tested in a program to divert youth from processing by the juvenile justice system. The program matched undergraduate student advocates with youth in jeopardy of court appearance. The results indicated that project youth had fewer contacts with the police, the contacts were less serious, and fewer petitions were filed than in the control group. Second-year follow-up showed that project youth were more likely to be in school and have better attendance records than the control group (Davidson et al., 1977).

TRENDS AND ISSUES

There are indications that the decade of the 1990s may be a time of large-scale coalition advocacy in behalf of children (Kamerman, 1989). Private citizens, legislators, and other policy makers are acknowledging in new ways that children are in current danger and will be increasingly so in the future if corrective actions are not taken. Losses for children in the 1980s of the Reagan administration have been documented: curtailment in eligibility for programs that serve children of poor families, such as AFDC, Food Stamps, and Medicaid; lowered expenditures for child welfare programs with dire effects for the child welfare system and the children it serves; loss of low-income housing that has resulted in homelessness for many thousands of children and their parents. Overall, programs for poor children were seriously hurt (Edelman, 1987; Kamerman, 1984).

In contrast to the years following President Nixon's veto of federal legislation for child care, today's public readiness to provide child care programs for working parents is a signal of the realities of new thought and commitment. More than twelve states have passed some form of legislation for parental leave from work for parents who need to be at home to care for their children—after a birth or when other family emergencies arise. Similar legislation is being discussed in other states in an effort to meet the requirements of working parents for a workplace more responsive to their needs. Pressure for a children's agenda within today's pattern of family life has accelerated to the point that "a melange of concerns about children seems to be driving a national public debate" (Kamerman, 1989, p. 375).

There has been a significant growth in the last ten years of state-based, individual citizen groups with a state policy focus. An Association of Child Advocates has a membership of eighty organizations in forty-one states (Fleming, 1986). The Massachusetts Advocacy Center, a statewide advocacy group established in the dynamic advocacy years of the 1960s, has continued to be an effective organization for change (Massachusetts, 1988). Around the country, monitoring of government and public policies, policy analyses, and search for solutions has taken the form of proactive advocacy (Lardie, 1989). At the federal level, beginning in 1983,

the House of Representatives' Select Committee on Children, Youth, and Families has held hearings and published a series of reports based on federal statistics and the testimony of a wide range of citizens, professionals, and other experts in the area of childhood and child welfare services.

Media attention to problems of children, youth, and their families has played a significant role in the new interest in change for children. Television, newspapers, journals of opinion, popular magazines, and films have publicized in different ways the problems of homelessness, the stark effects of poverty on children, teenage pregnancy, the dangers for youth in a drug culture, the growing rate of HIV-infection and AIDS in children, the plight of children moving around in the foster care system or waiting for a permanent home through adoption as they grow older, physical abuse of children of all ages, neglect that goes unaddressed throughout a child's growing-up years—all these are portrayed for public consumption. In addition, exposure of the deficits in schooling for millions of youth has alarmed representatives of industry who face a shortage of skilled labor in the 1990s and into the next century. Much of the publicity has drawn attention to the inadequacies of the child welfare system, which in turn are reflective of the conditions in the society (Meyer, 1987).

Politicians are not unaware of these vibrations. The declaration by New York's Governor Mario Cuomo that the 1990s will be "the decade of the child" is not only political rhetoric; it can also be viewed as a response to expressions of dissatisfaction across the country with respect to children and families.

Nevertheless, federal and state legislation in behalf of children will not come easily. Forecasts of the decade of the 1990s have suggested a continued shrinking of resources and a concomitant increase in competition for those that are available. Within government, advocacy offices are vulnerable to budget cutting as public agencies are asked to do more with less. Without doubt, many decisions will be reached on the basis of finances. In such a milieu, the need for action on behalf of children (illustrated repeatedly throughout this text) will be critical. Advocacy will be needed to ensure that legislation reflects the needs of youth and that resources are allocated to services for children and families. Monitoring legislation, building coalitions, testifying in Congress and state capitals, and becoming active in political campaigns will be necessary. Parents, youth, and other citizens need encouragement to express their views about the status of child and family life, risks they see, and the changes they want in order to strengthen

> *"Children will not stay in the public spotlight unless we keep them there. The media provides an effective vehicle."* (CDF Reports, *1988a, quoting M. W. Edelman, p. 6)*

and maintain strong family life and maximum opportunity for children and youth. The significant issue is "how the politics of children will be shaped, and how and when the political will for change will emerge" (Kamerman, 1989, p. 385).

FOR STUDY AND DISCUSSION

1. How can children and youth be given an opportunity to help define the problems and issues that are advocated in their behalf?
2. Select a problem facing a group of children or youth in your state or community. Apply the steps in the multiple strategy model of advocacy to this problem.
3. Debate the merits of a variety of persons acting as children's advocates. Include lawyers, social workers, college students, parents, teachers, etc. A list of qualifications for advocates should emanate from such a discussion.
4. Discuss the limits on the extent to which agency child welfare workers can act as advocates.
5. Responsibility for the neglect of today's youth is broadly shared. Discuss ways in which society could reshape its attitudes and priorities to help children and youth with their problems.

FOR ADDITIONAL STUDY

Coates, R. B. (1989). Social work advocacy in juvenile justice: Conceptual underpinnings and practice. In A. R. Roberts, (Ed.), *Juvenile justice: Policies, programs, and services.* Chicago: Dorsey Press.

Costin, L. B. (1983). *Two sisters for social justice. A biography of Grace and Edith Abbott.* Urbana, IL: University of Illinois Press.

Edelman, M. W. (1987). *Families in peril: An agenda for social change.* Cambridge, MA: Harvard University Press.

Friedman, R. (Ed.). (1989). *Advocacy on behalf of children with serious emotional problems.* Springfield, IL: Charles C Thomas.

Mnookin, R. H. (Ed.). (1985). *In the interest of children: Advocacy, law reform, and public policy.* New York: Freeman.

Polier, J. W. (1989). *Juvenile justice in double jeopardy. The distanced community and vengeful retribution.* Hillsdale, NJ: Lawrence Erlbaum Associates.

Schorr, L. B. (1988). *Within our reach. Breaking the cycle of disadvantage.* New York: Doubleday (Anchor Press).

References

AAPC's framework for advocacy. (1988/1989). *Protecting Children, 5*(4), 3–9.

Abbott, E. (1910). *Women in industry. A study in American economic history*. New York: Appleton. Appendix A, *Early history of child labor in the United States*.

Abbott, E., & Breckinridge, S. P. (1917). *Truancy and non-attendance in the Chicago Schools: A study of the compulsory education and child labor legislation of Illinois.* Chicago: University of Chicago Press.

Abbott, G. (1938a). *The child and the state* (Vol. 1). Chicago: University of Chicago Press.

Abbott, G. (1938b). *The child and the state* (Vol. 2). Chicago: University of Chicago Press.

Abrahamse, A. F., Morrison, P. A., & Waite, L. J. (1988). *Beyond stereotypes: Who becomes a teenage mother?* Santa Monica, CA: Rand Corporation.

Abused children in America: Victims of official neglect. A report of the Select Committee on Children, Youth, and Families, U.S. House of Representatives (1987). Washington, DC: U.S. Government Printing Office.

Adams, G., & Pittman, K. (1988). *Adolescent and young adult fathers: Problems and solutions.* Washington, DC: Children's Defense Fund, Adolescent Pregnancy Prevention Clearinghouse.

Addams, J. (1909). *The spirit of youth and the city streets.* New York: Macmillan.

Addams, J. (1935). *My friend, Julia Lathrop.* New York: Macmillan.

Adolescent maltreatment: Issues and program models. (1984). U.S. Department of Health and Human Services (DHHS Publication No. [OHDS] 84-30339). Washington, DC: U.S. Government Printing Office.

Adoption Assistance and Child Welfare Act of 1980. (P.L. No. 96–272, 94 Stat. 515) (Codified in scattered sections of 42 U.S.C.)

Adoption Resource Exchange of North America. (1967). New York: Child Welfare League of America.

Advisory Council on Public Welfare. (1966). *Having the power, we have the duty.* Washington, DC: U.S. Department of Health, Education, and Welfare.

Agopian, M. W. (1984). The impact on children of abduction by parents. *Child Welfare, 63*(6), 511–519.

AIDS reported as no. 9 killer of children. (1988, December 20), *New York Times,* p. 10.

Ainsworth, M. D. (1962). The effects of maternal deprivation: A review of findings and controversy in the context of research strategy. In *Deprivation of maternal care: A reassessment of its effects.* Geneva: World Health Organization, Public Health Papers no. 14.

Alan Guttmacher Institute. (1981). *Teenage pregnancy: The problem that hasn't gone away.* New York: Alan Guttmacher Institute.

Allen, A., & Morton, A. (1961). *This is your child.* London: Routledge & Kegan Paul.

Allen, M., Bonner, K., & Greenan, L. (1988). Federal legislative support for independent living. *Child Welfare, 67*(6), 515–527.

Allen, M., & Pittman, K. (1986). *Welfare and teen pregnancy: What do we know? What do we do?* Washington, DC: Children's Defense Fund, Adolescent Pregnancy Prevention Clearinghouse.

Allen-Hagen, Barbara. (1988, October). Public juvenile facilities, 1987: Children in custody. *Juvenile Justice Bulletin,* pp. 1–8.

Allerhand, M. E., Weber, R. E., & Haug, M. (1966). *Adaptation and adaptability: The Bellefaire follow-up study.* New York: Child Welfare League of America.

Alsop, R. (1989). The reasonable efforts requirement in protective services policy. *Protecting Children, 6*(2), 3–6.

Alter, C. F. (1985). Decision-making factors in cases of child neglect. *Child Welfare, 64*(2), 99–111.

Amatruda, C. S., & Baldwin, J. V. (1951). *Journal of Pediatrics, 38*(2), 208–212.

American Association for Protecting Children, Inc. (1986). *Highlights of official child neglect and abuse reporting 1984.* Denver: American Humane Association.

American Bar Association. (1981). *Protecting children through the legal system.* Washington, DC: Author.

American Friends Service Committee. (1976). *School days, Saturdays, Sundays, and fiestas: Children who work in commercial agriculture.* Philadelphia: Author.

American Humane Association. (1963). *Guidelines for legislation to protect the battered child.* Denver: American Humane Association, Children's Division.

American Humane Association. (1984). *Trends in officially reported child neglect and abuse.* Denver: American Humane Association, Child Protection Division.

American Indian and Alaskan native education. (1981). Washington, DC: U.S. Department of the Interior, Bureau of Indian Affairs.

American Public Welfare Association. (1973). *The interstate compact on the placement of children.* Washington, DC: Author.

American Public Welfare Association. (1988). *Foster care basic maintenance rates.* Washington, DC: Author.

Anderson, D. B., & Schoen, D. F. (1985). Diversion programs: Effect of stigmatization on juvenile/status offenders. *Juvenile & Family Court Journal, 36*(2), 13–25.

Anderson, S. (1988). *Foster home retention survey: Findings from former foster parents in 10 Bay Area counties.* Bay Area: Community Task Force on Homes for Children.

Annotated directory of selected family-based service programs. (1986). Oakdale, IA: National Resource Center on Family Based Services, University of Iowa, School of Social Work.

Antler, S. (1985). The social policy context of child welfare. In J. Laird & A. Hartman (Eds.), *A handbook of child welfare* (pp. 77–99). New York: Macmillan.

Arizona Social Service Bureau. (1974). *Foster care evaluation program.* Phoenix: Department of Economic Security.

Ashby, L. (1984). *Saving the waifs: Reformers and dependent children, 1890–1917.* Philadelphia: Temple University Press.

A smarter way to aid the working poor. (1988, July 11). *New York Times,* p. 20.

Association for Regulatory Administration in Human Services. (1988). *A licensing curriculum.* Richmond, VA: Author.

Attneave, C. (1982). American Indians and Alaska native families: Emigrants in their own homeland. In M. McGoldrick, J. Pearce, & J. Giordano (Eds.), *Ethnicity and family therapy* (pp. 55–83). New York: Guilford Press.

Attorney General's Task Force on Family Violence. (1984). *Final report.* (U.S. Department of Justice). In D. J. Besharov. (1987). *Child abuse: A police guide.* Washington, DC: American Bar Association's National Legal Resource Center for Child Advocacy and Protection and the Police Foundation.

Austin, L. N. (1948). Some psychoanalytic principles underlying casework with children. In E. Clifton & F. Hollis (Eds.), *Child therapy: A casework symposium.* New York: Family Service Association of America.

Bachrach, C. A. (1986). Adoption plans, adopted children and adoptive mothers. *Journal of marriage and the family, 48,* 243–253.

Bailey, E. H. (1890). Country homes for dependent children. In *Proceedings of the national conference of charities and correction.* Boston: George H. Ellis.

Bailey v. Drexel Furniture Co., 259 U.S. 20 (1922).

Baird, C. (1988). Development of risk assessment indices for the Alaska Department of Health and Social Services. In T. Tatara (Ed.), *Validation research in CPS assessment: Three recent studies.* (Occasional Monograph Series of APWA's R&D Department No. 2.) Washington, DC: American Public Welfare Association, CPS Risk Assessment Project.

Baird, S. C., & Neuenfeldt, D. (1988, July). Assessing potential for abuse and neglect. *The National Council on Crime and Delinquency: Focus.*

Bakan, D. (1979). Slaughter of the innocents. In D. G. Gil (Ed.), *Child abuse and violence* (pp. 138–144). New York: AMS Press.

Baker, N. C. (1978). *Baby selling: The scandal of black-market adoption*. New York: Vanguard.

Baker v. Owen, 96 S.Ct. 210 (1975).

Balassone, M. (1988). Multiple pregnancies among adolescents: Incidence and correlates. *Health and Social Work, 13*(4), 266–276.

Balcerzak, E. A. (1990). *Group care of children: Toward the year 2000*. Washington, DC: Child Welfare League of America.

Bandler, L. S. (1967). Casework—A process of socialization: Gains, limitations, conclusions. In E. Pavenstedt (Ed.), *The drifters: Children of disorganized lower-class families*. Boston: Little, Brown.

Bane, M. J. (1979). Marital disruption and the lives of children. In O. C. Moles & G. Lewinger (Eds.), *Divorce and separation* (pp. 276–286). New York: Basic Books.

Barbaro, F. (1979). The case against family policy. *Social Work. 24*(6), 447–456.

Barden, J. C. (1990, February 5). Toll of troubled families: Flood of homeless youth. *New York Times,* A1, B7.

Barnes, M. E., Jr. (1967, February). The concept of "parental force." *Child Welfare, 46,* 89–94.

Barrett, R. S. (1929). *The care of the unmarried mother*. Alexandria, VA: National Florence Crittenton Mission.

Barringer, F. (1990, August 17). After an 18-year decline, teen-age births are up. *New York Times, 1, 9.*

Barth, R. P. (1986a). *Social and cognitive treatment of children and adolescents*. San Francisco: Jossey-Bass.

Barth, R. P. (1986b). Emancipation services for adolescents in foster care. *Social Work, 31*(3), 165–171.

Barth, R. P. (1987). Adolescent mothers' beliefs about open adoption. *Social Casework, 68*(6), 323–331.

Barth, R. P., & Berry, M. (1988). *Adoption and disruption: Rates, risks, and responses*. New York: Aldine De Gruyter.

Barth, R. P., Blythe, B. J., Schinke, S. P., & Schilling, R. F. (1983). Self-control training with maltreating parents. *Child Welfare, 62*(4), 313–324.

Barth, R. P., Claycomb, M., & Loomis, A. (1988, Fall). Services to adolescent fathers. *Health and Social Work, 13,* 277–287.

Bassuk, E., & Rubin, L. (1987). Homeless children: A neglected population. *American Journal of Orthopsychiatry, 57*(2), 279–286.

Baumann, A. M. (1963). A follow-up study of the "telling process" in adoption. *Smith College Studies in Social Work, 34*(1).

Bean, S. (1971). The parents' center project: A multiservice approach to the prevention of child abuse. *Child Welfare, 50,* 277–282.

Beck, B. M., (1987, August 6). Mandatory mistake. *New York Times,* p. 22.

Beck, D. F., & Jones, M. A. (1973). *Progress on family problems*. New York: Family Service Association of America.

Beck, R., & Butler, J. (1974). An interview with Marian Wright Edelman. *Harvard Educational Review, 44*(1).

Beemsterboer, M. J. (1960). Benevolence in the star chamber. *Journal of Criminal Law, Criminology, and Political Science, 50,* 464–475.

Beer, E. S. (1938). *The day nursery*. New York: Dutton.

Beezley, P., Martin, H., & Alexander, H. (1974). Comprehensive family oriented therapy. In R. E. Helfer & C. H. Kempe (Eds.), *The battered child* (2nd ed.). Chicago: University of Chicago Press.

Begab, M. J., & Goldberg, H. L. (1962, January–February). Guardianship for the mentally retarded. *Children, 9,* 21–25.

Bell, C. J. (1978). Accessibility to adoption records: Influences on agency policy. *Dissertation Abstracts International* (University Microfilms).

Bell, C. J. (1985). Consent issues in inter-country adoption. *Children's Legal Rights Journal, 6*(3), 2–8.

Bell, C. J. (1986). Adoptive pregnancy: Legal and social work issues. *Child Welfare, 65*(5), 421–436.

Bell, C. J. (1988). Working with child witnesses. *Public Welfare, 46*(1), 5–13.

Bell, W. (1965). *Aid to dependent children*. New York: Columbia University Press.

Bellotti v. Baird, 99 S.Ct. (1979).

Bellucci, M. T. (1972, February). Group treatment of mothers in child protection cases. *Child Welfare, 51,* 110–116.

Belsky, J. (1980, April). Child maltreatment: An ecologial integration. *American Psychologist, 35,* 320–335.

Belsky, J. (1987). The role of the genetic counselor in fetal alcohol syndrome prevention. *Birth Defects, 23*(6), 111–114.

Benton, B., Field, T., & Miller, R. (1978). *Social services: Federal legislation vs. state implementation.* Washington, DC: Urban Institute.

Berdie, J., & Wexler, S. (1984). Preliminary research on selected adolescent maltreatment issues: An analysis of supplemental data from the four adolescent maltreatment projects. In *Adolescent maltreatment: Issues and program models* (DHHS Publication No. OHDS 84-30339). Washington, DC: U.S. Government Printing Office.

Berger, D. K., Rolon, Y., Sachs, J., & Wilson, B. (1989, February). Child abuse and neglect: An instrument to assist with case referral decision making. *Health and Social Work,* pp. 60-73.

Berger, N. (1967). *The rights of children and young people.* London: Cobden Trust, pp. 1-2.

Berliner, L., & Barbieri, M. K. (1984). The testimony of the child victim of sexual assault. *Journal of Social Issue, 40*(2), 125-137.

Bernard, J. (1966). *Marriage and family among Negroes.* Englewood Cliffs, NJ: Prentice-Hall, pp. 50-55.

Bernstein, R. (1960, July). Are we still stereotyping the unmarried mother? *Social Work, 5.*

Bernstein, R. (1963, March–April). Gaps in services to unmarried mothers. *Children, 10,* 50-51.

Berreuta-Clement, J. R., Schweinhart, L. J., Barnett, W. S., Epstein, A. S., & Weikart, D. P. (1984). *Changed lives, the effects of the Perry Preschool Program on youths through age 19.* Ypsilanti, MI: High/Scope Press.

Berry, M. (1988). A review of parent training programs in child welfare. *Social Service Review, 62*(2), 302-322.

Berry, M., & Barth, R. P. (1990). A study of disrupted adoptive placements of adolescents. *Child Welfare, 69*(3), 209-225.

Besharov, D. J. (1984, Spring). Liability in child welfare. *Public Welfare, 42.*

Besharov, D. J. (1985). "Doing something" about child abuse: The need to narrow the grounds for state intervention. *Harvard Journal of Law and Public Policy, 8*(3), 539-589.

Besharov, D. J. (1987, Winter). Contending with overblown expectations: CPS cannot be all things to all people. *Public Welfare, 45,* 7-11.

Billingsley, A., & Giovannoni, J. (1970). Research perspectives on interracial adoption. In R. R. Miller (Ed.), *Race, Research, and Reason: Social Work Perspectives* (pp. 57-77). New York: National Association of Social Workers.

Billingsley, A., & Giovannoni, J. M. (1972). *Children of the storm: Black children and American child welfare.* New York: Harcourt Brace Jovanovich.

Binder, G., & Class, N. E. (1958). The nature of welfare licensing laws. *Social Casework, 39,* 267.

Bird, J. R., Conlin, M. L., & Frank, G. (1984). Children in trouble: The juvenile justice system. In R. M. Horowitz & H. A. Davidson (Eds.), *Legal rights of children* (pp. 461-514). Colorado Springs: McGraw-Hill.

Births to the unwed found to have risen by 50% in 10 years. (1981, October 26). *New York Times,* pp. 1, 13.

Black, H. C. (1979). *Black's law dictionary* (5th ed.). St. Paul, MN: West.

Black, R., & Mayer, J. (1980). Parents with special problems: Alcoholism and opiate addiction. In C. H. Kempe & R. E. Helfer (Eds.), *The battered child* (pp. 104-114). Chicago: University of Chicago Press.

Blakesley, C. L. (1988). Custody and visitation. In L. D. Wardle, C. L. Blakesley, & J. Y. Parker (Eds.), *Family law: Principles, policy and practice* (Ch. 39). Deerfield, IL: Callaghan.

Block, N. M. (1981). Toward reducing recidivism in foster care. *Child Welfare, 60*(9), 597-610.

Bloom, B. S., Davis, A., & Hess, R. (1965). *Compensatory education for cultural deprivation.* New York: Holt, Rinehart and Winston.

Blumenthal, K., & Weinberg, A. (1983). Issues concerning parental visiting of children in foster care. In M. Hardin (Ed.), *Foster children in the courts* (pp. 372-398). Boston: Butterworth Legal.

Board of State Charities of Massachusetts. (1869). *Sixth annual report.*

Boehm, B. (1958). *Deterrents to the adoption of children in foster care.* New York: Child Welfare League of America.

Boehm, B. (1964, November). The community and the social agency define neglect. *Child Welfare, 43.*

Boehm, B. (1970). *The child in foster care.* In R. H. Bremner (Ed.). (1974). Children and youth in America: A documentary history. (Vol. 3, Pts. 5-7, 1933-1973). Cambridge, MA: Harvard University Press, pp. 673-677.

Boffey, P. M. (1988, September 20). Homeless plight

angers scientist experts. *New York Times,* pp. 1, 12.

Bolton, F. G. (1980). *The pregnant adolescent: Problems of premature parenthood.* Beverly Hills, CA: Sage.

Borgman, R. (1981). The consequences and parental rights termination for abused and neglected children. *Child Welfare. 60*(6), 391–304.

Borgotta, E. F., & Fanshel, D. (1965). *Behavioral characteristics of children known to psychiatric outpatient clinics.* New York: Child Welfare League of America.

Bourguignon, J. P., & Watson, K. W. (1987). After adoption: A manual for professionals working with adoptive families. Post-Placement Post-Legal Adoption Services Project for Special Needs Children and Their Families: Federal Grant #90-CO–02871. Chicago: Illinois Department of Children and Family Services.

Bovet, L. (1951). *Psychiatric aspects of juvenile delinquency.* Geneva: World Health Organization.

Bowen, G. L. (1987, June). Single fathers in the Air Force. *Social Casework,* pp. 339–344.

Bowlby, J. (1951). *Maternal care and mental health.* New York: World Health Organization.

Bowlby, J. (1961). Separation anxiety: A critical review of the literature. *Journal of Child Psychology and Psychiatry, 1*(2), 251–269.

Boyd, L. H., & Perry, L. L. (1978). Is foster parent training worthwhile? *Social Service Review, 52*(2), 275–296.

Boyne, J. (1978). A mental health note in adoption of school age and teenage children. *Child Welfare, 57*(3).

Boyne, J., Denby, L., Kettering, J. R., & Wheeler, W. (1983). *The shadow of success: A statistical analysis of outcomes of adoptions of hard-to-place children.* Westfield, NJ: Spaulding for Children.

Brace, C. L. (1872). *The dangerous classes of New York and twenty years' work among them.* New York: Wynkoop and Hallenbeck.

Bradbury, D. E., & Oettinger, K. B. (1962). *Five decades of action for children. A history of the Children's Bureau.* Washington, DC: U.S. Government Printing Office.

Bradley, T. (1966). An exploration of caseworkers' perceptions of adoptive applicants. *Child Welfare, 45*(8).

Bradley, T. (1967). *An exploration of caseworkers'*

perceptions of adoptive applicants. New York: Child Welfare League of America.

Brandwein, R. A., Brown, C. A., & Fox, E. M. (1974). Women and children last: The social situation of divorced mothers and their families. *Journal of Marriage and the Family, 36*(3), 498–514.

Branscombe, M. (1953, February). Basic policies and principles of public child care services: An underlying philosophy. *Child Welfare, 31* [Special issue].

Breckinridge, S. P. (1914). Some aspects of the public schools from a social worker's point of view. *Journal of Proceedings and Addresses of the National Education Association.* Ann Arbor, MI: National Education Association.

Breckinridge, S. P. (1934). *The family and the state.* Chicago: University of Chicago Press.

Breckinridge, S. P., & Abbott, E. (1912). The delinquent child and the home. New York: Russell Sage Foundation.

Bredekamp, S. (Ed.). (1987). *Accreditation criteria and procedure.* Washington, DC: National Academy of Early Childhood Programs.

Bremner, R. H. (Ed.). (1970). *Children and youth in America: A documentary history* (Vol. 1, 1600–1865). Cambridge, MA: Harvard University Press.

Bremner, R. H. (Ed.). (1971). *Children and youth in America. A documentary history* (Vol. 2, 1866–1932). Cambridge, MA: Harvard University Press.

Bremner, R. H. (Ed.). (1973). *Children and youth in America. A documentary history* (Vol. 3, Pts. 1–4, 1933–1973). Cambridge, MA: Harvard University Press.

Bremner, R. H. (Ed.). (1974). *Children and youth in America. A documentary history*(Vol. 3, Pts. 5–7, 1933–1973). Cambridge, MA: Harvard University Press.

Brenner, R. F. (1951). *A follow-up study of adoptive families.* New York: Child Adoption Research Committee.

Bresee, P., Stearns, G. B., Bess, B. H., & Packer, L. S. (1986). Allegations of child sexual abuse in child custody disputes: A therapeutic assessment model. *Americal Journal of Orthopsychiatry, 56*(4), 560–569.

Briar, S. (1963). Clinical judgments in foster care placement. *Child Welfare, 42*(4), 161–168.

Brieland, D. (1959). *An experimental study of the se-*

lection of adoptive parents at intake. New York: Child Welfare League of America.

Brieland, D. (1984). Selection of adoptive parents. In P. Sachdev (Ed.), *Adoption: Issues and Trends* (pp. 65–85). Toronto: Butterworths.

Brieland, D., & Lemmon, J. (1977). *Social work and the law.* St. Paul, MN: West.

Brieland, D., & Lemmon, J. A. (1985). *Social Work and the law.* St. Paul, MN: West.

Brodzinsky, D. M., Singer, L. M., & Braff, A. M. (1984). Children's understanding of adoption. *Child Development, 55*(3) 869–878.

Bross, D., Krugman, R., Lenherr, M., Rosenberg, D., & Schmitt, B. (1988). (Eds.). *The New Child Protection Team Handbook.* New York: Garland.

Bross, D. C., & Munson, M. M. (1980). Alternative models of legal representation for children. *Oklahoma City University Law Review, 5,* 561–618.

Brown, D. (1982). *The step-family: A growing challenge for social work.* Norwich: University of East Anglia.

Brown, E. G. (1970). *Selection of adoptive parents: A videotape study.* Unpublished doctoral dissertation, University of Chicago, School of Social Service Administration, Chicago.

Brown, E. G., & Brieland, D. (1975). Adoptive screening: New data, new dilemmas. *Social Work, 21,* 291–295.

Brown, F. H. (1988). The postdivorce family. In B. Carter & M. McGoldrick (Eds.), *The changing family life cycle: A framework for family therapy* (2nd ed., pp. 371–398). New York: Gardner Press.

Brown, G. E. (Ed.). (1968). *The multi-problem dilemma.* Metuchen, NJ: Scarecrow Press.

Brown, L. (1987, Winter). Seeking a national consensus. *Public Welfare, 45,* 12–17.

Bryant, H. D., Billingsley, A., Kerry, G. A., Leefman, W. V., Merrill, E. J., Senecal, G. R., & Walsh, B. G. (1963, March). Physical abuse of children—An agency study. *Child Welfare, 42.*

Bryce, M. E., & Ehlert, R. C. (1971). 144 foster children. *Child Welfare, 50*(9), 499–503.

Bucholz, E. S., & Gol, B. (1986). More than playing house: A developmental perspective on the strengths in teenage motherhood. *American Journal of Orthopsychiatry, 56,* 347–359.

Bullard, D. M., Jr., Galser, H. H., Heagarty, M. C., & Pivchik, E. C. (1967, July). Failure to thrive in the "neglected" child. *American Journal of Orthopsychiatry, 37,* 686–687.

Bumpass, L. L. (1984). Children and marital disruption: A replication and update. *Demography, 21*(1), 71–82.

Burgess, M. E., & Price, D. O. (1963). *An American dependency challenge.* Chicago: American Public Welfare Association.

Burkhart, K. W. (1975). *The Child and the law: Helping the status offender.* New York: Public Affairs Committee.

Burns, E. (Ed.). (1956). *Social security and public policy.* New York: McGraw-Hill.

Burns, E. (Ed.). (1968). *Children's allowances and the economic welfare of children.* New York: Citizens Committee for Children for New York.

Burud, S. L., Aschbacher, P. R., & McCroskey, J. (1984). *Employer-supported child care. Investing in human resources.* Boston: Auburn House.

Buzawa, D. (1977, December 22). Personal communication. Washington, DC: ARENA.

Bye, L. (1959). *Profile of unwed pregnancy today.* Unpublished paper presented at the National Conference of Social Welfare.

Caban v. Mohammed, 441 U.S. 380, 99 S.Ct. 1760, 60 L.Ed.2d 297 (1979).

Calburn, W. E., & Magura, S. (1978). Administrative case review for foster children. *Social work research and abstracts, 14*(1), 34–40.

California Citizens' Adoptions Committee (1965). *Serving children in need of adoption.* Los Angeles: Author.

Cardozo, B. (1921). *The nature of the judicial process.* New Haven: Yale University Press.

Carey v. Population Service International et al., 431 U.S. 678, 52 L.Ed.2d 675, 97 S.Ct. 2010 (1977).

Carrera, J. (1987). Aid to families with dependent children. *Encyclopedia of Social Work* (pp. 126–132). New York: National Association of Social Workers.

Carroll, C. A., & Haase, C. C. (1987). The function of protective services in child abuse and neglect. In R. E. Helfer, & R. S. Kempe (Eds.), *The battered child* (4th ed., pp. 137–151). Chicago: University of Chicago Press.

Carter v. Kaufman, 8 Ca.App.3d 783, 87 Ca. Rptr. 678 (1970), *cert. denied,* 402 U.S. 964 (1971) (Black, J. dissenting in separate opinion at 402 U.S. 954, 959).

Cartoof, V. G. (1978). Postpartum services for adolescent mothers. *Child Welfare, 57*(10), 660–666.

Cassetty, J. H. (1982). Child support: New focus for social work practice. *Social Work, 27*(6), 504–515.

Caulfield, B. A., & Horowitz, R. M. (1987). *Child abuse and the law: A legal primer for social workers* (2nd ed.). Chicago: National Committee for Prevention of Child Abuse.

Cautley, P. W. (1980). *New foster parents.* New York: Human Sciences.

Cavanaugh, D. N., et al. (1977). *Migrant child welfare: A state of the field study of child welfare services for migrant children and their families who are in-stream, home based, or settled out. Executive summary* (Publication No. (OHDS) 78–30117). Washington, DC: U.S. Department of Health, Education, and Welfare, National Center for Child Advocacy, Children's Bureau, Office of Child Development.

CDF Reports. (1985). Another look at adoption issues. *Monthly Newsletter of the Children's Defense Fund, 7*(6), 1.

CDF Reports. (1987a). *Monthly Newsletter of the Children's Defense Fund, 8*(10), 11.

CDF Reports. (1987b). Child Care: A time to act. *Monthly Newsletter of the Children's Defense Fund, 9*(5).

CDF Reports. (1988a). A new look at inner-city poverty. An interview with Dr. William J. Wilson. *Monthly Newsletter of the Children's Defense Fund, 9*(8), 3–4, 6.

CDF Reports. (1988b). An interview with Dr. Sheila Kamerman. *Monthly Newsletter of the Children's Defense Fund, 10*(2), 1, 6–7.

CDF Reports. (1988c). *Monthly Newsletter of the Children's Defense Fund, 10*(3), 3.

CDF Reports. (1988d). The neglected challenge of teen pregnancy prevention: Reaching teenage boys. *Monthly Newsletter of the Children's Defense Fund, 10*(4), 1.

CDF Reports. (1988e). Congress defers action on ABC. . . . *Monthly Newsletter of the Children's Defense Fund, 10*(5).

CDF Reports. (1989a). Welfare reform in the states. The stage is set for crucial choices. *Monthly Newsletter of the Children's Defense Fund, 10*(9), 1, 3–6.

CDF Reports. (1989b). Education in the 1990s: A conversation with David Hornbeck. *Monthly Newsletter of the Children's Defense Fund, 11,* 1–8.

CDF Reports. (1990). Notes from the President. *Monthly Newsletter of the Children's Defense Fund, 11*(6), 8.

Center for Law and Education, Inc. (1988, August). U.S. Supreme court limits authority of school officials to exclude disabled students. *Newsnotes 40,* 1, 4.

Chambers, C. A. (1963). *Seedtime of reform. American social service and social action, 1918–1933.* Minneapolis: University of Minnesota Press.

Chambers, D. E. (1970). Willingness to adopt atypical children. *Child Welfare, 49*(5), 275–279.

Chappell, B. (1975). One agency's periodic review in foster care—The South Carolina story. *Child Welfare, 54*(7), 477–486.

Chasnoff, R. J., Burns, W. J., Schnoll, S. H., & Burns, K. A. (1985). Cocaine use in pregnancy. *New England Journal of Medicine, 313,* 666–669.

Chavez, L. (1987, July 17). Women's movement, its ideals accepted, faces subtler issues. *New York Times,* p. 8.

Cheney, K. B. (1966, May–June). Safeguarding legal rights in providing protective services. *Children, 13,* 86–92.

Chesney-Lind, M. (1988). Girls in jail. *Crime & Delinquency, 54,* 151–168.

Child Adoption Service of the State Charities Aid Association. (1960). *Adoptability: A study of 100 children in foster care.* New York: Author.

Children at the center. Final report of the national day care study, executive summary. (1979). Cambridge, MA: Abt Associates.

Children's Bureau. (1919). Minimum standards for child welfare, adopted by the Washington and Regional Conference on Child Welfare (Publication No. 62). Washington, DC: U.S. Government Printing Office.

Children's Bureau. (1921a). *Administration of the first federal child-labor law* (Publication No. 78). Washington, DC: Children's Bureau.

Children's Bureau. (1921b). *Standards of legal protection for children born out of wedlock: A report of regional conferences held under the auspices of the U.S. Children's Bureau and the inter-city conference on illegitimacy* (Publication No. 77). Washington, DC: U.S. Government Printing Office.

Children's Bureau. (1922). *Children in an anthracite*

coal-mining district (Publication No. 106). Washington, DC: Children's Bureau. In G. Abbott. (1938). The child and the state (Vol. 1). Chicago: University of Chicago Press, pp. 377–382.

Children's Bureau. (1926). Foster home care for dependent children (Publication No. 136). Washington, DC: U.S. Government Printing Office.

Children's Bureau. (1938, July). Legislation and regulations relating to separation of babies from their mothers. The Child, 3, 19–21.

Children's Bureau. (1961). Legislative guide for the termination of parental responsibilities and the adoption of children (Publication No. 394). Washington, DC: U.S. Government Printing Office.

Children's Bureau. (1962). Five decades of action for children: A history of the Children's Bureau (Publication No. 358). Washington, DC: U.S. Government Printing Office.

Children's Bureau. (1963). The abused child—Principles and suggested language for legislation on reporting of the physically abused child. Washington, DC: U.S. Government Printing Office.

Children's Bureau. (1964). Report on day care. U.S. Department of Health, Education and Welfare. (Welfare Report No. 14). Washington, DC: U.S. Government Printing Office.

Children's Defense Fund. (1974). Children out of school in America. Washington, DC: Author.

Children's Defense Fund. (1975). School suspensions: Are they helping children? Washington, DC: Author.

Children's Defense Fund of the Washington Research Project. (1976). Children in adult jails. Washington, DC: Children's Defense Fund.

Children's Defense Fund. (1987a). A children's defense budget. FY 1988. An analysis of our nation's investment in children. Washington, DC: Author.

Children's Defense Fund. (1987b). Child care: The time is now. Washington, DC: Author.

Children's Defense Fund. (1987c). Opportunities for prevention: Building after-school and summer programs for young adolescents. Washington, DC: Author.

Children's Defense Fund. (1988). Teenage pregnancy: An advocate's guide to the numbers. Washington, DC: Children's Defense Fund, Adolescent Pregnancy Prevention Clearinghouse.

Children's Defense Fund. (1989). A vision for America's future. An agenda for the 1990s. A children's defense budget. Washington, DC: Author.

Children's Defense Fund. (1990). Children 1990. A report card, briefing book, and action primer. Washington, DC: Author.

Children waiting. (1972). Sacramento: California State Agency of Health and Welfare, Department of Social Welfare, State Social Welfare Board.

Children without homes. (1978). Washington, DC: Children's Defense Fund.

Child welfare in 25 states: An overview. (1976). (Publication No. [OHD] 76–30090). Washington, DC: U.S. Department of Health Education and Welfare.

Child Welfare League of America. (1959). Standards for homemaker service for children. New York: Child Welfare League of America.

Child Welfare League of America. (1960a). Adoption of Oriental children by American white families: An interdisciplinary symposium. New York: Author.

Child Welfare League of America. (1960b). Standards for child protective services. New York: Child Welfare League of America.

Child Welfare League of America. (1960c). Standards for day care service. New York: Author.

Child Welfare League of America. (1967). Adoption resource exchange of North America. New York: Author.

Child Welfare League of America. (1968). Standards for adoption service (rev. ed.). New York: Author.

Child Welfare League of America. (1972). Standards for adoption service (rev. ed.). New York: Author.

Child Welfare League of America. (1974). CWLA Adoption statistics—January–June, 1974, compared with July–December, 1973: Summary of findings. New York: Author.

Child Welfare League of America. (1977). 1976 ARENA annual report. ARENA News. New York: Author.

Child Welfare League of America. (1981). Statement on child advocacy. New York: Author.

Child Welfare League of America. (1982a). CWLA standards for residential centers for children. New York: Author.

Child Welfare League of America. (1982b). Foster

parenting: An integrative review of the literature. *Child Welfare, 46*(7).

Child Welfare League of America. (1984a). *Standards for organization and administration for all child welfare services.* New York: Author.

Child Welfare League of America. (1984b). *Standards for service for children and families in their own homes* (rev. ed.). New York: Child Welfare League of America.

Child Welfare League of America. (1988a). *Report of the CWLA task force on children and HIV infection. Initial guidelines.* Washington, DC: Author.

Child Welfare League of America. (1988b). *Standards for adoption services.* Washington, DC: Author.

Child Welfare League of America. (1989a). *Report of the CWLA task force on children and HIV infection.* Washington, DC: Author.

Child Welfare League of America. (1989b). *The state of adoption in America.* Washington, DC: Author.

Child Welfare League of America. (1990). *Children '90. 70 years of speaking out for children.* Washington, DC: Author.

Child Welfare League of America standards for independent living. (1989). Silver Spring, MD: Child Welfare League of America.

Chilman, C. S. (1978). *Adolescent sexuality in a changing American society: Social and psychological perspectives* (U.S. Department of Health, Education, and Welfare, NIH Publication No. 79-1426). Washington, DC: U.S. Government Printing Office.

Chilman, C. S. (1980). Social and psychological research concerning adolescent childbearing: 1970–1980. *Journal of Marriage and the Family, 42*(4), 794–805.

Chimezie, A. (1977). Bold but irrelevant: Grow and Shapiro on transracial adoption. *Child Welfare, 56*(2).

Christoffel, K., Liu, K., & Stamler, J. (1981). Epidemiology of fatal child abuse: International mortality data. *Journal of Chronic Diseases, 34,* 57–64.

Clark, H. H. (1968). The law of domestic relations in the United States. St. Paul, MN: West.

Class, N. E. (1963). Some comments on the Child Welfare League of America standards for protective service. *Child Welfare, 42,* 139–147.

Class, N. E. (1968a). *Licensing of child care facilities by state welfare departments* (Children's Bureau Publication No. 462). Washington, DC: U.S. Government Printing Office.

Class, N. E. (1968b, September–October). Licensing for child care—A preventive welfare service. *Children, 15,* 188–192.

Class, N. E. (1981, November 5). *A policy planning paper on issues in the prohibition of corporal punishment in child day care licensing standards.* Paper presented at the National Association of Education for Young Children, Detroit.

Class, N. E. (1982, November 7). Personal communication.

Class, N. E., & Norris, S. A. (1981). *The public regulation of child day care centers by health department regulatory standards.* Topeka: Kansas Department of Health and Environment.

Cloward, R. A., & Elman, R. M. (1967). The storefront on Stanton Street: Advocacy in the ghetto. In G. Brager & F. P. Purcell (Eds.), *Community action against poverty.* New Haven, CT: College and University Press.

Cloward, R. A., & Jones, J. A. (1963). Social class: Educational attitudes and participation. In H. Passow (Ed.), *Education in depressed areas.* New York: Columbia University Teachers College Press.

Coates, R. B. (1989). *Social work advocacy in juvenile justice: Conceptual underpinnings and practice.* In A. R. Roberts (Ed.), *Juvenile justice: Policies, programs, and servces.* Chicago: Dorsey Press.

Coates, R. B., Miller, A. D., & Ohlin, L. E. (1978). *Diversity in a youth correctional system: Handling delinquents in Massachusetts.* Cambridge, MA: Ballinger.

Cohen, D. J., & Zigler, E. (n.d.). *Federal day care standards: Rationale and recommendations.* Mimeographed.

Cohen, W. J. (1977). Social insurance. In *Encyclopedia of social work* (pp. 1361–1362). New York: National Association of Social Workers.

Cohen, W. J., & Ball, R. M. (1962). Public welfare amendments of 1962. *Social Security Bulletin, 25*(10).

Cohn, A. H., (1987a, June). How do we deal with research findings? *Journal of Interpersonal Violence, 228–232.*

Cohn, A. H. (1987b). Our national priorities for prevention. In R. E. Helfer & R. S. Kempe (Eds.),

The battered child (4th ed., pp. 444–455). Chicago: University of Chicago Press.

Cohn, A. H., & Birch, T. L. (1988). Building resources for prevention programs. In D. C. Bross et al. (Eds.), *The new child protection team handbook* (pp. 598–615). New York: Garland.

Cole, E. S. (1987). Adoption. In A. Minahan (Ed.), *Encyclopedia of social work* (Vol. 1, 18th ed.). Silver Spring, MD: National Association of Social Workers.

Coleman, J. S. (1966). *Equality of educational opportunity*. Washington, DC: U.S. Government Printing Office.

Coleman, S. H. (1924). *Humane society leaders in America*. Albany, NY: The American Humane Association.

Coles, R. (1971). *Children of crisis, Vol. 2. Migrants, sharecroppers, mountaineers*. Boston: Little, Brown.

Colley, L., Culbertson, R. G., & Latessa, E. J. (1987). Juvenile probation officers: A job analysis. *Juvenile & Family Court Journal, 38*(1), 1–12.

Collins, A. H., & Watson, E. L. (1976). *Family day care*. Boston: Beacon Press.

Colvin, R. W. (1962). Toward the development of a foster parent attitude test. In *Quantitative approaches to parent selection* (pp. 45–46). New York: Child Welfare League of America.

Commonwealth v. Fisher, 213 Pa. 48, 53–56 (1905).

Comptroller General. (1973). *Social services: Do they help welfare recipients achieve self-support or reduced dependency?* Washington, DC: U.S. Department of Health, Education and Welfare, Social and Rehabilitation Service.

Comptroller General. (1983). *Report to the Congress of the United States: Analysis of migration characteristics of children served under the migrant educational program*. Washington, DC: Author.

Conant, J. (1961). *Slums and suburbs*. New York: McGraw Hill.

Condelli, L. (1988). *National evaluation of the impact of guardians* ad litem *in child abuse or neglect judicial proceedings*. Washington, DC: Administration for Children, Youth and Families.

Conte, J. (1984). The justice system and sexual abuse of children. *Social Service Review, 58*(4), 556–568.

Cooper, S. P. (1976). *History of the federal interagency day care requirements*. Paper prepared for U.S. Department of Health, Education, and Welfare, Washington, DC.

Costin, L. B. (n.d.). *"The cruelty." Rescuing the victims of child abuse, 1874–1960*. Unpublished manuscript.

Costin, L. B. (1953). Implications of psychological testing for adoptive placements. *Journal of Social Casework, 34*(2), 68–73.

Costin, L. B. (1954). The history-giving interview in adoption procedures. *Journal of social casework, 35*(11), 393–400.

Costin, L. B. (1983). *Two sisters for social justice: A biography of Grace and Edith Abbott*. Urbana, IL: University of Illinois Press.

Costin, L. B. (1985a). Introduction. In L. Costin (Ed.), *Child Welfare, 64*(3): *Special Issue: Toward a Feminist Approach to Child Welfare* (pp. 197–201).

Costin, L. B. (1985b). Protective behaviors. *Social Work in Education, 7*(4), 210–211.

Cowan, E. A., & Stout, E. (1939). A comparative study of the adjustment made by foster children after complete and partial breaks in continuity of home environment. *American Journal of Orthopsychiatry, 9*(2).

Coyne, A., & Brown, M. E. (1985). Developmentally disabled children can be adopted. *Child Welfare, 64*(6), 607–615.

Craft, J. L., Epley, S. W., & Clarkson, C. D. (1980). Factors influencing legal dispositions in child abuse investigations. *Journal of Social Science Research, 4*(1), 31–46.

Cross, T. L. (1986). Drawing on cultural tradition in Indian child welfare practice. *Social Casework, 67*, 283–289.

Crumidy, P. M., & Jacobziner, H. (1966, August). A study of young unmarried mothers who kept their babies. *American Journal of Public Health, 56*, 1242–1251.

C.S.R. Study of adoption subsidy. (1983). Washington, DC: C.R.S.

Currie, E. (1982). Fighting crime. *Working Papers, 9*(4).

Curtis, P. A. (1986). The dialectics of open versus closed adoption of infants. *Child Welfare, 65*(5), 437–445.

Dahl, A. S., Cowgill, K. M., & Asmundsson, R. (1987). Life in remarriage families. *Social Work, 32*(1), 40–49.

Dall, A. (1977). Subsidized adoption in New York City. In *Adoption of the older foster child*. New

York: New York State Council of Voluntary Child Care Agencies.

D'Amico, S. A. (1986). The development and evaluation of a court-connected juvenile mediation program. *Juvenile & Family Court Journal, 37*(5), 7–13.

Danzinger, S., & Nichols-Casebolt, A. (1987–1988). Teen parents and child support: Eligibility, participation, and payment. *Journal of Social Service Research, 11*(2/3), 1–20.

Daro, D., & Mitchel, L. (1989). *Child abuse fatalities continue to rise: The results of the 1988 annual fifty state survey* (Working paper number 808). Chicago: National Committee for Prevention of Child Abuse, National Center on Child Abuse Prevention Research.

Datta, L. E. (1969). *A report on evaluation studies of project Head Start.* Paper presented at the 1969 Annual Convention of the American Psychological Association, Washington, DC.

Davidson, H. A., & Gerlach, K. (1984). Child custody disputes: The child's perspective. In R. M. Horowitz & H. A. Davidson (Eds.), *Legal rights of children* (pp. 232–261). Colorado Springs: Shepard's/McGraw-Hill.

Davidson, W. S., & Rapp, C. A. (1976). Advocacy in the juvenile justice system. *Social Work, 3,* 225–233.

Davidson, W. S., & Seidman, E. (1974). Studies of behavior modification and juvenile delinquency. *Psychological Bulletin, 81*(12), 998–1011.

Davidson, W. S., Seidman, E., Rappaport, J., Rapp, C. A., Rhodes, W., & Herring, J. (1977). The diversion of juvenile offenders: Some empirical light on the subject. *Social Work Research and Abstracts, 13*(2), 40–49.

Davidson, W. S., & Wolfred, T. R. (1977). Evaluation of a community-based behavior modification program for prevention of delinquency: The failure of success. *Community Mental Health Journal, 13*(4), 296–306.

Davis, A. L. (1948, December). Attitudes toward minority groups: Their effect on social services for unmarried mothers. *The Child, 13,* 82–85.

Davis, L. E., & Proctor, E. K. (1989). *Race, gender, and class: Guidelines for practice with individuals, families and groups.* Englewood Cliffs, NJ: Prentice Hall.

Davis, R., & Douck, P. (1955). Crucial importance of adoption home study. *Child Welfare, 34.*

Davis, S. M., & Schwartz, M. D. (1987). *Children's rights and the law.* Lexington, MA: Lexington Books/D. C. Heath.

DCFS out-of-state placements reduced. (1976, November 9). *Champaign-Urbana News Gazette,* p. 3.

de Anda, D., & Becerra, R. (1984). Support networks for adolescent mothers. *Social Casework, 65,* 172–181.

DeAngelo, A. J. (1988). Diversion programs in the juvenile justice system: An alternative method of treatment for juvenile offenders. *Juvenile & Family Court Journal, 39*(1), 21–28.

Deardurff, D. D. (1986). Representing the interests of the abused and neglected child: The guardian *ad litem* and access to confidential information. *University of Dayton Law Review, 11*(3).

Deasy, L. C., & Quinn, O. W. (1962). The urban Negro and adoption of children. *Child Welfare, 41*(9), 400–407.

de Blasio, F. (1988, Fall). A time to question SBCs. *Health and Social Work, 13,* 305–307.

Debo, A. (1940). *And still the waters run.* Princeton, NJ: Princeton University Press.

De Francis, V. (1987). Landmarks in the development of CPS. *Protecting Children, 4*(3), 3–5.

De Fries, Z., Jenkins, S., & Williams, E. C. (1965). Foster family care for disturbed children. A non-sentimental view. *Child Welfare, 44*(2).

Delaney, J. J. (1976). New concepts of the family court. In R. E. Helfer & C. H. Kempe (Eds.), *Child abuse and neglect, the family and community.* Cambridge, MA: Ballinger.

Delaware Code Ann. 13, Ch. 9, 911 (1953).

Department of Labor, Wage and Hours Division. (1982, July 16). Fair labor standards act. Child labor regulation No. 3; employment of 14 and 15 year olds, proposed rule. *Federal Register* (Pt. 7), *47,* 137, 30959–31260.

De Schweinitz, E., & De Schweinitz, K. (1964). The place of authority in the protective function of the public welfare agency. *Child Welfare, 43*(6), 286–291.

DeShaney v. Winnebago County Department of Social Services, 109 S.Ct. 998 (1989).

Deykin, E. Y., Campbell, L., & Patti, P. (1984). The postadoption experience of surrendering parents. *American Journal of Orthopsychiatry, 54*(2), 271–280.

Deykin, E. Y., Patti, P., & Ryan, J. (1988). Fathers

of adopted children: A study of the impact of child surrender on birthfathers. *American Journal of Orthopsychiatry, 58*(2), 240–248.

Dietrich, G. (1982). Indian Child Welfare Act: Ideas for implementation. *Child Abuse and Neglect, 6*(2).

Dionne, E. J. (1989, July 4). On both sides, advocates predict a 50-state battle. *New York Times,* p. 1, 9.

Divine-Hawkins, P. (1981). *Family day care in the United States, Executive summary, National day care home study final report* (Publication No. [OHDS] 80-30287). Washington, DC: U.S. Department of Health and Human Services.

Dobbert, D. L. (1987). Positive contingency probation management. *Juvenile & Family Court Journal, 38*(1), 29–33.

Dodson, D. (1983). Advocating at periodic review proceedings. In M. Hardin (Ed.), *Foster children in the Courts* (pp. 86–127). Boston: Butterworth Legal.

Dodson, G. D. (1984). Legal rights of adolescents: Restrictions on liberty, emancipation, and status offenses. In H. A. Davidson & R. M. Horowitz (Eds.), *Children and the law* (pp. 114–176). Washington, DC: Young Lawyers Division, The American Bar Association; The National Legal Resources Center for Child Advocacy and Protection.

Dorris, K., & Dorsey, P. (1989). Whose rights are we protecting, anyway? *Children Today, 18*(3), 6–8.

Downs, S. W. (1989). Foster parents of mentally retarded and physically handicapped children. In J. Hudson, et al. (Eds.), *Specialist foster family care: A normalizing experience.* New York: The Haworth Press.

Downs, S. W. (1990). Recruiting and retaining foster parents of adolescents. In A. Maluccio et al, (Eds.), *Preparing for life after foster care: The crucial role of foster parents.* Washington DC: The Child Welfare League of America.

Downs, S. W. (in press). Foster parents' length of tenure: demographic, motivational, and agency factors. *Journal of Sociology and Social Welfare.*

Downs, S. W., & Nahan, N. (in press). A neighborhood based family support program for self-referred and maltreating families. *Public Welfare.*

Downs, S. W., and Sherraden, M. (1983). The orphan asylum in the nineteenth century. *Social Service Review, 57*(2), 272–290.

Draughon, M. (1975). Stepmother's model of identification in relation to mourning the child. *Psychological Reports, 36,* 183–189.

Drury, L. (n.d.). *Illegitimacy as a child welfare problem: Part 3.* (Children's Bureau Publication No. 128).

Dukette, R. (1984). Value issues in present-day adoption. *Child Welfare. 63*(3), 233–244.

Dukette, R., & Thompson, T. G. (1959). *Adoptive resources for Negro children.* New York: Child Welfare League of America.

Duquette, D. N. (1983). Collaboration between lawyers and mental health professionals: Making it work. In M. Hardin (Ed.), *Foster children in the courts* (pp. 489–517). Chicago: American Bar Association.

Duquette, D. N. (1988a). Legal interventions. In K. C. Faller, *Child sexual abuse: An interdisciplinary manual for diagnosis, case management, and treatment.* New York: Columbia University Press.

Duquette, D. N. (1988b). Child advocacy 1988: Lessons learned. In H. A. Davidson & R. M. Horowitz (Eds.), *Child and the law* (pp. 244–264). Washington, DC: American Bar Association and National Legal Resource Center for Child Advocacy and Protection.

Duva, J., & Raley, G. (1988). *Transitional difficulties of out-of-home youth.* Washington, DC: Youth and America's Future: William T. Grant Foundation Commission on Work, Family and Citizenship.

Edelman, M. W. (1987). *Families in peril: An agenda for social change.* Cambridge, MA: Harvard University Press.

Edmonton, Canada. (1988). *Report on adoption.* Edmonton, Canada, Department of Public Welfare. Mimeographed.

Edwards, Judge L. (1985, Spring). A proposal for the appointment of counsel for children in marital dissolution actions. In M. Bloom & J. Buffaloe (Eds.), *The Newsletter.* San Diego: California Chapter of Family and Conciliation Courts.

Eisenberg, L. (1962). The sins of the fathers: Urban decay and social pathology. *American Journal of Orthopsychiatry, 32*(1), 5–17.

Eitzen, T. (1985). A child's right to independent representation in a custody dispute: A unique legal situation, a necessarily broad standard, the child's constitutional rights, the role of the attorney whose client is the child. *Family Law Quarterly, 19*(1), 53–76.

Ellrod, F. E., Jr., & Melaney, D. H. (1950, Winter). Juvenile justice: Treatment or travesty. *University of Pittsburgh Law Review, 11,* 277–287.

Elmer, E. (1967). *Children in jeopardy.* Pittsburgh: University of Pittsburgh Press.

Elonen, A. S., & Schwartz, E. M. (1969). A longitudinal study of emotional, social and academic functioning of adopted children. *Social Welfare, 48*(2).

Elson, A. (1962). Juvenile courts and due process. In M. K. Rosenheim (Ed.), *Justice for the child* (pp. 95–117). New York: Free Press.

Emlen, A. C. (1973). Slogans, slots, and slander: The myth of day care need. *American Journal of Orthopsychiatry, 43*(1).

Emlen, A. C. (1978). *Overcoming barriers to planning for children in foster care.* Washington, DC: U.S. Government Printing Office.

Engel, M., Marsden, G., & Woodaman, S. (1968). Orientation to work in children. *American Journal of Orthopsychiatry, 38*(1), 137–143.

Epstein, E. F. (1982). International adoption: The need for a guardianship provision. *Boston University International Law Journal, 1,* 225–248.

Epstein, I. (1981, Summer). Advocates on advocacy: An exploratory study. *Social Work Research & Abstracts.*

Escalona, S. K. (1967). Mental health, the educational process and the schools. *American Journal of Orthopsychiatry, 37*(1), 2.

Escobedo v. Illinois, 378 U.S. 478 (1964).

Excerpts from the court's ruling on Minnesota's abortion law. From the opinion of Justice Stevens. (1990, June 26). *New York Times,* p. 13.

Ex parte Loving, 178 M. 194, 202 (1903).

Fairweather, M. E. (1952). Early placement in adoption. *Child Welfare, 31*(3), 3–8.

Falk, L. L. (1970). A comparative study of transracial and inracial adoptions. *Child Welfare, 49*(2), 82–88.

Faller, K. C. (1988a). *Child sexual abuse: An interdisciplinary manual for diagnosis, case management, and treatment.* New York: Columbia University Press.

Faller, K. C. (1988b). Criteria for judging the credibility of children's statements about their sexual abuse. *Child Welfare, 67*(5), 389–401.

Faller, K. C. (1988c). Decision-making in cases of intrafamilial child sexual abuse. *American Journal of Orthopsychiatry, 58*(1), 121–128.

Famularo, R., Stone, K., Barnum, R., & Wharton, R. (1986). Alcoholism and severe child maltreatment. *American Journal of Orthopsychiatry, 56*(3), 481–485.

Fanshel, D. (1957). *A study in Negro adoption.* New York: Child Welfare League of America.

Fanshel, D. (1961a). Specializations within the foster parent role: A research report, Pt. 1. *Child Welfare, 40*(3), 17–21; *40*(4), 19–23.

Fanshel, D. (1961b). Specializations within the foster parent role: A research report, Pt. 2. *Child Welfare, 40*(4), 19–23.

Fanshel, D. (1963). Commentary on "clinical judgement in foster care placement." *Child Welfare, 42.*

Fanshel, D. (1966). Child Welfare. In H. E. Maas, (Ed.), *Five fields of social service: reviews of research,* (pp. 85–143.) New York: National Association of Social Workers.

Fanshel, D. (1970). The role of foster parents in the future of foster care. In H. D. Stone (Ed.), *Foster care in question* (pp. 228–240). New York: Child Welfare League of America.

Fanshel, D. (1972). *Far from the reservation: The transracial adoption of American Indian children.* Metuchen, NJ: Scarecrow Press.

Fanshel, D. (1975a). Parental visiting of children in foster care: Key to discharge. *Social Service Review, 49*(4), 493–514.

Fanshel, D. (1975b). Parental failure and consequences for children: The drug-abusing mother whose children are in foster care. *American Journal of Public Health, 65*(6), 604–612.

Fanshel, D. (1976, May). *The impact of research on social policy: Foster care of children as a case example.* Paper presented on the 40th anniversary celebration of the School of Social Work, University of Hawaii, Honolulu.

Fanshel, D. (1981). Decision-making under uncertainty: Foster care for abusive or neglected children? *American Journal of Public Health, 71*(7), 685–686.

Fanshel, D. (1982). *On the road to permanency: An expanded data base for service to children in foster care.* New York: Child Welfare League of America, Columbia University School of Social Work.

Fanshel, D., Finch, S. J., & Grundy, J. F. (1987).

Collection of data relating to adoption and foster care. Washington, DC: Technical Appendix to the Report of the Advisory Committee on Adoption and Foster Care Information, Administration for Children, Youth and Families, U.S. Department of Health and Human Services.

Fanshel, D., Finch, S. J., & Grundy, J. F. (1989a). Modes of exit from foster family care and adjustment at time of departure of children with unstable life histories. *Child Welfare, 68*(4), 391–402.

Fanshel, D., Finch, S. J., & Grundy, J. F. (1989b). Foster children in life-course perspective: The Casey Family Program experience. *Child Welfare, 68*(5), 467–478.

Fanshel, D., & Grundy, J. (1975). *Computerized data for children in foster care: first analyses from a management information service in New York City.* New York: Child Welfare Information Services.

Fanshel, D., & Shinn, E. B. (1978). *Children in foster care: A longitudinal investigation.* New York: Columbia University Press.

Farber, E. A., & Egeland, B. (1982). Developmental consequences of out-of-home care for infants in a low-income population. In E. F. Zigler, & E. W. Gordon (Eds.), *Day care. Scientific and social policy issues.* Boston: Auburn House.

Farber, M. A. (1969, April 8). Head Start report held "full of holes." *New York Times,* p. 5.

Farmer, J. (1969). *Senate hearings on Headstart Child Development Act* (Pt. 1, 91st Cong., 1st Sess.).

Federal Interagency Day Care Requirements (FIDCR). (1968). Department of Health, Education and Welfare Publication No. 938–038. Washington, DC: U.S. Government Printing Office.

Feigelman, W., & Silverman, A. R. (1977). Single parent adoptions. *Social Casework, 58,* 418–25.

Feigelman, W., & Silverman, A. R. (1984). The long-term effects of transracial adoption. *Social Service Review, 58*(4), 588–602.

Fein, E., & Knaut, S. A. (1986). Crisis intervention and support: Working with the police. *Social Casework, 67,* (5) 276–282.

Fein, E., Maluccio, A. N., Hamilton, V. J., & Ward, D. E. (1983). After foster care: Outcomes of permanency planning for children. *Child Welfare, 62*(6), 485–558.

Feld, B. C. (1987). The Juvenile court meets the principle of the offense: Legislative changes in juvenile waiver statutes. *Journal of Criminal Law & Criminology, 78*(3), 471–533.

Feldman, K. W. (1987). Child abuse by burning. In R. E. Helfer & R. S. Kempe, (Eds.), *The battered child* (4th ed., pp. 197–213). Chicago: University of Chicago Press.

Fellner, I. W. (1968). Recruiting adoptive applicants. *Social Work. 13*(1).

Felt, J. P. (1965). *Hostages of fortune: Child labor reform in New York State.* Syracuse, NY: Syracuse University Press.

Felt, S. K. (1983). The effects of neglect on children and implications for treatment. In C. M. Trainor (Ed.)., *The dilemma of child neglect: Identification and treatment* (pp. 15–27). Denver: American Humane Association, Children's Division.

Festinger, T. B. (1975). The New York court review of children in foster care. *Child Welfare, 54*(4), 211–245.

Festinger, T. B. (1976). The impact of the New York court review of children in foster care: A follow-up report. *Child Welfare, 55*(8), 515–544.

Festinger, T. B. (1983). *No one ever asked us . . . A postscript to foster care.* New York: Columbia University Press.

Festinger, T. B. (1986). *Necessary risk—A study of adoptions and disrupted adoptive placements.* Washington, DC: Child Welfare League of America.

Figueira-McDonough, J. (1985a). Discrimination or sex differences? Criteria for evaluating the juvenile justice system's handling of minor offenses. *Crime & Delinquency, 33*(2), 403–424.

Figueira-McDonough, J. (1985b). Are girls different? Gender discrepancies between delinquent behavior and control. *Child Welfare, 64*(3), 273–289.

Fimmen, M. D., & Mietus, K. J. (1988). *An empirical analysis of the impact of joint training upon child welfare practitioners* (DHHS Award No. 05CT1022/01). Macomb, IL: Western Illinois University.

Finch, J., Fanshel, D., & Grundy, J. F. (1990). *Data collection in adoption and foster care: A description of the state of the art in developing the capacity for obtaining organized information for policy analysis, program planning and practice.* Washington, DC: Child Welfare League of America.

Finkelhor, D. (1979). *Sexually victimized children.* New York: Free Press.

Finkelhor, D. (1984). *Child sexual abuse: New theory and research.* New York: Free Press.

Finkelhor, D., et al. (1988). *Sexual abuse in day care: A national study. Executive summary.* Durham: Family Research Laboratory, University of New Hampshire.

Fischer, J. (1973). Is casework effective? A review. *Social Work, 18*(1), 5–20.

Fiske, E. B. (1988, April 27). 35 pages that shook the U.S. education world. *New York Times,* p. 24.

Fjeld, S. P., Newsom, L., & Fjeld, R. M. (1981, May). Delinquents and status offenders: The similarity of differences. *Juvenile & Family Court Journal, 32.*

Fleiss, B. H. (1962). *The relationship of the Mayor's Committee on Wartime Care of Children to day care in New York City.* Unpublished doctoral dissertation, New York University.

Fleming, D. (1986). Child advocacy grows up. *Youth Policy, 8*(11), 5–8.

Flexner, B., & Baldwin, R. N. (1914). *Juvenile courts and probation.* New York: Century.

Flexner, B., & Oppenheimer, R. (1922). *The legal aspect of the juvenile court* (Children's Bureau Publication No. 99). Washington, DC: Children's Bureau.

Flicker, B. D. (1977). *Standards for juvenile justice: A summary and analysis* (Institute of Judicial Administration and American Bar Association, Juvenile Justice Standards Project). Cambridge, MA: Ballinger.

Folks, H. (1911). *The care of destitute, neglected, and delinquent children.* New York: Macmillan.

Foresman, L., Martin, N., Safier, R., & Scherer, L. (1963, March). The team approach in Protective Service. *Child Welfare, 42,* 135–138.

Forest, I. (1927). *Pre-school education: A historical and critical study.* New York: Macmillan.

Forsythe, P. (1987). Redefining child protective services. *Protecting Children, 4*(3), 12–16.

Fradkin, H. E. (1962). Disposition dilemmas of American juvenile courts. In M. K. Rosenheim (Ed.), *Justice for the child.* (pp. 123–126). New York: Free Press.

Fraley, Y. L. (1984). The family support center: Early intervention for high-risk parents and children. In *Perspectives on Child Maltreatment in the Mid '80s.* U.S. Department of Health and Human Services (DHHS Publication No. [OHDS] 84–30338).

Washington, DC: U.S. Government Printing Office.

Franek, C. C. (1980). Children's rights after the Supreme Court's decision on Parham v. J. L. and J. R. *Child Welfare, 59*(6).

Frank, M. (1983). Parenting education as an approach to treating neglecting families. In C. M. Trainor (Ed.), *The dilemma of child neglect: Identification and treatment.* Denver: American Humane Association.

Frankel, H. (1988). Family-centered, home-based services in child protection: A review of the research. *Social Service Review, 62*(1), 137–157.

Franklin, D. L. (1988). Race, class, and adolescent pregnancy: An ecological analysis. *American Journal of Orthopsychiatry, 58*(3), 339–354.

Franklin, D. S., & Massarik, F. (1969). The adoption of children with medical conditions (Pts. 1, 2, 3). *Child Welfare, 48*(8), 459–467; (9), 533–539; (10), 595–601.

Fraser, B., & Martin, H. P. (1976). An advocate for the abused child. In H. P. Martin (Ed.), *The abused child.* Cambridge, MA: Ballinger.

Fraser, G. G. (1972, April 10). Blacks condemn mixed adoptions. *New York Times.*

Fraser, C. G. (1937). *The licensing of boarding homes, maternity homes, and child welfare agencies.* Social Service Monographs. Chicago: University of Chicago Press.

Freebury, A. (1988). *Proceedings. Policy directions for foster and residential care licensing.* Portland, ME: National Child Welfare Resource Center for Management and Administration.

Freebury, A. (1989, April 15). Personal communication.

Freeman, E. M. (1990). The black family's life cycle: Operationalizing a strengths perspective. In S. M. L. Logan, E. M. Freeman, & R. G. McRoy (Eds.), *Social work practice with black families* (pp. 55–72). White Plains, NY: Longman.

Freeman, E. M., & Pennekamp, M. (1988). *Social work practice. Toward a child, family, school, community perspective.* Springfield, IL: C. C. Thomas.

Freeman, M. D. (1984). Subsidized adoption. In P. Bean (Ed.), *Adoption essays in social policy, law and sociology* (pp. 203–226). London and New York: Tavistock.

Freitag, M. (1990, February 5). Doing grown-ups'

work: Child labor laws flouted. *New York Times,* p. 12.

Freud, C. (1955). Meaning of separation to parents and children as seen in child placement. *Public Welfare, 13*(1), 13–17, 25.

Freund, E. (1935). Licensing. In *Encyclopedia of the social sciences* (Vol. 9). Chicago: University of Chicago Press.

Fricke, H. (1965). Interracial adoption: The little revolution. *Social Work, 10*(3), 92–97.

Friedman, R. (Ed.). (1989). *Advocacy on behalf of children with serious emotional problems.* Springfield, IL: C. C. Thomas.

Friedrich, W., & Boriskin, J. (1976). The role of the child in abuse: A review of literature. *American Journal of Orthopsychiatry, 46*(4), 580–590.

Friesen, B., Griesbach, J., Jacobs, J., Katz-Leavy, J., & Olson, D. (1988). Improving services for families. *Children Today, 17*(4), 18–22.

Fritz, M. (1986). Parents anonymous: Helping clients to accept professional services, a personal opinion. *Child Abuse & Neglect, 10*(1), 121–125.

Fromm, E. (1941). *Escape from freedom.* New York: Farrar and Rinehart.

Furstenberg, F. F. (1976). *Unplanned parenthood: The social consequences of teenage childbearing.* New York: Free Press.

Furstenberg, F. F. (1980). Burdens and benefits: The impact of early childbearing on the family. *Journal of Social Issues, 36*(1), 64–87.

Furstenberg, F. F., & Harris, K. M. (1990, April 6). *The disappearing father? Divorce and the waning significance of biological parenthood.* Paper presented at the Albany Conference on Demographic Perspectives on the American Family: Patterns and Prospects.

Galambos, N. L., & Garbarino, J. (1983). Identifying the missing links in the study of latchkey children. *Children Today, 12*(4), 2–4, 40–41.

Galaway, B. (1988). Crime victim and offender mediation as a social work strategy. *Social Service Review, 62*(4), 668–683.

Gallant, C. B. (1982). *Mediation in special education disputes.* Washington, DC: National Association of Social Workers.

Gallay, G. (1963). Interracial adoption. *Canadian Welfare, 39*(6).

Gamble, T. J., & Zigler, E. (1986). Effects of infant day care: Another look at the evidence. *American Journal of Orthopsychiatry, 56*(1), 26–42.

Gambrill, E. D., & Stein, T. J. (1981). Decision making and case management: Achieving continuity of care for children in out-of-home placement. In A. N. Maluccio & P. A. Sinanoglu (Eds.), *The challenge of partnership: Working with parents of children in foster care* (pp. 109–134). Washington, DC: Child Welfare League of America.

Garbarino, J., & Ebata, A. (1983). The significance of ethnic and cultural differences in child maltreatment. *Journal of Marriage and the Family, 45,* 773–783.

Garbarino, J., & Gilliam, G. (1980). *Understanding abusive families.* Lexington, MA: Heath.

Garbarino, J., & Jacobson, N. (1978). Youth helping youth in cases of maltreatment of adolescents. *Child Welfare, 17*(8), 505–510.

Garbarino, J., Sebes, J., & Schellenbach, C. (1984). Families at risk for destructive parent-child relations in adolescence. *Child Development, 55,* 174–183.

Garbarino, J., & Sherman, D. (1980). High-risk neighborhoods and high-risk families: The human ecology of child maltreatment. *Child Development, 51,* 188–198.

Garfinkel, I., & McLanahan, S. S. (1986). *Single mothers and their children.* Washington, DC: Urban Institute Press.

Garfinkel, I., & Sorenson, A. (1982). Sweden's child support system: Lessons for the United States. *Social Work, 27*(6), 509–515.

Geis, G. (1958, February). Publicity and juvenile court proceedings. *Rocky Mountain Law Review, 30,* 101–126.

Geismar, L. (1973). *555 families: A social psychological study of young families in transition.* New Brunswick, NJ: Transaction.

Geismar, L., & LaSorte, M. A. (1964). *Understanding the multiproblem family.* New York: Association Press.

Gelles, R. J. (1984). Parental child snatching: A preliminary estimate of the national incidence. *Journal of Marriage and the Family, 46*(3), 735–739.

Genden, J. K. (1976). Separate legal representation for children: Protecting the rights and interests of minors in judicial proceedings. *Harvard Civil Rights-Liberties Law Review, 11*(3), 565–595.

Gershenson, C. (1990, June 11). Personal communication. Washington, DC: Center for the Study of Social Policy.

Gershenson, C., & Kresh, E. (1986). School enrollment status of children receiving child welfare services at home or in foster care. *Child Welfare Research Note #15.* Washington, DC: Office of Human Development Services.

Gershenson, C., Maza, P. & Fucillo, A. (1983–1984). *Child welfare research notes, Nos. 1–6.* Washington, DC: U.S. Department of Health and Human Services, Administration for Children, Youth and Families, Children's Bureau.

Gesell, A. (1923a, November). Public school provision for exceptional children. *Annals of the American Academy of Political and Social Science, 98,* 73–81.

Gesell, A. (1923b). *The preschool child from the standpoint of public hygiene and education.* Boston: Houghton Mifflin.

Gibbens, T. C. N., & Walker, A. (1956, April). Violent cruelty to children. *British Journal of Delinquency, 6,* 260–277.

Gideon v. Wainwright, 372 U.S. 335 (1963).

Gil, D. (1964). Developing routine follow-up procedures for child welfare services. *Child Welfare, 43*(5), 229–240.

Gil, D. G. (1968). Legally reported child abuse: A nationwide survey. In National Conference on Social Welfare, *Social Work Practice.* New York: Columbia University Press.

Gil, D. G. (1970). *Violence against children: Physical child abuse in the United States.* Cambridge, MA: Harvard University Press.

Gil, D. G. (1981). The United States versus child abuse. In L. H. Pelton (Ed.), *The social context of child abuse and neglect.* New York: Human Sciences Press.

Gil, D. G. (1985). The ideological context of child welfare. In J. Laird & A. Hartman (Eds.), *A handbook of child welfare* (pp. 11–33). New York: Macmillan.

Gilbert, N., & Specht (1976). Advocacy and professional ethics. *Social Work, 21*(4), 288–293.

Gill, M. M., & Amadio, C. M. (1983). Social work and law in a foster care/adoption program. *Child Welfare, 62*(5), 455–467.

Giovannoni, J. M. (1987). Children. In *Encyclopedia of social work* (pp. 242–254). Washington, DC: National Association of Social Workers.

Giovannoni, J. M., & Becerra, R. M. (1979). *Defining child abuse.* New York: Free Press.

Giovannoni, J. M., & Billingsley, A. (1970, April). Child neglect among the poor: A study of parental adequacy in families of three ethnic groups. *Child Welfare, 49,* 196–204.

Girls Clubs of America. (1988). *Facts and reflections on girls and substance abuse.* New York: Author.

Gitlin, H. J. (1987, November 3). The rights of fathers of illegitimate children in adoption hearings. *Chicago Daily Law Bulletin,* pp. 2, 20.

Gittis, L. (1988). A multidisciplinary model for representing the child in neglect and abuse proceedings in juvenile court. In H. A. Davidson & R. M. Horowitz (Eds.), *Children and the law* (pp. 221–243). Washington, DC: American Bar Association/National Legal Resource Center for Child Advocacy and Protection.

Glueck, S., & Glueck, E. T. (1934). *One thousand juvenile delinquents.* Cambridge: Harvard University Press.

Goldfarb, W. (1945). Effects of psychological deprivation in infancy and subsequent stimulation. *American Journal of Psychiatry, 102,* 18–33.

Goldring, H., & Tutleman, J. (1970). *Adoption failures at the Los Angeles County Department of Adoptions.* Unpublished master's thesis, University of Southern California.

Goldstein, B., & Oldham, J. (1979). *Children and work. A study of socialization.* New Brunswick, NJ: Transaction Books.

Goldstein, J., Freud, A., & Solnit, A. J. (1973). *Beyond the best interests of the child.* New York: Free Press.

Goldstein, J., Freud, A., & Solnit, A. J. (1979). *Before the best interests of the child.* New York: Free Press.

Goleman, D. (1988, September 22). Studies of latchkey children say effects need not be bad. *New York Times,* pp. 1, 25.

Gomez v. Perez, 409 U.S. 535 (1973).

Gordon, L. (1988). *Heroes of their own lives: The politics and history of family violence.* New York: Viking.

Goss v. Lopez, 95 S. Ct. 729 (1975).

Gothard, S. (1989). Power in the court: The social worker as an expert witness. *Social Work, 34*(1), 65–67.

Gottesfeld, H. (1970). *In loco parentis: A study of perceived role values in foster home care.* New York: Jewish Child Care Association of New York.

Gould, K. H. (1991). Limiting change is not enough: A minority perspective on child welfare issues. In

S. S. Chipunger, B. R. Leashore, & Everette, J. E. (Eds.), *Scorned children: An Africentric perspective on child welfare.* New Brunswick, NJ: Rutgers University Press.

Graham, L. B. (1957). Children from Japan in American adoptive homes. In *Casework papers, 1957.* New York: Family Service Association of America.

Gray, E., & Coolsen, P. (1987). How do kids really feel about being home alone? *Children Today, 16*(4), 30–32.

Greenblatt, B. (1977). *Responsibility for child care: The changing roles of family and state in child development.* San Francisco, CA: Jossey-Bass.

Greenhouse, L. (1988a, June 6). Despite support, a child care bill fails to emerge. *New York Times,* p. 8.

Greenhouse, L. (1988b, September 8). Church-state debate blocks day care bill. *New York Times,* p. 14.

Greenhouse, L. (1989a, March 9). Justices' rulings have a ripple effect on the law. *New York Times,* p. 14.

Greenhouse, L. (1989b, July 4). Change in course. *New York Times,* pp. 1, 8.

Greenhouse, L. (1990a, June 26). States may require girls to notify parents before having abortion. *New York Times,* p. 1, 13.

Greenhouse, L. (1990b, June 28). Child abuse trials can use television. *New York Times,* A1, A12, A13.

Greenleigh Associates. (1960). *Facts, fallacies and future: A study of the Aid to Dependent Children Program of Cook County, Illinois.* New York: Greenleigh Associates.

Greif, G. L. (1985). *Single fathers.* Lexington, MA: Lexington Books.

Gross, J. (1988, February 13). Cocaine and AIDS in New York cause rise in infant deaths. *New York Times,* pp. 1, 10.

Grotevant, H. D. (1988). The rise and fall of transracial adoption: Science meets politics (Review of *Transracial adoptees and their families: A study of identity and commitment*). *Contemporary Psychology, 33,* 853–855.

Grow, L. J. (1979). Today's unmarried mothers: The choices have changed. *Child Welfare, 58*(6), 363–371.

Grow, L. J., & Shapiro, D. (1974). *Black children,*

white parents: A study of transracial adoption.* New York: Child Welfare League of America.

Gruber, A. R. (1973). *Foster home care in Massachusetts.* Boston: Governor's Commission on Adoption and Foster care.

Gula, M. (1964). *Agency operated group homes* (Children's Bureau Publication No. 416). Washington, DC: Children's Bureau.

Gurdin, P., & Anderson, G. R. (1987). Quality care for ill children: AIDS-specialized foster family homes. *Child Welfare, 66*(4), 291–302.

Gusfield, J. (1963). *Symbolic crusade: Status politics and the American temperance movement.* Urbana, IL: University of Illinois Press.

Gutierrez, M. J. (1987). Teenage pregnancy and the Puerto Rican family. In M. Lindblad-Goldberg (Ed.), *Clinical issues in single-parent households* (pp. 73–84). Rockville, MD: Aspen.

Guttenberg, M. (1966). The parallel institutions of the poverty act: Evaluating their effect on unemployed youth and on existing institutions. *American Journal of Orthopsychiatry, 36*(7).

Haas, W. (1959, July). Reaching out—A dynamic concept in casework. *Social Work, 4,* 41–45.

Hagen, C. (1965, May). *Basic values in adoption.* Paper presented at the meeting of the Adoptive Parents Committee of New York, New York.

Hall, E. H., & King, G. C. (1982). Working with the strengths of black families. *Child Welfare, 61*(8), 536–544.

Hall, M. (1978, September). Lesbian families: Cultural and clinical issues. *Social Work, 23,* 380–385.

Hall, M., DeLaCruz, A., & Russell, P. (1984). Working with neglecting families. In *Perspectives on child maltreatment in the mid '80s* (DHHS Publication No. [OHDS] 84-30338, pp. 41–44). Washington, DC: U.S. Government Printing Office.

Halliday, S. B. (1861). *The little street sweeper: Or life among the poor.* New York: Phinney, Blakemont and Mason.

Hamilton, A. (1791). On the employment of children. *American State Papers, Documents, Legislative and Executive of the Congress of the United States from the First Session of the First to the Third Session of the Thirteenth Congress, Inclusive, Class III, Finance* (1832). In G. Abbott (1938). *The child and the state* (Vol. 1). Chicago: University of Chicago Press, pp. 276–277.

Hammer v. Dagenhart, 247 U.S. 251, 268 (1918).

Handler, J. F. (1965). The Juvenile court and the adversary system: Problems of function and form. *Wisconsin Law Review, 7,* 7–51.

Handler, J., & Rosenheim, M. K. (1966, Spring). Privacy in welfare: Public assistance and juvenile justice. *Law and Contemporary Problems, 31,* 377–409.

Hardin, M. (1983). Legal placement options to achieve permanence for children in foster care. In M. Hardin (Ed.), *Foster children in the courts* (pp. 128–192). Foster Care Project/National Legal Resource Center for Child Advocacy and Protection/American Bar Association. Boston: Butterworth Legal.

Hardin, M. (1985). Families, children, and the law. In J. Laird & A. Hartman (Eds.), *A handbook of child welfare* (pp. 213–236). New York: Macmillan.

Hardin, M. (1986–1987). Guardians *ad litem* for child victims in criminal proceedings. *Journal of Family Law/University of Louisville School of Law, 25*(4), 687–728.

Hardin, M. (1989). The judicial determination of reasonable efforts: How and why. *Protecting Children, 6*(2), 7–11.

Hardin, M. A., & Shalleck, A. (1984). Children living apart from their parents. In R. M. Horowitz & H. A. Davidson (Eds.), *Legal rights of children* (pp. 353–421). Colorado Springs: McGraw-Hill.

Haring, B. L. (1976). *Adoption Statistics: Annual data, January 1–December 31, 1975: submitted by 41 voluntary and 16 public agencies* (Publication No. X-9). New York: Child Welfare League of America.

Harold, N. (1988, Fall). School-based clients effectively meet needs of adolescents. *Health and Social Work,* pp. 303–305.

Harrington, M. (1987). Poverty in America today. Testimony before the Senate Committee on Labor and Human Services. *American Family, 10*(11), 1–3.

Harris, D. V. (1988). Renewing our commitment to child welfare. *Social Work, 33*(6), 483–484.

Hartman, A. (1979). *Finding families: An ecological approach to family assessment in adoption.* Beverly Hills, CA: Sage.

Hartman, A. (1981). The family: A central focus for practice. *Social Work, 26*(1).

Hartman, A. (1984). *Working with adoptive families beyond placement.* New York: Child Welfare League of America.

Hartman, A. (1989). Homelessness: Public iussue and private trouble. *Social Work, 34*(6), 483.

Hartman, W. et al. (1971). *A study of children in foster care 15 months.* Springfield, IL: Department of Children and Family Services.

Harvard Educational Review. (1985, May). Editorial, 55, p. v.

Harvard Educational Review. (1989, November). Editorial, 57, pp. vi–viii.

Hawkins, J. D., Jenson, J. M., Catalano, R. F., & Lishner, D. M. (1988). Delinquency and drug abuse: Implications for social services. *Social Service Review, 62*(2), 258–284.

Hawks, D. (1988). *Development of national health and safety performance standards for out-of-home child care programs. Project overview.* Washington, DC: American Public Health Association.

Hayes, C. D. (Ed.). (1982). *Making policies for children. A study of the federal process.* Washington, DC: National Academy Press.

Hayes, R. M. (1989). Homeless children. In *Caring for America's children. Proceedings of the Academy of Political Science, 37*(2), 58–69.

Hearings before the Subcommittee on Children, Family, Drugs and Alcoholism of the Committee on Labor and Human Resources. 100th Cong. (1987, June 11). *First session on examining initiatives needed to meet the demand for quality and affordable child care in the United States.* Washington, DC: U.S. Government Printing Office.

Heath, P. A., & MacKinnon, C. (1988). Factors related to the social competence of children in single-parent families. *Journal of Divorce, 11*(3/4), 49–66).

Heck, R. O., Pindur, W., & Wells, D. K. (1985). The juvenile serious habitual offender/drug involved program: A means to implement recommendations of the National Council of Juvenile and Family Court Judges. *Juvenile & Family Court Journal, 36,* 27–37.

Helfer, R. (1976). Basic issues concerning prediction. In R. Helfer & C. Kempe (Eds.), *Child abuse and neglect: The family and the community.* Cambridge, MA: Ballinger.

Helfer, R. (1980). Developmental deficits which limit interpersonal skills. In C. Kempe & R. Helfer

(Eds.), *The battered child* (3rd ed.). Chicago: University of Chicago Press.

Helfer, R. (1987). Litany of the smoldering neglect of children. In R. E. Helfer & R. S. Kempe (Eds.), *The battered child* (4th ed.). Chicago: University of Chicago Press.

Helfer, R. E., & Kempe, R. S. (1987). *The battered child* (4th ed.). Chicago: University of Chicago Press.

Heller, E. (1966). Applications by married parents for adoptive placements of their in-wedlock children. *Child Welfare, 45*(7), 404–409.

Henry, D. (1981, February 24). "Divorcing" parents from child. *New York Times,* p. 24.

Herbers, J. (1969, April 15). Director defends Head Start saying it aids pupils. *New York Times,* p. 4.

Herbers, J. (1982, July 20). Poverty rate termed highest since '67. *New York Times,* p. 11.

Herman, M., Sadofsky, S., & Rosenberg, B. (Eds.). (1968). *Work, youth and unemployment.* New York: Thomas Y. Crowell.

Herstein, N. (1964). What is a group home? *Child Welfare, 43*(8), 403–414, 433.

Herzog, E. (1964, August). Cooperative research and demonstration reports, unwed motherhood: Personal and social consequences. *Welfare in Review, 2,* 20–22.

Herzog, E., & Sudia, C. E. (1968). Fatherless homes—A review of the research. *Children, 15*(5), 179–181.

Herzog, E., & Sudia, C. (1973). Children in fatherless families. In B. M. Caldwell & H. Riccuiti (Eds.), *Review of Child Development Research, 3,* 141–232.

Hildenbrand, W. S., et al. (1979). *Child protective services entering the 1980s: A nationwide survey.* Englewood, CO: American Humane Association.

Hines, P. M., & Boyd-Franklin, N. (1982). Black families. In M. McGoldrick, J. Pearce, & J. Giordano (Eds.), *Ethnicity and family therapy* (pp. 84–107). New York: Guilford Press.

H. L. v. Matheson et al., 450 US. 398, 67 L.Ed.2d 388 (1981).

Hobbs, N., Dokecki, P. R., Hoover-Dempey, K. V., & Weeks, K. H. (1984). *Strengthening families.* San Francisco: Jossey-Bass.

Hodges, W. L., & Spicker, H. H. (1967). The effects of preschool experiences on culturally deprived children. *Young Children, 22*(7).

Hodgson v. Minnesota. (June 25, 1990, Doc. No., 89-1125).

Hoeffer, B. (1978). Single mothers and their children: Challenging traditional concepts of the American family. In A. Brandt et al. (Eds.), *Current practices in psychiatric nursing.* St. Louis, MO: Mosby.

Hoff, P. M. (1980). Child snatching: The destructive game of hide and seek. *Children's Legal Rights Journal, 1*(4), 5.

Hofferth, S. L., & Phillips, D. A. (1987). Child care in the United States. *Journal of Marriage and the Family, 49*(3), 559–571.

Holman, R. (1966). The foster child and self knowledge. *Case Conference, 12*(9), 295–298.

Holt, J. (1964). *How children fail.* New York: Pitman.

Honig v. Doe, 108 S. Ct. 592. (1988).

Horowitz, B., & Wintermute, W. (1978). Use of an emergency fund in protective services casework. *Child Welfare, 17*(7).

Horowitz, R. M., & Davidson, H. A. (Eds.). (1984). *Legal rights of children.* Colorado Springs: Shepard's/McGraw-Hill.

Hoshino, G. (1977). Public assistance and supplementary security income: Social Services. In *Encyclopedia of social work* (pp. 1150–1155). New York: National Association of Social Workers.

Huffman, M. (1980). Family life education service delivery for the divorced family. In *The many dimensions of family practice: Proceedings of the North American Symposium on Family Practice.* New York: Jason Aronson.

Hughes, D., Johnson, K., Rosenbaum, S., & Liu, J. (1989). *The health of America's children: Maternal and child health data book.* Washington, DC: Children's Defense Fund, Adolescent Pregnancy Prevention, Prenatal Care Campaign.

Hughes, E., Ferguson, D. H., & Gula, M. (1962). *Licensing a dynamic for change.* New York: Child Welfare League of America.

Hunt, J. M. (1964). The psychological basis for using preschool enrichment as an antidote for cultural deprivation. *The Merrill-Palmer Quarterly of Behavior and Development, 10*(3), 209–248.

Hunt, J. M. (1969). Black genes—white environment. *Trans-action, 6*(7), 20–21.

Hutchings, J. R. (1988). Pediatric AIDS: An overview. *Children Today, 17*(3), 4–7.

Hutchinson, D. (1943). *In quest of foster parents: A*

point of view on homefinding. New York: Columbia University Press.

Hutchinson, J. R. (1986). Progress towards change: The National Resource Center on Family Based Services. *Children Today, 15*(6), 6–7.

Idaho v. Wright (1990, June 27). 58 U. S. L. R. W. 5036.

Immerman v. Immerman, 176 Cal. App. 2d 122, 1 Cal. Rptr. 298 (1959).

Independent living progress report. (1987, Summer). *Fostering Ideas,* pp. 1, 6.

Indian education: A national tragedy: A national challenge. (1969). Washington, DC: Committee on Labor and Public Welfare, Special Subcommittee on Indian Education; U.S. Senate, 91st Cong., 1st Sess.

Infausto, F. (1969). Perspective on adoption. *Progress in Family Law: The Annals of the American Academy of Political and Social Science* (Vol. 383).

Ingraham v. Wright, 96 S.Ct. 2200 (1977).

In re Gault, 387 U.S., 87 S.Ct. 1428, 18 L.Ed.2d 527 (1967).

In re Phillip B., 92 Cal. App. 3d 796, 156 Cal. Rptr. 48 (1957).

In re Winship, 397 U.S. 358 (1970).

Inspector General, U.S. Department of Health, Education, and Welfare, Office of the Secretary. (1979, August 31). Service delivery assessment report on domestic violence. Mimeographed draft.

Institute of Judicial Administration, American Bar Association Juvenile Justice Standards Project. (1977). *Standards relating to abuse and neglect.* Cambridge, MA: Ballinger.

Institute of Judicial Administration and American Bar Association. (1980). *Juvenile justice standards: Standards relating to court organization and administration.* Cambridge, MA: Ballinger.

Institute of Medicine. (1988). *Homelessness, health, and human needs.* Washington, DC: National Academy Press/Author.

Interagency Task Force on Adoption. (1988, March 31). *America's waiting children: A report to the President.* Washington DC: United States Office of Personnel Management.

Iowa Department of Social Services. (1973). *Foster care survey.* Des Moines: Department of Social Services, Bureau of Family and Adult Services, Division of Research and Statistics.

Ives, L. S. (1864, November 23). Lecture presented to the Cooper Institute, New York City. Cited in H. W. Thurston (1930), *The dependent child* (pp. 126–127). New York: Columbia University.

Jackson, A. (1984). Child neglect: An overview. In *Perspectives on child maltreatment in the mid '80s* (DHHS Publication No. [OHDS] 84030338, pp. 15–17). Washington, DC: U.S. Government Printing Office.

Jacobs, M. (1980). Foster parent training: An opportunity for skills enrichment and empowerment. *Child Welfare, 59*(10), 615–624.

Jaffee, B., & Fanshel, D. (1970). *How they fared in adoption: A follow-up study.* New York: Columbia University Press.

Jambor, H. A. (1964). Theory and practice in agency participation in the formulation of child care licensing standards. *Child Welfare, 43,* 521–528, 538.

Jenkins, S., & Norman, E. (1972). *Filial Deprivation and Foster Care.* New York: Columbia University.

Jenkins, S., & Norman, E. (1975). *Beyond placement: Mothers view foster care.* New York: Columbia University Press.

Jenkins, S., & Sauber, M. (1966). *Paths to children placement: Family situations prior to foster care.* New York: Department of Welfare and the Community Council of Greater New York.

Jeter, H. R. (1963). *Children, problems and services in child welfare programs.* (Children's Bureau Publication No. 403). Washington, DC: Children's Bureau.

Jimenez v. Weinberger, 417 U.S. 628 (1974).

Joe, T., & Yu, P. (1986). The "flip-side" of black families headed by women: The economic status of black men. In R. Staples (Ed.), *The black family: Essays and studies.* Belmont, CA: Wadsworth.

Joffe, C. E. (1977). *Friendly intruders. Child care professionals and family life.* Berkeley: University of California Press.

Johnson, B., & Morse, H. A. (1968, July–August). Injured children and their parents. *Children, 15.*

Johnson, B. B. (1981). The Indian Child Welfare Act of 1978: Implications for practice. *Child Welfare, 60*(7), 435–446.

Johnson, D. (1989, March 15). Wisconsin weighs 2-tier welfare to keep the poor from moving in. *New York Times,* pp. 1, 14.

Johnson, K. (1988). *Teens and AIDS: Opportunities for prevention*. Washington, DC: Children's Defense Fund.

Johnson, K., & Sum, H. (1987). *Declining earnings of young men: Their relation to poverty, teen pregnancy, and family formation*. Washington, DC: Adolescent Pregnancy Clearinghouse, Children's Defense Fund.

Johnson, W., & Clancy, T. (1988). A study to find improved methods of screening and disposing of reports of child maltreatment in the emergency response program in Alameda County, California. In T. Tatara (Ed.), *Validation research in CPS risk assessment: Three recent studies*. Washington, DC: American Public Welfare Association.

Johnson, W., & L'Esperance, J. (1984). Predicting the recurrence of child abuse. *Social Work Research and Abstracts, 20*(2) 21-26.

Joint Commission on Mental Health of children. (1970). *Crisis in child mental health: Challenge for the 1970s: Report of the Joint Commission on mental health of children*. New York: Harper & Row.

Jolowicz, A. R. (1946, November). *The hidden parent*. Paper presented at the New York State Conference of Social Welfare. New York: Federal Security Agency, Social Security Administration, Children's Bureau.

Jones, B. M. (1964, March). A demonstration homemaker project. *Child Welfare, 43,* 133-136.

Jones, D., & Alexander, H. (1987). Treating the abusive family within the family care system. In R. E. Helfer & R. S. Kempe (Eds.), *The battered child* (4th ed., pp. 339-359). Chicago: University of Chicago Press.

Jones, D. P., & McGraw, J. M. (1987). Reliable and ficticious accounts of sexual abuse of children. *Journal of Interpersonal Violence, 2,* 27-45.

Jones, J. Y. (1975). *Subsidized adoption. United States Congress Adoptions and Foster Care Hearings, Subcommittees on Children and Youth, U.S. Senate*. Washington, DC: U.S. Government Printing Office.

Jones, M. A. (1976). *The sealed adoption record controversy: Report of a survey of agency policy, practice and opinions*. New York: Child Welfare League of America.

Jones, M. A. (1985). *A second chance for families: Five years later follow-up of a program to prevent foster care*. New York: Research Center, Child Welfare League of America.

Jones, M. A. (1987). *Parental lack of supervision: Nature and consequence of a major child neglect problem*. Washington, DC: Child Welfare League of America.

Jones, M. A., Magura, S., & Shyne, A. W. (1981). Effective practice with families in protective and preventive services: What works? *Child Welfare, 60*(2).

Jones, M. A., Neuman, R., & Shyne, A. W. (1976). *A second chance for families*. New York: Child Welfare League of America.

Jones, M. L. (1978). Stopping foster care drift: A review of legislation and special programs. *Child Welfare, 57*(9), pp. 571-580.

Jones, M. L. (1979). Preparing the school age child for adoption. *Child Welfare, 58*(1), 27-34.

Joubert, J. (1842). *Pensées* (Katherine Lyttleton, Trans.). In R. T. Tripp (1970), *International thesaurus of quotations*. New York: Crowell.

Journal of the Senate of the Commonwealth of Pennsylvania Session of 1837-1838 Which Commenced at Harrisburg, on the Fifth Day of December, 1837. *Child labor in Pennsylvania in 1838*. In G. Abbott. (1938). *The child and the state* (Vol. 1). Chicago: University of Chicago Press, p. 281.

Julian, V., Mohr, C., & Lapp, J. (1983). Father-daughter incest: A descriptive analysis. In W. M. Holder (Ed.), *Sexual abuse of children: Implications for treatment*. Englewood, CO: American Humane Association, Child Protection Division.

Jung, C. G. (1935). *The integration of the personality*. New York: Farrar & Rinehart.

Justice, B., & Justice, R. (1976). *The abusing family*. New York: Human Services Press.

Juvenile Justice and Delinquency Prevention Act of 1974 and 1977, 88 Stat. 1121, 42 U.S.C. 3723.

Kadushin, A. (1962). A study of adoptive parents of hard-to-place children. *Social Casework, 53*(5), 227-233.

Kadushin, A. (1970). *Adopting older children*. New York: Columbia University Press.

Kadushin, A. (1977). Child welfare: Adoption and foster care. In *Encyclopedia of social work* (18th ed., pp. 114-125).

Kadushin, A. (1978a). Children in adoptive homes. In H. S. Maas, *Social service research. Reviews of studies.* Washington, DC: National Association of Social Workers.

Kadushin, A. (1978b). Children in foster families and institutions. In H. S. Maas (Ed.), *Social service research: Review of studies* (pp. 90–148). Washington, DC: National Association of Social Workers.

Kadushin, A. (1984). Principles, values and assumptions underlying adoption practice. In P. Sachdev (Ed.), *Adoption: Current Issues and Trends* (pp. 3–14). Toronto, Canada: Butterworths.

Kadushin, A. (1987). Child welfare services. In *Encyclopedia of social work* (18th ed., pp. 265–275). Washington, DC: National Association of Social Workers.

Kadushin, A. (1988). *Child welfare services* (4th ed.). New York: Macmillan.

Kadushin, A. J., & Seidl, F. (1971). Adoption failure. A social work postmortem. *Social Work, 16*(2), 32–37.

Kaersvang, E. (1972). *Attention house informational manual.* Boulder, CO: Attention.

Kagan, R. M., & Reid, W. J. (1986). Critical factors in the adoption of emotionally disturbed youths. *Child Welfare, 65*(1), 63–72.

Kagan, S. L., & Glennon, T. (1982). Considering proprietary child care. In E. F. Zigler & E. W. Gordon (Eds.), *Day care: Scientific and social policy issues.* Boston: Auburn House.

Kahn, A. J. (1953). *A court for children.* New York: Columbia University Press.

Kahn, A. J. (1965). The societal context of social work practice. *Social Work, 10*(4), 145–155.

Kahn, A. J. (1977). Child welfare. In *Encyclopedia of social work* (Vol. 1, pp. 101–114). Washington, DC: National Association of Social Workers.

Kahn, A. J. (1988). The ABC legislative approach should be renewed in 1989. *CDF Reports, 10*(6).

Kahn, A. J., & Kamerman, S. B. (1987). *Child care. Facing the hard choices.* Dover, MA: Auburn House.

Kahn, A. J., Kamerman, S. B., & McGowan, B. G. (1972). *Child advocacy: Report of a national baseline study.* New York: Columbia University Press.

Kamerman, S. B. (1980). *Parenting in an unresponsive society. Managing work and family Life.* New York: Free Press.

Kamerman, S. B. (1984). *Children and their families: The impact of the Reagan administration and the choices for social work.* New Brunswick, NJ: Rutgers University School of Social Work.

Kamerman, S. B. (1989). Toward a child policy decade. *Child Welfare, 68*(4), 371–388.

Kamerman, S. B., & Kahn, A. J. (1988). *Mothers alone, strategies for a time of change.* Dover, MA: Auburn House.

Kamerman, S. B., & Kahn, A. J. (1989). *Social services for children, youth and families in the United States.* New York: Columbia University School of Social Work (Annie E. Casey Foundation).

Kaminer, B., Crowe, A., & Budde-Giltner, L. (1988). The prevalence and characteristics of multidisciplinary teams for child abuse and neglect: A national survey. In D. Bross et al. (Eds.), *The new child protection team handbook* (pp. 548–567). New York: Garland.

Kammerer, P. (1918). *The unmarried mother.* Boston: Little, Brown.

Kaplan, S. (1958). Support from absent fathers in aid to dependent children. *Social Security Bulletin, 21*(12), 3–13.

Karger, H. J., & Stoesz, D. (1989). Welfare reform: Maximum feasible exaggeration. *Tikkun 4*(2), 23–25, 118–122.

Katz, S. V., McGrath, M., & Howe, R. (1975). *Child neglect laws in America.* Chicago: American Bar Association, Section on Family Law.

Kaufman, I. (1963). Psychodynamics of protective casework. In H. J. Parad & R. R. Miller (Eds.), *Ego-oriented: Problems and perspectives.* New York: Family Service Association of America.

Kaufman, J., & Zigler, E. (1987). Do abused children become abusive parents? *American Journal of Orthopsychiatry, 57*(2), 186–192.

Kaufman v. Carter, 402 U.S. 954, 959 (1971). (Black, J., dissenting from a denial of certiorari). Cited in D. J. Besharov, (1985), "Doing something" about child abuse: The need to narrow the grounds for state intervention. *Harvard Journal of Law and Public Policy, 8*(3), 539–589.

Keeping families together: The case for family preservation. (1985). New York: Edna McConnell Clark Foundation.

Kelley, F. (1895). Annual report of the chief factory inspector in Illinois. In E. Abbott, & S. P. Breckinridge, (1917), *Truancy and non-attendance to the Chicago Schools: A study of the compulsory education and child labor legislation of Illinois.* Chicago: University of Chicago Press.

Kelly, J. B., & Wallerstein, J. S. (1976). The effect of parental divorce experiences of the child in early latency. *American Journal of Orthopsychiatry, 46*(1), 20–32.

Kelly, J. B., & Wallerstein, J. S. (1977). Brief interventions with children in divorcing families. *American Journal of Orthopsychiatry, 47,* 22–29.

Kelly, R., & Ramsey, S. (1982–1983). Do attorneys for children in protection proceedings make a difference? A study of the impact of representation under conditions of high judicial intervention. *Journal of Family Law, 21*(3), 405–445.

Kempe, C. H., Silverman, F. N., Steele, B. T., Droegemueller, W., & Silver, H. K. (1962, July). The battered child syndrome. *Journal of the American Medical Association, 181.*

Kempe, R. S. (1987). A developmental approach to the treatment of the abused child. In R. E. Helfer & R. S. Kempe (Eds.), *The battered child* (4th ed., pp. 360–381). Chicago: University of Chicago Press.

Keniston, K. (1977). All our children: *The American family under pressure.* New York: Harcourt Brace Jovanovich.

Kennedy, J. F. (1962). *Message from the President of the United States: Public welfare program* (87th Cong., 2d Sess., H. R. Doc. no. 325). Washington, DC: U.S. Government Printing Office.

Kent v. United States, 383 U.S. 541, 555–556 (1966).

Kerner, O. (1968). *Report of the national advisory commission on civil disorders.* New York: Bantam Books.

Kessel, J. A., & Robbins, S. P. (1984). The Indian Child Welfare Act: Dilemmas and needs. *Child Welfare, 63*(3), 225–232.

Ketcham, O. W. (1962). The unfulfilled promise of the American juvenile court. In M. K. Rosenheim (Ed.), *Justice for the child.* New York: Free Press.

Keyserling, M. D. (1972). *Windows on day care.* New York: National Council of Jewish Women.

Kihss, P. (1969, April 16). Two educators here praise Head Start programs. *New York Times,* p. 4.

Kilborn, P. T. (1990a, February 8). Tougher enforcement of child labor laws is vowed. *New York Times,* p. 14.

Kilborn, P. T. (1990b, March 15). Child labor violators sought in nationwide raids. *New York Times,* p. 8.

Kim, B. C., Okamura, A. I., Ozawa, N., & Forrest, V. (1981). *Women in shadows: A handbook for service providers working with Asian wives of U.S. military personnel.* LaJolla, CA: National Committee concerned with Asian Wives of U.S. Servicemen.

Kim, C., & Carroll, T. G. (1975). Intercountry adoption of South Korean orphans: A lawyer's guide. *Journal of Family Law, 14*(2), 223–253.

Kim, D. S. (1977). How they fared in American homes: A follow-up study of adopted Korean children in the United States. *Children Today, 6*(2), 2–36.

Kimmich, M. H. (1985). *America's children. Who cares?* Washington, DC: Urban Institute.

King v. Smith, 392 U.S. 309, 88 S. Ct. 2128 (1968).

Kinsey, C. A., et al. (1948). *Sexual behavior in the human male.* Philadelphia: Saunders.

Kinsey, C. A., et al. (1953). *Sexual behavior in the human female.* Philadelphia: Saunders.

Kirk, H. D. (1964). *Shared Fate.* New York: Free Press.

Kirk, H. D. (1981). *Adoptive kinship: A modern institution in need of reform.* Toronto: Ben-Simon.

Kirp, D. L. (1974). Student classification, public policy and the court. *Harvard Educational Review, 44*(1), 7–52.

Klapmuts, N. (1972). *Children's rights: The legal rights of minors in conflict with law or social custom.* Hackensack, NJ: National Council on Crime and Delinquency.

Kleinman, J., Rosenberg, E., & Whiteside, M. (1979). Common developmental tasks in forming reconstituted families. *Journal of Marital and Family Therapy, 5* (2), 79–86.

Klemesrud, J. (1972, April 12). Furor over whites adopting blacks. *New York Times.*

Klerman, L., & Jekel, J. (1977). *School-age mothers: Problems, programs and policy.* Hamden, MA: Shoestring Press.

Knitzer, J. E. (1976). Child advocacy: A perspective. *American Journal of Orthopsychiatry, 46*(2), 200–216.

Koerin, B. (1979). Authority in child protective services. *Child Welfare, 58*(10), 650–657.

Konopka, G. (1966). *The adolescent girl in conflict.* Englewood Cliffs, NJ: Prentice-Hall.

Korbin, J. E. (1987). Child abuse and neglect: The cultural context. In R. E. Helfer & R. S. Kempe (Eds.), *The battered child* (4th ed., pp. 23–41). Chicago: University of Chicago Press.

Kornitzer, M., (1968). *Adoption and family life.* New York: Humanities Press.

Kornitzer, M., & Rowe, J. (1968, May). *Casework*

implications in the study of children reclaimed or returned before final adoption. Surrey, UK: Standing Conference of Societies Registered for Adoption. Mimeographed.

Kozol, J. (1967). *Death at an early age.* Boston: Houghton Mifflin

Kozol, J. (1988a, January 25). A reporter at large: The homeless and their children (Pt. 1). *New Yorker,* pp. 65–84.

Kozol, J. (1988b, February 1). A reporter at large: The homeless and their children (Pt. 2). *New Yorker,* pp. 36–67.

Kraft, A. D., Palombo, J., Mitchell, D. L., Woods, P. K., & Schmidt, A. W. (1985a). Some theoretical considerations on confidential adoptions, Pt. 1: The birth mother. *Child & Adolescent Social Work, 2*(1).

Kraft, A. D., Palombo, J., Mitchell, D. L., Woods, P. K., & Schmidt, A. W. (1985b). Some theoretical considerations on confidential adoptions, Pt. 2: The adoptive parent. *Child & Adolescent Social Work, 2*(2).

Kraft, A. D., Palombo, J., Mitchell, D. L., Woods, P. K., Schmidt, A. W., & Tucker, N. G. (1985c). Some theoretical considerations on confidential adoptions, Pt. 3: The adopted child. *Child & Adolescent Social Work, 2*(3).

Kraus, J. (1971). Predicting success of foster placement for school-age children. *Social Work, 16*(1).

Krause, H. (1981) *Child support in America: The legal perspective.* Charlottesville, VA: Michie.

Krause, H. (1983). *Family law. Cases and materials.* St. Paul, MN: West.

Krause, H. D. (1986). *Family law in a nutshell.* St. Paul, MN: West.

Krisberg, B., Schwartz, R. M., Litsky, P., & Austin, J. (1986). The watershed of juvenile justice reform. *Crime & Delinquency 32*(1), 3–38.

Kurdek, L. A. (1988). Social support of divorced single mothers and their children. *Journal of Divorce, 11*(3/4), 167–188.

Kutchins, H., & Kutchins, S. (1978). Advocacy and social work. In G. H. Weber & G. J. McCall (Eds.). *Social scientists as advocates* (pp. 13–48). Beverly Hills, CA: Sage.

Lacy, G., & Johnson, C. (1989). *State youth employment iniatives: A resource guide and framework for action.* Washington, DC: Children's Defense Fund.

Lacy, G., Johnson, C., & Heffernan, D. (1989).

Tackling the youth employment problem. Washington, DC: Adolescent Pregnancy Prevention Clearinghouse, Children's Defense Fund.

Ladner, J. (1985). Adolescent pregnancy: A national problem. *New Directions, 12,* 16–21.

Lahti, J. et al. (1978). *A follow-up study of the Oregon project.* Portland, OR: Regional Research Institute for Human Services.

Laird, J. (1985). An ecological approach to child welfare. In C. Germaine, (Ed.), *Social work practice: people and environments.* New York: Columbia University Press.

Laird, J., & Hartman, A. (1985). *A handbook of child welfare. Context, knowledge, and practice.* New York: Free Press.

Lamarine, R. J. (1988). Alcohol abuse among Native Americans. *Journal of Community Health, 13*(3), 143–155.

Lambert, B. (1989, July 17). AIDS abandoning growing generation of needy orphans. *New York Times,* pp. 1, 22.

Landwirth, J. (1987). Fetal abuse and neglect: An emerging controversy. *Pediatrics, 79*(4), 508–514.

Lardie, J. (1989, September 29). Personal communication. Executive Director of Association of Child Advocates.

Lathrop, J. C. (1925). The background of the juvenile court in Illinois. *The child, the clinic, and the court.* New York: New Republic.

Lawder, E. A. (1966). Quasi-adoption. *Children, 13*(1).

Lawder, E. A. (1969). *A follow-up study of adoptions: Postplacement functioning of adoption families.* New York: Child Welfare League of America.

Lawder, E. A., Poulin, J. E., & Andrews, R. G. (1986). A study of 185 foster children 5 years after placement. *Child Welfare, 65*(3), 241–251.

Lawrence, S. (1989. July 17). Personal communication. Philadelphia: Exchange Services, National Adoption Center.

Leader, A. L. (1969). Current and future issues in family therapy. *Social Service Review, 43*(1).

League of Women Voters of Illinois (1981). *Out of the shadows . . . A citizen's view of the juvenile court in Illinois.* Chicago: League of Women Voters.

Leashore, B. R. (1984–1985). Demystifying legal guardianship: An unexplored option for depen-

dent children. *Journal of Family Law/University of Louisville School of Law, 23*(3), 391–400.

Ledbetter v. Taylor, 818 F. 2nd 791 (11th Cir. 1987) (en banc).

Lee, P. R. (1923). Changes in social thought and standards which affect the family. In *Proceedings of the National Conference of Social Work*. Chicago: University of Chicago Press.

Lefkowitz, M. (1969). Personal communication to A. Kadushin. Los Angeles: Children's Home Society of California.

Lerman, A. C., Wolkomir, B., & Posner, W. (1943). *Three papers on homefinding*. New York: Jewish Child Care Association of New York.

Levin, M. M., & Sarri, R. C. (1974). *Juvenile delinquency: A comparative analysis of legal codes in the United States*. Ann Arbor: University of Michigan, National Assessment of Juvenile Corrections.

Levine, R. (1964). Treatment in the home. *Social Work, 9*(1), 19–28.

Levinton, S. A., & Johnston, B. H. (1975). *The Job Corps: A social experiment that works*. Baltimore: Johns Hopkins University Press.

Levy v. Louisiana, 391 U.S. 68 (1968).

Lewin, E. (1981). Lesbianism and motherhood: Implications for child custody. *Human Organization, 40*(1), 6–14.

Lewin, T. (1988a, August 24). Black churches: New mission on family. *New York Times,* pp. 1, 9.

Lewin, T. (1988b, November 25). New law compels sweeping changes in child support. *New York Times,* pp. 1, 8.

Lewin T. (1989, October 18). Study finds high turnover in child care workers. *New York Times,* p. 9.

Lewis, H. (1961). Child rearing practices among low-income families. *Casework papers*. New York: Family Service Association of America, National Conference on Social Welfare.

Lewis, K. (1978, November–December). On reducing the snatching syndrome. *Children Today,* pp. 19–21.

Lewis, M. R. (1974). Day care under the Social Security Act. *Social Service Review, 48*(3).

Lewis, O. (1966). The culture of poverty. *Scientific American, 215*(4), 19–25.

Leyendecker, G. (1958). Generic and specific factors in casework with unmarried mothers. In *Services to unmarried mothers* (pp. 3–17). New York: Child Welfare League of America.

Licensing standards for day care homes. (1985). Springfield: State of Illinois Department of Children and Family Services.

Licensing standards for foster families homes. (1987). Springfield: State of Illinois Department of Children and Family Services.

Liggett, I. (1958). Community aspects: What guardianship means to the child. In *The child at law* (Report of the Twenty-eighth Ross Pediatric Research Conference). Columbus, OH: Ross Laboratories.

Light, H. K., & Martin, R. E. (1986). American Indian families. *Journal of American Indian Education, 26*(1), 1–5.

Lindblad-Goldberg, M. (1987). The assessment of social networks in black, low-income single-parent families. In M. Lindblad-Goldberg (Ed.), *Clinical issues in single-parent households* (pp. 39–46). Rockville, MD: Aspen.

Linder, E. W., Mattis, M. C., & Rogers, J. R. (1983). *When churches mind the children. A study of day care in local parishes*. Ypsilanti, MI: High/Scope Press.

Lindsey, E. (1914). The juvenile court movement from a lawyer's standpoint. *Annals of the American Academy of Political and Social Science, 52,* 140–148.

Linn, J. W. (1935). *Jane Addams: A biography*. New York: Appleton-Century.

Linnell, T., Zieman, G. L., Romano, P. (1984). Treating abusive families in heterogeneous parent groups. *Family Therapy, 11*(1), 79–85.

Listening to America's families: Action for the 80's. The report to the President, Congress, and families of the nation. (1980). Washington, DC: U.S. Government Printing Office.

Littner, N. (1978). The art of being a foster parent. *Child Welfare, 57*(1), 3–12.

Long, K. A. (1986, January). Cultural considerations in the assessment of intrafamilial abuse. *American Journal of Orthopsychiatry, 56,* 131–136.

Long, T. J., & Long, L. (1983). *Handbook for latchkey children and their parents*. New York: Arbor House.

Lorenzi, M. E., Klerman. L. V., & Jekel, J. F. (1977). School-age parents: How permanent a relationship? *Adolescence, 12*(45), 13–22.

Los Angeles County Department of Adoptions.

(1967). *Biennial report 1965–67*. Los Angeles: Author.

Lou, H. H. (1927). *Juvenile courts in the United States*. Chapel Hill: University of North Carolina Press.

Lounsbury, J. W., & Hall, D. G. (1976). Supervision and consultation conflicts in the day-care licensing role. *Social Service Review, 50*(3).

Lourie, N. V., & Brody, S. J. (1970). Implications of recent U.S. Supreme Court decisions on residence requirements. *Public Welfare, 28*(1), 45–51.

Lowrey, L. G. (1940). Personality distortion and early institutional care. *American Journal of Orthopsychiatry, 10*, 576–785.

Lufton, R. C. (1982). Myths and realities of crisis intervention. *Social Casework, 63*, 276–285.

Lundberg, E. O. (1947). *Unto the least of these: Social services for children*. New York: Appleton-Century-Crofts.

Lystad, M. H. (1979). Violence at home. A review of the literature. In D. G. Gil (Ed.), *Child abuse and violence*. New York: AMS Press.

Maas, H. S. (1960). The successful adoptive parent applicant. *Social Work, 5*(1), 14–20.

Maas, H. S. (1963). The young adult adjustment of twenty wartime residential nursery children. *Child Welfare, 42*(2), 57–72.

Maas, H. S. (1969). Children in long term foster care. *Child Welfare, 48*(6), 331–334.

Maas, H. S., & Engler, R. E. (1959). *Children in need of parents*. New York: Columbia University.

Mack, J. W. (1909–1910). The juvenile court. *Harvard Law Review, 23*.

Madison, B. Q. (1966). Adoption: Yesterday, today, and tomorrow—Part 1. *Child Welfare, 45*(5).

Magazino, C. J. (1983). Services to children and families at risk of separation. In B. McGowan & W. Meezam (Eds.), *Child welfare: Current dilemmas, future directions* (pp. 211–254).

Magura, S., & Moses, B. (1986). The child well-being scales. In *Outcome measures for child welfare services*. Washington, DC: Child Welfare League of America.

Magura, S., Moses, B., & Jones, M. A. (1987). *Assessing risk and measuring risk scales*. Washington, DC: Child Welfare League of America.

Making reasonable efforts: Steps for keeping families together. (n. d.). National Council of Juvenile and Family Court Judges, Child Welfare League of America, Youth Law Center, National Center for Youth Law.

Maluccio, A. N., & Marlow, W. D. (1972). Residential treatment of emotionally disturbed children: A review of the literature. *Social Service Review, 46*(2), 230–251.

Maluccio, A. N., & Marlow, W. D. (1974, January). The case for the contract. *Social Work, 17*, 28–36.

Maluccio, A. N., & Sinanoglu, P. A. (Eds.). (1981). *The challenge of partnership: Working with parents of children in foster care*. New York: Child Welfare League of America.

Mansnerus, L. (1989, October 5). Private adoptions aided by expanding network. *New York Times*, p. 1.

Maraude, A. (1980). The Chicano family: Reanalysis of conflicting views. In A. Skolnick (Ed.), *The family in transition* (3rd ed., pp. 479–493). Boston: Little, Brown.

Margolick, D. (1990, July 4). Lesbians' custody fights test family law frontier. *New York Times*, pp. 1, 10.

Marin, R. C. (1969). *A comprehensive program for multi-problem families—Report on a four-year controlled experiment*. Puerto Rico: University of Puerto Rico, Institute of Caribbean Studies.

Markey, J. P. (1988). The labor market problems of today's high school dropouts. *Monthly Labor Review, 111*(6), 36–43.

Martin, A., & Baenen, N. (1987). School-age mothers' attitudes toward parenthood and father involvement. *Family Therapy, 14*(2), 97–102.

Martin, E. P., & Martin, J. M. (1978). *The black extended family*. Chicago: University of Chicago Press.

Martin, H. (Ed.). (1976). *The abused child: A multidisciplinary approach to developmental issues and treatment* (pp. 27–41). Cambridge, MA: Ballinger.

Maryland v. Craig (1990, June 27). 58 U. S. L. R. W. 5044.

Massachusetts Advocacy Center. (1988). *Purpose and activities of the Massachusetts Advocacy Center*. Boston: Author.

Mastria, E. O., Mastria, M. A., & Harkins, J. C. (1979, April). Treatment of child abuse by behavioral intervention: A case report. *Child Welfare, 58*, 253–262.

Masurofsky, M. (1975, June). The Title I migrant program: Passivity perpetuates a non-system of education for migrant children. *Inequality in Education, 21,* 11–24.

Mathews, J. (1990, May 18). Working off welfare: Study sees state treasuries as major beneficiaries. *Washington Post,* p. A4.

Mauro v. Ritchie, 3 D.C. 147 (1827).

Mayer, A. B. (1965). *Day care as a social instrument: A policy paper.* New York: Columbia University School of Social Work.

Mayhall, P. D., & Norgard, K. E. (1983). *Child abuse and neglect: Sharing responsibility.* New York: Wiley.

McCabe, A. (1967). *The pursuit of promise.* New York: Community Service Society.

McCabe, A., et al. (1965). *Forty forgotten families: A study of young AFDC families.* New York: Community Service Society of New York.

McCrea, R. C. (1910). *The humane movement—A descriptive survey.* Prepared for the Henry Bergh Foundation for the Promotion of Human Education. New York: Columbia University Press.

McCune, S. D., & Skoler, D. L. (1965, April). Juvenile court judges in the United States: Part I: A national profile. *Crime and delinquency, 2,* 121–131.

McDonald, T., Hornby, H., Palmer, M., & Bessey, W. (1988). *Risk assessment models: A comparative analysis.* Portland: University of Southern Maine, Center for Research and Advanced Study, National Child Welfare Resource Center for Management and Administration.

McDonough, J. (1976). Structural and staff characteristics of juvenile courts. In R. Sarri & Y. Hasenfeld (Eds.), *Brought to justice? Juveniles, the courts, and the law.* Ann Arbor: University of Michigan, National Assessment of Juvenile Corrections.

McGoldrick, M., & Carter, B. (1988). Forming a remarried family. In B. Carter & M. McGoldrick (Eds.), *The changing family life cycle: A framework for family therapy* (pp. 399–429). New York: Gardner Press.

McGowan, B. (1989). A neighborhood-based, comprehensive, child and family service. In S. Kamerman & A. J. Kahn, *Social services for children, youth and families in the United States* (pp. 248–254). New York: Columbia University School of Social Work/Annie E. Casey Foundation.

McKeany, M. (1960). *The absent father and public policy in the program of aid to dependent children.* Berkeley: University of California Press.

McKeiver v. Pennsylvania, 403 U.S. 538 (1971).

McMillan, M. (1919). *The nursery school.* New York: Dutton.

McRoy, R. G., Grotevant, H. D., & White, K. L. (1988a). *Openness in adoption. New practices, new issues.* New York: Praeger.

McRoy, R. G., Grotevant, H. D., & Zurcher, L. A., Jr. (1988b). *Emotional disturbance in adopted adolescents: Origins and development.* New York: Praeger.

McRoy, R. G., & Zurcher, L. A. (1983). *Transracial and inracial adoptees. The adolescent years.* Springfield, IL: Charles C. Thomas.

Mech, E. V. (1965). Trends in adoption research. In *Perspectives on adoption research.* New York: Child Welfare League of America.

Mech, E. V. (1970). Decision analysis in foster care practice. In H. D. Stone (Ed.), *Foster care in question.* New York: Child Welfare League of America.

Mech, E. V. (1984, April 24). *Statement on orientation of pregnancy counselors toward adoption.* Before the Subcommittee on Family and Human Services of the Committee on Labor and Human Relations. U.S. Senate.

Mech, E. V. (1985). Parental visiting and foster placement. *Child Welfare, 64*(1), 67–72.

Mech, E. V. (1988a). *Final report summary for an inventory-based counseling model for communicating adoption to pregnant adolescents* (Grant #APH00018). Office of Adolescent Pregnancy Programs, Office of Population Affairs, Public Health Service, Department of Health and Human Services.

Mech, E. V. (Ed.). (1988b). Independent living services for at-risk adolescents [Special issue]. *Child Welfare, 62*(6).

Mech, E. V. (1988c). Preparing foster adolescents for self-support: A new challenge for child welfare services. *Child Welfare, 67*(6), 487–495.

Meek, L. H. (1937). Preschool children. In R. H. Kurtz (Ed.), *Social work yearbook 1937.* New York: Russell Sage Foundation.

Meezan, W., Katz, S., & Russo, E. M. (1978a). *Adoptions without agencies: A study of independent adoptions.* New York: Child Welfare League of America.

Meezan, W., Katz, S., & Russo, E. M. (1978b). Independent adoptions. *Child Welfare, 57*(7).

Meezan, W., & Shireman, J. F. (1985). *Care and*

commitment: Foster parent adoption decisions. Albany: State University of New York.

Meier, E. B. (1964). Child neglect. In N. E. Cohen (Ed.), *Social work and social work problems.* New York: National Association of Social Workers.

Meier, E. G. (1965). Current circumstances of former foster children. *Child Welfare, 44*(4), 196–206.

Meigs, G. L. (1917). *Maternal mortality from all conditions connected with childbirth in the United States and certain other countries* (Publication No. 19). Washington, DC: Children's Bureau.

Melton, G. B. (1983). *Child advocacy: Psychological issues and interventions.* New York: Plenum Press.

Mencher, S. (1960). The concept of authority and social casework. In *Casework papers, 1960.* New York: Family Service Association of America.

Mercer, J. R. (1974). A policy statement on assessment procedures and the rights of children. *Harvard Educational Review, 44*(1), 125–140.

Merrill, E. J. (1962). Physical abuse of children—an agency study. In *protecting the battered child.* Denver: American Humane Association, Children's Division.

Meyer, C. H. (1968). Child welfare and licensing practice. *Social Service Review.* 42, 344–354.

Meyer, C. H. (1972). Review of *When parents fail. Children Today, 1,* 28.

Meyer, C. H. (1984). Can foster care be saved? *Social Work, 29*(6), 499.

Meyer, C. H. (1985). The institutional context of child welfare. In J. Laird and A. Hartman, (Eds.), *Handbook of child welfare.* New York: Macmillan.

Meyer, C. H. (1987). *The future of social work practice: A public response or a private enterprise.* New Brunswick, NJ: School of Social Work, Rutgers University.

Michaels, R. (1947). Casework considerations in rejecting the adoption application. *Journal of Social Casework, 28*(10).

Michel, S. (1986). *Children's interests/mother's rights: Women, professionals and the American family. 1920–1945.* Unpublished doctoral dissertation, American Civilization, Brown University, Providence, RI.

Michel, S. (1988, January). The nineteenth century origins of the American child care policy. Unpublished paper, Women's Studies, History and Literature, Howard University, Washington, DC.

Miller, J. L., & Whittaker, J. K. (1988). Social services and social support: Blended programs for families at risk of child maltreatment. *Child Welfare, 68*(2), 161–174.

Miller, J. S., Williams, K. M., English, D. J., & Olmstead, J. (1987). *Risk assessment in child protection: A review of the literature* (Occasional monograph series of APWA's R&D Department No. 1). Washington, DC: American Public Welfare Association, CPS Risk Assessment Project.

Miller, L. F., & Moorman, J. E. (1989). Married couple families with children. In U.S. Department of Commerce, Bureau of the Census, *Studies in Marriage and the Family, Current Population Reports* (Special Studies Series P–23, No. 162, pp. 27–38). Washington, DC: U.S. Government Printing Office.

Miller, S. H. (1984). The relationship between adolescent childbearing and child maltreatment. *Child Welfare, 63*(6), 553–557.

Mills v. Habluetzel, 456, U.S. 91 (1982).

Milner, J., & Wimberly, R. (1980). Prediction and explanation of child abuse. *Journal of Clinical Psychology, 36,* 875–884.

Milner, J. L. (1987). An ecological perspective on duration of foster care. *Child Welfare, 66*(2), 113–123.

Milowe, I. D., & Lourie, R. S. (1964, December). The child's role in the battered child syndrome. *Journal of Pediatrics, 65,* 1079–1081.

Milton, C. H., Pierce, C., Lyons, M., & Hippensteel, B. (1977). *Little sisters and the law.* Washington, DC: American Bar Association, Female Offender Resource Center.

Minimum safeguards in adoption. (1938). New York: Child Welfare League of America.

Minuchin, S., et al. (1967). *Families of the slums.* New York: Basic Books.

Miranda v. Arizona, 384 U.S. 436 (1966).

Mitchel, L. (1987). *Child abuse and neglect fatalities: A review of the problem and strategies for reform* (Working paper number 838). Chicago: National Committee for Prevention of Child Abuse, National Center on Child Abuse Prevention Research.

Mitchell. M. M. (1969). Transracial adoptions: Philosophy and practice. *Child Welfare, 48*(10), 613–619.

Mnookin, R. H. (1973). Foster care—In whose best

interest? *Harvard Educational Review, 43*(40), 599–638.

Mnookin, R. H. (Ed). (1985). *In the interest of children: Advocacy, law reform, and public policy.* New York: Freeman.

Morales v. Turman, 380 F. Supp. 53 E.D. Tex. (1974).

Morgan, G. (1987). *The national state of child care regulation, 1986.* Watertown, MA: Work/Family Directions.

Morgan, G. C. (1971). *Regulation of early childhood programs.* Washington, DC: Day Care and Child Development Council of America.

Morris, M. G., & Gould, R. W. (1963). Role reversal: A concept in dealing with the neglected/battered-child syndrome. In *The neglected/battered child syndrome.* New York: Child Welfare League of America.

Morris, M. G., Gould, R. W., & Mathews, P. J. (1964, March–April). Toward prevention of child abuse. *Children, 11,* 55–60.

Morrison, H. S. (1950). Research study in an adoptive program. *Child Welfare, 29*(7), 7–13.

Moss, S. Z. (1963). Authority—An enabling factor in casework with neglectful parents. *Child Welfare, 42*(8), 385–391.

Mott, P. E. (1976). *Meeting human needs: The social and political history of Title XX.* Columbus, OH: National Conference on Social Welfare.

Moynihan, D. P. (1987, August 6). Some welfare reform beats no welfare reform. *New York Times,* p. 22.

Mulford, R. M. (1958, October). Emotional neglect of children: A challenge to protective services. *Child Welfare, 37,* 19–24.

Mulford, R. M. (1971). Protective services for children. In *Encyclopedia of social work* (16th ed.). New York: National Association of Social Work.

Mullen, E., Chazin, R., & Feldstein, D. (1970). *Preventing chronic dependency.* New York: Community Service Society.

Munns, J. M., & Copenhaver (1989). *The state of adoption in America.* Washington, DC: Child Welfare League of America.

Myren, R. A., & Swanson, L. D. (1962). *Police work with children: Perspectives and principles* (Children's Bureau Publication No. 399). Washington, DC: Children's Bureau.

Nathanson, M., Baird, A., & Jemail, J. (1986). Family functioning and the adolescent mother: A systems approach. *Adolescence, 21*(84), 827–841.

National Association of Public Child Welfare Administrators. (1988). *Guidelines for a model system of protective services for abused and neglected children and their families.* Washington, DC: American Public Welfare Association.

National Association of Social Workers. (1976). *Report on survey of social work services in schools.* Washington, DC: Author.

National Association of Social Workers (1987, November). Foster care and adoption policy statement. NASW Delegate Assembly (pp. 1–4). Washington, DC: Author.

National Commission on Excellence in Education. (1983). *A nation at risk. The imperative for educational reform.* Washington, DC: U.S. Department of Education.

National Committee for Adoption. (1982). *Children from other lands.* Unpublished mimeographed draft. Washington, DC: Author.

National Committee for Adoption. (1985). *Adoption factbook: United States data, issues, regulations and resources.* Washington, DC: Author.

National Committee for Adoption. (1989). *Adoption factbook. United States data, issues, regulations and resources.* Washington, DC: Author.

National Committee for Prevention of Child Abuse. (1989, May). *NCPCA memorandum.* Chicago: Author.

National Council of the Churches of Christ in the U.S.A. Commission on Social Welfare. (1965). *Religious factors in child adoptions. A study document.* Author.

National Council of Juvenile and Family Court Judges. (1984, Summer). The Juvenile court and serious offenders: 38 recommendations [Special issue]. *Juvenile & Family Court Journal.*

National Probation and Parole Association. (1957). *Guides for juvenile court judges.* New York: National Probation and Parole Association.

National Resource Center on Family-Based Services. (1982, Spring). Minority concerns and the family based approach to care. *Prevention Report,* pp. 1–3.

Nejelski, P. (1976). Diversion: Unleashing the hound of heaven? In M. K. Rosenheim (Ed.). *Pursuing justice for the child* (pp. 94–118). Chicago: University of Chicago Press.

Nelson, B. J. (1984). *Making an issue of child abuse:*

Political agenda setting. Chicago: University of Chicago Press.

Nelson, J. R., Jr. (1982). The federal interagency day care requirements. In C. D. Hayes, (Ed.), (1982). *Making policies for children. A study of the federal process* (pp. 751–805). Washington, DC: National Academy Press.

Nelson, K., et al. (1988). *Family based services: Factors contributing to success and failure in family based child welfare services: Final report.* Iowa City: National Resource Center on Family Based Services, University of Iowa School of Social Work.

Nelson, K.A. (1985). *On the frontier of adoption: A study of special-needs adoptive families.* New York: Child Welfare League of America.

Neraas, N. (1983, November). The non-lawyer guardian *ad litem* in child abuse and neglect proceedings: The King County, Washington experience. *Washington Law Review, 58,* 853–870.

Nettleton, C. A., & Cline, D. W. (1975). Dating patterns, sexual relationships, and use of contraception of 700 unwed mothers during a two-year period following delivery. *Adolescence, 10*(37), 45–57.

New Jersey Welfare Rights Organization v. Cahill, 411 U.S. 619 (1973).

Newman, J. F. (1990, January 9). Children in the groves. *New York Times,* p. 23.

New uniform act on paternity approved by ABA House Delegates. (1989, February 18). *The Family Law Reporter, 15*(17), 1207–1208.

New York State. (1912). Preliminary Report of the Factory Investigating Commission. In G. Abbott (1938), *The child and the state* (Vol. 1, pp. 362–364). Chicago: University of Chicago Press.

New York Times. (1976, April 7). p. 5.

New York Times Illustrated Weekly Magazine. (1898, February 20). P. 2.

Nichols-Casebolt, A. M. (1988). Black families headed by single mothers: Growing numbers and increasing poverty. *Social Work, 33*(4), 306–312.

Nichols-Casebolt, A. M., & McClure, J. (1989). Social work support for welfare reform: The latest surrender in the war on poverty. *Social Work, 34*(1), 77–80.

Nieburg, P., Marks, J. S., McLaren, N. M., & Remington, P. L. (1985). The fetal tobacco syndrome. *Journal of the American Medical Association, 253*(20), 2998–2999.

Nieden, M. Z. (1951). The influence of constitution and environment upon the development of adopted children. *Journal of Psychology, 31*(1), 91–95.

Nixon, R. M. (1971, December 10). Veto message on the Comprehensive Development bill. Washington, DC: Author.

Noble, L. S., & Euster, S. D. (1981). Foster parent input: A crucial element in training. *Child Welfare, 60*(1), 35–42.

Nobles, W. G. (1988). American family life: An instrument of culture. In H. P. McAdoo (Ed.), *Black families* (2nd ed., pp. 44–53). Beverly Hills, CA: Sage.

Nordlie, E. B., & Reed, S. C. (1962). Follow-up on adoption counseling for children of possible racial admixture. *Child Welfare, 41*(7), 297–304, 327.

North American Post-Legal Adoption Committee. (1984). *Model statement. Post-Legal adoption services.* Author.

Nurse, S. M. (1964, October). Familial patterns of parents who abuse their children. *Smith College Studies in Social Work, 35.*

Nutt, A. S. (1949). Juvenile and domestic relations court. In *1949 Social work yearbook* (pp. 270–276). New York: Russell Sage Foundation.

O'Byrne, K., & Bellucci, M. T. (1982). Subsidized adoption: One county's program. *Child Welfare, 61*(3).

O'Connor v. Donaldson, 422 U.S. 563 S.Ct. 2486, 45 E. Ed.2d 396 (1975).

Office of Economic Opportunity. (1968, March). *Project Head Start fact sheet.* Washington, DC: U.S. Government Printing Office.

Office of Economic Opportunity. (1968, August). *Headstart newsletter, special issue.* Washington, DC: U.S. Government Printing Office.

Ohio v. Akron Center for Reproductive Health. (1990, June 25). Doc. No. 88–805.

Olds, D. L., Henderson, C., Chamberlin, R., & Tatelbaum, R. (1986). Preventing child abuse and neglect: A randomized trial of nurse home visitation. *Pediatrics, 78*(1), 65–78.

Olds, D. L., Henderson, C., Tatelbaum, R., & Chamberlin, R. (1988). Improving the life-course of socially disadvantaged mothers: A randomized trial of nurse home visitation. *American Journal of Public Health, 78*(11), 1436–1445.

Olsen, L. J. (1982). Predicting the permanence status

of children in foster care. *Social Work Research & Abstracts, 18,* 9–20.

"One Church, One Child" plan by Chicago cleric boosts Black adoptions. (1984, October 15). *Jet,* p. 22.

Oppel, W. C., & Royston, A. B. (1971). Teenage births: Some social, psychological, and physical sequelae. *American Journal of Public Health, 61*(4).

Oppenheimer, J. J. (1925). *The visiting teacher movement with special reference to administrative relationships* (2nd ed.). New York: Joint Committee on Methods of Preventing Delinquency.

Ortiz, C. G., & Vazquez-Nuttall, E. (1987). Adolescent pregnancy: Effects of family support, education, and religion on the decision to carry or terminate among Puerto Rican teenagers. *Adolescence, 22*(88), 897–917.

Osili, A. J., & Parker, F. A. (1957, January 24). *A follow-up study of fifty unmarried Negro mothers in action Aid-to-Dependent-Children cases in the Marion County Department of Public Welfare.* Indianapolis: Marion County, Indiana, Department of Public Welfare.

Ozawa, M. N. (1984). The 1983 amendments to the social security act: The issue of intergenerational equity. *Social Work, 29*(2), 131–137.

Paget, N. W. (1967, July). Emergency parent—A protective service to children in crisis. *Child Welfare, 46,* 403–407.

Palmer, M. (n.d.). *Risk assessment models: A comparative analysis* (quoting a source by *ACTION for Child Protection*). Portland: University of Southern Maine, National Child Welfare Resource Center for Management and Administration, p. 1.

Pannor, R., & Baran, A. (1984). Open adoption as standard practice. *Child Welfare, 63*(3), 245–250.

Pappenfort, D. M., & Kilpatrick, D.M. (1969). Child-caring institutions, 1966: Selected findings from the national survey of children's residential institutions. *Social Service Review, 43*(4), 449–450.

Pappenfort, D. M., Kilpatrick, D. M., & Roberts, R. W. (Eds.). (1973). *Child caring: Social policy and the institution.* Chicago: Aldine.

Pappenfort, D. M., & Young, T. W. (1980, December). *Use of secure detention for juveniles and alternatives to its use: A national study of juvenile detention.* U.S. Department of Justice, Law En-forcement Assistance Administration, Office of Juvenile Justice and Delinquency Prevention. Washington, DC: U.S. Government Printing Office.

Paquin, G. (1987–1988). Protecting the interests of children in divorce mediation. *Journal of Family Law/University of Louisville School of Law, 26*(2), 279–315.

Paradise, V. I. (1922). *Child labor and the work of mothers in oyster and shrimp canning on the Gulf Coast.* Children's Bureau Publication No. 98. Washington, DC: Children's Bureau. In G. Abbott. (1938). *The child and the state* (Vol. 1, pp. 370–376). Chicago: University of Chicago Press.

Parham v. J. R., 442 U.S. 584, 61 L.Ed.2d 101, 99 S.Ct. 2493 (1979).

Parke, R. D., Power, T. G., & Fisher, T. (1980). The adolescent father's impact on the mother and child. *Journal of Social Issues, 36*(1).

Parsons, T. (1954). *Essays in sociological theory* (rev. ed.). Chicago: Free Press of Glencoe.

Pasztor, E. M., Clarren, J., Timberlake, E. N., & Bayless, L. (1986). Stepping out of foster care into independent living. *Children Today, 15*(2), 32–35.

Patton, J. M. (1968). *Orphan voyage.* New York: Vantage Press.

Paul, J. L. (1977a). The need for advocacy. In J. L. Paul, G. R. Neufeld, & J. W. Pelosi (Eds.), *Child advocacy within the system.* Syracuse, NY: Syracuse University Press.

Paul, J. L. (1977b). Advocacy program development. In J. L. Paul, G. R. Neufeld, & J. W. Pelosi (Eds.), *Child advocacy within the system.* Syracuse, NY: Syracuse University Press.

Paul, J. L. (1977c). A framework for understanding child advocacy. In J. L. Paul, G. R. Neufeld, & J. W. Pelosi (Eds.), *Child advocacy within the system* (pp. 11–31). Syracuse, NY: Syracuse University Press.

Paul, J. L., Neufeld, G. R., & Pelosi, J. W. (Eds.). (1977). *Child advocacy within the system.* Syracuse, NY: Syracuse University Press.

Paulsen, M. G. (1965). Constitutional problems of utilizing a religious factor in adoption placements of children. In D. H. Oaks (Ed.), *The war between church and state.* Chicago: University of Chicago Press.

Paulsen, M. G. (1966a). Juvenile courts, family

courts, and the poor man. In J. Tenbroek (Ed.), *The law of the poor*. San Francisco: Chandler.

Paulsen, M. G. (1966b, March–April). Legal protections against child abuse. *Children, 13,* 43–48.

Paulsen, M. G. (1974). *The law and abused children*. In R. E. Helfer & C. H. Kempe (Eds.), *The battered child* (2nd ed., pp. 153–178). Chicago: University of Chicago Press.

Pavenstedt, E. (Ed.). (1967). *The drifters: Children of disorganized lower-class families*. Boston: Little, Brown.

Payne, G. H. (1916). *The child in human progress*. New York: G. P. Putnam's Sons.

Pear, R. (1988, December 28). U.S. pensions found to lift many of poor. *New York Times,* pp. 1, 12.

Pear, R. (1990, August 20). Welfare on rise, signaling a slump in economy of U.S. *The New York Times.* p. 1, 10.

Pecora, P., Carlson, I., Reese, S., & Bartholomew, G. (1986–1987, Winter). Developing and implementing risk assessment systems in Child Protective Services. *Protecting Children, 3,* 8–10, 15.

Pecora, P., Delewski, C. H., Booth, C., Haapala, D., and Kinney, J. (1985). Home-based, family-centered services: The impact of training on worker attitudes. *Child Welfare, 64*(5), 529–540.

Pedgeon, M. (1953). *Employed mothers and child care*. Bulletin 246. Washington, DC: Women's Bureau.

Pelosi, J. W., Taylor, D., & Paul, J. L. (1977). Child advocacy in state government. In J. L. Paul, G. R. Neufeld, & J. W. Pelosi (Eds.), *Child advocacy within the system*. Syracuse, NY: Syracuse University Press.

Pennsylvania Association for Retarded Children v. Commonwealth of Pennsylvania, 334 F. Aupp. 1257, E.D. Pa. (1971).

Perlman, H. H. (1964). Unmarried mothers. In N. E. Cohen (Ed.), *Social work and social problems* (pp. 270–320). New York: National Association of Social Workers.

Pettibone, J. M., Swisher, R. G., Weiland, K. H., Wolf, C. E., & White, J. L. (1981). *Major issues in juvenile justice information and training: Services to children in juvenile courts: The judicial-executive controversy*. U.S. Department of Justice, National Institute for Juvenile Justice and Delinquency Prevention, Office of Juvenile Justice and Delinquency. Washington, DC: U.S. Government Printing Office.

Phear, W. P. (1985, March). Parent-child mediation: Four states, four models. *Mediation Quarterly, 7* 35–45.

Phillips, M., Haring, B., & Shyne, A. W. (1972). *A model for intake decisions in child welfare*. New York: Child Welfare League of America.

Phillips, M., Shyne, A. W., Sherman, E., & Haring, B. (1971). *Factors associated with placement decisions in child welfare*. New York: Child Welfare League of America.

Philp, A. G., & Timms, N. (1957). *The problem of "The Problem Family."* London: Family Service Units.

Phipps-Yonas, S. (1980). Teenage pregnancy and motherhood: A review of the literature. *American Journal of Orthopsychiatry, 50*(3), 403–431.

Piaget, J. (1952). *The origins of intelligence in children* (M. Cook, Trans.). New York: International Universities Press.

Pierce, L. H., & Hauck, V. B. (1981). A model establishing a community-based foster group home. *Child Welfare, 60*(7), 477.

Pinderhughes, E. (1982). Afro-American families and the victim system. In M. McGoldrick, J. Pearce, and J. Giordano (Eds.), *Ethnicity and family therapy* (pp. 108–122). New York: Guilford Press.

Pittman, K., & Adams, G. (1988). *What about the boys? Teenage pregnancy prevention strategies*. Washington, DC: Children's Defense Fund, Adolescent Pregnancy Prevention Clearinghouse.

Pittman, K., & Govan, C. (1986). *Model programs: Preventing adolescent pregnancy and building youth self-sufficiency*. Washington, DC: Children's Defense Fund, Adolescent Pregnancy Prevention Clearinghouse.

Pittman, K., Taylor, S., & O'Brien, R. (1989). *The lessons of multi-site initiatives serving high-risk youths*. Washington, DC: Children's Defense Fund, Adolescent Pregnancy Prevention Clearinghouse.

Planned Parenthood Association of Champaign County *Newsletter,* July 1982, p. 1.

Planned Parenthood of Central Missouri v. Danforth, 96 S.Ct. 2843 (1976).

Plantz, M. C., Hubbell, R., Barrett, B. J., & Dobrec, A. (1989). Indian child welfare: A status report. *Children Today, 18*(1), 24–29.

Platt, A. M. (1969). *The child savers: The invention*

of delinquency. Chicago: University of Chicago Press.

Plyer et al. v. J. and R. Doe et al. (1982, June 15). *United States Law Week, 50*(48), 4650–4664.

Poertner, J., & Rapp, C.A. (1980). Information system design in foster care. *Social Work, 25*(2), 114–121.

Polansky, N. A., Ammons, P. W., & Gaudin, J. M. (1985). Loneliness and isolation in child neglect. *Social Casework, 66,* 38–47.

Polansky, N. A., Borman, R. D., & De Saix, C. (1972). *Roots of futility.* San Francisco: Jossey-Bass.

Polansky, N. A., Chalmers, M. A., Buttenwieser, E., & Williams, D. P. (1981). *Damaged parents: An anatomy of child neglect.* Chicago: University of Chicago Press.

Polansky, N. A., Hally, C., & Polansky, N. F. (1975). *Profile of neglect: A survey of the state of knowledge of child neglect* (DHEW Publication No. SRS 76–23037). Washington, DC: U.S. Government Printing Office.

Polansky, N. A., & Polansky, N. F. (1968). The current status of child abuse and child neglect in this country, report to the Joint Commission on Mental Health for Children.

Polansky, N. A., & Williams, D. P. (1978, January). Class orientations to child neglect. *Social Work, 23,* 397–401.

Polenz, G. D. (1970). *Supervision and consultation in child care licensing: special reference to children's institutions.* Unpublished doctoral dissertation, University of Southern California.

Polier, J. W. (1964). *A view from the bench.* New York: National Council on Crime and Delinquency.

Polier, J. W. (1974, October 3). Banished children. *New York Times,* p. 4.

Polier, J. W. (1975). Myths and realities in the search for juvenile justice. *Harvard Educational Review, 44*(1), 112–124.

Polier, J. W. (1989). *Juvenile justice in double jeopardy. The distanced community and vengeful retribution.* Hillsdale, NJ: Lawrence Erlbaum Associates.

Pollack, S. L. (1981). The hired farm working force of 1979. *Agricultural Economic Reports (No. 473).* Washington, DC: U.S. Department of Agriculture.

Polsky, H. (1962). *Cottage six.* New York: Wiley Science Editions.

Pound, R. (1923). *Interpretations of legal history.* New York: Macmillan.

Pound, R. (1950). The juvenile court in the service state. In *1949 Yearbook.* New York: National Probation and Parole Association.

Powell, T. J. (1979, February). Interpreting Parents Anonymous as a source of help for those with child abuse problems. *Child Welfare, 58.*

President's Commission on Law Enforcement and Administration of Justice, (1967). *Task force report: Juvenile delinquency and youth crime: Report on juvenile justice and consultants' papers.* Washington, DC: Author.

Pringle, M. L. K. (1967). *Adoption—Facts and fallacies.* London: Longmans, Green.

Proceedings of the conference on the care of dependent children (1909, January 25–26). (60th Cong., 2d. Sess., S. Doc. No. 721). Washington, DC: U.S. Government Printing Office.

Proch, K. (1980). *Adoptions by foster parents.* Unpublished doctoral dissertation, University of Illinois, Urbana-Champaign.

Proch, K. (1981). Foster parents as preferred adoptive parents: Practice implications. *Child Welfare, 60*(9), 617–626.

Proch, K., & Howard, J. A. (1986). Parental visiting of children in foster care. *Social Work, 31*(3), 178–181.

Proch, K., & Taber, M. A. (1987). Alienated adolescents in foster care. *Social Work Research and Abstracts, 23*(2), 9–13.

Provence, S. (1967). *Guide for the care of infants in groups.* New York: Child Welfare League of America.

Quillon v. Walcott, 98 S. Ct. 549 (1978).

Ramsey, P. (1959). The legal imputation of religion to an infant in adoption proceedings. *New York University Law Review, 34.*

Randolph, L. A., & Gesche, M. (1986). Black adolescent pregnancy: Prevention and management. *Journal of Community Health, 11*(1), 10–18.

Rapp, C. A. (1982). The effect of family support services on placement decisions. *Social work research and abstracts, 18*(1), 21–28.

Rathbun, C., McLaughlin, H., & Garland, J. A. (1964). *Later adjustments of children following radical separation from family and culture.* Paper presented at the American Orthopsychiatric Association, Chicago.

Ratterman, D., Dodson, D., & Hardin, M. (1987). *Reasonable efforts to prevent foster placement: A guide to implementation.* Washington, DC: American Bar Association.

Rawlings, S. W. (1989). Single-parents and their children. In U.S. Department of Commerce, Bureau of the Census, *Studies in Marriage and the Family, Current Population Reports* (Special studies series P-23, No. 162 pp. 13-25). Washington, DC: U.S. Government Printing Office.

Ray-Bettineski, C. (1978). Court appointed special advocates: The guardian *ad litem* for abused and neglected children. *Juvenile and Family Court Journal, 29*(3), 65-70.

Raynor, L. (1980). *The adopted child comes of age.* London: Allen & Unwin.

Real welfare reform at last. (1988, October 1). *New York Times,* p. 14.

Reamer, F. G., & Shireman, C. H. (1981). Alternatives to the juvenile justice system: Their development and the current "state of the art." *Juvenile and Family Court Journal, 32*(2), 25-40.

Red Horse, J. G. (1980). Family structure and value orientation in American Indians. *Social Casework, 61,* 462-467.

Reed, R. (1934). *The illegitimate family in New York City.* New York: Columbia University Press.

Report and other papers on subject of laws for relief and settlement of poor. (1824, January). *Assembly Journal,* pp. 386-399. Reprinted in S. P. Breckinridge (1927), *Public welfare administration in the United States: Select documents.* Chicago: University of Chicago Press.

Report of Select senate committee to visit charitable and penal institutions, 1857 (New York Senate Document No. 8). Reprinted in S. P. Breckinridge. (1927). *Public welfare administration in the United States: Select documents.* Chicago: University of Chicago Press.

Report of the Commission. (1914). New York: State Commission on Relief for Widowed Mothers.

Reppucci, N. D., & Haugaard, J. J. (1989). Prevention of child sexual abuse: Myth and reality. *American Psychologist, 44*(10), 1266-1275.

Rest, E. R., & Watson, K. W. (1984). Growing up in foster care. *Child Welfare, 63*(4), 291-306.

Rheinstein, M. (1958). Historical survey of the law of parent and child. In *The Child at law* (Report of the Twenty-eighth Ross Pediatric Research Conference). Columbus, OH: Ross Laboratories.

Richan, W. C. (1978). Personnel issues in child welfare. In *Child welfare strategy in the coming years* (Publication No. 78-30158). Washington, DC: Children's Bureau.

Riday, E. (1969). Supply and demand in adoption. *Child Welfare, 48*(8).

Riegel, B. (1968). Group meetings with adolescents in child welfare. *Child Welfare, 47,* 417-418, 427.

Riessman, F. (1962). *The culturally deprived child.* New York: Harper & Row.

Rights of the child, The. (1968). *New Society, 11*(278), 10.

Riley, P. V. (1971). Family advocacy: Case to cause and back to case. *Child Welfare, 50*(7).

Ripple, L. (1953). *Social work studies of unmarried parenthood as affected by contemporary treatment formulations 1920-1940.* Unpublished doctoral dissertation, University of Chicago.

Ripple, L. (1968). A follow-up study of adopted children. *Social Service Review, 42*(4), 479-499.

Roberts, M. (1979). Reciprocal nature of parent-infant interaction: Implications for child maltreatment. *Child Welfare, 58*(6).

Robert Wood Johnson Foundation (1988). *Serving handicapped children: A special report.* Author.

Robinson, B. E. (1988). Teenage pregnancy from the father's perspective. *American Journal of Orthopsychiatry, 58*(1), 46-51.

Robinson, J. F. (1950). Arranging resident psychiatric treatment with foster children. *Quarterly Journal of Child Behavior, 2,* 176-184.

Rodham, H. (1973). Children under the law. *Harvard Educational Review, 43*(4).

Rodman, H., Pratto, D. J., & Nelson, R. S. (1985). Child care arrangements and children's functioning: A comparison of self-care and adult care of children. *Developmental Psychology, 21*(3), 413-418.

Roe v. Wade, 410 U.S. 113, S.Ct. 705, 35 L.Ed.2d 147 (1973).

Rose, J. A. (1962). A re-evaluation of the concept of separation for child welfare. *Child Welfare, 41*(10), 444-458.

Rose, S. J. (1989). *Child neglect: A definition perspective.* Unpublished doctoral dissertation. Chicago: University of Illinois Jane Addams College of Social Work.

Rosenberg, D. A. (1988). Recent issues in child maltreatment. In D. C. Bross et al. (Eds.), *The new child protection team handbook* (pp. 113–125). New York: Garland.

Rosenberg, D. A., & Gary, N. (1988). Sexual abuse of children. In D. C. Bross et al. (Eds.), *The new child protection team handbook*. New York: Garland.

Rosenberg, J., & Pierce, W. (1987). Adoption practice today: The current judicial boundaries. *The Family Law Reporter, 13*(42), 3025–3030.

Rosenberg, R., & Donohue, A. M. (1925). *The welfare of infants of illegitimate birth in Baltimore* (Children's Bureau Publication No. 144). Washington, DC: Children's Bureau.

Rosenheim, J. K. (Ed.). (1962). *Justice for the child.* New York: Free Press.

Rosewater, A. (1989). Caring for America's children. Child and family trends: Beyond the numbers. *Proceedings of the Academy of Political Science, 37*(2), 4–10.

Ross, H., & Sawhill, I. (1975). *Time of transition: The growth of families headed by women.* Washington, DC: Urban Institute.

Rothchild, A. (1974). An agency evaluates its foster care service. *Child Welfare, 53*(1), 42–50.

Rothman, J., (1974). Introduction. In F. M. Cox, J. L. Erlich, J., Rothman & J. E. Tropman (Eds.), *Strategies of community organization.* Itasca, IL: Peacock.

Rothman, J., Gant, L. M., & Hnat, S. A. (1985). Mexican-American family culture. *Social Service Review, 59*(2), 197–215.

Rowe, R. (1989, January–February). Preventing infant mortality: An investment in the nation's future. *Children Today, 18,* 16–20.

Rubin, L. (1987). A feminist response to Lasch. *Tikkun, 1*(2), 89–91.

Rubin, S. (1952, November–December). Protecting the child in juvenile court. *Journal of Criminal Law, Criminology and Police Science, 43,* 425–440.

Ruderman, F. A. (1968). *Child care and working mothers: A study of arrangements for daytime care of children.* New York: Child Welfare League of America.

Rudoff, A., & Piliavin, I. (1969). An aid to needy children program: A study of types and responses to casework services. *Community Mental Health Journal, 5*(3), 447–463.

Russell, A. B., & Trainor, C. M. (1984). *Trends in child abuse and neglect: A national perspective.* Denver: American Association for Protecting Children, American Human Association.

Russell, D. (1983). The incidence and prevalence of intrafamilial and extrafamilial sexual abuse of female children. *Child Abuse and Neglect: The International Journal, 7,* 133–146.

Rutter, M. (1982). Social-emotional consequences of day care for preschool children. In E. F. Zigler & E. W. Gordon (Eds.), *Day care. Scientific and social policy issues* pp. 3–32). Boston: Auburn House.

Ryan, P. (1987, Summer). Recruitment and retention. *Fostering Ideas,* pp. 1–8.

Sachdev, P. (Ed.). (1984a). *Adoption: Current issues and trends.* Toronto: Butterworths.

Sachdev, P. (1984b). Adoption outlook: projection for the future. In P. Sachdev (Ed.), *Adoption: Current issues and trends.* Toronto: Butterworths.

Sager, C. J., Steer, H., Crohn, H., Rodstein, E., & Walker, E. (1980). Remarriage revisited. *Family and Child Mental Health Journal, 6*(1).

Sahd, D. (1983). Psychological assessment of sexually abusing families and treatment implications. In W. M. Holder (Ed.), *Sexual abuse of children: Implications for treatment.* Englewood, CO: American Humane Association, Child Protection Division.

Sale, J. S. (1973). Family day care: One alternative in the delivery of developmental services in early childhood. *American Journal of Orthopsychiatry, 43*(1).

Salomone, R. C. (1989). Children versus the state: The status of students' constitutional rights. *Proceedings of the Academy of Political Science, 37*(2), 182–200.

Saluter, A. F. (1989). Singleness in America. In U.S. Department of Commerce, Bureau of the Census, *Studies in Marriage and the Family, Current Population Reports* (Special Studies Series P-23, No. 162, pp. 1–10). Washington, DC: U.S. Government Printing Office.

Sandberg, D. N. (1989). *The child abuse—delinquency connection.* Lexington, MA: Lexington Books.

Sanger, C. (1985). *Day care center licensing and religious exemptions: An overview for providers.* San Francisco: Child Care Law Center.

Santosky v. Kramer, 102 S.Ct. 1388 (1982).

Sarri, R. C. (1974). *Under lock and key: Juveniles in*

jails and detention. Ann Arbor: University of Michigan, National Assessment of Juvenile Corrections.

Sarri, R. C. (1976). Service technologies: Diversion, probation, and detention. In R. Sarri & Y. Hasenfeld (Eds.), *Brought to justice? Juveniles, the courts, and the law* (pp. 160–166). Ann Arbor: University of Michigan, National Assessment of Juvenile Corrections.

Sarri, R. C. (1983). Gender issues in juvenile justice. *Crime & Delinquency, 29*(3), 381–397.

Sarri, R. C. (1985). *Juvenile justice as child welfare.* In J. Laird and A. Hartman. *A handbook of child welfare. Context, knowledge, and practice* (pp. 489–513). New York: Free Press.

Sarri, R. C., & Hasenfeld, Y. (Eds.). (1976). *Brought to justice? Juveniles, the courts, and the law.* Ann Arbor: University of Michigan, National Assessment of Juvenile Corrections.

Sauber, M., & Rubinstein, E. (1965). *Experiences of the unwed mother as a parent.* New York: Community Council of Greater New York.

Savage, B. D. (1987). *Child support and teen parents.* Washington, DC: Adolescent Pregnancy Clearinghouse, Children's Defense Fund.

Scarr, S., Phillips, D., & McCartney, K. (1990). Facts, fantasies and the future of child care in the United States. *Psychological Science, 1*(1), 26–35.

Scarr, S., & Weinberg, R. A. (1976). I.Q. test performance of black children adopted by white families. *American Psychologist, 31*(10), 726–739.

Schafer, W. E., & Polk K. (1967). Delinquency and the schools. In President's Commission on Law Enforcement and Administration of Justice, *Task force report: Juvenile delinquency and youth crime: Report on juvenile justice and consultants' papers.* Washington, DC: Government Printing Office.

Schall, Commissioner of New York City Department of Juvenile Justice v. Martin et al., 467 S.Ct. 253 (1984).

Schapiro, M. (1956). *A study of adoption practices* (Vol. 1). New York: Child Welfare League of America.

Schechter, M. D. (1960). Observations on adopted children. *A.M.A. Archives of General Psychiatry, 3,* 21–32.

Schechter Poultry Corp. v. United States, 295 U.S. 495 (1935).

Schene, P. (1987, June). Is child abuse decreasing? *Journal of Interpersonal Violence, 2*(2), 225–232.

Schene, P., & Bond, K. (Eds.). (1989) *Research issues in risk assessment for child protection.* Denver: American Association for Protecting Children, American Humane Society.

Schlesinger, A. M., Jr. (1959). *The age of Roosevelt: The coming of the new deal.* Boston: Houghton Mifflin.

Schmidt, W. E. (1987). Spanking in school: A tradition is under fire. *New York Times,* pp. 1, 14.

Schmitt, B. D. (1988a). Failure to thrive: The medical evaluation. In D. C. Bross et al. (Eds.), *The new child protection team handbook* (pp. 82–101). New York: Garland.

Schmitt, B. D. (1988b). Physical abuse: The medical evaluation. In D. C. Bross et al. (Eds.), *The new child protection team handbook* (pp. 49–65). New York: Garland.

Schorr, A. L. (1966). *Poor kids.* New York: Basic Books.

Schorr, A. L. (1974). *Slums and the social insecurity.* (Research report No. 1). Washington, DC: U.S. Department of Health, Education, and Welfare, Social Security Administration, Division of Research and Statistics.

Schorr, L. B. (1988). *Within our reach. Breaking the cycle of disadvantage.* New York: Doubleday (Anchor Press).

Schultz, L. L., & Cohen, F. (1976). Isolationism in juvenile court jurisprudence. In M. K. Rosenheim (Ed.), *Pursuing justice for the child.* Chicago: University of Chicago Press.

Schwartz, R. K. (1987). A new role for the guardian ad litem. *Ohio State Journal on Dispute Resolution, 3*(1), 117–185.

Scope of the problem. (1974, Winter). *Indian Family Defense.*

Sebold, J. (1987). Indicators of child sexual abuse in males. *Social Casework, 68*(2), 75–80.

Secretariat to the Association of Administrators of the Interstate Compact on Adoption and Medical Assistance, Inc. (1988). *A guide to the interstate compact on adoption and medical assistance.* Washington, DC: American Public Welfare Association.

Seitz, V., Rosenbaum, L., & Apfel, N. (1985). Effects of family support intervention: A ten-year follow-up. *Child Development, 56,* 376–391.

Selinske, J. (1983, Summer). Protecting CPS clients and workers. *Public Welfare, 41,* 30–35.

Shaffer, G. L. (1977). Subsidized adoption: A fifty-state survey, 1976. In G. L. Shaffer, *Subsidized adoption: An alternative to long term foster care.* Unpublished doctoral dissertation, University of Illinois, Urbana-Champaign.

Shames, M. (1964, January). Use of homemaker service in families that neglect their children. *Social Work, 9,* 12–18.

Shapiro, D. (1966). *Social distance and illegitimacy: A comparative study of attitudes and values.* Unpublished doctoral dissertation, Columbia University, New York City.

Shapiro, D. (1967). Attitudes, values, and unwed motherhood. In *Unmarried parenthood: Clues to agency and community action* (pp. 52–63). New York: National Council on Illegitimacy.

Shapiro, D. (1976). *Agencies and foster care.* New York: Columbia University.

Shapiro, D. (1979). *Parents and protectors: A study in child abuse and neglect.* New York: Child Welfare League of America.

Shapiro, D. (1984). Fostering and adoption: Converging roles for substitute parents. In P. Sachdev (Ed.), *Adoption: Current issues and trends* (pp. 267–286). Toronto: Butterworths.

Shapiro, D., & Grow, L. J. (1977). Not so bold and not so irrelevant: A reply to Chimezie. *Child Welfare, 56*(2), 86–92.

Shapiro v. Thompson, 394 U.S. 618, 89 C. Ct., 618 (1969).

Shelley v. Westbrooke, 1 Jacob 266 (1817).

Shepherd, R. E. (1988). Adult prosecution of juvenile offenders. In H. A. Davidson & R. M. Horowitz (Eds.), *Children and the law* (pp. 424–439). Washington, DC: Young Lawyers Division, American Bar Association; National Legal Resource Center for Child Advocacy and Protection.

Sheridan, W. H. (1966). *Standards for juvenile and family courts* (Publication No. 437). Washington, DC: Children's Bureau.

Shireman, J. F., & Johnson, P. R. (1975) *Adoption: Three Alternatives—A comparative study of three alternative forms of adoptive placements. Phase I.* Chicago: Chicago Child Care Society.

Shireman, J. F., & Johnson, P. R. (1976). Single persons as adoptive parents. *Social Service Review, 50*(2), 103–116.

Shireman, J. F., & Johnson, P. R. (1980). *Adoption:*
Three alternatives, Pt. 2. Chicago: Child Care Society.

Shireman, J. F., & Johnson, P. R. (1986). A longitudinal study of black adoptions: Single parent, transracial, and traditional. *Social Work, 31,* 172–176.

Shribman, D. (1982a, July 28). Child labor rules: Oliver Twist or Adam Smith? *New York Times,* p. 11.

Shribman, D. (1982b, July 29). Work proposals on youth assailed. *New York Times,* p. 13.

Shribman, D. (1982c, July 22). Job opportunities—For children. *New York Times,* p. 16.

Shyne, A. (1980). Who are the children? A national overview of services. *Social Work Research and Abstracts, 16*(1), 26–33.

Shyne, A. W., & Schroeder, A. W. (1978). *National study of social services to children and their families.* Rockville, MD: Westat.

Siegel, A. E., & Haas, M. B. (1963). The working mother: A review of research. *Child Development, 34*(3), 126–166.

Silberman, C. E. (1971). *Crisis in the classroom.* New York: Random House.

Silverstein, L. (1981). A critical review of current research on infant day care. In S. B. Kamerman & A. S. Kahn (Eds.), *Child care, family benefits, and working parents. A study in comparative policy* (Appendix A, pp. 265–313). New York: Columbia University Press.

Simon, R. J., & Altstein, H. (1977). *Transracial adoption.* New York: Wiley.

Simon, R. J., & Altstein, H. (1981). *Transracial adoption: A follow-up.* Lexington, MA: Lexington Books.

Simon, R. J., & Altstein, H. (1987). *Transracial adoptees and their families: A study of identity and commitment.* New York: Praeger.

Sims, A. R. (1988). Independent living services for youths in foster care. *Social Work, 33*(6), 539–542.

Singer, J. D., & Butler, J. A. (1987). The education for all handicapped children act: Schools as agents of social reform. *Harvard Educational Review, 57*(2), 125–152.

Siu, S., & Hogan, P. T. (1989). Public child welfare: The need for clinical social work. *Social Work, 34*(5), 423–428.

Skeels, H. M. (1965). Effects of adoption on children from institutions. *Children, 12*(1), 33–34.

Slingerland, W. H. (1919). *Child-placing in families.* New York: Russell Sage Foundation.

Smeeding, T. M., & Torrey, B. B. (1988, November). Poor children in rich countries. *Science, 242,* 873–877.

Smith, A. D. (1955). *The right to life.* New Haven, CT: College and University Press.

Smith, A. K. (1951). *Juvenile court laws in foreign countries* (Publication No. 328). Washington, DC: Children's Bureau.

Smith, A. M. (1989, June 21, 26). Statistics as of 3/31/89. Chicago: Adoption Information Center of Illinois (AICI).

Smith, C. P., Berkman, D. J., Fraser, W. M., & Sutton, J. (1980). *Jurisdiction and the elusive status offender: A comparison of involvement in delinquent behavior and status offenses.* U.S. Department of Justice, Law Enforcement Assistance Administration, Office of Juvenile Justice and Delinquency Prevention. Washington, DC: U.S. Government Printing Office.

Smith, K. C. (1974). A profile of juvenile court judges in the United States. *Juvenile Justice, 25*(2), 27–38.

Smith, S. R. (1989). The changing politics of child welfare services: New roles for the government and the nonprofit sectors. *Child Welfare, 68*(3), 289–299.

Snipp, C. M. (1986). The changing political and economic status of the American Indians: From captive nations to internal colonies. *American Journal of Economics and Sociology, 45*(2), 145–157.

Snyder, H. N. (1987). A national portrait of juvenile court caseloads: A summary of *Delinquency in the United States 1983. Juvenile & Family Court Journal, 38*(1), 39–53.

Social Security amendments of 1972. (1972, September 26). (To accompany H.R. 1 to amend the Social Security Act). (Senate Report No. 92-1230, 92d Cong., 2d Sess., pp. 490–493). Washington, DC: U.S. Senate Committee on Finance.

Social Security Bulletin. (1982). *45*(3), p. 1.

Soffen, J. (1962). The impact of a group educational program for foster parents. *Child Welfare, 41*(5), 195–201.

Sokoloff, B., Carlin, J., & Pham, H. (1984). Five-year follow-up of Vietnamese refugee children in the United States. *Clinical Pediatrics, 23*(10), 565–570.

Solender, E. K. (1976). The guardian *ad litem:* A valuable representative or an illusory safeguard? *Texas Tech Law Review, 7*(3).

Solomon, B. B. (1985). Assessment, service, and black families. In S. S. Gray, A. Hartman, & E. S. Saalberg (Eds.), *Empowering the black family* (pp. 9–20). Ann Arbor: University of Michigan, National Child Welfare Training Center.

Sorosky, A. D., Baran, A., & Pannor, R. (1984). *The adoption triangle: The effects of the sealed record on adoptees, birth parents and adoptive parents.* Garden City, NY: Anchor Press/Doubleday.

Sorosky, A. D., Baran, A., & Pannor, R. (1989). *The adoption triangle: Sealed or opened records: How they affect adoptees, birth parents, and adoptive parents.* San Antonio: Corona.

Source materials. (1963). Searching homes of public assistance recipients: The issues under the social security act. *Social Service Review, 37*(3).

Spencer, M. E. (1987). Post-legal adoption services: A lifelong commitment. *Journal of Social Work and Human Sexuality, 6*(1), 155–167.

Spendlove, D. C. (1978). Custodial day care on military bases. *Health and Social Work, 3*(4), 113–130.

Spicer, E. (1980). American Indians. In S. Thernstrom, A. Orlov, & O. Handlin (Eds.), *Harvard encyclopedia of American ethnic groups.* Cambridge, MA: Harvard University Press.

Spitz, R. A. (1945). Hospitalism: An inquiry into the genesis of psychiatric conditions in early childhood. In Fenichel et al. (Eds.), *The psychoanalytic study of the child* (Vol. 1, pp. 53–74). New York: International Universities Press.

Stack, C. (1974). *All our kin: Strategies for survival in a Black community.* New York: Harper & Row.

Standards relating to the juvenile probation function: Intake and predisposition investigative services. (1980). Recommended by the IJA/ABA Joint Commission on Juvenile Justice Standards. Cambridge, MA: Ballinger.

Standards relating to police handling of juvenile problems. (1980). Recommended by the IJA/ABA Joint Commission on Juvenile Justice Standards. Cambridge, MA: Ballinger.

Stanley v. Illinois, 405 U.S. 645, 92 S.Ct. 1208, 31 L.Ed. 2d 551 (1972).

Stanton, H. R. (1956). Mother love in foster homes. *Marriage and Family Living, 18*(4), 301–307.

A statement of principles and policies on public child welfare. (1950). *Child Welfare, 29*(12).

State of Illinois, Department of Child and Family

Services. (1985). *Licensing standards for day care homes.* Springfield: Author.

State of Illinois, Department of Child and Family Services. (1987). *Licensing standards for foster family homes.* Springfield: Author.

State of Michigan, Department of Social Services, Bureau of Regulatory Service. (1977). *Demonstration project for the registration of family day care homes, Final Report.* Lansing: Author.

Statutes of California, Chap. 281. sec. 1407, 1408 (1931).

St. Denis, G. C. (1969). *Interracial adoptions in Minnesota: Self-concepts and child rearing attitudes of Caucasian parents who have adopted Negro children.* Unpublished doctoral dissertation, University of Minnesota, Minneapolis/St. Paul.

Steele, B. (1975). Psychodynamic factors in child abuse. In C. Kempe & R. Helfer (Eds.), *The battered child.* Chicago: University of Chicago Press.

Steele, B. (1980). Psychodynamic factors in child abuse. In C. H. Kempe & R. Helfer (Eds.), *The battered child* (3rd ed., pp. 49–85). Chicago: University of Chicago Press.

Steele, B. (1987). Psychyodynamic factors in child abuse. In R. E. Helfer & R. S. Kempe (Eds.), *The battered child* (4th ed., pp. 81–114). Chicago: University of Chicago Press.

Steele, Z. (1942). *Angel in top hat.* New York: Harper & Brothers.

Stehno, S. M. (1982). Differential treatment of minority children in service systems. *Social Work, 27*(1), 39–45.

Stehno, S. M. (1986). Family-centered child welfare services: New life for a historic idea. *Child Welfare, 65*(3), 231–239.

Stein, T. (1976). Early intervention in foster care. *Public Welfare, 34*(2), 38–44.

Stein, T. J. (1984). The child abuse prevention and treatment act. *Social Service Review, 58* (June), 302–314.

Stein, T. J. (1987). Foster care for children. In *Encyclopedia of social work.* (pp. 639–650). Washington, DC: National Association of Social Workers.

Stein, T. J., & Gambrill, E. D. (1977). Facilitating decision making in foster care: The Alameda project. *Social Service Review, 51*(3), 502–513.

Stein, T. J., Gambrill, E. D., & Wiltse, K. T. (1974). Foster care: The use of contracts. *Public Welfare, 32*(4), 20–25.

Stein, T. J., Gambrill, E. D., & Wiltse, K. T. (1978).

Children in foster homes—achieving continuity of care. New York: Praeger.

Stein, T. J., & Rzepnicki, T. L. (1983). *Decision-making at child welfare intake: A handbook for practitioners.* New York: Child Welfare League of America.

Stein, T. J., & Rzepnicki, T. L. (1984). *Decision making in child welfare services: Intake and planning.* Boston: Kluwer-Nijhoff.

Steinberg, L. (1986). Latchkey children and susceptibility to peer pressure: An ecological analysis. *Developmental Psychology, 22*(4), 433–439.

Steiner, G. Y. (1966). *Social insecurity: The politics of welfare.* Chicago: Rand McNally.

Steiner, G. Y. (1976). *The children's cause.* Washington, DC: Brookings Institute.

Steiner, G. Y. (1981). *The futility of family policy.* Washington, DC: Brookings Institute.

Steinman, S. (1984). Joint custody: What we know, what we have yet to learn, and the judicial and legislative implications. In J. Folberg (Ed.), *Joint custody and shared parenting* (pp. 111–127). Washington, DC: Bureau of National Affairs/Association of Family and Conciliation Courts.

Stevens, W. K. (1988, June 22). Economics, politics and sociology converge to bring a historic change within reach. *New York Times,* p. 1.

Stewart, J. J., Vockell, E. L., & Ray, R. E. (1986). Decreasing court appearances of juvenile status offenders. *Social Casework, 67*(2), 74–79.

Stockburger, C. (1976, June). Child labor in agriculture. *Inequality in Education, 21,* 25–32.

Stoltz, L. M. (1960). Effects of maternal employment on children: Evidence from research. *Child Development, 31*(4).

Stone, D. J., & Cohn, A. H. (1984). Stop talking about child abuse. In *Perspectives on child maltreatment in the mid '80s* (DHHS Publication No. [OHDS] 84-30338). Washington, DC: U.S. Government Printing Office.

Stone, H. D. (1987). *Ready, set, go: An agency guide to independent living.* Washington, DC: Child Welfare League of America.

Stone, L. J., & Church, J. (1984). *Childhood and adolescence. A psychology of the growing person* (5th ed.). New York: Random House.

Straus, M. & Gelles, R. (1986). Societal change and change in family violence from 1975 to 1985 as revealed by two national surveys. *Journal of Marriage and the Family, 48*(3), 465–479.

Straus, M., & Gelles, R. (1987). The costs of family violence. *Public Health Reports, 102*(6), p. 640.

Straus, M., Gelles, R., & Steinmetz, S. (1980). *Behind closed doors: Violence in the American family.* Garden City, NY: Anchor/Doubleday.

Straus, M. A., & Kantor, G. K. (1987). Stress and child abuse. In R. E. Helfer & R. S. Kempe (Eds.), *The battered child* (4th ed., pp. 42–59). Chicago: University of Chicago Press.

Strean, H. S. (1978). Social work and clinical social workers. In *Clinical Social Work: Theory and Practice* (pp. 1–40). New York: Free Press.

Stroul, B. A., & Friedman, R. M. (1988). Principles for a system of care. *Children Today, 17*(4), 11–15.

Stuart, A. (1986). Rescuing children: Reforms in the child support payment system. *Social Service Review, 60*(2), 201–217.

Stuart, R. B. (1977). *Truth or treatment: How and when psychotherapy fails.* Champaign, IL: Research Press.

Studt, E. (1954, June). An outline for study of social authority factors in social casework. *Social Casework, 35,* 231–238.

Study findings: National study of the incidence and severity of child abuse and neglect. (1979). (DHHS Publication No. OHDS 81-30325.) Washington, DC: U.S. Government Printing Office.

Study findings: Study of national incidence and prevalence of child abuse and neglect. (1988). Washington, DC: U.S. Government Printing Office.

Stumbras, B. (1971). Administrative issues in enforcement of regulation. In I. R. Winogrond (Ed.), *Delivery of services in a regulated society: Proceedings of the second Milwaukee Institute on a social welfare issue of the day.* Milwaukee: University of Wisconsin at Milwaukee, School of Social Work.

Sudia, C. (1986). Preventing out-of-home placement of children: The first step to permanency planning. *Children Today, 15*(6), 6–7.

Sullivan, M., Spasser, M., & Penner, L. (1975). *The Bowen Center Project.* Chicago: Juvenile Protective Association.

Sunley, R. (1963). Early nineteenth-century American literature on child rearing. In M. Mead & M. Wolfenstein (Eds.), *Childhood in contemporary cultures.* Chicago: University of Chicago Press.

Sussman, E., Trickett, P., Iannotti, R., Hollenbeck, B., & Zahn-Waxler, C. (1985). Child rearing patterns in depressed, abusive, and normal mothers. *American Journal of Orthopsychiatry, 55*(2), 237–251.

Sussman, M. B. (1971). Family. In *Encyclopedia of social work* (16th ed., pp. 329–340). Washington, DC: National Association of Social Work.

Sweeny, D. M., Gasbarro, D. T., & Gluck, M. R. (1963). A descriptive study of adopted children seen in a child guidance center. *Child Welfare, 42*(7), 345–349.

Tatara, T. (1987). *A summary of the highlights of the National Roundtable on CPS Risk Assessment and Family Systems Assessment.* Washington, DC: American Public Welfare Association.

Tatara, T., Morgan, H., & Portner, H. (1986). Scan: Providing preventive services in an urban setting. *Children Today, 15,* 17–20.

Taylor, D. A., & Starr, P. (1967). Foster parenting: An integrative review of the literature. *Child Welfare, 46*(7).

Taylor, H. B. (1935). *Law of guardian and ward.* Chicago: University of Chicago Press.

Taylor, H. B. (1966). Guardianship or "permanent placement" of children. In J. Tenbroek (Ed.), *The law of the poor* (pp. 417–423). San Francisco: Chandler.

Ten Broeck, E., & Barth, R. P. (1986). Learning the hard way: A pilot permanency planning program. *Child Welfare, 65,* 281–94.

Terpstra, J. (1985, June). *Coming to terms with terms in licensing, or, do you mean what I know?* Paper presented at the meeting of the Association for Regulatory Administration in Human Services, Richmond, VA.

Terpstra, J. (1989). Day care standards and licensing. *Child Welfare, 68*(4), 437–442.

Tessman, I. (1978). *Children of parting parents.* New York: Jason Aronson.

Theis, S. V. S. (1924). *How foster children turn out.* New York: State Charities Aid Association.

Thernstrom, S., Orlov, A., & Handlin, O. (Eds). (1980). *Harvard encyclopedia of American ethnic groups.* Cambridge, MA: Harvard University Press.

Thomas, C. W. (1976, October). Are status offenders really so different? A comparative and longitudinal assessment. *Crime and Delinquency, 22,* 438–55.

Thomas, G. (1975). *A community oriented evaluation of the effectiveness of child caring institutions* (p. 106). Athens, GA: Regional Institute of Social Welfare Research.

Thompson, M. S. (1986). The influences of supportive relations on the psychological well-being of teenage mothers. *Social Forces, 64*(4), 1006–1024.

Thompson v. Oklahoma, 108 S.Ct. 2687 (1988).

A threshold is crossed on mothers who work. (1988, July 16). *New York Times,* p. 12.

Thurston, H. W. (1930). *The dependent child.* New York: Columbia University Press.

Timms, V. (1962). *Casework in the child care service.* London: Butterworth.

Tomkins, C. (1989, March 27). Profiles: Marian Wright Edelman: A sense of urgency. *New Yorker,* pp. 48–50, 54, 56, 60, 61–64, 66, 67–74.

Tourse, P., & Gundersen, L. (1988). Adopting and fostering children with AIDS: Policies in progress. *Children Today, 17,* 15–19.

Toussieng, P. W. (1962). Thoughts regarding the etiology of psychological difficulties in adopted children. *Child Welfare, 41*(2), 59–65.

Townshend, Mrs. (1909). *The case for school nurseries. Tract number 145.* London: Fabian Society.

Tracy, E. M., & Whittaker, J. K. (1987). The evidence base for social support interventions in child and family practice: Emerging issues for research and practice. *Children and Youth Services Review, 9,* 249–270.

Trasler, G. (1960). *In place of parents.* London: Routledge & Kegan Paul.

Traverse, J., Glantz, F., & Coelen, C. (1979). *Children at the center.* Cambridge, MA: Abt Associates.

Tremitière, B. T. (1984, July). *A break in commitment.* York, PA: Tressler-Lutheran Service Association.

Trimble v. Gordon, 430 U.S. 762 (1977).

Triseliotis, J. (1973). *In search of origins: The experiences of adopted people.* London: Routledge & Kegan Paul.

Turitz, Z. R., & Smith, R. (1965). Child Welfare. In *Encyclopedia of social work* (pp. 137–145). New York: National Association of Social Workers.

Twenty-fourth annual report, 1888, Boston Children's Aid Society. (1930). Cited in H. W. Thurston, *The dependent child* (pp. 185–186). New York: Columbia University Press.

U.N. Assembly approves doctrine to guard children's rights. (1989, November 21). *New York Times,* p. 9.

Unger, C., Dwarshuis, G., & Johnson, E. (1977). *Chaos, madness and unpredictability.* Chelsea, MI: Spaulding for Children.

U.S. Children's Bureau. (1921). *A demonstration of the first federal child-labor law* (Publication No. 78). Washington, DC: U.S. Government Printing Office. In G. Abbott. (1938). *The child and the state* (Vol. 1). Chicago: University of Chicago Press, p. 465.

U.S. Children's Bureau. (1933). *Mothers' aid, 1931* (Publication No. 220). Washington, DC: U.S. Government Printing Office.

U.S. Children's Bureau, Division of Research. (1964). Psychiatric problems among adopted children. *Child Welfare, 43*(3).

U.S. Congress (1975, April, July). Adoption and foster care. Hearings before the Subcommittee on Children and Youth of the Committee on Labor and Public Welfare. U.S. Senate. Washington D. C.: U.S. Government Printing Office.

U.S. Department of Commerce, Bureau of the Census. (1976). *Statistical abstract of the United States* (97th ed.). Washington, DC: U.S. Government Printing Office.

U.S. Department of Commerce, Bureau of the Census. (1987a). After school care of the school-age child. (*Current population reports,* Series P-23, 149). Washington, DC: U.S. Government Printing Office.

U.S. Department of Commerce, Bureau of the Census. (1987b). *Who's minding the kids? Child care arrangements: Winter 1984–85.* (*Current Population Reports,* Series P-70, 9). Washington, DC: U.S. Government Printing Office.

U.S. Department of Commerce, Bureau of the Census. (1989). *Statistical abstract of the United States* (109th ed.). Washington, DC: U.S. Government Printing Office.

U.S. Department of Health and Human Services, Children's Bureau (1979). DHHS Publication No. (OHDS) 81-30325. Washington, DC: DHHS.

U.S. Department of Health and Human Services. (1980) *Adoption project for handicapped children: Ohio District II.* Washington D. C.: DHHS.

U.S. Department of Health and Human Services, National Center on Child Abuse (1988). *Study findings: Study of national incidence and prevalence of child abuse and neglect.* Washington, DC: U.S. Government Printing Office.

U.S. Department of Health, Education, and Welfare (1963). *Guides to state welfare agencies for the development of day care services.* Washington, D.C.: U.S. Government Printing Office.

U.S. Department of Health, Education and Welfare.

(1971a). *Abstracts of state day care licensing requirements, Part 1: Family day care homes and group homes; Part 2: Day care centers* (DHEW Publications Nos. [OCD] 72–11 and 72–12.). Washington, DC: Author.

U.S. Department of Health, Education and Welfare. (1971b). *Day care licensing study: summary report on phase 1: State and local day care licensing requirements* (DHEW Publication No. [OCD] 00–08). Washington, DC: Author.

U.S. Department of Health, Education and Welfare. (1972). *Models for day care licensing.* (DHEW Publication No. [OCD] 00–00). Washington, DC: Author.

U.S. Department of Health, Education and Welfare. (1975). *Model state subsidized adoption act and regulations.* Washington, DC: U.S. Government Printing Office.

U.S. Department of Health, Education and Welfare. (1976). *Subsidized adoption in America* (Publication No. [OHD] 76–30087). Washington, DC: U.S. Government Printing Office.

U.S. Department of Health, Education, and Welfare. (1978, February 17). *The appropriateness of federal interagency day care requirements. (FIDCR), v. 1: An overview of the study and findings.* Washington, DC: U.S. Government Printing Office.

U.S. Department of Health, Education, and Welfare, Office of Economic Opportunity, and U.S. Department of Labor. (1968). *Federal interagency day care requirements* (DHEW Publication No. 938–038). Washington, DC: Government Printing Office.

U.S. Department of Labor. (1966). *Manpower report of the president and a report on manpower requirements, resources, utilization and training.* Washington, DC: Author.

U.S. Department of Labor. (1988, August). *Labor force statistics derived from the current population survey, 1948–1987* (Bulletin 2307). Washington, DC: Bureau of Labor Statistics.

U.S. Department of Labor, Bureau of Labor Statistics. (1982, August). *Employment and Earnings, 29*(8), table A-33. Washington, DC: U.S. Department of Labor, Bureau of Labor Statistics.

U.S. Federal Works Agency. (1947). *Final report on the WPA program, (1935–1943).* Washington, DC: U.S. Government Printing Office.

U.S. Office of Economic Opportunity. (1968, March). *Project Head Start Fact Sheet.*

U.S. Office of Economic Opportunity. (1968, August). *Head Start Newsletter,* Special Issue.

U.S. Office of Education and the Office of Economic Opportunity. (1966). *Education: An answer to poverty.* Washington, DC: U.S. Government Printing Office.

U.S. Select Committee on Children, Youth, and Families. (1989, November). *No place to call home: Discarded children in America.* Washington DC: House of Representatives, 101st Cong. 1st Sess.

U.S. Senate Committee on Children and Youth. Hearings before the subcommittee on Labor and Public Welfare. (1975). *Adoption and foster care.* Washington, DC: U.S. Senate, 94th Cong., 1st Sess.

U.S. Senate Committee on Labor and Public Welfare. (1975, December 1). Washington, DC: Subcommittee on Children and Youth and the House of Representatives Select Subcommittee on Education.

Valentine, D. P., Acuff, D. S., Freeman, M. L., & Andreas, T. (1984). Defining child maltreatment: A multidisciplinary overview. *Child Welfare, 63*(6), 497–509.

Valk, M. (1957). *Korean-American children in American adoptive homes.* New York: Child Welfare League of America.

Vandell, D. L., & Corasaniti, M. A. (1988). The relation between third graders' after-school care and social, academic, and emotional functioning. *Child Development 59*(4), 868–875.

Vandell, D. L., Henderson, V. K., & Wilson, K. S. (1986). A longitudinal study of children with day-care experiences of varying quality. *Child Development, 59*(5), 1286–1292.

Van Meter, M. J. (1986). An alternative to foster care for victims of child abuse/neglect: A university-based program. *Child Abuse & Neglect, 10*(1), 79–84.

Vasaly, S. M. (1976). *Foster care in five states: A synthesis and analysis of studies from Arizona, California, Iowa, Massachusetts, and Vermont.* Washington, DC: George Washington University, Social Research Group.

Vecchiolla, F. J., & Maza, P. L. (1989). *Pregnant and parenting adolescents: A study of services.*

Washington, DC: Child Welfare League of America.

Vinter, R. D. (1967). The juvenile court as an institution. In *Task force report: Juvenile delinquency and youth crime: Report on juvenile justice and consultants' papers.* Washington, DC: U.S. President's Commission on Law Enforcement and Administration of Justice, Task Force on Juvenile Delinquency.

Vinter, R. D., & Sarri, R. C. (1965). Malperformance in the public schools. A group work approach. *Social Work, 10*(1), 3–13.

Visher, E., & Visher, J. S. (1978). Common problems of step-parents and their spouses. *American Journal of Orthopsychiatry, 48*(2).

Visher, E. B., & Visher, J. S. (1979). *Stepfamilies: A guide to working with stepparents and stepchildren.* New York: Brunner Mazel.

Wald, L. D. (1915). *The house on Henry Street.* New York: Henry Holt.

Wald, M. S. (1975, April). State intervention on behalf of neglected children: A search for realistic standards. *Stanford Law Review, 27.*

Wald, M. S. (1976). State intervention on behalf of "neglected" children: Standards for removal of children from their homes, monitoring the status of children in foster care and termination of parental rights. *Stanford Law Review, 28,* 625–706.

Wald, M. S., Carlsmith, J. M., & Liederman, P. H. (1988). *Protecting abused and neglected children.* Stanford, CA: Stanford University Press.

Wald, M. S., Carlsmith, J. M., Leiderman, P. H., deSales French, R., & Smith, C. (1985). *Protecting abused/neglected children: A comparison of home and foster placement.* Stanford: Stanford University, Center for Study of Youth Development.

Waldinger, G. (1982). Subsidized adoption: How paid parents view it. *Social Work, 27*(6).

Waldinger, G. (1988). *Aging out of foster care: Los Angeles county's independent living program* (Final Report-Year One presented to Department of Children's Services). Los Angeles: UCLA School of Social Welfare, Center for Child and Family Policy Studies.

Wallerstein, J. S. (1986). Women after divorce: Preliminary report from a ten-year follow-up. *American Journal of Orthopsychiatry, 56*(1), 65–77.

Wallerstein, J. S., & Kelly, J. B. (1980). *Surviving the breakup: How children and parents cope with divorce.* London: Grant McIntyre.

Ward, M. (1979). The relationship between parents and caseworker in adoption. *Social Casework, 60*(2), 96–103.

Ward, M. (1981). Parental bonding in older child adoptions. *Child Welfare, 60*(1).

Ward, M. (1984). Sibling ties in foster care and adoption. *Child Welfare, 63*(4), 321–332.

Watson, K. (1987, March 19). *Adoption policy.* Presentation at the Annual Conference of the Child Welfare League of America, Inc., Washington, DC.

Wattenberg, E. (1977). Characteristics of family day care providers. *Child Welfare, 56,*(3) 211–219.

Wattenberg, E. (1980). Family day care: Out of the shadows and into the spotlight. *Marriage and Family Review, 3,* 36–62.

Wattenberg, E. (1985). In a different light: A feminist perspective on the role of mothers in father-daughter incest. *Child Welfare, 64*(3), 203–211.

Wattenberg, E. (1987). Establishing paternity for nonmarital children. *Public Welfare, 45*(3), 8–13.

Wattenberg, E. (1990). Unmarried fathers: Perplexing questions. *Children Today, 19*(2), 25–30.

Weaver, E. T. (1977). *Public assistance and supplementary security income* (pp. 1121–1135). New York: National Association of Social Workers.

Weber, D. E. (1978). Neighborhood entry in group home development. *Child Welfare, 57*(10), 627–642.

Weber, G. H., & McCall, G. J. (Eds.). (1978). *Social scientists as advocates.* Beverly Hills, CA: Sage.

Weber, M. W. (1988, Summer). A framework for consistent decisionmaking in child protective services. *Protecting Children, 5,* 10–12.

Weber v. Aetna Casualty & Surety Co., 406 U.S. 164 (1972).

Webster-Stratton, C. (1985). Comparison of abusive and non-abusive families with conduct-disordered children. *American Journal of Orthopsychiatry, 55*(1), 59–69.

Webster v. Reproductive Health Service, 492 U.S. , 106 L.Ed.2d 410, 109 S.Ct. 3040 (1989).

Weidell, R. (1980). Unsealing sealed birth certificates in Minnesota. *Child Welfare, 59*(2), 113–119.

Weil, R. H. (1984). International adoptions: The quiet migration. *International Migration Review, 18*(2). 276–293.

Weinhaus, L. (1980–1981). Substantive rights of the

unwed fathers: The boundaries are defined. *Journal of Family Law, 19*(3), 445–461.

Weiner, L. (1985). *From working girl to working mother. The female labor force in the United States 1820–1980.* Chapel Hill: University of North Carolina Press.

Weinstein, E. A. (1960). *The Self-Image of the Foster Child.* New York: Russell Sage Foundation.

Weis, J. G., Sakumato, K., Sederstrom, J., & Seiss, C. (1980). *Reports of the national juvenile justice assessment centers: Jurisdiction and the elusive status offender: A comparison of involvement in delinquent behavior and status offenses.* U.S. Department of Justice, Law Enforcement Assistance Administration, Office of Juvenile Justice and Delinquency Prevention. Washington, DC: U.S. Government Printing Office.

Weissman, I. (1949). *Guardianship: A way of fulfilling public responsibility for children* (Publication No. 330). Washington, DC: Children's Bureau.

Weitzman, L. J. (1985). *The divorce revolution.* New York: Free Press.

Welbourn, A., & Mazuryk, G. (1980). Inter-agency intervention: An innovative therapeutic program for abuse prone mothers. *Child Abuse & Neglect, 4,* 199–203.

Wellesley v. Wellesley, 2 Russ. 1 (1827).

Wells, S. J., Stein, T. J., Fluke, J., & Downing, J. (1989). Screening in child protective services. *Social Work, 34*(1), 45–48.

Welter, M. (1965). *Comparison of adopted older foreign born and American children.* New York: International Social Services.

Werry, J. S., & Wollersheim, J. P. (1967). Behavior Therapy with children: A broad overview. *Journal of the American Academy of Child Psychiatry, 6,* 347–352.

Westat, Inc. (1986). *Independent living services for youth in substitute care* (Contract No. 105–84–1814). Washington, DC: Department of Health and Human Services.

Westinghouse Learning Corporation. (1969, April). *The impact of Head Start: An evaluation of the effects of Head Start experience on children's cognitive and affective development.* Athens: Ohio University.

Whipple, G. M. (Ed.). (1929). *The twenty-eighth yearbook of the National Society for the Study of Education. Preschool and parental education.* Bloomington, IL: Public School Publishing.

White House Conference 1930. (1931). New York: Century.

Whiting, L. (1977). The central registry for child abuse cases: Rethinking basic assumptions. *Child Welfare, 56,* 761–767.

Whittaker, J. K. (1977). Child welfare: Residential treatment. In *The Encyclopedia of Social Work.* New York: National Association of Social Workers.

Whittaker, J. K. (1981). Family involvement in residential treatment: A support system for parents. In A. N. Maluccio & P. A. Sinanoglu (Eds.), *The challenge of partnership: Working with parents of children in foster care* (pp. 67–88). New York: Child Welfare League of America/University of Connecticut School of Social Work.

Whittaker, J. K. (1987). Group care for children. In A. Minahan (Ed.), *Encyclopedia of social work* (18th ed., pp. 672–682). Silver Spring, MD: National Association of Social Workers.

Whittaker, J. K., Overstreet, E. J., Grasso, A., Tripodi, T., & Boylan, F. (1988). Multiple indicators of success in residential youth care and treatment. *American Journal of Orthopsychiatry, 58*(1), 143–147.

Wickenden, E., & Bell, W. (1961). *Public welfare: Time for a change.* New York: Columbia University Press.

Wilensky, H. L., & Lebeaux, C. N. (1958). *Industrial society and social welfare.* New York: Russell Sage Foundation.

Wilkenson, I. (1987, June 26). Infant mortality: Frightful odds in inner city. *New York Times,* pp. 1, 14.

Will, M. (1988). Family support: Perspectives on the provision of family support services. In *Focal Point* (The Bulletin of the Research and Training Center to Improve Services for seriously emotionally handicapped children and their families, Regional Research Institute for Human Services, Portland, Oregon), *2*(3), 1–2.

Williams, C. W. (1980). *Guardianship: A minimally used resource for California's dependent children: A study in policy: 1895–1978.* Unpublished doctoral dissertation. University of Southern California, Los Angeles.

William T. Grant Foundation Commission on Work, Family and Citizenship. (1988). *The forgotten half. Pathways to success for America's youth and young families.* Washington, DC: William T.

Grant Foundation Commission on Work, Family and Citizenship.

Wilson, W. J. (1988). A new look at inner-city poverty. *CDF Reports, 9*(8). 3–4, 6.

Wiltse, K. T. (1963). Orthopsychiatric programs for socially deprived groups. *American Journal of Orthopsychiatry, 33*(5), 806–813.

Wiltse, K. T., & Gambrill, E. (1974). Foster care, 1973. A reappraisal. *Public Welfare, 32*(1), 7–15.

Wingard, D. (1987). Trends and characteristics of California adoptions: 1964–1982. *Child Welfare, 66*(4), 303–314.

Winget, W. G. (1982). The dilemma of affordable child care. In E. Zigler & E. Gordon (Eds.), *Day care: Scientific and policy issues.* Boston: Auburn House.

Winsted, L. (1989, April 12). Personal communication.

Wisconsin v. Yoder, 406 U.S. 205, 92 S.Ct. 1526, 32 L.Ed. 2d 15 (1972).

Wisdom, WIC. (1987, October 14). *New York Times,* p. 26.

Withey, V., Anderson, R., & Lauderdal, M. (1980, December). Volunteers as mentors for abusing parents: A natural helping relationship. *Child Welfare, 59.*

Witmer, H., Herzog, E., Weinstein, E. A., & Sullivan, M. E. (1963). *Independent adoptions: A follow-up study.* New York: Russell Sage Foundation.

Witte, E. E. (1963). *The development of the social security act.* Madison: University of Wisconsin Press.

Wittenborn, J. R. (1957). *The placement of adoptive children.* Springfield, IL: Charles C. Thomas.

Wolfe, D. (1985). Child-abusive parents: An empirical review and analysis. *Psychological Bulletin, 97*(3), 462–482.

Wolins, M. (1968, December). Licensing and recent developments in foster care. *Child Welfare, 47,* 570–582, 614.

Wolins, M., & Piliavin, I. (1964). *Institution or foster family: A century of debate.* New York: Child Welfare League of America.

Wolkend, S., & Kozaruk, A. (1983). The adoption of children with medical handicaps. *Adoption and Fostering, 7*(1), 32–35.

Wolock, I. (1982). Community characteristics and staff judgements in child abuse and neglect cases. *Social Work Research and Abstracts, 18*(2), 9–15.

Wolock, I., & Horowitz, B. (1984). Child maltreatment as a social problem: The neglect of neglect. *American Journal of Orthopsychiatry, 54*(4), 530–543.

Wood, L., Herring, A. E., & Hunt, R. (1989). *On their own: the needs of youth in transition.* Elizabeth, NJ: Association for the Advancement of the Mentally Handicapped.

Woodruff, G., & Sterzin, E. D. (1988, May–June). The transagency approach: A model for serving children with HIV infection and their families. *Children Today, 17,* 9–14.

Woods, F. J., & Lancaster, A. C. (1962). Cultural factors in Negro adoptive parenthood. *Social Work, 7*(4), 14–21.

Wood v. Strickland, 95 S Ct. 992, (1975).

Wyatt v. Stickney, 344 F. Supp. 373 (M. D. Ala.) (1972).

Yarrow, L. J. (1961). Maternal deprivation. Toward an empirical and conceptual re-evaluation. *Psychological Bulletin, 58*(6), pp. 459–490.

Young, A. T., Berkman, B., & Rehr, H. (1975). Parental influence on pregnant adolescents. *Social Work, 20*(5), 387–391.

Young, A. T., Berkman, B., & Rehr, H. (1980). Teenage parenting: Social determinants and consequences. *Journal of Social Issues, 36*(1).

Young, L. (1964). *Wednesday's children: A study of neglect-abuse.* New York: McGraw-Hill.

Young, L. R. (1966, July). An interim report on an experimental program of protective service. *Child Welfare, 45,* 373–381, 387.

Zabin, L., Kantner, J., & Zelnik, M. (1979). The risk of adolescent pregnancy in the first months of intercourse. *Family Planning Perspectives, 11*(4), 215–222.

Zelizer, V. A. (1985). *Pricing the priceless child: The changing social value of children.* New York: Basic Books.

Zelnik, M., & Kantner, J. (1977). Sexual and contraceptive experience of young unmarried women in the United States 1976 and 1971. *Family Planning Perspectives, 9*(2), 55–71.

Zelnik, M., & Kantner, J. (1978). Contraceptive patterns and premarital pregnancy among women aged 15–19 in 1976. *Family Planning Perspectives, 10*(3), 133–142.

Zigler, E. (1985). Assessing Head Start at 20: An invited commentary. *American Journal of Orthopsychiatry, 55*(4), 603–609.

Zigler, E., & Black, K. B. (1989). America's family support movement: Strengths and limitations. *American Journal of Orthopsychiatry, 59*(1), 6–19.

Zigler, E., & Gordon, E. (Eds.). (1982). *Day Care: Scientific and policy issues.* Boston: Auburn House.

Zigler, E., & Valentine, J. (1979). *Project Headstart. A legacy of the war on poverty.* New York: Free Press.

Zigler, E. F., & Frank, L. (1988). *The parental leave crisis.* New Haven: Yale University Press.

Zimrim, H. (1984). Do nothing but do something: The effect of human contact with the parent on abusive behavior. *British Journal of Social Work, 14,* 475–485.

Zober, E., & Taber, M. (1965, July). The child welfare agency as parent. *Child Welfare, 44,* 387–401.

Zuravin, S. (1985). Housing and child maltreatment: Is there a connection? *Children Today, 14*(6), 8–13.

Zuravin, S. (1988). Child maltreatment and teenage first births: A relationship mediated by chronic sociodemographic stress? *American Journal of Orthopsychiatry, 58*(1), 91–103.

Zuravin, S. (1989, Fall). Child neglect research findings: Some implications for the delivery of child protective services. *Protecting Children, 6,* 13–18.

Name Index

Subject Index